Andrew B. Davidson

The Book of the Prophet Ezekiel

With notes and introduction

Andrew B. Davidson

The Book of the Prophet Ezekiel
With notes and introduction

ISBN/EAN: 9783337037390

Printed in Europe, USA, Canada, Australia, Japan

Cover: Foto ©Lupo / pixelio.de

More available books at **www.hansebooks.com**

The Cambridge Bible for Schools and Colleges.

GENERAL EDITOR:—J. J. S. PEROWNE, D.D.
BISHOP OF WORCESTER.

THE BOOK OF THE PROPHET

EZEKIEL,

WITH NOTES AND INTRODUCTION

BY

THE REV. A. B. DAVIDSON, D.D., LL.D.

EDITED FOR THE SYNDICS OF THE UNIVERSITY PRESS.

CAMBRIDGE:
AT THE UNIVERSITY PRESS.
1892

Cambridge
PRINTED BY C. J. CLAY M.A. AND SONS
AT THE UNIVERSITY PRESS

PREFACE
BY THE GENERAL EDITOR.

THE General Editor of *The Cambridge Bible for Schools* thinks it right to say that he does not hold himself responsible either for the interpretation of particular passages which the Editors of the several Books have adopted, or for any opinion on points of doctrine that they may have expressed. In the New Testament more especially questions arise of the deepest theological import, on which the ablest and most conscientious interpreters have differed and always will differ. His aim has been in all such cases to leave each Contributor to the unfettered exercise of his own judgment, only taking care that mere controversy should as far as possible be avoided. He has contented himself chiefly with a careful revision of the notes, with pointing out omissions, with suggesting occasionally a reconsideration of some question, or a fuller treatment of difficult passages, and the like.

Beyond this he has not attempted to interfere, feeling it better that each Commentary should have its own individual character, and being convinced that freshness and variety of treatment are more than a compensation for any lack of uniformity in the Series.

PREFATORY NOTE.

THE Book of Ezekiel is less suited than most others to be the subject of merely popular annotation. The state of the Text is such that frequent references to it as well as to the Versions are unavoidable. It was no part of the purpose of the following Notes to construct a Text; the thing aimed at has been to shew the general meaning of the Book, and, if possible, the connexion of its parts with one another; but the readings of the LXX. have generally been adduced when they presented any important deviation from the Hebrew. In the later chapters the MS. of which the Greek is a translation was in many instances more correct than that of which the present Hebrew is a copy.

Such aids as were available have been used, and obligations are acknowledged to a number of works, besides those named at the end of the Introduction. A number of passages in the Text have baffled the ingenuity of the best scholars, and appear to be incurably confused. Other parts of the Book are rendered obscure by allusions not now understood. And altogether the student of the Book must take leave of his task with a certain sense of defeat.

THE EDITOR.

CONTENTS.

		PAGES
I. INTRODUCTION.		
Chapter I.	The Book of Ezekiel...............	ix—xvii
Chapter II.	Ezekiel's History and Prophetic Work	xvii—xxxi
Chapter III.	Jehovah, God of Israel	xxxi—xliii
Chapter IV.	Israel, the People of the Lord......	xliii—lv
II. TEXT AND NOTES................................		1—361
INDEX		363

*** The Text adopted in this Edition is that of Dr Scrivener's *Cambridge Paragraph Bible.* A few variations from the ordinary Text, chiefly in the spelling of certain words, and in the use of italics, will be noticed. For the principles adopted by Dr Scrivener as regards the printing of the Text see his Introduction to the *Paragraph Bible,* published by the Cambridge University Press.

INTRODUCTION.

CHAPTER I.

The Book of Ezekiel.

The Book of Ezekiel is simpler and more perspicuous in its arrangement than any other of the great prophetical books. It was probably committed to writing late in the prophet's life, and, unlike the prophecies of Isaiah, which were given out piecemeal, was issued in its complete form at once. The prophecies are disposed upon the whole in chronological order, though the book may contain much that was never actually spoken, and even the prophecies that were orally delivered may have undergone considerable modification under the pen of the prophet when reproducing them. None of the prophets shews any anxiety to record his discourses in the precise form in which he delivered them. The aim of the prophets in their writings was not literary but practical, as it was in their speeches. It was their purpose to influence the minds of the people when they spoke, and this was equally their purpose when they wrote, and, if in the interval the circumstances of the people had to some extent changed, they did not hesitate to accommodate their former discourses to the new situation.

The book of Ezekiel is occupied with two great themes: the destruction of the city and nation; and the reconstitution of the people and their eternal peace. The book thus falls into two equal divisions of 24 chapters each:—

First Division, ch. i.—xxiv., Prophecies of the destruction of the city and nation, its certainty and necessity.

Second Division, ch. xxv.—xlviii., Prophecies of the restoration of the people, their regeneration and eternal peace as the people of the Lord.

These prophecies are for the most part symbolical actions, of which the explanation is added; or allegories and riddles, the meaning of which is read to the people. Though a good many actual events are referred to, the book contains little that is historical. It is rather a book of general principles. These principles are all but deductions from the prophet's conception of Jehovah, God of Israel and God over all. In this respect Ezekiel resembles the author of Is. xl—lxvi, though he has neither the breadth of sympathy nor the glow of emotion that distinguish the Evangelist of the Old Testament.

First Division, ch. i.—xxiv. Prophecies of the destruction of the nation.

First section, ch. i.—iii. 21. The prophet's consecration to his calling, and first period of his ministry (July 592 B.C.).

(1) Ch. i. Vision of Jehovah, the God of Israel, who calls and sends him.

(2) Ch. ii. 1—iii. 9. His mission to Israel as a prophet. His inspiration, under the symbol of eating the roll of a book presented to him in the hand of Jehovah.

(3) Ch. iii. 10—21. He goes to the Exiles, and when among them receives a clearer view of his mission, which is to be a watchman to warn every individual person, the wicked that he may turn from his evil, and the righteous lest he fall from his righteousness.

The theophany of ch. i. is a vision of Jehovah as he is in himself (final note to the Chapter). The appointment of the prophet to be a watchman is not a change on his original appointment to be a prophet, it is a more precise definition of it. The prophet of this age is a watchman, a warner of individual men. For the old order has changed, the state is disappearing, and only individuals remain out of which the new and eternal kingdom of the Lord has to be reconstructed (note on iii. 16). On the general meaning of the whole section cf. note on iii. 21.

Second section, ch. iii. 22—vii. 27. Symbolical prophecies of the overthrow of the city and state. (Under foregoing date.)

(1) Ch. iii. 22—27. Change in the prophet's procedure: he is commanded to cease for a time from being a public reprover.

(2) Ch. iv. Symbols of the siege of the city, the terrible scarcity within it, and of the people's bearing their iniquity in exile.

(3) Ch. v. Further symbols of the fate of the inhabitants: a third shall die of famine; a third fall by the sword around the city, and a third be scattered among the nations, still pursued by the sword.

(4) Ch. vi. Prophecy of destruction on the mountains, the mountain-land of Israel, where idolatries everywhere prevailed.

(5) Ch. vii. Dirge over the downfall of the city and nation.

Third section, ch. viii.—xi. More precise symbolical prophecies of the destruction of the city and people at Jehovah's own hand, because of the idolatrous pollution of his house (Aug. 591 B.C.).

(1) Ch. viii. The multiplied idolatries in the Temple: the image of jealousy in the court; the worshippers in the chambers of imagery; the women wailing for Tammuz; and the sun-worship between the Temple and the altar (cf. final note to the ch.).

(2) Ch. ix. Symbol of the slaughter of the idolatrous people. A messenger from the Lord passes through the city putting a mark on the forehead of all who bewail the evils that prevail, and he is followed by divine executioners who slay all not so sealed.

(3) Ch. x. Symbol of the destruction of the city by fire from God.

(4) Ch. xi. Symbol of the Lord's departure from his House, and abandonment of the city to the fury of her enemies.

Fourth section, ch. xii.—xix. The same theme of the certainty of the destruction of the nation, with proofs of its moral necessity. (Without date, but later than preceding.)

(1) Ch. xii. 1—20. The unbelief of the people is new signs must be given them. Symbolical prophecy, or the attempted escape of the king, and his capture by the Chaldeans.

(2) Ch. xii. 21—28. The people's unbelief is partly due to their observation of the character of prophecy. But the popular imagination that prophecies of evil fail to come true, or refer to the distant future, shall receive a speedy and terrible refutation.

(3) Ch. xiii., xiv. These delusions of the people are fostered by the false prophets, who prophesy only of prosperity. The prophets who deceive and those who are deceived by them shall perish together.

(4) Ch. xv. But will the Lord destroy the nation of Israel, the vine of his planting?—The nation of Israel among the nations is like the vine branch among the trees. Good for little when whole, what is it good for now when half-burnt in the fire? Only to be flung again into the fire and wholly consumed.

(5) Ch. xvi. Parable of the foundling child who became the faithless wife. Let Israel's history be judged. What has it been but one persistent course of ingratitude and unfaithfulness to Jehovah? Her chastisement cannot be deferred.

(6) Ch. xvii. And must not Zedekiah's perfidy against the king of Babylon, and his breaking the oath of Jehovah be punished? He has brought ruin both on himself and on the kingdom. Yet the Lord will set up a new kingdom on the land of Israel, into which all nations shall be gathered.

(7) Ch. xviii. The principles of this kingdom: the righteous shall live in his righteousness and the sinner die in his sin. The Lord hath no pleasure in the death of him that dieth. None shall perish for the sins of another: neither does any man lie under a ban from his own past life. Therefore let every man repent that he may live (cf. final note to the ch.).

(8) Ch. xix. Lament over Judah and her royal house.

Fifth section, ch. xx—xxiii. Concluding prophecies demonstrating the necessity of Israel's destruction. (Aug. 590 B.C.)

(1) Ch. xx. That which has preserved Israel from destruction at every stage of her history, and that which has given her a history, has been Jehovah's regard for his own name—lest it should be profaned among the nations.

(2) Ch. xxi. But now his threats uttered long ago must take effect. The sword of the Lord is whetted and furbished against Jerusalem.

(3) Ch. xxii. The aggravated sins of all classes of the people: the royal house, the priests, the prophets, and the people of the land.

(4) Ch. xxiii. New exposure of the life-long immoralities of the two adulterous women, Oholah and Oholibah (Samaria and Jerusalem).

After a silence of several years the military movements of Nebuchadnezzar drew a new and final oracle from the prophet against Jerusalem, Jan. 587 B.C., the time when Nebuchadnezzar began to invest the city.

(5) Ch. xxiv. Final symbol of the siege and the dispersion of the people, and of their purification from evil amidst the afflictions of the exile. A rusted caldron is set upon the fire that its contents may be seethed and pulled out indiscriminately (the siege and dispersion), and that its brass may glow and its rust and foulness may be molten and purged away.

Second Division, ch. xxv.—xlviii. Prophecies of the restoration and reconstruction of the nation (xxv.—xxxix); and vision of the final and perfect state of Israel as the people of the Lord (ch. xl. *seq.*).

First section, ch. xxv.—xxxii. Prophecies concerning the nations.

These prophecies occupy the place in the prophet's book proper to their contents. They are an introduction to the positive prophecies of the restoration of Israel. The judgments on the nations prepare the way for the restitution of the people. The purpose and effect of them is to make Jehovah, God of Israel, and God over all, known to the nations, so that they shall no more vex or seduce his people, as they have done in the past (ch. xxviii. 25, 26); and no more lift themselves up in pride of heart against the one living God (cf. introductory note to ch. xxv.). The prophet does not pursue the destiny of the nations further, nor state how much their recognition of Jehovah implies. But cf. final notes, ch. xvi.

(1) Ch. xxv. Judgment on the smaller nations around Israel, and revelation to them of Jehovah—Ammon, Moab, Edom and the Philistines.

(2) Ch. xxvi.—xxviii. 19. Judgment on Tyre for her pride of heart, and on the prince of Tyre, who said, I am God!

(3) Ch. xxviii. 20—26. Judgment on Sidon that it may no more be a pricking briar to the house of Israel.

(4) Ch. xxix.—xxxii. Judgments on Egypt. It shall be humbled and reduced to be a base kingdom, that it may no more be a delusive stay to the house of Israel, nor seduce them from trust in Jehovah alone.

Second section, ch. xxxiii.—xxxix. Positive prophecies of the restoration of the people, and reconstitution of the kingdom of the Lord.

(1) Ch. xxxiii. The place of the prophet in preparing for the kingdom. He is a watchman, warning every individual soul that by repentance and righteousness it may live. The conditions of entering the new kingdom and of life are altogether moral, and each man shall enter it for himself (cf. final note to the ch.).

(2) Ch. xxxiv. The Ruler. The former evil shepherds, who fed themselves and not the flock, shall be removed; Jehovah himself will take in hand the feeding of his flock, and will set up one shepherd over them, even his servant David, to feed them for ever.

(3) Ch. xxxv.—xxxvi. The Land. The land of the Lord, rescued from the grasp of Edom and the nations who have usurped it, shall be given again to Israel for ever; it shall be luxuriant in fertility and teem with people.—The principle that moves the Lord to do these things for Israel is regard to his holy name, even that he may reveal himself, as he truly is, to mankind. His forgiveness and regeneration of the people, who shall henceforth be led by his spirit (xxxvi. 16—38, cf. final note).

(4) Ch. xxxvii. The People. Thus the nation, now dead, shall be reawakened into life and restored. In the restitution Ephraim and Judah shall no more be divided, but shall have one king, even David, over them for ever.

Thus the restitution of the people is complete, and their holiness as the people of the Lord perfect. Jehovah sanctifies them by dwelling among them; the people know that he is their God, and the nations know that he sanctifies them (xxxvii. 28). So far that which is the purpose of all history has been attained: Jehovah has been revealed both to his people and to the nations. The nations, however, who have learned to know Jehovah, whether from his judgments lighting on themselves (xxv.—xxxii.), or from their observation of the principles on which he rules his people, are the nations who have long been on the stage of history and played their parts beside Israel. There are far-off peoples lying in the ends of the earth who have not heard Jehovah's fame nor seen his glory. One great act in the drama of history has still to be performed. He who is God alone is known to the world as the God of Israel, and it is only through Israel that he can reveal himself to all. These distant peoples shall come up from the ends of the earth, and, like other nations, also touch on Israel, and then shall the glory of the Lord be revealed and all flesh shall see it together. History as the prophet conceives it, whether of Israel or of the nations, is Jehovah's revelation of himself to mankind; every movement of it carries this burden, "Ye shall know that I am the Lord." The wave of history pauses on the shore when Jehovah's glory rises on the uttermost ends of the earth.

(5) ch. xxxviii., xxxix. Invasion of Israel in the latter day by Gog and all the nations lying in the far-off corners of the earth. The Lord's defence of his people, now that they are holy and true, reveals to the nations not only his power but his nature, and the principles on which he rules his people and the world. He is known to the ends of the earth.

Third section, ch. xl.—xlviii. A vision of the final glory and peace of the redeemed people of the Lord.

Preceding prophecies described the redemption and restoration of the people (xxxiii.—xxxvii.); the present section gives a picture of the condition of the people thus for ever redeemed. The background of the picture is the whole preceding part of the book. The last words of ch. i.—xxxix. are, "And I will hide my face from them no more; for I have poured out my spirit on the house of Israel, saith the Lord God." The people are all righteous, led by the spirit of the Lord, and knowing that Jehovah is their God. The passage does not describe how salvation is to be attained, for the salvation is realized and enjoyed; it describes the state and life of the people now that their redemption is come. The fact that the subject of the passage is the *final* blessedness of the people accounts for the supernatural elements in the picture. But both the natural and the supernatural features of the people's condition are to be understood literally. The Temple, the services and the like are meant in a real sense, and no less literally meant is the supernatural presence of Jehovah in his House, the transfiguration of nature, the turning of the desert into a garden, and the sweetening of the waters of the Dead Sea (cf. introductory note to ch. xl.).

(1) ch. xl. 1—xliii. 27. Account of the Temple buildings. (*a*) ch. xl. 1—27, description of the outer gateway and outer court. (*b*) ch. xl. 28—47, the inner gateway and inner court. (*c*) ch. xl. 48—xli. 26, the house itself with its annexed buildings. (*d*) ch. xlii., other buildings in the inner court, and dimensions of the whole. (*e*) ch. xliii. 1—12, entry of Jehovah into his House. (*f*) ch. xliii. 13—27, the altar of burnt-offering, and the rites consecrating it.

(2) ch. xliv.—xlvi. Ordinances regarding the Temple. (*a*) ch. xliv., those who shall minister in the house, priests and Levites. (*b*) ch. xlv. 1—17, revenues of priests, Levites and prince; the duties devolving on the prince in upholding the ritual. (*c*) ch. xlv. 18—xlvi. 24, the special and daily services in the Temple; the special offerings of the prince.

(3) ch. xlvii., xlviii. The boundaries of the holy land, and new disposition of the tribes within it. (*a*) ch. xlvii., the life-

giving stream issuing from the Temple; the boundaries of the holy land. (*b*) ch. xlviii., disposition of the tribes in the land; dimensions and gates of the holy city.

CHAPTER II.

Ezekiel's History and Prophetic Work.

EZEKIEL was the son of Buzi, of whom nothing further is known. This name has some resemblance to the word "to despise," and a rabbinical fancy interprets it of Jeremiah, "the despised," making Ezekiel the lineal descendant of this prophet, as he is his child in thought and faith. Ezekiel is styled the priest, and in all probability he was of the family of Zadok. The priests had already in this age attained to great influence; they were the aristocracy, standing next to the royal family (xxii. 25, 26). It is not certain whether Ezekiel had actually been engaged in priestly duties before his captivity, though it is not unlikely, both from the name priest applied to him and from the minute acquaintance which he shews with the Temple, its dimensions and furniture, and with the sacerdotal rites. The passage iv. 14 is not certain evidence, as the prohibition to eat carrion was binding on all the people (Ex. xxii. 31, though some consider this verse a later insertion). The age at which priests undertook their duties is not clearly stated in the Law. Ezekiel began to prophesy five years after the captivity of Jehoiachin (597 B.C.), and he states that this was in the thirtieth year. If this statement referred to his age he would have been grown up to manhood some years before his exile, but the words are obscure (notes on i. 1—3). It is doubtful if the statement of Josephus (*Ant.* x. 6, 3) that he was carried captive "when a youth" has any ground beyond the historian's own fancy. The evidence points in a different direction. In several passages the prophet's "house" is mentioned (iii. 24, xii. 3 *seq.*); the "elders" occasionally assemble there (viii. 1, xiv. 1, xx. 1), and according to xxiv. 18 he was married. Reuss is hardly right in regarding his wife and her death as fictions; the language used implies that she was a real person and that her death occurred as stated, though, as usual, the prophet employed the incident for didactic purposes, and some of the details may be creations of his idealism; for it is characteristic of him that real events float before his eye in a moral atmosphere, which magnifies them and gives them an outline which is ideal only. The uncompromising attitude taken up by him towards his fellow captives is a thing hardly to be expected from a mere youth (Jer. i. 6); and even in the earliest part of his Book his views appear fully formed, and his convictions regarding the impending fate of his country unalterably fixed. The weight due to the last fact, however, may not be so great, because the Book was written at an advanced period of life, and even the earlier parts of it may be coloured with reflections of a later time.

The period at which the prophet's youth was passed was rich in influences that must have powerfully affected him. Though too young to take part in the reform of Josiah (620), or perhaps to remember it, he grew up in the midst of the changes which it had introduced, and probably learned to estimate previous history from the point of view which it gave him. The tragic events which followed one another closely at this epoch, such as the death of Josiah (608), the exile of Jehoahaz to Egypt and of Jehoiachin to Babylon, made a lasting impression on his mind. The last event formed the chief landmark of his life, and that not solely because his own history was so closely connected with it; and how deeply the fate of the two young princes touched him, and how well he could sympathise with the country's sorrow over it, a sorrow recorded also by Jeremiah (xxii. 10), is seen in his Elegy on the princes of Israel (ch. xix.). He has a fondness for historical study, and no history is to him without a moral; and silently the events of this time were writing principles upon his mind to which in after years he was to give forcible enough expression.

It was not, however, merely the silent teaching of events from which Ezekiel learned. He had a master interpreting events to him to whose influence every page of his prophecies bears witness. Jeremiah, indeed, may not have been Ezekiel's only master; there were other prophets of the time likeminded with him, such as that Urijah whom Jehoiakim dragged from his hiding-place in Egypt and slew with the sword (Jer. xxvi.), and perhaps others of whose names no record has been kept, for it is almost an accident, and only because his fate cast light on the history of Jeremiah in a moment of peril, that the name of Urijah has been preserved. There were also priests who cherished the same aspirations as these prophets, and pursued in their own province the same ends. It is not without significance that Jeremiah no less than Ezekiel was of a priestly family, and that too a rural one, for it was not in the capital alone that true religion had its representatives— like Micah Urijah was a prophet of the country, being of Kirjath-jearim (Jer. xxvi. 20). And among Ezekiel's predecessors in the priesthood and also among his contemporaries there were some who, if they had spoken to the world, would have spoken in the same manner as he did, for the favourable judgment which he passes on the Zadokite priests (xliv. 15) is not altogether due to mere caste prejudice.

Still the teaching and life of Jeremiah was probably the most powerful influence under which the young priest grew up. It would, no doubt, be a mistake to ascribe every idea in Ezekiel which coincides with Jeremiah's teaching to the influence of that prophet. There is a common circle of thoughts and feelings which even the greatest minds share with those of their own age. Striking out some new conceptions, and opening up some lines of advancement which mark an epoch, the chief elements of their faith and life are common to them with others of their day and have been inherited from the past. The surprise with which we read Jeremiah might be lessened if the means of comparing him with others were not so narrow as the paucity of writers in the century before the exile causes it to be. At any rate his influence upon the language and thought of Ezekiel can readily be observed. It could hardly have been otherwise. For thirty years before Ezekiel's captivity Jeremiah had been a prophet, speaking in the courts and chambers of the temple and in the streets of Jerusalem, and having such a history as made him the most prominent figure of the day. Ezekiel was familiar with his history and had listened to his words from his infancy. Many of his prophecies had circulated in writing for a number of years previous to the captivity of Jehoiachin which Ezekiel shared, and the constant intercourse between Jerusalem and the exiles kept the prophet of the Chebar well informed regarding the course of events at home, and the views which prominent persons there took of them (xi. 2 *seq.*, xvii. &c.).

In the year 597 B.C. Nebuchadnezzar took Jerusalem and carried into captivity the young king Jehoiachin, the flower of the population including many priests, Ezekiel among them, as well as a multitude of other citizens, particularly craftsmen. Ezekiel with a community of other exiles was settled at Tel-Abib by the river Chebar—not to be identified with the Chabor which falls into the Euphrates near Carchemish, but some stream or canal in Babylonia proper; and five years later he was called to occupy among them the place of a "watchman" (592 B.C.). How large the community was does not appear, nor what kind of place Tel-Abib was, for the references of the prophet to walls (xii. 7, xxxiii. 30) hardly justify the conclusion that it was a walled town. The community appears to have been left, as was usually the case, to regulate its internal affairs and govern itself according to its own mind. The prophet repeatedly mentions the "elders," and though he calls them elders of Judah (viii. 1) or Israel (xiv. 1, xx. 1), he identifies them with the captivity (xi. 25), of which they must have been the heads and representatives. The lot of the exiles might in some cases be hard, but there is no evidence that they were harshly treated by their conquerors or suffered want. When the prophet speaks of famine he refers to Canaan (xxxvi. 29, 30, xxxiv. 27, 28), and the phrase "made servants of them" (xxxiv. 27) has more a national than an individual reference, like such expressions as "prison houses" in the second part of Isaiah (xlii. 22). The exiles possessed houses (iii. 24, xxxiii. 30), and there is no allusion to persecution from their heathen neighbours. Cf. Jer. xxix. 5 *seq.*

The picture, if it can be called so, which the prophet gives of the life of the exiles and their circumstances is singularly colourless. His interests were exclusively religious, and any insight which he affords us is into the religious condition of his fellow-captives, from whose mouth he occasionally quotes an expression very suggestive as to their state of mind (xii. 22, 27, xviii. 2, 25, 29, xx. 49, xxxiii. 10, 30, xxxvii. 11). His own mind was occupied with the largest conceptions, and the exiles were to his eye representatives of a larger subject. When bidden go to "them of the captivity" he felt sent to the "house of Israel" (ii. 3, iii. 4), and while addressing his fellow exiles he fancies before him the people in Canaan or the nation scattered abroad throughout the world. This identification of the exiles with the people as a whole, and this occupation of the prophet's mind with great national interests, makes it difficult to know how far in his apparent addresses to the exiles he is touching upon their actual practices. Nothing is more likely than that the captives continued the evil courses in which they had grown up at home, so far as this was possible in a foreign land. They certainly shared in the fanaticism or optimism of those left in the country, and heard with incredulity the prophet's predictions of the speedy downfall of the city (xii. 22, 26 *seq.*). It is known from Jeremiah (xxix. 8) that there were false prophets among the exiles who confirmed them in their delusive hopes, and Ezekiel might refer to these prophets in such passages as ch. xiii, xiv. But such language as "ye have not gone up into the breach" (xiii. 5), "I sought for a man that should stand in the breach before me for the land" (xxii. 30), shews that it is the circumstances of the nation as a whole and not those of the exiles that occupy the prophet's attention. The same appears from such expressions as those in xiv. 7, "every one of the house of Israel, or of the strangers that sojourn in Israel, that layeth his idols on his heart." In one passage (xx. 32) the people are represented as resolving to adopt the religion of the nations, "We will be as the nations, to serve wood and stone;" and such a spirit might very naturally reveal itself among the exiles surrounded by heathen neighbours. But probable as this is, the chapter is a review of the nation's history, and the language may be little more than the prophet's interpretation of the spirit shewn by the people all through its history. It is only on rare occasions that he draws any distinction between the exiles and those remaining in the land. When he does so he shares the feeling of Jeremiah (ch. xxiv, xxix. 16 *seq.*) that the flower of the people had been carried into captivity with Jehoiachin, and that the hope of the nation lay in them (xi. 14—21). But usually the exiles are regarded as the representatives of the house of Israel; the "elders" are the elders of Judah or Israel, and when addressing them the prophet desires to speak in the ears of all his countrymen; just as it is the fate of Jerusalem (iv.—xi.), the history of the nation (xvi, xx, xxiii), and its future destinies (xxxiii.—xxxvii.), that form the theme of his discourse. The idea that the prophet's office was limited to the exiles, among whom he was a sort of pastor, with a cure of souls, is supported by nothing in the Book.

It would be a mistake, however, to press this general bearing of Ezekiel's mission, and his preoccupation with the destinies of the house of Israel as a whole, so far as to infer from it that he had no actual prophetic ministry among the exiles; that he was a writer simply, unused to the life of men—a solitary theorist, whose "stuff for removing" (xii. 4), if he had brought it forth, would have been little more than an inkhorn; and that the form of oral address which he gives his words is a mere literary artifice. It may not be allowable to assume that his operations among the exiles were literally altogether such as he describes them, but, apart from his own representations, several things afford evidence indirectly that he did exercise a ministry of some kind and of some duration. In ch. xx. 49 (Heb. xxi. 5), when commanded to prophesy of the great conflagration which the Lord would kindle in the field of the south, he exclaims, "Ah Lord God! they say of me, Is he not a speaker of parables?" And in xxxiii. 30 he is represented as being the subject of conversation among the people: "The children of thy people talk of thee by the walls and in the doors of the houses, saying, Come, and hear what is the word that cometh forth from the Lord." These incidental allusions imply that the prophet had a manner which the people had learned to recognise and to discount, and that they were in the habit of meeting to consult him. The frequent assembling of the elders before him implies the same thing. It is true that these elders are very subordinate figures; they are mentioned and then the discourse passes on to the "house of Israel" or even the strangers that sojourn in Israel, but they cannot be wholly fictitious, or (to speak with Reuss) mere "dummies." Again, though it may be true that the prophet's book was written as it now is at a late period, and though its present form suggests careful planning, all passages relating to the destruction of Jerusalem and the principles of Jehovah's government and the attributes of his nature illustrated by it being embraced in the first part, and the second part being devoted to the Restoration and the illustrations of Jehovah's purposes which it affords, the fact that in the first part there are many promises of restitution is evidence of actual oral communication (xi. 14—20, xvi. 52—63, xvii. 22—24, xx. 39—44). These consolatory passages naturally arise out of the preceding threatenings, as in other prophets, if these were actually spoken, while in an orderly dogmatic treatise they would have been postponed to the second part of the book. The passage xxix. 17—20 possibly implies that the prophet felt his predictions against Tyre to have received a less literal fulfilment than was expected from them. If so, his retention of the predictions without change affords ground for believing that upon the whole he has reproduced his discourses with fidelity. The severe, even harsh tone pervading the early part of the book is evidence to the same effect. It is scarcely conceivable that the prophet should have adopted such a tone after the fall of the city unless he had been reproducing in the main what he had spoken before it. And in like manner the people's mind, buoyant and impatient of the prophet's anticipations of disaster in the first half of the book, appears prostrated and plunged into despair in the second (xxxiii. 10). It is beyond belief that so many circumstances, all harmonious if real, should be nothing but elaborate fictions.

It cannot be assumed that the prophet's exercise of his office was just literally such as it is represented. Circumstances of actual occurrence are idealized by him and made the expressions of general conceptions and principles, and it is not always possible to distinguish between events which were actual but are idealized, and things which are purely creations of the symbolizing imagination (note on xi. 13). The prophet appears to have entered on his mission with his convictions in regard to the fate of his country fixed. He clearly foresaw the downfall of the state. But like all the prophets he was assured of the reconstitution of the kingdom of God on a securer basis. It is for this chiefly that he is appointed to labour (ch. xxxiii.); and this position suggests to him from the beginning the nature of his prophetic calling, which is to be a "watchman" to warn every individual man (note iii. 16). It is probable that the first section of the book (ch. i.—iii. 21) covers the earliest period of his ministry. After this a change of procedure, occasioned by the incredulity of the people, appears to have been adopted by him; he ceased to be a public reprover, confining himself to the instruction of those who visited him in his house (iii. 22—27, note, p. 26). The meaning of this so-called "silence" is obscure; it was only comparative, though it is represented as lasting till tidings arrived of the fall of the city (xxiv. 27, xxxiii. 22), when, his anticipations being verified, his mouth was again opened. Little is said of the prophet after this beyond mention of occasional visits from the elders. But, though the book may contain a good deal that was never publicly spoken, and though, being edited after the events foretold had occurred, the predictions in it may even have received in some parts a certain colour from the fulfilment, it may be assumed that the main contents of the oral addresses are faithfully reproduced in it; and the passage xx. 49 is warrant for supposing that the more striking peculiarities of the prophet's manner are truly reflected.

The prophet's style, though stately and polished, is less

INTRODUCTION. xxv

elevated and more prosaic than that of the earlier prophets, though he occasionally rises into wild and irregular poetry (ch. vii., xxi.), and in particular affects the *Ḳinah* or Lament (ch. xix., xxvi. 17, xxxii. 17). His language begins to shew incorrectness, though some of the faults may be due to the very depraved state of the text; and his diction has a certain luxuriance, which must sometimes be called redundancy, unless we may infer from the more sober text of the LXX. that many of the cumulative phrases are glosses with which the Heb. text has been overgrown (note, vi. 6). The frequent recurrence of the same phrases produces a feeling of monotony, though the repetition appears due to mannerism and the ascendancy of certain ideas in the prophet's mind quite as much as to defective literary skill. The expression "child of man" (ii. 1) occurs nearly a hundred times, and others very frequently, such as "idols" (block-gods, vi. 4); "the mountains of Israel" (vi. 2 &c.), a phrase found in no other writer (cf. Is. xiv. 25); "appease my fury" (v. 13, &c.); "stumbling-block of iniquity" (vii. 19); "rebellious house" (ii. 5, and often in ch. i.—xxiv. cf. xliv. 6); "desolate in the midst of the countries that are desolate" (xxix. 12, xxx. 7); "the time of the iniquity of the end" (xxi. 25, &c.); "the Lord Jehovah" (ii. 4, and extremely often, though much seldomer in LXX.); "I Jehovah have spoken it" (v. 13, &c.); and the characteristic "they (ye) shall know that I am Jehovah" (vi. 7, &c.), language by which Ezekiel expresses his conception of the purpose and issue of all history, whether it be the dispersion and restoration of his own people or the commotions and changes that take place among the nations.

There are three things in particular which are characteristic of the Book: symbolical figures, symbolical actions, and visions. The three seem all due to the same cast of mind, and are related to one another, being all more or less the creations of an imagination or phantasy always grandiose and often beautiful. One of the finest of the ideal symbols appears in the Elegy on the princes of Israel (ch. xix.), in which the nation is represented as a mother lioness rearing her whelps, one after another of which when they had learned to catch the prey was taken by the nations in their pit and caged in captivity. There is a touch of pathos, rare in the prophet, when in reference to the captive prince he speaks of the young lion's voice being no more heard on the mountains of Israel. Of singular beauty also is the representation of the merchant city Tyre, rising out of the waters on her island rock, under the symbol of a gallant ship moored in the seas (ch. xxvii.). Her mast is a cedar of Lebanon, her sail fine byssus of Egypt, her decks of teak inlaid with ivory. All the ships of Tarshish attend on her and pour into her the richest products of the nations to form her cargo. But she is broken by the east wind and founders in the heart of the seas, to the dismay and inconsolable grief of all seafaring men. If the author of the Apocalypse be a purer poet than Ezekiel, the prophet has given him his inspiration and furnished him with materials for his most splendid creations. Again, though marked by a breadth which offends against modern taste, the allegory of the foundling child which became the faithless wife is powerful, and, when the details are forgotten and only the general idea kept in mind, even beautiful as well as true. An outcast infant, exposed in the open field and weltering in her blood, was seen by the pitying eye of a passer by. Rescued and nourished she grew up to the fairest womanhood and became the wife of her benefactor, who heaped on her every gift that could please or elevate. But the ways into which he led her were too lofty to be understood, and the atmosphere around too pure for her to breathe; the old inborn nature (her father was the Amorite and her mother a Hittite) was still there beneath all the refinements for which it had no taste, and at last it asserted itself in shameless depravity and insatiable lewdness. Other figures are the familiar one of Israel as a vine (ch. xv.), to which a pathetic turn is given by a studious silence regarding its fruit; that of Egypt as the crocodile, a semi-mythical monster, fouling his waters in his restless energy, but dragged out by the hook of Jehovah and flung upon the land, his carcase filling the valleys and his blood the water-courses; and that of Nebuchadnezzar as a great speckled eagle with long pinions, hovering over Lebanon and cropping its highest branches. It is the prophet's manner to develop his symbols into a multitude of details, which sometimes has the effect of obscuring the brilliancy of the central conception.

Though scarcely, with Ewald, to be called "learned," Ezekiel has a knowledge of designing and architecture (ch. xl. *seq.*), and his acquaintance with foreign lands and their natural and industrial products is wide. In this respect he comes nearest to the author of Job, though the latter delights rather to dwell on the phenomena of nature, the luxuriant vegetation of the Nile valley, the wild creatures of the desert, and the monstrous creations of the waters, while Ezekiel is more attracted by the precious stones and metals which various lands are famed for, and by the rich fabrics produced by human skill (ch. xxvii.). Naturally, his imagination luxuriates in mythological tradition, especially of a weird kind, such as tales of the "mighty" which were of old (ch. xxxii.), legends of paradise, the garden of God (xxviii.), and impressions of the popular mind regarding Sheòl the abode of the dead.

The prophet's symbolical actions have been variously understood. It is beyond doubt that actions of this kind were occasionally performed by prophets. Zedekiah made him "horns of iron" wherewith to push (1 Kings xxii. 11). Jeremiah put a yoke upon his own neck, which Hananiah broke from off him (Jer. xxviii. 2, 10). The symbolical act, ch. li. 59—64, may also have been literally executed, as well as that in xix. 10. Whether his act in hiding his girdle (ch. xiii.) was real or not may be doubtful, and the same doubt exists in regard to Isaiah's walking naked and barefoot (ch. xxi.); the fact that the sign was continued for three years rather tells against a literal performance of it; and it may be held certain that Jeremiah did not send yokes to the kings of Edom and Moab (Jer. xxvii. 3). It is possible that Ezekiel may in some cases have had recourse to this forcible way of impressing his teaching. Some of the actions described might well have been performed, such as joining two sticks together into one to represent the future union under one king of Judah and Israel (xxxvii. 15 *seq.*). He might also have refrained from all outward mourning on the death of his wife, as a sign of the silent grief under which the people would pine away when tidings reached them of the destruction of the city and the death of all dear to them (xxiv. 15 *seq.*). But on the other hand how could the prophet "eat his bread with quaking and drink his water with trembling" as a sign to the house of Israel? (xii. 18). And can it be seriously supposed that he actually took a sharp sword as a razor and shaved off the hair of his head and beard, burning a third of it in the city (what city?), smiting a third of it with the sword about the walls, and scattering the remaining third to the winds? (v. 1 *seq.*). Such actions, and others like them, could not have been performed, and this fact casts doubt on the literality even of those which were possible. Even if 190 days be the true reading in iv. 5, it is most improbable that the prophet should have lain on his side immoveable for half a year, and it appears impossible when other actions had to be done simultaneously. The hypothesis of Klostermann[1] hardly deserves mention. This writer supposes that the prophet lay on his side because he was a cataleptic and temporarily paralysed, that he prophesied against Jerusalem with outstretched arm because his arm could not be withdrawn, being convulsively rigid, and that he was "dumb" because struck with morbid *alalia*. It is surprising that some reputable scholars should seem half inclined to accept this explanation[2]. They perhaps have the feeling that such an interpretation is more reverential to Scripture. But we need to remind ourselves, as Job reminded his friends, that superstition is not religion (Job xiii. 7—12, xxi. 22). The Book itself appears to teach us how to interpret the most of the symbolical actions. In xxiv. 3 the symbol of setting the caldron on the fire is called uttering a parable (cf. xx. 49). The act of graving a hand at the parting of the ways (xxi. 19) must certainly be interpreted in the same

---

[1] *Stud. u. Krit.*, 1877.
[2] Orelli, *Kurzgef. Kommentar;* Valeton, *Viertal Voorlezingen;* Gautier, *La Mission du Prophète Ezéchiel.* See on the other side Kuenen, *Onderzoek*, ii. p. 268.

way, and, though there may be room for hesitation in regard to some of them, probably the actions as a whole. They were imagined merely. They passed through the prophet's mind. He lived in this ideal sphere; he went through the actions in his phantasy, and they appeared to him to carry the same effects as if they had been performed[1].

The vision is a mental operation of the same kind, though higher. The simplest and most beautiful of them all is the vision of the dry bones and their resurrection (ch. xxxvii.). Three elements are observable in it: first, certain truths and ideas in the prophet's mind, truths not new but often expressed elsewhere, at least partially, such as the idea of the people's restoration. Secondly, the operation on these truths of the prophet's mental genius, giving them a unity, throwing them into a physical form, and making them stand out before the eye of his phantasy as if presented to him from without. And thirdly, there may be a certain literary embellishment. This last element is most conspicuous in the visions of the Cherubim (ch. i.) and of the new Temple (ch. xl. *seq.*)[2]. But it must be maintained that the second element, the constructive operation of the phantasy, was always present, and that the visions are not mere literary invention. Occasionally, however, the prophet does use the vision, like other things, in an ideal way, bringing considerable stretches of his own prophetic work under the outline of a single vision, as in ch. i.—iii. 21 and ch. viii.—xi. (cf. note, iii. 21). Ezekiel felt such visions as that in ch. xxxvii. to be a revelation of God. And from whence else could his assurance of the people's restoration have come? There was nothing in the state of the world and the nations to suggest it, and everything

[1] In regard to ch. iv. 1—3 Calvin remarks, Hoc fuit puerile spectaculum, nisi a Deo jussus fuisset Propheta sic agere. But that which would be puerile unless commanded by God remains puerile in itself, and the sound sense of men will conclude that God did not command it.

[2] The difference between Isaiah's knowledge of God and that of Ezekiel, and consequently the greater detail of the latter in ch. i. compared with Is. vi., is very prettily expressed by Abarbanel, who says that Ezekiel was a villager who saw the divine Majesty but rarely and therefore minutely described it, while Isaiah dwelt in the capital and was familiar with the great King.

in the past history of the people and their present condition to make it seem impossible (xxxiii. 10). The singular struggle between hope and fear revealed in Lam. iii. 21 *seq.* is typical of the state of mind even of those in whose hearts hope was not dead; and the very energy of the utterance in Is. l. 4—8 is evidence of the obstacles which faith had to overcome.

Between the latest date in ch. i.—xxxix. and the date of ch. xl. *seq.* there is an interval of thirteen years. Ch. i.—xxxix. may be supposed to have been composed a considerable time before ch. xl. *seq.* The latter chapters are quite unique in a prophetic book, while the contents of the earlier part do not differ from those of other prophetic writings. The difference of the two parts may have suggested to Josephus (*Ant.* x. 5, 1) the idea that Ezekiel wrote *two* books, unless, indeed, the words he uses should apply rather to Jeremiah. Although ch. i.—xxxix. form the background to ch. xl.—xlviii., a certain change in the prophet's view seems to have taken place in the interval, particularly in regard to the *rôle* of the Prince. The passage xxix. 17—21 is a later insertion dated two years after ch. xl. After this date (570 B.C.) nothing is known of the prophet. Tradition asserts that he met his death in Babylonia at the hands of a prince of his people whom he had upbraided for his idolatrous practices[1].

The contention of some scholars that the Book is later than the exile and pseudepigraphic has not met with any wide acceptance. Zunz[2] would place it in the Persian period (c. 440—400 B.C.). The view of Geiger[3] is similar; while Seinecke[4], who identifies Gog with Antiochus Epiphanes, brings the Book as low as the Maccabean age.

Ezekiel was received into the Canon along with the other prophetical books. The date of the canonising of the Prophets is uncertain, though it must have been prior to 200 B.C. (Prol.

---

[1] For this and other traditions cf. Knobel, *Prophetismus*, p. 301.
[2] *Gottesdienst. Vorträge*, p. 157, and *Zeit. Deut. Morg. Ges.*, vol. xxvii., p. 676.
[3] *Urschrift*, p. 23.
[4] *Gesch. d. V. Is.* i. 138, quoted in Kuen., *Onderz.*, ii. 315.

INTRODUCTION. xxxi

to Ecclus., and Ch. xlix. 8, Dan. ix. 2). The differences between the ritual details in ch. xl. *seq.* and the Law naturally created difficulties, which, however, do not seem to have been widely felt, as no scholar's name or school is mentioned in connexion with them. Hananiah ben Hezekiah, of blessed memory (a contemporary of Gamaliel the master of St Paul), resolutely grappled with them; he had 300 measures of lamp-oil brought him, and betaking himself to an upper room he sat and reconciled the differences, of which no more was heard[1].

CHAPTER III.

JEHOVAH, GOD OF ISRAEL.

EZEKIEL'S general doctrine of God does not differ materially from that of other prophets of the same age, such as Jeremiah and Isaiah xl. *sq.*, though the character of his mind causes him to bring some divine attributes into more prominence than others, and his education as a priest leads him to a way of thinking or at least to the use of a kind of phraseology not observed in other prophets.

His conception of Jehovah appears in the "visions of God" which he describes (ch. i., viii., x., xliii.). These visions were all alike, and they reveal his general impression of that which Jehovah is. The fourfold nature of the cherubim, of their faces and wings and of the wheels, all forming a chariot moving in every direction alike, and with the velocity suggested by the wings and wheels, symbolizes the omnipresence of Jehovah, while the eyes of which the whole was full are a token of his omniscience. The throne above the firmament on which he sat indicates that he is King in heaven, God over all, omnipotent. The divine being himself appeared as of human

---

[1] See Buhl, *Kanon und Text*, p. 30 (Transl., p. 24, 30). Wildeboer, *Het Ontstaan van den Kanon*, p. 59. Bleek, 4 Ed., p. 551.

form, while his nature was light, of such brightness that fire fitly represented him only from the loins downwards, from the loins upwards the effulgence was something purer and more dazzling, and he was surrounded by a brightness like that of the rainbow in the day of rain. This "glory," which contains himself within it (x. 4, 18, xliii. 5, 6), is that which is manifested to men (final note, ch. i.).

The name by which the prophet calls the God of Israel is Jehovah, or the Lord Jehovah. Whether the name Lord expresses something judicial or no may be uncertain, it expresses at least something sovereign (Is. vi. 1, 5); but the other name Jehovah now in Ezekiel's age expresses the idea of God absolutely. Jehovah has all power: the nations as well as Israel are in his hand. He brought Israel out of Egypt, and gave them the good land of Canaan, and he will disperse them among the nations, delivering them over to the king of Babylon; but yet again he will recover them out of the hand of those who have served themselves of them, and save them with an everlasting salvation. With the same omnipotence he rules among the nations. His judgments fall upon the peoples around Israel, Ammon, Moab and Edom, whose name he causes to perish among the nations; but they light also on Tyre and even upon Egypt, which he gives into the hand of Nebuchadnezzar. He breaks the arm of Pharaoh and strikes the sword out of his hand, putting his own sword into the hand of Nebuchadnezzar. He brandishes his sword in the eyes of all the nations, while creation shudders and the waters of the great deep stand motionless. He puts his hook in the jaws of Gog, and brings him up from the ends of the earth, revealing himself to the most distant lands and the far-off islands of the sea. He reverses the past, bringing again the captivity of Sodom and her daughters. He sends forth his life-giving spirit, and the nation that was dead and its bones scattered feels the breath of life and rises to its feet a great army. His rule of the nations is the judgment of the nations; and his verdict upon a nation is seen in the last act which it plays upon the stage of history and is eternal (xxxii. 17 *sq.*).

At the sight of his glory the prophet fell upon his face, but it is not Jehovah's will that his servants should be overborne by his majesty (Job ix. 32—35, xiii. 21), and he says to the prophet "stand upon thy feet that I may speak with thee" (ii. 1). Though profoundly devout and but a "child of man" in the presence of Jehovah, the prophet is far from regarding God as a mere transcendent majesty and abstract omnipotence. He is the living God. He has "a likeness as the appearance of a man" (i. 26). He has "a mighty hand and a stretched out arm" (xx. 33), a "face" (vii. 22, xiv. 8, xv. 7, xxxix. 23, 24), a "mouth" (iii. 17, cf. xxii. 21), "eyes" and "ears" (viii. 18), his fury comes up into his "nostrils" (xxxviii. 18), and the sanctuary is the place of the "soles of his feet" (xliii. 7; cf. Is. lx. 13). These representations in Ezekiel mean neither more nor less than they do in other prophets, such as Is. xl.—lxvi.; they are not to be dwelt upon individually but taken together, and when thus combined they express the idea of a living personality possessing all the powers of personal being. Even when the prophet represents Jehovah's judgments as executed by the mediation of divine messengers (ch. ix.), or when he interposes a "man" between God and himself (xl. 3 *sq.*), this is due to his tendency to personify rather than to any feeling of the distance of God from men or the world, as appears from xliii. 5—7.

Again, Jehovah appears in the prophet endowed with all the attributes and emotions of moral being. He expresses his own consciousness of that which he is by using his own name, as when he says, "Ye shall know that I am Jehovah;" and his sense of himself when injured, as it is when his people worship other gods or when the nations touch that which is his, oppressing his people or usurping his land, reacts and manifests itself as "jealousy." He pities the outcast infant weltering in its blood and bids it live (xvi. 6), and the little children passed through the fire to Molech, whom he calls "my children" (xvi. 21). He has compassion on "his sheep," broken or lost and scattered on the mountains through the selfishness of hirelings who feed themselves and not the flock, and he binds up that of them which was broken, and strengthens that which was sick (xxxiv. 16). His "soul" is "alienated" from his people (xxiii. 18), whose uncleannesses he "loathes" (xxxvi. 17). His "anger" is kindled by their ways, he pours out his "fury" upon them and "appeases" it in their punishment. Yet he has no pleasure in the death of the wicked; his will is that men should live (xviii. 23, xxxiii. 11). He is conscious of being God alone, and directs all history, whether of his people or the nations, towards one goal, the revealing of himself as that which he is to the eyes of mankind. If he sends afflictions on his people it is that he may break their whorish heart and their eyes (vi. 9), and when his chastisements fail he forgives for his name's sake (xxxvi. 22; cf. Is. xlviii. 9), brings himself near and dwells by his spirit in men's hearts (xxxvi. 27), even tabernacling in a visible form among them for ever, so that the name of the new Jerusalem to all generations is, *The Lord is there* (xlviii. 35).

His relation to his people or the prophet is not that of one distant or unapproachable. Being King in Israel,—and he expresses his resolution to be King over them yet in truth (xx. 33),—he gives them statutes and judgments. Yet these are "good," they are "statutes of life" (xxxiii. 15), which if a man do he shall live by them (xx. 11). In like manner he communicates his word to the prophet, commanding him to receive it and not be rebellious like the rebellious house (ii. 8). The prophet represents his inspiration under the symbol of eating the roll of a book, but why this symbol should imply a more "mechanical" idea of inspiration than the language of Jer., "Behold I have put my *words* in thy mouth" (i. 9), does not appear. Though the roll was written on the front and on the back with lamentation and woe, it was in the prophet's mouth "as honey for sweetness" (iii. 3). The same joy in Jehovah's service even amidst persecutions was felt by Jeremiah: "Thy words were found and I did eat them; they were the joy and rejoicing of my heart, for I am called by thy name" (xv. 16). Sympathy with Jehovah in his alienation from the people because of their evil is expressed by both prophets, "I sat alone

INTRODUCTION. xxxv

because of thy hand, for thou hast filled me with indignation" (Jer. xv. 17, and in a more violent form vi. 11; cf. Ez. iii. 14). Both prophets have such fellowship with Jehovah that they can venture to intercede for the people, though they are repulsed with the answer that the time for intercession has gone by, "Though Moses and Samuel stood before me my mind could not be toward this people; cast them out of my sight" (Jer. xv. 1; Ez. ix. 8, xi. 13).

Jehovah is God over all, and the self-exaltation of peoples or their rulers in any place of the world, as when the prince of Tyre says, I am God, or when the Pharaoh says, My river is mine, I have made it, is an offence against the majesty of him who is alone exalted. What might be called moral forces are no less subservient to his will and ruled by him than those that are physical. The prophet, indeed, represents Jehovah as the Author of all that occurs, whether on the stage of history or in the minds of men. Even the evil that men do is in many instances ascribed to him, without men, however, being thereby relieved of responsibility for it. In one aspect men's deeds are their own, in another they are occasioned by God. Jerusalem sets her bloodshed on a bare rock, without covering it; but from another point of view it is the Lord himself who sets it on a bare rock "that it might cause fury to come up, to take vengeance" (xxiv. 7). A prophet allows himself to be enticed, and entering into the purposes of the people—whitewashing the wall which they build—speaks such a prophetic word as fosters their delusive hopes. It is the Lord that deceives this prophet that both he and those whom he deludes may perish together (xiv. 10). The laws given to the people were "good," statutes of life. But the people neglected and disobeyed them, they perverted their meaning, extending the law of the offering of the firstborn even to children, whom they burnt in the fire. This perversion was caused by God himself; he gave them laws that were not good, that he might destroy them (xx. 25, 26). Evil things come into the mind of Gog, he devises an evil device, saying, "I will go up against them that are quiet, to take the spoil, and to take the prey." It is Jehovah that puts hooks in his jaws and brings him forth; "I will bring thee against my land, that the nations may know me, when I shall be sanctified in thee" (xxxviii. 4, 10, 16).

These representations in Ezekiel are similar to others in Scripture, and, no doubt, raise difficult questions. Perhaps two things may be said in general: first, Jehovah is nowhere represented as causing nations or men to do evil acts, which they are not also represented as doing of their own accord and with evil intent; and secondly, Jehovah is nowhere represented as the author of sin in such a sense that he causes an innocent mind to sin. He adds to the sin of one already sinful for wider purposes which he has in view. The instances of Pharaoh, the Amorites (Deut. ii. 30; Josh. xi. 20; cf. Gen. xv. 16; Lev. xviii. 24, 25), Saul (1 Sam. xxvi. 19), Ahab (1 K. xxii. 20), Israel (Is. vi. 9, xxix. 10, lxiii. 17, cf. lxiv. 5, 6; Ez. xx. 25, 26), the false prophets (Ez. xiv. 9), Gog (Ez. xxxviii.) are all of this kind. They are so clearly of this kind that none of them needs discussion except the case of Saul's persecution of David. The words of David are, "If the Lord hath stirred thee up against me let him smell an offering." David's view appears to be that Saul's persecution of him is due to an aberration with which the king has been struck by Jehovah. This aberration is a punishment for some previous unwitting offence, and he advises an atoning offering that the offence may be forgiven and the aberration removed. The aphorism *quem deus vult perdere prius dementat* may have its application in Scripture, but there at least the previous question needs to be carefully raised, Whom does God will to destroy? It is always assumed that they are evil men, either in themselves or as the adversaries of Jehovah or of his people. On broader grounds the propriety or justice of this assumption may in some cases appear to need investigation. But, the assumption being made, God appears as the author of sin only in a secondary and very modified sense. He uses sin already existing, punishes it with delusion and worse sin, laying a stumbling-block before the sinner, over which he falls and perishes (Jer. vi. 21; Ez. iii. 20)[1].

[1] The Essay of Dr J. C. Matthes, Oorsprong der Zonde, *Theol.*

The view has been suggested that to the prophet's mind the prevailing characteristic of Jehovah is his justice—Jehovah is "the rigidly just one;" and that this conception of Jehovah's justice is but the reflection of the prophet's own "scrupulous and precise character." Jehovah's punctilious righteousness appears in his way of dealing with different classes of men, ch. xiv. 12—20, xviii., xxxiii. 10—20; and the prophet's own scrupulous and somewhat pedantic nature in the way he feels the responsibilities of his office as watchman, ch. iii. 16—21, xxxiii. 1—9[1]. This representation appears to invert the true order, putting that first which is last. The prophet's conception of his office is a reflection, if there be reflection in the case, of his idea of the divine method of dealing with men. It is because God will deal with each man individually that the prophet feels he must warn each separately. The reality of his office and of his sense of responsibility in the discharge of it being admitted, his statements about himself are in the main an indirect way of impressing upon men the true nature of their relations to God and of the method in which he will treat them (initial note to xxxiii.). And the point of view from which passages like ch. xviii. and xxxiii. are to be looked at is scarcely that of the divine rectitude merely (final notes to xviii.).

There are several expressions used by Ezekiel of interest in connexion with his conceptions of God. They are the words frequently spoken by the Lord, (1) "Ye (they) shall know that I am Jehovah;" (2) "I will be sanctified (shew myself holy) in you (them);" and (3), "I wrought for my name's sake, that it should not be profaned in the sight of the nations." From the occasional combination of these phrases together it appears that they differ little from one another in meaning; thus: "I will magnify myself and sanctify myself, and I will make myself known in the eyes of many nations; and they shall know that I am Jehovah" (xxxviii. 23). "And my holy name will I make known in the midst of Israel; and the nations shall know

Tijds., 1890, p. 225, appears to overlook the previous assumption referred to.
[1] Kuenen, *Modern Review*, Oct. 1884.

that I am Jehovah, the Holy One in Israel" (xxxix. 7). "I will be jealous for my holy name" (xxxix. 25). "That the nations may know me when I shall be sanctified in thee, O Gog, before their eyes" (xxxviii. 16). "And the nations shall know that I am Jehovah, when I shall be sanctified in you (Israel) before their eyes" (xxxvi. 23).

In the words spoken by the Lord, "Ye shall know that I am Jehovah," the term "Jehovah" expresses the speaker's own consciousness of that which he is. The language is frequently used towards the nations: his judgments on them reveal to them that he is Jehovah, or they learn the same truth from observation of his restoration and protection of Israel (the former, xxv. 5, 7, 11, 17, xxvi. 6, xxviii. 22, 23, xxix. 9, xxx. 19, xxxv. 9, 15, xxxviii. 16, 23, xxxix. 6, 7; and the latter, xxxvi. 23, 36). The phrase is also addressed to Israel, both in connexion with judgments and in connexion with blessings such as restoration and final peace (the former, vi. 7, 10, 14, vii. 4, 27, xi. 10, 12, xii. 15, 16, 20, xiii. 9, 23, xv. 7, xx. 38, xxiv. 24; and the other, xx. 42, 44, xxviii. 26, xxxiv. 27, 30, xxxvi. 11, 38, xxxvii. 13). The words mean more than that those addressed shall learn that it is "Jehovah" who inflicts the judgment or confers the blessing upon them; they mean that they shall learn to know the nature of Him who is dealing with them, or at least his nature on some side of his being. This appears from an occasional variation in the expression: "Ye shall know that I am Jehovah God" (xiii. 9, xxiii. 49, xxiv. 24, xxix. 16, cf. xxviii. 26). The term "Jehovah," however, is not a mere synonym for "God;" it appears always to carry a historical element in it. When addressed to the nations it connotes "the God of Israel;" and when addressed to Israel it carries a reminder of that which they have been told of him by his servants the prophets, or that which they have learned of him from his presence in their history. How much is suggested by the name "Jehovah" must perhaps be learned from each particular passage. When spoken to the nations in general it may suggest his power, and that he will not leave injuries done to his people unrequited; in some cases it may imply that he is

God over all, as when the words are spoken in regard to the Pharaoh (xxix. 9). Indeed, as the language is used now in Ezekiel we should probably not be far wrong in putting into the term "Jehovah" when spoken by the Lord himself the meaning which it would have if used by the prophet, and to him certainly "Jehovah," the God of Israel, is he who is God alone, and who, in righteousness and power and all other attributes, is that which one who is God alone is—although in each several passage where the word is used some special divine attribute may be more particularly suggested.

The expression "I will be sanctified," or, "sanctify myself," or, "shew myself holy" (or, get me sanctifying), does not differ materially from the phrase just discussed. In modern usage the term "holy" has drifted away from its proper sense and lost its original comprehensive meaning. The word is an adj. derived from a neut. verb which probably expressed some physical idea, though the idea is not now recoverable. Whatever the idea was the term "holy" was very early felt to be an appropriate epithet for deity, not as expressing any particular attribute but rather the general notion of godhead. Jehovah swears by his "holiness" or by "himself" without difference of meaning (Am. iv. 2, vi. 8). The term was so much appropriated to the divine that when coupled with the word "god" or "gods" it became a mere otiose epithet, "the holy gods" meaning nothing more than "the gods" (Dan. iv. 8, 9, 18, v. 11, cf. v. 14; Inscrip. of Eshmunazar). In Israel the epithet is transferred to Jehovah, who is the Holy One of Israel, or, *in* Israel (xxxix. 7), or the Holy One, or even Holy One, almost as a proper name (Prov. xxx. 3; Is. xl. 25; cf. Josh. xxiv. 19).

It appears to be a secondary use, though also very early, when the term was applied to that which belongs to the sphere of deity, which lies near God's presence or has come into it (Ex. iii. 5; Numb. xvi. 37, 38), or which belongs to him, whether as part of himself or as his property. Hence his arm, his spirit are "holy;" and so his house, city, hill, people, land, and the like; his sabbath, his offerings, and his ministers. Hence the angels, belonging to the sphere of deity, are the "holy ones"

(Job v. 1). The word in this sense is applied both to things and men, and expresses primarily not a quality but a relation. But naturally, just as the idea of godhead would always carry some attribute or perhaps several with it, so that which was considered the possession of God or near him, whether things or men, would also be considered to have certain characteristics. These characteristics would be regulated by that which God was thought to be. Things repulsive to his nature could not be his nor come near him, and could not be "holy;" neither could men unlike him in character, or in any physical condition repugnant to his nature. But things and men that were his shared his "holiness" and could be "profaned," such as his sabbaths or his holy princes (Ez. vii. 22, 24, xx. 16; Is. xliii. 28).

The term "holy" applied to Jehovah is very elastic, and may embrace much or little, one thing or another. To call Jehovah "holy" tells nothing in regard to him further than that he is God, with the attributes of God. The idea has to be distinguished from the details brought at different times under it. There might be included under the idea the sole godhead of Jehovah; such natural attributes of deity as power, manifested in the rule of nature (Ex. xv. 1, 11), or in judgments on the enemies of his people (Ez. xxviii. 22, xxxviii. 16, 23, xxxix. 7); moral attributes, as punitive righteousness (Is. v. 16), or ethical purity (Lev. xix. 2); and finally physical or what might be called æsthetic purity (Lev. xi. 44 *seq.*, xx. 25, 26; Ez. xliii. 7, 9, cf. initial note to xl.—xlviii., last par.). When Jehovah reveals himself as that which he is, or in any of his attributes and aspects of that which he is, he "sanctifies" himself. Hence to "magnify" or "glorify" himself or set his glory among the nations are particulars coming under the more general "sanctify" (xxxviii. 23, xxxix. 21). In like manner men "sanctify" Jehovah when they recognise that which he is or ascribe to him his true nature (xxxvi. 23; Is. viii. 13). On the other hand when the iniquities of his people constrain him to act in such a way as to disguise any of his great attributes, such as his power, in the eyes of the nations, so that they misinterpret his being, his holy name is "profaned," as on the contrary he is "sanctified" in the

INTRODUCTION. xli

eyes of the nations by the restoration of his people and their defence when restored and righteous (xxxvi. 23, xxxviii. 16).

The phrase, "I wrought for my name's sake, lest it should be profaned among the nations," has a meaning but little different. The expression is chiefly used in reference to Israel and its destinies. It contains the prophet's philosophy of history. History, particularly that of Israel in the face of the nations, is Jehovah operating for his name's sake. It is his regard for his name that explains Israel's history, that, indeed, has given her a history, for otherwise she would many a time have been cut off for her iniquities. The "name" of God here is not the mere word "Jehovah," neither is it what might be called his "reputation," though both are included in it. The idea of the prophet is suggested by the fact that he who is God alone and over all is known to the world as Jehovah, God of Israel. He whom the peoples of mankind know as the God of Israel has the consciousness of being true God, and wills to reveal himself to all mankind (Is. xlii. 8, xliii. 10, xliv. 8, xlv. 21—24). Within Israel he can reveal himself as he is in himself; to the nations he must reveal himself as that which the God of Israel is. He who knows himself as God alone (Is. xliv. 8) has become historically God of Israel, has begun his revelation of himself to the world thus, and will thus carry it to an end till he is known to all the earth. Therefore he cannot destroy Israel, for this would undo the first steps of his great purpose already taken, and efface from the minds of the nations the knowledge of him which they have received by his redemption of his people in their sight (xx. 9, 14, 22; cf. Deut. ix. 28, 29, xxxii. 26, 27; Num. xiv. 15, 16; Ex. xxxii. 11, 12). Henceforth his "name," the name of him who knows himself to be God alone, is inseparably linked with the destinies of Israel. Within Israel his revelation of himself as he is went on, though thwarted by the rebelliousness of the people. Eventually their want of receptiveness was so great that they had to be rejected for a time and cast out of Jehovah's land. In the world of the nations without this was a retrograde movement. Unable to conceive of a moral rule of his people by Jehovah, the nations concluded that he was without power to protect them (xxxvi. 20). Thus his name was profaned; the knowledge which the nations had of him was obscured. It was perhaps not among the nations only that Jehovah's name had suffered an eclipse: the feet of many in Israel also well-nigh slipped. It took time for them to accommodate themselves to what had happened. It was only when they were enabled to read their past history in a new light, the light shed on it by the prophets, that their minds came to rest. But this new reading both gave them a profounder knowledge of Jehovah and awakened a new enthusiasm for the future. And Jehovah's recovery of his people from all lands not only restored the prestige of his power among the nations, but taught them the deeper moral principles of his rule (xxxix. 23), as it sealed to Israel the ancient truths which they had heard concerning him (xx. 42—44, xxxvi. 11, 37, xxxix. 28, 29).

The prophet's idea is a large one, and might comprehend more than he fills into it. It is that God's revelation of himself is historical; that he becomes the God of one people with whose destinies his name is linked; that his rule of this people in their history, its progress and final issues, the way he leads them and that into which at the last he fashions them, is his revelation of himself to the eyes of mankind.

The conception that Jehovah acts only for his own name's sake, to sanctify his great name, is capable of being set in a repellent light. It seems to make the divine being egoistic, and his own sense of himself the source of all his operations. The way too in which he brings the nations to know that he is Jehovah, through judgments mainly, invests the idea with additional harshness. The conception is not found in the earlier prophets, but is familiar in the age of Ezekiel. Perhaps two things, if considered, would help to explain the prophet's idea. One is his lofty conception of Jehovah, God alone and over all, and his profound reverence before him. The "child of man" cannot conceive the motive of Jehovah's operations to be found anywhere but in himself. But that name for whose sake he works is a "great name" (xxxvi. 23), and a "holy name" (xxxix. 25), it is that of him who is God. The prophet thinks of Jehovah as one of his predecessors did: "For Jehovah your God, he is God of gods, and Lord of lords, the great God, the mighty and the terrible, which regardeth not persons, nor taketh a reward" (Deut. x. 17). And other prophets of his age, very unlike him, move among similar thoughts: "my glory will I not give to another" (Is. xlii. 8, xlv. 23); "for mine own sake will I do it; for how should my name be profaned" (Is. xlviii. 11).

And the second thing is this: the conception arose out of the conflicts of the time. There were antagonisms within Israel, and more powerful antagonisms without, between Israel and the nations. These conflicts on the stage of history were but the visible forms taken by a conflict of principles, of religions, of Jehovah God with the idolatries of which the nations of the earth were the embodiments. The prophet could not help drawing up this antagonism into his conception of God; and not unnaturally he reflected his own feeling upon the mind of God, and conceived him thinking of himself as he thought of him. If it was but half a truth, it was perhaps the half needful for the age. When the fulness of time was come the centre of divine motive was shifted, "God so loved the world." Coming from the bosom of the Father and knowing him, the Son's mind was altogether absorbed in the positive truth, the stream of which was so broad and deep that all antagonisms were buried beneath it.

CHAPTER IV.

Israel, the People of the Lord.

THE tone of the prophet towards the people in the early part of his book is severe and threatening, though the threats are here and there relieved with consoling promises and a brighter outlook (xi. 16 *seq.*, xvi. 53 *seq.*, xvii. 22 *seq.*, xxi. 27). In the second half he adopts a kindlier tone. In both parts his teaching agrees in many things with that of his predecessors, particularly Jeremiah.

It is surprising how much the two prophets have in common. Both enter upon their office with opinions already formed of the people to whom they are sent, and with the expectation of opposition from them (Jer. i. 19); those around Ezekiel are thorns and briars and he dwells among scorpions (ii. 6); they are impudent and stiffhearted (ii. 4). Both receive assurance of divine assistance in their contention with them: "I have made thy face hard against their faces...harder than flint have I made thy forehead" (iii. 8, 9; Jer. i. 8, 17, 18, xv. 20; Is. l. 7). Both sympathise with the anger of Jehovah in his controversy with his people and share it, being filled with "indignation" (iii. 14; Jer. vi. 11, xv. 17), and keep aloof from the people, refusing to enter into their sorrow or joy, for a doom from heaven hangs over them (iii. 26, cf. xxiv. 15—27; Jer. xvi. 5 *seq.*). Israel is a "rebellious house," and their rebellion has been continuous throughout their history, "they have rebelled they and their fathers unto this very day" (ii. 3, ch. xvi., xx.); "from the day that your fathers came forth out of Egypt unto this day, I have sent unto you my servants the prophets; yet they hearkened not unto me, they did worse than their fathers" (Jer. vii. 25). Both assert that Jerusalem has outbidden Samaria in wickedness (xvi. 47, 51, xxiii. 11; Jer. iii. 11, xvi. 12), and that both peoples have been more perverse than the heathen (v. 6, xvi. 48; Jer. ii. 11). The degeneracy has infected all classes and persons, it is in vain to look for a "man" in the streets of Jerusalem: "I sought for a man among them to stand in the gap before me for the land, but I found none" (xxii. 30; Jer. v. 1).

In one respect Ezekiel appears to exceed his predecessors in the condemnation of his people: he recognises no good time in Israel's history. To older prophets a halo surrounded Israel's earliest time, though it soon faded away: "I found Israel like grapes in the wilderness; but they came to Baal-Peor and consecrated themselves unto the shame, and became abominable like that which they loved" (Hos. ix. 10); "I remember of thee the kindness of thy youth, when thou wentest after me in the wilderness" (Jer. ii. 2). And Isaiah even speaks of Jerusalem as at one time "the faithful city," though in his own day she had become an harlot (i. 21). Jeremiah appears to date the declension from the settlement in Canaan (ii. 5—7, 21, cf. Is. v. 2; Mic. vi. 3), and Ezekiel agrees with him that at that time the people sank into deeper degeneracy, seizing the occasion presented by the Canaanite shrines to add to their provocation and blasphemy (xvi. 15 *seq.*, xx. 28; Deut. xii. 2). But he goes further, pushing the people's idolatries back as far as the wilderness (xx. 24), and even into an earlier time: "Son of man, there were two women...and they committed whoredoms in Egypt" (xxiii. 2). Jerusalem came of tainted blood: her father was the Amorite, and her mother an Hittite (xvi. 3). The history of Israel in Egypt is told so briefly in the Pent. that no corroboration of the prophet's idea is found, which, however, has everything in its favour (on xx. 7, 8); and for the wilderness the oldest part of the Pent. supports him (Ex. xxxii., cf. Deut. ix. 6, and often). The revelation of Jehovah was not first made to Israel in Egypt, Jacob was his "servant" (xxviii. 25, xxxvii. 25), as well as Abraham (xxxiii. 24); and the prophet supposes the state of the people in Egypt to be very much their state in his own day: they knew Jehovah, but they had abandoned him for idols which they refused to forsake (xx. 5). It is possible that Ezekiel may judge the past history of his people from the point of view of his own attainment in religious knowledge; he may regard the worship at the high places, though meant by the people for service of Jehovah, as nothing better than Canaanitish heathenism; and looking at the darker side of the people's history and regarding the nation as a moral personality (xx. 30—44), he may not advert to much that deserved to be excepted from his sweeping charge of apostasy. The nature of the prophetic discourse has always to be taken into account. Its object was to shew to Jacob his transgressions (Mic. iii. 8; Jer. xxviii. 8). The judgment of the prophets on the people in every age was not a comparative but an absolute one. They condemn the people because they fall short of the ideal which they themselves perceive to be true. They also represent this shortcoming as a declension and forsaking of a position formerly attained. This latter part of the prophetic judgment has been thought by many to be scarcely historical: their own ideal which they contrast with the popular religion is always true, but their verdict on the people, it is thought, would have been fairer if, instead of charging them with declension, they had blamed them for backwardness and slowness of attainment. The written history of Israel is so greatly occupied with external events that it affords little insight into the religious condition of the people before the prophetic age, but the unanimous feeling of the prophets as to the past must have a historical ground. Ezekiel's judgment on Jerusalem (ch. xvi.) finds a parallel in a singular passage in Jer. xxxii. 30—35: "For this city hath been to me a provocation of mine anger and my fury from the day that they built it unto this day."

Further, the two prophets are in agreement on much else, the details of the people's sin and the issue of it. Both name the chief sin of Israel "whoredom," as had been common since Hosea, though Isaiah uses the metaphor only once (i. 21); and the figures by which Ezekiel describes it, realistic and repulsive enough though they be, in nothing exceed those used by Jeremiah (xvi. 25, 34, xxiii. 8, 17, 20, 40; Jer. ii. 23, 24, iii. 2, v. 7, 8, xiii. 27). Apart from figure, this whoredom or infidelity to Jehovah, includes two things, idolatry and alliances with foreign states, those "lovers" on whom Israel and Judah doted (xxiii. 5, 16; Jer. iv. 30). The idolatry was partly real, a worship of "other gods" (Jer. xvi. 11), the Baals or shame (xi. 13), the host of heaven (Jer. xix. 13; Ez. viii. 16), and the queen of heaven (Jer. vii. 18, xliv. 17 *seq.* cf. Ez. viii. 14). It is not certain to what deities the small shrines were erected which were to be found in every street and at the head of every way (xvi. 24, 25). Jer. xi. 13 appears to call them altars to the shame or Baal, though it might be inferred from Ez. xvi. 23 that they were dedicated to deities not native to Canaan. Besides this, however, both prophets stigmatise with the same odious name the whole service at the rural altars, on the high hills and under the evergreen trees, with its accessories of images, sun-pillars and asheras (vi. 6; Jer. ii. 20, iii. 2, 6). It is not the mere localities nor the number of the altars that arouses their aversion; it is the nature of the worship and its evil memories (Hos. iv. 13, 14; Am. ii. 7), for Ezekiel regards the rural shrines as a survival of Canaanitish paganism (xx. 27, 28). The images or block-gods (vi. 4) standing in these shrines were probably in many instances figures of Jehovah, for since the verdict of Hosea on the calf-image (viii. 6), "A workman made it, it is no God," little if any distinction was drawn between such images and others (Is. ii. 8, xvii. 8, xxx. 22). Both prophets name these objects of worship "abominations," and represent them as being placed in the house of the Lord to defile it (Jer. vii. 30, xix. 4; Ez. viii. 3 *seq.*), and as polluting the land (Jer. xvi. 18). Since Hosea foreign alliances had been stigmatised as "hiring lovers" (viii. 9, 10), and both the later prophets adopt the phraseology (xvi. 37, xxiii. 9, 22; Jer. xxx. 14; cf. Lam. i. 19). From the earliest times the prophets regard these alliances as due to a false conception of the nature of the kingdom of the Lord, and as evidence of mistrust in Jehovah (Is. vii. 9, x. 20, 21, xxx. 15, xxxi. 1); and, naturally, they were opposed to them for another reason, because the customs and idolatries of the foreign nations followed in their train (Is. ii. 6, cf. on xvi. 23 *seq.*; initial note to xxiii., and final note to xvi.).

In other details the two prophets are in harmony: they both reprobate the "bloodshed" of which Jerusalem is guilty. This "blood" was partly judicial murders (ix. 9, xxii. 6; Jer. vii. 6, xxii. 3), partly that shed in partizan conflicts within the city (xi. 7), but especially the child murder of later days (xvi. 20, 36, xx. 26; Jer. vii. 31, xxxii. 35, cf. notes on xvi. 20, xx. 25). Jerusalem is "the bloody city" (xxiv. 6, xxii. 3, 4, &c.); she has set her blood upon a rock and it cries for vengeance (xxiv. 7; Job xvi. 18). But both prophets enter into greater details regarding the sins of the people than earlier prophets were wont to do, though Jeremiah adheres more to the ancient custom of denouncing civil wrongs (vii. 5 *seq.*, xxii. 1—5), while Ezekiel descends lower and exposes the social abominations of his day (ch. xviii., xxii., xxiii., cf. Jer. ix. 2—9). In these descriptions (e.g. xxii. 1—13) he shews affinities with some parts of the Law, particularly the small code, Lev. xvii.—xxvi., and reveals how deeply the taint of Canaanitish impurity had infected the moral life of Israel, though it may not be easy to say whether what he describes be a recent outbreak of immorality due to the decaying vigour of the national life and the moral paralysis rapidly advancing to its heart, or whether the conscience of the teachers of Israel was only now awakening to the enormity of vices that had long been prevalent.—On the prophet's moral ideal compared with others cf. on xviii. 9.

The sin of Israel is universal, infecting all classes, the royal house, the priests, the prophets and the people of the land (xxii. 23—31). The time for intercession has gone by; the sword of the Lord is whetted for the slaughter (xxi.); Jerusalem, the rusted caldron, must be set upon the fire that its contents may be seethed, and that its brass may glow and its rust be molten away (xxiv.). When the catastrophe came, verifying the prophet's anticipations, his mouth was opened. The people perceived that the view taken of their history by their prophetic teachers, from Amos downwards, was just, and that they were true interpreters of the mind of their God. So the old era was closed. The prophet had now to inaugurate the new.

Like all other prophets Ezekiel, though he sees the destruction of the state to be necessary, believes in its restitution. And this restitution will be the operation of Jehovah. A complete section of his prophecies (xxxiii.—xxxvii.) is devoted to this future, in which all its details are set forth; but even in the earlier part of his Book many allusions to it occur. As early as ch. xi. the exiles are consoled with the promise: "I will gather you from the peoples and give you the land of Israel. And I will put a new spirit within you, and I will be your God" (xi. 17—20). And in xvi. 60 a new and everlasting covenant is promised to Jerusalem, under which she shall not only be restored herself, but receive her sisters Samaria and Sodom for daughters.

As in other prophets these prophecies of restitution assume a

Messianic form, a universal kingdom being promised to the house of David: "I will take of the lofty top of the cedar...in the mountain of the height of Israel will I plant it; and under it shall dwell all fowl of every wing" (xvii. 22—24). In xxi. 27 the Messiah is alluded to in the words "till he come whose right it is" (the ref. in xxix. 21 is more general, to the restoration of Israel). The passages xxxiv. 23 *seq.*, and xxxvii. 24 *seq.* are even more explicit. In the restitution the two kingdoms shall be reunited, with one shepherd over the two peoples, even the Lord's servant David (Am. ix. 11; Hos. iii. 5; Jer. xxxiii. 15). David shall be their prince for ever (xxxvii. 24, 25; Is. ix. 7). In these passages "prince" and "king" are used without distinction, and as the Messianic king is called "David" it is probable (Jer. xxiii. 5—8) that there is allusion to the Davidic house, though "David" might mean one in the spirit and power of David (cf. on xxxiv. 23, xxxvii. 25). In all these passages Ezekiel's representations are quite parallel to those of other prophets. In ch. xl. *seq.* the "prince" seems to play a more subordinate *rôle*, though there his functions in the worship of the restored community are specially referred to. Ch. xxxiii.—xxxvii. describe the reconstitution of the kingdom on all its sides: the culmination of the monarchy in the Messiah (xxxiv.); the recovery of the land and its transfiguration (xxxv., xxxvi.); the regeneration of the people, with the redemptive principles which it illustrates, such as will leave eternal impressions on the people's mind (xxxvi.); and the re-awakening of the dead nation into life and the union of all the disjointed members of the north and of the south into one living subject again, as seen in the grandiose vision of the dry bones (xxxvii.).

The conditions on man's part of entering this new kingdom appear to be stated in such passages as xviii. and xxxiii. The object of the prophet here is scarcely to vindicate the strict retributive righteousness of God or to shew how this righteousness operates at all times. The passages refer more to the future than to the present, more to how God is about to deal with men than to how he has dealt with them; and there is a certain ideal element in the delineation, as there is in all prophetic references to the coming kingdom of the Lord. Of course the general principle is sometimes stated that the righteous will be spared and the wicked perish (ix.), though in other places the judgment is represented as sweeping away all indiscriminately (xx. 45 *seq.*); and ch. xiv. 12 *seq.* depends on Jer. xv. 1 *seq.*, and is meant to shew that the wicked will no longer be spared for the sake of the righteous rather than to exemplify the strict retributive righteousness of God.

That the reference in these chapters is to the future, a future somewhat indefinite and ideal, is probable both from the parallel passage in Jeremiah and from the prophet's own language. It is in the ideal times of Israel restored that the proverb, "The fathers ate sour grapes and the children's teeth are set on edge," shall no more have currency (Jer. xxxi. 27 *seq.*); and Ezekiel's language is similar, "As I live, saith the Lord, it shall no longer be permitted to you to use this proverb in Israel" (xviii. 3). The prophet stands before a new age, and it is its principles that he reveals. His purpose is practical, to meet the conditions of the people's mind, and to awaken them to a new moral activity, in preparation for the sifting and crisis that shall try every individual mind (xxxiii. 1—6). His principles but form the background to his exhortation to repentance. He attaches them to two expressions which he had heard from the mouths of the people: "The fathers ate sour grapes and the children's teeth are set on edge" (xviii. 2), and, "Our iniquities be upon us and we pine away in them, how then shall we live?" (xxxiii. 10). To the one, which means that men are inexorably involved in the sins of their people or forefathers, he opposes the principle that every individual mind stands in immediate relation to God, and none shall perish for the sins of another, the soul that sinneth shall die; and to the other, which means that the evil past of life is irremediable, he opposes the principle that God has no pleasure in the death of the sinner, there is place for repentance. The last principle is developed with a certain theoretical completeness, which means no more, however, than that man has moral freedom to do good or evil, that he who is righteous may become a sinner, and that the sinner may turn from his evil, and that men will be judged not according to that which they have been but according to that which they are. The real point upon which the prophet's mind is operating is the spiritual relation of the individual mind to God; but like others he may not be able to keep this distinct from the external condition of the person, or as he calls it "life" or "death." At the same time the future and ideal time to which he applies his principles exonerates him from the charge of teaching a doctrine false to everyday experience (cf. notes on xviii. and xxxiii.).

This emancipation of the individual soul, whether from a doom inherited from a former generation or from one entailed on it by its own evil past, was perhaps the greatest contribution made by Ezekiel to the religious life and thought of his time. He probably reached his individualism by reflection on such events as the downfall of the state, leaving now no place for religion except in the individual mind, and on the sentiments which he heard expressed by men around him. His contemporary Jeremiah reached the same truth from another direction, from his own experience of the *inwardness* of the relation of God to men. The very nature of this relation required that the religious subject should be the individual mind.

Yet, as in the case of other prophets, Ezekiel no sooner states the conditions on man's part of entering the new kingdom than he seems to desert them. Jeremiah, after demanding of the people a radical reformation (iv. 3), pauses to ask himself, Can the Ethiopian change his skin? and his hope at last is in a divine operation: "I will write my law in their hearts...and their sin will I remember no more" (xxxi. 31—34). The transition in Ezekiel from ch. xxxiii. to ch. xxxvi. is similar. It was the hope of the prophets that the fires of the exile would purify the people, and that they would come out as silver tried in the furnace. They are constrained to confess that this hope has been disappointed: Israel will be saved, but only by Jehovah working for his name's sake (Is. xliii. 25, xlviii. 10, 11).

Ezekiel perhaps hardly saw so much of the exile as to reason in this way, but his conclusion in xxxvi. 24—29 is the same. This remarkable passage has no parallel in the Old Testament, and reads like a fragment of a Pauline epistle (final note on xxxvi.). The doctrine of the spirit of God receives fuller development in it than anywhere else in the Old Testament. Only one thing is wanting to complete this doctrine on its practical side, a statement of the means which the spirit shall use in his operations (John xvi. 14). Of singular beauty are the prophet's references to the eternal impressions which God's goodness in their history will leave on the mind of his people (xxxvi. 31, 32, xvi. 61, 63, xx. 42—44, xxxix. 26 *seq.*). Like that of Hosea and others Ezekiel's eschatology occupies itself chiefly with the destinies of Israel; the place of the nations in the regenerated world is not dwelt upon. How much is implied in the oft-repeated words, "They shall know that I am Jehovah," is not clear. Profounder conceptions of the relations of Jehovah to the nations are at least touched upon in ch. xvi. (final notes); and in one passage it is foretold that the nations will seek refuge under the rule of the Messiah (ch. xvii. 23).

The final section (xl. *seq.*) is an ideal picture of the perfection and eternal peace of Israel restored. It has been remarked that in these chapters Ezekiel supplies a programme for the subsequent development of Judaism. It is possible that a subsequent generation imposed his ideal of Israel's final state upon the historical restoration that took place under Zerubbabel and under Ezra. But such a thing was not the prophet's idea, and never came into his mind. In his view Israel's development reaches its culmination in the restoration itself, and the regeneration of the people accompanying it (cf. Is. lx.). The ritual observances which he enjoins are not the "statutes of life" elsewhere spoken of. These statutes are the moral requirements of the decalogue, practically carried out so as to exclude idolatry and the impurities often referred to (ch. xxii.); and the fulfilment of these statutes is ensured by the moral regeneration wrought by God upon the people (xi. 18—20, xvi. 60—63, xxxvi. 25 *seq.*: cf. initial note to xl. *seq.*).

INTRODUCTION.   liii

The points of contact between Ezekiel and the ritual Law have raised many interesting though complicated questions of criticism, upon which this is not the place to enter. The questions mainly relate to the age of the Law in its present written form as this has to be determined by the antiquity of some of the practices contained in it, e.g. the day of Atonement (Lev. xvi., cf. Ez. xlv. 18—20), the distinction of Priests and Levites within the tribe of Levi (Ez. xliv., cf. Deut. xviii. 1, 6—8; 2 K. xxiii. 8, 9), and the High-priesthood (on xliv. 22). Inferences from comparison of Ezekiel with the Law have to be drawn with caution, for it is evident that the prophet handles with freedom institutions certainly older than his own time. The feast of weeks (Ex. xxiii. 16, xxxiv. 22) forms no element in his calendar; the law of the offering of the firstlings of the flock is dispensed with by him; there is no gilding in his Temple, and no wine in his sacrificial libations. His reconstruction of the courts of the Temple is altogether new; and so is his provision in the "oblation" of land for the maintenance of priests, Levites and prince. On any hypothesis of priority the differences in details between him and the Law may be easiest explained by supposing that, while the sacrifices in general and the ideas which they expressed were fixed and current, the particulars, such as the kind of victims and the number of them, the precise quantity of meal, oil and the like, were held non-essential and alterable when a change would better express the idea. The prince is left to regulate some of these things at his own discretion (xlvi. 7, 11). The affinities of Ezekiel with the small code, Lev. xvii.—xxvi., are remarkable both in subject and in some parts in phraseology (Lev. xxvi.). The differences, however, are too important to admit the view that he is the author of this code; and the question whether he had some parts of it at least before him in a written form is a very complicated one.

Of more interest than the question, What amount of the Law was known to Ezekiel in writing? is the other, How much of it was familiar to him in practice? It is evident that the ritual as it appears in his Book had long been a matter of consuetudinary law. He is familiar not only with burnt, peace and meat offerings, but with sin and trespass offerings (xlv. 17). All these are spoken of as things customary and well understood (xlii. 13, xliv. 29—31); even the praxis of the trespass offering is so much a thing familiar that no rules are laid down in regard to it (xlvi. 20). The sin and trespass offerings are little if at all alluded to in the ancient extra-ritual literature, but the argument from silence is a precarious one, for Ezekiel himself, when not precise, uses the comprehensive phraseology "burnt offerings and peace offerings" (xliii. 27). The people's dues to the priests are also so much customary that no rules are needful to regulate them (xliv. 30). Ezekiel is no more a "legislator" than he is the founder of the Temple.

The affinities in language between Ezekiel and the ritual law are scarcely literary, they arise from the fact that the writers move among the same class of conceptions, and, in Ezekiel's case at least, from the fact that these conceptions have long ago created for themselves a distinct phraseology. The question of interest is, how ancient the conceptions are. In the literature outside the Law little light is cast on the history of the priesthood or ritual or on the class of conceptions prevailing in priestly circles. The prophets, while furnishing abundant evidence of the existence of a sumptuous ritual, shew little sympathy for it, and reveal more the popular perversion of priestly conceptions than their legitimate meaning. Sparse as historical allusions are they suffice to shew the antiquity of the conceptions, e.g. the sacredness of blood (1 Sam. xiv. 33), the distinctions of clean and unclean (1 Sam. xxi. 4), and the atoning virtue of sacrifice (1 Sam. iii. 14, xxvi. 19). It is evident that two streams of thought, both issuing from a fountain as high up as the very origin of the nation, ran side by side down the whole history of the people, the prophetic and the priestly. In the one Jehovah is a moral ruler, a righteous king and judge, who punishes iniquity judicially or forgives sins freely of his mercy. In the other he is a person dwelling among his people in a house, a holy being or nature, sensitive to every uncleanness in all that is near him, and requiring its removal by lustrations and atonement. Those cherishing the latter circle of conceptions might be as zealous for the Lord of hosts as the prophets. And the developments of the national history would extend their conceptions and lead to the amplification of practices embodying them just as they extended the conceptions of the prophets. A growth of priestly ideas is quite as probable as a growth of prophetic ideas. That the streams ran apart is no evidence that they were not equally ancient and always contemporaneous, for we see Jeremiah and Ezekiel both flourishing in one age. At one point in the history the prophetic stream was swelled by an inflow from the priestly, as is seen in Deuteronomy, and from the Restoration downwards both streams appear to coalesce[1].

[1] Commentaries referred to in the following notes are, Hävernick, 1843, Hitzig, 1847, Ewald, 1868 (Trans. 1880), Keil, Trans. 1876, Reuss, 1876, Smend, 1880. Cornill, *Das Buch des Proph. Ezechiel*, 1886, a reconstruction of the Text. Schrader, *Die Keilinschriften und das Alte Test.*, is referred to as *KAT* (now translated by Whitehouse). Boettcher, *Proben Alttest. Schrifterklärung*, 1833, and *Aehrenlese*, vol. 2, 1864. Besides the valuable discussions in Driver, *Introduction*, 1891, and in Kuenen, *Onderzoek*, II. 1889, the following are contributions to the exposition of Ezekiel: Cornill, *Der Prophet Ezechiel*, 1882; Kühn, *Ezechiel's Gesicht vom Tempel*, 1882; Plumptre, "Ezekiel: an Ideal Biography," *Expositor*, 1884; Valeton, *Viertal Voorlezingen* (third lecture), 1886; Arndt, *Die Stellung Ezechiel's*, 1886; Meulenbelt, *De Prediking van den Profeet Ezechiel*, 1888; Gautier, *La Mission du Prophète Ezéchiel*, 1891. Horst, *Leviticus xvii.—xxvi. und Hezekiel*, 1881 (critical). Also the Essays of Klostermann, *Stud. u. Krit.*, 1877, and Kuenen, *Modern Review*, 1884.

THE BOOK OF THE PROPHET
EZEKIEL.

Now it came to pass in the thirtieth year, in the fourth 1
month, in the fifth *day* of the month, as I *was* among

FIRST DIVISION, CH. I.—XXIV., PROPHECIES OF THE DESTRUCTION OF THE KINGDOM.

FIRST SECTION. CH. I.—III. 21.

THE section consists of two divisions: First, Ch. I. inaugural vision of Jehovah; second, Ch. II.—III. 21, the various steps by which Jehovah, thus seen, initiated the prophet into his work.

The inaugural vision Ch. i. has two parts; (1) *vv.* 1—3, definition of the time and place of the appearance of the vision of God; and (2) *vv.* 4 —28, description of the vision itself, with its influence upon the prophet. 1—3. The manifestation of Jehovah was made to the prophet in the thirtieth year, in the fourth month, on the fifth day of the month, and in the midst of the captives by the river Chebar (*v.* 1); or, it was on the fifth of the month, in the fifth year of the captivity of king Jehoiachin, and in the land of the Chaldeans, by the river Chebar (*vv.* 2, 3). *Vv.* 1—3 appear to contain two superscriptions, one in *v.* 1, in which the prophet speaks in the first person, and which is syntactically connected with *v.* 4 *seq.*; and one in *vv.* 2, 3, in which the prophet is spoken of, his name and descent and priestly rank stated, and the thirtieth year of *v.* 1 identified with the fifth year of the captivity of Jehoiachin. The language in *v.* 1 is precisely similar to almost all the other specifications of time in the Book, e.g. viii. 1, xx. 1, xxiv. 1, xxvi. 1, xxix. 1, 17, xxx. 20, xxxi. 1, xxxii. 1, 17, xxxiii. 21, xl. 1. In two cases the phrase "and it came to pass" is not used (xxix. 1, xl. 1). If the verse stood alone the natural inference from the other dates would be that the year was the thirtieth of Jehoiachin's captivity, as in other cases, or as it is put in two instances "our captivity" (xxxiii. 21, xl. 1). The latest date mentioned in the Book is the 27th year of the captivity (xxix. 17), and it has been conjectured that *v.* 1 refers to another prophecy or vision three years later, and that *vv.* 2, 3 form the real heading. Against this, however, is (1) that the specification of circumstances and place in *v.* 1 is natural in an introductory statement, but not to be expected in any other. In point of fact it nowhere occurs after

the captives by the river of Chebar, *that* the heavens were
2 opened, and I saw visions of God. In the fifth *day* of the
month, which *was* the fifth year of king Jehoiachin's cap-

the introductory visions by which the prophet received his commission,
except in references to these visions (x. 15, 20, 22, xliii. 3). And (2)
the words "which was the fifth year" *v.* 2 evidently refer to some year
already mentioned, which is now said to coincide with the fifth of
Jehoiachin's captivity. The two parts of the superscription are
awkwardly connected, but neither of them can be wanted, though it is
quite possible that they do not appear in their original form.

The thirtieth year might refer to some event or era from which
Ezekiel reckoned. (1) As such an event the discovery of the Book of the
Law and Josiah's consequent reformation of worship (621 B.C.) already
occurred to the Chaldee translator. Between this date and 592, the
fifth year of Jehoiachin's captivity there is a period of 29 years. There
is, however, no other instance of such a kind of reckoning, nor any
evidence that the discovery in Josiah's eighteenth year was ever regarded
as an era. (2) That the prophet should refer to a Babylonian era is quite
possible, seeing he lived in Babylonia. But no such era has been
discovered. The beginning of the reign of Nabopolassar, when Babylon
became independent of Assyria, is usually dated in 625; and the fifth
year of Jehoiachin's captivity would be the thirty-third year of such an
era. (3) It is possible that the prophet might refer to the year of his
own age. The conjecture that Ezekiel, being a priest, would have
entered upon office in his thirtieth year, and that his prophetic call
coincided with this date, has little to support it, as the age at which
priests might undertake office is nowhere fixed in the Law; and the
reference to the year of the prophet's age in *v.* 1 would be extremely unnatural. Neither is there much probability in the suggestion (Klostermann, *Stud. u. Krit.* 1877) that *v.* 1 is a fragment of a longer passage
in which the prophet's history before his call was narrated. In such a
case reference to the thirtieth year of his age would certainly lose its
strangeness, but such a history would be without example, as a prophet's
life always opens with his call.

the river of Chebar] Not to be identified with the Chabor (2 Kings
xvii. 6) which falls into the Euphrates at Circesium. More probably
the Chebar was some stream much further south in Babylonia proper
(2 Kings xxiv. 15; Jer. xxix. 15, 20).

heavens were opened] In his trance the prophet saw the heavens
opened (*v.* 3).

visions of God] Might be visions given by God, or visions in which
God was seen. The expression is probably to be taken somewhat
generally, as meaning heavenly or divine visions (viii. 3).

2. *fifth year...Jehoiachin*] Jehoiachin, son of Jehoiakim and grand-
son of Josiah, reigned only three months and ten days. He is also
styled Jeconiah or Coniah, Jer. xxii. 24 *seq.*, xxiv. 1, xxvii. 20; 2 Kings
xxiv. 8. His captivity dates B.C. 597, and Ezekiel's call 592, six years
before the fall of Jerusalem.

tivity, the word of the LORD came expressly unto Ezekiel the 3
priest, the son of Buzi, in the land of the Chaldeans by the
river Chebar; and the hand of the LORD was there upon
him.

And I looked, and behold, a whirlwind came out of the 4
north, a great cloud, and a fire infolding itself, and a bright-

3. *came expressly*] Omit *expressly*. The name Ezekiel probably means "God is strong." Nothing further is known of Ezekiel or of his father Buzi. The designation "priest" appears to apply to Ezekiel, not to his father. As the prophet excludes all Levites from priestly office except the "sons of Zadok" (xl. 46, xliii. 19, xliv. 15, 16), it may be inferred that he belonged himself to this family. It appears from Jer. xxix. 1 *seq.* that among the captives carried away with Jehoiachin were both priests and prophets.

hand of the Lord] the prophetic ecstasy.

4—28. THE THEOPHANY, OR, VISION OF GOD.

This is described first generally, as a whirlwind and great cloud coming from the North, with a luminous splendour around it, due to a fire sending out continuous flashes within it (*v.* 4).

Secondly, more particularly that is described which appeared within the storm-cloud (*vv.* 5—28). This was the chariot of God, in which he rode, descending to the earth and moving from one place to another (cf. ch. x.). This chariot is represented as foursided. On each of the four sides was a living creature of human shape, with outstretched wings. Also on each of the four sides, beside each of the living creatures there was a wheel. The living creatures are not represented as having any platform or basement under them on which they stand; the wheels are usually said to be "beside" them, in ch. x. 2 "under" them. The wheels are to be conceived as at right angles to each of the four sides of the chariot, presenting their rims to the four points of the compass.

Above the heads of the four living creatures, or over their wings when horizontally expanded, was a firmament of crystal. Above the firmament was the appearance of a throne. And upon the throne the appearance of one like fire, encircled with a glory which was like the rainbow in the day of rain.

4. God appears in cloud and storm: clouds and darkness are round about him, Ex. ix. 24; 1 Kings xix. 11; Job xxxviii. 1; Ps. l. 3.

out of the north] In Ps. xxix. the theophany also comes from the north, and passes southward to the desert. The idea of the prophet can hardly be that the "place" or abode of God, from which he now comes, is situated in the northern part of the earth, for he saw "the heavens opened" (*v.* 1). In other places he refers to Eden, the garden of God (xxviii. 13, xxxi. 8, 9) for which he appears also to use the name "mount of God" (ch. xxviii. 14, 16), though without indicating any locality for it, but it would be very precarious to bring these passages

ness *was* about it, and out of the midst thereof as the colour
5 of amber, out of the midst of the fire. Also out of the

into any connexion with the present one. When Jehovah leaves the city (ch. xi. 23) his glory passes out by the East gate and stands over the "mountain which is on the East side of the city," the mount of Olives; and when he returns to the new temple he enters by the same east gate, which therefore is to remain for ever shut (xliii. 2, xliv. 2). In Is. xiv. 13 the king of Babylon resolves to seat himself in the mount of assembly, in the recesses of the north, above the stars of God; but whatever this passage means it has no reference to the God of Israel. On the other hand the idea that the theophany appears to come from the north because the north was the region from which the enemies of Israel, the instruments of God's vengeance, were to advance, is altogether to be rejected. The theophany here is not a manifestation of God specially in the character of an avenger or judge; he does not appear to the prophet as inflamed with anger. The theophany no doubt expresses the prophet's conception of God, but it is his conception of God as he is in himself and in his nature, not as he is in preparation for any signal act of judgment. This is conclusively shewn by the fact that the theophany here, and that when Jehovah appears for the destruction of Jerusalem (ch. viii.—xi.), and when he again appears to enter the new Jerusalem and make his abode in the new temple (ch. xliii.) are all identical, according to the statement of the prophet: "and the appearance was like the vision which I saw when I (? he) came to destroy the city, and like the vision that I saw by the river Chebar" (xliii. 3).

a fire infolding itself] lit. *taking hold of itself*. The meaning appears to be that the fire incessantly gave out flames or flashes. The expression is suggested by the zigzag, chainlike flash of the thunderbolt.

brightness was *about it*], i.e. about the whole phenomenon of storm and cloud; though a great cloud it was illuminated all round by the continuous flashing of fire within it.

colour of amber] Perhaps *look, glance* (Heb. eye) of amber. The word rendered "amber" is of uncertain meaning. LXX. renders *elektron*, which probably was some very brilliant metal, usually supposed to be an amalgam of gold and silver.

out of the midst of the fire] The words seem an explanation of the preceding phrase "out of the midst thereof." But this phrase more naturally refers to the whole phenomenon, as in *v.* 5. The words are wanting in LXX. and may be a gloss. If genuine they might go along with amber: like amber out of the midst of fire, as Rev. i. 15, "like fine brass burning in a furnace." This is not quite natural, neither is it natural to take "fire" here in a general sense of the great light caused by the fire (*v.* 13, ch. x. 2, 6). Probably the words are a marginal gloss referring the expression "out of the midst thereof" to the fire, while in fact it refers to the whole whirlwind and cloud. The prophet immediately proceeds to describe in detail the four living creatures, the wheels, the firmament and throne. No one of these can be the thing compared to electrum, because each of them is compared to something else. It

midst thereof *came* the likeness of four living creatures. And this *was* their appearance; they had the likeness of a man. And *every* one had four faces, and every one had four wings. 6 And their feet *were* straight feet; and the sole of their feet 7

seems that the combined effect produced by these, the look of the whole manifestation *within* the tempestuous cloud, the chariot, living creatures and the like, was a splendour like that of electrum. When the prophet looked more narrowly the general splendour resolved itself into these individual things, living creatures, wheels and so on.

5—14. THE FOUR LIVING CREATURES.

These are described as having in general the human form; they were erect and had apparently two feet (*vv.* 5, 7); they had four faces, one looking each way: the face of a man, a lion, an ox and an eagle (*v.* 10). The man's face was the front face of each, and met the eye of the beholder who looked at the chariot on any of its four sides, and thus when the chariot moved in any direction the creature on that side had the appearance of an advancing man. The living creatures had each four wings, one pair being used in flight, and the other pair covering the body (*vv.* 6, 11). The two pairs of wings were probably at right angles to one another, one pair belonging to the front and back sides and the other pair to the two lateral sides, for it is said that they had human hands under their wings on their four sides (*v.* 8). They had thus four hands or arms like those of men. Their feet, that is, their limbs were straight like those of men, but their feet proper were round like those of a calf (*v.* 7). When in motion each creature expanded one pair of wings, that is the wings on the right and left of the front face; the expanded wings of the four thus formed a square, the tips of the wings of each creature touching those of two of its fellows on the right and on the left (*v.* 11). When the living creatures stood still their wings dropped (*v.* 24).

5. *out of the midst thereof*] Most naturally, out of the midst of the whole phenomenon of the tempestuous fiery cloud, though it might be out of that splendour which was like electrum. Four "living creatures," as Rev. iv., there unfortunately rendered "beasts."

6. *had four faces*] These were a man's in front of each, an eagle's opposite to this at the back of each; a lion's on the right hand of each, and the face of an ox on the left of each. Thus four different faces were presented in each direction, so that in whatever direction the whole moved, while a man's face was presented first, those of a lion, an ox and an eagle were also encountered. In this view the four living creatures made up one creature, and each of the four was in small that which the four were combined.

7. *straight feet*] "Feet" here means limbs. These appear to have been two in number, though this is not expressly stated. The foot itself was round, or as much so as that of a calf. The word "straight" applied to the limbs means strictly "even," i.e. probably without pro-

was like the sole of a calf's foot: and they sparkled like the
8 colour of burnished brass. And *they had* the hands of a
man under their wings on their four sides; and they four
9 had their faces and their wings. Their wings *were* joined
one to another; they turned not when they went; they went
10 every one straight forward. As for the likeness of their
faces, they four had the face of a man, and the face of a
lion, on the right side: and they four had the face of an ox
on the left side; they four also had the face of an eagle.
11 Thus *were* their faces: and their wings *were* stretched up-

tuberance or knot such as a knee-joint would be. The living creature
did not need to turn, and its leg was without joints.

they sparkled...burnished brass] that is, the limbs of the creature, not
the living creature itself, Dan. x. 6, "his arms and his feet like in colour
to burnished brass" (Rev. i. 15). "Colour" (lit. eye) is probably
"glance" (*v.* 4).

8. Each living creature appears to have had four hands or arms, cf.
ch. x. 21. The last words of *v.* 8 must be joined with *v.* 9: "and their
faces and their wings, of them four—their wings were joined one to
another; they turned not when they went, they went every one straightforward." The meaning is that as each creature with his outstretched
wings formed one side of the square his wings touched or were joined to
those of two other creatures, one on his right and another on his left.
The words "they turned not" refer to the faces. The above sentence
is very awkward, and the whole is given by LXX. in a much shorter
form: *v.* 8 and the faces of them four *v.* 9 turned not when they went,
they went every one straightforward. The clauses in *v.* 9 (Heb.) correspond respectively to *vv.* 11, 12.

10. Read as R. V., *and as for the likeness of their faces: they had the
face of a man; and they four had the face of a lion on the right side*, &c.
The right side is that of the living creature, not of the beholder.

11. *Thus* were *their faces*] This rendering is perhaps just possible,
particularly if present text in xlvii. 17, 18, 19 be accepted (which most
scholars, however, alter according to *v.* 20). The words are rather to
be omitted (with LXX.); or "inwards" (penīmah) is to be read for
"their faces" (penêhem) with Wellh. and attached to *v.* 10—*the face
of an eagle inwards*, i.e. towards the centre of the chariot. The same
change is required ch. xl. 22, 26.

wings were *stretched upward*] Or, **and their wings were outstretched
above.** This was their appearance when in flight; each creature stretched out one pair of wings above, while the other pair covered its body.
The wings being expanded horizontally would be nearly on a level with
the head of the living creature, hence the "firmament" is said to be
over the heads of the living creatures or over their expanded wings (*vv.* 22,
23). The next clause reads literally: *everyone* (of the living creatures)
had two wings joining everyone (of the living creatures to the others).

ward; two *wings* of every one *were* joined one to another, and two covered their bodies. And they went every one 12 straight forward: whither the spirit was to go, they went; *and* they turned not when they went. As for the likeness 13 of the living creatures, their appearance *was* like burning coals of fire, *and* like the appearance of lamps: it went up and down among the living creatures; and the fire was bright, and out of the fire went forth lightning. And the 14 living creatures ran and returned as the appearance of a flash of lightning.

If the text be correct it states somewhat elliptically what is said with more precision in *v.* 23 (cf. *v.* 9), viz. that the tips of the expanded wings of one creature touched the tips of the wings of two other creatures, on his right and on his left.

12. *went straight forward*] i.e. in the direction to which the living creature's face was turned. The chariot had four sides facing the four quarters of the heavens; on each side of the chariot was a living creature whose principal face, the human, looked in the same direction as the side of the chariot on which it stood. Thus the whole, the chariot and living creatures, presented exactly the same front to each of the four directions, and there was no need to "turn." See what is said of the wheels, *v.* 15 *seq*.

whither the spirit was to go] The "spirit" is the directing impulse. It did not belong to the individual living creatures but to the whole manifestation composed of living creatures, wheels, and the like.

13. A slight correction of the text after LXX. is necessary in this verse, which should read as R.V. marg., **and in the midst of the living creatures was an appearance like burning coals of fire, like the appearance of torches**. The description of the living creatures themselves was finished in *v.* 12; in this verse the prophet refers to the fire that was between them (ch. x. 2, 6 *seq*.). The whole phenomenon represents not only a chariot on which Jehovah rides, but also a throne on which he sits and a place where he abides. Hence as in Is. vi. there is an altar with fire. With the idea of Isaiah, however, the prophet has combined the other that coals of fire accompany the manifestation of Jehovah (Ps. xviii. 13), and the altar fire gives out flashes like the lightning. This again has suggested the combinations in Rev. vi. 9, viii. 3—5.

14. Jerome testifies that this verse was not found in LXX. The verse both in regard to terminology and construction is untranslateable. The word rendered "ran" has no existence, and that translated "flash of lightning" is equally unknown. Attempts have been made to amend the verse by substituting for "ran" a real word, "went out" (yaço for raço), and the ordinary word "lightning" for the unknown term so rendered (baraḳ for bazaḳ). But such a movement to and fro

15 Now as I beheld the living creatures, behold one wheel upon the earth by the living creatures, with his four faces. 16 The appearance of the wheels and their work *was* like unto the colour of a beryl: and they four had one likeness: and their appearance and their work *was* as it were a wheel in

or backwards and forwards of the living creatures is not suggested by anything said of them hitherto or afterwards; they could not move without a movement of the whole chariot, and such a darting about like lightning offends against that which is becoming in the divine manifestation. The verse is probably a marginal amplification of *v.* 13, due to the error which had already crept into that verse, making it apply to the living creatures instead of to the fire between them.

15—21. THE FOUR WHEELS.

The prophet saw four wheels beside the four living creatures, one wheel beside each creature. The wheels touched the ground, and were all alike, having the appearance of tarshish-stone. The construction of each appeared as if a wheel were within a wheel, that is, each of the four wheels looked like two wheels, cutting each other at right angles. In this way each of the four wheels had a rim or circumference facing each of the four directions, just as the living creature had a face looking in each direction, so that toward whatever quarter the chariot moved *four* wheels seemed to be running in that direction. Their felloes were full of eyes. The movements of the wheels corresponded entirely with those of the living creatures, they went, rose, or stood still according as the living creatures did. The wheels were not inanimate, but part of the living chariot of God; the "spirit" of the living creature was also in the wheels.

15. *beheld the living creatures*] lit. *and I saw the living creatures and behold.* LXX. reads, *and I saw and behold*—precisely as ch. viii. 2, x. 1, 9.

by the living creatures] **beside**, as R.V.

with his four faces] lit. *according to,* or, *at his four faces.* LXX. reads, *to these four*, as *v.* 10, which is simpler. In the present text the "four faces" must be those of each one of the living creatures. The general sense appears to be that for each face of the individual living creature there was a wheel. The appearance would be so if the wheel really seemed two wheels cutting one another transversely. The position of the living creature was above the wheel, though the rim of the wheel might be higher than his feet (x. 2).

16. *the colour of a beryl*] Heb. *tarshish-stone,* so named from Tartessus in Spain, in which country it was found. It is the chrysolite of the ancients, the topaz of the moderns, a stone of a golden colour. Colour is "glance." The words "and their work" in first clause, and "and their appearance" in second clause are wanting in LXX.

wheel in the middle of a wheel] This was their work or construction; *each* of the four wheels (ch. x. 10) had this appearance. What seems

the middle of a wheel. When they went, they went upon 17
their four sides: *and* they turned not when they went. As 18
for their rings, they were so high that they were dreadful;
and their rings *were* full *of* eyes round about them four. And 19
when the living creatures went, the wheels went by them:
and when the living creatures were lift up from the earth,
the wheels were lift up. Whithersoever the spirit was to go, 20
they went, thither *was their* spirit to go; and the wheels
were lifted up over against them: for the spirit of the living
creature *was* in the wheels. When those went, *these* went; 21

meant is that the wheels had such a construction that they could run not only, say, east and west, as an ordinary wheel, but also (without turning) north and south. This could be in no other way than by each wheel being double, consisting of two wheels cutting one another in planes at right angles. Thus in whatever direction the chariot moved four wheels appeared to be running in that direction.

17. *they turned not when they went*] Of course they ran round on their axle, but each wheel was of such a kind that it had a rim facing all four directions, and could run in any direction. *On* their four sides should rather be, **toward**.

18. *so high that they were dreadful*] lit. *as for their rings, there was height to them and there was fear to them;* R.V. they were high and dreadful. The word "fear," however, nowhere means terribleness but always terror. Ps. xc. 11, "thy fear" is the fear due to thee, or, the fear inspired by thee. The statement also that the rings or felloes were high has little meaning, as in any case the living creatures were higher, and is strangely expressed. The text is possibly in some disorder. The main point of the verse is that the rings or felloes were full of eyes round about.

full of *eyes*] as R.V. **they four had their rings full of eyes round about.** The eye is the expression of life and intelligence (ch. x. 12).

19—21. The movement of the wheels corresponded with that of the living creatures. They were animated by the same spirit as the creatures, and were part of the whole living phenomenon. In the Book of Enoch "wheels" (Ophannim) are a class of angels, named along with Seraphim and Cherubim, ch. lxi. 10; lxx. 7.

20. *thither* was their *spirit to go*] Rather, **the** spirit, i.e. the general spirit moving the whole manifestation. The words are wanting in LXX., and are possibly an accidental repetition of those in the beginning of the verse; or they are a somewhat loose and elliptical repetition attached to "they went," in which case they should rather be rendered, *whither* the spirit was to go.

spirit of the living creature] The marg. "spirit of life" is to be deleted. The "living creature" is hardly the complex being formed by the four living creatures; the four were exactly alike, and the term is used generically (*v.* 22, ch. x. 20) to express the kind of creature.

and when those stood, *these* stood; and when those were lifted up from the earth, the wheels were lifted up over against them: for the spirit of the living creature *was* in the
22 wheels. And the likeness of the firmament upon the heads of the living creature *was* as the colour of the terrible
23 crystal, stretched forth over their heads above. And under the firmament *were* their wings straight, the one toward the other: every one had two, which covered on this *side*, and every one had two, which covered on that *side*, their bodies.

22—28. THE FIRMAMENT, AND THRONE, AND GLORY OF GOD.

Over the heads and outstretched wings of the four living creatures there appeared a firmament like crystal (*vv.* 22—25); and above the firmament an appearance as of a throne, like a sapphire stone; and upon the throne the appearance of a man (*v.* 26). From his loins upwards he had the appearance of glancing amber (electrum), and from his loins downwards of fire; and there was a splendour around him like that of the rainbow in the day of rain (*vv.* 25—28).

22. *And the likeness of the firmament*] Rather: **and there was a likeness over the heads of the living creature** (of) **a firmament.** The term "firmament" has come from the LXX. (stereōma) through the Vulgate. The verb is used of the creation of the earth, Is. xlii. 5; xliv. 24; Ps. cxxxvi. 6, and once, Job xxxvii. 18, of the creation of the heavens; and the noun is always used of the heavens. In the above passages LXX. renders "make strong," and the noun "firmament." The word "firmament" occurs only in Gen. i.; Ezek. i., x. 1; Ps. xix. 1, cl. 1; Dan. xii. 3.

the terrible crystal] Cf. Ex. xxiv. 10, "and they saw the God of Israel, and there was under his feet as it were a pavework of sapphire stone, and as it were the very heaven for clearness." In Rev. iv., which is largely indebted to Ezek. i., the crystal firmament here becomes "a sea of glass like unto crystal" (*v.* 6). The word "terrible" is wanting in LXX., which reads also *as* a firmament in the first clause.

23. were *their wings straight*] "straight" is even, level, and the reference appears to be to the upper side of the wings stretched out horizontally under the firmament. It is not meant that the firmament *rested* on the wings or heads of the living creatures, it was over them.

the one toward the other] A repetition of the statement that the outspread wings of one creature touched those of the other creatures; see *vv.* 9, 11.

on this side...on that side] In these rather obscure words "this side," "that side" do not refer to the "sides" of the individual creature, but to the positions of the different creatures, and might be rendered, "here... there," or, "respectively...respectively." It is doubtful, however, if the words can have this meaning. Probably the rendering should be: *every one had two covering them, and every one had two covering*

And when they went, I heard the noise of their wings, like 24 the noise of great waters, as the voice of the Almighty, the voice of speech, as the noise of a host: when they stood, they let down their wings. And there was a voice from the 25 firmament that *was* over their heads, when they stood, *and* had let down their wings.

And above the firmament that *was* over their heads *was* 26 *them*, even *their bodies*—the words "their bodies" giving a more exact definition of "covering them." Cf. Is. xi. 9. The statement is repeated in order to distribute it over each of the creatures, although the *and* before the repetition is less usual (ch. iv. 6, xlvi. 21). LXX. reads simply: every one had two, covering their bodies.

24. The sound of the wings of the living creatures when in flight was as the noise of many waters, as the thunder, or, as the roar of a host.

voice of the Almighty] that is, the thunder, Ps. xxix. 3; Job xxxvii. 4. The comparison to waters occurs again, ch. xliii. 2, and that to the voice of the Almighty, ch. x. 5 (God Almighty). The name Almighty (Heb. *shaddai*, of uncertain derivation) occurs alone chiefly in poetical pieces, e.g. about thirty times in Job, a few times in prophecy (Is. xiii. 6 = Joel i. 15; Ezek. i. 24) and in the idyl of Ruth (i. 20, 21); but in prose has the word "God" (El) prefixed to it (Gen. xvii. 1).

the voice of speech] Rather: **noise of tumult**, as Jer. xi. 16, where the word appears to occur again. The rendering "speech," though that of the ancient versions, assumes a different pronunciation. As to noise of a "host" cf. Is. xvii. 12, Joel ii. 5. LXX. omits all the comparisons except the first, as in ch. xliii. 2, unless Jerome is to be followed, who vindicates here for LXX. what is usually ascribed to Theodotion.

25. *from the firmament*] Rather: **above the firmament**, as R.V. The voice must be that of him who sat above the firmament. This voice might be supposed to command the movement or halting of the chariot, though such a voice seems nowhere else referred to. The verse repeats the last words of the preceding verse and otherwise is almost identical in words with the following one, and possibly it may not be original.

they stood, and *had let down*] Render as *v.* 24, *when they stood, they let down* their wings. The last words might be rendered: *their wings dropped;* so *v.* 24.

26—28. THE THRONE AND GLORY OF HIM WHO SAT ON IT.

Above the firmament was the appearance of a throne, like a sapphire stone; and on the throne the appearance of one sitting, from his loins upwards like amber, and from his loins downwards like fire. And round about him was a glory like the rainbow in the day of rain.

26. The rendering of LXX. makes the sapphire stone different from

the likeness of a throne, as the appearance of a sapphire stone: and upon the likeness of the throne *was* the likeness
27 as the appearance of a man above upon it. And I saw as the colour of amber, as the appearance of fire round about within it, from the appearance of his loins even upward, and from the appearance of his loins even downward, I saw as it were the appearance of fire, and it had brightness round
28 about. As the appearance of the bow that is in the cloud in the day of rain, so *was* the appearance of the brightness round about. This *was* the appearance of the likeness of the glory of the Lord. And when I saw *it*, I fell upon my face, and I heard a voice of one that spake.

the throne, the former being the ground on which the throne was placed. A special pavement, however, above the firmament, on which the throne was set is scarcely to be expected and is hardly the meaning of Ex. xxiv. 10. Comp. Ez. x. 1.

27. *the colour of amber*] the glance (lit. eye). See *v.* 4.

fire round about within it] This is the natural sense, but "round about" and "within it" seem to contradict one another. The rendering "fire that is enclosed round about," and therefore brighter by contrast with what surrounds it (Hitz.), expresses a thought more ingenious than probable, and assumes an unlikely construction. The clause is wanting in LXX.

it had brightness round about] Rather: **and a brightness round about him**, viz. him who sat on the throne (*v.* 28).

28. The prophet speaks with great reverence. What he saw was the "appearance" of a throne and of one sitting on it and of a rainbow; he does not venture to say that he saw these things themselves. The rainbow is an element borrowed from the theophany in the storm cloud. It expresses the glory surrounding the throne of God. The traditional idea that the rainbow is the token of covenant grace has little to support it. The rainbow in the cloud was a memorial of God's covenant with nature that he would not again destroy the world with a flood, it had no relation to any covenant of redemption.

the glory of the Lord] probably refers to the particular glory of the appearance sitting on the throne and the rainbow colours around him, not to the whole manifestation embracing the cherubim and wheels. The "glory of the Lord" is described as leaving the cherubim and standing elsewhere, e.g. ch. ix. 3, x. 4. At the sight of this glory the prophet fell upon his face.

That which ch. i. presents is a theophany, a manifestation of God to the prophet. It is not a vision of the cherubim nor of anything else, but of God. The cherubim, wheels, firmament and throne are all subordinate, they have no meaning in themselves, they merely help to suggest what God is who thus manifests himself.

The vision is a composite one, made up of a number of elements drawn from several sources. There is first the idea that God moves and descends to the earth upon the cherubim (Ps. xviii. 10, civ. 3); he is borne upon them. It is possible that the storm-cloud on which Jehovah rode and in which his presence was enshrouded became personified into a being, which bore him on its wings. Cf. Is. xix. 1. But if this was the origin of the idea of the cherub, the conception of the cherubim as "living creatures" had become established long before the time of this prophet, as appears from Gen. iii. 24. The cherubim being thus the means of Jehovah's manifesting himself, that on which he was borne and moved, wherever they were seen Jehovah was known to be present. They were the means and the tokens of his manifestation. Hence two great cherubims were placed by Solomon in the Debîr, or innermost shrine of the temple. On these Jehovah was enthroned: he dwelt or sat upon the cherubim (Ps. xcix. 1, lxxx. 1).

Again in Isaiah's vision of "the King, the Lord of hosts" (ch. vi.) there is naturally a palace and a throne. The palace, though the heavenly one, is the counterpart of the earthly one or temple, and has a hearth or altar fire. Both the fire and the throne reappear in Ezekiel's vision in an amplified form. The fire is no more a mere hearth from which a hot coal might be taken, it shoots forth flames and thunderbolts. This is a combination of the phenomena of the theophany in the thunderstorm with the representation of Isaiah. Similarly Isaiah's idea of Jehovah's throne being in the heavenly temple has been amplified by Ezekiel with various details. There was seen by him the appearance of a firmament like crystal, and above the firmament the appearance of a throne like a sapphire stone. Jehovah in his manifestation carries heaven, the place of his abode with him. Further his throne is surrounded by the glories of the rainbow, another element borrowed from the theophany in nature. In this way there is in the vision a combination of the theophany in nature with Jehovah's self-manifestation to men among his people in redemption.

And finally according to his manner the prophet has descended to elaborate details in describing the various elements of the manifestation, the cherubim, the wheels and the like. In all the prophet's symbols throughout his Book the idea is first and the symbol but the expression of it. In the present case, however, the whole phenomenon is a vision of God, and the ideas which the symbols express are ideas in regard to God. This is evident so far as the wheels, the firmament, the throne and the like are concerned. But the same is true of the cherubim. These are hardly yet independent beings, with a significance belonging to themselves. They are still half in the region of symbol, and what meaning they have has to be transferred to God, whose movements they mediate, just as much as that of the wheels or the flashing fire. At a later time the "wheels" were represented as beings and in the Book of Enoch are a class of angels.

It may be assumed that in the prophet's mind each detail of the symbolism expressed some idea, though it may not be possible now to interpret the details with certainty. The firmament and throne represent Jehovah as God of heaven, God alone over all, the omnipotent. The fourfold character of the living creatures, their wings, and the wheels which moved in all directions, and presented the same face to every quarter, suggest the power of Jehovah to be everywhere present. The wheels, called whirl or whirling thing (ch. x. 13), may have been suggested by the sweeping whirlwind and tempest in which Jehovah moves. The conception of velocity which they express does not differ greatly from that of ubiquity expressed by their number. The eyes of which they and the living creature were full are symbols of life and intelligence. That the faces of each creature are four is but part of the larger general conception that the creatures are four in number. The four faces, that of a man, a lion, an ox, and an eagle or vulture are the highest types of animal life. It is possible that to the prophet's mind these types represented four different attributes. Probably the cherubim in the temple had the human face, though this is not expressly stated. The prophet represents those carved on the walls of the new temple as having two faces, those of a man and a young lion (ch. xli. 18). Jehovah is frequently compared to a lion. He is also called by a name which may be an epithet of the ox. The symbol of the ox was a familiar one, 1 Kings vii. 25, 29, 36, x. 19. Ezekiel may have been familiar with the mixed animal forms seen in the Assyrian temples, though it is scarcely necessary to suppose him influenced by these. The multiplication of details in his symbols is so characteristic of him that he may be credited with the creation of the four faces himself, just as of the four hands and four wings of the cherub. Cf. Is. vi. 2. The derivation and meaning of the word cherub is uncertain. It has been supposed that the word has been found in Assyrian, but this also is not quite certain. See Schrader *KAT* on Gen. iii. 24. Cf. the art. in *Encyc. Brit.* (Cheyne); Riehm in his *Bible Dictionary*, and *Stud. u. Krit.*, 1871, also his paper, "De Natura &c. Cheruborum," 1864. And, *Die Lehre des A. Test. über die Cherubim*, von J. Nikel, Bres. 1890.

CH. II. 1—III. 21. THE STEPS OF THE PROPHET'S INITIATION INTO HIS MISSION BY JEHOVAH WHO HAD THUS APPEARED TO HIM.

The points touched upon are the character of those to whom he is sent, and the position he is to take in regard to them; and his dependence upon Jehovah for all that he is to speak and in all that he is to do. The passage has these divisions:—

(1) Ch. ii. 1—7. The character of those to whom the prophet is sent. They are the rebellious house of Israel, who have rebelled against Jehovah, they and their fathers unto this day. The prophet is not to fear them but speak Jehovah's words unto them.

(2) Ch. ii. 8—iii. 3. Symbolical representation of the communication of Jehovah's words to the prophet. He is commanded to eat the roll of a book presented to him in Jehovah's hand.

(3) Ch. iii. 4—9. Thus furnished with the words of the Lord, the prophet is commissioned to go to the house of Israel. He is not sent to foreign nations, which would not understand him, but to the house of Israel. They will understand but will not listen.

(4) Ch. iii. 10—15. Particularly he is sent to them of the captivity of Tel-abib.

(5) Ch. iii. 16—21. Now among the exiles there is brought home to

vv. 1—4.] EZEKIEL, II. 15

And he said unto me, Son of man, stand upon thy feet, 2
and I will speak unto thee. And the spirit entered into me 2
when he spake unto me, and set me upon my feet, that I
heard him that spake unto me. And he said unto me, Son 3
of man, I send thee to the children of Israel, to a rebellious
nation that hath rebelled against me: they and their fathers
have transgressed against me, *even* unto this very day. For 4
they are impudent children and stiff hearted. I do send thee

his mind the precise nature of the office he is to fill; he is to be a
"watchman," warning everyone—the sinner that he may turn from his
sin, and the righteous lest he fall from his righteousness.

1—7. THE REBELLIOUS PEOPLE TO WHOM THE PROPHET IS SENT.

1. *Son of man*] Better, **child of man.** The phrase is used over
ninety times, and expresses the contrast between the prophet, as one of
mankind, and the majesty of God, whose glory he had just seen.
   stand upon thy feet] At the sight of the great glory of God the prophet had fallen to the ground (ch. i. 28). He is bidden stand on his
feet. Not paralysis before him is desired by God, but reasonable
service. The prophet's falling down was natural, yet a condition unfit
for God's purposes, and not desired by him to continue. Those whom
he calls to his service are his fellow-workers, who may look upon his
face. It is man erect, man in his manhood, with whom God will have
fellowship and with whom he will speak—stand upon thy feet "that I
may speak with thee."
   2. *And the spirit*] Perhaps, **and sp'rit.** It is not said directly to be
the spirit of God, though in a sense this is meant. Spirit is strength,
or, rather the source of strength and life; a power or energy entered into
the prophet and set him on his feet. But this power was external to
him and came from God. While God desires man to stand erect before
him and be man, it is only spirit from God that enables man to take this
right place.
   3. *to a rebellious nation*] Rather, **nations.** First the people are
called the children of Israel, then described more particularly as "nations," the reference being either to the two houses of Israel, the north
and south, or to the people as a whole considered as consisting of larger
divisions (Ps. cvi. 5) as "peoples" is used elsewhere (Hos. x. 14; Deut.
xxxiii. 19). There hardly lies in "nations" any suggestion that they
were as the "heathen." The general character of the people is
described as "rebellious;" and they had "rebelled" continuously
throughout all their history, they and their fathers; cf. ch. xvi. 23.
Israel is a moral person, with an unbroken identity all through its
history; and its disposition has been uniformly disobedient—it is a
rebellious house.
   4. *for* they are *impudent children*] Rather, **and the children are
impudent and stiffhearted, to whom I send thee.** The "children"

unto them; and thou shalt say unto them, Thus saith the
5 Lord God. And they, whether they will hear, or whether
they will forbear, (for they *are* a rebellious house,) yet shall
6 know that there hath been a prophet among them. And
thou, son of man, be not afraid of them, neither be afraid of
their words, though briars and thorns *be* with thee, and thou
dost dwell among scorpions: be not afraid of their words,
nor be dismayed at their looks, though they *be* a rebellious

are the present generation, who are like their fathers. Outwardly they
are "impudent," lit. *hard in face*, resolute and whose eyes do not quail
before one that opposes them; and within they are *strong of heart*,
unyielding and stubborn in will and feeling. The word here used of
the face is said of the heart, ch. iii. 7, and the term applied to the
heart is said of the face and forehead, ch. iii. 8. More often the term
used of the face is applied to the neck, "stiffnecked" (Ex. xxxiii. 3).
For the idea comp. Is. xlviii. 4, "I knew that thou art obstinate, and
thy neck is an iron sinew, and thy brow brass."

Thus saith the Lord God] lit. the Lord Jehovah. The word "Jehovah" was pronounced *Adonai*, "Lord," and when Adonai, Lord, actually stood in the text, Jehovah was pronounced God, *Elohim*. In A.V. "God" is then printed in small capitals. This is what the prophet shall say on his part: "Thus saith the Lord Jehovah;" he shall announce himself a prophet from Jehovah, bearing his word. And the people shall eventually know that a prophet has been among them (*v.* 5). By various omissions LXX. reads *vv.* 3, 4 in a shorter form: Son of man I send thee to the house of Israel, who provoke me; who have provoked me they and their fathers unto this day, *v.* 4 and thou shalt say unto them, &c. This reading certainly reflects a more natural Hebrew sentence than our present text.

5. *for they* are *a rebellious house*] Whether they hear or whether they forbear—and they will forbear, for they are a rebellious house—yet shall they know that a prophet has been among them. The future shall bring this home to them. They shall see the prophet's words come to pass, and shall know that a true messenger from the Lord spoke to them. The true prophet, the man who has anything to announce from God, may assure himself that, however he be received when he speaks, in the long run he shall receive his due and be recognized for what he was.

6. Thorns and briars, that pierce and wound, and scorpions, that strike and sting, are figures for intractable and injurious men. The prophet must understand their character and not fear them.

though they be *a rebellious*] Rather: **for they are.** Stubborn opposition and injurious words may be expected of them; such conduct has always characterized them, for they are a rebellious house. Be not deceived by them nor dismayed before them, as if they were in the right and not thou; thou art in the right, and thou shalt speak my words to them (*v.* 7).

house. And thou shalt speak my words unto them, whether 7
they will hear, or whether they will forbear: for they *are*
most rebellious. But thou, son of man, hear what I say 8
unto thee ; Be not thou rebellious like *that* rebellious house:
open thy mouth, and eat that I give thee.

8.—III. 3. THE PROPHET'S INSPIRATION.

Being commanded to speak God's words to the people, the prophet is next assured by a symbol, a book given him to eat, that God's words shall be given him.

8. *be not rebellious*] In addition to the positive command, "hear what I say unto thee," the prophet is warned not to refuse and be rebellious like the house of Israel. There was need for this double peremptoriness of the command. The instinctive act of men before any great undertaking of the kind set before the prophet is to shrink from it. Jonah fled that he might escape from the task laid on him; Moses and Jeremiah both entreated that they might be relieved of it. The work was both arduous and painful: painful because it was against his own people that the prophet had to speak ; and arduous because leading to opposition and persecution. There is no easy situation in God's service. Had the prophet refused the great commission he would have rebelled like Israel. And no doubt Israel's rebellion was also from an arduous and painful commission, whether we regard its task to have been to walk before God as his people, or to be the prophet of Jehovah to the nations, being entrusted as Ezekiel was with his word. In both Israel may be said to all appearance to have failed. Yet not wholly: the Servant of the Lord, the true Israel of God, existing all throughout the history of the outward Israel, could say, "the Lord opened mine ear, and I was not rebellious, nor turned away back" (Is. l. 5).

The command to hear and not be rebellious is hardly to be confined to the act of eating the Book, but refers rather to the whole ministry of the prophet, although, considering that the Book was a symbol of all God's words to him, and his eating it a symbol of his receiving them, the sense in either case is the same (cf. *v.* 10).

The passage suggests: (1) the divine source of that which the prophet was to say and has said—"eat that I give thee" (*v.* 8), "a hand stretched out and in it a book" (*v.* 9), "he made me eat that roll of a book" (iii. 2). (2) The definiteness of it: it was a roll of a book (ii. 9), although its contents were large, the roll being written both in front of the page and on the back. This was unusual, rolls being generally written only on one side. The idea is reproduced, Rev. v. 1. (3) The nature of the contents—"lamentation and mourning and woe" (ii. 10). The prophet was made well aware of the nature of the contents as well as of their extent, "he spread the roll before me" (ii. 10). (4) The prophet made the Book his own, he "did eat it," and it "filled" him (iii. 3). And having eaten it it was in his mouth as honey for sweetness. The sweetness was not due to this, that, though the Book contained bitter things at the first, at the end it was filled with promises which

9 And when I looked, behold, a hand *was* sent unto me;
10 and lo, a roll of a book *was* therein; and he spread it before me; and it *was* written within and without: and *there was*
3 written therein lamentations, and mourning, and woe. Moreover he said unto me, Son of man, eat that thou findest; eat
2 this roll, and go speak unto the house of Israel. So I
3 opened my mouth, and he caused me to eat that roll. And he said unto me, Son of man, cause thy belly to eat, and fill thy bowels with this roll that I give thee. Then did I eat *it;* and it was in my mouth as honey for sweetness.

4 And he said unto me, Son of man, go, get thee unto the
5 house of Israel, and speak with my words unto them. For

were sweet, for there was written thereon lamentation and woe; it was due rather to this that the things written were from God, whose bitter word is sweet. "Thy words were found and I did eat them; and thy word was unto me the joy and rejoicing of mine heart, for I am called by thy name (am thine and thy servant) Jehovah, God of hosts," Jer. xv. 16. Cf. Ps. xix. 10; Rev. x. 8—11.

The prophet's idea of what we call his inspiration is perhaps more precise and stringent than that of Isaiah. In the inaugural vision of the latter prophet (ch. vi.), "there flew one of the seraphim having a live coal in his hand,...and he laid it on my mouth and said, Lo, this hath touched thy lips and thine iniquity is taken away." Immediately on this an impulse seized the prophet to enter upon the service of God: I said, Here am I, send me. The forgiveness of sin and moral purity, carrying with it sympathy with the great King and the ministering spirits around him, and elevating the man into that exalted sphere of life, seemed enough to Isaiah to constitute him a prophet. There was in him a strength and power of character which needed only the removal of the moral hindrance to set them free. But both Jeremiah and Ezekiel were weaker men. Ezekiel as is usual with him makes Jeremiah his model, and he can hardly be said to go beyond that prophet: "The Lord said unto me, whatsoever I command thee that shalt thou speak. Then the Lord put forth his hand and touched my mouth. And the Lord said unto me, Behold I have put my words in thy mouth," Jer. i. 7—9. Both the later prophets represent themselves as receiving not merely the "word" but the "words" of Jehovah.

4—9. THE PROPHET SHALL BE STRENGTHENED TO PERFORM HIS HARD TASK.

Having taken in the "words" of the Lord (*v.* 4) there opens up before the prophet a general view of the mission he is sent upon. It is an arduous one. The difficulties are not of a superficial kind. He is not sent to foreign nations, who would not understand his words, but to Israel. They can well understand, but they will not listen. Their

thou *art* not sent to a people of a strange speech and of a
hard language, *but* to the house of Israel; not to many 6
people of a strange speech and of a hard language, whose
words thou canst not understand. Surely, had I sent thee
to them, they would have hearkened unto thee. But the 7
house of Israel will not hearken unto thee; for they will not
hearken unto me: for all the house of Israel *are* impudent
and hardhearted. Behold, I have made thy face strong 8
against their faces, and thy forehead strong against their foreheads. As an adamant harder than flint have I made thy 9
forehead: fear them not, neither be dismayed at their looks,
though they *be* a rebellious house. Moreover he said unto 10

refusal to listen unto him is but an example of their life-long refusal to
listen unto God. They are resolute and obstinate in their disobedience,
but the prophet shall be made more resolute than they.

5. *a strange speech*] lit. *deep of lip* (or speech) *and heavy of tongue.*
The former expression perhaps refers to the inarticulateness with which,
to one unacquainted with their language, foreigners appear to speak;
and the other to the thickness of their utterance. The first half of the
expression occurs again Is. xxxiii. 19, a people of deep speech, so that
thou canst not perceive; and the second half is said of Moses, Ex. iv. 10.

6. *many people*] Rather: **peoples**, i.e. different foreign nations.

Surely, had I sent thee] More exactly: **surely if I sent thee...they
would hearken.** There is some difficulty about the construction, but
the sense is sufficiently clear. The heathen have a greater susceptibility
for the truth than Israel, which has acted more wickedly than the
nations (ch. v. 6, 7, xvi. 48, 51. Cf. Jer. ii. 10, 11). Others would
render: but I send thee to them (Israel), *they* will understand thee.
The last words, however, cannot mean "understand thee;" they mean
"hearken unto thee," as *v.* 7, where the phrase is the same.

7. *impudent and hardhearted*] See on ch. ii. 4.

9. *harder than flint*] Cf. Jer. v. 3, "they have made their faces
harder than a rock; they have refused to return."

though they be *a rebellious*] Rather: **for they are.** See ch. ii. 6.
What gave the prophet invincible courage in the face of the opposition
of the people was in the main the assurance that he was sent of God,
that God was with him, and that his word was given him to speak.
Comp. Is. l. 7, "For the Lord Jehovah will help me, therefore shall I
not be confounded; therefore have I set my face like a flint, and I know
that I shall not be ashamed."

10—15. The Prophet's Particular Mission to the Exiles at Tel Abib.

Though Ezekiel's mission, like that of all the prophets, was to the
house of Israel as a whole (*v.* 5), yet immediately his work lay among the

me, Son of man, all my words that I shall speak unto thee
11 receive in thine heart, and hear with thine ears. And go, get thee to them of the captivity, unto the children of thy people, and speak unto them, and tell them, Thus saith the Lord GOD; whether they will hear, or whether they will for-
12 bear. Then the spirit took me up, and I heard behind me a voice of a great rushing, *saying*, Blessed *be* the glory of the

captives in the midst of whom he lived. It is remarkable, however, how little reference is made in his prophecies to the particular circumstances of the exiles. The attention of the prophet, as well as those around him in captivity, seems to have been engrossed by the events occurring in Palestine, and especially in the capital. And the truths spoken by him, though uttered in the ears of the exiles, bear reference to all Israel. Though he occasionally draws a distinction between those left in the land and the exiles carried away with Jehoiachin, of whom he was one (ch. xi. 15), in general he regards the exiles as representatives of Israel, and feels when addressing them that he is speaking to the whole house of Israel. In the gradual defining of his task more clearly these exiles are now referred to. He is bidden go to them of the captivity (*v.* 11), and he came to them of the captivity to Tel Abib. And now that he is entering upon his ministry there comes to him: (1) the command anew to hear and receive into his heart the words that God shall speak to him (*v.* 10). (2) next the command to announce himself as a prophet of the Lord: thus saith the Lord (*v.* 11). And (3) with this command comes the sense of the divine impulse carrying him forward to his service: then the spirit lifted me up...and I came to them of the captivity (*vv.* 12, 14, 15).

12. *the spirit took me up*] See on ii. 2. This "lifting up" by the spirit must be interpreted according to ch. viii. 1—3, it was part of the trance. The great theophany or vision of God in ch. i. was not an external phenomenon which the prophet beheld with his actual eyes, it was a vision which he saw, being in a trance. The same is true of all the words heard by him, and all the actions done in ch. ii., iii., they took place in the spirit, not outwardly. See after *v.* 21.

I heard behind me] The prophet had been in the presence of the theophany (ch. i.) during all that has hitherto been narrated (ch. ii. 1—iii. 12), and thus when he was lifted up and carried away it seemed to him that he left the theophany *behind* him.

a great rushing] The word is used of an earthquake, and of the roar of battle (Is. ix. 5, confused noise); also of the rattling of chariots (Jer. xlvii. 3; Nah. iii. 2). In ch. xxxvii. 7 it is said of the sound of the coming together of the dry bones, but it appears nowhere employed of the noise caused by voices speaking.

Blessed be *the glory of the Lord*] According to the present text these words were uttered with a sound like "a great rushing," though no intimation is given who they were who uttered the words. But (1) the

Lord from his place. *I heard* also the noise of the wings 13
of the living creatures that touched one another, and the
noise of the wheels over against them, and a noise of a great
rushing. So the spirit lifted me up, and took me away, and 14
I went in bitterness, in the heat of my spirit; but the hand
of the Lord was strong upon me.

Then I came to them of the captivity *at* Tel-abib, that 15
dwelt by the river of Chebar, and I sat where they sat, and

phrase "blessed be the glory of the Lord" has no parallel; and it is hardly admissible to take the "glory of the Lord" as equivalent to "the Lord" or "the name of the Lord" or even his "glorious name" (Ps. lxxii. 19). Even the fact that the "glory" is distinct from the divine chariot, which it may leave (ch. ix. 3), and that a voice may come from where it is (xliii. 6) is hardly sufficient to justify such an expression. (2) It is natural to take the "great rushing" of this verse to be the same as that in v. 13, where it is the roar of the wings of the living creatures and the wheels when the chariot is in motion. (3) With the present text the exclamation "Blessed," &c., might come from the cherubim. There is no other passage in the prophet where the cherubim are represented as praising God, although the seraphim do so in Is. vi., and the living creatures in Rev. iv., and this might possibly be the meaning, particularly as the reading "Blessed," &c., is the only one known to the versions. Luzzatto, and independently of him Hitzig, proposed to read: *when* the glory of the Lord *rose up* from its place; cf. ch. x. 5, 19, xi. 22, 23. The reading implies a change of only one letter.

13. I heard *also the noise*] More fairly: **and the noise.** The words seem to state the cause of the great rushing sound in v. 12, it came from the wings of the living creatures touching one another when they flew, and from the wheels. Cf. ch. i. 9, 11, 23.

14. *in bitterness*] i.e. indignation, or anger, Judg. xviii. 25 (angry fellows), 2 Sam. xvii. 8. Similarly "heat of spirit" is fury or wrath. The prophet was lifted up into sympathy with God and shared his righteous indignation against Israel. Again Jeremiah is his model: "Therefore I am full of the fury of the Lord; I am weary with holding in: Pour it out upon the children in the street and upon the assembly of young men together," Jer. vi. 11. LXX. omits "bitterness."

but the hand] Rather: **and** (or, for) the hand. See on ch. i. 3. Cf. Jer. xv. 17, "I sat not in the assembly of them that make merry, nor rejoiced; I sat alone because of thy hand; for thou hast filled me with indignation."

15. The name Tel-abib means possibly, Hill of corn-ears, or shortly, Cornhill; but see against this Frd. Del. *Heb. Lang.* p. 16. Names compounded with the word Tel, hill, are very common. The place is not otherwise known.

and I sat where they sat] This is the Heb. marg. (Ķri); the text is as R.V., "and to where they dwelt." The passage is almost certainly cor-

16 remained there astonished among them seven days. And it came to pass at the end of seven days, that the word of

rupt. Most probably the words: "that dwelt by the river Chebar, and" should be omitted: then I came to them of the captivity **to Tel-abib where they dwelt**; and I sat there astonied among them seven days.

astonished among them] R. V. *astonied*, i.e. dumb and motionless. Ezr. ix. 3, 4, "And when I heard this word I rent my garment and my mantle, and sat down astonied," Dan. ix. 27, xi. 31. There was enough in the prophet's circumstances to produce a conflict of feelings in his mind—the sin of Israel, who were yet his own people; the task before which he stood, and his close and awful communications with heaven. The simple feeling of bitterness and indignation which filled his mind when he newly left the presence of God became broken into a tumult of feelings when he saw the face of men. Zeal for God becomes tempered and humanized in actual service. Ezekiel felt himself a prophet a moment ago, now he feels himself a watchman (*v.* 17 *seq.*). Comp. the pathetic story of Samuel and Saul, 1 Sam. xv. 25—31.

seven days] Job's friends "sat down with him upon the ground seven days and seven nights; and none spake a word unto him; for they saw that the affliction was very great." The week was the first large division of time, and the long period of motionless silence expresses the strength of the prophet's emotions. Ezra sat in stupor only until the evening.

16—21. MORE PRECISE DEFINITION OF THE PROPHET'S APPOINTMENT: HE IS SET TO BE A WATCHMAN.

So soon as the prophet is face to face with the exiles, and is able to see the sphere and materials of his work, he receives a more precise account of his position—he is appointed a watchman or sentinel. The watchman stands on his watch-tower to observe, and his office therefore is to *warn*, should danger be seen approaching. Is. xxi. 6, "Thus saith the Lord, Go set a watchman, let him declare what he seeth." Jer. vi. 17, "Also I set watchmen over you and said, Hearken to the sound of the trumpet, but they said, We will not hearken;" Hab. ii. 1; comp. 2 Kings ix. 17—20. The appointment of Ezekiel as watchman was not a change upon his original appointment as "prophet" (ch. ii. 5), it is only a more precise definition of it. The term, which had already been used by Jer. (vi. 17), expresses the duties and part of a prophet of this age. Ezekiel entered on his prophetic career with his ideas as to the course of events to come fixed and matured. The fall of Jerusalem was a certainty. And his true place was in the midst of a people whom this great calamity had overtaken. The destruction of the state was not the end of Israel or of the kingdom of God. Israel would be gathered again, and the kingdom of God reconstituted. But it would be on new principles. God would no more deal with men in the lump and as a state, he would deal separately with each individual soul (ch. xviii.). The destruction of the former state, however, was not the final judgment. Before the new kingdom of God arose men would have to pass through a new crisis, and to pass through it as individual persons, and the issue

the LORD came unto me, saying, Son of man, I have made 17
thee a watchman unto the house of Israel: therefore hear
the word at my mouth, and give them warning from me.
When I say unto the wicked, Thou shalt surely die; and 18
thou givest him not warning, nor speakest to warn the
wicked from his wicked way, to save his life; the same
wicked *man* shall die in his iniquity; but his blood will I
require at thine hand. Yet if thou warn the wicked, and he 19
turn not from his wickedness, nor from his wicked way, he
shall die in his iniquity; but thou hast delivered thy soul.
Again, When a righteous *man* doth turn from his righteous- 20
ness, and commit iniquity, and I lay a stumbling-block

of this crisis would be "life" or "death" to them. It is in this full
sense that Ezekiel speaks of the wicked dying and the righteous living.
To "live" is to be preserved and enter the new kingdom of God, to
"die" is to perish in the crisis and be excluded from it. The idea of
a "watchman" implies danger imminent (ch. xxxiii. 1—6), and the
coming crisis is the ideal danger before the prophet's mind. Hence the
part of the watchman is to warn men in regard to this coming sifting of
individual souls, and to prepare them for it. The idea is part of the
prophet's individualism, his teaching regarding the freedom and responsibility to God of the individual mind (ch. xviii., xxxiii.). Hence
the watchman warns all classes of men, the wicked that he may turn
from his evil lest he "die," and the righteous that he may be confirmed
in his righteousness and "live." The watchman's place is behind the
destruction of the old state and in front of the new and final kingdom of
God, for the reconstruction of which he labours. This place is given
him in ch. xxxiii.

18. *When I say unto the wicked*] The watchman spies danger approaching, so the prophet receives intimation from the Lord (*v.* 17).
This intimation given to the prophet is represented as a threat spoken
directly to the wicked. If the prophet as a watchman perceive this
danger of death to the wicked and fails to warn him, the wicked shall
die for his own sin indeed, but his blood will be upon the watchman.
He that fails to save life kills; and blood will be required of him, of
every man's hand the blood of his brother. Prov. xxiv. 11, 12,
"Deliver them that are carried away unto death...If thou sayest, Behold, we knew not this, Doth not he that weigheth the hearts consider
it?"

in his iniquity] Perhaps: *through* his iniquity. It is of the nature
of sin that it is made the instrument of its own punishment, Job viii. 4.
"Warning" will naturally be of many kinds, suitable to those warned;
some may be deterred and others allured from their evil.

20. *I lay a stumbling-block*] i.e. something over which he shall fall
and perish; Lev. xix. 14, "Nor put a stumbling-block before the blind."
When God prepares such a stumbling-block for the righteous who has

before him, he shall die; because thou hast not given him warning, he shall die in his sin, and his righteousness which he hath done shall not be remembered; but his blood will 21 I require at thine hand. Nevertheless if thou warn the righteous *man*, that the righteous sin not, and he doth not sin, he shall surely live, because he is warned; also thou hast delivered thy soul.

sinned, unless he is warned he will fall and be broken, and his blood will be on the prophet.

21. The case of the righteous is even more complex and perilous for the watchman than that of the wicked, though it might not be thought so. The wicked has to be warned to turn from his evil, and so has the righteous if he sins. But the righteous has also to be warned, in ways that are suitable, lest he fall into evil. Only when the righteous is seen maintaining his righteousness unto the end can the watchman feel that he has delivered his own soul in regard to him. Like a ship laden with a precious freight he has to be anxiously piloted into the haven.

This passage, ch. i. 1—iii. 21, is not quite easy to estimate. There are two questions suggested by it, viz., first, how does the prophet represent the occurrences? and secondly, how is his representation to be interpreted? In answer to the first question, it is evident that all narrated from ch. i. 1 to iii. 12 or iii. 15 belongs to the prophet's trance. The vision of God in ch. i. and his inspiration under the symbol of eating a book, as also his commission generally, all belong to the sphere of ecstatic experience. This is manifest so far as the great Theophany of ch. i. is concerned; but all that follows, ch. ii. 1—iii. 12, was transacted in the presence of this Theophany, and like it must be regarded as part of the trance or ecstasy. In iii. 12, however, it is said that the vision of God went up from him, and if this were to be interpreted as ch. xi. 24, 25, where the same vision of God departed from him and he reported all he had seen during it to them of the captivity, we might suppose that the ecstasy was over. In ch. iii. 15, it is said that he came to them of the captivity. It is added, however, that the spirit took him up and carried him there, that he sat among the captives dumb seven days, and that the hand of the Lord was strong upon him. All these expressions are usual to describe prophetic ecstasy, e.g. viii. 3, xxxvii. 1, xl. 2. In the passage ch. xxxiii. 22, "the hand of the Lord" might describe something less than the full ecstasy, though this is not certain. After the prophet's statement that he came to them of the captivity to Tel-abib, we might have expected some account of his ministry among them, but nothing of this is given; what follows is a more precise definition of his office, which is to be that of a watchman. The representation appears to be that the place by the river Chebar where the vision of God was seen by him was at some distance from Tel-abib, and that when the vision went up from him he "came" to the captives at that place. This "coming," however, is described as being taken up and carried by the spirit, terms usual to describe prophetic ecstasy, and it almost seems that the prophet does not strictly distinguish between what he did in the spirit, in vision, and what he did bodily and in reality.

If the last remark be true, it may suggest how the prophet's representation is to be interpreted. On the one hand the extent and variety of the incidents represented as occurring in the trance, the things seen and heard, the prophet's emotions and the like, hardly form any argument against the literal reality of the account. The rapidity of the mind's operation in such conditions is well known. Naturally the thoughts of God and of the people and of himself and all the general ideas described as presenting themselves in the vision are not to be regarded as absolutely new to the prophet's mind. They had many times before occurred to him, at least separately and in fragments. But now in a more exalted frame of mind than usual they are reproduced in connexion with one another and with a power to influence the mind to action which they had not before possessed. This is how the inaugural vision of all the prophets, Isaiah (vi.) and Jeremiah (i.) as well as Ezekiel are to be understood. It is probable that the prophet was subject to trances, for the vision is but a higher form of the mental condition which clothes its thoughts in symbols, and this symbolism is characteristic of the whole Book.

On the other hand the presumption is that the various incidents described did not occur precisely as represented. It is probable that these three chapters cover the earliest part of the prophet's ministry, extending over a considerable period. But in the first place he has condensed the events and experiences of this period, the thoughts and feelings which he had in his intercourse with the exiles and the reception he met with at their hands, into the present brief statement. And secondly, he has thrown the experiences of this period into a symbolical form; the thought of God, of the divine majesty and greatness, which filled his mind at first and constantly, is presented under the form of the Theophany (ch. i.) always present with him. The feeling that he was a true prophet of God, commissioned to declare his will, and that the divine presence was always with him is symbolised in the other actions which follow (ii. iii.). At a later time looking back over this early period, recalling his vivid sense of God, of his presence with him directing all he did and inspiring all his words, he has presented the religious meaning of the period under the symbol of a trance in which he was in the immediate presence of God (cf. viii.—xi.).

SECOND SECTION. CH. III. 22—VII. 27.

The second section of the Book contains these parts:

(1) Ch. iii. 22—27. A preface in which the prophet is commanded to confine himself to his own house, and abandon for a time his public ministry.

(2) Ch. iv. 1—v. 4. A series of symbols representing the siege of Jerusalem, the scarcity during it, the pollution of the people in exile among the nations, and the terrible fate of the inhabitants on the capture of the city.

And the hand of the LORD was there upon me; and he

(3) Ch. v. 5—17. Exposition of these symbols.
(4) Ch. vi. Prophecy against the mountains of Israel, the seats of Idolatry.
(5) Ch. vii. Dirge over the downfall of the state.

CH. III. 22—27. THE PROPHET ABANDONS PUBLIC EXERCISE OF HIS MINISTRY.

The verses form the preface to ch. iv.—xxiv., all the prophecies that bear upon the fate of Jerusalem and its inhabitants, up to its fall. The prophet under the "hand" of God goes out into the "valley," and the same Theophany appears to him as at the first by the river Chebar. He is in communication with the same great God, and all his actions are determined by his commands. According to the interpretation put upon ch. i. 1—iii. 21 above, he had exercised his office of watchman among the people, speaking to them publicly in the name of the Lord, for some time. Possibly the time was not very long, for this passage comes in under the same general date as all that preceded it. His ministry had met with resistance; the people would not hear, as he had anticipated. A public ministry among them was fruitless; the burden of his preaching to them was distasteful. He warned them against their idolatries, from which they would not turn; and foretold the downfall of their city and country, a thing which they heard with an incredulous ear and would have none of. Therefore the prophet feels instructed of God to cease to be a public "reprover" (*v.* 26) for a time. The people refuse to believe his words when he speaks of the downfall of their beloved city, they will be constrained to believe events when they happen; and then the prophet, his word being confirmed, will speak with boldness, his mouth will be opened, and he will be able to impress upon more ready listeners the lessons of God's righteous providence. His silence meantime is not an absolute one, it is only a change of method; but this so-called silence continues till the actual destruction of the city. In ch. xxiv. 27, it is said, "in that day (when tidings come of the city's fall) shall thy mouth be opened and thou shalt speak and be no more dumb, and they shall know that I am the Lord;" and in ch. xxxiii. 21 *seq.*, when those that escaped came bringing tidings, saying, the city is fallen, it is said: "then my mouth was opened, and I was no more dumb." No motive is assigned for the change in his prophetic method, beyond the unwillingness of the people to listen, "for they are a rebellious house" (*v.* 26). At the same time as a prophet of the restoration with its new principles (ch. xviii., xxxiii.), a watchman appointed to speak no more to the state but to individual men, his ministry proper could not commence till the state had fallen. See note on ch. iii. 17.

22. *the hand of the Lord*] A trance or ecstasy from the Lord. It is probable that the prophet's retiring to the "valley" was merely transacted in vision. He felt himself transported away from the presence of

said unto me, Arise, go forth into the plain, and I will there talk with thee. Then I arose, and went forth into the plain: 23 and behold, the glory of the LORD stood there, as the glory which I saw by the river of Chebar: and I fell on my face. Then the spirit entered into me, and set me upon my feet, 24 and spake with me, and said unto me, Go, shut thyself within thine house. But thou, O son of man, behold, they 25 shall put bands upon thee, and shall bind thee with them, and thou shalt not go out among them: and I will make 26 thy tongue cleave to the roof of thy mouth, that thou shalt be dumb, and shalt not be to them a reprover: for they *are* a rebellious house. But when I speak with thee, I will open 27 thy mouth, and thou shalt say unto them, Thus saith the Lord GOD; He that heareth, let him hear; and he that forbeareth, let him forbear: for they *are* a rebellious house.

men to some lonely retreat, and there the glory of the Lord seemed again to stand before him (cf. ch. viii. 1—3).

into the plain] R.V. marg. *the valley*. This is scarcely a general term, meaning the plain country in opposition to Tel-Abib, where the exiles dwelt; some particular place in the neighbourhood called the "valley" is meant. According to *v.* 23 the place was not identical with the other by the river Chebar, where the Vision of God first appeared to the prophet. Cf. ch. xxxvii. 1 *seq.*

24. *shut thyself within thy house*] The words are not to be pressed to mean more than abstention from the exercise of his ministry in public. Cf. ch. viii. 1, xi. 25, xiv. 1 &c.

25. *they shall put bands upon thee*] that is, the exiles, as the words "thou shalt not go out among them" imply. The expression can hardly be merely equivalent to the *pass.*, "cords shall be put upon thee" (Sep. Vulg.). The language is a figure for the restraint of opposition (ch. iv. 8).

26. *I will make thy tongue cleave*] The restraint imposed by the opposition of the people is acquiesced in by God, it is part of his purpose. His providence will meantime be the best teacher of the people. The prophet's "dumbness," however, is compatible with much speaking at least by signs to those who will hear. He is "dumb" in the sense of the Psalmist, "I was dumb, not opening my mouth, because thou didst it" (Ps. xxxix. 9; Is. liii. 7; cf. Ezek. xxiv. 27, xxxiii. 22).

27. Eventually the prophet's mouth will be opened, his word will be confirmed, and he will no more have to speak to incredulous ears. (Comp. ch. xxix. 21). During the existence of the kingdom all the prophets from Amos downward had stood in opposition to the mass of the people. Their teaching whether on religion or on policy ran counter to the inclinations of the multitude. The fall of the state, however, which they had so unanimously predicted gave them consideration in the eyes of the people, and led even the unthinking masses to feel that they were true interpreters of the mind of God and of his government. Passages like ch. xxxiii. 10, "Our transgressions and our sins are upon us, and we pine away in them; how then should we live?" shew the change taking place in the people's thoughts, and how they were coming round to take that view of their history which this prophet, as well as his predecessors, had so persistently inculcated. It is not easy to form any clear conception of the prophet's ministry during the years preceding the fall of the state, but such passages as the above suggest the kind of thoughts which he expresses under the symbols of "dumbness" and "opening of the mouth." It is unnecessary to say that the "binding" of the prophet here (*v*. 25), which continues till the fall of Jerusalem, is quite different from the binding in ch. iv. 8, which lasts only for a period of days, and is a symbol of Israel bearing its iniquity in exile.

CH. IV. 1—V. 4. SYMBOLICAL ACTIONS REPRESENTING THE SIEGE AND CAPTURE OF JERUSALEM, AND THE FATE OF THE INHABITANTS—THEIR SLAUGHTER AROUND THE CITY AND DISPERSION AMONG THE NATIONS.

(1) Ch. iv. 1—3. Symbol of the siege of Jerusalem.
(2) Ch. iv. 4—8. Symbol of the people's bearing their iniquity in the siege and exile.
(3) Ch. iv. 9—17. Symbol of scarcity during the siege, and pollution among the nations.
(4) Ch. v. 1—4. Symbol of the slaughter of the inhabitants around the city on its capture, and their dispersion over the world.

The following symbols seem as much designed for the prophet himself as for the people. He is commanded of God to perform them. They represent the thoughts which under the inspiration of God filled his mind at this time, regarding the fate of the city and the state. His thoughts as well as those of the captives around him are occupied with Jerusalem, for Jerusalem is almost Israel. Being far from it and from its inhabitants his imagination is fertile in devising means to bring it before him. Sometimes he portrays a picture of it on a brick, and sometimes he is carried by a lock of his head through the air and set down in the midst of it, in order to behold its iniquities (ch. viii. 1). Though some of the symbols here might have been actually represented, others could not, such as lying on his side immoveable for many days (iv. 4—8), and probably none of them were actually performed. The prophet no more drew a sketch of Jerusalem upon a brick than he was carried by the hair of his head from the Chebar to Palestine. At the same time there is more than mere literary artifice. The symbols stood actually before his imagination, and the narration of them to the people would convey the same instruction as the actual representation of them (*v*. 3, cf. ch. xi. 25). The three symbolical actions (ch. iv.) must go on simultaneously, viz. the siege, the lying on his side or bearing iniquity, and eating bread by measure and in pollution. For the three are the same thing under different aspects; first the actual siege, then the mean-

vv. 1—3.] EZEKIEL, IV. 29

Thou also, son of man, take thee a tile, and lay it before 4
thee, and pourtray upon it *the* city, *even* Jerusalem: and 2
lay siege against it, and build a fort against it, and cast a
mount against it; set the camp also against it, and set
battering rams against it round about. Moreover take thou 3

ing of this, God's judgment for sin, and finally some of the ways in
which this judgment is felt, straitness of food and water, and dispersion
and defilement among the nations.

CH. IV. 1—3. SYMBOLICAL SIEGE OF JERUSALEM.

The prophet is commanded to take a brick (it is to be supposed still
soft) and portray on it a city, even Jerusalem. Around the city he is
to draw representations of siege operations, towers, a mound, camps
and battering-rams. Between him and the city he is to set an iron
plate to represent an iron wall. The determination of the besiegers is
shewn by his attitude, he sets his face against the city. All this is
symbol of a hard siege, carried on with great determination and apparatus against a lofty city.

1. *take thee a tile*] or, brick. The brick would be such as those
found in the ruins of the cities of Mesopotamia, covered with figures and
inscriptions, engraved on them when still moist. Libraries of such bricks
have been found by explorers in this region, and deciphered. For *the*
city read a city.

2. *a fort against it*] The word is always used in the sing., though
sometimes rightly rendered *forts* (2 Kings xxv. 1), as the term is the
name of a *class* of offensive siege works. The work was probably a
species of tower, of which a number might be erected "round about"
the walls (2 Kings xxv. 1), and was used as a station for archers, or to
discharge projectiles from (cf. LXX. ch. xvii. 17). Towers of this kind,
manned by archers are seen on the Assyrian bas-reliefs. Layard, *Nin.
and Bab.* p. 149.

cast a mount] The "mount" or mound was an embankment raised
till the besiegers standing on it were on a level with the top of the wall
and able to command the streets of the city, cf. Lam. iv. 18. See Is.
xxxvii. 33; Jer. vi. 6, xxxii. 24.

set the camp] set camps, detachments of soldiery.

battering *rams*] These were beams of wood with a head of iron,
suspended by chains or ropes from a cross plank, and swung with great
force by a number of men against the walls to batter them down. The
term "round about" indicates that they were applied to different parts
of the wall, perhaps where it might be thought weakest. It is not
probable that the siege works were also engraved upon the brick. The
latter rather by its elevation above the ground represented the city, and
the siege works would be upon the ground, if we are to suppose them
anywhere. But as the whole is a creation of the imagination it may be
doubtful if the prophet was so precise or consistent as to put to himself
the question where the siege works were placed.

unto thee an iron pan, and set it *for* a wall of iron between thee and the city: and set thy face against it, and it shall be besieged, and thou shalt lay siege against it. This *shall be a sign to the house of Israel.*

4 Lie thou also upon thy left side, and lay the iniquity of

3. *an iron pan*] As marg. *plate*, i.e. griddle on which cakes were fired (Lev. ii. 5). This common article the prophet is to set up between him and the city to represent an iron wall. As the plate is said to be an iron wall between him and the city it is most natural to interpret it of the powerful fortifications of Jerusalem (Ew.). It might, however, be a symbol of the implacable and iron severity of the siege, which itself but shews the inexorable grasp which the judgment of God has taken of the city. The word *it* in the end of the verse refers to the city; and the prophet plays the rôle of besieger.

All this is a sign to the house of Israel of what shall come to pass. Comp. ch. xii. 11.

4—6. SYMBOL OF THE PEOPLE'S BEARING THEIR INIQUITY.

In the former symbol the prophet carried on the siege, representing the besiegers; here he changes his part and represents the besieged. This symbol is shewn contemporaneously with the former, of which it is but the inner side. He is commanded to lie first on his left side for a great number of days; thus he bears the iniquity of the Northern Kingdom. To bear the iniquity means to endure the punishment due to it. When the prophet is said to bear the iniquity of Israel, the meaning is that in his action he is a sign or symbol of the house of Israel bearing its iniquity. Lying on his side, held down as with cords (*v.* 8) and unable to turn he represents Israel pressed down and held in the grasp of the punishment of its iniquity. The left side represents the Kingdom of Israel, which lay to the left or north. The number of days during which the prophet lies on his side corresponds to the number of years during which Israel shall be bound under the weight of its iniquity (*v.* 5). Secondly, having finished the days for the Northern Kingdom the prophet has to lie on his right side forty days to represent Judah also bearing its iniquity for forty years. The right side is suitable to Judah, which lay on the south or right. The prophet being unable to lie on both sides at once has to lie first on one and then on the other. It is obvious, however, that the symbolism here is not quite exact. Israel and Judah bear the penalty of their iniquity for part of the time simultaneously. The period of bearing iniquity ends for both at the same moment, when both are restored together as the prophet hopes. Consequently Judah's forty years are concurrent with the last forty years of Israel's chastisement. The whole period is not $390+40=430$, but 390 in all for Israel and the last 40 of that period for Judah. See on *v.* 6.

4. *lay the iniquity...upon it*] The meaning seems to be that as when one lies on his side it bears his weight, so this laying of the prophet's weight upon his side is a symbol of the weight of punishment

the house of Israel upon it: *according to* the number of the days that thou shalt lie upon it thou shalt bear their iniquity. For I have laid upon thee the years of their iniquity, according to the number of the days, three hundred and ninety days: so shalt thou bear the iniquity of the house of Israel. And when thou hast accomplished them, lie again on thy right side, and thou shalt bear the iniquity of the house of Judah forty days: I have appointed thee each day for a

which shall be laid on Israel for its iniquity. Others propose to alter the pointing and read: *and I will lay* the iniquity of the house of Israel *upon thee*. The alteration is unnecessary.

thou shalt bear their iniquity] To "bear iniquity" is a standing expression meaning to bear the punishment of iniquity. Possibly the word actually means "punishment of iniquity" in such phrases. The prophet does not bear the iniquity of Israel *instead* of Israel, as the servant of the Lord in Is. liii., his act is entirely symbolical, representing how Israel shall bear its iniquity.

5. Read with R.V., **for I have appointed the years of their iniquity to be unto thee a number of days,** even 390 days. The number of years during which the people shall bear their iniquity is symbolized by the number of days during which Ezekiel lies on his side, as is said explicitly in *v.* 6 "a day for a year."

6. In *v.* 5 the number of days for Israel is stated to be 390, and in *v.* 6 the number for Judah 40. The number 390 creates a difficulty. Several things have to be borne in mind. 1. To bear iniquity means to bear the penalty of it. The period of bearing iniquity, therefore, does not refer to the time of sinning but to the time of being punished for sin. Consequently any allusion to the period of the *duration* of the Northern Kingdom is excluded. 2. The representation in this prophet, as in all the prophets, is that the overthrow of the state is due to the sin of the people, and this overthrow with the continued state of the Exile and its hardships is the punishment of the people's sin. To be subdued by the heathen and driven into exile is for the people to have to bear their iniquity. Hence restoration is impossible until the iniquity of the people is paid off, or atoned in suffering (Is. xl. 2). Israel's bearing of iniquity comes to an end with the Restoration: "Cry unto her that her warfare is accomplished, her iniquity pardoned." 3. It is the view of all the prophets, Ezekiel included, that the Restoration will embrace all the existing captives both of the North and South, every one called by Jehovah's name (Is. xliii. 6, 7; cf. Is. xi. 12 *seq.*; Jer. iii. 12, 18; Ezek. xxxvii. 16 *seq.* &c.). And this restoration is final. 4. It follows from all this that the periods during which Israel and Judah bear their iniquity terminate simultaneously. Israel bears iniquity longer than Judah because it began to bear earlier. It is evident (cf. *v.* 9) that the whole period of bearing iniquity in exile is 390 years, not 390+40 or 430, but 350+40, the 40 years of Judah running parallel to the last 40 of Israel. The period of 40 years for Judah's exile is confirmed by

7 year. Therefore thou shalt set thy face toward the siege of Jerusalem, and thine arm *shall be* uncovered, and thou shalt
8 prophesy against it. And behold, I will lay bands upon thee, and thou shalt not turn thee from one side to another, till thou hast ended the days of thy siege.

ch. xxix. 11—14, where it is said that Egypt shall be carried into captivity 40 years by Nebuchadnezzar, and at the end of that period restored, though not to its former greatness. Forty years is the period of Chaldean supremacy; at the end of that period Babylon shall fall, a new world arise, and the captive nations shall be restored. Now the prophet cannot possibly have supposed that Israel went into exile 350 years before Judah. From the fall of Samaria (722) to the destruction of Jerusalem (586) is only 136 years. In *v.* 5 LXX. reads 190 (so *v.* 9); in *v.* 4 the reading is 150, which probably is an addition (Field's *Hex.*). The number 190 is probably the original one. It is not quite certain from what point the prophet computed, whether from the fall of Samaria (722), which is most natural, or from the deportation of the Northern tribes by Tiglath Pileser twelve years earlier; as he spoke also before the fall of Jerusalem even this point may be somewhat indefinite. Most probably he used general and round numbers, computing the time which Israel had already passed in captivity at 150 years, to which, if the 40 years still to be undergone in common with Judah be added, the whole period is 190 years.

Verses 7, 8 recapitulate *vv.* 1—6: *v.* 7, *vv.* 1—3, and *v.* 8, *vv.* 4—6. Verses 1—6 form one passage describing first the siege (*vv.* 1—3), and secondly the rigours of the siege, which are prolonged into exile (*vv.* 4—6). While enduring these hardships in siege and exile the people are bearing their iniquity. The apparent incongruity of the prophet's playing two rôles, that of besieger (*vv.* 1—3), and that of being besieged (*vv.* 4—6), could hardly be avoided if both things were to be represented.

7. *Therefore thou shalt set*] With R.V., **and thou shalt set...with thine arm uncovered.** In this verse the prophet resumes *vv.* 1—3, representing the besiegers; he sets his face towards the siege, presses it steadily and with determination; his arm is bare—the instrument with which he works unentangled and effective (Is. lii. 10); and he prophesies against the city, for all that is done to Jerusalem is but the irresistible word of the Lord against it taking effect.

8. *from one side to another*] lit. *from thy side to thy side.* Here the prophet represents those pressed by the rigours of the siege, as in *vv.* 4—6. The "days of thy siege" most naturally means the days of thy suffering siege (ch. v. 2).

9—17. SYMBOL OF SCARCITY DURING THE SIEGE AND POLLUTION IN THE DISPERSION FROM HAVING TO EAT UNCLEAN THINGS AMONG THE GENTILES.

The passage continues *v.* 8. The prophet is commanded (while lying immovably on his side in siege) to take of all kinds of grain,

Take thou also unto thee wheat, and barley, and beans, 9
and lentiles, and millet, and fitches, and put them in one
vessel, and make thee bread thereof, *according to* the number
of the days that thou shalt lie upon thy side, three hundred
and ninety days shalt thou eat thereof. And thy meat 10
which thou shalt eat *shall be* by weight, twenty shekels a
day: from time to time shalt thou eat it. Thou shalt drink 11
also water by measure, the sixth *part* of a hin: from time to
time shalt thou drink. And thou shalt eat it *as* barley 12
cakes, and thou shalt bake it with dung that cometh out of

coarse as well as fine, of everything that will still hunger, and cast them into one vessel. These are to be baked into cakes and fired with hot ashes of men's dung, though on the prophet's entreaty a relaxation of this repulsive condition is granted and he is allowed to substitute the dung of cows. These cakes are to be eaten sparingly in small quantity from time to time, and water drunk with them sparingly. And this use of the cakes so prepared is to continue all the time that the prophet lies on his side. These actions symbolize first, great scarcity and straitness during the siege (*vv.* 16, 17); and secondly, pollution from eating unclean things in the exile among the nations (*v.* 13).

9. *and fitches*] So Vulg. *viciam*, vetches. Others *spelt*, as marg. and R.V. Bread was usually made of wheat, the addition of the other coarser materials and their mixture indicate the straits to which men will be reduced in the siege and perhaps after the fall of the city; cf. Lam. v. 6, 10, "We gave the hand to the Egyptians and to the Assyrians to be satisfied with bread...Our skin was black like an oven because of the terrible famine." It is not certain that a mixture of various kinds of grain was regarded as a thing unclean, though the Law forbade sowing a field with divers sorts of seed, Lev. xix. 19; cf. Deut. xxii. 9.

three hundred and ninety] Probably 190 should be read as in *v.* 5. The language here shews that the 190 (or, 390) was the whole number, and that the 40 for Judah were not additional but included.

10. *twenty shekels a day*] Twenty shekels might be eight or nine ounces. In this country two pounds of bread is held an ordinary allowance.

11. *sixth* part *of a hin*] The hin was rather less than a gallon, and the sixth part under a quart. Both the bread and water were to be consumed from time to time, always in unsatisfying quantities.

12. It was customary in the East to use the dung of animals when perfectly dried as fuel. The hot ashes remaining from it are perfectly clean, and retaining their glow for a considerable time were used for firing cakes upon or under. See Wetzstein in Del. *Job*, p. 261 (Trans. i. p. 377). Whether the Hebrews would have considered such fuel unclean is not certain (cf. Lev. v. 3, vii. 21; Deut. xxiii. 13); the material for firing which the prophet is commanded to use would certainly be

13 man, in their sight. And the LORD said, Even thus shall the children of Israel eat their defiled bread among the
14 Gentiles, whither I will drive them. Then said I, Ah Lord GOD, behold, my soul *hath* not *been* polluted: for from my youth up even till now have I not eaten *of* that which dieth of itself, or is torn in pieces; neither came there abominable
15 flesh into my mouth. Then he said unto me, Lo, I have given thee cow's dung for man's dung, and thou shalt pre-
16 pare thy bread therewith. Moreover he said unto me, Son of man, behold, I will break the staff of bread in Jerusalem:

unclean (Deut. xxiii. 13) as well as loathsome. The command is explained in *v.* 13.

13. *eat their defiled bread*] Rather: **eat their bread unclean.** This is the meaning of the symbol: the food which the people shall eat among the nations will be unclean. In a pathetic passage of Hosea it is said: "they shall not dwell in the Lord's land; but Ephraim shall eat unclean food in Assyria. They shall not pour out wine offerings to the Lord, neither shall their sacrifices be pleasing unto him; their bread shall be unto them as the bread of mourners, all that eat thereof shall be polluted; for their bread shall be for their appetite; it shall not come into the house of the Lord" (ch. ix. 3, 4 R.V. marg.). A foreign land was in itself unclean (Am. vii. 17), no presence of Jehovah sanctified it; all food eaten in it was also common for it was not hallowed by part of it being brought into the house of the Lord and offered to him. Food eaten among the heathen was as the bread of mourners in Israel, all who partook of it were polluted. But as the words of the prophet suggest (*v.* 14) in addition to this general uncleanness the people were forced in their straits or induced to eat many things actually prohibited by the Law, such as that which died of itself or was torn by wild beasts (ch. xliv. 31; Lev. xvii. 15; Deut. xiv. 21. Comp. Is. lxv. 4). And it is natural that in the sore famine during the siege such unclean food was eaten, as indeed more terrible practices prevailed (ch. v. 10). Verse 13 appears in a shorter form in LXX., but there is no reason to regard the whole verse as a gloss.

14. *abominable flesh*] This word "abomination" is applied to the sacrificial flesh kept over till the third day (Lev. vii. 18, xix. 7), and in Is. lxv. 4 broth of "abominations" is coupled with swine's flesh. The meaning seems to be "carrion." The word occurs only these four times.

16, 17. Explanation of the symbol of eating bread by measure (*vv.* 10, 11).

16. *the staff of bread*] i.e. the staff which bread is; a common figure, ch. v. 16; Lev. xxvi. 26; Is. iii. 1; Ps. cv. 16.

It is scarcely necessary to say that the symbolical actions of this chapter were not actually performed. They naturally passed through the mind of the prophet as described, but so far as others were con-

and they shall eat bread by weight, and with care; and they shall drink water by measure, and with astonishment: that 17 they may want bread and water, and be astonied one with another, and consume away for their iniquity.

cerned they were merely narrated. The truth expressed by the symbolical action was as plain when the action was merely described as it would have been had the action been performed and seen. It is evident that the actions referred to here could not have been performed because they are represented as being done simultaneously. It is while he presses the siege with arm uncovered that the prophet also lies on his side held down by bands, bearing the sin of the people (*vv.* 5, 7, 8), and it is while lying immoveable in this condition that he prepares cakes upon the coals and eats them (*vv.* 8, 9). The prophet's symbols merely express an idea; it is only when supposed to be actually performed that inconsistencies appear.

The siege and the hardships of it prolonged into the exile—the people's bearing their sin—are the two chief ideas of the chapter. These are of course contemporaneous with one another so far, but they are spoken of separately in *vv.* 1—6, the siege in *vv.* 1—3, and the hardships of it and the exile in *vv.* 4—6. But from *v.* 7 onwards they are somewhat mixed together. Cornill reconstructs the chapter in a very drastic way with the view of keeping the two things, the siege and the exile, distinct throughout. He groups the verses as follows: first, bearing the sin of the people, i.e. the exile with its uncleanness, *vv.* 4—6, 8 (7 is a gloss), 9, 12—15; and secondly, the siege with its scarcity, *vv.* 1—3, 10, 11, 16, 17. This reconstruction of the text is too violent to have any probability. A different suggestion was made by Well. (*Hist.* p. 273, note), to the effect that in *v.* 9, 390 is the right reading (though erroneously transferred also to *v.* 5 for 190), and that the reference is exclusively to the siege, which the prophet calculated would last so long. Further, the prophet's lying on his side and being bound with bands, *v.* 8, is a different thing from his lying on his side, *v.* 5. In *v.* 5 he represented the bondage of the exile, in *v.* 8 *seq.* the straitness of the siege. This view requires that *v.* 13, which interprets *v.* 8 *seq.* of eating unclean food in the dispersion, should be struck out as a gloss. The verse certainly appears in a shorter form in LXX., though there seems no ground for considering it wholly interpolated. And it is more natural that the repulsive symbol of *v.* 12 should refer to the fact that all food eaten in exile was unclean rather than to uncleanness due to scarcity of fuel during the siege. The introduction too of a literal number of 390 days among other numbers of days which are symbolical is scarcely probable.

CH. V. 1—4. SYMBOL SHEWING THE FATE OF THE POPULATION DURING THE SIEGE AND AFTER IT, AND THEIR DISPERSION AMONG THE NATIONS.

The prophet is commanded to take a sharp sword and use it as a barber's razor. With this he is to shave off the hair of his head and

5 And thou, son of man, take thee a sharp knife, take thee a barber's rasor, and cause *it* to pass upon thine head and upon thy beard: then take thee balances to weigh, and 2 divide *the hair*. Thou shalt burn with fire a third *part* in the midst of the city, when the days of the siege are fulfilled: and thou shalt take a third *part*, *and* smite about it with a knife: and a third *part* thou shalt scatter in the 3 wind; and I will draw out a sword after them. Thou shalt also take thereof a few in number, and bind them in thy

beard. He is then to take balances in order accurately to weigh the hair into three parts. One third is to be burned in the fire within the city; a second third is to be cut to pieces with the sword round about the city; and the last third is to be strewn to all the winds, and pursued by the sword. Of these last a few were to be taken and bound in the skirts of the prophet's garment; though of these again some were to be thrown into the fire and consumed. The sense of the symbol is clear; a third part of the population shall be consumed by pestilence and famine within the city (*v.* 12); a third shall fall by the sword round about the city, on its capture; and a third shall be scattered among all nations, pursued by the sword. Of these a few shall meantime escape, but shall be subjected anew to consuming judgments.

1. *a sharp knife*] lit. sword. The term may suggest the devouring divine sword, ch. xxi. 8 *seq*.

take thee a barber's rasor] With R.V., **as a barber's razor shalt thou take it unto thee.** Two weapons are not to be taken, the sword is to be used as a razor. Isaiah (ch. vii. 20) had already said: "In that day shall the Lord shave with the razor that is hired, even with the king of Assyria, the beard and the hair of the feet." The land is likened to a man; the enemy sweeps off the population clean as the razor does the hair of the body.

balances to weigh] The divine justice is accurate, assigning to each part its destined chastisement; Jer. xv. 2, "Such as are for death to death; and such as are for the sword to the sword; and such as are for the famine to the famine; and such as are for the captivity to the captivity."

2. *third* part *in the midst of the city*] If we could suppose that the prophet were strict in his symbolism the "city" here would be that graven upon the brick (ch. iv. 1). There is no reason to suppose that he has this in his mind.

smite about it with a knife] Rather: **and smite it with the sword round about it**, i.e. around the city (*v.* 12). This is the fate of many of those who seek to escape before and after the capture of the city.

draw out a sword] Comp. Jer. ix. 16, "I will scatter them among the heathen...and will send the sword after them." Lam. i. 3, "Judah dwelleth among the heathen, she findeth no rest; all her pursuers overtook her between the straits." The phrase again Lev. xxvi. 33.

3. *few in number*] Or, "by number,"—accurately numbering them. (Is. xl. 26.) Of those dispersed a few shall meantime be preserved.

skirts. Then take of them again, and cast them into the 4
midst of the fire, and burn them in the fire; *for* thereof shall
a fire come forth into all the house of Israel.

Thus saith the Lord GOD; This *is* Jerusalem: I have set 5
it in the midst of the nations and countries *that are* round
about her. And she hath changed my judgments into 6
wickedness more than the nations, and my statutes more

4. Yet of those preserved some shall be cast into the fire and consumed.
thereof shall a fire] **therefrom**, i.e. from that remnant which is subjected to new consumption in the fire. The "fire" that goes out from this remnant must be destructive, not purifying, as in xix. 14 (cf. Jud. ix. 15; Ezek. xv. 5, xxx. 9, xxxix. 6), but the meaning is not quite clear. It is the prophet's belief that those left in the city after the captivity of Jehoiachin were more debased and wicked than those already carried away (ch. ix. 9, xi. 15). When the city is destroyed and its inhabitants come as captives among the former exiles, these when they see their wickedness will be comforted over the fall of Jerusalem, acknowledging that it was inevitable (ch. xiv. 22). Further Jehovah expresses his determination that he *shall* yet subdue Israel unto him and rule over them, though this implies purging out from among them the rebels, as of old in the wilderness of the Exodus (ch. xx. 33—38). And the prophet feels himself a watchman (ch. iii. 17); an approaching judgment looms before him, which all the people, each one for himself, will have to pass through. And the idea may be that the judgment, beginning with the inhabitants of Jerusalem, shall spread from them over the whole house of Israel.

5—17. EXPLANATION OF THE FOUR PRECEDING SYMBOLS.

Jerusalem, set in the midst of the nations and favoured of God above them all, has even exceeded them in wickedness (*vv.* 5, 6). Therefore God's judgments upon her shall be unparalleled in severity, first in the horrors of the siege, and secondly in the terrible miseries of pestilence, famine and blood that shall follow it (*vv.* 7—17).

5. *This* is *Jerusalem*] Or, *this Jerusalem*—I set it! (Ex. xxxii. 1; Ezek. xl. 45). Jerusalem is placed emphatically at the head of the sentence; the thoughts which the name suggests are then developed in the succeeding clauses.

countries that are round] Rather: **nations; and countries are round about her.** The geographical position of Jerusalem in the midst of the nations, distinct from them all, was but the external side of the exclusive favours bestowed on her by God. She should have been distinguished above the nations in righteousness, but her corruption was become deeper than theirs. Comp. on the idea of the central position of Jerusalem and Canaan, ch. xxxviii. 12—"the navel of the earth."

6. Read: **And she hath rebelled against my judgments to do wickedness more than the nations, and against my statutes.** "Judg-

than the countries that *are* round about her: for they have refused my judgments, and my statutes, they have not 7 walked in them. Therefore thus saith the Lord God; Because ye multiplied more than the nations that *are* round about you, *and* have not walked in my statutes, neither have kept my judgments, neither have done according to the judgments of the nations that *are* round 8 about you; therefore thus saith the Lord God; Behold, I, even I, *am* against thee, and will execute judgments 9 in the midst of thee in the sight of the nations. And I will do in thee that which I have not done, and whereunto I will not do any more the like, because of all

ments" is ordinances; and "they" refers to the people, who compose Jerusalem.

7—17. Because she has surpassed the nations in evil, her chastisements shall be without example in severity.

Because ye multiplied] R.V. *because ye are turbulent*. Both renderings assume an otherwise unknown verb, supposed to be derived from the noun "multitude," "tumult," &c. The existence of such a verb is improbable. The suggestion of Boett. followed by Corn. *because ye rebelled* (hamroth) is perhaps best, as *v*. 6 is then resumed. The sense of R.V. could be got by a very slight change (hamoth), cf. xxii. 5, last words; Am. iii. 9.

neither...according to the judgments] that is, the ordinances and practices of the nations. Others with Syr. would omit the neg.: *but have done according to....* The charge of the prophet, however, is that Israel had exceeded the nations in wickedness; cf. xvi. 47, 48; Jer. ii. 10, 11, "Hath a nation changed their gods, which yet are no gods?"

8. *in the sight of the nations*] The nations saw Israel's wickedness, and they shall also see her judgments, and they shall know that Jehovah is God alone.

9. *that which I have not done*] This is no mere rhetorical threat. It is possible that the miseries of the siege and exile were no greater than those endured by other nations in those days, but the same miseries may be felt more acutely. Israel was a nation fervidly patriotic, and patriotism was inspired by the glow of religion; it was also for that time a nation highly cultured; and moreover its calamities were felt to come from the hand of its own God. The feelings of the godly Israelite after the fall of the city corresponded to the prophet's words here before its fall: "Ho! all ye that pass by, behold and see if there be any sorrow like unto my sorrow which is done unto me, wherewith the Lord hath afflicted me in the day of his fierce anger" (Lam. i. 12). "See O Lord and behold, To whom hast thou done thus?" (Lam. ii. 20). "For the punishment of the daughter of my people is greater than the punishment

thine abominations. Therefore the fathers shall eat the 10
sons in the midst of thee, and the sons shall eat their fathers;
and I will execute judgments in thee, and the whole remnant of thee will I scatter into all the winds. Wherefore, as 11
I live, saith the Lord GOD; Surely, because thou hast defiled my sanctuary with all thy detestable things, and with
all thine abominations, therefore will I also diminish *thee;*
neither shall mine eye spare, neither will I have any pity.
A third *part* of thee shall die with the pestilence, and with 12
famine shall they be consumed in the midst of thee: and a
third *part* shall fall by the sword round about thee; and I
will scatter a third *part* into all the winds, and I will draw
out a sword after them. Thus shall mine anger be accom- 13
plished, and I will cause my fury to rest upon them, and I
will be comforted: and they shall know that I the LORD
have spoken *it* in my zeal, when I have accomplished my

of Sodom, which was overthrown in a moment, and no hands were laid
on her" (Lam. iv. 6).

10. *the fathers shall eat the sons*] Neither is this, as it might be,
a generality merely to suggest severe straitness. Lam. iv. 10, "The
hands of the pitiful women have sodden their own children, they were
their meat in the destruction of the daughter of my people." See
the story 2 Kings vi. 24—29; cf. Lev. xxvi. 29; Deut. xxviii. 53; Jer.
xix. 9; Lam. ii. 20.

11. *defiled my sanctuary*] The commentary on this is supplied by
ch. viii.

will I also diminish thee] The word is so rendered ch. xvi. 27,
where, however, an object follows the verb. The balance of clauses
here: I also will—and mine eye shall not spare: I also will not pity,
appears to shew that the word expresses one idea along with the
words "mine eye shall not spare." This can hardly be expressed
otherwise than: I also will withdraw mine eye and it shall not spare;
I also will have no pity. For the phrase "withdraw the eye" cf.
Job xxxvi. 7. In ch. xxiv. 14 a similar word occurs, but there with
the negative. Targ. Vulg. render "hew down," but this kind of
reading (*d* for *r*) is too familiar to be of any value. Perhaps the
reading might be: I also am *against thee* and mine eye shall not spare,
(form of "against thee" as xxi. 8, cf. here *v.* 8). Cf. ch. viii. 18.

12. Explanation of the symbol *vv.* 1—4.

13. *my fury to rest upon them*] Rather: **will quiet** (assuage, or,
appease) **my fury**. Zech. vi. 8, "have quieted my spirit in the North
country." The phrase again, ch. xvi. 42, xxi. 17, xxiv. 13.

I will be comforted] i.e. appeased by the vengeance taken on the
people's sins, cf. Is. i. 24 (the word is for hithnehamti).

in my zeal] The word, usually rendered "jealousy," expresses the

14 fury in them. Moreover I will make thee waste, and a reproach among the nations that *are* round about thee, in 15 the sight of all that pass by. So it shall be a reproach and a taunt, an instruction and an astonishment unto the nations that *are* round about thee, when I shall execute judgments in thee in anger and in fury and in furious rebukes. I the 16 LORD have spoken *it*. When I shall send upon them the evil arrows of famine, which shall be for *their* destruction, *and* which I will send to destroy you: and I *will* increase 17 the famine upon you, and will break your staff of bread: so will I send upon you famine and evil beasts, and they shall bereave thee; and pestilence and blood shall pass through thee; and I will bring the sword upon thee. I the LORD have spoken *it*.

heat of any passion, here resentment, ch. xvi. 38, 42, xxiii. 25, xxxvi. 5, 6, xxxviii. 19. Cf. ch. ii. 5, vi. 10, xxiv. 22.

14. *reproach among the nations*] Lam. ii. 15, 16, "All that pass by clap their hands at thee, they hiss and wag their head at the daughter of Jerusalem, saying, Is this the city that they called the perfection of beauty?"

15. *So it shall be*] So shall she be, i.e. Jerusalem. The ancient versions, however, give: *and thou shalt be*.

an instruction] i.e. a lesson of warning, cf. ch. xxiii. 48, "that all women may be taught (take warning) not to do after your lewdness." Cf. Deut. xxix. 23 *seq.*

16. *arrows of famine*] Cf. Deut. xxxii. 23, 24.

shall be for their destruction] as R.V., **that are for** destruction.

I will *increase*] lit. *add*, i.e. send famine upon famine upon you. On "staff of bread" cf. ch. iv. 14.

17. *evil beasts*] The three great plagues often specified are, famine, pestilence and sword (ch. xiv. 13, 17, 19), to which a fourth is sometimes added, evil beasts (ch. xiv. 15, 21, xxxiii. 27, xxxiv. 25; Lev. xxvi. 22; Deut. xxxii. 24).

In the above verses the cumulative expressions are often wanting in LXX. e.g. *v.* 11 the words "and with all thine abominations." Differences of this kind do not affect the sense, and it is unnecessary to notice them in detail.

CH. VI. PROPHECY AGAINST THE MOUNTAINS OF ISRAEL, THE SEATS OF HER IDOLATRY.

Ch. iv. v. were directed chiefly against Jerusalem, because she had rebelled against the statutes of the Lord (ch. v. 6) and because she had polluted his sanctuary with her abominations (ch. v. 11). Therefore the arrows of Jehovah's judgments shall come upon her, famine, pestilence and sword. For the same reason his judgments must over-

And the word of the LORD came unto me, saying, Son of 6
man, set thy face towards the mountains of Israel, and 2
prophesy against them, and say, Ye mountains of Israel, 3
hear the word of the Lord GOD; Thus saith the Lord GOD
to the mountains, and to the hills, to the rivers, and to the
valleys; Behold, I, *even* I, *will* bring a sword upon you, and
I will destroy your high places. And your altars shall be 4

take the land, especially the mountains, on which the high places were situated, where the idolatries and false worship were practised.

(1) *vv.* 1—7. The high places, altars and sun-images shall be utterly destroyed; the carcases of the worshippers shall fall before the idols, and their bones be scattered about them.

(2) *vv.* 8—10. A remnant shall escape and shall remember the Lord among the nations whither they are scattered, and shall loathe themselves for all the evils which they have done; and they shall know that he who spake to them was Jehovah, God alone.

(3) *vv.* 11—14. Renewal of the threat of destruction with every expression of scorn and hatred on the prophet's part for the people's doings. They shall know when their slain fall down and lie around their altars that Jehovah has done it.

2. *Son of man*] See on ch. ii. 1.

mountains of Israel] i.e. the mountain-land of Israel, but with special reference to the mountains as the seats of idolatrous worship.

3. *to the rivers*] the **ravines**; the gorges where there were streams and thick trees, and where idolatrous worship was practised (ch. xxxv. 8, xxxvi. 4, 6), cf. Is. lvii. 5, "that slay the children in the valleys (a different word) under the clefts of the rocks; among the smooth stones of the valley is thy portion; they, they are thy lot; even to them hast thou poured a drink offering, thou hast offered an oblation" (Jer. ii. 23).

your high places] The word properly means a height or hill (ch. xxxvi. 2), then a sanctuary situated on such a height (1 Sam. ix. 13), and finally any sanctuary (Is. xvi. 12, and so in Moabitish, Moab-stone, l. 3), particularly in Israel the rural sanctuaries. These sanctuaries had probably been mainly Canaanitish (Deut. xii. 2; Lev. xxvi. 30), but had been adopted by Israel and devoted to the service of Jehovah (ch. xx. 28). Along with the sanctuaries themselves no doubt much of the native religious practice was also adopted. After a long struggle these rural high places were abolished by Josiah, and public service of Jehovah confined to the temple at Jerusalem, though they grew up again under Manasseh. Even the worship of Jehovah at such sanctuaries would be very corrupt, and in the last years of the kingdom the worship of other deities was no doubt also practised. This prophet condemns all worship at the high places as "abominations." This does not appear to be with him a question of mere locality or number of sanctuaries; he considers the high places to be Canaanitish and the service at them no worship of Jehovah.

desolate, and your images shall be broken: and I will cast
5 down your slain *men* before your idols. And I will lay the
dead carcases of the children of Israel before their idols;
6 and I will scatter your bones round about your altars. In
all your dwelling places the cities shall be laid waste, and
the high places shall be desolate; that your altars may be
laid waste and made desolate, and your idols may be broken
and cease, and your images may be cut down, and your
7 works may be abolished. And the slain shall fall in the
midst of you, and ye shall know that I *am* the LORD.

4. *your images*] As marg., sun-images, i.e. symbols of the sungod, probably in the shape of a pyramid or obelisk. They stood beside the altars. So again *v.* 6.
your idols] The term used is an opprobrious or contemptuous epithet, applied to idols, though its precise meaning is doubtful. Most probably it means *block*-gods; though others connect it with the word dung (ch. iv. 12) and render dung-gods, which is less probable. The term occurs in Ez. nearly 40 times, otherwise Lev. xxvi. 30; Deut. xxix. 17; Jer. l. 2; 1 Kings xv. 12, xxi. 26; 2 Kings xvii. 12, xxi. 11, 21, xxiii. 24. These idols were probably of Jehovah for the most part.
5. The same had already been threatened by Jer. viii. 1, 2.
6. *your works*] the works of your hands, the idols. All the cumulative phrases in the verse are wanting in LXX. viz. "and made desolate," "and cease," "and your works may be abolished." The term "abolished" is lit. "blotted out." The rendering "made desolate" is probably right, though as spelled the word might mean "suffer" or "be punished," R.V. marg., "bear their guilt." The apparatus of worship in the prophet's time comprehended (1) the high place, the general name for the sanctuary, which might be a building of various degrees of simplicity or splendour, or perhaps a mere tent; (2) the altar, an essential of course of every high place; (3) the obelisk or sun-pillar, and (4) the idol, with which probably most of the rural high places were provided, as Is. ii. 8 says, Their land also is full of idols; they worship the work of their own hands. Cf. Jer. ii. 27, 28, who complains that their gods (which he describes as "stocks" and "stones") were as numerous as their cities. With this religious inventory may be compared that given by Hosea iii. 5. Ezekiel does not mention the Ashera, except in the form of the "evergreen tree" (ch. vi. 13).
7. *I* am *the LORD*] The term Jehovah is used in the later prophets to mean the true and only God. In this prophet the purpose and the effect of all the judgments on Israel is that they may know that he who inflicts them is Jehovah—God alone. The same is the purpose and effect of his judgments on the heathen—*these* learn also the same truth. But further, the redemption of Israel reveals this truth to the

Yet will I leave a remnant, that ye may have *some* that 8
shall escape the sword among the nations, when ye shall be
scattered through the countries. And they that escape of 9
you shall remember me among the nations whither they
shall be carried captives, because I am broken with their
whorish heart, which hath departed from me, and with their
eyes, which go a whoring after their idols: and they shall
lothe themselves for the evils which they have committed in
all their abominations. And they shall know that I *am* the 10
LORD, *and that* I have not said in vain that *I* would do this
evil unto them.

Thus saith the Lord GOD; Smite with thine hand, and 11
heathen fully. When the idols were cut down to the ground and the
bones of their worshippers lay scattered around them, the futility of
serving them could not but be perceived; Jer. ii. 28, "where are thy
gods that thou hast made? let them arise if they can save thee in the
time of thy trouble." Cf. Hos. ii. 7; Is. lvii. 12, 13.

8—10. A REMNANT SHALL BE PRESERVED, AND SHALL REMEMBER
THE LORD AMONG THE NATIONS WHITHER THEY ARE SCATTERED.

8. *that ye may have*] R.V. *in that ye shall have some* is better.
The original reads very awkwardly, and in LXX. the words: "yet
will I leave a remnant" are wanting. *V.* 9 seems the apodosis of *v.* 8,
*and when ye shall have them that escape the sword...*9 *then shall they
that escape of you remember.*

9. *because I am broken*] R.V. *how that I have been broken* with
their whorish heart. Such a sense as "been broken with" is altogether
impossible; and the middle sense " break for myself" is equally to be
rejected. The natural sense is: they shall remember (think of) me...*when
I have broken.* Their idolatrous heart shall be broken with their calamities, and then shall they return unto the Lord; Hos. ii. 7, "I will
return unto my first husband, for then was it better with me than now."
The present reading has probably arisen from the similar word "carried
captive" being in the copyist's mind.

and with their eyes] Read: **when I have broken their whorish
heart...and their eyes.** The harshness of the zeugma, "and their eyes,"
is relieved by the distance from " break " and the metaphorical nature of
the expression. Cf. the phrase "lifted up his eyes towards the idols,"
ch. xviii. 6, 12, 15, xx. 24, xxxiii. 25.

lothe themselves] Lit. *their faces;* a use of "face" for self, not uncommon in the later language, ch. xx. 43, xxxvi. 31; Job xxiii. 17.

11—17. RENEWAL OF THE THREAT OF DESTRUCTION BECAUSE OF
IDOLATRY.

11. *Smite with thine hand*] Ch. xxv. 6, "Because thou (Ammon)
hast clapped thine hands and stamped with the feet, and rejoiced with

stamp with thy foot, and say, Alas for all the evil abominations of the house of Israel: for they shall fall by the sword,
12 by the famine, and by the pestilence. *He* that *is* far off shall die of the pestilence; and *he* that *is* near shall fall by the sword; and he that remaineth and is besieged shall die by the famine: thus will I accomplish my fury upon them.
13 Then shall ye know that I *am* the Lord, when their slain *men* shall be among their idols round about their altars, upon every high hill, in all the tops of the mountains, and under every green tree, and under every thick oak, the place where
14 they did offer sweet savour to all their idols. So will I stretch out mine hand upon them, and make the land desolate, yea, more desolate than the wilderness towards Diblath, in all their habitations: and they shall know that I *am* the Lord.

all the despite of thy soul against the land of Israel." The gestures are those of scorn and ill-will, and of rejoicing over another's misfortune; ch. xxii. 13; Job xxvii. 23. In ch. xxi. 17 the same gesture is attributed to Jehovah.

Alas for all] Rather: **Ha**! for all. The interjection seems a shorter form of that used elsewhere, as ch. xxv. 3, "Because thou (Ammon) saidst, Aha! for my sanctuary, when it was destroyed, and for the land of Israel, when it was desolate." The prophet hates and scorns the evil practices of Israel so deeply, that he rejoices at the vengeance about to overtake them. The grammatical anomaly in "evil abominations of" is obviated in LXX. by omission of "evil."

12. *and is besieged*] **and he that is besieged.** In LXX. the previous "he that remaineth" is wanting. With this omission "he that is besieged" might stand, cf. ch. vii. 15, "he that is in the city, famine shall devour him." Otherwise the sense seems rather as in R.V. marg. *preserved*, as Is. xlix. 6.

13. Comp. *v.* 7 on the effect of these judgments on the minds of the people. On "idols," cf. *v.* 4. The cumulative phrases "in all the tops of the mountains," and "under every thick oak" are wanting in LXX.; and so "he that remaineth" *v.* 12. For *oak* rather **terebinth**.

sweet savour] Is said of the smoke or steam of the sacrificial fat burnt upon the altar, ch. xvi. 19, xx. 28, 41, and often in the ritual laws of the Pentateuch.

14. *desolate, yea, more desolate*] Rather: **desolate and waste** (ch. xxxiii. 28, 29, xxxv. 3) more than the wilderness of Diblah. The comparative "more than," however, is not probable. Moreover a wilderness of Diblah is unknown; Diblathaim besides being in Moab could not be called desert. The construction is difficult, but probably the reading should be: *from the wilderness to Riblah*, i.e. from south to north. Riblah was situated on the northern border of the country

Moreover the word of the Lord came unto me, saying, 7
Also, thou son of man, thus saith the Lord God unto the 2
land of Israel; An end, the end is come upon the four
corners of the land. Now *is* the end *come* upon thee, and I 3
will send mine anger upon thee, and will judge thee according to thy ways, and will recompense upon thee all thine
abominations. And mine eye shall not spare thee, neither 4
will I have pity: but I will recompense thy ways upon thee,
and thine abominations shall be in the midst of thee: and
ye shall know that I *am* the Lord.

(Numb. xxxiv. 11); it is said to be in "the land of Hamath," Jer. lii. 9, 27 (where by the converse substitution of *d* for *r*, LXX. reads Diblah). A few MSS. read Riblah. It must be acknowledged that this way of designating the whole extent of the land from S. to N. is nowhere else employed, the northern limit being usually expressed by "the entering in of Hamath."

Ch. VII. Dirge over the downfall of the kingdom of Judah.

The passage is probably in some confusion; *vv*. 8, 9 are virtually a repetition of *vv*. 3, 4. In LXX. *vv*. 3, 4 stand immediately after *vv*. 8, 9, and have the appearance of being a duplicate. In other respects the text is very difficult, and in several places no longer presents the original reading. The chapter appears to have two divisions:—

First, *vv*. 1—13, announcement that the end of the state is come, in a series of interjectional sentences, and

Secondly, *vv*. 14—27, a picture of its dissolution, in language somewhat calmer and more connected.

First, announcement of the end, in three short strophes:

(1) *vv*. 1—4. The end is come upon the four corners of the land.
(2) *vv*. 5—9. The end is come upon the inhabitants of the land.
(3) *vv*. 10—13. The ruin is common and universal. Persons and possessions alike perish.

1—4. The end is come upon the whole land, unsparing destruction from the Lord.

This destruction is the fruit of the abominations of the people, their idolatries and crimes (*v*. 23). They shall know when it overtakes them that he who inflicts it is Jehovah, God alone.

2. *v*. 2 might read: unto the land of Israel an end! the end is come upon, &c. Cf. Am. viii. 2.

3. *send mine anger*] Is an unusual form of expression.

will recompense] **Bring** or **put**. Chastisement is but sin assuming another form, a form which it inevitably takes.

4. *mine eye shall not spare*] So *v*. 9, ch. v. 11, viii. 18, ix. 10. From their calamities the people shall learn not only that he that

5 Thus saith the Lord God; An evil, an only evil, behold,
6 is come. An end is come, the end is come: it watcheth
7 for thee; behold, it is come. The morning is come unto
thee, O thou that dwellest in the land: the time is come,
the day of trouble *is* near, and not the sounding again of
8 the mountains. Now will I shortly pour out my fury upon
thee, and accomplish mine anger upon thee: and I will
judge thee according to thy ways, and will recompense thee

inflicts them is their God, whom they called Jehovah (a thing which they were slow to learn, Am. iii. 2, v. 18), but also what the nature of that God is—that he is Jehovah, the true and righteous God (a thing which they were even slower to learn), cf. *v.* 27, ch. vi. 7, xii. 20, &c.

5—7. THE DIRGE TAKES A FRESH TURN, ANNOUNCING IN NEARLY THE SAME WORDS THAT THE END IS COME UPON THE INHABITANTS OF THE LAND.

5. *an only evil*] Lit. *one evil*, scarcely a "unique" evil, to which there is nothing like, but an evil which is "one" and final, 1 Sam. xxvi. 8; Hagg. ii. 6, "Yet once, it is a little while, and I will shake the heavens and the earth" (Heb. xii. 26).

6. *it watcheth*] Rather: **it awaketh for thee.** The word forms an alliteration with "end" (Ḳêç, heḳîç), and suggests that the vengeance slumbering long is now ready to fall on them. A similar paronomasia in Am. viii. 2, between "end" and "summer fruit," and in Jer. i. 11, between "almond tree" and "be wakeful."

7. *The morning is come*] The sense "morning" is that which a similar word has in Aramaic; but the dawn or morning is always used of the breaking in of felicity not of calamity (cf. Is. viii. 20). The term occurs in Is. xxviii. 5 in the sense of crown or chaplet, probably from the idea of encircling, going a round or circuit (Judg. vii. 3, R.V. marg.), and it has been conjectured that the word may have the sense of "turn" (vicem), naturally with the meaning "calamitous turn," misfortune or fate (as da'irah in Arab.). So Abulwalid followed by most moderns (R.V. *doom*). Dukes quotes a Chaldee proverb of Sirach in which another form of the word has the sense of *times* (a hundred times, *Blumenlese*, p. 80). LXX. does not recognise the word either here or in *v.* 10.

the day of trouble] Rather: **the day is near, even tumult, and not joyful shouting upon the mountains**, as R.V. This rendering assumes that the word translated "joyful shouting" is another form of the term rendered "shouting" (vintage shouting) Is. xvi. 9, 10; Jer. xlviii. 33—"the shouting is no vintage shouting" but tumult of invasion (Lam. ii. 22).

8, 9. Verses 8, 9 are virtually *vv.* 3, 4 repeated, except that *v.* 9 ends with the words: that I am Jehovah that smiteth. The order of *vv.* 1—9 in LXX. differs from the Heb. thus: *vv.* 1, 2, 6 the end is come, 7 unto thee O inhabitant of the land, &c., 8, 9, 3, 4. This order is certainly not original, because *vv.* 3, 4, being virtually the same as 8, 9 cannot

for all thine abominations. And mine eye shall not spare, 9
neither will I have pity: I will recompense thee according
to thy ways and thine abominations *that* are in the midst of
thee; and ye shall know that I *am* the LORD that smiteth.
Behold the day, behold, it is come: the morning is gone 10
forth; the rod hath blossomed, pride hath budded. Vio- 11
lence is risen up into a rod of wickedness: none of them
shall remain, nor of their multitude, nor of any of theirs:
neither *shall there be* wailing for them. The time is come, 12

have followed these verses immediately. It is probable that 3, 4 and 8, 9 are duplicates and that they should stand only once. On the other hand they might be regarded as a kind of refrain, first to the judgment on the land (*vv.* 3, 4) and then to the judgment on the inhabitants (*vv.* 8, 9); if so the pronouns in 8, 9 should possibly be read in the *masculine*,

10—13. THE RUIN IS UNIVERSAL, OVERTAKING ALL CLASSES.

10. *morning is gone forth*] Rather: **is come forth,**—the figure of a plant springing up; Job xiv. 2, "man cometh forth like a flower." On "morning" see *v.* 7; R.V. *doom* as there.

rod hath blossomed] i.e. sprouted and grown so as to become a rod. The general scope of the passage seems to imply that the "rod" here is that by which Israel shall be chastised. In Jer. l. 31 Babylon is named "pride" (R.V. marg.), and the words "pride has budded" may serve to explain "the rod has blossomed." If the pride were that which the rod was to humble the words would better be attached to the next verse.

11. "Violence" must be that in Israel, not that of the enemy. This violence has risen up so as to be, or to bring down a rod of wickedness, i.e. a rod due to wickedness or in chastisement of it (*v.* 23). All this, however, is language very unnatural.

The rest of *v.* 11 is very obscure, and the text certainly corrupt. The general sense conveyed when the words *shall remain* (A.V.) are inserted is that Israel and her multitude and her possessions shall be wholly swept away.

nor of any of theirs] Ges. conjectured: *nor of their wealth*, so R.V.

wailing for them] Ges. conjectured: *magnificence*, so R.V. *neither shall there be eminency* among them. Both words rendered "wealth" and "eminency" are entirely unknown; the former is probably no word at all but a false repetition of the previous expression "none of them;" if it be a word the natural rendering is that of Ew., moaning or sighing (*v.* 16 of doves), or unquietness. For the word "eminency" recourse is had to the Arab., generally a precarious proceeding. LXX. renders no account of either of the words. In his reconstruction of the text Corn. follows LXX. generally to the end of *v.* 9; *vv.* 10, 11 he emends thus: "Behold the crown (as Is. xxviii. 5) is come forth, the sceptre blossoms; but the crown shall wither 11 and the sceptre fade; what are

the day draweth near: let not the buyer rejoice, nor the seller mourn: for wrath *is* upon all the multitude thereof.
13 For the seller shall not return to that which is sold, although they were yet alive: for the vision *is* touching the whole multitude thereof, *which* shall not return; neither shall any strengthen himself in the iniquity of his life.

they, and what their multitude?" The crown and sceptre are those of Israel. The emendation may be left to itself.

12. The inhabitants shall be overwhelmed in a common ruin, in which all social relations shall be forgotten—the buyer shall not rejoice nor the seller sorrow. A universal "wrath" shall be on all classes, involving them in a common destruction. Cf. Is. xxiv. 2, "It shall be as with the buyer so with the seller, as with the lender so with the borrower," &c.

13. *return to that which is sold*] Sales, particularly of real property, were usually temporary, the subjects sold being redeemable. When they were redeemed the seller would "return to that which was sold." By the Law real property returned to the original owner at the year of freedom. This hope is vain: the coming calamity shall obliterate all titles. Others conjecture that the prophet has before his mind the case of the captives carried away with Jehoiachin, who were compelled to make forced sales of their property before going into exile, and who longed to return to claim what was theirs.

although they were yet alive] Or, **while they are**; i.e. never, so long as they live.

for the vision] Instead of "vision" *wrath* should be read: **for wrath is upon all the multitude thereof**," as *vv.* 12, 14. Probably the clause: "for the vision (wrath)...not return" should be omitted as accidental repetition of previous words.

strengthen himself...his life] Perhaps: *neither shall any one keep hold of his life* (maintain his life) *in his iniquity*. Those driven out shall not return, and those remaining shall die in their sins. Or if there be no reference to those two classes the statements are general: none shall return to his possessions, and none shall live in his iniquity.

14—27. PICTURE OF THE DISSOLUTION OF THE STATE.

(1) *vv.* 14—18. The trumpet shall sound the alarm, but none shall prepare himself for the battle. The sword shall devour without and famine consume within. A paralysing terror shall seize upon all.

(2) *vv.* 19—22. They shall cast their gold and silver into the streets, for it cannot buy wherewith to appease their hunger. Their wealth which was their pride and which they used to further their abominations shall become the prey of the invader.

(3) *vv.* 23—27. The city is full of violence therefore it shall be given over to the worst of the heathen. Perplexity and stupefaction shall seize king and people, priest and prophet alike. They shall know Jehovah when his judgments overtake them.

They have blown the trumpet, even to make all ready; 14
but none goeth to the battle: for my wrath *is* upon all the
multitude thereof. The sword *is* without, and the pestilence 15
and the famine within: he that *is* in the field shall die with
the sword; and he that *is* in the city, famine and pestilence
shall devour him. But they that escape of them shall 16
escape, and shall be on the mountains like doves of the
valleys, all of them mourning, every one for his iniquity.
All hands shall be feeble, and all knees shall be weak *as* 17
water. They shall also gird *themselves* with sackcloth, and 18
horror shall cover them; and shame *shall be* upon all faces,
and baldness upon all their heads. They shall cast their 19

14—18. FRUITLESSNESS OF THE DEFENCE.

14. Preparations for the defence are made but there is no courage to face the enemy, for the wrath of God upon them predetermines their defeat.

even to make all ready] Rather: **and have made** (inf. abs.).

15. Comp. Lam. i. 20.

16. Read: **and when** (if) **they that escape of them shall escape, they shall be upon the mountains.**

mourning] This refers to the doves: the fugitives shall be on the mountains (seeking refuge) like doves of the valleys, all of which mourn. Is. lix. 11, We moan all like bears, and mourn sore like doves; xxxviii. 14, Like a swallow so did I chatter, I did mourn as a dove. The Arabic poets often refer to the mourning of the dove or ring-dove (Ḳumrî) as being like their own. See the citations of Ahlwardt, Chalef el Aḥmar, p. 102 seq. Similarly in the Babylonian Penitential Psalms (Zimmern), Ps. i. 10, Like doves do I mourn; on sighs I feed myself; Ps. vi. 4, vii. 10.

for his iniquity] Or, **in**; in the consciousness of it and its consequences.

17. The description returns from the condition of the fugitives to that of the besieged. Prostration and despair seizes them. The figures of the hands "hanging down," and the knees becoming "water" are expressive of complete paralysis of strength. LXX. Hitz. interpret the latter phrase literally. Cf. ch. xxi. 7; Is. xiii. 7; Jer. vi. 24.

18. *horror shall cover them*] Or, **trembling**, terror, Job xxi. 6. It shall take such hold of them that it shall be all over them, like a garment covering them. Cf. Is. lix. 17, he was clad with zeal as a cloke; Ps. lv. 6.

baldness] A sign of mourning: Is. xv. 2, On all heads shall be baldness; Mic. i. 16, Enlarge thy baldness like the vulture. This tonsure in token of mourning, common among many nations of antiquity, was confined among the Hebrews to shaving the front part of the head (Deut. xiv. 1), and was forbidden by the Law in the case of priests (Lev. xxi. 5,

silver in the streets, and their gold shall be removed: their silver and their gold shall not be able to deliver them in the day of the wrath of the LORD: they shall not satisfy their souls, neither fill their bowels: because it is the stumblingblock of their iniquity.

20 As for the beauty of his ornament, he set it in majesty: but they made the images of their abominations *and* of their detestable things therein: therefore have I set it far from 21 them. And I will give it into the hands of the strangers for a prey, and to the wicked of the earth for a spoil; and they 22 shall pollute it. My face will I turn also from them, and they shall pollute my secret *place*: for the robbers shall enter

cf. Ezek. xliv. 20), and of the whole people (Deut. xiv. 1), cf. Am. viii. 10; Jer. xvi. 6; Lev. xix. 27.

19. Amidst the famine they cast their silver and gold away in the streets, it cannot procure them food. On the horrors of famine during the siege of Jerusalem, comp. Lam. iv. 4, 8—10, ii. 11, 12, 19, 20, i. 11.

gold shall be removed] Rather: **shall be a thing unclean**, lit. uncleanness. The term refers properly to female impurity, and is the strongest expression for "object of abhorrence;" cf. ch. xxxvi. 17, where the people's idolatries are in Jehovah's eyes as a woman's impurity. Lev. xx. 21.

is the stumblingblock] **hath been**. Their gold and silver has been to them something on which they have stumbled and fallen, i.e. a cause of their sinning; cf. ch. xiv. 3, xliv. 12.

20. Read: **and the beauty of their ornament they turned into pride, and they made the images...thereof; therefore will I make it unto them a thing unclean**. The thing spoken of is still their silver and gold; this they not only turned into pride, but made also images of it. Hos. ii. 8, I multiplied unto her silver and gold, which they used for Baal; viii. 4, Of their silver and gold have they made them idols, that they might be cut off. Cf. ch. xvi. 11; 2 Sam. i. 24; Jer. iv. 30.

21. Because of this abuse of their silver and gold in making it into idols it shall become the prey of the Chaldeans, who shall profane it, turning it from a sacred to a common use. In a certain sense all that was in Israel was sacred, and the mere fact of the heathen taking possession of it profaned it. Hos. x. 6, It (the calf) shall be carried unto Assyria for a present to king Jareb; cf. Is. xlvi. 1, 2; Mic. i. 7.

22. The enemy shall penetrate into the temple and profane it.

turn...from them] This most naturally refers to Israel, from whom the Lord will turn his face in anger, cf. *v.* 11. It might refer to the invader, whom the Lord will not behold but permit to work his will, cf. Lam. ii. 3.

secret place] Is probably the temple (Lam. ii. 1); less natural would be the city. The word "secret," however, is not to be referred

into it, and defile it. Make a chain: for the land is full *of* 23
bloody crimes, and the city is full *of* violence. Wherefore I 24
will bring the worst of the heathen, and they shall possess
their houses: I will also make the pomp of the strong to
cease; and their holy places shall be defiled. Destruction 25
cometh; and they shall seek peace, and *there shall be* none.
Mischief shall come upon mischief, and rumour shall be 26
upon rumour; then shall they seek a vision of the prophet;
but the law shall perish from the priest, and counsel from
the ancients. The king shall mourn, and the prince shall be 27
clothed with desolation, and the hands of the people of the

to the *arcanum* of the Most Holy place; the meaning is "my precious thing."

for the robbers] **and robbers**; the Chaldean pillagers. The words "pollute" and "defile" are the same; better, **profane**.

23. *Make a chain*] **the** chain. The chain could only be for binding the captives to carry them into exile. In Is. xl. 19 a similar word is used for the silver chains with which the idols were fastened to the wall lest they should totter or fall; and in Nah. iii. 10 the verb is rendered "were bound" with chains (another word, Jer. xl. 1). If the reading be correct the sense is not doubtful. It must be confessed, however, that nothing in the text suggests any reference to chains. LXX. connects with the preceding (so Syr.) and reads: and they shall work disorder (defilement). Corn. suggests two inf. abs. (after xxiii. 46), viz. raze and empty out! (cf. Ps. cxxxvii. 7; Is. xxiv. 1). Curiously neither of the words is used by Ezekiel. The present reading is scarcely original.

24. *worst of the heathen*] Cf. xxviii. 7, xxx. 11, the terrible of the nations. Jer. vi. 23; Hab. i. 7.

the pomp of the strong] Or, **pride**. In xxiv. 21 the pride of their strength, and so LXX. here. Cf. xxxiii. 28; Lev. xxvi. 19. The spelling of "sanctuaries" is an Aramaism.

25. *Destruction cometh*] Or, **anguish**.

26. *Mischief...upon mischief*] i.e. calamity upon calamity; and "rumour" of misfortune upon rumour. Jer. iv. 20; Is. xxviii. 19.

but the law] **and** the law. It is implied in seeking a vision from the prophet that no vision is granted; and the law, i.e. decision or judgment, sought from the priest, ceases; neither can the elders give any counsel. The same three classes of advisers, viz. prophets, priests, and elders or wise men are spoken of Jer. xviii. 18. All sources of revelation are dumb. Cf. Lam. ii. 9, The law is no more, her prophets also find no vision from the Lord. Ps. lxxiv. 9; Mic. iii. 6.

27. *king shall mourn*] 2 Sam. xix. 1. The "prince" is Ezekiel's usual term for the chief civil ruler, and princes for those of the royal house. The clause "the king shall mourn" is wanting in LXX. On "clothed with desolation," i.e. utterly appalled, cf. *v.* 18, xxvi. 16.

4—2

land shall be troubled: I will do unto them after their way, and according to their deserts will I judge them; and they shall know that I *am* the LORD.

according to their deserts] lit. *judgments*, i.e. practices and deeds, as ch. v. 7, xi. 12 (manners). All that should defend and save the state, from the king to the people of the land, shall be paralysed and helpless. The Lord will judge them according to their doings and they shall know that he is Jehovah.

THIRD SECTION. CH. VIII.—XI. NEW VISIONS OF JEHOVAH'S WITHDRAWAL FROM HIS HOUSE, AND THE APPROACHING DESTRUCTION OF JERUSALEM.

On the fifth day of the sixth month of the sixth year of the Captivity of Jehoiachin (B.C. 591) the prophet sat in his house and the elders of the exile sat before him. Moved by their words or by their presence he fell into a trance and was transported by the spirit to Jerusalem, where a series of events passed before his view.

First, ch. viii., a vision of the idolatries practised by all classes in the house of the Lord.

Secondly, ch. ix., a vision of the messengers of divine vengeance, and the slaughter of the inhabitants of the city.

Thirdly, ch. x., a vision of the destruction of the city itself by fire from God, with a new description of the cherubim.

Fourthly, ch. xi., a vision of the internal condition of the city, the counsels and thoughts of the leaders. Then the departure of Jehovah from the city, and renewal of the threat of destruction, but with a promise of restoration to those already in exile.

Finally, awaking out of his trance, the prophet narrates the proceeding revelations to the exiles (ch. xi. 25).

CH. VIII. THE MANIFOLD IDOLATRIES OF ISRAEL, WHEREBY THEY PROFANE THE HOUSE OF THE LORD, CAUSING HIM TO WITHDRAW FROM IT.

Four idolatrous scenes pass before the prophet's view.

(1) *vv.* 1—6. He is shewn an image, called the image of jealousy, situated apparently in the outer court, but near the gateway leading to the inner court.

(2) *vv.* 7—11, the secret idolatries practised by the elders in the chambers of the gateway.

(3) *vv.* 12—13, the lamentation for Tammuz or Adonis engaged in by the women.

(4) *vv.* 15—18, sun-worship practised in front of the temple in the inner court.

1—3. The trance in presence of the elders. The prophet, abiding in his house (ch. iii. 25), was visited by the elders of the captivity among whom he dwelt. They probably came to consult him regarding the affairs at home and the prospects of the city. Thrown into a state of

And it came to pass in the sixth year, in the sixth *month*, 8
in the fifth *day* of the month, as I sat in mine house, and
the elders of Judah sat before me, that the hand of the Lord
GOD fell there upon me. Then I beheld, and lo, a likeness 2
as the appearance of fire: from the appearance of his loins
even downward, fire; and from his loins even upward, as

excitation by their words or by their presence he fell into a trance. The vision of the God of Israel again appeared to him, for this thought of Jehovah chiefly occupied his mind and led to all his other thoughts, and he was carried away in the spirit to Jerusalem; and there the manifold idolatries of the people were shewn him. Two chief thoughts appear expressed by the symbolism; first, by making the "glory" of Jehovah appear in Jerusalem the prophet points the contrast between the glorious God whom the people had abandoned and the debased forms of worship to which they had addicted themselves, and also implies that this worship was done in the face of Jehovah, "to provoke the eyes of his glory" (Is. iii. 8); and secondly, when Jehovah himself shews the idolatrous practices of the people, we see, what is characteristic of the prophet, the effort to throw himself into the consciousness, so to speak, of Jehovah, and look out at things from *his* mind, he being who he is. It would be a mistake to regard the details here given as due entirely to literary artifice; there is no doubt a foundation of reality under them, though when in after years the prophet reflected on the facts and recorded them he gave them great expansion and embellishment.

1. *the sixth* month] The first vision of the prophet was in the fifth year of Jehoiachin's captivity and in the fourth month (i. 1); the present one a year and two months later. LXX. reads *fifth* month, and many modern scholars accept this reading, arguing that the Heb. date is due to some copyist or reader who wished to leave room for the number of days during which the prophet had to lie on his side (ch. iv. 5, 9). The copyist must have been an indifferent arithmetician, for 7 (iii. 15) + 390 + 40 (ch. iv. 5, 6) = 437, while a lunar year and two months, 354 + 59 = 413 days. The discrepancies between the Heb. and LXX. dates are not easy to explain.

elders of Judah] Ch. xiv. 1, "Certain of the elders of Israel." The meaning appears from ch. xi. 25, "So I spake to them of the captivity all the things which the Lord had shewed me." The community at Tel Abib were probably permitted to have a certain internal government of their own. In the "elders" before him the prophet sees represented not so much the captivity as the whole "house of Israel." On "hand of the Lord," cf. ch. i. 3.

2. *as the appearance of fire*] More naturally, the appearance of a man, as LXX., cf. ch. i. 26, 27, "the appearance of a man" (a different word, however), where the description is the same, viz. fire from the loins downwards and amber from the loins upwards. The prophet speaks with reverential vagueness of God—"a likeness as the appearance of a man," and "he put forth the likeness of a hand."

3 the appearance of brightness, as the colour of amber. And he put forth the form of a hand, and took me by a lock of mine head; and the spirit lift me up between the earth and the heaven, and brought me in the visions of God to Jerusalem, to the door of the inner gate that looketh toward the north; where *was* the seat of the image of jealousy, which

3. He does not even say that it was the divine hand that carried him; **spirit** carried him, the form of the divine hand was merely symbolical.

the visions of God] i.e. shewn him by God, ch. i. 1.

door of the inner gate] Rather: door of **the gate of the inner court** looking toward the north, i.e. the northern gate of the inner court. The word "inner" is wanting in LXX. The general opinion has been that the prophet was set down in the inner court, at the *inner* door of the northern gateway into that court. The term "door," however, seems in usage to mean the outside entrance; and if the prophet had stood in the inner court he would have had to look northward through the gateway in order to see the image of jealousy, which was certainly not in the inner court. It is more natural to suppose him set down in the outer court, in front of the gateway leading into the inner court. In front of this gateway, in the outer court, stood the image of jealousy, near the entrance. Having seen this the prophet is next brought *into* the gateway (*v.* 7), where he enters the chamber of imagery, some one of the cells in the gateway building. From there he is carried outside the sacred enclosure altogether to the north door of the outer court (*v.* 14), where he finds the women bewailing Tammuz. And finally he is transported into the inner court where he beholds the sun-worship practised in front of the temple-house itself. Previous to this he had not been in the inner court, for when being shewn the idolatries he is always taken to the precise place where they are practised.

image of jealousy] Not an image of "jealousy" itself, considered as a deity, but an image which because it provoked to jealousy was named image of jealousy. The "jealousy" of God is a violent emotion or resentment arising from the feeling of being injured (Deut. xxxii. 21). It is uncertain what this image was. The word occurs again, Deut. iv. 16, in the sense of similitude or "figure," and in Phenician with the meaning of "statue," e.g. in an inscription from Idalion (*Corp. Ins. Sem.*, vol. I. 88, 3, 7, &c.). According to 2 Kings xxi. 7 Manasseh put a graven image of Ashera in the house of the Lord, which Josiah brought out and burnt (2 K. xxiii. 6; 2 Chron. xxxiii. 7, 15). In earlier times the Ashera (A.V. grove) was a tree or pole planted beside an altar. It is not quite certain whether the pole or stock was a substitute for the evergreen tree, when this could not be had, or whether like the sun-image it was the symbol of a goddess. In later times the term seems used as the name of a goddess. The expression "in the house of the Lord" is hardly to be pressed so far as to imply that Manasseh placed the Ashera in the temple proper, "house" is used of the whole temple

provoketh to jealousy. And behold, the glory of the God of 4 Israel *was* there, according to the vision that I saw in the plain.

Then said he unto me, Son of man, lift up thine eyes now 5 the way towards the north. So I lift up mine eyes the way toward the north, and behold, northward at the gate of the altar this image of jealousy in the entry. He said further- 6 more unto me, Son of man, seest thou what they do? *even* the great abominations that the house of Israel committeth here, that *I* should go far off from my sanctuary? but turn thee yet again, *and* thou shalt see great*er* abominations. And he brought me to the door of the court; and when I 7

buildings, including the courts. The image here may be this Ashera, whether we are to suppose it replaced after Josiah had burnt it, or whether the prophet be here taking a comprehensive view of the idolatries of Israel, including the time of Manasseh. In 2 Kings xxiii. 11 reference is made to the horses of the sun placed "at the entering of the house of the Lord," but these would scarcely be called an "image."

4. The glory of the Lord was that seen by the prophet at the Chebar (ch. i.). This glory expressed the prophet's conception of Jehovah. And this Jehovah is here, in contrast with the deities worshipped by the people, and beholding their worship.

5. *gate of the altar*] Is probably the northern inner gate. The northern entrance was the most frequented, partly because the royal palace and buildings lay to the south and east, and the west was closed by the buildings of the temple itself. In Lev. i. 4 the sacrificial victims are commanded to be slaughtered on the north side of the altar.

in the entry] The image was situated on the north of the altar gate, and the words in or at the entry are to be taken somewhat generally. The words are wanting in LXX.

6. I *should go far off*] i.e. withdraw. These abominations defiled Jehovah's sanctuary, the place of his abode, causing him to abandon it. His withdrawal is symbolized ch. xi. 1, 22, 23.

turn thee...again...see] Rather: **thou shalt again see** greater abominations; so *vv.* 13, 15.

7—12. THE SECRET IDOLATRY OF THE ELDERS.

7. *the door of the court*] i.e. the outside entrance of the gateway into the inner court. Placed at first near the entrance the prophet is now brought to the gateway itself, either unto some chamber within it or some building attached to it, cf. xl. 44. In the wall of this building he observed a hole, through which he dug and entered a chamber, on the walls of which were portrayed all manner of creatures, and in the chamber were seventy elders offering incense to the imagery on the walls.

8 looked, behold a hole in the wall. Then said he unto me, Son of man, dig now in the wall: and when I had digged in 9 the wall, behold a door. And he said unto me, Go in, and 10 behold the wicked abominations that they do here. So I went in and saw; and behold every form of creeping things, and abominable beasts, and all the idols of the house of

behold a hole] The symbolism is not very clear. The "hole" is meant to suggest that entrance into the chamber was obtained secretly by those who practised their rites there. The words are wanting in LXX.
   8. The words "in the wall" are wanting both times in LXX.
   9. The word "wicked" is wanting in LXX.
   10. The construction is difficult: lit. "and behold every likeness (*v.* 3; Deut. iv. 17, 18) of creeping things and beasts (cattle), abomination, and all," &c., the term "abomination" being descriptive both of creeping things and beasts. The term "beasts" is employed of the larger domestic animals, though also of the beasts of prey; it seems nowhere used of the smaller vermin. On the other hand the word "abomination" is chiefly used in regard to the smaller creatures that swarm, whether in the waters or on the land, in the latter case winged and creeping things being included (Lev. xi.), and nowhere of the animals called "beasts." LXX. omits "likeness of creeping things and beasts," and it is possible that these words are a marginal gloss explanatory of "abomination." It has usually been supposed that the reference is to the debased forms of Egyptian superstition. This is possible, for the other practices mentioned, the lamentation for Tammuz and the sun-worship came from abroad. Israel appears to have fallen into the idolatries of the nations about her when she came under their influence, particularly when they became paramount over her, and their gods were thought to be stronger than her own God. The Egyptian influence had been powerful from the days of Isaiah downwards, and even after the battle of Carchemish (B.C. 604) the hope of Egyptian support induced Jehoiakim in his last years and Zedekiah toward the close of his reign to renounce their allegiance to Babylon. On the other hand the practices here mentioned may be rather a revival of ancient superstitions which, during the prosperity of the kingdom and amidst the vigour of the national religion, had fallen into disuse or maintained themselves only as a secret cult, but which, amidst the disasters of the time, when Jehovah appeared to have forsaken the land and men looked to every quarter for aid, again became prevalent (see W. R. Smith, *Religion of the Semites*, p. 338). If the LXX. reading be followed the passage may have less significance than has been attributed to it.
   and all the idols] the block-gods, see ch. vi. 4. The fact that the "idols," which according to ch. vi. (*vv.* 4, 6, 9, 13) are to be found over all the mountains of Israel, are represented as portrayed upon the wall is peculiar, and suggests that the whole is symbolical. In

Israel, pourtrayed upon the wall round about. And there 11 stood before them seventy men of the ancients of the house of Israel, and in the midst of them stood Jaazaniah the son of Shaphan, with every man his censer in his hand; and a thick cloud of incense went up. Then said he unto me, 12 Son of man, hast thou seen what the ancients of the house of Israel do in the dark, every man in the chambers of his imagery? for they say, The LORD seeth us not; the LORD hath forsaken the earth. He said also unto me, Turn thee 13 yet again, *and* thou shalt see great*er* abominations that they do.

Then he brought me to the door of the gate of the LORD'S 14 house which *was* towards the north; and behold, there sat

ch. xxiii. 14 Jerusalem sees images of the Chaldeans portrayed upon the wall and falls in love with them, but such portraits can hardly have been a reality.

11. *seventy men of the ancients*] i.e. of the *elders*. The seventy were not any court such as the later Sanhedrim, but merely seventy men representing the elders of Israel (Ex. xxiv. 1; Numb. xi. 16, 24, 25). The elders were the leaders of the people, and probably here represent them. Prominent among these elders was Jaazaniah the son of Shaphan. There is no reason to suppose the name fictitious. Shaphan the scribe was the person who read the Book of the Law found in the temple to king Josiah (2 Kings xxii. 10). A son of his son Ahikam acted along with him and was a protector of Jeremiah (Jer. xxxix. 14), and another son is mentioned (Jer. xxxvi. 10) as having a chamber in the upper court where Baruch read Jeremiah's roll in the ears of the people. If Jaazaniah was a son of this Shaphan he pursued a different course from his father and brothers.

12. *the chambers of his imagery*] Or, **his chambers of imagery**. The language implies that there were many chambers of imagery, and again suggests that the scene was symbolical. For "ancients" **elders**. On "imagery" Lev. xxvi. 1; Numb. xxxiii. 52.

forsaken the earth] Rather: **the land**. The multiplied calamities of later years suggested that Jehovah no more protected the country (ch. ix. 9). This was possibly the feeling of the elders and people in some moods, but in other moods they spoke differently. In ch. xi. 15 they say to those already in exile, "Get you far from the Lord! unto us is this land given in possession."

13. *Turn thee yet again*] See *v.* 6.

14. THE WOMEN BEWAILING TAMMUZ.

14. *gate of the LORD's house*] i.e. outside the whole temple buildings to the north gate of the outer court; cf. ch. x. 19, xi. 1. The term "house" embraces all the temple buildings (Jer. xxxv. 4). The

15 women weeping for Tammuz. Then said he unto me, Hast thou seen *this*, O son of man? turn thee yet again, *and* thou
16 shalt see greater abominations than these. And he brought me into the inner court of the Lord's house, and behold, *at* the door of the temple of the Lord, between the porch and the altar, *were* about five and twenty men, *with* their backs toward the temple of the Lord, and their faces towards the

women may have been seen sitting outside the gate, or they may have been in some of the chambers of the outer gateway. Of course the temple building in Ezekiel's time did not quite correspond to his ideal sketch in ch. xl. seq., but there were no doubt chambers at that time connected with both gateways (Jer. xxxv. 2, 4, xxxvi. 10, 12, 20, 21, cf. xxvi. 10; 2 Kings xxiii. 11). Tammuz is identical with Adonis. The latter name, *Adon*, "Lord," is not a proper name, being applicable to any great god, but when the myth found its way to Greece, the word became a proper name. The name Tammuz is Babylonian Dumu-zi, Dûzi, said to signify "son of life," and to indicate the eternal youth of the sun-god (cf. Fried. Del. in Baer's *Ezek.*; Schrader, *KAT.* on Ezek. viii. 14; Sayce, *Hibbert Lect.* iv.). The story of the death of Tammuz is said to be a solar myth, having reference to the death of the sun-god. The explanations given by Assyrian scholars are not very clear. Sometimes the death is said to be that which he undergoes each night, sometimes that which he undergoes when he expires before the touch of winter, and sometimes the death is that of the lusty, life-giving vernal god, who perishes along with all life on earth amidst the summer fires which he himself has kindled. The town of Gebal or Byblos, eight miles north of Beirut, was the great seat of the Adonis worship in Phenicia. It is possible that the cult passed westward from Babylonia, but it may be that in Syria the rites had an independent origin and a different meaning, and that it was not till later that they were interpreted in the sense of the Babylonian myth (W. R. Smith, *Religion of the Semites*, index under Adonis). It was probably from Phenicia that the worship entered Judæa. Milton's interpretation of the rites may not quite exhaust their meaning:

> the love tale
> Infected Zion's daughters with like heat;
> Whose wanton passions in the sacred porch
> Ezekiel saw.

Such myths may originally be only beautiful nature poetry, but we are so allied to nature that we see our feelings reflected in her, as on the other hand her moods repeat themselves in us. Particularly in times of decay and loss the sadder aspects of nature intensify our own feeling by presenting to our minds a universal decay in which we and all things are involved. It is only the sorrowful side of the Tammuz rite that the prophet refers to.

15. *turn thee yet again*] See *v.* 6 end.

east; and they worshipped the sun towards the east. Then 17 he said unto me, Hast thou seen *this*, O son of man? Is it a light thing to the house of Judah that *they* commit the abominations which they commit here? for they have filled the land *with* violence, and have returned to provoke me to anger: and lo, they put the branch to their nose. Therefore 18 will I also deal in fury: mine eye shall not spare, neither will I have pity: and though they cry in mine ears *with* a loud voice, *yet* will I not hear them.

16. THE SUN-WORSHIPPERS IN THE INNER COURT.

16. *about five and twenty*] LXX., about twenty. These men were seen adoring the sun with their faces to the east, and their backs to the temple house. Their position between the temple and the altar seems to imply that they were priests (Joel ii. 17), and it is not decisive against this view that they are called "elders" in ch. ix. 6, for Jer. xix. 1 refers to "the elders of the priests." They may be supposed representatives of the priesthood.

worshipped the sun] The worship of the sun, the queen of heaven, and the host of heaven, was adopted by Israel from their eastern conquerors: cf. 2 Kings xxiii. 5, 11; Jer. xliv. 17; Job xxxi. 26; Deut. iv. 19. (The Heb. is to be read mishtahavim.)

17. *Is it a light thing*] Probably: is it too light a thing for the house of Judah to commit...that they have filled: cf. Is. xlix. 6; ch. ix. 9.

the branch to their nose] This is supposed to be part of the ceremonies of their sun-worship. It is said that the Persian sun-worshippers held before them a branch or bunch of date, pomegranate or tamarisk tree, or according to some of the Homa tree, probably that their breath might not contaminate the glory of the rising deity. The word "nose" might mean face (Gen. iii. 19), but why not "mouth?" And this distinctively Persian rite is hardly probable at so early a date in Israel. Also the reference to idolatry seemed concluded, for it is asked whether these idolatries were not enough, that they had also filled the land with blood. LXX. has given a general sense, "and behold these are as mockers," probably regarding the words as a proverbial phrase.

18. These abominations will assuredly bring down the unsparing chastisements of heaven. The phrase "shall not spare nor pity" is common in the prophet, ch. v. 11, vii. 4, 9, ix. 5, 10.

cry...with a loud voice] Comp. ch. xi. 13, and for the general idea of vain appeal to heaven, Is. i. 15; Jer. xi. 11; Prov. i. 28.

This passage contains much that is difficult to estimate. The fact that the things described were seen in the "visions of God," the symbolical form in which Jehovah appeared, and the analogy of chh. ix, x, lead to the conclusion that there is at least an ideal and symbolical element in the representation of the idolatries practised in the temple.

The view of Hitz., Kuen. (*Onderz.* II. 278) that the idolatrous practices are to be taken literally but referred to the time of Manasseh is not natural. The prophet would hardly be shewn things once but no longer in existence, though of course he might take a continuous view of Israel's practice, as he often does. The tense in *v.* 17 "which they have committed here" is scarcely evidence for a former generation. It is not easy to say how far the representation that the idolatrous usages were practised *in* the temple is to be taken literally. Such practices are not referred to by Jeremiah nor other prophets of the time. It is possible that the chambers and cells about the gateways, which appear in some cases to have belonged to private persons, may have been used for illegitimate purposes, but that sun-worship was actually practised between the temple and the altar has little probability. And the scene in the chamber of imagery is obviously ideal. The prophet certainly desires to shew that idolatry both public and in private was practised by all classes, the elders representing the nation, the women, and perhaps also the priests; and that these idolatries were not only the old native ones of Israel, but new imports at this period from all the nations around. The representation, however, that such things were done *in* the temple may rather be ideal. The temple was the dwelling-place of Jehovah, and every impurity done not only there but in the land and in the houses of the people was felt in the place of his abode, which it defiled, causing him to withdraw from it (*v.* 6, cf. Lev. xv. 31, xx. 3; Num. xix. 13, 20; and the elaborate precautions to guard against defilement adopted in ch. xl.—xlviii). On the other hand those privileged to dwell in the land or have access to the temple are spoken of as dwelling *in* the house, Ps. xxiii. 6, xxvii. 4, lxxxiv. 5 &c. See preliminary remarks to the chapter.

CH. IX. FIRST ACT OF THE DIVINE JUDGMENT, SLAUGHTER OF THE INHABITANTS OF THE CITY.

Ch. viii. presented a picture of the enormities practised by the inhabitants of the land and of the city, their religious debasement in contrast with the glory of Jehovah. The description was meant to lead up to the conclusion expressed in the end of the chapter, "Therefore will I deal in fury, mine eye shall not spare, neither will I have pity" (ch. viii. 18). Now is shewn the first act of the execution of this threat.

(1) *vv.* 1—3. A loud cry proceeded from the glory of the Lord, Bring hither the executioners of the city! and forthwith are seen approaching from the northern gate of the temple six men, each with his weapon of destruction in his hand, and a seventh clad in linen garments, with a writer's inkhorn at his girdle. The seven take up their position between the house and the brazen altar.

(2) *vv.* 4—6. Ere this the glory of the Lord which was over the cherubim had risen, or now rose, and stood over the threshold of the temple. From there a cry came to the man clothed in linen to go forth into the city and put a mark upon the foreheads of those who mourned over the evils done in the midst of it, and to the six others to follow him and slay indiscriminately all not so sealed, and to begin at the house of the Lord.

He cried also in mine ears *with* a loud voice, saying, 9
Cause them that have charge over the city to draw near,
even every man *with* his destroying weapon in his hand.
And behold, six men came from the way of the higher gate, 2

(3) *vv.* 7—10. Immediately the work of slaughter commences, beginning with the elders before the house (ch. viii. 16). From there the destroying angels move outwards, polluting the courts with dead, and pass into the city. The prophet is left alone, conscious only of the work going on without. This work fills his mind with such a conception of the wrath of God that it seems to him the whole remnant of Israel must perish before it. He falls on his face and intercedes for them, but is answered that the sin is great, and must be unsparingly chastised.

(4) *v.* 11. While his intercession is repelled, the man clad in linen garments returns, announcing the fulfilment of the commands given to him and his fellows.

1. *that have charge over the city*] Lit. either the "oversights" (overseers), or the "visitations" (visitants) of the city. The latter is most natural, "visitations" being said for "those who visit," that is, the executioners (Jer. lii. 11). Cf. Is. lx. 17 (officers). The verb may be rendered as A.V. Bring near, or Draw near (ch. xxxvi. 8; Job xxxi. 37). The *perf.*, the executioners are at hand, is less suitable to the loud cry, and the immediate appearance of the seven men seems in response to the summons.

2. *six men*] The symbolism represents the judgment of God as executed by supernatural agents, immediately under his command. These agents are called "men," having the human form to the eyes of the prophet (cf. ch. xl. 3, xliii. 6). Six of the men had instruments of destruction in their hands, and the seventh was clothed in linen garments with an inkhorn at his girdle. The inkhorn consisted of a case for holding the reed pens, with an inkholder attached near the mouth of the case. These inkhorns are carried in the girdle, and those worn by high officials are often of silver, richly chased and ornamented. The purpose of the inkhorn appears in *v.* 4. The linen garments mark the man's divine sanctity and eminence, not priestly rank (Ew.); the high angel, Dan. x. 5, xii. 6, was so clothed, as were the seven angels having the vials of wrath, the last plagues of judgment upon the world, Rev. xv. 6. The seven men entering the inner court proceeded until they stood beside the brazen altar, in front of the house, whither the glory of the Lord had moved from the cherubim (*v.* 3).

the higher gate] Or, upper. What this gate was is not quite clear. It is usually held to be the same gate of the inner court already mentioned, ch. viii. 3, 5. In Ezekiel's new temple the inner court is higher than the outer, and a flight of steps leads to the gate from the level of the outer court, but probably in the old temple the courts were much on a level. In 2 Kings xv. 35, Jotham is said to have built the "upper gate" of the house of the Lord. This gate seems identical with the upper Benjamin gate, Jer. xx. 2, probably also with the "new

which lieth toward the north, and every man a slaughter weapon in his hand; and one man among them *was* clothed *with* linen, with a writer's inkhorn by his side: and they went ₃ in, and stood beside the brasen altar. And the glory of the God of Israel was gone up from the cherub, whereupon he was, to the threshold of the house. And he called to the man clothed *with* linen, which *had* the writer's inkhorn by ₄ his side; and the LORD said unto him, Go through the midst of the city through the midst of Jerusalem, and set a mark upon the foreheads of the men that sigh and that cry for all the abominations that be done in the midst thereof.

gate," Jer. xxvi. 10, xxxvi. 10. In the last passage this new gate is said to be in the "upper court," which can hardly be the inner court, but rather a small court which lay at the northern extremity of the outer court, and was elevated some feet above the latter. (See plan in *Encycl. Brit.*, Art. Temple.) At all events the "men" came from the north side of the house into the inner court. The abominations of the people are represented as practised on the north side (ch. viii.), and the instruments of God's vengeance approach from the same quarter.

the brasen altar] This is again obscure. It is said in 1 Kings viii. 64 that the brazen altar was too small to receive the burnt-offerings and the fat of Solomon's holocausts, and that the king consecrated the middle of the court, and there burnt his offerings. Ahaz caused his priest Uriah to "build" an altar after the pattern of the altar which he saw in Damascus. This new altar must have been of stone, terminating at the top in a platform or hearth for burning the fat and sacrifices upon; and somewhat after this model the altar in Ezekiel's new temple is to be constructed (ch. xliii. 13—17). The altar of Ahaz appears to have been placed in the middle of the court, further from the house than the original position of the brazen altar; and it is added that Ahaz removed the brazen altar from its former place, and set it on the north side of his new altar (2 Kings xvi. 14). This sense is given both by the Heb. and LXX., though the texts differ in some points. The Heb. reading is not quite natural, and as construed by some it says nothing of a removal of the brazen altar from its former place. (See W. R. Smith, *Rel. of Sem.*, p. 466 *seq.*) The seven men took up their position either in the middle of the court in the vicinity of the altar place, or considerably nearer the house than the altar of burnt-offering.

3. *from the cherub*] See at the end of ch. x.

4—7. COMMAND TO SEAL THOSE TO BE SPARED, AND TO SLAY WITHOUT DISTINCTION ALL OTHERS.

4. *set a mark*] The word is *Tav*, the last letter of the alphabet, the old form of which was a cross. The term is used here as in Job xxxi. 35, of a mark in general, though perhaps the Tav or cross was the sim-

And to the others he said in mine hearing, Go ye after him 5
through the city, and smite: let not your eye spare, neither
have ye pity: slay utterly old *and* young, both maids, and 6
little children, and women: but come not near any man
upon whom *is* the mark; and begin at my sanctuary. Then
they began at the ancient men which *were* before the house.
And he said unto them, Defile the house, and fill the courts 7
with the slain: go ye forth. And they went forth, and slew
in the city.

And it came to pass, while they were slaying them, and I 8
was left, that I fell upon my face, and cried, and said, Ah
Lord GOD, *wilt* thou destroy all the residue of Israel in thy

plest form the mark could take. The passage is imitated, Rev. vii.,
though the mark there is the name of God. All who mourned over the
abominations done in Jerusalem were to be thus sealed and spared.

5. The other executioners were to follow the footsteps of the seventh
man, and slay without discrimination all not marked by him.

6. *begin at my sanctuary*] Judgment begins at the house of God.
The Lord had returned for a moment to the place of his abode in the
temple, and from there the judgment went forth; Am. i. 2, "The Lord
shall roar out of Zion and give forth his voice from Jerusalem." There
he was most present, there most fully known, there if possible most
forgotten and provoked, and there his holiness and godhead will assert
themselves with most terribleness against the sins of men.

the ancient men] *the elders*, those mentioned, ch. viii. 16.

7. *Defile the house*] The "house" embraces the temple house and
its precincts, including the courts. The presence of dead in the courts
defiled the whole.

v. 8—10. INTERCESSION OF THE PROPHET.

and I was left] The executioners passed out of the inner court,
leaving only dead behind them, and the prophet was left alone (Is. xlix.
21. The anomalous form is to be read impf.). The terrible outbreak of
the Divine wrath seemed to forebode the extinction of all the remnant
of Israel, and the prophet fell on his face, appealing to the Lord on
their behalf. The "residue" suggests the many calamities that had
already befallen the people, wearing them down to only a few men
(Is. xli. 14, comp. the prophet's own figure of the half-burnt brand, ch.
xv.), and the threat of a fire going out upon all the house of Israel
seemed about to be realized (ch. v. 4). The prophet passes from one
state of feeling to another. Sometimes he is in sympathy with the
divine resentment, and is himself full of fury against the sinful people
(ch. iii. 14), and of a scorn that rejoices at their coming chastisements
(ch. vi. 11), but when the judgments of God are abroad before his eyes
he is appalled at their severity, and his pity for men overcomes his religious zeal (ch. xi. 13).

9 pouring out of thy fury upon Jerusalem? Then said he unto me, The iniquity of the house of Israel and Judah *is* exceeding great, and the land is full *of* blood, and the city full *of* perverseness: for they say, The LORD hath forsaken
10 the earth, and the LORD seeth not. And *as for* me also, mine eye shall not spare, neither will I have pity, *but* I will
11 recompense their way upon their head. And behold, the man clothed with linen, which *had* the inkhorn by his side, reported the matter, saying, I have done as thou hast commanded me.

9. *full* of *perverseness*] As marg., *wresting of judgment*, or turning the innocent out of the way (Am. ii. 7). The Divine answer is inexorable. Two evils are stated, and the deeper cause of them: violence unto bloodshed, and the perversion of justice, the cause of both being the feeling that Jehovah had forsaken the land. The language shews the strange length to which the hard fate of Israel had brought men—Jehovah had abandoned his land. Possibly these persons concluded that he had retired, being overcome by deities stronger than himself; even the godly were driven to conclude that he had ceased to interest himself in his people (Is. xl. 27, xlix. 14). And with the departure of Jehovah, the righteous God, all moral restraints were relaxed. The persons who here speak had probably been obstinate opponents of the prophets, but the passage shews that the prophetic preaching of Jehovah's righteousness, even when to appearance unheeded, had lodged itself in the consciences of men.

10. Cf. ch. v. 11, vii. 4, viii. 18.

11. The man clad in linen returns, announcing the execution of Jehovah's commands.

CH. X. SECOND ACT OF THE DIVINE JUDGMENT, THE SCATTERING OF FIRE FROM GOD UPON THE CITY.

The connexion between this chapter and the last is not quite close, otherwise ch. x. 2 would have stood at the beginning. Unobserved by the prophet or at least unmentioned by him the glory had returned from the threshold of the house (ch. ix. 3), and the Lord again sat upon the throne above the cherubim (ch. i. 26).

(1) *vv*. 1—3. From his place above the cherubim the Lord commanded the man clothed with linen garments to approach the fire within the wheelwork and take coals from it to scatter over the city—a symbol of the divine judgment on Jerusalem, on which fire from God would fall as on Sodom. The man advanced towards the cherubim.

(2) *vv*. 4—8. Meanwhile the glory of the Lord again left the cherubim, and stood over the threshold of the house, the cloud filling the temple and the brilliancy lighting up the inner court. The chief angel had approached the chariot and the cherub took coals from between the wheelwork, putting them into the hands of the angel, who went forth.

Then I looked, and behold, in the firmament that *was* 10
above the head of the cherubims there appeared over them
as it were a sapphire stone, as the appearance of the likeness
of a throne. And he spake unto the man clothed with 2
linen, and said, Go in between the wheels, *even* under the
cherub, and fill thine hand *with* coals of fire from between
the cherubims, and scatter *them* over the city. And he went
in in my sight. Now the cherubims stood on the right side 3
of the house, when the man went in; and the cloud filled
the inner court. Then the glory of the LORD went up from 4
the cherub, *and stood* over the threshold of the house; and
the house was filled with the cloud, and the court was full
of the brightness of the LORD's glory. And the sound of 5
the cherubims' wings was heard *even* to the utter court, as

The actual strewing of the fire upon the city, though assumed, is not
described.
(3) *vv*. 9—17. Renewed description of the cherubim.
(4) *vv*. 18—22. Return of the divine glory from the threshold of the
house to the cherubim, and movement of the whole manifestation from
the inner court to the outside of the eastern gate of the outer court
(*vv*. 18—19). Finally the prophet lays stress upon the identity of the
cherubim seen here with those which he saw by the river Chebar
(*vv*. 20—22).

1. *in the firmament*] **upon** or **above**. *V*. 4 assumes that the glory
of the Lord had returned from the threshold of the house, where it
stood (ch. ix. 3), and again appeared above the cherubim. The fact
was either unremarked by the prophet or at least has not been mentioned by him. On the firmament and throne, cf. ch. i. 26 *seq*.

2. *between the wheels*] The word is singular and occurs again *v*. 13,
being used as a collective to describe the whole wheel-work. There
were four wheels (a different word) which are called here collectively
wheelwork, lit. whirling. The word is used of the whirlwind or tempest
(Ps. lxxvii. 18), but also of chariot wheels (Is. v. 28; Ezek. xxiii. 24,
xxvi. 10).

3. *the right side of the house*] i.e. on the south of the temple proper.
It is difficult to see any significance in the position of the cherubim,
except that the south side of the house was more in the direction of the
city than either the north or east side, and the west side was closed by
buildings.

4. *Then the glory went up*] This can hardly be rendered, and...*had
gone up;* consequently the implication in *v*. 1 that the glory had
returned to the cherubim from the threshold is confirmed.

5. *sound of the cherubims' wings*] It is to be supposed that some
movement of the living creatures' wings accompanied the rising of the
divine glory from above them, as it is said that when they stood their

6 the voice of the Almighty God when he speaketh. And it came to pass, *that* when he had commanded the man clothed with linen, saying, Take fire from between the wheels, from between the cherubims; then he went in, and stood beside
7 the wheels. And *one* cherub stretched forth his hand from between the cherubims unto the fire that *was* between the cherubims, and took *thereof*, and put *it* into the hands of *him that was* clothed with linen: who took *it*, and went out.
8 And there appeared in the cherubims the form of a man's
9 hand under their wings. And when I looked, behold the four wheels by the cherubims, one wheel by one cherub, and another wheel by another cherub: and the appearance
10 of the wheels *was* as the colour of a beryl stone. And *as for* their appearances, they four had one likeness, as if a
11 wheel had been in the midst of a wheel. When they went, they went upon their four sides; they turned not as they went, but *to* the place whither the head looked they followed

wings dropped (i. 24). The language of *v*. 18 (cf. ix. 3) excludes the supposition that the cherubim as well as the glory moved towards the threshold (Ew.). Jehovah's "speaking" is the thunder (ch. i. 24), but the statement that the sound was heard in the outer court is strange, as the distance was not great. In Ezekiel's day, however, the outer court had not the symmetry which he gives it in his final vision but extended to a considerable distance from the house, and may have been regarded as including the royal buildings (see the plans *Ency. Brit.*, and Stade's *Hist.*, vol. I.).

6. On the fire between the cherubim, cf. i. 13.

7. *and* one *cherub*] lit. the cherub; the one on the side approached by the man. The cherubim interposed to hand the fire to the man in linen garments, who received it and went forth (Job i. 12, ii. 7). The symbolism is suggested by Is. vi. 6.

8. On the "hands" of the cherubim, cf. ch. i. 8.

Instead of depicting the conflagration of the city, which would have been impossible, the prophet's attention is anew drawn to the cherubim, and a fresh description of the living creatures and of the divine chariot follows.

9. *the four wheels*] Omit: *the*. The description is somewhat more exact than that given ch. i. 15. A "beryl stone," i.e. Tarshishstone, ch. i. 16.

10. Cf. ch. i. 16.

11. Ch. i. 17.

the head looked] i.e. the front of the chariot. The word is hardly to be rendered the principal, or foremost, referring to the wheels. Cf. ch. i. 12, 17.

it; they turned not as they went. And their whole body, 12 and their backs, and their hands, and their wings, and the wheels, *were* full *of* eyes round about, *even* the wheels that they four had. As for the wheels, it was cried unto them in 13 my hearing, O wheel. And *every* one had four faces: the 14 first face *was* the face of a cherub, and the second face *was* the face of a man, and the third the face of a lion, and the

12. *their whole body*] Lit. *flesh*, a strange term to be used of the living creatures. LXX. omits. The word "backs" is used of the felloes of the wheels in ch. i. 18, and in this verse the living creatures and the wheels are confused together.

wheels that they four had] More naturally: even their four wheels, lit. even they four, their wheels, where "they" anticipates "wheels."

13. *in my hearing, O wheel*] Rather as mar., **They were called in my hearing Wheel**, R.V., whirling *wheels*. Cf. *vv.* 2, 6 where the word (galgal) is used by the divine speaker.

14. The verse, which LXX. omits, is difficult. The words rendered "first face" might have that sense or the sense "one face" at a pinch, but mean naturally "face of the first;" and those rendered "the second face" can hardly mean anything but "the face of the second," for it is precarious to extend constructions like Jer. xlvi. 2 "the year of the fourth" (year) = the fourth year, to other words than "year." The easiest course would be to omit the word "face" before "first" and "second," as in fact it does not stand before "third" and "fourth;" or perhaps it might be enough to omit it before "second" and assume that the anomalous constr. "one face" (Lev. xxiv. 22; 2 Kings xii. 10) had led to the insertion of "face" before "the second."

face of a cherub] Of **the** cherub. As the other faces were those of a man, a lion, and an eagle, this face must be that of the ox (ch. i. 10). Why should this be called the face of the cherub? It is said that the winged bulls at the portals of Assyrian temples are called cherubs in Assyrian (Fried. Del. *Paradies*, p. 153, Lenormant, *Les origines de l'histoire*, p. 118), but these winged bulls have not the face of an ox but that of a man, and there is no probability that in Israel the cherubs in the temple were ox-faced.

It seems possible to explain the verse only by making some suppositions which may appear rather artificial, viz. first that the prophet looking at the phenomenon of the chariot and four creatures as a whole saw four faces presented to him, one (and a different one) by each of the creatures, and that he named the faces which were thus presented to him. We should then translate "the face of the first," "the face of the second" &c., though this seems opposed to the meaning of the first words of the verse. And secondly, that he assumes the side of the chariot presented to him not to be the front, but regards the side looking in another direction as the front or head. His view of the chariot is taken when it rose and proceeded eastward (*v.* 19); and he regards the side of the chariot turned to the east as the front, and

15 fourth the face of an eagle. And the cherubims were lifted up. This *is* the living creature that I saw by the river of
16 Chebar. And when the cherubims went, the wheels went by them: and when the cherubims lift up their wings to mount up from the earth, the same wheels also turned not
17 from beside them. When they stood, *these* stood; and when they were lifted up, *these* lift up themselves *also:* for the spirit of the living creature *was* in them.
18 Then the glory of the LORD departed from off the thresh-
19 old of the house, and stood over the cherubims. And the cherubims lift up their wings, and mounted up from the earth in my sight: when they went out, the wheels also *were* besides them, and *every one* stood *at* the door of the east gate of the LORD'S house; and the glory of the God of
20 Israel *was* over them above. This *is* the living creature that I saw under the God of Israel by the river of Chebar;
21 and I knew that they *were the* cherubims. Every one had

he calls the cherub which led the movement to the east *the* cherub. Further at this moment the chariot and cherubim were standing on the south side of the house (*v*. 3), and the prophet's position was probably near the house and thus to the north or left of the phenomenon. Now the ox-face of all the cherubs was on their left (ch. i. 10), that is, in the case of a cherub leading the movement eastward, toward the north where the prophet presumably was standing. Thus he would see the ox-face of the first cherub (whose human face was eastward, leading the whole chariot). He would also see the man's face of the cherub on the side of the chariot facing himself, the lion's face of the cherub who stood on the west side of the chariot, and the eagle's face of the cherub on the south side of the chariot, for all the eagle-faces looked inward to the centre of the chariot. This is the order followed in the verse.

15. *were lifted up*] The prophet identifies the manifestation with that seen at the Chebar when he perceives its movement. The verse is resumed in *v*. 19.

16, 17. Cf. ch. i. 19.

17. *lift up themselves*] **Were lifted up** with them.

18. The glory of the Lord returns from the threshold of the house to the cherubim, and these mount up and remove outside the precincts of the temple altogether, and stand within the city at the eastern gateway of the outward court.

19. every one *stood* at *the door*] Rather: *they stood*, lit. *it*, viz. the whole manifestation.

20. were the *cherubims*] **Were cherubim.** The remark that he knew that the living creatures were cherubim is of very great difficulty. It would scarcely be in the sense of the prophet to suppose that he learned that the living creatures were cherubim from hearing them so

four faces apiece, and every one four wings; and the likeness of the hands of a man *was* under their wings. And the likeness of their faces *was* the same faces which I saw by the river of Chebar, their appearances and themselves: they went every one straight forward.

called by the divine speaker (*vv.* 2, 6) because previous to this he himself has so called them (ch. ix. 3). The meaning is rather that this third vision of them (ch. i. and ch. iii. 23) with its details and movements revealed to him that the creatures were cherubim. But admitting that the prophet had visions we can hardly escape the conclusion that the details of the phenomenon of the cherubim repose upon reflection. This reflection may have preceded the visions and been reproduced in them, but where did he find the elements that entered into his combination? Were they not derived from the temple largely, though also from the storm-cloud? Could he be unaware of the source whence he derived them? It is possible that in the excitation of the vision he did not recall the processes of his own reflection. Or may it be that we are straining the word "knew" when we understand it in the sense of *learned*, came to know? This is the natural sense to put upon it in this Book, and up to this time the prophet has not used the name cherubim.

The derivation of the word cherub is obscure. If Assyrian scholars are right the name is Babylonian, and is found given to the colossal winged bulls (called at other times shidu, Heb. *shêd*) which guard the portals of palaces and temples in Babylonia. The word (Kirubu) is said to have the sense of "great" (Schrader, *KAT.* on Gen. iii. 24, Del. *Paradies*, p. 150 seq.). But though the name be common to Babylonian and Hebrew, and though originally the idea expressed by the name may have been the same in both, the usage as known from Babylonian literature marks the end of a long development, and that in Hebrew marks the end of another long and independent development, and any attempt to control or explain the one by the other must be made with caution.

The narrative and essential part of Ch. x. lies in *vv.* 2, 3, 4, 6, 7, 18, 19; the rest is annotation suggested by points in the narrative, in which ch. i. is repeated without anything essential being added to it. A second description of the cherubim after ch. i. looks unnecessary, and Cornill would excide *vv.* 8—17 entirely. There may be occasional glosses in these verses, but no reason exists for cutting them out which does not equally apply to *vv.* 20—22. The whole description of the divine chariot has an appearance of artificiality to us now, but in Ezekiel we have a peculiar mind, and it is safer to content ourselves with saying that we do not altogether understand the importance which he attaches to the phenomenon of the chariot and the living creatures.

11 Moreover the spirit lift me up, and brought me unto the

CH. XI. THREAT OF DESTRUCTION AGAINST THE PEOPLE, ESPECIALLY THE WAR PARTY IN JERUSALEM, WITH PROMISE OF RESTORATION TO THE EXILES.

Though the symbolism in ch. ix. x., shewing the slaughter of the inhabitants and the burning of the city, might have seemed exhaustive, there were thoughts in men's minds which had to be met, and issues to which reference had to be made. The city was thought impregnably strong, and Jehovah's presence would protect it. The prophet symbolizes the departure of Jehovah from it, and warns those who trust to its strength that their trust is vain. Yet the fall of the city is not the last act in Israel's history; the "house of Israel" is wider than the population of Jerusalem, and towards the larger Israel Jehovah has purposes of mercy. He will restore them to their ancient heritage, where they shall serve him in a land purified from all its uncleanness.

In ch. x. 18 it was stated that the glory of the Lord left the threshold of the house and returned to the cherubims, and in ch. x. 19 that the whole manifestation removed from the inner court and stood at the eastern entrance to the outer court of the temple. The prophet also is transported to the same place (ch. xi. 1). At the entrance to the gateway he sees twenty-five men, among them two who are named, princes of the people. The twenty-five represent the rulers of the city and the leaders of the inhabitants.

(1) *vv.* 2—12. These men are represented as plotting evil enterprizes, that is, of rebellion against the king of Babylon. They are not unaware of the danger they incur, but are confident in the protection which the well fortified city will afford them—it is the pot and they are the flesh, which the fire cannot reach. The prophet receives command to prophesy against them, and declare that their confidence is vain. The city shall not protect them; they shall be dragged out of it and slain on the borders of the land, far away from it.

(2) *vv.* 13—21. While the prophet was delivering this threat one of the two princes named died. Filled with terror at the certainty with which the word of God takes effect, the prophet fell down to intercede that the remnant of Israel might not be destroyed. He is reminded that though Jerusalem fall his fellow exiles remain and all the house of Israel. These exiles were despised by the people of Jerusalem and denied any share in the inheritance of the land; but though the Lord had scattered them he would yet bring them to their ancient home, giving them a new heart to serve him.

(3) *vv.* 22—25. Finally the divine manifestation rose from the city and stood over the Mount of Olives. The prophet was carried back to Chaldæa; the hand of the Lord was lifted from him, and he awoke out of his vision, the contents of which he narrated to them of the captivity.

1—12. THE MEN THAT PLOT EVIL.

1. The gate referred to is the outer eastern gate; the position taken up by the cherubim and glory was outside the temple precincts wholly.

east gate of the LORD'S house, which looketh eastward: and behold at the door of the gate five and twenty men; among whom I saw Jaazaniah the son of Azur, and Pelatiah the son of Benaiah, princes of the people. Then said he unto 2 me, Son of man, these *are* the men that devise mischief, and give wicked counsel in this city: which say, *It is* not 3 near; *let us* build houses: this *city is* the caldron, and we

Jaazaniah and Pelatiah are named "princes of the people." Possibly they were more prominent members of the ruling party. It is the manner of the prophet to introduce elements of reality into his symbolical pictures (cf. ch. xxiv. 16 *seq.*), and it is unnecessary to regard these two personages as fictitious or seek for some symbolical meaning in their names. A different Jaazaniah was mentioned in ch. viii. 11. The twenty-five men here are not to be identified with those in ch. viii. 16; they are rulers and leaders of the people (*v.* 2).

2. *give wicked counsel*] lit. *who counsel evil counsel.* The evil counsel probably refers to the revolutionary enterprizes of these men against the authority of Babylon, which the prophet severely condemns (ch. xvii.). The city was divided into factions, one part holding with Babylon and another with Egypt, while some were for peace on any terms. The consequence of these divisions was much bloodshed within the city (*v.* 6). It is probable that the schemes of these plotters were only being hatched (*v.* 5); it was not till some time later that the steps now meditated were actually taken.

3. It is *not near;* let us *build*] Rather as R.V. **The time to build houses is not near,** lit. *the building of houses is not near.* The phrase "to build houses" is to be taken as in ch. xxviii. 26, "And they shall dwell with confidence therein, and shall build houses and plant vineyards and shall dwell with confidence." To build houses is a sign and a consequence of a time of peace and security (Is. lxv. 21; Jer. xxix. 5, 28). These agitators desire to turn men's minds away from peaceful occupations, and make them contemplate other measures, assuring them that when war comes the strong city will be their salvation—it is the pot which will protect the flesh from the fire around it. Others, e.g. Ew., take the phrase interrogatively: Is not the building of houses near? This, however, hardly corresponds to the situation, which is not one of war which it is hoped will speedily pass over, but one of contemplated rebellion. LXX. renders: Have not the houses been recently built? it is the pot &c.; so Corn. This gives a closer connexion to the two halves of the verse, but "houses" could hardly have the sense of fortifications, nor does the phrase naturally express the meaning that the damage done to the city when last captured (under Jehoiachin) had been fully repaired.

this city is *the caldron*] lit. it is the caldron or pot. The phrase implies two things, the danger of fire around, and that the strong city will prove a protection to those within it. These revolutionary spirits are aware of the risks they run, but with a certain grimness

4 *be* the flesh. Therefore prophesy against them, prophesy, O
5 son of man. And the Spirit of the LORD fell upon me, and
said unto me, Speak; Thus saith the LORD; Thus have ye
said, O house of Israel: for I know the things that come
6 into your mind, *every one of* them. Ye have multiplied your
slain in this city, and ye have filled the streets thereof *with*
7 the slain. Therefore thus saith the Lord GOD; Your slain
whom ye have laid in the midst of it, they *are* the flesh, and
this *city is* the caldron: but *I* will bring you forth out of the
8 midst of it. Ye have feared the sword; and I will bring a
9 sword upon you, saith the Lord GOD. And I will bring you
out of the midst thereof, and deliver you into the hands of
10 strangers, and will execute judgments among you. Ye shall
fall by the sword; I will judge you in the border of Israel;
11 and ye shall know that I *am* the LORD. This *city* shall not
be your caldron, neither shall ye be the flesh in the midst
12 thereof; *but* I will judge you in the border of Israel: and
ye shall know that I *am* the LORD: for ye have not walked

of humour they make light of them. The figure here is somewhat
different from that of the boiling pot for war common in the Arabic
poets.

4. The prophet felt called to prophesy against these men—and all
this is part of the vision. See on ch. iii. 21.

5. *things that come into your mind*] i.e. your projects. Apparently
as yet the rebellion was no more than a plan which was being hatched.

6. Comp. ch. xxii. 25, vii. 23. Those opposed to the schemes of
the ruling party, or suspected of opposition, were openly or on various
pretexts cut off.

7. Those slain in the midst of Jerusalem will be the only "flesh"
that will remain in the pot. The living conspirators who think they
shall be safe shall be dragged forth and judged far away from the pro-
tecting city, on the borders of Israel. The figure of the pot and flesh is
used differently in ch. xxiv. (The Heb. is probably to be spelled so as
to give the meaning "I will bring you forth.")

8. *have feared*] **Ye fear.** The language of the ruling class, in spite
of its recklessness (*v.* 3), betrays the consciousness of the risks they
incur; and their fears shall be more than verified.

9. *hands of strangers*] i.e. foreign conquerors, the Babylonians.

10. *in the border of Israel*] far away from the city, which they hoped
would protect them. Cf. Jer. lii. 26, "So Nebuzaradan, the captain
of the guard took them and brought them to the king of Babylon to
Riblah; and he smote them and put them to death in Riblah, in the
land of Hamath." 2 Kings xxv. 18 *seq.*

11, 12. *vv.* 11, 12 are wanting in LXX.

in my statutes, neither executed my judgments, but have done after the manners of the heathen that *are* round about you.

13 And it came to pass, when I prophesied, that Pelatiah the son of Benaiah died. Then fell I down upon my face, and cried *with* a loud voice, and said, Ah Lord God, *wilt* thou make a full end of the remnant of Israel? 14 Again the word of the Lord came unto me, saying, 15 Son of man, thy brethren, *even* thy brethren, the men of thy kindred, and all the house of Israel wholly, *are* they unto whom the inhabit-

13. While Ezekiel was uttering this prophecy Pelatiah fell down dead, and the prophet seemed to see in the event the coming destruction of all the remnant of Israel before the wrath of God, and fell on his face to intercede for them. This incident is exceedingly difficult to estimate. The prophet tells us that all the occurrences in ch. viii.—xi. were done in vision. Unfortunately this does not justify us in assuming that the death of Pelatiah was a mere symbolical death, and no reality. For the "vision" is in great measure a mere *schema* under which the prophet groups much that had reality, such as his own thoughts, his discourses to the people, and probably actual events happening in Jerusalem. But in grouping the events under the *schema* of the vision he idealises them, making them expressive of general conceptions and principles, and it is impossible to distinguish between things which were actual but are idealised, and things which are purely creations of the symbolizing imagination. It is possible that Ezekiel prophesied against these princes in Jerusalem (ch. xi. 4), as Jeremiah did against the false prophets in Babylon, whom a horrible fate overtook (Jer. xxix. 21), and against Hananiah (Jer. xxviii. 15 *seq.*), and it is possible that soon afterwards Pelatiah suddenly died, and that these real occurrences have been drawn by the prophet under his *schema* of the vision. On the other hand the death of Pelatiah may be merely symbolical, to shew with what certainty the word of God takes effect, the symbol being modelled on Jeremiah's prophecy against Hananiah.

a full end] See on ch. ix. 8.

14 *seq.* The answer of the Lord to the prophet's intercession. The destruction of the inhabitants of Jerusalem is not the end of Israel. The Israel in exile is the Israel whom the Lord regards and will yet restore.

15. *the men of thy kindred*] Lit. *the men of thy redemption*. This could only mean, the men to be redeemed, or delivered, by thy intercession—the men for whom thou shouldst pray. Such a sense is difficult to draw from the words. In usage the term has not the meaning of "kindred." Probably the word should be so read as to mean "exile"— *the men of thy exile*, i.e. thy fellow captives.

are they unto whom] It is better to regard the first words in the verse down to "wholly" as exclamations: "thy brethren, thy brethren, thy fellow exiles, and all the house of Israel, all of it! they unto whom..."

ants of Jerusalem have said, Get ye far from the LORD:
16 unto us is this land given in possession. Therefore say,
Thus saith the Lord GOD; Although I have cast them far
off among the heathen, and although I have scattered them
among the countries, yet will I be to them as a little sanc-
17 tuary in the countries where they shall come. Therefore
say, Thus saith the Lord GOD; I will even gather you from
the people, and assemble you out of the countries where ye

The sentence is not strictly grammatical, but the exclamations give an answer to the prophet's anxious question, "wilt thou make a full end of the remnant of Israel?" (*v.* 13). The destruction of them of Jerusalem is no full end; the fellow-exiles of the prophet and all the house of Israel scattered abroad (ch. iv. 4, xxxvi. 16) remain. The second half of the verse is loosely attached to the first—*they to whom*, &c.

Get ye far from the LORD] A slight alteration in a point would give the sense: of whom...have said (say), *They are far* from the Lord. The change is hardly necessary. Those left were in possession of the temple, the abode of Jehovah, and had the assurance of his presence, in which those gone forth had no part, for to go into a foreign land was to come under the dominion of other gods, according to the words of David, "For they have driven me out this day from having part in the inheritance of the Lord, saying, Go serve other gods" (1 Sam. xxvi. 19, cf. Deut. iv. 28, xxviii. 36, 64; Jer. xvi. 13; Hos. ix. 3). See ch. viii. 12, ix. 9, for the expression of a different mood of feeling.

is this land given] is **the** land. Comp. the expression of similar pretensions, ch. xxxiii. 24.

16 *seq.* Answer of Jehovah. It is true he has scattered the exiles among the nations; but he will again gather them.

16. *yet will I be to them*] Rather: and **have been to them for a sanctuary but little** in the countries where they are come. The expression "for a sanctuary but little" refers to the taunt of the dwellers in Jerusalem that the exiles were far from the sanctuary and had no part in Jehovah. It is true that he had not been to the exiles in great measure that which a "sanctuary" is, viz. a presence of Jehovah, a sanctification, and a religious joy. It is doubtful if "sanctuary" has anywhere (even Is. viii. 14) the meaning of asylum, protection; the sanctuary is the abode of Jehovah, and his presence there sanctifies those in the midst of whom he dwells. The exiles longed to be near the sanctuary and mourned their distance from it (Ps. lxxxiv., cxxxvii.); while those left in the land boasted of the possession of it and looked on the exiles as outcasts.

17—20. But this time of privation for the exiles shall come to an end. They shall be gathered out of the countries, and the land of Israel given to them; from which they shall remove all its abominations. They shall receive a new heart to walk in the Lord's commandments; and he shall be their God and they his people.

have been scattered, and I will give you the land of Israel. And they shall come thither, and they shall take away all 18 the detestable things thereof and all the abominations thereof from thence. And I will give them one heart, and I will 19 put a new spirit within you; and I will take the stony heart out of their flesh, and will give them a heart of flesh: that 20 they may walk in my statutes, and keep mine ordinances, and do them: and they shall be my people, and I will be their God. But *as for them* whose heart walketh after the 21 heart of their detestable things and their abominations, I will recompense their way upon their own heads, saith the Lord God.

give you the land of Israel] Those left in the country said: The land is given unto us. They shall be cast out and the land again given to those now in exile. The flower of the nation had been carried away in the captivity of Jehoiachin. Both Jeremiah and Ezekiel regard the exiles as the hope of the nation and speak bitterly against the population remaining at home; comp. the former's parable of the very naughty figs (ch. xxiv.), and the latter's scornful questions, ch. xxxiii. 24—26. Cp. ch. xxviii. 25, xxxiv. 13, xxxvi. 24.

18. *shall take away*] i.e. remove. Cf. ch. xxxvii. 22, 23. The "detestable things" are the false gods (1 K. xi. 5, 7; 2 K. xxiii. 13), and all the accompaniments of the debased worship (cf. ch. xxxiii. 25, 26).

19. *give them one heart*] Cf. Jer. xxxii. 38, "And they shall be my people and I will be their God, and I will give them one heart and one way, that they may fear me for ever." LXX. "another" heart (*r* for *d*). Some MSS., Targ. and Syr. read *new*, which is the prophet's own term, ch. xxxvi. 26. Both "another" and "new" form a better antithesis to "stony heart" than "one" does. The old stony heart, unimpressible and obstinate, shall be taken away, and a heart of "flesh," sensitive and responsive to the touch of Jehovah, shall be given them.

20. *shall be my people*] Then shall the covenant between the Lord and Israel be fully realized, for this is the idea of the covenant, that he should be their God and they his people, ch. xxxvi. 28, xxxvii. 27; Jer. xxxi. 33.

21. But those who cleave to their abominations shall receive the recompense of their ways—there is no peace saith the Lord to the wicked (Is. xlviii. 22).

The language "whose heart walketh *after the heart of* their detestable things" is without parallel or meaning; elsewhere it is: whose heart walketh after their idols (ch. xx. 16, xxxiii. 31, after their covetousness). A different class of persons is referred to from those spoken of in *vv.* 17—20, either the population in Jerusalem or more naturally those in general who follow idols. The text requires some amendment: but as for those whose heart goeth after their detestable things... their way will I recompense.

22 Then did the cherubims lift up their wings, and the wheels besides them; and the glory of the God of Israel *was* over them above. 23 And the glory of the Lord went up from the midst of the city, and stood upon the mountain which *is* on the east side of the city. 24 Afterwards the spirit took me up, and brought me in vision by the Spirit of God into Chaldea, to them of the captivity. So the vision that I had seen went up from me. 25 Then I spake unto them of the captivity all the things that the Lord had shewed me.

vv. **22—25.** The manifestation of Jehovah rises from over the city and moves eastward to the Mount of Olives. The city is abandoned by Jehovah (Hos. v. 15). The prophet does not pursue the movement further. The glory passes out by the eastern gate, by which also it returns into the new temple (ch. xliii. 1—4). The prophet is carried back by the spirit to the captivity; to which he narrates all he had seen.

Fourth Section, Ch. XII.—XIX. The necessity of Israel's destruction.

The preceding symbols, such as those in ch. iv.—xii. and ch. viii.—xi., had foreshewn the certainty of the nation's fall, a new series of discourses demonstrate the necessity of it. Many thoughts and considerations occurred to men's minds which invalidated the force of the prophet's threats and disinclined them to receive them, or at least left them in hesitation. They had been for long familiar with threats of judgment, but the threatened storm had passed over. There were also men who saw into the future as well as Ezekiel, who, however, discerned no signs of approaching calamity, but foretold peace and security. And further, was not Israel the people of Jehovah, whom he could not cast away? In a new series of discourses the prophet disposes of such considerations, adding also positive reasons which demonstrate the moral necessity of the nation's removal. The section has these divisions—

(1) ch. xii. 1—20. Symbol of the king's secret flight and capture.

(2) ch. xii. 21—28. The popular delusion that prophecies of evil failed to come true, or referred to the distant future, shall receive a speedy and terrible refutation.

(3) ch. xiii., xiv. The prophets who foster such delusions and preach peace, prophesy out of their own heart and lie. The deceivers and those deceived by them shall perish together.

(4) ch. xv. Will the Lord destroy the nation of Israel, his own people?—Israel among the nations is like the vinebranch among the trees: what was it ever good for? Particularly, what is it good for now when half-burnt in the fire? Only to be flung again into the fire and wholly consumed.

(5) ch. xvi. Let the history of Jerusalem be judged and estimated !

12 The word of the LORD also came unto me, saying, Son of
2 man, thou dwellest in the midst of a rebellious house, which
have eyes to see, and see not; they have ears to hear, and
hear not: for they *are* a rebellious house. Therefore thou **3**

Has it not been a persistent course of ingratitude and unfaithfulness? Can the issue of it be anything but destruction?

(6) ch. xvii. And the perfidy of Zedekiah against the king of Babylon, must it not be chastised?

(7) ch. xviii. The principles of the divine government.

(8) ch. xix. Dirge over Judah and her royal house.

CH. XII. SYMBOL OF THE FLIGHT AND CAPTURE OF THE KING.

The passage is without date, but the signs were subsequent to those already described. The first part, *vv.* 1—20, is rather of the nature of a preface, repeating the certainty of the downfall of the city and nation, while all that follows up to ch. xix. supports this certainty by shewing the moral necessity of Israel's destruction.

(1) *vv.* 1—2. An introduction characterizing the house of Israel as blind and unable to discern the signs of the times, and therefore in need of new proofs to convince them.

(2) *vv.* 3—7. A symbolical action, prefiguring the fate of the king and people on the capture of the city.

(3) *vv.* 8—16. Exposition of the symbol: the failure of Zedekiah's attempt at resistance, his flight and capture, exile and death in Babylon, with the dispersion of the people into all lands.

(4) *vv.* 17—20. A new symbol of the life of anguish and terror which the people shall lead under the foreign invaders.

(5) *vv.* 21—25. Warning against a proverb current in Israel to the effect that "visions," that is, prophecies of evil, did not come true.

(6) *vv.* 26—28. Warning against a less blameable form of unbelief, the idea that prophecies, such as those now given, referred to a distant time, and that it would be long ere they were fulfilled.

2. The people of Israel among whom the prophet dwells is a rebellious house (ch. ii. 3, 6, 7, 8, iii. 26, 27). His former signs meet with no belief from them. They have eyes but see not: they behold events and history with their bodily eyes, but fail to discern the moral meaning in them. Events are just events to them, the nature of the God who animates the events remains undiscovered by them (Is. vi. 9, xlii. 20; Jer. v. 21; Mark viii. 18). And the signs and words of the prophet make no impression on them; they say, "Doth he not speak parables?" (ch. xx. 49). Therefore new signs must be given them (*v.* 4).

3—7. SYMBOLICAL ACTION, PREFIGURING THE ESCAPE AND CAPTURE OF THE FUGITIVES.

The details of the symbol seem to be as follows: First, the prophet prepares "stuff for removing"—such articles as one meaning to escape would carry with him. These things being prepared, he brings them

son of man, prepare thee stuff for removing, and remove by day in their sight; and thou shalt remove from thy place to another place in their sight: it may be they will consider, 4 though they *be* a rebellious house. Then shalt thou bring forth thy stuff by day in their sight, as stuff for removing: and thou shalt go forth at even in their sight, as they that 5 go forth into captivity. Dig thou through the wall in their 6 sight, and carry out thereby. In their sight shalt thou bear

out. It is not said where he deposits them; it would be in some place convenient to make his escape from, in the vicinity of the wall of the city. These things he does before the eyes of the people during daylight. His action represents the conduct of persons in a besieged city, whose movements are free within the city; hence this part of the action is done openly (*vv.* 3, 4). Secondly, these preparations having been made by day, the prophet himself goes out in the even, in the darkness, and digs through the wall, making his escape at the opening, and carrying on his shoulder the articles which he had prepared to take with him in his flight. Besides doing this in the darkness he covers his face. In doing all this he is a "sign" to the house of Israel: in this way shall the king and those with him seek to escape into exile from the enemy when the city is about to fall into their hands (*vv.* 4—7).

3. *stuff for removing*] Lit. articles of exile, i.e. such articles as one carries with him when going as a fugitive into exile.

and remove by day] Lit. remove as into exile. The word is wanting in LXX., which reads: prepare for thyself articles of exile by day in their sight. This is more natural.

remove from thy place] The words seem to describe generally the whole symbolical action which the prophet is to perform.

though they be *a rebellious*] **for they are.**

4. *Then shalt thou bring*] **And thou shalt.** The prophet is to bring forth the articles which he had prepared, depositing them in some convenient place in readiness to carry with him when he escapes.

and thou shalt go forth] Possibly: and thou shalt go forth thyself, as R.V. The second half of *v.* 4 is to be connected with *v.* 5, describing the prophet's action so far as it symbolizes what refers to the *persons* of the fugitives.

5. *Dig through the wall*] Naturally the "wall" is not the wall of his house, but the city wall. He brought out his articles of flight by day, making them ready for the night-time when he was to escape through the wall. It is absurd to suppose, as is usually done, that he carried his things back into the house, and digged through the wall of his house in the evening. This would mar the action and be ridiculous. The "wall" is the city wall. The question whether Tel Abib was a walled place is of no importance, because the actions were probably not actually performed.

6. The verse refers to the prophet's going out through the city wall,

it upon *thy* shoulders, *and* carry *it* forth in the twilight: thou shalt cover thy face, that thou see not the ground: for I have set thee *for* a sign unto the house of Israel. And I 7 did so as I was commanded: I brought forth my stuff by day, as stuff for captivity, and in the even I digged through the wall with mine hand; I brought *it* forth in the twilight, *and* I bare *it* upon *my* shoulder in their sight.

And in the morning came the word of the LORD unto me, 8 saying, Son of man, hath not the house of Israel, the re- 9 bellious house, said unto thee, What doest thou? Say thou 10 unto them, Thus saith the Lord GOD; This burden *concerneth* the prince in Jerusalem, and all the house of Israel

bearing on his shoulder the bundle of articles he carried with him in his flight.

in the twilight] in the **darkness**. So *v.* 7. The word again only Gen. xv. 17.

cover thy face] This might be to disguise himself, but the next words "thou shalt not see the land" (ground) seem to require a different sense. Cf. *vv.* 12, 13.

a sign unto...Israel] A typical sign, as explained *v.* 11, "As I have done so shall it be done unto them." Comp. ch. xxiv. 24, 27; Is. viii. 18; xx. 3; Zech. iii. 8.

7. *with mine hand*] lit. *with hand*, i.e. by force, Is. xxviii. 2. LXX. omits.

in the twilight] the **darkness**, as *v.* 6, so *v.* 12.

vv. 8—16. Exposition of the symbol.

The action of the prophet is a representation of what shall happen in the last days of the siege. The king and those about him shall prepare for flight; they shall go out secretly through the walls, but shall be captured and brought to Babylon.

8, 9. *in the morning*] This circumstance might seem to imply that the prophet really performed the actions described. But though in this case performance of the action was not an impossibility it was probably only narrated (see on ch. iv.). The natural sequel of the action (supposing it done), the curiosity of the people, is described, just as the action itself was, as if it had literally been shewn.

10, 11. The general meaning of these verses is clear enough—the prophet's action is a representation of what shall happen in Jerusalem in the case of prince and people, but *v.* 10 is very obscure, and probably not in its original form.

This burden concerneth *the prince*] lit. *the prince* (is) *this burden* in Jerusalem. The term "burden" has also the sense of "oracle," but Ez. does not use it in this sense and there is no reason to find any play upon the word as Jer. xxiii. 33. The allusion can only be to the last words of *v.* 7—I *bare it* upon my shoulder; and the meaning would be: this bearing or loading has reference to the prince (*v.* 12). With this

11 that *are* among them. Say, I *am* your sign: like as I have done, so shall it be done unto them: they shall remove *and*
12 go into captivity. And the prince that *is* among them shall bear upon *his* shoulder in the twilight, and shall go forth: they shall dig through the wall to carry out thereby: he shall cover his face, that he see not the ground with *his* eyes.
13 My net also will I spread upon him, and he shall be taken in my snare: and I will bring him to Babylon *to* the land of the Chaldeans; yet shall he not see it, though he shall die

sense the following words must run: and all the house of Israel which are in the midst of it (Jerusalem—with a change of one letter). The objection to this that if the relative were subject the pronoun would not be expressed after it (Hitz., Keil) is worthless. But there are other objections more valid: "all the house of Israel" could hardly be used of the inhabitants of Jerusalem, the phrase usually refers to the larger Israel, existing in all places. R.V. "this burden *concerneth* the prince...and all the house of Israel among whom they are;" but *concerneth* is said of the "prince" and of "all the house of Israel" in different senses. Notwithstanding the objections to it the easiest course is to read: *in the midst of it* (Jerusalem) as above. Corn. omits the verse as a gloss.

11. *I* am *your sign*] i.e. a sign to you—the exiles, to whom he is speaking; while done "to them" refers to the inhabitants of Jerusalem. Cf. *v.* 6.

12. *shoulder in the twilight, and shall*] The balance of clauses requires: shall bear upon his shoulder; in the darkness shall he go forth (or, carry forth—a slight change of reading, which obviates the unnatural *and*).

that he see not the ground] Rather as R.V., **because he shall not see the land.**

with his *eyes*] Lit. *by eyesight himself.* The language is unnatural. LXX. "that he may not be seen by eye, and he himself shall not see the land." Whether original or not this rendering combines the two ideas expressed by "covering the face," viz. that of disguise (Job xxiv. 15), and that of inability to see (Job ix. 24). The prophet clearly foresaw the fall of the city and the captivity of the king, and he may have threatened the king with a chastisement for his rebellion which, though barbarous, was not unusual in that age. If he did so it is still probable that afterwards when composing his Book he made the references to the putting out of the king's eyes more distinct (*v.* 13).

13. The king's flight shall be unavailing; he shall be captured and brought blinded to Babylon, where he shall die. As the Lord fought against Jerusalem in the siege, so it is he that ensures the capture of the king. It is in his net that he is ensnared and taken; Hos. vii. 12, "when they go, I will spread my net upon them; I will bring them down as the fowls of heaven." Cf. Ez. xvii. 20; xxxii. 3.

yet shall he not see it] The eyes of Zedekiah were put out by Nebuchadnezzar at Riblah. 2 Kings xxv. 5 *seq.*; Jer. lii. 8, 11.

there. And I will scatter toward every wind all that *are* 14
about him to help him, and all his bands; and I will draw
out the sword after them. And they shall know that I *am* 15
the LORD, when I shall scatter them among the nations, and
disperse them in the countries. But I will leave a few men 16
of them from the sword, from the famine, and from the
pestilence; that they may declare all their abominations
among the heathen whither they come; and they shall know
that I *am* the LORD.

Moreover the word of the LORD came to me, saying, Son 17
of man, eat thy bread with quaking, and drink thy water 18
with trembling and with carefulness; and say unto the 19
people of the land, Thus saith the Lord GOD, of the inhabitants of Jerusalem, *and* of the land of Israel; They shall eat
their bread with carefulness, and drink their water with
astonishment, that her land may be desolate from all that is
therein, because of the violence of all them that dwell
therein. And the cities that are inhabited shall be laid 20
waste, and the land shall be desolate; and ye shall know
that I *am* the LORD.

And the word of the LORD came unto me, saying, Son of 21 22

14—16. All the armies and aids of the king shall be dispersed and pursued with the sword. They shall be scattered among the nations, and their history shall bring to their knowledge what Jehovah, their God, truly is. A remnant of them shall be spared among the nations that they make known to them their abominations, and these also shall learn what the God of Israel is. Jerusalem and Israel is set in the midst of the nations round about (ch. v. 5), its history is a drama enacted before the eyes of mankind, and the drama when finished will reveal, not only to Israel but the nations of the world, Jehovah in his fulness. Cf. ch. xiv. 22, 23, xvii. 24, xx. 9, xxxviii. 23, xxxix. 23; Is. v. 16; Jer. xxii. 8.

17—20. A new symbol of the terror and violence and desolation about to come upon the land.

18. It is obvious that this symbol could not have been actually performed. Cf. ch. iv. 16.

19. *Jerusalem* and *of the land*] Rather: Jerusalem **in** (lit. upon) the land.

because of the violence] The punishment of violence is violence. The internal wrong and oppression shall be avenged by a crushing violence and destruction from without. Am. iii. 9—11. The phrase "desolate from all that is therein," lit. *from its fulness*, means desolate and emptied of its fulness.

man, what *is* that proverb *that* ye have in the land of Israel, saying, The days are prolonged, and every vision faileth? 23 Tell them therefore, Thus saith the Lord GOD; I will make this proverb to cease, and they shall no more use it as a proverb in Israel; but say unto them, The days are at hand, 24 and the effect of every vision. For there shall be no more

21—28. WARNING AGAINST DESPISING OF PROPHECY.

The prophet felt that such threats as those just uttered (*vv.* 1—20) were neglected and little thought of. People disposed of such prophecies by saying that they did not come true; or, if they did not go so far, by saying that they referred to the distant future. Ezekiel warns them that Jehovah's threatenings bear upon the present time, and that they shall be fulfilled.

22. *The days are prolonged*] i.e. time passes and becomes long. The words are a generalization upon the fact that prophecies of judgment are not fulfilled; time goes on and "every vision faileth," remains a dead threat. LXX. omits "every," giving even a more comprehensive sense. The reference is specially to prophecies of judgment, and there was room for misapprehension in regard to these, because being drawn forth by moral evils existing when they were uttered, they were of the nature of threats, the object of which was to bring the people to repentance, and thus prevent their own fulfilment. For the same reason they were often of a general character, and thus when their fulfilment was postponed or when they were not literally fulfilled, men judged that they were merely uttered in the air. The moral purpose and consequently the contingent character of prophecy is expressly taught in Jer. xviii., and was well understood by intelligent persons in Israel, as appears from the reasoning of the princes in regard to the prophecy of Micah, Jer. xxvi. 17—19.

23. Judgment had been so often threatened and so often deferred that the failure of prophecy to realize itself became a proverb. Too superficial to apprehend the meaning of its postponement these scoffers made light of the threatened judgment (2 Pet. iii. 3, 9). Now they shall be undeceived. For similar popular sentiments, cf. Jer. v. 13, 14, xvii. 15.

the effect of every vision] Lit. *the word*—the contents, of every vision.

24. Another thing which robbed the word of the true prophets, who threatened judgment, of its force was the fact that there were other prophets who spoke in a contrary sense, preaching peace and security. Prophets, though alike speaking in the name of Jehovah, contradicted one another, and the people, even if anxious to know the truth, had no criterion whereby to judge between them. The scene between Jeremiah and Hananiah (Jer. xxviii.) is very instructive as to the condition in which the people were left. There was nothing in Jeremiah to shew him to be a true prophet, and nothing in Hananiah

any vain vision nor flattering divination within the house of Israel. For I *am* the LORD: I will speak, and the word 25 that I shall speak shall come to pass; it shall be no more prolonged: for in your days, O rebellious house, will I say the word, and will perform it, saith the Lord GOD.

Again the word of the LORD came to me, saying, Son of 26 man, behold, *they of* the house of Israel say, The vision that 27 he seeth *is* for many days *to come*, and he prophesieth of the times *that are* far off. Therefore say unto them, Thus saith 28

to prove him false. Truth and falsehood could be distinguished in those days in no other way than now: he who has to distinguish must find the criterion in himself—he that is of the truth heareth my voice. The people believed that Jehovah spoke by prophets, but by which prophets, whether Jeremiah or his opponents, they had to decide out of their own hearts, and not unnaturally (Mic. ii. 11) they despised Jeremiah as a false prophet and held to his opponents (Jer. xviii. 18).

no more...flattering divination] These false prophecies of peace shall cease, for the same judgment which confirms the true prophecy shall annihilate the false. The term "divination" was employed of the methods of reaching the mind of the deity used by the native populations of Canaan (Deut. xviii. 10; 1 Sam. vi. 2). They were such appliances as lots, arrows, and other methods of augury (Ezek. xxi. 21). Possibly these methods had in some degree passed into use in Israel, and were employed by a low prophecy. In true prophecy these mechanical arts were discarded: Jehovah spoke to the mind of the prophet in his mind. Here, however, the word "divination" is used of the oracles of the prophets who were false, even though not employing any external arts of augury. Their prophecy is called "flattering," lit. *smooth*, because it promised immunity from trouble and disaster. Cf. Jer. xiv. 14.

25. *for I* am *the LORD*] Rather: **for I the Lord will speak.** Lit. for I the Lord will speak what word I shall speak, and it shall come to pass. The sense is given by A.V. The word which the Lord speaks to this generation shall be fulfilled before it pass away.

26—28. If others did not go so far as to disregard prophecy altogether, they concluded that the prophecies bore reference to the future, and that the judgments threatened would not come in their day (Is. xxxix. 8). This also was an inference not unnatural. The prophecies of the true prophets were moral and designed even when threatening to turn men away from their sins, and thus in a manner to frustrate their own fulfilment. They were not absolute predictions, but conditional threats, which might be averted on repentance and amendment (Jonah; Jer. xviii.; Joel ii. 14). And in point of fact the most terrible threatenings of judgment were connected with the "day of the Lord," which might be supposed not very near (Is. v. 18, 19). Cf. on *v.* 22; Hab. ii. 3.

the Lord God; There shall none of my words be prolonged any more, but the word which I have spoken shall be done, saith the Lord God.

13 And the word of the Lord came unto me, saying, Son of 2 man, prophesy against the prophets of Israel that prophesy, and say thou unto them that prophesy out of their own 3 hearts, Hear ye the word of the Lord; thus saith the Lord

28. *word which I have spoken*] which **I shall speak**, lit. what word I shall speak. Cf. for construction, Jer. xiv. 1, xlvi. 1; Am. v. 1.

Ch. XIII. Against the false prophets and prophetesses.

The passage is an expansion of ch. xii. 24, and has three main parts: first, *vv.* 1—9 denunciation of the prophets as persons who help forward the downfall of the state, as foxes among the ruins only undermine that which is still standing. Secondly, *vv.* 10—16 denunciation of them under another graphic figure—they are persons who whitewash the tottering wall which the people build. Thirdly, *vv.* 17—23 denunciation of the prophetesses who ensnare souls.

1—9. The lying prophets are like foxes among the ruins.

(1) *vv.* 1—3. The inspiration of these prophets is not from the spirit of God but from their own heart.

(2) *vv.* 4, 5. Consequently so far as the state was concerned they were like foxes among the ruins; they burrowed among these and only helped to bring down what might still be standing.

(3) *vv.* 6, 7. They deceived the people, and were self-deceived. They prophesied lies, and looked that God would establish their lies.

(4) *vv.* 8, 9. Therefore destruction shall overtake them. The people of the Lord, when the day of chastisement has passed, shall be again a people in their own land, but the names of these prophets shall not be found among them.

2. *prophets of Israel that prophesy*] There seems a kind of sarcasm on "prophets of Israel,"—those whom Israel accepts and delights to regard as prophets (Mic. ii. 11); and a similar sarcasm in "that prophesy." They prophesied and that without limit: their mouths were always full of "thus saith the Lord" (*v.* 6). LXX., however, reads rather differently. Jer. xviii. 18 shews how the people regarded their prophets; they had faith in them and believed that Jehovah spoke by them, while such men as Jeremiah they judged to be false prophets: Come, let us devise devices against Jeremiah, for the law shall not perish from the priest, nor counsel from the wise, *nor the word from the prophet*. Cf. Jer. xliii. 2.

their own hearts] The inspiration of these prophets came from their own hearts or minds—their own thoughts and hopes, and judgment upon the situation in which they were placed. They had nothing higher than human wisdom, while the inspiration of the true prophet came from the spirit of God.

God; Woe unto the foolish prophets, that follow their own

3. *foolish prophets*] The word, not used again by Ezekiel, is rather a moral term, meaning destitute of that wisdom the beginning of which is the fear of the Lord (Ps. xiii. 1). Jeremiah charges the prophets of his day with shameful vices, "They commit adultery with their neighbours' wives" (Jer. xxix. 23, cf. xxiii. 14, and *pass.*); but, without supposing that all the "false" prophets were so bad, it characterized them in general that they were superficial men in a moral sense. Their notions of religion and life were not high or strict, and hence they saw nothing in the condition of the people or the state calling for the judgment of God, and prophesied "peace." This was what distinguished them from Jeremiah and other prophets whom we call "true." Micah says in opposition to them: "I am full of power by the spirit of the Lord to declare unto Jacob his transgression and to Israel his sin" (ch. iii. 8); and Jeremiah goes so far as to declare it to be the mark of a true prophet that he threatens judgment upon the nation (Jer. xxviii. 8, 9). A true prophet is one by whom the Lord speaks, and a "false" prophet (the expression is not used in the Old Testament, though the prophets are said to speak "falsely") is one by whom he does not speak. This is true: but the converse has also its truth—the Lord did not speak by these prophets because they were "false" (1 Kings xxii. 6 *seq.*). There is a spirit of false prophecy as well as a spirit of true prophecy. The spirit of true prophecy is the spirit of the theocracy and of the religion of Jehovah, the spirit that comprehends its principles, sympathises with its lofty morality, understands its aims, and therefore can perceive the true means to be used for fulfilling them. The spirit of false prophecy is the untheocratic spirit, which, even when speaking in the name of Jehovah, has not entered with any profoundness into the nature and aims of his kingdom, and consequently misapprehends the means needful to further it. In his encounters with the prophets of his day Jeremiah opposes them in three spheres: that of policy; that of morals; and that of personal experience. In policy the genuine prophets had some fixed principles, all arising out of the idea that the kingdom of the Lord was not a kingdom of this world. Hence they opposed military preparation (Ps. xx. 7), riding on horses and building of fenced cities (Hos. xiv. 3; Mic. v. 10, 11; Is. xxxi. 1), and counselled trust in Jehovah (Is. vii. 9, x. 20, 21, xvii. 7, xxx. 15). These prophets were moving forward (often unconsciously) towards that conception of the kingdom of God which has been realized in the "Church;" and external providence was shaping the history of the nation on lines parallel to this conception, which eventually received form by the destruction of the state and the reduction of the people to be a mere religious community. The false prophets, on the other hand, desired their country to be a military power among the powers around, they advocated alliances with the Eastern empires and with Egypt, and relied on their national strength (Am. vi. 13). Again, the true prophets had a stringent personal and state morality (see above). In their view the true cause of the destruction of the state was its immoralities. But the false prophets had no

4 spirit, and have seen nothing! O Israel, thy prophets are
5 like the foxes in the deserts. Ye have not gone up into the
gaps, neither made up the hedge for the house of Israel to

such deep moral convictions, and seeing nothing unwonted or alarming in the condition of things, prophesied of "peace." They were not necessarily irreligious men, but their religion had no truer insight into the nature of the God of Israel than that of the common people (Am. v. 18); hence they pointed to the Temple as the house of the Lord, which he must protect; while Jeremiah told them that they had made it "a cave of robbers," in which they thought themselves safe after committing their crimes, and threatened it with the fate of Shiloh (Jer. vii., xxvi.). And finally Jeremiah expresses his conviction that the prophets whom he opposed did not stand in the same relation to the Lord as he did; they had not his experiences of the word of the Lord, into whose counsel (Am. iii. 7) they had not been admitted, and they were without that fellowship of mind with the mind of Jehovah which was the true source of prophecy (Jer. xxiii. *pass.*). Hence he satirizes their pretended supernatural "dreams," and charges them from conscious want of any true prophetic word with "stealing" words from one another. Cf. *vv.* 6, 7 and ch. xiv.

their own spirit] The term is used in opposition to the "spirit" of the Lord which inspired the true prophet, who is called "a man of the spirit" (Hos. ix. 7). As distinct from heart "spirit" is rather the force or power moving the prophet. In early times the prophets were the subjects of considerable excitation; and looking on them thus powerfully affected men recognised the influence of the spirit of God upon them.

and have seen nothing] Rather: and (go after) **that which they have not seen**. They did not see, though no doubt they thought they saw. They were self-deceived.

4. *foxes in the deserts*] in **the waste places**, i.e. ruins. The prophets are like foxes; ruins are congenial to them; a condition of decay is their proper sphere; there they can burrow as their instincts prompt them. The main idea, however, is that their operations only increase the devastation and undermine and bring down anything that may yet be standing. In a declining and disastrous time the minds of men are excited and feed on the wildest schemes, and feeling themselves helpless they readily turn to those who pretend to speak to them in God's name. And it only adds to their ruin when those to whom they turn have no higher wisdom than themselves.

5. *gone up into the gaps*] Or, *breaches*. Ezekiel turning to the prophets themselves uses "ye"—a frequent change of person in animated speech.

made up the hedge] Or, *fence*, R.V. If they had been true prophets they would have done two things: stood in the breach, and made a wall of defence for Israel. Without figure: these prophets knew neither what measures to adopt to stop the way of the invading dangers, nor what protective methods to recommend that the state

stand in the battle in the day of the LORD. They have seen 6 vanity and lying divination, saying, The LORD saith, and the LORD hath not sent them: and they have made *others* to hope that *they* would confirm the word. Have ye not seen 7 a vain vision, and have ye not spoken a lying divination, whereas ye say, The LORD saith *it;* albeit I have not spoken? Therefore thus saith the Lord GOD; Because ye 8 have spoken vanity, and seen lies, therefore behold, I *am*

might be successfully defended. They are hardly charged with want of personal courage when it is said they go not up into the breach; rather they wanted wisdom and insight, they had no measures to suggest which would repair or protect the fortunes of the people. Another prophet with more pathos describes the incompetence of Israel's leaders in the day of her distress: "there was none to guide her among all the sons which she had brought forth; neither was there any to take her by the hand of all the sons that she had brought up" (Is. li. 18). No doubt the one measure to adopt was repentance and trust in the Lord; Am. v. 14, "Seek good, and not evil...and so the Lord, the God of hosts, shall be with you, as ye say."

6, 7. THEIR PROPHECIES ARE FALSE: THEY ARE SELF-DECEIVED.

6. *have made* others *to hope*] Rather: **they have hoped for the confirmation** of the word. The usual sense of the verb is to "hope;" only in a single passage (Ps. cxix. 49) does it appear to mean to "cause to hope." The false prophets looked for the confirmation (in fulfilment) of their prophecies and visions—they were self-deceived, not consciously false. Prophecy being an inward thing, a speaking by the spirit in the mind and to the mind, there was no external criterion, and while the true prophet had the witness in himself that he was true, the false prophet might not be aware that he was false (Jer. xxiii. 21, 31). It is an interesting question what kind of mental experience the true prophet had, which verified to him his own genuineness.

vv. 8, 9. Chastisement from Jehovah upon these prophets.

Because these prophets speak falsely Jehovah is against them, for he is the living and the true (*v.* 8); but that which God is against must speedily feel the effects of his opposition—his hand will be upon them (*v.* 9). There is no inert, inoperative opposition on God's part. The sweep of his operation is so vast that its movement may be unperceived, as the earth appears to stand still, though moving with inconceivable rapidity, but its effect will become apparent.

9. The punishment is described in three steps, which form a climax. At present these prophets possess influence, they are counsellors and leaders; when Israel is a nation again upon her own land they shall have no place in the council of the people—read **council** for assembly as marg. Now they occupy a high place in the roll of citizens, and have names distinguished; then their names shall not be written in the writing (i.e. the book or register-roll) of the house of Israel;

9 against you, saith the Lord GOD. And mine hand shall be upon the prophets that see vanity, and that divine lies: they shall not be in the assembly of my people, neither shall they be written in the writing of the house of Israel, neither shall they enter into the land of Israel; and ye shall know that I 10 *am* the Lord GOD. Because, even because they have seduced my people, saying, Peace; and *there was* no peace; and one built up a wall, and lo, others daubed it *with* un- 11 tempered *morter:* say unto them which daub *it with* untempered *morter,* that it shall fall: there shall be an overflowing shower; and ye, O great hailstones, shall fall; and a stormy

cf. Ezr. ii. 62; Is. iv. 3. And finally, they shall not have a place in the land at all—Israel shall return, while they shall perish. Jeremiah had already used the same language in regard to Shemaiah, a prophet who misled the exiles, Jer. xxix. 32.

10—16. THE PROPHETS WHITEWASH THE TOTTERING WALL WHICH THE PEOPLE BUILD.

10. *Because, even because*] A solemn and emphatic introduction of the offence of the prophets; ch. xxxvi. 3; Lev. xxvi. 43.

seduced] Or, **led astray.**

peace; and there was *no peace*] "Peace" includes security and prosperity; cf. Mic. iii. 5; Jer. vi. 14, viii. 11, xxiii. 17.

and one built up a wall] Rather: **and it** (the people) **buildeth up a wall, and behold they** (the prophets) **daub it with whitewash,** or plaster. The word for "wall" (occurring only here) is not the usual one, though similar to the one common in Arab.; in usage it may have meant "a slight wall," as marg., or a partition. The figure incisively describes the futile projects of the people, and the feeble flattery and approval of the prophets. When a weak man cannot originate anything himself, he acquires a certain credit (at least in his own eyes) by strong approval of the schemes of others, saying, Right! I give it my cordial approval, and indeed would have suggested it. What made the prophets whitewash the wall which the people built was partly the feeling that from the place they occupied they must do something, and maintain their credit as leaders even when being led; and partly perhaps that having no higher wisdom than the mass they quite honestly approved their policy. Being sharers with them in the spirit of the time they readily acquiesced in their enterprises.

11 *seq.* Threat of destruction under the figure of a hailstorm, which shall sweep away the wall and those who daub it with whited plaster.

11. *and ye, O great hailstones*] The apostrophe to the hailstones is rather unnatural. A different pointing gives the sense, *and I will cause great hailstones to fall,* but the construction is altogether improbable. Jer. viii. 13, is not in point.

wind shall rent *it*. Lo, when the wall is fallen, shall it not 12 be said unto you, Where *is* the daubing where*with* ye have daubed *it?* Therefore thus saith the Lord GOD; I will 13 even rent *it with* a stormy wind in my fury; and there shall be an overflowing shower in mine anger, and great hailstones in *my* fury to consume *it*. So will I break down the wall 14 that ye have daubed *with* untempered *morter*, and bring it down to the ground, so that the foundation thereof shall be discovered, and it shall fall, and ye shall be consumed in the midst thereof: and ye shall know that I *am* the LORD. Thus 15 will I accomplish my wrath upon the wall, and upon them that have daubed it *with* untempered *morter*, and will say unto you, The wall *is* no *more*, neither they that daubed it; *to wit*, the prophets of Israel which prophesy concerning 16 Jerusalem, and which see visions of peace for her, and *there is* no peace, saith the Lord GOD.

Likewise thou son of man, set thy face against the 17 daughters of thy people, which prophesy out of their own heart; and prophesy thou against them, and say, Thus saith 18

wind shall rent it] Or, a strong wind **shall break forth.**
12. Confusion of the false prophets.
13. *rent* it with *a stormy wind*] Rather: **cause a** stormy wind **to break forth.**
14. *shall be discovered*] i.e. uncovered, laid bare. The prophets shall be destroyed in the ruins of the wall (Am. ix. 1). The figure tends in these words to be replaced by the reality, namely, Jerusalem and its downfall.
16. to wit, *the prophets*] This construction puts "the prophets" in apposition with the last words of *v.* 15 "they that daubed it." The words may be taken as an address: Ye prophets of Israel &c.

17—23. DENUNCIATION OF THE FALSE PROPHETESSES.

Female prophets were not unknown in Israel whether in earlier or later times, as Deborah (Judg. iv. 3) and Huldah (2 Kings xxii. 14). The prophetesses referred to here were like the prophets, prophesying out of their own heart (*v.* 17). Their prophesying was by some species of divination, which they used in order to obtain oracles. The methods of divination practised are somewhat obscure: they bound fillets upon the joints and threw cloths or veils over the heads of those who consulted them. By these means they "hunted" souls; they saved souls alive that should not live and slew souls that should not die (*v.* 19), or as expressed otherwise, they made the heart of the righteous sad and strengthened the hands of the wicked (*v.* 22). In other words

the Lord God; Woe to *the women* that sew pillows to all armholes, and make kerchiefs upon the head of every stature to hunt souls! Will ye hunt the souls of my people, and will
19 ye save the souls alive *that come* unto you? And will ye pollute me among my people for handfuls of barley and for pieces of bread, to slay the souls that should not die, and to save the souls alive that should not live, by your lying to my

like the false prophets they misled the people, promising life to the ungodly and prophesying disaster to those who were righteous.

18. *pillows to all armholes*] Probably: **fillets** or bands **to all joints of the hand.** Heb. appears to read "my hands," which is no doubt an error of transcription; none of the ancient versions reproduces the reading. The term rendered "kerchiefs" probably means veils or coverings to the head, which fell down over the whole body, and were adapted in size to the person to be covered, whether young or old. The language is to be understood literally, and not as a metaphor, with the meaning, to lull into ease and security. Ephrem Syrus already considered the reference to be to amulets worn on the arms, from which responses were brought forth, and the translation cited in the Hexapla as the "Hebrew" renders "phylacteries." Fried. Del. (Baer's *Ezek.*, pp. xii., xiii.) quotes a Babylonian formula of incantation in which reference is made to such fillets and cloths.

souls alive that come *unto you*] Lit., *save souls alive for yourselves*, i.e. to your advantage or profit. R.V. marg., souls *that are yours*, may represent a sense not unusually put upon the words; *your own souls*—by the earnings of false prophecy.

19. *and will ye pollute*] Rather, directly: and **ye profane me.** To "profane" the Lord is to bring him down from the high sphere of purity or truth or power, where men's thoughts should place him, into the region of the impure, the false or unworthy—the sphere of the common (ch. xx. 39). To "profane" is the opposite of to "sanctify."

for handfuls of barley] may signify, for mean and trifling hire. Others think that the offerings may be described which were presented in order to obtain the oracular response. In this case the rendering would be: *with* handfuls of barley (see W. R. Smith, *Journal of Philology*, vol. XIII.). But comp. 1 Sam. ii. 36; 2 Kings xxiii. 9 with 1 Sam. ix. 8; 1 Kings xiv. 3; 2 Kings iv. 42; Mic. iii. 5. In Jer. xliv. 15 the women are represented as baking cakes to be offered to the queen of heaven.

the souls that should not die] The righteous; cf. *v.* 22, ye have made the heart of the righteous sad. The meaning appears to be that the tendency and direction of their prophecies, like those of the false prophets, was in support of the wicked and adverse to those likeminded with the true prophets. They "slay" by their prophetic word (Hos. vi. 5; Jer. i. 10, I have set thee to pluck up &c.) when they threaten evil; and so they make the heart sad (faint and despondent) of those whom the Lord hath not made sad.

people that hear *your* lies? Wherefore thus saith the Lord 20
God; Behold, I *am* against your pillows, where*with* ye there
hunt the souls to make *them* fly, and I will tear them from
your arms, and will let the souls go, *even* the souls that ye
hunt to make *them* fly. Your kerchiefs also will I tear, and 21
deliver my people out of your hand, and they shall be no
more in your hand to be hunted; and ye shall know that I
am the LORD. Because *with* lies *ye* have made the heart of 22
the righteous sad, whom I have not made sad; and strengthened the hands of the wicked, that *he* should not return from
his wicked way, by promising him life: therefore ye shall 23
see no more vanity, nor divine divinations: for I will deliver
my people out of your hand: and ye shall know that I *am*
the LORD.

vv. 20—23. Chastisement of the prophetesses.
*where*with *ye there hunt*] Or, *where* (or, wherein) ye hunt. A
slight change of reading gives, wherewith ye hunt (Targ. Syr.).
to make them *fly*] Or, as R.V. marg. *like birds* (Ew.). LXX. omits.
For "pillows" as above *fillets*. The expression "from your arms" is
not to be forced so as to imply that the bands or fillets were bound
upon the arms of the prophetesses themselves (cf. *v.* 18).
even the souls that ye hunt] The reading here is no doubt corrupt.
The easiest change is to read: I will let the souls go, whose life (naph-
shām) ye hunt as birds; cf. Prov. vi. 26 "the adulteress hunteth for the
precious life." Cornill makes the excellent suggestion: "I will let the
souls go *free* [reading othān hophshim] that ye hunt."
22. *heart of the righteous sad*] Or, discourage the heart of the
righteous—opposed to "strengthen the hands" of the wicked. The
word rendered "made sad" or pained in the end of the clause might
have been expected.
by promising him life] Rather: **and be saved alive**; lit. so as to
save him alive. The agent is not expressed.
23. The judgment of God is at hand which shall make an end of
all false prophecy and divination. Ch. xii. 24; Mic. iii. 6, 7; Am.
viii. 11. The issue of these judgments shall be that Jehovah shall be
known in truth.

CH. XIV. ANSWER TO IDOLATERS WHO INQUIRE OF THE LORD.

In ch. xiii. Ezekiel had denounced the false prophets who led the
people astray, and had threatened them with extirpation from the
community of the Lord. But the question of false prophecy is not
yet exhausted. It has another side. It is true that false prophets
mislead the people, but it is equally true that it is to a wrong-minded
people that the existence of false prophets is due. The strong current
of perverse inclination in the people sweeps the prophet away before

14 Then came certain of the elders of Israel unto me, and
2 sat before me. And the word of the Lord came unto me,
3 saying, Son of man, these men have set up their idols in
their heart, and put the stumblingblock of their iniquity
before their face: should I be inquired of at all by them?

it; he is enticed, and entering into the mind of the people, gives such prophecies as coincide with their desires. The evil of false prophecy is due to a deeper and more pervasive evil than itself; it is indeed a judgment from God upon the fundamental sin of the people, their idolatry (*v.* 9). Therefore the true prophet has only one answer to give to the people who consult him—Put away your idolatries. The chapter has two parts:

First, *vv.* 1—11. There shall no answer be given by the prophet to idolaters who inquire through him but the answer, "Put away your idolatries or look for the judgment of God." If a prophet lets himself be enticed to answer the people after their mind, he and they shall perish together.

Secondly, *vv.* 12—23. The principle of the Divine judgment. The presence of righteous men among a sinful people shall not save the sinners; the righteous shall deliver only their own souls.

1—11. ANSWER TO IDOLATERS WHO INQUIRE OF THE LORD.

1. *elders of Israel*] That is, in point of fact, elders of the exiles; but in them the prophet sees representatives of the house of Israel both at home and abroad (*vv.* 4, 7), and when addressing them he feels himself speaking to his people in all places. Cf. ch. viii. 1, xx. 1. These elders came and sat before him. It is scarcely probable that their presence was due to the prophet's words in ch. xiii., denouncing their false prophets. It might no doubt be supposed that they were perplexed by these denunciations, and, not knowing whom to believe, waited on the prophet for some further enlightenment. It is more likely that their thoughts were occupied about Jerusalem and the future of their country, and that they hoped to hear something more from Ezekiel on these subjects.

3. *set up their idols in*] Lit. *have laid their idols upon their heart*, which appears to mean, laid them on their minds, busied their thoughts and filled their affections with them.

stumblingblock of their iniquity] The reference is still to the idols. Stumblingblock of iniquity is that over which one falls and commits iniquity, see on ch. vii. 19.

before their face] i.e. have placed them in their view, or, so as to follow them; cf. *v.* 6 "turn away your faces from all your abominations;" Ps. xvi. 8, ci. 3. The language is figurative, and does not imply literal setting-up of idols.

should I be inquired of] Or, shall I let myself be inquired of? that is, shall I give an answer (through the prophet)? cf. Is. lxv. 1, where "inquired of" is parallel to "was found."

Therefore speak unto them, and say unto them, Thus saith 4
the Lord GOD; Every man of the house of Israel that setteth
up his idols in his heart, and putteth the stumblingblock of
his iniquity before his face, and cometh to the prophet; I
the LORD will answer him that cometh according to the
multitude of his idols; that *I* may take the house of Israel 5
in their own heart, because they are all estranged from me
through their idols. Therefore say unto the house of Israel, 6
Thus saith the Lord GOD; Repent, and turn *yourselves* from
your idols; and turn away your faces from all your abominations. For every one of the house of Israel, or of the 7
stranger that sojourneth in Israel, which separateth himself
from me, and setteth up his idols in his heart, and putteth
the stumblingblock of his iniquity before his face, and
cometh to a prophet to inquire of him concerning me; I the
LORD will answer him by myself; and I will set my face 8

4. The Lord will answer such men directly through himself, by involving them in the consequences of their own idolatries and destroying them.
setteth up his idols] Cf. *v.* 3.
will answer him that cometh] If this reading be adopted, the rendering must be, I the Lord will answer him; he cometh in the multitude—a meaning which has no probability. The present text reads, I will answer him according to it, (i.e. the iniquity, or the stumbling-block) (even) according to the multitude, &c. In *v.* 7, where the same expression occurs, the reading is, "I will answer him *by myself;*" and the present passage had better be assimilated to *v.* 7. What is meant by the Lord's answering "through himself" is stated *v.* 8, "I will set my face against that man." The answer will be given in acts of judgment.
according to the multitude] The divine chastisement will be heavy, proportionate to the gross idolatry.
5. *take...in their own heart*] The sinner's sin is like a snare in which he is captured and destroyed; sin carries its own retribution in itself (Job viii. 4). The phrase "take them in their own heart" is explained by the words that follow, "because they are all estranged from me through their idols." Their "heart" is the idolatrous direction of their thoughts and affections; in this they shall be taken (*vv.* 3, 4, 7).
6. The *prophet* is not permitted to give an answer to any inquiries of such men. Jehovah will answer them through himself (*v.* 7); the message which the prophet has to deliver is, repentance or destruction!
7. *every one...sojourneth in Israel*] Comp. Lev. xvii. 8, 10, 13, xx. 2, and remark on *v.* 1 above. On "setteth up" cf. *v.* 3.
answer him by myself] Or, through myself, directly in deeds.

against that man, and will make him a sign and a proverb, and I will cut him off from the midst of my people; and ye 9 shall know that I *am* the LORD. And if the prophet be deceived when he hath spoken a thing, I the LORD have deceived that prophet, and I will stretch out my hand upon him, and will destroy him from the midst of my people 10 Israel. And they shall bear the punishment of their iniquity: the punishment of the prophet shall be even as the punish-

8. Jehovah's answer to the idolatrous inquirer: he will make him a sign and a proverb, and cut him off from his people.

make him a sign] This is the traditional reading (Baer's *Ezek.*—hiph. of *sîm*, cf. xxi. 16; Job iv. 20). R.V. follows a different text. On "sign" &c. cf. Numb. xxvi. 10; Deut. xxviii. 37.

9—11. FATE OF THE PROPHET WHO GIVES AN ANSWER TO IDOLATROUS INQUIRERS: HE AND THEY SHALL PERISH TOGETHER.

9. *be deceived when he hath spoken*] Rather, be deceived (or, enticed) **and speak a word**, i.e. a prophetic word, ch. xii. 25 *seq*. The meaning appears to be: if the prophet, entering into the "heart" of the idolaters, the circle and direction of their thoughts, and the general spirit which animates them, gives them a prophetic oracle which coincides with the line of their thoughts, and thus helps to foster their delusions, that prophet himself has been seduced or enticed; and it is the Lord who has enticed him. The passage has a resemblance to 1 Kings xxii. 20. There a lying spirit came forth from the Lord and entered into the prophets of Ahab and deceived them, so that they entered into the designs of the wicked king and gave an answer favourable to him. Here it is the Lord himself who entices the prophet. In both cases this enticement or deception was in punishment for previous sin. Ezekiel does not appear to reflect upon the point whether the prophet before being deceived was true or false. The "prophet" became false when deceived, when he entered into the spirit and purposes of the idolaters, and spoke a word to them in the line of their sinful conduct and hopes. And this word merely hardened them in their mind and was a step towards taking them in their own heart (*v.* 5).

10. Both the people and prophet shall perish together; the punishment of the one shall be as that of the other. Already Jer. xiv. 15, 16, xxvii. 15.

The passage rests on such general assumptions as these: 1. That the principles of the constitution of Israel are known, and the fundamental one is, thou shalt have no other gods before Me. Probably Ezekiel interpreted this first principle as Hosea did, including among "other gods" not only gods different from Jehovah, but images or representations of Jehovah himself (Hos. viii. 6). Men's first duty was to be true to this principle; cf. the summary proceeding advocated in Deut. xiii. 2.

ment of him that seeketh *unto him;* that the house of Israel 11
may go no more astray from me, neither be polluted any
more with all their transgressions; but that they may be my
people, and I may be their God, saith the Lord GOD.

The word of the LORD came again to me, saying, Son of 12, 13

To those who sin against this fundamental article of religion all other religious offices and ordinances, so far from being beneficial, are made by God a means of destruction. The preaching of the true prophets only hardens (Is. vi.); or prophecy may be turned into false prophecy. The man who wittingly commits sin had better keep clear of religious ordinances and performances. And the "prophet" (even the modern one) had better keep clear of wicked men, lest he should be used as the instrument of their punishment and perish with them. See on iii. 20.

11. Yet all these judgments of God have a far-off merciful end in view. They are a blast of fire and of judgment to consume the sin of the people (Is. iv. 4), and when the tempest is overpast the sky rises clear behind—that the house of Israel go no more astray...but that they may be My people and I may be their God.

12—23. THE PRESENCE OF RIGHTEOUS MEN AMONG A SINFUL PEOPLE WILL NOT SAVE THE SINNERS.

The passage may be in answer to thoughts which the prophet felt might rise in the minds of those to whom he spoke. He threatened destruction to people and prophets alike, a destruction indiscriminate and universal. Were not these threats exaggerations? Were they in harmony with God's former ways of dealing with his people? Would he slay the righteous with the wicked? would he not rather spare the wicked on the intercession of the righteous and for their sake, as often in former times? (Gen. xviii. 23; Num. xiv. 15). To this the prophet replies after Jer. xv. that righteous men among the people shall not avert God's judgment, they shall only save their own souls.

(1) *vv.* 12—20. A supposition is put that God brings any one of his four great judgments, famine, evil beasts, sword or pestilence, upon a land to destroy it. Though these three men, Noah, Daniel and Job were in that land, they should by their righteousness save neither sons nor daughters, only their own souls.

(2) *vv.* 21—23. Application to Jerusalem. Much less shall the righteous save the wicked when the Lord shall bring all his four sore judgments together upon Jerusalem. And if a remnant be spared and carried into all lands, this apparent exception will only confirm and impress the principle by shewing to all how inevitable the utter destruction of Jerusalem was on account of its wickedness, and that God in his righteousness could deal in no other way with it. And thus the exiles when they see the way and doings of those that escape from Jerusalem will be comforted for its fall, and their minds will be lifted up into a higher sympathy with God in his acts of righteousness.

On the prophet's own sympathy, cf. ch. iii. 14.

vv. 12—14. Famine.

man, when the land sinneth against me by trespassing grievously, then will I stretch out mine hand upon it, and will break the staff of the bread thereof, and will send famine
14 upon it, and will cut off man and beast from it: though these three men, Noah, Daniel, and Job, were in it, they should deliver *but* their own souls by their righteousness,
15 saith the Lord GOD. If I cause noisome beasts to pass through the land, and they spoil it, so that it be desolate, that
16 no man may pass through because of the beasts: *though* these three men *were* in it, *as* I live, saith the Lord GOD, they shall deliver neither sons nor daughters; they only
17 shall be delivered, but the land shall be desolate. Or *if* I

13. *when the land*] Rather: a land. The whole of *v.* 13 is supposition: when a land sinneth...and I stretch...and break...and send... and cut off.

14. *these three men*] By Jeremiah the Lord had already said: "though Moses and Samuel stood before me, yet my mind could not be toward this people"(Jer. xv. 1). The history of Noah had been written, and was well known long before the time of Ezekiel. He is referred to by other prophets, e.g. Is. liv. 9, "This is as the waters of Noah unto me." It is scarcely probable, however, that the prophet owed his knowledge of Daniel and Job to the books which now exist under their names. They are more likely great traditional names, familiar to the prophet and his people, which the authors of our present books appropriated and used for their own purposes of edification. It is scarcely natural that the prophet should name Daniel if he was a contemporary of his own living at the court of Babylon. He refers here to his piety, and in ch. xxviii. 3 to his wisdom. These references are quite suitable to the Daniel known to us from the book of that name, but of course the picture of Daniel drawn in the book may contain traits taken from tradition, or even from Ezekiel. In all probability the Book of Job is posterior to the time of Ezekiel. On "staff of bread," cf. ch. iv. 16, v. 16; Lev. xxvi. 26.

vv. 15, 16. Noisome, i.e. hurtful, beasts. Lev. xxvi. 22.

16. *neither sons nor daughters*] There is no support in the words for the idea of Hävernick that the three names, Noah, Daniel and Job form a climax, inasmuch as Noah saved his children, Daniel only his three fellow-exiles, while Job could deliver neither son nor daughter, though every week he interceded and made atonement for them. This idea is false to the sense of the Book of Job, for Job's children are nowhere represented by the author of the book as having been cut off for their sins, though naturally Job's "friends" put this construction upon their death (ch. viii. 4). The prophet does not appear to have in view any historical details in the lives of these three men; he refers to the men themselves as great saints famous in the traditions of his people.

vv. 17, 18. Sword and war. Lev. xxvi. 25.

bring a sword upon that land, and say, Sword, go through the land; so that I cut off man and beast from it: though 18 these three men *were* in it, *as* I live, saith the Lord GOD, they shall deliver neither sons nor daughters, but they only shall be delivered themselves. Or *if* I send a pestilence 19 into that land, and pour out my fury upon it in blood, to cut off from it man and beast: though Noah, Daniel, and 20 Job, *were* in it, *as* I live, saith the Lord GOD, they shall deliver neither son nor daughter; they shall *but* deliver their own souls by their righteousness. For thus saith the Lord 21 GOD; How much more when I send my four sore judgements upon Jerusalem, the sword, and the famine, and the noisome beast, and the pestilence, to cut off from it man and beast? Yet behold, therein shall be left a remnant that shall be 22 brought forth, *both* sons and daughters: behold, they *shall*

17. *say, Sword, go through*] This rendering assumes a grammatical anomaly. Rather, **the sword shall go** through.

vv. 19, 20. The pestilence.

19. *my fury upon it in blood*] The term "blood" is almost a synonym for "death;" cf. Ps. xxx. 9, "What profit is there in my blood, in my going down to the pit?" Ch. v. 17. On the Babylonian idea of "four" plagues, cf. Del. *Parad.* p. 146.

vv. 21—23. Application to Jerusalem.

21. *How much more*] If when a single judgment is sent upon a land the wicked shall not be spared for the sake of the righteous, how much more shall this not happen when the wickedness of the land is so great that God's four sore judgments together fall upon it, as they shall fall upon Jerusalem? Ch. v. 17, xxxiii. 27, 22. Yet the history of Jerusalem may seem an exception. It is an exception for a wider purpose.

22. *behold, therein shall be left*] Rather: **and behold, should there be left** therein a remnant. After "behold" the verb is hypothetical, as often, e.g. ch. xiii. 12, xv. 4. If some of the wicked in Jerusalem escape it is with a special design, viz. that those spared should reveal their great wickedness to the earlier exiles among whom they shall come, and thus shew how inevitable the destruction of the city was.

that shall be brought forth] The ancient versions read the active (hiph.) participle here: *that shall bring forth* sons and daughters. In *vv.* 18, 20 it is said that the three great saints named should save neither sons nor daughters; and here some would be spoken of who brought out sons and daughters. It is very doubtful if this pointed antithesis was in the mind of the prophet. His point is that if some in Jerusalem, men and women, escape, notwithstanding the principle that the righteous shall not save the wicked, it is for a special purpose, viz. to shew to the earlier exiles the great wickedness of Jerusalem, and thus comfort them over its fall. Both Jeremiah and Ezekiel regard the exiles carried away

come forth unto you, and ye shall see their way and their doings: and ye shall be comforted concerning the evil that I have brought upon Jerusalem, *even* concerning all that I
23 have brought upon it. And they shall comfort you, when ye see their ways and their doings: and ye shall know that I have not done without cause all that I have done in it, saith the Lord God.

under Jehoiachin as the flower of the nation (Jer. xxiv.), and those left behind as the dregs of the people. Of course it was the persons of rank and influence that were carried captive, while those left behind were the meanest, least educated and probably most idolatrous (Jer. xxiv. 8—10, xxix. 16—20).

their way and their doings] Their evil "way" of life, and their gross idolatries.

comforted concerning the evil] The exiles of the days of Jehoiachin and those of earlier times, whose thoughts were keenly occupied with Jerusalem and its fate (ch. xxiv. 25), shall be comforted for its destruction when they see the way and doings of the new exiles. So corrupt and gross in their iniquities shall these appear to them that they will feel that no other fate than that which has befallen it was possible for Jerusalem; and that "not without cause" has Jehovah overthrown it (*v.* 22). Cf. on "comforted" ch. xxxii. 31.

In the passage *vv.* 12—23 questions are not raised what "land" it is that Jehovah will bring his plagues of famine, sword and the like upon, nor when he will bring them. The cases supposed are merely illustrations of the principle that the righteous shall not save the wicked. And the application to Jerusalem is what the prophet has in view. See on ch. xviii.

Ch. XV. The vine tree among the other trees of the forest.

The chapter pursues the same general line of thought as ch. xiv. 12—23, and ch. xvi. In ch. xiv. 12—23 the prophet had replied to a feeling that might arise in men's minds that Jehovah would spare the sinners of the people for the sake of the righteous. Here he replies to another thought—were these predictions of wholesale destruction upon Israel, the people of the Lord, and Jerusalem where he had placed his name, probable? Other nations might perish, but Israel was the Lord's heritage, the vine of his planting. The prophet accepts the idea of the vine and replies to it.

Like Isaiah's song of the vineyard (Is. v.) the passage has two parts, first, the similitude of the vine, *vv.* 1—5; and secondly, the application to Israel, *vv.* 6—8.

Founding on old similitudes the prophet assumes that Israel is the vine, and compares it as a tree or as wood with the other trees of the forest. It is as wood that it is put in comparison with the trees. He

And the word of the Lord came unto me, saying, Son of 15 man, What is the vine tree more than any tree, *or than* a 2 branch which is among the trees of the forest? Shall wood 3 be taken thereof to do *any* work? or will *men* take a pin of it to hang any vessel thereon? Behold, it is cast into the 4 fire for fuel; the fire devoureth both the ends of it, and the midst of it is burnt. Is it meet for *any* work? Behold, 5 when it was whole, it was meet for no work: how much less shall it be meet yet for *any* work, when the fire hath devoured it, and it is burned? Therefore thus saith the Lord 6 God; As the vine tree among the trees of the forest, which

is studiously silent in regard to the fruit of the vine. This, which gave the vine its preeminence (Judg. ix. 13), cannot be touched upon, for it does not exist. It is the wood of the vine only that can be compared with the other trees of the forest, the feeble, creeping plant with the lofty trees around it. Judah never had any pretensions to be a powerful state, or to enter into competition in wealth or military resources with the kingdoms round about. As a tree among the trees, a state among the states, what was it good for? And especially now what is it good for, when it has already been in the fire, its ends consumed and its heart charred? What is it fit for, or need it expect, but to be flung again into the fire and wholly consumed?

  2. or than *a branch*] Perhaps: the vine-branch which is,—the words taking up "the vine tree" of previous clause. Owing to the verb the natural sense is: *what shall be* made of *the wood of the vine among all wood, the vine branch* that is among the trees of the forest? Cf. *v.* 3. With the comparative sense the accents should be disregarded: *what is the wood of the vine more than any wood of the branch* which is &c. On Israel as the vine cf. Gen. xlix. 22; Is. v. 1; Deut. xxxii. 32; Jer. ii. 21; Ezek. xvii. 5, xix. 10; Ps. lxxx.; Hos. x. 1.

  3. Uselessness of the wood of the vine.

  to do any *work*] i.e. use for any work or purpose. The words may mean, to make it into any work or article of workmanship. It has too little firmness even to be made into a pin to hang any article upon.

  4. A hypothetical sentence: Behold, when it hath been cast into the fire for fuel, when the fire hath devoured both the ends of it, and the midst of it is charred, will it be meet for any work? This part of the similitude is borrowed from the actual instance of Israel. As it is Jerusalem, including Judah, that is compared to the vine, the burning of the ends and scorching of the middle probably refers to the calamities sustained by that kingdom, such as the captivity under Jehoiachin and other severe reverses.

  5. *meet for no work*] Lit., *it could not be made into*, or, *used for* any work; how much less, when the fire hath devoured it and it is charred, shall it be any more used for, or made into any work.

I have given to the fire for fuel, so will I give the inhabitants of Jerusalem. And I will set my face against them; they shall go out from *one* fire, and *another* fire shall devour them; and ye shall know that I *am* the LORD, when I set my face against them. And I will make the land desolate, because they have committed a trespass, saith the Lord GOD.

6—8. APPLICATION OF THE FIGURE TO JERUSALEM.

6. *which I have given*] The reference is to the supposition in *v.* 4. It is nowhere said in the passage that the vinewood is fit only for fuel, nor that it has been appointed (when created by God) to be burnt; *v.* 4 is a supposition that in a particular case it has been flung into the fire for fuel, and its ends burnt, and the inference is drawn that, good for little when whole, much less will it be good for anything in that condition. The use of the first person "I have given" is peculiar. Cornill suggests "it has been given," considering "I have given" which follows immediately to have been the source of the error.

so will I give] Lit., *so have I given*. The comparison is not between Jerusalem and a vine when whole, but between Jerusalem and a vine with its two ends burnt. Naturally the supposition is made that the vinewood flung into the fire has been plucked out after having been burnt and charred, and the question is asked, Is it good for anything now? This is the condition of Jerusalem: it has been given into the fire for fuel, plucked out of it, as it were, half-burnt; is it good for anything?

7. *go out from one fire*] Rather: **they have come out of the fire, but the fire** shall devour them. They are in the condition of a brand that has been plucked for a moment from the fire (*vv*. 4, 5), but they shall be plunged again into it to be burnt. Only scathed and charred as yet, they shall be wholly consumed.

I am the Lord] The object of these chastisements is that they may know that he who inflicts them is Jehovah, and what Jehovah is; and this shall be the result of them.

8. The figure of "burning" in the fire is expressed in literal language: the land shall be made a desolation. Like his predecessor Jeremiah, the prophet sets little store by the existence of Israel as a state or kingdom among other states. Israel's mission is religious, not political. See on ch. xiii. 3.

CH. XVI. THE FOUNDLING CHILD WHO BECAME THE FAITHLESS WIFE.

The prophet continues to pursue his demonstration of the inevitableness of Jerusalem's destruction. In ch. xiii. xiv. he swept away the delusive hopes with which the prophets of Israel filled her imagination; and in ch. xv. he shewed how little the fact that Israel was the people of the Lord was fitted to inspire confidence, as other prophets had shewed before him (Am. iii. 2). In the present passage it is the positive proof

Again the word of the LORD came unto me, saying, Son 16
of man, cause Jerusalem to know her abominations, and say, 2
Thus saith the Lord GOD unto Jerusalem; Thy birth and 3
thy nativity *is* of the land of Canaan; thy father *was* an

of the necessity of Israel's destruction that he exhibits—her persistent unfaithfulness to Jehovah through all her history, and her forgetfulness of his goodness. He has to "shew to Jerusalem all her abominations" (*v.* 2). This is done in the allegory of the foundling child who became the faithless wife of her benefactor. Though marked by a breadth with which modern taste is unfamiliar the allegory is powerful. And when the details are forgotten and only the general conception remains in the mind, the prophet's creation is felt to be artistically beautiful as well as true. An outcast infant exposed in the open field and weltering in its blood was seen by the pitying eye of a passer by. Rescued and nourished she grew up to the fairest womanhood, and became the wife of her benefactor, who lavished on her all that could delight and elevate. But the ways into which he led her were too lofty to be understood, and the atmosphere around her too pure for her to breathe; the old inborn nature (her father was the Amorite and her mother a Hittite) was still there beneath all the refinements for which it had no taste, and at last it asserted itself in shameless depravity and insatiable lewdness.

This moral history of Israel has these divisions:

(1) *vv.* 1—7. The exposed infant adopted and reared to womanhood.
(2) *vv.* 8—14. The foundling, now grown up to be a fair woman, taken in marriage by her benefactor.
(3) *vv.* 15—34. Her numerous infidelities.
(4) *vv.* 35—58. Punishment of the adulterous wife.
(5) *vv.* 59—63. Her receiving again.

1—7. THE EXPOSED CHILD RESCUED AND ADOPTED BY JEHOVAH— HIS TAKING TO HIMSELF THE FAMILY OF ISRAEL IN THE EARLY PATRIARCHAL TIMES.

2. *cause Jerusalem to know*] The object of the chapter is to impress on Israel the necessity of the Divine judgment because of her persistent idolatry through all her history (ch. xx. 4, xxii. 2, xxiii. 36). Jerusalem, which is spoken to throughout, represents the kingdom of Judah, and even the whole family of Israel in its early history.

3. *Thy birth...land of Canaan*] of **the Canaanite.** "Birth" is *origin* (ch. xxi. 30, xxix. 14), the figure being taken from a mine or a quarry, cf. Is. li. 1, "Look unto the rock whence ye are hewn, and to the hole of the pit whence ye are digged." When Jerusalem's origin is said to be from the land of the Canaanite several references seem combined, e.g. the fact that Jerusalem was a Canaanite city; that Israel first became a family in Canaan (*v.* 4); and that having originated there its moral character corresponded to its Canaanite origin and had cleaved to it all through its history.

4 Amorite, and thy mother a Hittite. And *as for* thy nativity, in the day thou wast born thy navel was not cut, neither wast thou washed in water to supple *thee;* thou wast not 5 salted at all, nor swaddled at all. None eye pitied thee, to do any of these unto thee, to have compassion upon thee; but thou wast cast out in the open field, to the lothing of thy person, in the day that thou wast born.

6 And when I passed by thee, and saw thee polluted in thine own blood, I said unto thee *when thou wast* in thy blood, Live; yea, I said unto thee *when thou wast* in thy 7 blood, Live. I have caused thee to multiply as the bud of

an Amorite] **the** Amorite. The Amorites and Hittites are named as the two chief Canaanitish peoples, the whole population being sometimes called the Amorites (Gen. xv. 16; Am. ii. 9), and at other times the Hittites (Josh. i. 4). Jerusalem has the one for father, and the other for mother (*v.* 45).

4. as for *thy nativity*] The circumstances of thy birth were these, as follows. The family of Israel, represented by Jerusalem, is compared to an exposed infant, for whom the things absolutely necessary to preserve its life were not done. The reference is to the history of the family in Canaan, and in its descent to Egypt, when it was feeble, unprotected and in danger of perishing.

to supple thee] The word is otherwise unknown. Targ. "for purification," probably guessed, but some such sense is required. Fried. Del. refers to an Assyrian root signifying *to wash.*

wast not salted at all] An ancient custom was to rub the newborn infant with salt—"tenera infantium corpora...solent ab obstetricibus sale contingi ut sicciora sint et restringantur," Jerome. The ceremony was probably partly religious as well as healthful.

5. None of the offices necessary to preserve the life of the child were performed; no pitying eye looked on it, no affectionate hand did aught for it; it was even thrown out in the open field. It was too common a custom among ancient nations to expose children; among the Arabs female children were buried alive (*Kor.* 81. 8).

to the lothing of thy person] Rather, **because of the utter loathing of thee**; lit. the loathing of thy soul. Cf. *v.* 45.

6. *And when I passed*] More pathetic in the Heb. order: and I passed by thee and saw thee.

polluted] **weltering**; wallowing or struggling.

when thou wast in thy blood] The meaning may be: "I said unto thee, In thy blood live!" i.e. in spite of thy blood; although unclean and loathsome, live! Jehovah's pitying eye looked through that which might repel, and saved. The repetition (which LXX., however, omits) may emphasise the great act of Jehovah's pity.

7. *have caused...multiply*] Lit. as marg. *made thee a myriad.* This idea of multiplication in *number* deserts the figure, introducing the notion

the field, and thou hast increased and waxen great, and thou art come to excellent ornaments: *thy* breasts are fashioned, and thine hair is grown, whereas thou *wast* naked and bare. Now when I passed by thee, and looked upon thee, behold, 8 thy time *was* the time of love; and I spread my skirt over thee, and covered thy nakedness: yea, I sware unto thee,

of the numerical increase of the people (Ex. i. 7; Deut. x. 22, xxxiii. 17). The rest of the verse, however, continues the figure of the child growing up to womanhood. For "myriad" LXX. has "do thou grow" (imper.). This is not natural, but probably some word signifying "growth" should be read, "I gave thee growth like the herb of the field; and thou didst grow and wax great."

thou art come...ornaments] Thou **didst come** to excellent ornament, lit. ornament of ornaments. The connexion requires that "ornament" should mean graces and beauties of the person. The word has nowhere else this sense, being always employed of such ornaments as jewelry which are worn (*v.* 11). The rendering "beauty of cheeks" (Hitz.) rests upon the supposed sense of Ps. xxxii. 9, ciii. 5. In Is. lxiv. 6 a word somewhat similar occurs: *filthy* (i.e. menstruous) garment, and several scholars (J. D. Michaelis, Cornill) assume this sense here. This requires considerable alteration of the text, which already lay before LXX. (though *r* was read for *d*, as often). Neither is *v.* 22 in favour of it.

are fashioned] Better past tenses: **were fashioned...was grown**, but thou **wast**.

The passage is an allegorical description of the early history of the family of Israel, their struggles for existence in Canaan, their descent into Egypt, the oppressions suffered there, and the Lord's care and protection of them (Ex. iii. 7, 9; Ps. cv. 12 *seq*.). The unattractive character of the early patriarchal history as written in Genesis is plain enough (Gen. xxix.—xxxi., xxxviii.). This unattractive character is set forth in the blood and pollution of the new-born infant, and the Lord's care of them in their dependent and defenceless condition under the figure of his pity and adoption of the outcast child. The truth conveyed in the allegory is more delicately expressed by another writer: "The Lord did not set his love upon you, nor choose you, because ye were more in number than any people; for ye were the fewest of all peoples; but because the Lord loved you" (Deut. vii. 7, 8).

8—14. THE CHILD, NOW AN ADULT VIRGIN, TAKEN TO HIMSELF IN MARRIAGE BY JEHOVAH :—THE REDEMPTION OF THE PEOPLE FROM EGYPT, AND COVENANT WITH THEM AT SINAI TO BE THEIR GOD.

8. *Now when I passed*] Better in continuance of the historical narrative, **and I passed by**.

the time of love] The outcast child was now a marriageable woman.

spread my skirt] Cf. Ruth iii. 9—a figure for marriage.

and entered into a covenant with thee, saith the Lord God, and thou becamest mine. Then washed I thee with water; yea, I throughly washed away thy blood from thee, and I anointed thee with oil. I clothed thee also with broidered work, and shod thee *with* badgers' *skin*, and I girded thee about with fine linen, and I covered thee *with* silk. I decked thee also *with* ornaments, and I put bracelets upon thine hands, and a chain on thy neck. And I put a jewel on thy forehead, and earrings in thine ears, and a beautiful crown upon thine head. Thus wast thou decked *with* gold

a covenant with thee] The marriage relation is a covenant, Prov. ii. 17; Mal. ii. 14. On the "oath," cf. *v.* 59.

thou becamest mine] She became his wife, Ruth iv. 13; Hos. iii. 3.

9. Purifications before marriage. Whether "blood" be used somewhat generally to indicate the uncleanness of her infancy still cleaving to her, or in a more specific sense, may be uncertain (*v.* 7). Ruth iii. 3; Esth. ii. 12.

10. The costly clothing.

broidered work] Ps. xlv. 14; Judg. v. 30. The word might mean work of various colours (Ex. xxvi. 36). So *vv.* 13, 18.

badgers' skin] According to most, skin of the sea-cow or manati, an animal allied to the dolphin, and found in the Red Sea. The name is found in Assyrian; the Assyrian kings crossed the Euphrates in ships made of the skin of this animal, and Salmaneser pursued his foes on lake Van in such ships. These facts suggest that the skins were readily procured not only in Mesopotamia but even in Armenia, and that some land animal must have furnished them. On these grounds Fried. Del. (*Prolegomena*, p. 78) decides for the *wether*. See Dill. on Ex. xxv. 5.

fine linen] i.e. byssus. It was not certain whether the byssus was cotton or linen, or both. It was worn by the priests (Ex. xxxix. 27), and by persons of rank (Gen. xli. 42). The "girding" or binding here can hardly refer to the headdress (Ex. xxix. 9), because in *v.* 13 the "clothing" is said to be of fine linen (cf. *v.* 12 for headdress).

covered thee with *silk*] The word again only in *v.* 13. It may be doubtful if silk was worn as early as the time of the prophet. The LXX. and ancients thought of some very thin and delicate material. The kind of garment was probably some large wrapper or veil covering the whole person.

vv. 11, 12. Her ornaments.

11. On bracelets, cf. Gen. xxiv. 22, 47. On chain or necklace, Gen. xli. 42; Prov. i. 9, iii. 3.

12. *on thy forehead*] Rather: a ring **on thy nose**, Is. iii. 21. The nose-ring was a jewel placed on the outside of the nostril. Cf. Judg. viii. 24 (where read, nose-rings). Gen. xxiv. 47. On earrings, Numb. xxxi. 50.

a beautiful crown] so ch. xxiii. 42; in Is. lxii. 3 rendered "a crown of glory." The word does not suggest royalty (xxiii. 42).

13. Her delicate fare and beauty.

and silver; and thy raiment *was of* fine linen, and silk, and broidered work; thou didst eat fine flour, and honey, and oil: and thou wast exceeding beautiful, and thou didst prosper into a kingdom. And thy renown went forth among 14 the heathen for thy beauty: for it *was* perfect through my comeliness, which I had put upon thee, saith the Lord God.

fine flour] This was used in offerings at the altar (*v.* 19), and was probably the food of persons of refinement and rank. Cf. Ps. lxxxi. 16, "I should have fed them also with the finest of the wheat, and with honey out of the rock should I satisfy thee;" Ps. cxlvii. 14; Deut. xxxii. 13, 14.

exceeding beautiful] The beauty is less that of the mere city (Ps. xlviii. 2) than of the personified state or people (*v.* 14).

prosper into a kingdom] Or, **attain to royal estate.** The reference is not to the mere historical fact that a monarchy arose in Israel under Saul or more permanently under David. It was Israel herself, personified as a woman, that attained to royalty, that is, to be an independent state among the states around, a queen among other queens. The words are wanting in LXX.

14. Her renown spread among the nations because of her beauty. In this is included partly the prosperity and success of the state, not without reference perhaps to the beauty of the city (Lam. ii. 15, the perfection of beauty, the joy of the whole earth, Ps. l. 2), and of the land, which is often celebrated (ch. xx. 6, 15 the glory of all lands, cf. Dan. viii. 9, xi. 16, 41; Zech. vii. 14); and partly also the glory of a higher kind conferred on her by Jehovah and his presence, in the sense of Deut. iv. 6—8.

my comeliness] Or, **my adornment**; that given by me (*vv.* 10—13); hardly in the sense of Is. lx. 1, that Jerusalem's beauty was only a reflection of the glory of Jehovah, who was in the midst of her.

These verses allegorically set forth the second period of Israel's history: her redemption by Jehovah from Egypt, his covenant with her to be her God, his leading her into the promised land, and making her the paramount power there, and loading her with all the riches of that good land. Other prophets with more simplicity have celebrated this early time, "I remember of thee the kindness of thy youth, the love of thine espousals; how thou wentest after me in the wilderness, in a land not sown" (Jer. ii. 2); "I found Israel like grapes in the wilderness; I saw your fathers as the firstripe on the fig tree at her first season" (Hos. ix. 10; cf. Deut. xxxii. 10).

15—34. THE WIFE'S INFIDELITIES—ISRAEL'S IDOLATRIES AND IDOLATROUS ALLIANCES WITH FOREIGN NATIONS.

The idolatries of Israel are represented figuratively as a wife's infidelities against her husband, as had been common in the prophets since Hosea, particularly in Jeremiah (in Isaiah only the single passage ch. i. 21). These idolatries seem presented in two stages: *vv.* 15—22,

15 But thou didst trust in thine own beauty, and playedst the harlot because of thy renown, and pouredst out thy forni-
16 cations on every one that passed by; his it was. And of thy garments thou didst take, and deckedst thy high places with divers colours, and playedst the harlot thereupon: *the*
17 *like things shall* not come, neither shall it be *so*. Thou hast also taken thy fair jewels of my gold and of my silver, which I had given thee, and madest to thyself images of men,

her addicting herself to the worship and religious customs of the Canaanites among whom she dwelt; and *vv.* 23—34, her alliances with foreign peoples and adoption of their religions.

15—22. All the gifts of Jehovah to her she took and bestowed on idols: her raiment (*vv.* 16, 18), her gold and silver (*v.* 17), and her delicate fare (*v.* 19). And as if this were a small matter, she sacrificed also the children which were Jehovah's to her idols (*vv.* 20, 21).

15. *because of thy renown*] In the consciousness of it. The consciousness of her beauty and renown removed from her mind the sense of dependence and responsibility, and she became vain in her own imaginations. Another prophet has expressed the same idea in regard to Babylon: "Thou saidst, I shall be a lady for ever, so that thou didst not lay these things to thy heart, neither didst consider the issue of them...thou hast said, None seeth me." (Is. xlvii. 7, 10). Hävern. quotes Ovid, *Fasti*, I. 419, *Fastus inest pulchris, sequiturque superbia formam.*

every one that passed by] A figure taken from the habit of harlots sitting by the wayside, Gen. xxxviii. 14; Jer. iii. 2, "By the ways thou hast sat for them as an Arab in the desert."

his it was] The prostitution was indiscriminate, Jer. iii. 2; cf. ch. xxiii. 40. The idea expressed is the ineradicable tendency of the people to adopt the religious customs of the nations with which age after age they came into connexion (*v.* 23 *seq.*). The phrase is peculiar and wanting in LXX.

16. She took of her "garments," the flax and the wool which Jehovah had given her to cover herself withal (Hos. ii. 9), and made tents upon the high places for the idols which she there worshipped. For "high places" cf. ch. vi. 3. The "high places decked with divers colours" (R. V.) might be tents, or the reference might be to hangings or carpets. In 2 Kings xxiii. 7 reference is made to women "who wove tents for Ashera;" cf. 1 Kings xiii. 32; 2 Kings xvii. 29.

like things shall not come] Or, *should not come.* An exclamation of dislike and abhorrence of the shameful practices just referred to. The rendering given can hardly be extracted from the words, which are probably corrupt in some way, though already read by LXX. (with a different vocalization). Comp. perhaps ch. xx. 29.

17. Cf. Hos. ii. 8, I multiplied unto her silver and gold, which they used for Baal.

images of men] Jerusalem being an unfaithful wife the idols are

and didst commit whoredom with them, and tookest thy 18
broidered garments, and coveredst them: and thou hast set
mine oil and mine incense before them. My meat also 19
which I gave thee, fine flour, and oil, and honey, *wherewith*
I fed thee, thou hast even set it before them for a sweet
savour: and *thus* it was, saith the Lord GOD. Moreover 20
thou hast taken thy sons and thy daughters, whom thou
hast borne unto me, and these hast thou sacrificed unto

"men." The images were of gods; and this prophet probably saw
little distinction between an image of Jehovah and that of any other
deity. It is likely that, apart from the calf-images, the symbols of
Jehovah as well as of the other gods were of the human form; cf. as
to the Teraphim, 1 Sam. xix. 13. The supposition hazarded by some
that the "male images" (marg.) were representations of the Phallus
has little to support it. It is true that Jerome considers the "gruesome
object" set up by Maacah the mother of Asa to be *simulacrum Priapi*
(2 Chron. xv. 16, cf. 1 Kings xv. 13), but this is mere conjecture;
and the passage Is. lvii. 8 is too obscure to be depended upon (cf. Prof.
W. R. Smith, *Rel. of Sem.* p. 437).
broidered...coveredst them] Cf. *v.* 10, 13. The practice of clothing
the idols is illustrated by Jer. x. 9, "There is silver beaten into plates
...blue and purple for their clothing; they are all the work of cunning
men."
hast set mine oil] **didst set.** The ref. is to the offerings made to
the idols. The Lord calls it "mine" because due to him, or rather
because given by him to Israel, Hos. ii. 8, "she did not know that
I gave her corn and wine and oil...I will take back my corn in the
time thereof."
19. *a sweet savour*] See on ch. vi. 13. The words "*and* thus
it was" emphasize what was done, with a tone of reprobation.

20 *seq.* THE SACRIFICE OF CHILDREN.

Jehovah is the husband of the idealized community, and the individual members are his children. Human sacrifices, though rare, were
not altogether unknown in early Israel, as the instance of Jephthah
proves (Judg. xi.). They were probably more common among the
Canaanites and neighbouring peoples, though perhaps even among
them resorted to only on occasions of great trial, in the hope of
appeasing the anger or securing the favour of the deity (cf. the tragic
story of the king of Moab, 2 Kings iii. 27). Instances of human
sacrifices do not occur in the early history of Israel, for neither the
slaughter of Agag (1 Sam. xv. 33) nor the hanging of seven descendants
of Saul (2 Sam. xxi.) comes strictly under the idea of a sacrifice; but
Ahaz king of Judah is said to have passed his son through the fire
(2 Kings xvi. 3), and the practice introduced by him was followed by
Manasseh (2 Kings xxi. 6), and must have spread among the people

them to be devoured. *Is this* of thy whoredoms a small
21 matter, that thou hast slain my children, and delivered
them to cause them to pass through *the fire* for them?
22 And in all thine abominations and thy whoredoms thou
hast not remembered the days of thy youth, when thou
23 wast naked and bare, *and* wast polluted in thy blood. And
it came to pass after all thy wickedness, (woe, woe unto
24 thee! saith the Lord God;) *that* thou hast also built unto
thee an eminent place, and hast made thee a high place in

(Jer. vii. 31, xix. 5, xxxii. 35). The phrase "to pass through the fire" might be taken to mean merely a lustration or purification by fire, not implying the death of the child. This cannot, however, have been the case, for this prophet uses the words sacrifice (*v.* 20) and slaughter (*v.* 21), and Jeremiah says the people built high places "to burn their children in the fire as burnt offerings to Baal" (ch. xix. 5). The child, of course, was not burnt alive, but slain like other sacrifices, and offered as a burnt offering. The practice was a widespread one in the East, 2 Kings xvii. 31. See further on ch. xx. 25 *seq.*

20. *to be devoured*] Namely, in the fire.

21. *hast...delivered them*] Or, **didst deliver** them up, in causing them, as R.V. The child passed into the possession of the deity when consumed in the fire.

22. So absorbed was Jerusalem in her infidelities that she remembered nothing of her early history, "the shame of her youth," nor the compassion shewed her by Jehovah. On "polluted" cf. *v.* 6.

23—34. Her infidelities with strangers from abroad, i.e. her alliances with idolatrous nations and adoption of their religious rites: Egypt (*vv.* 23—27), Assyria (*v.* 28), and Chaldea (*v.* 29 *seq.*). Hosea already stigmatized foreign alliances as whoredoms; it is not, however, so much the political aspect of these alliances as their religious consequences that Ezekiel reprobates. Such alliances were followed by the fashions and worship of the nations with which they were formed (Is. ii. 5 *seq.*). Naturally also when Israel became subject to the great eastern empires, the overwhelming influence of these states, with their customs and religions, was widely felt. The gods which had given them universal empire were introduced and worshipped. There appears to have been a great invasion of foreign idolatry in Judah in the declining years of the state, and the kingdom sank to a level in this respect to which the North had never fallen.

23. *after all thy wickedness*] The wickedness described in preceding verses as idolatries of Canaan; after this followed foreign idolatry. LXX. omits the words "woe, woe unto thee."

24. *an eminent place*] The term is used of the "back," the "boss" of a buckler, and the like, and means something elevated to some extent and probably arched; R.V. marg. *vaulted chamber*. It appears to be the same thing which is called a "high place" or rather: height, or elevated place, in this verse and *v.* 25 (a different word from that

every street. Thou hast built thy high place at every head 25 of the way, and hast made thy beauty to be abhorred, and hast opened thy feet to every one that passed by, and multiplied thy whoredoms. Thou hast also committed for- 26 nication with the Egyptians thy neighbours, great of flesh; and hast increased thy whoredoms, to provoke me to anger. Behold therefore, I have stretched out my hand over thee, 27 and have diminished thine ordinary *food*, and delivered thee unto the will of them that hate thee, the daughters of the Philistines, which are ashamed of thy lewd way. Thou 28

usually rendered "high place"). Small shrines must be meant, as they were put in every street, and at every head of the way. If the places were arches or vaults there is no reason to suppose that they were used for literal prostitution, as A.V. marg. suggests. The language is figurative for idolatry, Jer. ii. 20, iii. 2.

25. *thy high place*] See *v.* 24.

made...to be abhorred] This sense is doubtful; the word means to abominate, hence dishonour or disregard, or as we might say "prostitute thy beauty."

26. Egyptian idolatry.

hast also committed] **and** thou **didst commit**. The narrative tense should be used throughout.

great of flesh] In an obscene sense. Cf. ch. xxiii. 20. The expression is chosen probably to represent the brutality of the Egyptian idolatries, which in some ways were baser than those of any people.

27. *I have stretched*] I **stretched**...and **diminished**...them that **hated...were ashamed**. The reference appears to be to the distant times of the Philistine supremacy in the last days of the Judges.

thine ordinary food] Or, allotted portion, Ex. xxi. 10. The measure is one to which an offended husband might have recourse. Hos. ii. 9, "therefore will I take back my corn in the time thereof, and my wine in the season thereof."

daughters of the Philistines] i.e. the cities or small Philistine lordships. The clause might explain the phrase "diminished thy portion" —her territory was seized by her enemies.

which are ashamed] **were** ashamed. Cf. Am. iii. 9, "Publish ye in the palaces of Ashdod and say, Assemble ye on the mountains of Samaria, and behold what oppressions are in the midst thereof." Whether the prophet speaks of Egyptian idolatry in the early times of Israel's life from historical sources may be uncertain. Such idolatry at this period seems nowhere else spoken of; comp. the list Judg. x. 6. Possibly as he charges the people with idolatry in Egypt (ch. xx. 7; xxiii. 3, 8, 19, 21) they may not have shaken themselves clear of it even in the period of the Judges. The connexion of the country with Egypt was at all times very close.

28. Infidelity with Assyria.

The historical tense "didst play" is better. Already Am. v. 26

hast played the whore also with the Assyrians, because thou wast unsatiable; yea, thou hast played the harlot with 29 them, and yet couldest not be satisfied. Thou hast moreover multiplied thy fornication in the land of Canaan unto 30 Chaldea; and yet thou wast not satisfied herewith. How weak is thine heart, saith the Lord GOD, seeing thou doest all these *things*, the work of an imperious whorish woman; 31 in that thou buildest thine eminent place in the head of every way, and makest thine high place in every street; and hast not been as a harlot, in that *thou* scornest hire; 32 *but as* a wife that committeth adultery, *which* taketh

appears to mention the names of Assyrian gods, for the passage can hardly refer to any time but his own. Jer. ii. 18, 36.

29. Infidelities with the Chaldeans. Past tense is better: **didst** multiply.

in the land of Canaan] Rather: **with** (lit. unto) **the merchants' land, even Chaldea.** Again ch. xvii. 4, the land of traffic. With similar contempt Hosea (xii. 7) uses the term of Israel. Cf. Prov. xxxi. 24; Is. xlvii. 15.

30. *How weak is thine heart*] i.e. how passion-sick, consumed by desire. The term "heart" (*fem.*) occurs nowhere else, and the plur. (Ps. vii. 10; Prov. xv. 11) is hardly evidence for it (Ges.). LXX. renders: how shall I deal with thy daughter (exactly as Hos. xi. 9 how shall I deal with thee, Ephraim). Our present text lay before the translator: "with thy daughter" is "thy heart" with different points; and "weak" was probably read as part of verb "to fill" (spelled as Job viii. 21) and rendered freely. The text, however, may be faulty.

imperious...woman] Not positive: domineering; but negative: subject to no control, unbridled.

31. Recapitulation of the acts done in her unbridled licentiousness, with the addition of a trait shewing that her dissoluteness was without parallel—other harlots take hire, she gives it.

in that thou *scornest hire*] Rather: **hast not been as an harlot, that scoffeth at her hire** (R.V. marg.), lit. in scoffing at hire. The words describe a characteristic of harlots, not one of Jerusalem in which she is unlike them. On scoff or "mock at," cf. ch. xxii. 5; 2 Kings ii. 23; Hab. i. 10; Ps. xliv. 14; Jer. xx. 8, &c. The harlot mocks at her hire in order to augment it; Jerusalem does not desire hire, she rather offers it (*v.* 33).

32. Seems to break the connexion and has been regarded as a gloss. The words "instead of her husband" should be "under her husband," though her husband's (cf. xxiii. 5, when she was mine; Numb. v. 19). The clauses are probably exclamatory: A wife that committeth adultery! though her husband's (though married) she taketh strangers! It is also possible to take the language as an apostrophe: O adulterous wife, &c. LXX. read differently, and the verse is not without suspicion.

strangers instead of her husband. They give gifts to all 33
whores: but thou givest thy gifts to all thy lovers, and
hirest them, that *they* may come unto thee on every side
for thy whoredom. And the contrary is in thee from *other* 34
women in thy whoredoms, whereas none followeth thee to
commit whoredoms: and in that thou givest a reward, and
no reward is given unto thee, therefore thou art contrary.

Wherefore, O harlot, hear the word of the Lord: thus 35/36
saith the Lord God; Because thy filthiness was poured out,
and thy nakedness discovered through thy whoredoms with
thy lovers, and with all the idols of thy abominations, and
by the blood of thy children, which thou didst give unto
them; behold therefore, I will gather all thy lovers, with 37
whom thou hast taken pleasure, and all *them* that thou hast
loved, with all *them* that thou hast hated; I will even
gather them round about against thee, and will discover
thy nakedness unto them, that they may see all thy nakedness. And I will judge thee, as *women* that break wedlock 38
and shed blood are judged; and I will give thee blood in

34. *from* other *women*] Point thus: "from other women: in that thou committest whoredom, and none goeth a whoring after thee; and in that thou givest hire, and no hire is given unto thee; therefore thou art contrary." Hos. viii. 9, Ephraim hireth lovers; Jer. ii. 23—25, iii. 1, 2.

35—43. Punishment of the adulterous wife, and child-murderer.

This punishment is described in somewhat mixed figures: first, *vv.* 36—39, in a figure which tends to pass into a literal account of the destruction of Jerusalem; and secondly, *vv.* 40—43, in a figure suggested by the punishment of the ordinary adulteress.

36. *thy filthiness*] The parallelism "nakedness" requires some such sense; and so the Jewish tradition. The Heb. is the ordinary word for "brass," but any reference to "hire" or money here is out of the question. Cf. Dukes, *Spr. d. Mischnah*, p. 37. Geiger, *Urschrift*, p. 392. Somewhat differently Fried. Del. in Baer, *Ezek.*, p. xiv.

37. *all thy lovers*] The heathen nations whose alliance she sought, Hos. ii. 10.

taken pleasure] Lit. to whom thou hast been pleasing or sweet—with a sensual reference.

that thou hast hated] The nations with whom no alliances were formed, such as the Philistines.

38. *shed blood*] Reference to child murder, *vv.* 20, 36. Cf. ch. xxiii. 45; Lev. xx. 10; Deut. xxii. 22.

give thee blood in fury] Lit. make thee the blood of fury, i.e. bring

39 fury and jealousy. And I will also give thee into their hand, and they shall throw down thine eminent place, and shall break down thy high places: they shall strip thee also of thy clothes, and shall take thy fair jewels, and leave thee 40 naked and bare. They shall also bring up a company against thee, and they shall stone thee with stones, and 41 thrust thee through with their swords. And they shall burn thine houses with fire, and execute judgments upon thee in the sight of many women: and I will cause thee to cease from playing the harlot, and thou also shalt give no 42 hire any more. So will I make my fury towards thee to rest, and my jealousy shall depart from thee, and I will be 43 quiet, and will be no more angry. Because thou hast not remembered the days of thy youth, but hast fretted me in all these *things;* behold therefore, I also will recompense thy way upon *thine* head, saith the Lord GOD: and thou shalt not commit *this* lewdness above all thine abominations.

on thee the bloody death which fury and jealousy executes. On cons. cf. ch. xxvi. 21, xxxv. 6.

39. On "eminent place" and "high places," see *v.* 24.

strip thee...of thy clothes] Reference is probably to a barbarous practice of publicly exposing the adulteress, *v.* 37. Ch. xxiii. 26; Hos. ii. 10.

40. *a company against thee*] A congregation or public assembly of the people, at which the adulteress shall be tried and then executed; Lev. xx. 2; Deut. xxii. 21 (cf. 1 Kings xxi. 9—15), Prov. v. 8—14, I was almost in all evil (danger of death) in the midst of the congregation and assembly. The death of the adulteress was by stoning; Lev. xx. 10; Deut. xxii. 22; John viii. 5.

41. *thine houses with fire*] A summary method of punishment often adopted, as by the Philistines on Samson's father-in-law (Judg. xv. 6); threatened by Ephraim on Jephthah (Judg. xii. 1). Comp. also the summary act of Absalom against Joab for his inattention to the prince's messages (2 Sam. xiv. 30), cf. Josh. vii. 25.

sight of many women] The neighbouring states. There may be reference to a custom of making women witness the fate of the adulteress, that they might take warning.

42. *make my fury...to rest*] i.e. satisfy and appease it. Cf. ch. v. 13.

43. The verse concludes the whole passage *vv.* 35—43, summing up its meaning compendiously, cf. *v.* 22.

thou shalt not commit] The tense is *perf.*, which can hardly be taken as fut. perf., though the prophet does use the perf. in an uncommon way (ch. xiii. 11, xxiv. 5). The sentence can hardly be read interrogatively, without altering the text. LXX. read *and thus* for "and not":

Behold, every one that useth proverbs shall use *this* 44
proverb against thee, saying, As *is* the mother, *so is* her
daughter. Thou *art* thy mother's daughter, that lotheth 45
her husband and her children; and thou *art* the sister of
thy sisters, which lothed their husbands and their children:
your mother *was* a Hittite, and your father an Amorite.
And thine elder sister *is* Samaria, she and her daughters 46

and thus hast thou committed lewdness. The term "lewdness" is used by Ezekiel of sexual enormity, applied figuratively to idolatry (*v.* 27). "Lewdness" and "abominations" would not differ, except that the former was the quality characterizing the acts called abominations. In this case the clause must read: and thus hast thou committed lewdness in (amidst) all thine abominations; and the words would be a final summary of the preceding verses. "Lewdness," however, is used literally (ch. xxii. 9), and *v.* 45 seems to speak of literal unchastity. The clause might thus be attached to *v.* 44, and "lewdness" being distinguished from "abominations," we might read: lewdness in addition to all thine abominations. This distinction, however, is not natural. The proposal to read first person, and put the words into the mouth of Jehovah (Keil): I have not committed wickedness in all thine abominations (i.e. by winking at them and leaving them unpunished, Lev. xix. 29) is singularly inept.

44. A taunting proverb in regard to Jerusalem, the adulteress and child-murderer: she is the true daughter of her mother the Canaanite. The proverb or saying is probably to be restricted to the words: "As is her mother, so is her daughter." In *v.* 45 *seq.* the prophet speaks and addresses Jerusalem.

45. *that lotheth her husband*] In the sense of the allegory "lothing her husband" should mean changing her god for another; and in the case of Jerusalem and Samaria the charge is intelligible, Jehovah being the husband (ch. xxiii.). But such a charge could hardly be made against the Canaanites, the Hittite mother and Sodom (Jer. ii. 11). The prophet appears to desert the allegory, introducing real features into his description, and referring to actual adultery and unfaithfulness, which were characteristic of the Canaanite nations. Another interpretation, as old as Theodoret, considers Jehovah to be the "husband" even of the Hittite mother, heathen idolatries being infidelity to the true God. Such a reflexion is not natural to a prophet of this age, though a similar idea occurred to St Paul (Rom. i.). At the same time this prophet predicts the restoration of Sodom and its union to the people of the Lord. Cornill, considering the difficulties of interpretation as insuperable, strikes out the words as a gloss.

sister of thy sisters] The sisters of Jerusalem were Samaria and Sodom, and she had a genuine family likeness to them.

your mother] Your (plur.) refers to the three sisters.

46. *elder sister*] "elder" is lit. greater, and the reference is to the greater political importance and wider territory of Samaria; as on

that dwell at thy left hand: and thy younger sister, that dwelleth at thy right hand, *is* Sodom and her daughters. 47 Yet hast thou not walked after their ways, nor done after their abominations: but, as *if that were* a very little *thing*, 48 thou wast corrupted more than they in all thy ways. *As* I live, saith the Lord GOD, Sodom thy sister hath not done, she nor her daughters, as thou hast done, thou and thy 49 daughters. Behold, this was the iniquity of thy sister Sodom, pride, fulness of bread, and abundance of idleness was in her and in her daughters, neither did she strengthen 50 the hand of the poor and needy. And they were haughty, and committed abomination before me: therefore I took 51 them away as I saw *good*. Neither hath Samaria committed half of thy sins; but thou hast multiplied thine abominations more than they, and hast justified thy sisters in all

the other hand Sodom was smaller than Judah. In estimating the quarters of the heavens the beholder faced the east, having the north on his left, &c.

her daughters] i.e. subordinate towns.

47—51. The depravity of Jerusalem exceeded that of either of her sisters: Sodom (*v.* 48—50), Samaria (*v.* 51).

47. *as if that were a very little* thing] Or temporally: *but a little while, and then*, i.e. *speedily thou wast corrupted;* though there seems no reference to any actual period of righteousness, such as the times of David. (The strange word *ḳāṭ* is utterly unknown; any connexion with Ar. kaṭ *only*, or with an Assyr. word "a little," Fried. Del. p. xvi. is little probable. If the word be anything but an echo of preceding sounds it may be a fragment of the word "little," cf. Is. xvi. 14, xxix. 17.) Cf. ch. v. 6, 7.

48. Cf. Matt. x. 15, xi. 24.

49. *abundance of idleness*] **prosperous ease**, as R.V., lit. prosperity of quiet. Sodom lived in security and suffered no calamities, as Jer. xlviii. 11 says of Moab, "Moab has been at ease from his youth, and he hath settled on his lees; he hath not been emptied from vessel to vessel, neither hath he gone into captivity." On "fulness of bread" and consequent pride and forgetfulness of God cf. Deut. xxxii. 15; Hos. xiii. 6; Prov. xxx. 7.

strengthen the hand] Or, **take hold of** the hand, i.e. to help or rescue. Prosperity led to pride and inhumanity and then to abominations (*v.* 50).

50. *as I saw* good] Or, **when I saw** it. Gen. xviii. 21, I "will go down and see whether they have done according to the cry which is come up unto me."

51. *hast justified*] Jer. iii. 11, "Backsliding Israel hath justified thine abominations which thou hast done. Thou also, 52 which hast judged thy sisters, bear thine own shame for thy sins that thou hast committed more abominable than they: they are more righteous than thou: yea, be thou confounded also, and bear thy shame, in that thou hast justified thy sisters.

When I shall bring again their captivity, the captivity of 53 Sodom and her daughters, and the captivity of Samaria and her daughters, then *will I bring again* the captivity of thy captives in the midst of them: that thou mayest bear 54 thine own shame, and mayest be confounded in all that thou hast done, in that thou art a comfort unto them. When thy sisters, Sodom and her daughters, shall return 55

herself more than treacherous Judah." The abominations of Judah set Samaria and Sodom in a comparatively righteous light.

52. Point thus: "and thou also, which hast (in that thou hast) given judgment for (in behalf of) thy sisters, bear thy shame; through thy sins which thou hast committed more abominable than they, they are more righteous than thou." Jerusalem has "given judgment" or interposed (1 Sam. ii. 25) in behalf of her sisters in being more wicked than they—she has made them comparatively righteous. The phrase "bear thy shame" might mean "suffer in destruction the consequences of thy wickedness;" *vv.* 54, 61, 63, however, shew that the ref. is to the feeling of shame due to the fact that by the grossness of her abominations she has shewn her sisters to be more righteous than she (cf. xxxix. 26). The prophet assumes the exile and looks forward to the time of restoration. Sodom also and Samaria shall be restored as well as Jerusalem, and it is this that shall bring shame to her, for she shall feel that they whom she did not deign to mention because of their evil fame (*v.* 56) were not worse but better than herself.

53. Sodom and Samaria shall be restored, and Jerusalem along with them.

When I shall bring again] Rather; **and I will bring again.** The phrase "turn the captivity" probably means: turn the fortunes (lit. the turning) of one.

captivity of thy captives] Most moderns by a slight change of reading after LXX. render: and I will bring again thy captivity in the midst of them. Cf. Is. xix. 24, "In that day shall Israel be a third with Egypt and with Assyria, a blessing in the midst of the earth."

54. Read: "that thou mayest bear thy shame, and be ashamed because of all that thou hast done in comforting them." Jerusalem "comforted" Samaria and Sodom in surpassing them in wickedness, and causing them to feel less their own guilt, as also in causing their restoration.

55. *When thy sisters*] Better: **and** thy sisters...**and thou** and thy daughters. In this idea of the restoration of Israel's heathen neighbours

to their former estate, and Samaria and her daughters shall return to their former estate, then thou and thy daughters 56 shall return to your former estate. For thy sister Sodom was not mentioned by thy mouth in the day of thy pride, 57 before thy wickedness was discovered, as *at* the time of *thy* reproach of the daughters of Syria, and all *that are* round about her, the daughters of the Philistines, which despise 58 thee round about. Thou hast borne thy lewdness and 59 thine abominations, saith the LORD. For thus saith the Lord GOD; I will even deal with thee as thou hast done, which hast despised the oath in breaking the covenant. 60 Nevertheless I will remember my covenant with thee in

to their own land after being plucked up out of it Ezekiel as usual follows Jeremiah; cf. in general, Jer. xii. 14—17; Moab, ch. xlviii. 47, Ammon, xlix. 6, and Elam, xlix. 39.

56. Jerusalem did not deign to refer to Sodom on account of the wickedness and evil repute of the latter. Others interrogatively: Was not Sodom a report (a moral byword) in thy mouth? But the interrogative form is precarious.

57. *was discovered*] i.e. manifested. According to modes of thinking then prevalent calamity was the accepted proof of wickedness. Jerusalem's wickedness was laid bare when her great calamities fell upon her, Lam. i. 8, 9.

the time of thy *reproach*] Better, with R.V. **as at the time of the reproach** of the daughters of Syria—which is that which they cast upon Jerusalem, not conversely as A.V. The "time" must be the present, not any previous time, and the language expresses this awkwardly. LXX. read: as now thou art the reproach ("now" for "time," and either finding or inserting the pron. "thou"). The rendering: before thy wickedness was discovered *as* (it is) *now*, a reproach &c. (Hitz. Corn.), is scarcely a Heb. construction. It would be easiest to change "time" into "thou" (cf. the opposite change "which" into "ten" ch. xl. 49): as thou art the reproach.

Syria, and...round about her] The mention of Syria (Heb. Aram) is strange when the reference is to the downfall of Jerusalem. For Aram Syriac gives *Edom* (*d.* for *r*, cf. ch. xxvii. 16) which is more natural (cf. ch. xxxv. 12 *seq.*, xxv. 5, 12, 15). Vulg. reads, round about *thee*, while Syr. wants the whole phrase. The ref. is to Jerusalem in any case. Ezekiel nowhere else brings Syria into connexion with Israel.

which despise thee] Or, **do despite unto** thee; cf. ch. xxv. 15.

58. This and the preceding verses assume the destruction of Jerusalem, of which the prophet was fully assured.

59. The fall of Jerusalem, prophetically assumed in *v.* 58, is now directly threatened. On the "oath" cf. Deut. xxix. 12, 14.

60. The Lord will substitute for the old covenant which was broken

the days of thy youth, and I will establish unto thee an everlasting covenant. Then thou shalt remember thy ways, 61 and be ashamed, when thou shalt receive thy sisters, thine elder and thy younger: and I will give them unto thee for daughters, but not by thy covenant. And I will establish 62 my covenant with thee; and thou shalt know that I *am* the LORD: that thou mayest remember, and be confounded, 63 and never open thy mouth any more, because of thy shame, when I am pacified toward thee for all that thou hast done, saith the Lord GOD.

an "everlasting" covenant, cf. ch. xxxvii. 26; Is. liv. 9, 10, lv. 3; Jer. xxxi. 35, 36, xxxii. 40, xxxiii. 20—22. The covenant will be everlasting because he will forgive their sins (Jer. xxxi. 34), and write his law (*v.* 33), and put his fear (xxxii. 40) in their hearts; giving them a new heart and putting his spirit within them, Ezek. xxxvi. 26. On "days of thy youth" cf. Jer. ii. 2, and Is. liv. 6.

61. Sodom and Samaria, the sisters of Jerusalem, shall be restored also with her and given her for daughters. This restoration of her sinful sisters and her receiving them for daughters shall bring the sense of her own sin home to Jerusalem, and she shall be ashamed of all she has done.

not by thy covenant] This glory of receiving Samaria and Sodom and her other sister cities and nationalities for daughters shall not accrue to Jerusalem as the result of her former covenant with Jehovah, for that covenant of his she broke. It shall be like the new covenant itself, something altogether additional, an act of God's goodness in no way depending on former relations (*v.* 62).

62. *I will establish*] "*I*" is emphatic, in opposition to "not by thy covenant." The new covenant will shew that which Jehovah is better than all his chastisements.

63. *when I am pacified*] Better active: when **I forgive thee.** The word is the technical sacrificial word to "atone" or make atonement for. It probably means to "cover," though it is no more used in the physical sense but only in reference to sins or guilt. Hence when God is the agent this covering of sin is pardon, Jer. xviii. 23; Deut. xxi. 8 (be merciful to); 2 Chron. xxx. 18. The important point is to retain the active sense of the word. An act of God is described, not an effect produced upon his mind.

The great grace of Jehovah in restoring Jerusalem will humble and ashame her, when she remembers her past evil. What all chastisements could accomplish but indifferently, goodness will accomplish fully. Jerusalem will no more "open her mouth," but sit in abashed though glad silence before God. His goodness and her own sin will so fill her mind that the thoughts will be too deep for words. Formerly she accused God's providence, thinking she suffered for the iniquities of generations before her; formerly she boasted of her place before Jehovah, and her sister Sodom was not in her mouth. Now her mind will muse on other things.

Though the language and conceptions of Ezekiel are less familiar and natural to western minds than those of some of the other writers of Scripture, his thoughts are very elevated.

(1) The figure of the adulterous wife expresses the conviction, felt by him very strongly, that all through her history Israel had sinned against Jehovah, especially in the matter of his service. While former prophets like Amos and Hosea condemn the ritual and the manner of the worship because this implies a false conception of Jehovah, a conception so false as to correspond in no sense to Jehovah as he really is, Ezekiel condemns the worship at the high places as in itself false. He regards the high places as Canaanite shrines, and the service there is no service of Jehovah. And when he says that Jerusalem was unfaithful with Egypt, Assyria and Babylon, besides expressing his belief that the kingdom of Jehovah is not as one among the other kingdoms, he assails the strange infatuation which the people displayed in adopting the gods and rites of the nations with which in successive ages they entered into relation. What took place in regard to the worship of the Canaanites when Israel entered upon possession of that land, took place all down the history as they successively came under the influence of the great states around.

(2) When the prophet charges Jerusalem with outbidding Samaria and Sodom in wickedness, his judgment agrees with that of Jeremiah, and is founded partly on the fact that Jerusalem had fuller knowledge of Jehovah from her more extended history, and consequently her sin was greater than that of Samaria. The judgment, however, may also be partly based on objective grounds. So far as appears from the prophets Amos and Hosea idolatry in the strict sense was not greatly prevalent in the North. What prevailed was mainly a sensuous worship of Jehovah, due to false conceptions of his nature, which probably had arisen from a long syncretism with the idea and service of the Baals. But in the later history of Judah idolatry in the sense of the worship of gods different from Jehovah greatly prevailed. Neither does the cruel rite of child-sacrifice appear to have invaded the Northern Kingdom.

(3) It is, however, when the prophet brings the sin of Jerusalem into connexion with that of Samaria and Sodom, which it exceeded, and lifts that strange fact up into the region of divine thoughts and providential operations, that his ideas become most profound. The sin of Jerusalem, so great amidst all God's love and favour, reveals to himself the nature of sin and its power over men, and he remembers with compassion those heathen peoples, like Sodom, on whom his former judgments had so unsparingly fallen. His own people's fall causes him to take to his heart the Gentile world. The Apostle Paul touches the same or a kindred idea when he says: By their fall salvation is come unto the Gentiles; the casting away of them is the reconciling of the world (Rom. xi. 11, 12).

Again when the prophet says that Jerusalem "shall be ashamed in that she has justified her sisters," the thought is similar to that expressed by St Paul, "Salvation is come unto the Gentiles for to provoke them

And the word of the LORD came unto me, saying, Son

(Israel) to jealousy.' Cf. Deut. xxxii. 21. The sight of other peoples received by her God awakens Israel to the meaning of her own past, and to recollections of her former relations to God. Finally the receiving again of Israel and the incoming of the Gentile peoples like Sodom illustrate the manner of salvation, shewing it to be of grace, a grace that is stronger to overcome sin and awaken sorrow for it than all judgments—he hath shut up all into disobedience that he might have mercy upon all. Neither the prophet nor the apostle moves in the region of second causes; they lift up the whole movement of salvation into the region of the divine thoughts and compassions.

(4) The prophet predicts the restoration of Jerusalem, Samaria and Sodom, and that Jerusalem, though like a sister to them in wickedness, shall receive all these greater and smaller sisters as daughters. There shall then in the new kingdom of Jehovah be only one mother city, all other cities or peoples shall be her children. To the prophet's mind the identity of Samaria and Sodom remains even when they are destroyed, and they shall remember and turn to the Lord. There is in such passages, what is not unusual in Ezekiel, a struggle between the spiritual conception or fact and the external form in which he still feels it must be embodied. It is the spiritual conception of the conversion to Jehovah even of peoples like Sodom that fills his mind; but he is unable to give this expression in any other way than by saying that Sodom shall return to her former estate.

CH. XVII. THE TREACHEROUS VINEPLANT—KING ZEDEKIAH'S DISLOYALTY TO THE KING OF BABYLON.

The chapter is without date. Nebuchadnezzar appeared in Palestine in the ninth year of Zedekiah to punish his disloyalty and intrigues with Egypt. The present passage assumes this disloyalty and may be dated a year or two earlier (c. 590).

The chapter contains these divisions:
First, vv. 1—10. The riddle of the great eagle.
Secondly, vv. 11—21. Explanation of the riddle.
Thirdly, vv. 22—24. Promise that Jehovah will set up in Israel a kingdom that shall be universal.

1—10. THE RIDDLE OF THE GREAT EAGLE.

(1) vv. 1—4 introduction. The great, broadwinged, speckled eagle came to Lebanon, and broke off the top of the cedar, carrying it to the merchant-land, Babylon—the captivity of Jehoiachin by Nebuchadnezzar.

(2) vv. 5, 6. He took also of the seed of the land and planted it beside the waters that it might be a spreading vine, and might turn its branches towards him who had planted it—the elevation to the throne by Nebuchadnezzar of Zedekiah as a feudatory monarch.

(3) vv. 7, 8. There was another great eagle, and the vine bent its

of man, put forth a riddle, and speak a parable unto the
3 house of Israel; and say, Thus saith the Lord GOD; A
great eagle with great wings, longwinged, full *of* feathers,
which had divers colours, came unto Lebanon, and took
4 the highest branch of the cedar: he cropt off the top of his
young twigs, and carried it into a land of traffick; he set
5 it in a city of merchants. He took also of the seed of the
land, and planted it in a fruitful field; he placed *it* by great
6 waters, *and* set it *as* a willow tree. And it grew, and
became a spreading vine of low stature, whose branches
turned toward him, and the roots thereof were under him:
so it became a vine, and brought forth branches, and shot
7 forth sprigs. There was also another great eagle with great

roots and sent out its branches towards him—Zedekiah sought the
alliance and protection of the king of Egypt.
  (4) *vv*. 9, 10. Denunciation of the vine for its treachery. The east
wind shall blow on it and it shall wither.
  2. *a riddle*] As requiring interpretation; the passage is also called a
"parable," as containing a similitude or comparison. The eagle is
Nebuchadnezzar, king of Babylon. Conquerors are often compared to
the eagle, Deut. xxviii. 49; Is. xlvi. 11; Jer. iv. 13, xlviii. 40; Hos. viii.
1; Lam. iv. 19.
  3. *longwinged*] With long pinions. The eagle was also of "divers
colours" or speckled, with reference possibly to the very diverse nationalities included in the Babylonian empire.
  came unto Lebanon] The figure of the eagle coming to Lebanon and
cropping off the highest branch and top of the young twigs (*v*. 4) represents the carrying off of those highest in the land of Israel. Lebanon as
opposed to Babylon is the mountain of Palestine; the cedar, the tree of
Lebanon, appears to represent the royal Davidic house (*vv*. 12, 22), and
its highest branches king Jehoiachin and the princes who were carried
away to Babylon (*v*. 12). On "land of traffic" (*v*. 4), cf. ch. xvi. 29.
  5. Nebuchadnezzar then took Mattaniah, son of Josiah, and made
him king under the name of Zedekiah. The "seed of the land" is the
native royal house.
  he placed it] The unknown form so rendered might be a verb, cf.
Hos. xi. 3. LXX. omits; Ew. conjectures slip, or cutting. The comparison to the willow (the sense is not certain, the word not occurring
again) is suggested by the place where it was planted, beside great waters.
"Water" is the requisite of every tree in the East, and "great waters"
are the favourable conditions granted to Zedekiah. "They that drink
water" is a name for trees, ch. xxxi. 16.
  6. *of low stature*] This refers to the dependent nature of Zedekiah's
kingdom, as tributary to the lord superior. Cf. Is. xvi. 8: Hos. x. 1.
  whose branches turned] Or, **that its branches might turn**...and
the roots thereof **be**.

wings and many feathers: and behold, this vine did bend her roots towards him, and shot forth her branches toward him, that *he* might water it by the furrows of her plantation. It *was* planted in a good soil by great waters, that *it* might 8 bring forth branches, and that *it* might bear fruit, that *it* might be a goodly vine. Say thou, Thus saith the Lord 9 God; Shall it prosper? shall he not pull up the roots thereof, and cut off the fruit thereof, that it wither? it shall wither *in* all the leaves of her spring, even without great power or many people to pluck it up by the roots thereof. Yea behold, *being* planted, shall it prosper? shall it not 10 utterly wither, when the east wind toucheth it? it shall wither in the furrows where it grew.

Moreover the word of the Lord came unto me, saying, 11 Say now to the rebellious house, Know ye not what these 12 *things mean?* tell *them,* Behold, the king of Babylon is

7. The other great eagle, which however is not described with such imposing epithets as the former, is the king of Egypt. The vine bent its roots toward him—sought to draw nourishment from him.

by the furrows] Rather: **from the beds of its plantation**—i.e. where it was planted. The words are connected with "did bend her roots." The comparative sense: to water it more than the beds, has less probability; though it would express the uneasiness of Zedekiah and his vain political dreams.

8. The happy condition of Zedekiah's monarchy under the king of Babylon, had he been content with his subordinate role as a feudatory prince.

9. Threat of punishment because of his treachery. The vine shall be pulled up and utterly withered—Zedekiah's monarchy shall be taken away before the king of Babylon.

shall he not pull up] The subject is most naturally the king of Babylon, who planted it; the words might be used in the sense of the *pass.*: shall it not be pulled up?

it shall wither...her spring] As R.V., all her fresh springing leaves shall wither.

even without great power] It will be a light thing for the king of Babylon to pluck up this vine by the roots. Both the words and construction are peculiar; cf. *v.* 17.

10. Destruction under another figure, that of the east wind, before which vegetation crumbles into dust. Cf. ch. xix. 12; Hos. xiii. 15; Is. xxvii. 8, xl. 7; Job xxvii. 21.

11—21. Interpretation of the riddle.

12. *the rebellious house*] i.e. Israel, ch. ii. 5.
king of Babylon is come] Better past tenses throughout: **came**...and

come *to* Jerusalem, and hath taken the king thereof, and the princes thereof, and led them with him to Babylon;
13 and hath taken of the king's seed, and made a covenant with him, and hath taken an oath of him: he hath also
14 taken the mighty of the land: that the kingdom might be base, that *it* might not lift itself up, *but* that by keeping of
15 his covenant it might stand. But he rebelled against him in sending his ambassadors *into* Egypt, that *they* might give him horses and much people. Shall he prosper? shall he escape that doeth such *things?* or shall he break the cove-
16 nant, and be delivered? *As* I live, saith the Lord GOD, surely in the place *where* the king *dwelleth* that made him king, whose oath he despised, and whose covenant he brake, *even* with him in the midst of Babylon he shall die.
17 Neither shall Pharaoh with *his* mighty army and great

took; so *v.* 13 and **took**. On the captivity of Jehoiachin, cf. 2 Kings xxiv. 11 *seq*.; Jer. xxiv. 1, xxix. 1.

13. *the king's seed*] the **royal seed**, lit. seed of the kingdom. See on *v.* 5; cf. 2 Kings xxiv. 17; Jer. xxxvii. 1.

an oath of him] Cf. 2 Chron. xxxvi. 13.

he hath also taken] he **took also**. On "mighty of the land," cf. *v.* 12. Probably the more influential classes are included, those who if left might be uneasy under the yoke and likely to stir up revolt; cf. 2 Kings xxiv. 14, 15; Jer. xxix. 1, 2.

14. *might be base*] i.e. humble, and without pretension; cf. ch. xxix. 14. It was with this purpose that Nebuchadnezzar carried away the mighty of the land. He also hoped that the kingdom would "stand;" it was no doubt his policy to have a dependent, friendly state on the frontier of Egypt. The word "stand," however, may refer to the covenant: to keep his covenant, that it might stand.

15. Cf. 2 Kings xxiv. 20. The king of Egypt referred to was Pharaoh Hophra, Jer. xliv. 30, xxxvii. 5 *seq*. The indignation of Ezekiel against Zedekiah arises greatly from his regarding the subjection of Jerusalem to Babylon as a thing determined by Jehovah. Hence the covenant broken by Zedekiah is not merely the covenant of the king of Babylon but that of Jehovah (*v.* 19). The prophet follows Jeremiah. He had possibly read the words of the latter spoken in the beginning of the reign of Zedekiah, ch. xxvii. 9—17, "serve the king of Babylon and live;" and probably he had heard his words to the same effect spoken in the fourth year of Jehoiakim, ch. xxv. His advice to the exiles also was no doubt known to him, ch. xxix. 4.

16. Zedekiah, being carried to Babylon, shall die there.

17. The aid of Pharaoh shall be in vain; cf. Jer. xxxvii. 5, and the pathetic references to the hopes and disappointments of the besieged during the last days of Jerusalem in Lam. iv. 17.

company make for him in the war, by casting up mounts, and building forts, to cut off many persons: seeing he 18 despised the oath by breaking the covenant, when lo, he had given his hand, and hath done all these *things*, he shall not escape. Therefore thus saith the Lord GOD; *As* I 19 live, surely mine oath that he hath despised, and my covenant that he hath broken, even it will I recompense upon his own head. And I will spread my net upon him, and 20 he shall be taken in my snare, and I will bring him to Babylon, and will plead with him there *for* his trespass that he hath trespassed against me. And all his fugitives with 21 all his bands shall fall by the sword, and they that remain shall be scattered towards all winds: and ye shall know that I the LORD have spoken *it*.

Thus saith the Lord GOD; I will also take of the highest 22 branch of the high cedar, and will set *it;* I will crop off from the top of his young twigs a tender one, and will

On "mounts," &c., cf. ch. iv. 2.
20. *spread my net*] Cf. ch. xii. 13; Hos. vii. 12.
plead with him] i.e. there subject him to the consequences of his treachery, bringing it thereby to his knowledge that he is suffering the penalty of it, cf. xx. 35, 36, xxxviii. 22; Jer. ii. 35.
21. *all his fugitives*] The form of word does not otherwise occur, but has been so understood by some ancient versions. Others as Targ., Syr., assume a transposition of two letters and render: *his choice men;* and so many moderns (cf. ch. xxiii. 7; Dan. xi. 15). This last reading is found in a number of MSS. Cf. ch. v. 2, 12, vi. 10, 13, xii. 12 *seq.*

22—24. PROMISE OF A NEW AND UNIVERSAL MESSIANIC KINGDOM IN ISRAEL.

The attempt of the king of Babylon to set up a kingdom in Israel miscarried; he who set up the kingdom took it away. The shoot planted by him was smitten by the east wind and withered. But Jehovah himself will plant a shoot of the high cedar, the Davidic house, on a high mountain that all nations may see it (Is. ii. 2, xi. 10), even on the height of the mountain land of Israel, and it shall become a great cedar, so that all the fowls of heaven shall lodge in the branches of it. This kingdom shall be imposing and universal, and all peoples shall find protection under it. And then shall it be known that Jehovah is king among the nations, that kingdoms are in his hand, to set one up and pull another down; that he can make the green tree wither and the dry tree blossom and bear fruit.

22. *I will also take*] **I will take**—" I " emphatic. The figure refers to the house of David, cf. *vv.* 2, 3; Is. liii. 2.

23 plant *it* upon a high mountain and eminent: in the mountain of the height of Israel will I plant it: and it shall bring forth boughs, and bear fruit, and be a goodly cedar: and under it shall dwell all fowl of every wing; in the 24 shadow of the branches thereof shall they dwell. And all the trees of the field shall know that I the Lord have brought down the high tree, have exalted the low tree, have dried up the green tree, and have made the dry tree to flourish: I the Lord have spoken and have done *it*.

high mountain] This belongs partly to the figure of the cedar, but indicates also the conspicuousness to the eyes of the nations of this great cedar; Is. ii. 2.
23. *mountain of the height*] Cf. ch. xx. 40, xl. 2.
fowl of every wing] As fowls flock to a great tree so all peoples will put their trust in the shadow of this great monarchy in the land of Israel; ch. xxxi. 6; Dan. iv. 12; Matt. xiii. 32.
24. As this kingdom is compared to a cedar other kingdoms are likewise called trees; cf. ch. xxxi. 5, 8, 14, 16, 18. Kings and kingdoms are hardly distinguished, the kingdom is but the expression of the king. Then all shall know that this great result is the work of Jehovah, who worketh contrary to men's expectations; who overturneth till he come whose right it is to rule. Cf. 1 Sam ii. 4—8; Luk. i. 51—53.

CH. XVIII. THE MORAL FREEDOM AND RESPONSIBILITY OF THE INDIVIDUAL MAN BEFORE GOD.

This great idea is expressed in two parts:
First, *vv.* 1—20. The individual man is not involved in the sins and fate of his people or of his forefathers.
Secondly, *vv.* 21—32. Neither does he lie under the ban of his own previous life. His moral freedom raises him above both.
The prophet as usual attaches himself to the ideas of Jeremiah, who had prophesied that in the ideal days to come, those of the New Covenant, the perfect future that was about to dawn upon men, they should no more say, "The fathers ate sour grapes and the children's teeth are set on edge," but every one should die for his own iniquity (ch. xxxi. 29, 30). The outlook of Ezekiel is also in some measure ideal, and the principles which he enunciates must be judged in this light (ch. xxxiii.). His purpose is in the main practical. He desires to lay a basis for his exhortation "Turn yourselves from all your transgressions" (*vv.* 30—32). His exhortations are addressed to the individuals of the people, for he contemplates the end of the state and only individuals remain, and he has to face and settle questions that from the circumstances of the time had begun to exercise and perplex men's minds. The strokes that had fallen one after another upon the state might be deserved, when the state was considered a moral person that had sinned all through her history (ch. xvi.); but

And the word of the LORD came unto me again, saying, **18** the calamities that were deserved by the general mass fell with a crushing weight on many who had not been partakers in the sins that brought them down. The captives carried away under Jehoiachin were more righteous than those still left to inherit the mountains of Israel; and compared with the dark days of Manasseh even the generation subject to Zedekiah might think themselves better men. Such reflections made the people feel themselves involved as by a kind of fate in the deeds of their forefathers, a feeling which found expression in the proverb, "The fathers ate sour grapes, and the children's teeth are set on edge." This proverb might express various feelings as it came from different mouths. It might be uttered by some in self-exculpation, and in a satisfied, self-righteous tone; or it might be the expression of a perplexed condition of mind, which found God's providence dark, and went so far as well nigh to arraign the divine rectitude; or finally it might express the feeling of lying under a hopeless fate inherited from the past—a feeling which crushed out individual life and paralysed all personal effort after righteousness, and delivered over the mind to an inactivity of despair (ch. xxxiii. 10). These difficulties could not fail themselves to suggest their own solution. They were partly due to the consciousness, which circumstances were everywhere creating, of the worth of the individual soul; and their solution lay in pursuing this idea further and giving it clearer expression.

The prophet meets the state of the people's mind with two great principles from the mouth of the Lord: (1) "All souls are mine; as the soul of the father, so also the soul of the son is mine." Each soul is the Lord's, his relation to each is direct and immediate (*v.* 4). And (2) "I have no pleasure in the death of him that dieth," saith the Lord (*vv.* 23, 32).

And two conclusions follow from these principles: (1) "Each soul being immediately related to God, its destiny depends on this relation— the soul that sinneth shall die;" and (2) "Wherefore, turn yourselves and live" (*v.* 32). The emancipation of the individual soul is complete.

First, *vv.* 1—20. The individual soul shall not be involved in the sins and fate of its people or forefathers.

(1) *vv.* 1—5. Introduction. The current proverb that the children suffer the consequences of the sins of their fathers (*vv.* 1, 2). Answer of Jehovah: All souls are mine. None shall answer for the sins of another—the soul that sinneth shall die (*vv.* 3—5).

(2) *vv.* 6—20. Developement of this principle in three instances: first, a man who is upright, doing truth and righteousness—this man shall live (*vv.* 5—9). Secondly, if this righteous man beget a wicked son who doeth evil, this wicked son of a righteous father shall die (*vv.* 10—13). Thirdly, but if this wicked son of a righteous father himself beget a son who, seeing the evil of his father, avoids it and acts righteously, this righteous son of an evil father shall live (*vv.* 14—18). To restate the principle: the righteous shall live in his righteousness, and the wicked shall die in his own evil (*vv.* 19, 20).

2 What mean ye, that ye use this proverb concerning the land of Israel, saying, The fathers have eaten sour grapes, 3 and the children's teeth are set on edge? *As* I live, saith the Lord GOD, ye shall not have *occasion* any more to use 4 this proverb in Israel. Behold, all souls *are* mine; as the soul of the father, so also the soul of the son *is* mine: the soul that sinneth, it shall die.

5 But if a man be just, and do that which is lawful and

2. *concerning the land*] Rather, **in** the land, lit. upon: cf. *v.* 3 "in Israel."

fathers have eaten] Or, the fathers eat; the proverb being thrown into a general form. The proverb, already noticed by Jeremiah (ch. xxxi. 29, 30) means that the children suffer the consequences of the sins of their fathers. Sour or unripe grapes are occasionally eaten, and naturally the effect upon the eater's teeth is immediate—his teeth are set on edge, lit. blunted, the edge of them turned. Here, however, the effect is first felt by the children. Such feelings could not but arise in the troubled times of the fall of the state, when the righteous suffered with the wicked, and the most righteous were carried into exile, and just because they still clave to their own faith in the midst of heathenism endured severer sufferings than others who accommodated themselves to their circumstances. Soon after the fall of Jerusalem we hear the same complaint in literal terms: "The fathers sinned and are not, and we have borne their iniquities" (Lam. v. 7).

3. *ye shall not have* occasion] Or, **it shall not be permitted you.**

4. *all souls* are *mine*] i.e. every individual soul stands in immediate relation to God; Numb. xvi. 22, "O God, God of the spirits of all flesh, shall one man sin, and wilt thou be wroth with all the congregation?" All souls alike belong to God, and this "alike" guarantees the treatment of each by itself, the soul of the son no less than the soul of the father. According to former modes of thought the son had not personal independence, he belonged to the father, and was involved in the destiny of the father.

sinneth, it shall die] *It* and not another because of its sin. "Live" and "die" are used by the prophet of literal life and death, continuance in the world and removal from it. They have, however, a pregnant meaning arising from the other conceptions of the prophet. He feels himself and the people standing immediately before that perfect kingdom of the Lord which is about to come (ch. xxxiii., xxxvii), and "live" implies entering into the glory of this kingdom, while "die" implies deprivation of its blessedness; for of course, like all the Old Testament writers, Ezekiel considers the kingdom, even in its perfect condition, an earthly one.

5—20. DEVELOPEMENT OF THE PRINCIPLE IN THREE INSTANCES, CHOSEN SO AS TO EXHIBIT IT IN ITS MOST PARADOXICAL FORM.

5—9. The man that is righteous shall live. First, his righteousness

right, *and* hath not eaten upon the mountains, neither hath 6
lift up his eyes to the idols of the house of Israel, neither
hath defiled his neighbour's wife, neither hath come near to
a menstruous woman, and hath not oppressed any, *but* hath 7
restored *to* the debtor his pledge, hath spoiled none by
violence, hath given his bread to the hungry, and hath
covered the naked with a garment; he *that* hath not given 8
forth upon usury, neither hath taken any increase, *that* hath
withdrawn his hand from iniquity, hath executed true judgment between man and man, hath walked in my statutes, 9

is defined generally as doing judgment or right and justice, *v*. 5. Then it is analysed into: (1) religious duties, *v*. 6; (2) duties relating to marriage and the relations of men and women, *v*. 6; (3) duties to one's neighbour, *vv*. 7, 8; and (4) finally all these duties are brought under the conception of obedience to the commands of God, *v*. 9.

6. *eaten upon the mountains*] that is, sacrificed on the high places and partaken of the sacrificial meal following, token of fellowship as a guest with the idols there worshipped. The phrase occurs again *vv*. 11, 15, xxii. 9. In xxxiii. 25 the reading is, eaten *with the blood;* cf. Lev. xvii. 17, xix. 26; 1 Sam. xiv. 33. Sept. renders Lev. xix. 26, eaten *upon the mountains*, and it is possible that the same error of reading occurs here, and that xviii. 6, 11, 15, xxii. 9, should be assimilated to xxxiii. 25 (W. R. Smith, *Kinship*, p. 310).

lift up his eyes] In prayer to the idols, or trust in them, or perhaps generally, in acknowledgment of them. Ps. cxxi. 1, cxxiii. 1; Job xxxi. 26.

his neighbour's wife] Adultery is not seldom charged against the people by the prophets, especially Jeremiah, e.g. Jer. v. 8, ix. 2, xxix. 23; cf. Lev. xx. 10; Deut. xxii. 22. Note Job's claims for himself, ch. xxxi. 9. On the other impurity forbidden cf. Lev. xv. 24, xviii. 19.

7, 8. Duties to one's neighbour.

7. *hath not oppressed*] In *v*. 12 the opposite course reads: hath oppressed the poor and needy. Occasion of oppression would arise when the poor was in debt (Am. ii. 6, 7); or being unprotected he might be defrauded of his hire, Mal. iii. 5 (James v. 4). Cf. the claim made by Job, xxxi. 13.

to the debtor his pledge] This refers to the duty of returning to the debtor any pledge which was an article necessary to his existence or comfort, as a garment which was his cover by night. Ex. xxii. 26; Deut. xxiv. 6; cf. Job xxii. 6; Am. ii. 8. On the positive duties of feeding the hungry and clothing the naked cf. again the claims of Job, xxxi. 17—20.

8. On usury cf. the humane law, Lev. xxv. 35—37. The case supposed is that of lending to the poor, Ex. xxii. 25; Deut. xxiii. 20.

executed true judgment] When acting as judge, or as umpire between man and man.

and hath kept my judgments, to deal truly; he *is* just, he shall surely live, saith the Lord GOD.

10 If he beget a son *that is* a robber, a shedder of blood,
11 and *that* doeth the like to *any* one of these *things*, and

9. The man who acts thus (*vv.* 5—8) hath walked in God's statutes and he shall live. For "to deal truly," LXX. reads: *to do them*, by transposition of two letters, which is more natural.

With the ideal of a righteous man here given may be compared these others: Job's, ch. xxxi., perhaps the most inward in the Old Testament, Ps. xv.; Is. lviii. 5—7. Such ideals differ from ours principally in that they seem to consist of conduct exclusively external, while we express our ideal in terms of the thought and feelings. But first, when these external actions are enumerated it is always assumed that they proceed from a right condition of mind, of which they are the natural fruit. Hence the prophet says, "Make you a new heart, and a new spirit" (*v.* 31). The same assumption is made when God is spoken of as making men righteous by forgiveness, or by bestowing on them prosperity, the sign of righteousness. The mental state corresponding to this right relation to God is always regarded as present. And in point of fact the righteousness of God himself consists in righteous acts, just as the righteousness of man. The ancient mind fastened on the outward acts as revealing the inward state, while the modern mind goes directly to the internal condition. And secondly, moral conduct was never thought of as the result of a happy or pure disposition, or as the fruit of prevalent social custom, or obedience to laws called moral or natural; it was always regarded as obedience to divine commandment. Morals was part of religion. Every moral law was fulfilled in obedience to God; hence Jehovah says of this moral man, "he hath walked in my statutes, he shall live" (*v.* 9).

10—13. SECOND LINK IN THE CHAIN: THIS RIGHTEOUS MAN IS THE FATHER OF A VIOLENT SON WHO SHEDS BLOOD AND DOES EVIL; THE WICKED SON SHALL NOT LIVE BECAUSE OF THE RIGHTEOUSNESS OF HIS FATHER, HE SHALL DIE IN HIS OWN SIN.

10. *a robber*] a **man of violence**.

and that *doeth the like*] The text is difficult. LXX. reads: shedding blood, *and committing sins*, 11 *who hath not walked in the way of his righteous father*, but hath even eaten, &c. This text gives the general meaning of the Heb., of which it looks like a paraphrase. It is difficult to decide whether the last clause of *v.* 10 refers to the father or the son. The words in the place where they stand should refer to the wicked son, and so A.V., R.V., but if so they cannot be reconciled with *v.* 11. The words rendered "these *things*" (*v.* 10) and "those *duties*" (*v.* 11) are the same, viz. the things *vv.* 6—9, and cannot be regarded as things forbidden (*v.* 10) and things commanded (*v.* 11) at once. The unknown word *ach* occurring here (cf. *v.* 18, xxi. 20) is supposed to be the same as "only" (akh), but is probably a fragment of the word "one" due to an error of the copyist and should be neglected.

that doeth not any of those *duties*, but even hath eaten upon the mountains, and defiled his neighbour's wife, hath oppressed the poor and needy, hath spoiled by violence, hath not restored the pledge, and hath lift up his eyes to the idols, hath committed abomination, hath given forth upon usury, and hath taken increase: shall he then live? he shall not live: he hath done all these abominations; he shall surely die; his blood shall be upon him.

Now lo, *if* he beget a son, that seeth all his father's sins which he hath done, and considereth, and doeth not such like, *that* hath not eaten upon the mountains, neither hath lift up his eyes to the idols of the house of Israel, hath not defiled his neighbour's wife, neither hath oppressed any, hath not withholden the pledge, neither hath spoiled by violence, *but* hath given his bread to the hungry, and hath covered the naked with a garment, *that* hath taken off his hand from the poor, *that* hath not received usury nor increase, hath executed my judgments, hath walked in my statutes; he shall not die for the iniquity of his father, he shall surely live. *As for* his father, because he cruelly oppressed, spoiled *his* brother by violence, and did *that* which *is* not good among his people, lo, even he shall die in his iniquity.

11. *and that doeth not*] Fairer: *and he hath not done any of these things, but even hath eaten*, &c. The things which he hath not done are those in *vv*. 6—9 regarded as positive commandments. The words naturally refer to the wicked son. They are incompatible with those in the end of *v*. 10, if these be said of the son. Syr., feeling the incompatibility, omits. It is easier, however, to omit the words in *v*. 10, as a gloss from Lev. iv. 2, because the words "but even hath eaten" require a negative clause before them.

13. *shall surely die*] The formula common in the law, "shall surely be put to death," Lev. xx. 11; Ex. xxi. 15, xxii. 18.

his blood...upon him] He shall suffer the death due to his own deeds, ch. xxxiii. 4; Lev. xx. 9; 2 Sam. i. 16.

vv. 14—20. Third link in the chain of illustration: this unrighteous man on the other hand begets a son who, seeing his father's iniquities, is deterred by them and lives righteously. This son shall not die for the sins of his father, but live because of his own righteousness.

14. *and considereth*] Lit. *even seeth*, so *v*. 28. With a different punctuation the word would mean: *and feareth*, as R.V.

16. *withholden the pledge*] **taken aught to pledge**, as R.V.

17. *taken off his hand*] withdrawn his hand—so as not to injure or oppress—the poor. LXX. reads: from iniquity, but cf. ch. xx. 22.

18. *spoiled* his *brother*] LXX. omits "brother;" the word is that

19 Yet say ye, Why? doth not the son bear the iniquity of the father? When the son hath done that which is lawful and right, *and* hath kept all my statutes, and hath done
20 them, he shall surely live. The soul that sinneth, it shall die. The son shall not bear the iniquity of the father, neither shall the father bear the iniquity of the son: the righteousness of the righteous shall be upon him, and the
21 wickedness of the wicked shall be upon him. But if the wicked will turn from all his sins that he hath committed, and keep all my statutes, and do that which is lawful and right,
22 he shall surely live, he shall not die. All his transgressions that he hath committed, they shall not be mentioned unto him: in his righteousness that he hath done he shall live.
23 Have I any pleasure at all that the wicked should die? saith the Lord God: *and* not that he should return from his ways, and live?

referred to *v.* 10. Here "brother" might stand, though "neighbour" is the term elsewhere used (*vv.* 6, 11). The word "violence" or robbery has a different form *vv.* 7, 12.

19. *Yet say ye, Why?*] Rather: **and ye say, wherefore doth not the son bear...?** The prophet refers to the current view, and supposes it quoted as an objection to his principle. So long as the idea prevailed that the son was, so to speak, part of the father, it was natural to suppose that he should be included in the father's punishment; hence the people ask, Why doth the son not bear, lit. *bear part of, share in bearing* (so *v.* 20), the iniquity of the father? In opposition to this idea the prophet states his principle on both its sides, *vv.* 19, 20.

Secondly, *vv.* 21—32. As men shall not be involved in the sins of their people or their fathers, so the individual soul shall not lie under the ban of its own past.

The sinner who turneth from his evil and doeth righteousness shall live in his righteousness, *vv.* 21—23. And on the other hand, the righteous man who turneth away from his righteousness and doeth evil shall die in his evil, *v.* 24.

22. *mentioned unto him*] Or, **remembered in regard to him.**

23. The verse meets a feeling of despair both in regard to themselves and in regard to God which was beginning to take possession of the minds of some, perhaps many, among the people. The despair in regard to themselves is seen in ch. xxxiii. 10, 11, "We pine away in our iniquities, how should we live?" and the despair in regard to God, which is but another side of that in regard to themselves, is expressed in such passages as Lam. iii. 42—44, "We have rebelled and thou hast not pardoned...Thou hast covered thyself with a cloud that our prayer should not pass through." The Lord had brought the evil on them which he had purposed (Lam. ii. 8, 17), and it was final (Lam. ii. 9).

But when the righteous turneth away from his righteousness, 24 and committeth iniquity, *and* doeth according to all the abominations that the wicked *man* doeth, shall he live? All his righteousness that he hath done shall not be mentioned: in his trespass that he hath trespassed, and in his sin that he hath sinned, in them shall he die. Yet ye say, The way 25 of the Lord is not equal. Hear now, O house of Israel; Is not my way equal? are not your ways unequal? When a 26 righteous *man* turneth away from his righteousness, and committeth iniquity, and dieth in them; for his iniquity that he hath done shall he die. Again, when the wicked 27 *man* turneth away from his wickedness that he hath committed, and doeth that which is lawful and right, he shall save his soul alive. Because he considereth, and turneth 28

The same despondency, though softened in some measure by the lapse of time, appears in another prophet, Is. xl. 27—31, xlix. 14, "Zion hath said, The Lord hath forsaken me, and my Lord hath forgotten me." So long as the state existed the covenant might also be thought to remain, and the prophets could sustain the hearts of men by reminding them that the Lord was their God; but when the state fell and Israel was no more to appearance the people of Jehovah, they had to go behind the covenant and fall back on that unchanging nature of Jehovah which originated the covenant—that mercy which endureth for ever. The prevailing disposition of the mind of Jehovah was towards the salvation of men.

24. Although it would have sufficed for the prophet's purpose to assure the repentant sinner of God's forgiveness, he has a certain theoretical interest in the principle which he is insisting on which makes him develop it on the other side also.

25. *Yet ye say, The way...equal*] **And** ye say. The "way" of the Lord is the principle on which he acts, or his action on it, Is. lv. 8, cf. ch. xxxiii. 17, 20. The objection of the people may really have been expressed (cf. *v.* 19). The prophet's principle of the freedom of the individual and his independence was a novelty running counter to cherished notions of that age, notions corroborated by much that is seen in history and life. The instance of Korah, whose children perished with him for his sin, the case of Achan, whose transgression was imputed to the whole camp, the history of Jonathan, and no doubt multitudes of instances were familiar to the people where men were treated as bodies and the individuals shared the fate of the mass though personally innocent. To us now the prophet's principle is self-evident. Still even to us it is only a theoretical principle, and can be maintained against facts only by drawing a distinction, which the people in Israel had not yet learned to draw, between the spiritual relation of the mind to God and the external history of the individual. See end of chapter.

away from all his transgressions that he hath committed, he
29 shall surely live, he shall not die. Yet saith the house of
Israel, The way of the Lord is not equal. O house of Israel,
are not my ways equal? are not your ways unequal?
30 Therefore I will judge you, O house of Israel, every one
according to his ways, saith the Lord GOD. Repent, and
turn *yourselves* from all your transgressions; so iniquity shall
31 not be your ruin. Cast away from you all your transgressions, whereby ye have transgressed; and make you a new
heart and a new spirit: for why will ye die, O house of
32 Israel? For I have no pleasure in the death of him that
dieth, saith the Lord GOD: wherefore turn *yourselves*, and
live ye.

30—32. Exhortation to repentance founded on the principle that God will deal with every man according to the condition in which he is found.

30. *iniquity...your ruin*] More naturally: **that it (your transgressing) be not a stumbling block of iniquity to you.** The transgressions which they are called on to renounce are specially their idolatries, cf. ch. xiv. 3, vii. 19, xliv. 12.

31. *a new heart*] Cf. ch. xi. 19, xxxvi. 26; Jer. iv. 4, xxiv. 7; Ps. li. 7. The words are those of practical exhortation; to charge the prophet with assigning to man a power greater than that which Scripture in general allows to him is to distort his language. Cf. what he says on the other side regarding the divine operation on man, ch. xxxvi. 25—27, xi. 19.

32. The appeal to turn from evil sustained by reference to the prevailing nature of God. He is the God of salvation; his will is that men should live. The A.V. marg. to "turn yourselves (cf. *v.* 30) or *others*" is altogether false. The active form "turn" is either used intransitively, or yourselves (lit. your faces) is understood, cf. ch. xiv. 6.

(1) The place of the present chapter may be explained by connecting it with the Messianic prophecy immediately preceding (ch. xvii. 22 —24); the passage enunciates the principles and conditions of entering the perfect kingdom. The same principles are stated in two other passages, ch. iii. 16—21, and ch. xxxiii. 1—20. They are properly in place in the last passage. The prophet feels himself, however, essentially a prophet of the new age, and writing his Book after the fall of Jerusalem he may have expanded principles less fully developed at an earlier time. The age before which he stands is an ideal one, and principles realized but imperfectly now shall then have full prevalence (ch. xii. 16, xiv. 22).

(2) The principle which the prophet insists upon is not the strict retributive righteousness of God, but the moral freedom and independence of the individual person. The individual is not involved

in the destiny of his fathers or of his people; neither does he lie under an irrevocable doom pronounced over him by his past life. The immediate relation of every spirit to God and its moral freedom to break with its own past raises it above both these dooms. What Ezekiel teaches regarding God is that he hath no pleasure that the wicked should die. The prophet's whole purpose is practical, to strike off from the people the shackles of a despair that was settling upon them, whether they looked to themselves or to God. What he says of men is that each stands in immediate relation to God and shall live or die according as he repents or continues in his sin; and what he teaches of God is that in spite of the dark clouds of judgment behind which he seems now hidden his prevailing will is that men should live.

(3) The conception of the prophet is a complex or double one, having an internal and an external side. The inward element in the conception is the spiritual relation of the individual person to God; the outward element is the form "life" and "death" in which this internal relation is made manifest, rewarded or punished in God's treatment of the individual person. We perceive a cleavage taking place between these two elements. The principles enunciated by the prophet refer to the spiritual relation of the individual to God, and are true when limited to this. The individual shall not, in this sense, suffer for the sins of his people, nor the child for the sins of his father; and even his own past life does not weave an inexorable fate around him from which there is no escape. In all cases consequences evil enough may descend upon the son from the father, or upon himself from his own past life, but not this particular consequence. His moral freedom and independence raises him above these consequences, and brings him as an independent person into direct relation with God, over against others and even over against his former self. And this is really all that the prophet is teaching of new truth here. It is truth which the New Testament teaches, and which is the foundation of all morals. To charge the prophet with cutting up the individual human life into sections which have no moral relation to one another, or with teaching that a man shall live or die according to the condition in which he shall be found "for the moment" when the judgment overtakes him, is grossly to distort his language.

It may be true that the prophet has not yet been able fully to analyse his own complex conception and separate completely the spiritual relation of the mind to God from the person's external conditions. No Old Testament writer probably has been able to do this consciously and formally, although it is often done in principle and in moments of spiritual elevation (Ps. lxxiii. 23 *seq.*, xvii. 14, 15). But the ideal character of the age which the prophet feels to be about to dawn, and to which he applies his principles, marks an approach towards completing the distinction. This future though imminent ideal time, the time of the perfect kingdom of God, is that which corresponds to our idea of heaven, or another future world, in which external condition will perfectly correspond to spiritual state. The prophet's ideal world, in which spiritual relation would be perfectly bodied out externally, was still the earth. "Life" and "death," in

19 Moreover take thou up a lamentation for the princes of
2 Israel, and say, What *is* thy mother? A lioness: she lay
down among lions, she nourished her whelps among young

the ordinary use of these words, were the only means by which inward spiritual relations could find proper outward expression.

Ch. XIX. Dirge over the princes of Judah.

The elegy represents the princes of Judah as young lions, reared among lions by the mother lioness, but caught in pits by the nations and carried away. The mother lioness cannot of course be the natural mother of the princes, but rather the people, Judah itself. Two princes are lamented, one captured and carried to Egypt, viz. Jehoahaz, son and successor of Josiah (*vv.* 1—4); and another carried to Babylon, who must be Jehoiachin (*vv.* 5—9). The elegy does not appear to extend further. Verses 10—14 refer to Zedekiah, and are prophetic. They are connected in general idea with *vv.* 1—9, but the figure for the mother is now the vine.

The following table may be useful here.

       Josiah falls at Megiddo, B.C. 608.
       Jehoahaz his son reigned three months.
       Jehoiakim (son of Josiah), 608—597.
       Jehoiachin (his son) reigned 3 months.
       Zedekiah (son of Josiah), 597—586.
       Nebuchadnezzar besieges Jerusalem, 588.
       Fall of Jerusalem, 586.

The elegiac measure is maintained in *vv.* 1—8; it is somewhat disturbed in *v.* 9; while *vv.* 10—14 seem in the ordinary measure. The elegiac verse (which may be half or even third of a full verse) is divided by the cesura into two members of unequal length, the second being shorter, and falling with a mournful cadence.

1—4. Captivity of Jehoahaz in Egypt.

2. How was thy mother a lioness!—among the lions;
    In the midst of young lions she couched—she reared her whelps.
3. And she brought up one of her whelps—he grew a young lion;
    And he learned to catch the prey—he devoured men.
4. And the nations heard regarding him—he was taken in their pit;
    And they brought him with hooks—unto the land of Egypt.

1. *princes of Israel*] Probably with LXX. *prince*, as required by the pron. *thy* mother (*v.* 2). The "prince" is a general term for the king, applicable to one king after another. The lamentation is for the "king" of Judah, represented by one person after another. On "lament" cf. Jer. vii. 29.

2. *What* is *thy mother?*] Rather to be taken as an exclamation, as rendered above. The mother is the people Israel, a lioness among other lions—kings or states with royalty.

lions. And she brought up one of her whelps: it became a 3
young lion, and it learned to catch the prey; it devoured
men. The nations also heard of him; he was taken in their 4
pit, and they brought him with chains unto the land of
Egypt. Now when she saw that she had waited, *and* her hope 5
was lost, then she took another of her whelps, *and* made
him a young lion. And he went up and down among the 6

3. The first young lion is Jehoahaz, son of Josiah, carried to Egypt by Pharaoh Necho after the defeat of his father at Megiddo, 2 Kings xxiii. 31—35. Cf. the touching reference to him Jer. xxii. 10—12. He also bore the name of Shallum. Coming to the throne at the age of 23 he reigned only 3 months, and died in Egypt. Cf. Jer. v. 26.

4. *heard of him*] This might better be read: *raised a cry against him*, in the sense of Is. xxxi. 4; Jer. l. 29.

with chains] **hooks** (or, rings) as ch. xxix. 4, xxxviii. 4; cf. 2 Kings xix. 28.

5—8. Jehoiachin carried captive to Babylon.

The second young lion is Jehoiachin. The intermediate prince Jehoiakim could not be included in an elegy, because he died in peace. It is the princes of Israel whom foreign nations captured that are lamented. What is touched upon is more the humiliation and sorrow of Israel, the mother lioness, in her young lions being captured, than the fate of the two *persons*. The elegy is a national one, cf. on *v.* 1.

5. And she saw that she had waited—her hope was lost;
   And she took another of her whelps—she made him a young lion.
6. And he walked among the lions—he grew a young lion,
   And he learned to catch the prey—he devoured men.
7. And he broke down their palaces—he wasted their cities;
   And the land and its fulness was desolate—at the noise of his roaring.
8. Then the nations set themselves against him—on every side from the countries.
   And they spread their net over him—he was taken in their pit.

5. *that she had waited*] If "she" be subject some such sense as deceived, "disappointed" (Ew.) would be suitable, though to reach this sense by adding "in vain" to waited is hardly permissible. The subject might be "her hope," and waited might mean tarried, *delayed*. There might be reference to hope of the return of Jehoahaz, which appears to have been cherished, as Jeremiah takes occasion altogether to cut it off (Jer. xxii. 10—12). Corn. proposes "acted foolishly," but the word suggested is too strong (Num. xii. 11; Is. xix. 13; Jer. v. 4, l. 36).

6. Jehoiachin ascended the throne on the death of his father at the age of 18. He reigned only 3 months, when Nebuchadnezzar carried him away to Babylon, 2 Kings xxiv. 8 *sq.*

lions, he became a young lion, and learned to catch the
7 prey, *and* devoured men. And he knew their desolate palaces, and he laid waste their cities; and the land was desolate, and the fulness thereof, by the noise of his roaring.
8 Then the nations set against him on every side from the provinces, and spread their net over him: he was taken in
9 their pit. And they put him in ward in chains, and brought him to the king of Babylon: they brought him into holds, that his voice should no more be heard upon the mountains of Israel.
10 Thy mother *is* like a vine in thy blood, planted by the

7. *knew their desolate palaces*] R.V. *knew their palaces*. The word is usually "widows" as marg., but "palaces," Is. xiii. 22. Neither translation gives any sense. Better: he broke down their palaces, (change of *r* for *d*); or cf. Jer. ii. 15, 16 (marg. *fed on*), a passage very similar. If "widows" be read the verb would need to be altered to "multiplied," ch. xxii. 25, an important passage (Jer. xv. 8). Corn. (partly Hitz.): and he lay down in his den, he wasted the forests. This keeps up the figure, but requires serious alteration of the reading. Jer. ii. 15 shews that "young lions" may burn cities, and feed on the crown of the head.

8. *in their pit*] A well-known method of capturing dangerous beasts. The object to "set" may be voice or shout, *v*. 4, Jer. xii. 8.

9. *in chains*] See *v*. 4. The elegiac measure is not maintained in this verse. Possibly the original form of the verse has not been preserved. If the words "they brought him into holds" were omitted, an elegiac verse, though less regular, would be restored.

10—14. THE FATE OF ZEDEKIAH AND HIS COUNTRY, ON WHICH HE HAS BROUGHT RUIN.

Israel was once a spreading vine by great waters; her branches rose into the clouds, and her rods were rulers' sceptres—a powerful race of kings rose out of her. Now she is torn up and thrown down, carried into the wilderness, and planted in a dry and barren soil. A fire also has gone out from one of her strong rods which has consumed her. Her last prince, Zedekiah, has finally broken the state to pieces (cf. ch. xvii.).

10. is *like a vine*] **was** like, in contrast to "but now she is planted in the wilderness" (*v*. 13). The "prince" of Israel is addressed, not any individual prince, but the kingship or royalty by whomsoever represented. The mother, as before, is the people or nationality of Israel.

in thy blood] R.V. marg. refers to ch. xvi. 6, not wisely. LXX. read "on a pomegranate" (*brmn* for *bdmk*). Ew. suggests: "a vine of Carmel," Ges. "a vine of thy vineyard;" Corn. as usual "zu streichen." Others: "in thy likeness" "in thy thought," "in thy rest"—all without sense. More tolerable: "in her height" (rumah), *v*. 11.

waters: she was fruitful and full of branches by reason of many waters. And she had strong rods for the sceptres of them that bare rule, and her stature was exalted among the thick branches, and she appeared in her height with the multitude of her branches. But she was plucked up in fury, she was cast down to the ground, and the east wind dried up her fruit: her strong rods were broken and withered; the fire consumed them. And now she *is* planted in the wilderness, in a dry and thirsty ground. And the fire is gone out of a rod of her branches, *which* hath devoured her fruit, so that she hath no strong rod *to be* a sceptre to rule. This *is* a lamentation, and shall be for a lamentation.

11. *sceptres...bare rule*] Or, **for rulers' sceptres**, i.e. royal sceptres. Out of Israel this vine there rose powerful native kings.

among the thick branches] Or, into the clouds, cf. xxxi. 3, 10, 14. The phrase is designedly hyperbolical, to express the power of Israel in earlier times. Jer. xi. 16, 17.

appeared in her height] Lit. was seen—conspicuously and from afar.

12. Destruction of the vine, the nationality of Israel. The figures employed are usual, ch. xvii. 9, 10, xxxi. 12; Am. ix. 15.

13. The deportation of the people from their own land into conditions where national life cannot thrive.

14. The fire that consumed the vine went out from her own rods. The royal house brought destruction on the nation as well as on itself. Reference is to the rebellion of Zedekiah.

gone out of a rod] Possibly collective: out of the rods. The reference to Zedekiah is expressed generally in terms of the royal house.

shall be for a lamentation] Lit. *and is become a lamentation*. Sad enough is the history, ch. xxxii. 16. It is not necessary, however, to infer from this that the lamentation was written after the exile. The passage *vv*. 10—14 is prophetic, cf. Is. xlvii.; Jer. ix. 16—21. In the Book of Kings both Jehoahaz and Jehoiachin are said to have "done evil." A three months' reign afforded little scope for much mischief. Ezekiel's treatment of the young lions is ideal, and in the case of Jehoiachin the reference is rather to the evils which his attitude brought upon the country, than to any ravages which he wrought personally.

Ch. XX.—XXIV. Further predictions regarding the fall of Jerusalem.

These chapters pursue the same subject as occupied the prophet in previous chapters, the destruction of the state, though they appear to look at it from another point of view, and suggest another motive for it—Jehovah's regard to his own name.

First, ch. xx. Review of Israel's past history and emphasising of the principle which has given Israel a history and saved her from destruction, viz. Jehovah's regard to his own name.

138 EZEKIEL, XX. [vv. 1—5.

20 And it came to pass in the seventh year, in the fifth *month*, the tenth *day* of the month, *that* certain of the elders of Israel came to inquire of the LORD, and sat before me. 2,3 Then came the word of the LORD unto me, saying, Son of man, speak unto the elders of Israel, and say unto them, Thus saith the Lord GOD; Are ye come to inquire of me? *As* I live, saith the Lord GOD, I will not be inquired of by 4 you. Wilt thou judge them, son of man, wilt thou judge *them?* cause them to know the abominations of their fathers: 5 and say unto them, Thus saith the Lord GOD; In the day

Second, ch. xxi. But this same principle—regard to his name—requires Israel's dispersion now. Therefore the sword of the Lord is whetted against her.

Third, ch. xxii., xxiii. New exhibition of the sins of Israel.

Fourth, ch. xxiv. Final judgment on Jerusalem, under the figure of a rusted caldron set upon the fire to cleanse it.

ch. xx. has two divisions:

(1) *vv.* 1—29. The principle that has saved Israel from destruction and given her a history—Jehovah's respect to his own name.

(2) *vv.* 30—44. The same principle will rule what of Israel's history still lies in the future.

1—4. Introductory. Certain elders came to the prophet to enquire of the Lord, in the seventh year of the captivity of Jehoiachin and tenth day of the fifth month—Aug. 590 B.C., four years before Jerusalem fell.

3. *will not be inquired of*] The proposed enquiries of the elders probably related to something in the present; to such men no answer will be given except to read the lesson of Israel's history to them. For the history concerns them. They are one in spirit and conduct with Israel of the past, and the principles which have ruled the former history will rule also the history to come.

4. *wilt thou judge*] The interr. seems to have the sense of an impatient imperative, and the repetition gives stronger expression to the imperative, cf. ch. xxii. 2, xxiii. 36. "Judge" is explained by "cause them to know the abominations of their fathers." To rehearse the history of the fathers is to hold the mirror up to themselves.

5—29. REVIEW OF THE HISTORY OF THE FATHERS.

The principle that has ruled this history is that all through it Jehovah has acted for his name's sake. It is this principle that has given Israel a history, otherwise their sins would have cut them off. For his name's sake he spared the people in Egypt (*v.* 9), again in the wilderness (*v.* 14), and again the second generation there (*v.* 22). The history is reviewed in these divisions: *vv.* 5—10 Israel in Egypt; *vv.* 11—17 the people led out into the wilderness; *vv.* 18—26 the children of those who fell in the wilderness; and *vv.* 27—29 the people that entered Canaan.

when I chose Israel, and lifted up mine hand unto the seed of the house of Jacob, and made myself known unto them in the land of Egypt, when I lifted up mine hand unto them, saying, I *am* the LORD your God; in the day *that* I lifted 6 up mine hand unto them, to bring them forth of the land of Egypt into a land that I had espied for them, flowing with milk and honey, which *is* the glory of all lands: then said I 7 unto them, Cast ye away every man the abominations of his eyes, and defile not yourselves with the idols of Egypt: I *am* the LORD your God. But they rebelled against me, 8 and would not hearken unto me: they did not every man cast away the abominations of their eyes, neither did they forsake the idols of Egypt: then I said, *I* will pour out my

5. *when I chose Israel*] The choice or election of Israel is referred to only here in Ez., and also once in Jeremiah, xxxiii. 24. The idea is much insisted on in Is. xl.—lxvi. Already, however, Deut. vii. 6.
lifted up mine hand] i.e. sware, Ex. vi. 8; Numb. xiv. 30. The thing sworn is stated *v.* 6.
made myself known] Cf. Ex. iii. 6 *seq.*, vi. 3. He made himself known as Jehovah their God, whose nature his acts revealed, Ps. ciii. 7.
6. *the day* that *I lifted*] **On that day I lifted...7 and I said** unto them. On "milk and honey" cf. Ex. iii. 8; and on the idea of Canaan as the "glory" of all lands, a frequent judgment in late writings, cf. Jer. iii. 19; Dan. viii. 9; Ps. xlviii. 2.
7. *abominations of his eyes*] Those to which his eyes and desires were directed, the idols, cf. xviii. 6; Num. xv. 39. The prophet charges Israel with idolatry in Egypt (ch. xxiii. 3). Though history as we have it says little of such a thing, it may be assumed as certain, considering the people's receptivity to the worship of their neighbours throughout their history. The same view, Josh. xxiv. 14; cf. Lev. xviii. 3.
The question how far Jehovah was known and worshipped in Egypt is an obscure one. The name could not have been altogether unknown or the people could not have been rallied by Moses to his service nor induced to put themselves under his protection. That his worship, however, was mixed with impurities may be assumed. How far the people partook in the worship of Egyptian deities cannot be ascertained.
8. The history in Exodus narrates only the conflict of Israel with the Egyptians, being silent on internal struggles in Israel itself. The work of Moses in delivering his people must have extended over a period of time. His efforts in educating the people are entirely passed over in the history. The announcement, however, that Jehovah was the God of Israel implied casting away all other gods, and this principle, often expressed in his intercourse with the people, probably met with but slack acceptance. Ps. cvi. follows Ezek. closely, cf. *v.* 7.

fury upon them, to accomplish my anger against them in the
9 midst of the land of Egypt. But I wrought for my name's
sake, that *it* should not be polluted before the heathen,
among whom they *were*, in whose sight I made myself
known unto them, in bringing them forth out of the land of
10 Egypt. Wherefore I caused them to go forth out of the
11 land of Egypt, and brought them into the wilderness. And
I gave them my statutes, and shewed them my judgments,
12 which *if* a man do, he shall even live in them. Moreover

9. *for my name's sake*] This idea, very common in this prophet, also in Is. xl.—lxvi., does not appear in the earlier prophets, except Is. xxxvii. 35. Cf. however, Deut. ix. 28, 29; Jer. xiv. 7, 21; Is. xliii. 25, xlviii. 9, 11. Jehovah's name expresses that which he is, or has revealed himself to be, and the phrase does not differ from "for my own sake," cf. ch. xxxvi. 22, 32.

should not be polluted] Rather: **profaned**. The words explain, "for my name's sake," viz. lest it should be profaned among the nations. Deut. ix. 28, 29 suggests one way in which the name of Jehovah might be profaned among the nations. To "profane" is the opposite of to "sanctify." The one is to cherish any thoughts of Jehovah or to attribute any deed to him inconsistent with his being the one true God, or derogatory to him who is so. To "sanctify" him is to recognise him in thought and in act, particularly in worship, to be the one true God; to assign to him attributes and operations befitting his nature, and to live in such a way as those who are the people of Jehovah ought to live, for the manner of the people is reflected on the character of their God (Am. ii. 7). This is the way, at least, in which Ezek., with the conception of Jehovah which in his age he had reached, uses the terms "profane" and "sanctify."

11—17. The people delivered from Egypt and brought into the wilderness. There also Jehovah wrought for his name's sake.

10. First half of the verse is wanting in LXX.

11. *gave them...statutes*] Reference is to the Sinaitic legislation. The fact of the legislation is confirmed by the prophet, but his language "statutes and judgments" does not enable us to form an opinion how extensive it was, nor what particulars it embraced besides the law of the sabbath (*v.* 12), and of course the law that Jehovah was God alone of Israel, because he uses the phrase "statutes and judgments" very generally, for example of the conduct and principles of the people in the wilderness themselves (*v.* 18).

shall even live in them] Or, **shall live by** them. Obedience to them will issue in "life," the word being used in its natural sense, Deut. iv. 40, "thou shalt keep his statutes...that thou mayest prolong thy days upon the land," Deut. v. 16 (fifth commandment). The precepts of Jehovah given to the people were such that obedience to them would ensure prosperity and life, while disobedience would cause calamity and death, and this not only in the mere government of them by their God,

also I gave them my sabbaths, to be a sign between me and them, that *they* might know that I *am* the LORD that sanctify them. But the house of Israel rebelled against me in the wilderness: they walked not in my statutes, and they despised my judgments, which *if* a man do, he shall even live in them; and my sabbaths they greatly polluted: then I said, *I* would pour out my fury upon them in the wilderness, to consume them. But I wrought for my name's sake, that *it* should not be polluted before the heathen, in whose sight I brought them out. Yet also I lifted up my hand unto them in the wilderness, that *I* would not bring them into the land which I had given *them*, flowing with milk and honey, which *is* the glory of all lands; because they despised

but because the statutes were in themselves "good," cf. *v.* 25; Am. v. 14; Hos. viii. 3; Mic. iii. 2, vi. 8.

12. *my sabbaths*] The plural refers to the stated recurrence of the day; other festivals are not included.

to be a sign] The prophet does not speak of the Sabbath as an older institution than the exodus, though his language does not decide the point, as he refers merely to the connexion into which the day was brought with Israel's redemption (as Deut. v. 15) and made a "sign" to them of their relation to Jehovah. The people were commanded to "sanctify" the Sabbath, i.e. to dedicate it and keep it to the Lord. This dedication of a part of their time or life to Jehovah had a similar significance to the dedication of the first-fruits of the ground and the firstlings of their cattle; it was an acknowledgment that they were the Lord's. It was the response on their side to the operation of Jehovah on his side in "sanctifying" them, or making them his own possession (end of *v.*) Thus the Sabbath was a "sign" or visible token that he was their God and they his people (*v.* 20); Ex. xxxi. 13, 14; Is. lvi. 2, 4. This meaning of the Sabbath as a symbol of the religion of Jehovah explains the importance attached to keeping it particularly in the exile; its observance sustained the feeling of the people among the heathen that they were the people of Jehovah, Is. lvi. 2 *seq.*, lviii. 13; Neh. xiii. 19, cf. Jer. xvii. 21; Lev. xix. 3, xxvi. 2.

13. Provocation of the people in the wilderness. They rejected the statutes of Jehovah and "polluted," better: **profaned**, his sabbaths, i.e. failed to dedicate and keep them to Jehovah. The profanation is to be taken in a wider sense than the special instances of neglect, Ex. xvi. 27; Numb. xv. 32. This profanation of the Sabbath was oblivion of the covenant, cf. Am. viii. 5.

pour out my fury] Cf. Ex. xxxii. 10 seq.; Num. xiv. 11, 12, 29.

14, 15. For his name's sake Jehovah did not make a clean end of the people, nevertheless he sware that the generation that came out of Egypt should not enter into the land of promise, Num. xiv. 22, 23, 29; Deut. i. 35; Ps. xcv. 11.

my judgments, and walked not in my statutes, but polluted
17 my sabbaths: for their heart went after their idols. Nevertheless mine eye spared them from destroying them, neither
18 did I make an end of them in the wilderness. But I said unto their children in the wilderness, Walk ye not in the statutes of your fathers, neither observe their judgments,
19 nor defile yourselves with their idols: I *am* the LORD your God; walk in my statutes, and keep my judgments, and do
20 them; and hallow my sabbaths; and they shall be a sign between me and you, that *ye* may know that I *am* the LORD
21 your God. Notwithstanding the children rebelled against me: they walked not in my statutes, neither kept my judgments to do them, which *if* a man do, he shall even live in them; they polluted my sabbaths: then I said, *I* would pour out my fury upon them, to accomplish my anger against
22 them in the wilderness. Nevertheless I withdrew mine hand, and wrought for my name's sake, that *it* should not be polluted in the sight of the heathen, in whose sight I brought
23 them forth. I lifted up mine hand unto them also in the wilderness, that *I* would scatter them among the heathen,

16. *polluted my sabbaths*] **profaned.**
went after their idols] Ex. xxxii.; Num. xxv.; Hos. ix. 10. Am. v. 25 cannot be appealed to here.

17. Another motive besides regard for his own name moved Jehovah to spare Israel—pity for the sinners; cf. Ps. lxxviii. 38, "But he being full of compassion forgave their iniquity and destroyed them not; yea many a time he turned his anger away". Num. xiv. 20.

18—26. The second generation in the wilderness. These only imitated the sins of their fathers, Num. xxv. 1, 2; Deut. ix. 23, 24, xxxi. 27.

21. *polluted my sabbaths*] **profaned.**

22. *withdrew mine hand*] Lit. turned, or turned back his hand, outstretched to smite. The words are wanting in LXX., and in the other verses (*vv.* 9, 14) the phrase "I wrought for my name's sake" begins the verse. For be *polluted*, **profaned.**

23—26. Yet though he wrought for his name's sake not to destroy them their sins could not be altogether passed by. In two ways they were marked: Jehovah laid a heavy threat upon the people of dispersion among all nations, *vv.* 23, 24; and he gave them laws that were not good, that by following them they might be destroyed, *vv.* 25, 26.

23. *I lifted up...also*] **Moreover I lifted up**, lit. And I on my part, so *v.* 25.

scatter...among the heathen] The people entered Canaan laden with this heavy threat for their sins in the wilderness. Such threats were

and disperse them through the countries; because they had 24
not executed my judgments, but had despised my statutes,
and had polluted my sabbaths, and their eyes were after
their fathers' idols. Wherefore I gave them also statutes 25
that were not good, and judgments whereby they should not

always conditional, Jer. xviii., Jonah. This conditional character is
expressed in other passages where a similar idea occurs, Lev. xxvi. 33;
Deut. xxviii. 64. The prophet hardly means that the exile was due to
the people's sins in the wilderness, except in so far as the moral character of the people remained the same throughout down to the generation
then living. But cf. Ex. xxxii. 34.

25. *Wherefore I gave...also*] **Moreover also I gave,** see *v.* 23.

statutes...not good] These statutes are of a kind contrary to those
given before (*v.* 11) which were good. These points seem plain: 1.
The practice referred to is that of passing the firstborn male children
through the fire as a burnt-offering to the deity. 2. The law in Israel
was that all the male firstborn of men and the male firstlings of beasts
were the Lord's. The firstborn of men were to be redeemed, as also the
firstlings of unclean animals, but the firstlings of clean animals were
to be offered in sacrifice to Jehovah (Ex. xiii. 2, 12, 13, xxii.
29, cf. Num. iii. 46, 47, xviii. 15, 16). The law requiring the
sacrifice of the firstborn had become extended, so as to include
children. The practice was one prevailing among the peoples around
Israel, and probably it first crept into use in Israel and was then
justified by the law or custom relating to cattle, of which it might seem
a natural extension; but in Jeremiah vii. 31, xix. 5 Jehovah vehemently
protests that to command it never came into his mind. The question to
whom the children were offered, lit. passed over in the fire, is not quite
easy to decide. In passages where the practice is condemned it is
represented as a sacrifice to "the Molech," Lev. xviii. 21; Deut. xii. 31,
xviii. 10, or to the Baal, Jer. vii. 31, or generally, to the idols, Ezek.
xvi. 21; Ps. cvi. 38 (idols of Canaan). Though the spelling of the
name Molech is peculiar, the word probably means "the king" originally, just as the Baal means "the lord," both names being descriptive of
the same deity. In Is. lvii. 9 "the king" has the ordinary spelling.
Though borrowing the practice from the Canaanites it is probable that
in Israel the sacrifice was offered to Jehovah, particularly as the law
under which it was made was considered given by him. On the other
hand Jer., though repudiating this popular inference, speaks of the
offering as being made to Baal. The name "Baal," however, from
Hosea downwards is used somewhat laxly, including the images of
Jehovah, and all heathenish ceremonies in his service are called worship
of Baal. 3. This law is described as not good, one by which men
could not live. The effect of it was that men were polluted in their
gifts (*v.* 26), and the purpose of it was to destroy them. This evil law,
entailing this consequence, was a judicial punishment of them for their
former sins, just as the "deception" of the false prophets was, ch. xiv.
9. Whether the people, familiar with the Baal worship, drew the

26 live; and I polluted them in their own gifts, in that they caused to pass through *the fire* all that openeth the womb, that I might make them desolate, to the end that they might know that I *am* the LORD.
27 Therefore, son of man, speak unto the house of Israel, and say unto them, Thus saith the Lord GOD; Yet *in* this your fathers have blasphemed me, in that they have com-
28 mitted a trespass against me. *For* when I had brought them into the land, *for* the which I lifted up mine hand to

false inference from the law of the firstborn, or whether false teachers set the idea before them, is uncertain (Jer. viii. 8 appears to refer to written perversions of the law). The sacrifice of children was a practice that gained ground in the disastrous times before the exile (Hos. xiii. 2 has another meaning: men who sacrifice kiss calves; it is the irrationality of *men* kissing calves that the prophet mocks, not the enormity of human sacrifices). Ezekiel appears to regard the practice as ancient, as he connects it with the second generation in the wilderness. The instances noted in early history are transjordanic (Jephthah and king of Moab), and possibly, though the practice became aggravated only at a later period, the prophet may have considered that the people became acquainted with it on the other side of the Jordan.

26. *might make them desolate*] Or, **destroy them**; less probably: horrify them (ch. xxxii. 10). The train of thought is the same as that expressed in ch. xiv. 9. The penalty of sin is further delusion and worse sin, the end of which is death. The last clause "to the end... Lord" is wanting in LXX.

27—29. The people on their entry and in their abode in Canaan.

27. *Yet* in *this*] i.e. the following act, *v.* 28, cf. xxiii. 38.

have blasphemed] Past tense: **blasphemed**...they **committed**. The blasphemy is not in words, but in high-handed disregard of his commands, Num. xv. 30.

28. The prophet regards the worship on the high-places and under the evergreen trees as a Canaanitish usage adopted by Israel, as Deut. xii. At the same time Israel usually employed the altars or chapels which they found for the service of Jehovah; but naturally many corruptions would creep into such service, and it might become little different from a service of Baal. In the oldest prophets, Amos and Hosea, it is the *kind* of worship at the high-places that is condemned, the revelry and heathenish merrymaking (Hos. ix. 1), the sensuousness (Hos. viii. 13; Am. v. 21), and the false conception of deity implied in it (Hos. vi. 6). The mere localities or multitude of altars do not seem assailed, except that the more there were of them the more sin was committed, because the whole worship was sinful (Hos. viii. 11; Am. iv. 4). Later this impure worship was perceived to be inseparable from the high-places and these themselves came under condemnation. Ezekiel does not go further in his condemnation of the high hills and green trees than his predecessor Jeremiah (Jer. ii. 20, iii. 6).

give it to them, then they saw every high hill, and all the thick trees, and they offered there their sacrifices, and there they presented the provocation of their offering: there also they made their sweet savour, and poured out there their drink offerings. Then I said unto them, What *is* the high place whereunto ye go? And the name thereof is called Bamah unto this day. Wherefore say unto the

all the thick trees] Evergreen and umbrageous trees appear to have been regarded as abodes of deity.

offered...their sacrifices] Four words are employed: offerings of flesh, particularly the peace or thank-offerings; what is called their "offering" or oblation, a general word used of bloodless sacrifices as well as of others, possibly first-fruits and the like; their "sweet savour," usually said of the odour of the flesh or fat burnt upon the altar, but also of the odour of meal-offerings (ch. xvi. 19); and finally, drink-offerings. The clause "and there...provocation of their offering" is wanting in LXX. The term "offering" (Korban), found only in Lev., Numb., again in Ez. xl. 43 (see there).

29. The word *bamah*, "high-place," has no certain etymology, though often used and at an early period, e.g. in David's elegy on Saul (2 Sam. i. 19), and in Moabite (Mesha's inscrip.). The prophet here introduces a punning and contemptuous derivation of the word. Jehovah asks "what (*mah*) is the high place whereunto ye go (*ba*)," and the prophet seems to consider the word composed of these two syllables. Some have supposed that "go" has the sense of "go in," and that the allusion is to the immoralities practised on the high places (Am. ii. 7; Hos. iv. 13, 14). This idea does not seem expressed in the words; neither is there much probability in the conjecture that the words are borrowed by Ezek. from some older prophet (Ew.).

The prophet's view of the generation of the exodus differs from that of earlier prophets, e.g. Hos. ix. 10; Jer. ii. 2. The generation in the wilderness was probably not a homogeneous one, and the narratives which we possess represent its conduct as various at different times. Two views might be taken of it, and Ezek. as his manner is takes the severer view.

30—44. JEHOVAH'S REGARD TO HIS OWN NAME WILL FASHION THE HISTORY OF THE PEOPLE TO COME AS IT HAS FASHIONED THE PAST.

Having reviewed the past and shewn the elders their own picture in the doings of their fathers, and how the thing which has fashioned the history in the past has been Jehovah's regard for his own name, the prophet now comes to read to them the history of the future as the same regard of Jehovah to his name will model it.

First, *vv.* 30—34. The Lord will not give any answer to such enquirers who follow the ways of their fathers. But they may be assured that their resolution to assimilate themselves to the heathen and become

house of Israel, Thus saith the Lord God; Are ye polluted after the manner of your fathers? and commit ye whoredom after their abominations? For when *ye* offer your gifts, when *ye* make your sons to pass through the fire, ye pollute yourselves with all your idols, *even* unto *this* day: and shall I be inquired of by you, O house of Israel? *As* I live, saith the Lord God, I will not be inquired of by you.

32 And that which cometh into your mind shall not be at all, that ye say, We will be as the heathen, as the families 33 of the countries, to serve wood and stone. *As* I live, saith

like them worshippers of wood and stone shall not be permitted to have effect. Jehovah *will* assert his sovereignty over them, and will disentangle them out from among the heathen as he gathered their fathers from among the Egyptians.

Secondly, vv. 35—40. He will bring them out from the nations into the wilderness of the peoples, as he brought their fathers into the wilderness of Egypt, and will plead with them anew as he pleaded with their fathers in days long ago—and with the same result that the rebels among them shall fall in the wilderness, but the remnant shall again in the mountain height of Israel serve the Lord, who will accept them.

Thirdly, vv. 41—44. And from this restoration these things shall follow: 1. Jehovah shall be sanctified, seen to be God and acknowledged by the nations (v. 41). 2. Israel shall know what Jehovah is, when he fulfils his ancient promise to the fathers to give them this land (v. 42). 3. They shall then lay to heart their past doings and lothe themselves (v. 43). And 4. they shall see that not according to their evil has Jehovah dealt with them all through their history and in their restoration, but has wrought for his name's sake (v. 44).

30, 31. The Lord will not give himself to be enquired of by such men. What they desire to know about others or themselves they shall be left in ignorance of; but *he* has something to tell them regarding himself.

30. *Are ye polluted*] do ye pollute yourselves?

31. *For when...ye pollute*] Interrogatively: *and when...do ye pollute yourselves* unto this day?

32. The prophet regards the worship on the high-places as Canaanitish heathenism; but probably many of the exiles to whom he spoke were drifting into complete conformity with the nations among whom they were. Their minds were losing hold of their distinctiveness as the people of Jehovah. This practical assimilation to the heathen the prophet represents as a deliberate one, which in many cases it may have been—cf. the answer of the exiles in Egypt to Jeremiah, xliv. 15—19, also Jer. ii. 25.

to serve wood and stone] The service of the heathen is a service of wood and stone, Deut. iv. 28, xxviii. 36; Is. xxxvii. 19. The images were often of wood, plated with some precious metal (Is. xl. 20; Jer. x.

the Lord GOD, surely with a mighty hand, and with a stretched out arm, and with fury poured out, will I rule over you: and I will bring you out from the people, and 34 will gather you out of the countries wherein ye are scattered, with a mighty hand, and with a stretched out arm, and with fury poured out. And I will bring you into the wilderness 35 of the people, and there will I plead with you face to face. Like as I pleaded with your fathers in the wilderness of the 36 land of Egypt, so will I plead with you, saith the Lord GOD. And I will cause you to pass under the rod, and I 37

3; Is. xxx. 22), or of stone; often, however, of baser metal overlaid with gold or silver. It is the dead matter in opposition to Jehovah, the living God, that gives point to the antithesis. On "cometh into your mind" cf. xi. 5; Jer. vii. 31, xix. 5; Is. x. 7.

33. This resolution of the people to sink themselves among the heathen shall not stand; Jehovah *will* assert his sovereignty over them, amidst terrible manifestations of his power and anger.

rule over you] be or, **become king** over you. The mighty hand (Ex. xiii. 9; Deut. v. 15) and the stretched out arm (Ex. vi. 6; Deut. vii. 19, xi. 2, &c.), were turned at the exodus against their enemies, here partly at least they are directed upon the disobedient people themselves (v. 35).

34. *the people*] **peoples.** Though Israel was in captivity in the Babylonian empire, this empire embraced many peoples, the world as it was then known (cf. ch. xvii.) Formerly Israel was entangled among the Egyptians, now it is entangled among all nations; it shall now be gathered out as it was in the former age.

35. *of the people*] **peoples.** This wilderness of the peoples is the Syro-Babylonian wilderness, adjoining the peoples among whom they were dispersed; as that into which their fathers were brought was the wilderness of Egypt, i.e. adjoining Egypt. Is. xl. 1—11 also represents Jehovah as marching at the head of his people, redeemed from exile, through the wilderness from Babylon to Jerusalem. Ezek. may follow Hos. ii. 14, 15, but cf. Jer. xxxi. 2 *seq.*

plead...face to face] With no intermediaries, no heathen people on whose fellowship they could stay themselves, absolutely cut off from men and alone with their God (Hos. ii. 14). Jehovah's "pleading" or litigating is sometimes in terrible deeds (ch. xvii. 20), sometimes in words of reason (Is. i. 18; Mic. vi. 2 *seq.*). Gathered out from the nations and far from their seductive influences Israel will respond to the discipline of her God as in former days (Hos. ii. 15).

37. *to pass under the rod*] According to the usage of the language (Lev. xxvii. 32, cf. Jer. xxxiii. 13) the rod or staff here is that of the shepherd, which he uses in counting his flock. "The shepherds carried a staff (Ps. xxiii. 4; Mic. vii. 14; Zech. xi. 7) and used it in counting when they brought the beasts forth from the place where they were kept or made them go into it. It was customary to count the beasts every

38 will bring you into the bond of the covenant: and I will purge out from among you the rebels, and them that transgress against me: I will bring them forth out of the country where they sojourn, and they shall not enter into the land 39 of Israel: and ye shall know that I *am* the Lord. As for you, O house of Israel, thus saith the Lord God; Go ye, serve ye every one his idols, and hereafter *also*, if ye will not hearken unto me: but pollute ye my holy name 40 no more with your gifts, and with your idols. For in mine holy mountain, in the mountain of the height of Israel, saith the Lord God, there shall all the house of Israel, all of them in the land, serve me: there will I accept them, and there will I require your offerings, and the firstfruits 41 of your oblations, with all your holy *things*. I will accept you with *your* sweet savour, when I bring you out from the

day (Jer. xxxiii. 13), usually at evening when they came home (Theocr. VIII. 16; Virg. *Georg.* IV. 436), sometimes twice, morning and evening (Virg. *Ecl.* III. 34)," Dillm. on Lev. xxvii. 32.

bond of the covenant] The word "bond" is otherwise unknown. LXX. reads: and I will cause you to go in by number, i.e. probably in special or precise tale (Is. xl. 26; 1 Chr. ix. 28; Ezr. viii. 34). This carries on the figure of passing under the staff, and is amplified in *v.* 38. The word "covenant" is possibly a duplicate of the next word "purge" (*v.* 38). The expression "*by* or, *in number*" hardly of itself means *few* (cf. ch. v. 3), neither is the idea of fewness suitable here. Cf. Jer. iii. 14.

38. Describes the other side of the process from *v.* 37, the separating of the unworthy from among the people, ch. xxxiv. 17, 20.

and they shall not enter] But they. They shall be brought out but shall fall in the wilderness of the peoples as the rebellious generation aforetime fell in the wilderness of Egypt.

39. The present text must read: Go, serve ye every one his idols; but hereafter surely ye shall hearken unto me, and no more profane my holy name with your gifts (cf. *v.* 26), cf. xxiii. 38, 39. The ironical advice or concession refers to *vv.* 32, 33, cf. Am. iv. 4.

40. Resumes *vv.* 34—38, and carries these verses a step further—to the restoration (*v.* 41).

your offerings] Always rendered *oblations* in Ezek., except ch. xlviii. 8. The idea expressed by the word appears in ch. xlv. and xlviii., where it is used of the portion of the land devoted to special and sacred uses. "Firstfruits," marg. *chief*, i.e. the best of your offerings.

41. *you with* your *sweet savour*] Lit. *amidst*, or, *in* sweet savour (i.e. when I smell it) I will accept you. The expression is used literally of the sweet smoke of sacrifice, hardly figuratively of Jehovah's complaisance. R.V., *as* a sweet savour, is wholly improbable.

people, and gather you out of the countries wherein ye have been scattered; and I will be sanctified in you before the heathen. And ye shall know that I *am* the LORD, 42 when I shall bring you into the land of Israel, into the country *for* the which I lifted up mine hand to give it to your fathers. And there shall ye remember your ways, and 43 all your doings, wherein ye have been defiled; and ye shall lothe yourselves in your own sight for all your evils that ye have committed. And ye shall know that I *am* the 44 LORD, when I have wrought with you for my name's sake, not according to your wicked ways, nor according to your corrupt doings, O ye house of Israel, saith the Lord GOD.

Moreover the word of the LORD came unto me, saying, 45

be sanctified in you] Lit. get me sanctifying in (through) you in the sight of the heathen (or, shew myself holy). On the idea of "sanctify" cf. *v.* 9—be recognised as God. The dispersion of Jehovah's people derogated in the eyes of the heathen from his power (ch. xxxvi. 20); when they see his people restored the heathen will know that it was for their iniquity that they were cast out (ch. xxxix. 23), particularly when after restoration and purification they see them protected against the countless hosts of Gog by Jehovah's arm. Thus Jehovah will "through" his people, by his dealing with them in their restoration, approve himself as God—that which God is—in the sight of the heathen.

43. The goodness of Jehovah in restoring them shall fill their hearts with abhorrence of their own past doings, cf. xvi. 61.

lothe...in your own sight] Omit *in your own sight*, ch. vi. 9.

44. And the final issue of all shall be that the people will know that he is Jehovah. Jew and Gentile shall alike know that the God of Israel is God alone. Cf. Is. xl. 5 "the glory of the Lord shall be revealed and all flesh shall see it together," Ps. cii. 15, 16, 22.

vv. 45—49 belong to ch. xxi.

On the prophet's philosophy of history, his idea that history is Jehovah operating for "his name's sake," cf. Introduction.

CH. XX. 45—XXI. 32. THE AVENGING SWORD OF THE LORD.

The passage xx. 45—49 belongs to ch. xxi. (as in Heb.). The time to which the chapter is to be assigned is the early period of Nebuchadnezzar's movements westwards. The prophet foresees the coming desolation of Israel by the conqueror, which he expresses under the figure of a devouring fire, consuming all indiscriminately. The passage has two divisions, ch. xx. 45—xxi. 27, and xxi. 28—32.

First division. xx. 45—xxi. 27.

(1) xx. 45—49. A conflagration shall be lighted in the forest of the south, which shall consume all, the green tree and the dry.

(2) xxi. 1—5. Explanation: the sword of the Lord shall be on Jeru-

46 Son of man, set thy face toward the south, and drop *thy word* toward the south, and prophesy against the forest of
47 the south field; and say to the forest of the south, Hear the word of the LORD; Thus saith the Lord GOD; Behold, I *will* kindle a fire in thee, and it shall devour every green tree in thee, and every dry tree: the flaming flame shall not be quenched, and all faces from the south to the
48 north shall be burnt therein. And all flesh shall see that I the LORD have kindled it: it shall not be quenched.
49 Then said I, Ah Lord GOD, they say of me, Doth he not speak parables?

salem and her sanctuaries, and on the land of Israel. Righteous and wicked shall perish; and men shall know that the Lord hath drawn his sword.

(3) *vv.* 6, 7. Agitation of the prophet at the thought of the coming desolation: so shall all men be agitated and confounded.

(4) *vv.* 8—17. Song of the sword—the sword of the Lord whetted and furbished against Jerusalem.

(5) *vv.* 18—27. He who is the sword or wields it, the king of Babylon. The prophet returning to the point from which he started represents the king of Babylon hesitating whether to march against Ammon or Jerusalem. He consults the oracle and the lot comes out "Jerusalem."

xx. 45—49. Figure of a forest in which a great conflagration is kindled. The fire is unquenchable (*vv.* 47, 48), it devours all alike, the green tree and the dry (*v.* 47); all faces from north to south shall be scorched by it (*v.* 47); and all flesh shall see that it is the hand of the Lord which has kindled so great a flame (*v.* 48).

46. *the south*] Though the reference is to Judah and Jerusalem (xxi. 1—5), the term "south" hardly means the south of Palestine; rather the whole land of Palestine from the point of view of the prophet residing in the north. The "forest of the field" hardly refers to Lebanon, but belongs to the figure, which, however, Lebanon may have suggested (xvii. 3; Jer. xxii. 23). The "scorching" of all faces from north to south (*v.* 47) is also part of the figure, though powerfully expressing the effect on all who behold the great judgments on Israel. There may be, however, a certain mixture of figures, those whose faces are scorched being no other than those who, regarded as trees, are consumed—viz. all flesh from the south to the north in Israel (xxi. 3, 4).

the south field] **the field in the south**, the land of Israel (xxi. 3).

49. *speak parables*] or, similitudes—with the suggested idea that there lies no reality behind them (xii. 21—28). The prophet, indeed, cannot utter a statement plainly, he must throw it first into a figure; the same is true also of Isaiah, though the figures of the latter prophet are brief and pointed, while those of Ezek. are overloaded with details.

And the word of the LORD came unto me, saying, Son 21 of man, set thy face toward Jerusalem, and drop *thy word* 2 toward the holy places, and prophesy against the land of Israel, and say to the land of Israel, Thus saith the LORD; 3 Behold, I *am* against thee, and will draw forth my sword out of his sheath, and will cut off from thee the righteous and the wicked. Seeing then that I will cut off from thee 4 the righteous and the wicked, therefore shall my sword go forth out of his sheath against all flesh from the south *to* the north: that all flesh may know that I the LORD have 5 drawn forth my sword out of his sheath: it shall not return any more. Sigh therefore, thou son of man, with the 6 breaking of *thy* loins; and with bitterness sigh before their eyes. And it shall be, when they say unto thee, Wherefore 7 sighest thou? that thou shalt answer, For the tidings; because it cometh: and every heart shall melt, and all hands shall be feeble, and every spirit shall faint, and all knees shall be weak *as* water: behold, it cometh, and shall be brought to pass, saith the Lord GOD.

Again the word of the LORD came unto me, saying, Son 8 9

The words shew how the people took notice of the prophet's peculiarities, and how he himself was conscious of the impression his manner made. Cf. xxiv. 18.

XXI. 1—5. These verses, though still figurative, are plainer than the preceding, of which they furnish the explanation. The sword of the Lord is drawn finally from its sheath, to which it shall not return (*v*. 5); it is drawn against Jerusalem and its sanctuaries (*v*. 2); it shall slay indiscriminately righteous and wicked (*v*. 3, cf. xx. 47), and all flesh shall know that it is the sword of the Lord, and that it is his hand that wields it (*v*. 5).—Even to-day the study of Israel's history occupies men, and its lessons are not yet exhausted.

2. *the holy places*] Or, sanctuaries. These are not the rural sanctuaries or high places, but the holy buildings in Jerusalem (vii. 24; Lam. ii. 6).

6, 7. Agitation of the prophet at the tidings of the coming calamity. This agitation of his is only a symbol of the dismay and paralysis that shall overtake all when the calamity comes. On the figures in *v*. 7 cf. vii. 17.

7. *it cometh*] i.e. the overwhelming disaster. The words, "and... to pass" are wanting in LXX.

8—17. The destroying sword of the Lord. The violent agitation of the prophet at the thought of the coming destruction finds expression in a wild and irregular ode upon the sword of the Lord. The general sense of the poem is discernible, but as in ch. vii. the text is in several

of man, prophesy, and say, Thus saith the LORD; Say, A
10 sword, a sword is sharpened, and also furbished: it is
sharpened to make a sore slaughter; *it is* furbished that
it may glitter: should we then make mirth? it contemneth

places very obscure (e.g. *vv.* 10, 13). There appear to be four divisions:—

vv. 9—11. A sword is furbished that it may glitter terribly in the eyes of men (cf. xxxii. 10); it is sharpened for the slaughter—furbished and sharpened to give it into the hand of the slayer.

vv. 12, 13. The prophet must cry and howl and smite in wild excitement on his thigh, for the princes of Israel and the people are delivered over to the sword. His agitation is but the reflexion of the carnage which shall be witnessed.

vv. 14, 15. The sword is doubled and tripled; universal shall be the carnage.

vv. 16, 17. Wild apostrophe to the sword to execute its task in all directions. Sympathy of Jehovah with the terrible work.

10. *should we then make mirth*] lit., or shall we make mirth? These words with the rest to the end of the verse appear to have little meaning in the connexion. R.V. renders the whole: "shall we then make mirth? the rod of my son, it contemneth every tree." This is a literal rendering, the last words meaning probably that the rod (the sword of Babylon) with which Jehovah now chastises his son (the prince, or, people) contemneth (exceeds in severity) every tree, or, all wood, i.e. all rods of chastisement which are mere wood, for it is glittering steel. Some ingenuity is needed to extract the meaning, which, however, when extracted is difficult to harmonise with *v.* 13. The words "shall we then make mirth?" still appear meaningless. For "or" or "then" Frd. Del. would find some cohortative particle after the Assyr.,—ha! let us make mirth! the words being those of God (cf. *v.* 17), and the following words "contemneth every tree" meaning that in comparison with the rod he now uses all other rods of chastisement are only despicable, and useless for their purpose (*Zeit. f. Keilschriftforschung*, II. 4 p. 385). The text appears to be in disorder, and though many emendations have been proposed none of them is satisfactory. Ges., ..."glitter, against the prince of the tribe of my son (Judah), which despiseth all wood"—*prince* for "should we rejoice" (nasi' for nasis), and the idea being expressed that as Judah has hitherto despised all ordinary chastisements with the rod of wood the sword shall now be drawn against the prince. Ew., "no weak rod of my son, the softest of all wood"—the words "rod of my son" being a phrase from the mouth of fathers and meaning a gentle rod. Apart from the unnatural constructions and the strong Aramaisms assumed, the sense is feeble and improbable. Smend, "woe O prince! thou hast despised the rod, contemned every tree (all wood)"—rod and wood being used of chastening as before. LXX. reads: "ready (=furbished) for paralysing (enfeebling); slay, despise, set at nought every tree"! The imperatives are addressed to the sword. The words "for paralysing" may be a

the rod of my son, *as* every tree. And he hath given 11
it to be furbished, that *it* may be handled: this sword is
sharpened, and it *is* furbished, to give it into the hand of
the slayer. Cry and howl, son of man: for it shall be 12
upon my people, it *shall be* upon all the princes of Israel:
terrors by reason of the sword shall be upon my people:
smite therefore upon *thy* thigh. Because *it is* a trial, and 13

rendering of present Heb. read with Aramean sense; but "for" is read for "or." It is by no means certain that LXX. *found* imperatives, because it renders *v.* 9 also in the imperative. Partly following Sep. Corn., "for men who slay and plunder (lit. men of slaughter and plundering) who despise every stronghold"—viz. the Chaldeans, into whose hand the sword of the Lord is to be given. (Cf. Is. xxxiii. 8; Hab. i. 10.) This really gives a meaning, though it is gained at considerable cost, for some of the words assumed do not occur, the constructions are far from probable, and the changes of the text are serious. Further, in all the passage it is the sword itself that is dwelt upon and those whom it shall slay; those who are to wield it are only alluded to.

Scholars almost unanimously assume that there is ref. in the clause to former chastisement, hence "rod" and "all wood" are read in that sense. But such an idea seems little in place in the connexion; and the word rendered "rod" may mean sceptre or almost ruler (xix. 11, 14), and "every tree" may be taken of other sceptres. The assumption that "contemneth every tree" (all wood) means: exceeds in severity of punishment every rod, or looks down on every other chastening rod, feeling its own superiority as an instrument of punishment, is a very far-fetched one. It is certainly possible that the word "prince" (princes) lurks in the strange "shall we then rejoice?" (Ges. Sm.). The prince and royal house are alluded to repeatedly in the chapter, e.g. *vv.* 14, 25—27, 29. The rendering: "against the prince (princes), the sceptre of my son (that) despiseth all wood" (i.e. other sceptres, or royal powers, xix. 11, 14), is not very natural. The expression "my son," whether applied to the king or the people, has something unexpected about it in Ezek., though "my people" is used in the passage also (*v.* 12), and an undertone of pity, or at least a deep feeling of the terribleness of the coming calamity, runs through the passage. The words "shall we then make mirth?" can hardly stand in any case, even in this form: "or shall we make mirth (saying), The sceptre of my son contemneth all wood!" i.e. defies every other sceptre or royal power (*La Bible Annotée*). Any reference in the passage to Gen. xlix. 9 or 2 Sam. vii. 14 is without probability.

12. *terrors...the sword*] With R.V. **they** (the princes) **are delivered over to** the sword with my people.

smite upon thy *thigh*] A gesture implying despair or the sense of a terrible and irreparable evil happening, Jer. xxxi. 19.

13. *Because* it is *a trial*] Or, for there is a trial. So accented the

what if *the sword* contemn even the rod? it shall be no
more, saith the Lord God. Thou therefore, son of man,
prophesy, and smite *thine* hands together, and let the sword
be doubled the third time, the sword of the slain: it *is* the
sword of the great *men that are* slain, which entereth into
their privy chambers. I have set the point of the sword
against all their gates, that *their* heart may faint, and *their*
ruins be multiplied: ah, *it is* made bright, *it is* wrapt up for

word occurs again Is. xxviii. 16, a stone of trial (tried stone). The word might be read as a verb: for trial has been made. In any case reference is not to the "sword" nor the Babylonian conqueror who wields it, as if the meaning were: trial has been made of what it or he can do! Such a sense has no probability. The word must refer to those on whom the calamity is to fall.

and what if...be no more] The same difficulties recur here as in *v.* 10, and the translation will follow that adopted there. Ew., "for it has been tried—and what? is it also a soft rod?—that will not be, saith" &c.; i.e. the rod (the sword) has been tried, and it will be found no soft one. This is wholly improbable. Boett., "for (as to) trial, what (is to be effected) with that, when thou hast even contemned the rod?" (*Aehrenlese*, II. p. 174.) Others (Hitz., Corn.) point the word "trial" differently, and read: for with kindness what (should I accomplish)? &c.—which is quite destitute of probability. In spite of the grammatical harshness (cf. however *v.* 27) the construction followed in R.V. is perhaps the most probable: "for trial hath been made, and what if the sceptre (R. V. rod) that contemneth should be no more!"—reference being to the royal house of Judah which shall perish, cf. *vv.* 25—27, 29?

14. *doubled the third time*] The reading must mean: let the sword be doubled, tripled! lit. unto a third (sword), i.e. till it be three-fold. Of course there were not to be three swords or even two; what is called for is a double and triple intensity and operation of the one sword (cf. *v.* 16).

great men that are *slain*] Rather: **the great one that is slain**, i.e. doomed to be slain—ref. being to king Zedekiah, cf. *v.* 25. A different division of letters gives: the great sword of the slain (collective)—which is less probable as "slain" is *plur.* immediately before.

entereth...privy chambers] Rather: **which compasseth them about**—still descriptive of the sword.

15. *the point of the sword*] Or, **the glitter**, lit. whirl or swing. Others by changing a letter would read "slaughter," which Frd. Del. (Baer, *Ezek.*) by comparison of Assyr. considers the word to mean as it stands.

ruins be multiplied] Or, **stumbling-blocks**, Jer. vi. 21. Or, by a slight change in pointing: *those overthrown* may be multiplied; Jer. xviii. 23, cf. xlvi. 16.

wrapt up] **sharpened**, as marg.

the slaughter. Go thee one way or other, *either* on the 16
right hand, *or* on the left, whithersoever thy face *is* set. I 17
will also smite mine hands together, and I will cause my
fury to rest: I the LORD have said *it*.

The word of the LORD came unto me again, saying, Also, 18
thou son of man, appoint thee two ways, that the sword of 19
the king of Babylon may come: both twain shall come forth
out of one land: and choose thou a place, choose *it*, at the
head of the way to the city. Appoint a way, that the sword 20
may come to Rabbath of the Ammonites, and to Judah in
Jerusalem the defenced. For the king of Babylon stood at 21

16. Perhaps with R.V., "gather thee together, go to the right; set thyself in array, go to the left!" The sword is addressed by the Lord and bidden concentrate its force to smite on the right, and set itself on to slaughter on the left. Others by changes in the text find a command to the sword to smite in all the four directions (Boett.), which is more artificial.

thy face is set] Or, thine edge is appointed. Cf. same word "appointed" used of the sword, Jer. xlvii. 7, of the rod, Mic. vi. 9.

17. *smite mine hands*] The strong anthropomorphism suggests a tumult of emotion in the Divine mind, and sympathy with the terrible work.

cause my fury to rest] Appease, or, assuage my fury. Cf. ch. v. 13.

18—27. He who is, or who wields, the sword, the king of Babylon. The verses furnish the interpretation of the preceding passage.

18—27. The prophet is commanded to represent a way which parts into two ways. At the parting of the ways he is to set up two guideposts, the one pointing to Rabbah Ammon, the other to Jerusalem. The king of Babylon, coming to the parting of the ways, hesitates which he shall take. He consults the oracle, draws lots by means of the arrows, and the arrow that he draws out in his right hand is the one inscribed "Jerusalem."

19. *appoint thee two ways*] Or, *make* thee. The prophet is to make a representation of a way branching into two ways, i.e. the way from Babylon, which at a certain point parts into two, there being two possibilities before the king, either Rabbah or Jerusalem. Naturally the action was not performed in reality by the prophet.

choose thou a place] and **grave a hand, at the head of the way to** the (each) city **grave** it. The "hand" is the pointer or sign-post indicating direction. LXX. reads somewhat differently.

20. On Rabbah cf. xxv. 5.

in Jerusalem] **unto** Jerus. For "the defenced" LXX. reads: "in the midst of it," i.e. of Judah.

21. *for the king ...stood*] **standeth**. All the verbs had better be put in the present.

the parting of the way, at the head of the two ways, to use divination: he made *his* arrows bright, he consulted with 22 images, he looked in the liver. At his right hand was the divination for Jerusalem, to appoint captains, to open the mouth in the slaughter, to lift up the voice with shouting, to appoint *battering* rams against the gates, to cast a mount, 23 *and* to build a fort. And it shall be unto them as a false divination in their sight, to them that have sworn oaths:

made his *arrows bright*] he shaketh the arrows, he consulteth the teraphim, he looketh in the liver. These ceremonies explain the phrase "to use divination." The process has several parts: a sacrifice was offered to the deity or image, the liver of the animal apparently being inspected to see what intimations it suggested. Then arrows (among the Arabs they were pointless and unfeathered), inscribed with the names or things between which a decision was sought from the god (here Rabbah and Jerusalem), were cast into a vessel or bag; these were shaken and brought before the god from whom the decision was sought; one was then drawn, and the inscription it bore was the answer of the god to the alternative propounded for his settlement; in the present case the king's right hand drew out the arrow inscribed "Jerusalem." This method of divination by arrows was common among the Arabs (cf. Wellhausen, *Skizzen*, III. p. 127), and apparently also in Chaldea (Lenormant, *La Divination chez les Chaldéens*, ch. II. IV., Sayce, *Trans. Soc. Bib. Archæology*, vol. III. 145). It is related of the poet Imru'ulḳais that he used this method of divination to ascertain whether he should avenge his father's death or no, and the answer always coming out "no," he became enraged and breaking the arrows flung them in the god's face, telling him that if the case had been that of his own father he would not have given such a decision, and (in Arab fashion) applying many foul epithets to the god's mother.—The teraphim are the deities which Nebuchadnezzar carried with him, who gave the oracle. The *plur.* does not imply the use of more than one image.

22. *at his right hand*] in his right hand is the lot (or, oracle) "Jerusalem," to set battering rams, to open the mouth with a cry. Though "battering rams" occurs again in the verse the word can have no other sense, such as "captains." The word "cry" seems required by the parallel "shouting;" the letters have probably been transposed. On the apparatus of siege, cf. ch. iv. 2.

23. *to them...sworn oaths*] The words are obscure and wanting in LXX., and possibly are not original. Whether a gloss or no their purpose appears to be to explain why Israel considered this divination of the king's to be false, i.e. believed that he would not besiege or at least capture Jerusalem. The natural sense is: they have those who have sworn oaths (to them), i.e. allies, viz. the Egyptians, &c., who will frustrate and falsify Nebuchadnezzar's divination. Others: inasmuch as they (Israel) have sworn oaths to them (the Chaldeans). The construction is unnatural, and the sense without relevancy, because Israel

but he will call to remembrance the iniquity, that *they* may be taken. Therefore thus saith the Lord God; Be- 24 cause ye have made your iniquity to be remembered, in that your transgressions are discovered, so that in all your doings your sins do appear; because, *I say*, that ye are come to remembrance, ye shall be taken with the hand.

And thou, profane wicked prince of Israel, whose day is 25 come, when iniquity *shall have* an end, thus saith the Lord 26 God; Remove the diadem, and take off the crown: this *shall* not *be* the same: exalt *him that is* low, and abase *him that is* high. I will overturn, overturn, overturn it: and it 27 shall be no *more*, until he come whose right it is; and I will give it *him*.

had just broken its oath, a thing which Neb. came up to punish (ch. xvii.). Others still would change the pointing: they have weeks of weeks, i.e. weeks upon weeks—abundance of time to prepare for the siege, a sense feeble in the extreme.

he will call to remembrance] Or, **calleth.** The subject is most naturally Nebuchadnezzar, whose presence is an accusation before God of the king and people because of their breaking their allegiance to him (cf. ch. xvii.). The consequence of this accusation or bringing guilt to remembrance is that they shall be taken, i.e. captured, the city and people, by the foe. It is certainly possible that the clause "sworn oaths" may have been thrown in to explain this idea.

24. *so that in...appear*] Or, so that your sins do appear, even all your evil doings. Cf. xxix. 16.

25. *profane wicked prince*] Or, **and thou wicked one, who art to be slain, prince of Israel.** The sense "profane" is not quite certain, cf. *fem.*, Lev. xxi. 7, 14.

when iniquity...an end] **in the time of the iniquity of the end,** i.e. when iniquity shall receive its final chastisement—in the downfall of the state and captivity of the king. Cf. xxxv. 5.

26. The term "diadem" is used of the mitre of the high-priest, Ex. xxviii. 4. There can be no reference to the high-priest here, the passage refers exclusively to the royal house, which shall be discrowned.

this...the same] The somewhat enigmatical words mean probably: this is not that, i.e. the present royal house and régime is not that which shall be (the Messianic), as *v.* 27 explains. Or, this shall not remain this, i.e. what it is, it shall be removed and give place to something higher to come, *v.* 27.

exalt...that is high] **let that be exalted which is low, and that which is high be abased.** The words "overturn," &c., *v.* 27 explain the idea. The present order shall disappear, the high shall be abased and at last that which is humble shall be exalted, cf. xvii. 24.

27. *and it shall be no* more] Or, yea this—it shall not be (or, it is gone!). "This" does not refer to the condition introduced by the

28 And thou, son of man, prophesy and say, Thus saith the Lord God concerning the Ammonites, and concerning their reproach; even say thou, The sword, the sword *is* drawn: for the slaughter *it is* furbished, to consume because of the 29 glittering: whiles *they* see vanity unto thee, whiles *they* divine a lie unto thee, to bring thee upon the necks of *them*

overturning, but goes back and resumes the present condition of things, which shall be overturned till he comes who hath the right, the Messiah. On verb, cf. Is. xv. 6; Job vi. 21.

until he come...give it him] Rather: *and I will give it him*. He whose right it is, or, he who hath the right, is the Messiah. Reference is possibly to Gen. xlix. 10, where Ezek. read *shelloh* (whose), not as now Shiloh.

APPENDIX. 28—32. THREATENING PROPHECY AGAINST AMMON.

The passage is obscure, but several things seem evident. 1. In spite of the similarities between the language of *v.* 28 and that in *vv.* 9, 10, the sword here is that of Ammon. This is certain from the words *v.* 30 "return it to its sheath." 2. It is against Israel, not against the Chaldeans, that the Ammonites furbish and draw their sword. This appears from the words "concerning Ammon, and concerning their reproach" *v.* 28. Deceived by false prophecies they cherish purposes of conquest outside their own borders, which shall be far from being realized; on the contrary they shall be assailed in their own home and there annihilated (*v.* 25, cf. xxv. 4). History does not enable us to follow the progress of events. It is possible that simultaneously with Judah all the neighbouring peoples threw off the yoke of Babylon, so that it might be doubtful which of them Nebuchadnezzar would attack first (*vv.* 20, 21), but that in the course of events Ammon, true to its instincts, assumed an attitude hostile to Judah (cf. 2 Kings xxiv. 2). The date of the present passage is no doubt later than that of the rest of the chapter, and may owe some of its colour to events subsequent to the fall of Jerusalem. Cf. xxv. 1—7.

28. *the sword...is drawn*] Rather with disregard of the accents: **a sword, a sword is drawn for slaughter; it is furbished to the uttermost in order that it may glitter.**

to consume] Rather: **to the uttermost,** lit. as far as it can hold or receive. Corn. amends: to flash (*hahel* for *hakil*).

29. *they see vanity unto thee*] i.e. Ammon's soothsayers falsely hold out the prospect to it of victory and conquest.

bring thee upon the necks] The sense is doubtful, the phrase "bring, or, put, upon the necks" not occurring again. The "wicked, whose day is come, in the time of the iniquity of the end," can hardly be any other than the princes and people of Jerusalem, *v.* 25. 1. The clause "to bring thee," &c., might express the *contents* of the lying prophecy: they divine a lie and bring thee—they promise that thou shalt fall upon Israel, and conquer them. 2. The clause may express the *issue that are* slain of the wicked, whose day is come, when *their* iniquity *shall have* an end. Shall I cause *it* to return into his sheath? I will judge thee in the place where thou wast created, in the land of thy nativity. And I will pour out mine indignation upon thee, I will blow against thee in the fire of my wrath, and deliver thee into the hand of brutish men, *and* skilful to destroy. Thou shalt be for fuel to the fire; thy blood shall be in the midst of the land; thou shalt be no *more* remembered: for I the LORD have spoken *it*. 30 31 32

Moreover the word of the LORD came unto me, saying, 22

of the lying divination, the eventual issue of it in God's hand. These lying prophecies lead the Ammonites to enterprises or to purpose enterprizes the issue of which in God's hand (or, his judgment because of which) will be that they shall have a common fate with the princes and people of Jerusalem, upon whose necks (bodies) they shall be flung slain. 3. Others (Hitz. Corn.) would alter the text reading *it* (the sword) for *thee*, and connecting closely with *v*. 28: that it may glitter (whiles they divine a lie unto thee, &c.), in order to bring it (the sword) upon the necks, &c., i.e. assail and slay them with it. This is simpler, though against LXX.

upon the necks...wicked] More plainly: upon the necks of the wicked that are (to be) slain, i.e. the princes, &c. in Jerusalem, *v*. 25.

when their *iniquity...end*] **At the time of the iniquity** (or, punishment) **of the end**, cf. *v*. 25.

30. *Shall I...return*] **Return it into its sheath!** Ammon is commanded to put back his sword to its sheath; his dreams of conquests abroad are vain, he shall be visited and destroyed in his own land. On "nativity" cf. xvi. 3.

31. *brutish men*] i.e. wild and savage men. So in xxv. 4 it is the "men of the east," the children of the desert, who are to execute the judgment on Ammon.

skilful to destroy] lit. the smiths or forgers of destruction. Ewald's "smiths of hell," i.e. demons who forge in hell, is fanciful.

32. Cf. xxv. 10. Ammon shall perish in his own land.

CH. XXII. NEW INDICTMENT OF JERUSALEM.

The passage has three divisions:

First, *vv*. 1—12. The sins of Jerusalem, especially her two crying ones, idolatry and bloodshed (*vv*. 1—5); along with the dark catalogue of other offences (*v*. 6—12).

Secondly, *vv*. 13—22. Necessity and certainty of her judgment, which is stated first directly (*vv*. 13—16), and secondly under the figure of a smelting furnace (*vv*. 17—22).

Thirdly, *vv*. 23—31. Renewal of the indictment against all classes of the nation, from the prince to the people of the land.

2 Now, thou son of man, wilt thou judge, wilt thou judge the bloody city? yea, thou shalt shew her all her abominations.
3 Then say thou, Thus saith the Lord GOD, The city sheddeth blood in the midst of it, that her time may come, and
4 maketh idols against herself to defile *herself*. Thou art become guilty in thy blood that thou hast shed; and hast defiled *thyself* in thine idols which thou hast made; and thou hast caused thy days to draw near, and art come *even* unto thy years: therefore have I made thee a reproach unto
5 the heathen, and a mocking to all countries. *Those that be* near, and *those that be* far from thee, shall mock thee, *which*
6 *art* infamous *and* much vexed. Behold, the princes of Israel, every one were in thee to their power to shed blood.
7 In thee have they set light by father and mother: in the midst of thee have they dealt by oppression with the stranger: in thee have they vexed the fatherless and the
8 widow. Thou hast despised mine holy *things*, and hast
9 profaned my sabbaths. In thee are men that carry tales to

    2. *wilt thou judge*] See on ch. xx. 4, cf. xxiii. 36.
    yea, thou shalt shew] Rather: **then thou shalt cause her to know...**
v. 3 **and thou shalt say.**
    3. *the city sheddeth*] Rather as address: **city that sheddeth!** ch. xxiv. 6, 9. Her "time" is that of her chastisement, cf. xxx. 3 "the time of the heathen," Jer. xxvii. 7. So *v.* 4, "days" and "years," i.e. full number of thy years.
    against herself] Rather: **unto** herself, parallel to "in the midst of it."
    4. The "blood" is not only that of her children sacrificed to the idols, but judicial and other murders, cf. *vv.* 6, 9. Cf. xxiii. 37, xxiv. 6, 9.
    therefore have I made] prophetic perf., cf. "shall mock" *v.* 5.
    5. *much vexed*] **full of tumults**, Am. iii. 9, and on ch. v. 7.

    6—12. PARTICULAR ENUMERATION OF JERUSALEM'S SINS.

    6. The "princes" are those of the royal house.
    were...to their power] **have been high-handed in thee, to shed**. The meaning is not that they shed blood to the utmost of their power, but that they were arbitrary; their power, lit. *arm*, was the only law.
    7. "They" no more refers to the princes, but is said generally. On "father and mother" Ex. xx. 12; Deut. v. 16, xxvii. 16. On "stranger" ch. xviii. 18; Ex. xxii. 21. On "fatherless," Ex. xxii. 22.
    8. *Thou hast despised*] Jerusalem or the community is addressed, cf. *v.* 26, ch. xx. 13, 16, &c.
    9. Informers and false witnesses, Jer. ix. 3; Ex. xxiii. 1; Lev. xix. 16. Cf. ch. xviii. 6, 11.

shed blood: and in thee they eat upon the mountains: in the midst of thee they commit lewdness. In thee have they 10 discovered their father's nakedness: in thee have they humbled her that was set apart for pollution. And one 11 hath committed abomination with his neighbour's wife; and another hath lewdly defiled his daughter in law; and another in thee hath humbled his sister, his father's daughter. In thee have they taken gifts to shed blood; thou hast taken 12 usury and increase, and thou hast greedily gained of thy neighbours by extortion, and hast forgotten me, saith the Lord God. Behold therefore, I have smitten mine hand at 13 thy dishonest gain which thou hast made, and at thy blood which hath been in the midst of thee. Can thine heart 14 endure, or can thine hands be strong, in the days that I shall deal with thee? I the Lord have spoken *it*, and will do *it*. And I will scatter thee among the heathen, and 15 disperse thee in the countries, and will consume thy filthi-

commit lewdness] This clause should probably introduce the vices in *v.* 10. Idolatry is metaphorically "lewdness," but here it is not the community but individuals who are spoken of, cf. *v.* 11.

10. Lev. xviii. 7, xx. 11,—defiled their father's wife, i.e. their stepmother, or some of their father's concubines; cf. 2 Sam. xvi. 22.

set apart for pollution] **unclean from her impurity**, ch. xviii. 6; Lev. xviii. 19, xx. 18.

11. Lev. xviii. 20, xx. 10. Lev. xviii. 15, xx. 12. Lev. xviii. 9, xx. 17.

12. *taken gifts*] i.e. bribes, said of judges, Ex. xxiii. 8; Is. i. 23; Mic. iii. 11.—Cf. ch. xviii. 13, xxiii. 35.

by extortion] **oppression**, or violence, as *v.* 7. The vices here enumerated follow one another without any strict connexion. 1. The despotic conduct of the princes, whose power is their god (Hab. i. 11), *v.* 6. 2. Irreverence to parents, and want of compassion for the unprotected and helpless, *v.* 7. 3. Irreligion, *vv.* 8, 9. 4. Immoralities and incest, *vv.* 10, 11. And finally, greed of gain that overreaches and oppresses, *v.* 12. The picture is dark enough, and is unmistakeably that of a people whose decline is incurable, and its time at hand (*v.* 3), cf. Jer. v. 7, vi. 13, vii. 5, 6, xxii. 3; Hos. vii. 7; Mic. vi. 10.

13—22. THE JUDGMENT ON THESE VICES.

13. *smitten mine hand*] *clapped my hands*, cf. xxi. 14, 17, vi. 11. The gesture is expressive of violent agitation, though the agitation may be due to different emotions—here disdain and dislike.

14. Cf. xxi. 7, "every heart shall melt, and all hands shall be feeble."

15. Cf. ch. xxiii. 27, 28, xxxvi. 25, 29.

16 ness out of thee. And thou shalt take thine inheritance in thyself in the sight of the heathen, and thou shalt know that I *am* the LORD.

17,18 And the word of the LORD came unto me, saying, Son of man, the house of Israel is to me become dross: all they *are* brass, and tin, and iron, and lead, in the midst of the 19 furnace; they are *even the* dross *of* silver. Therefore thus saith the Lord GOD; Because ye are all become dross, behold therefore, I will gather you into the midst of Jeru-20 salem. *As they* gather silver, and brass, and iron, and lead, and tin, into the midst of the furnace, to blow the fire upon it, to melt *it;* so will I gather *you* in mine anger and in my 21 fury, and I will leave *you there*, and melt you. Yea, I will gather you, and blow upon you in the fire of my wrath, and 22 ye shall be melted in the midst thereof. As silver is melted in the midst of the furnace, so shall ye be melted in the

16. *take thine inheritance*] According to the points: and thou shalt be profaned in (through) thyself. The idea that Jehovah "profanes" his people by casting them out of their land is not uncommon, Is. xliii. 28, xlvii. 6, cf. Ezek. xxiv. 21 (xxviii. 16). It is doubtful if it be anywhere said that this casting out of the people is a profanation of them "in the sight of the heathen." On the other hand that phrase is often used when Jehovah himself, or his name, is spoken of as being profaned, ch. xx. 9, 14, 22. Particularly it is said that Israel's dispersion among the nations profaned Jehovah's name, ch. xxxvi. 20—23, and in xxxix. 7 Jehovah says, I will not pollute (let be polluted) my name any more (by the humiliation of his people). A slight change of reading gives: *and I will be* profaned in thee in the sight....The whole passage speaks of the chastisement of Israel, not of the purging away their uncleanness (*v.* 15), which is mentioned incidentally (cf. *v.* 22). This chastisement is dispersion among the nations, by which Jehovah is profaned and by which Israel learns to know that he who disperses them is the Lord. Corn. suggests: by which (uncleanness) I have been profaned in thee. Does the idea appear in the prophet that Jehovah was profaned in the eyes of the nations by Israel's idolatries?

17—22. Judgment on Israel under the figure of a smelting furnace. Israel is dross and base metal, which must be flung into the furnace.

18. *dross* of *silver*] In construction "silver" is in apposition with dross. For the figure cf. Is. i. 22, xlviii. 10; Jer. vi. 28—30; Mal. iii. 2, 3.

19. *midst of Jerusalem*] Cf. ch. xxiv.

22. The figure of the furnace expresses mainly the idea of the terrible trials approaching; it is not intimated that pure silver was obtained from the process. In a prophet toward the end of the exile Jehovah

midst thereof; and ye shall know that I the LORD have poured out my fury upon you.

And the word of the LORD came unto me, saying, Son of man, say unto her, Thou *art* the land that is not cleansed, nor rained upon in the day of indignation. *There is* a conspiracy of her prophets in the midst thereof, like a roaring lion ravening the prey; they have devoured souls; they have taken the treasure and precious things; they have made her many widows in the midst thereof. Her priests have violated my law, and have profaned mine holy *things:* they have put no difference between the holy and profane, neither have they shewed *difference* between the unclean and the clean, and have hid their eyes from my sabbaths, and I am profaned among them. Her princes in the midst thereof *are* like wolves ravening the prey, to shed blood, *and* to destroy souls, to get dishonest gain. And her

complains that his casting Israel into the furnace had been barren of result, Is. xlviii. 10.

vv. 23—31. New indictment of all classes of the nation: the royal house, *v*. 25; the priests, *v*. 26; the princes, *v*. 27; the prophets, *v*. 28, and the people of the land, *v*. 29. Among all the people not one is found to stand in the breach, therefore his wrath must be poured out upon them to the uttermost.

24. *the land...not cleansed*] A land. The words "not cleansed" are parallel to "not rained upon." In the east, however, raining upon is not a figure for cleansing, but for removing the curse and judgment, and blessing with fertility (Jer. iii. 3). LXX. has "not wetted by rain" here, which most moderns accept, cf. ch. xxxiv. 26; Lev. xxvi. 4; Deut. xi. 14; 1 Kings viii. 35, 36.

25. *conspiracy of her prophets*] More probably with LXX., **whose princes in the midst of her** are like...The prophets are spoken of *v*. 28. The "princes" are those of the royal house, ch. xix. 1, xxi. 12, xxii. 6, xlv. 8, 9; those called "princes" in v. 27 are the chiefs or heads of the people.

have taken the treasure] i.e. by violence from others, Jer. xx. 5.

her many widows] **her widows many.** Corr. *their palaces*, cf. ch. xix. 7, Jer. xxii. 13—17. The change is unnecessary, Jer. xv. 8.

26. The great influence possessed by the priests in this age appears from the place they occupy next the royal house. Jer. ii. 8, 26, iv. 9, viii. 1, xiii. 13, xxvi. 11.

between the holy and profane] ch. xliv. 23; Jer. xv. 19; Lev. x. 10.

27. *Her princes*] The "princes" here are the chiefs or leaders of the people, cf. Jer. xxvi. 10, xxxvi. 12.

get dishonest gain] Cf. Jer. vi. 13, viii. 10. The term is used pretty generally, of selfish advantage.

prophets have daubed them *with* untempered *morter*, seeing vanity, and divining lies unto them, saying, Thus saith the Lord GOD, when the LORD hath not spoken. The people of the land have used oppression, and exercised robbery, and have vexed the poor and needy: yea, they have oppressed the stranger wrongfully. And I sought for a man among them, that *should* make up the hedge, and stand in the gap before me for the land, that *I* should not destroy it: but I found none. Therefore have I poured out mine indignation upon them; I have consumed them with the fire of my wrath: their own way have I recompensed upon their heads, saith the Lord GOD.

28. *have daubed them*] daubed **for them**, seconding them. The persons called "princes" may be referred to, but not exclusively. Cf. ch. xiii. 10, and xiii. 6, 7.

29. *people of the land*] The phrase for the common people already, Jer. xxxvii. 2, and common in Ezek., vii. 27, xii. 19, &c. The "people of the land" is certainly subject here, cf. v. 7, ch. xviii. 12; Jer. xxiii. 34, xxvi. 7.

30. All classes (v. 25—29) are alike corrupt; a man to stand in the breach in behalf of the people is looked for in vain, cf. Jer. v. 1.

For "hedge" better **fence**, cf. on xiii. 5. A "man" here is not a man to intercede, but a man to interpose, to stem the tide of ruin and turn the fortunes of the people. The moral energies of the nation were wholly exhausted; it could no more put forth out of itself a saviour to retrieve its fortunes. Cf. Is. lix. 16, "and he saw that there was no man, and wondered that there was none to interpose" (Is. lxiii. 5).

31. *have I poured*] Prophetic perfect; the end is as good as come, vv. 3, 4. The result of this moral paralysis of the people must be its destruction. In the passages cited from Isaiah, written later and at a different juncture, the Lord himself interposes as saviour, there being none else.

CH. XXIII. HISTORY OF THE TWO ADULTEROUS WOMEN, OHOLAH AND OHOLIBAH—SAMARIA AND JERUSALEM.

The alliances and intrigues of Samaria and Jerusalem with foreign nations had been represented as infidelity to Jehovah since Hosea. These foreign alliances naturally carried foreign manners and worship in their train (Is. ii. 6). In Judah at least a great flood of idolatry from the east overflowed the country in the declining days of the kingdom, and to some extent this had been true of Israel also (Am. v. 26, 27). But apart from this from the earliest times the prophets conceive the kingdom of the Lord as something different in kind from the kingdoms of the nations: its essence consisted in fidelity to Jehovah, and its defence should have been left to him. Therefore when

23 The word of the LORD came again unto me, saying, Son
2 of man, there were two women, the daughters of one
3 mother: and they committed whoredoms in Egypt; they
committed whoredoms in their youth: there were their
breasts pressed, and there they bruised the teats of their
4 virginity. And the names of them *were* Aholah the elder,
and Aholibah her sister: and they were mine, and they bare
sons and daughters. Thus *were* their names; Samaria *is*
Aholah, and Jerusalem Aholibah.

the community of Jehovah sought alliances abroad for protection the
prophets detected in this alienation of mind from Jehovah, distrust
of his power and dissatisfaction with his rule. Already the conception
was taking possession of the prophetic mind that the kingdom of God
was not a state but what we now call a church.

The chapter reviews the history of Israel and Judah from the
beginning, and has these divisions:—

First, *vv.* 1—10. Infidelities of Samaria with Assyria and Egypt,
and the disastrous issue of them.

Secondly, *vv.* 11—21. Infidelities of Jerusalem with Assyria (11—13),
Babylon (14—18), and Egypt (19—21) successively.

Thirdly, *vv.* 22—35. Therefore her fate shall be like that of Samaria,
she shall drink to the dregs the cup which her sister drank.

Fourthly, *vv.* 36—49. A new description of the immoralities of
Oholah and Oholibah, with a fresh threat of punishment.

2. The two kingdoms are already called sisters, Jer. iii. 7. Cf.
Ez. xvi. 46.

3. The two kingdoms are represented ideally as already existing
in Egypt. This is not so far from the truth. The great tribes of
Judah and Ephraim from the first stood apart, and in their attitude
there lay already the germs of the two kingdoms, as appears in the
song of Deborah. On the idea of the prophet that idolatry was practised in Egypt, cf. ch. xx. 8, xvi. 26.

4. The name Oholah may mean "her tent," though not so pointed,
and Oholibah "my tent in her." Possibly the words mean "tent"
(or, tents) and "tent in her;" and the reference may be to the worship
practised on the high places in both kingdoms, cf. xvi. 16. It is
doubtful if the prophet means that Samaria had "her tent," i.e. a
sanctuary or worship of her own devising, while Jerusalem had Jehovah's tent or true sanctuary in her. Cf. the names Hephzi-bah, Is.
lxii. 4, and Oholibamah (high-place tent), Gen. xxxvi. 2. It was
common in the east to give sisters or brothers names almost the same,
as Hasan and Husein (little Hasan), the two sons of 'Ali, the son-in-
law of Muhammed.

they were mine] became mine, my wives, cf. xvi. 8, 20. It is curious
that Jehovah is represented as the husband of two sisters, a thing which
the law disallows, Lev. xviii. 18.

5   And Aholah played the harlot when she was mine; and she doted on her lovers, on the Assyrians *her* neighbours,
6 *which were* clothed with blue, captains and rulers, all of them desirable young men, horsemen riding upon horses.
7 Thus she committed her whoredoms with them, *with* all them *that were* the chosen men of Assyria, and with all *on* whom she doted: with all their idols she defiled herself.
8 Neither left she her whoredoms *brought* from Egypt: for in her youth they lay with her, and they bruised the breasts of
9 her virginity, and poured their whoredom upon her. Wherefore I have delivered her into the hand of her lovers, into
10 the hand of the Assyrians, upon whom she doted. These discovered her nakedness: they took her sons and her daughters, and slew her with the sword: and she became famous among women; for they had executed judgment upon her.

5—10. The intrigues of Samaria with Assyria.

5. *when she was mine*] **though my wife**, lit. under me.

Assyrians her *neighbours*] In xvi. 26 the Egyptians are called Israel's "neighbours," but the Assyrians could hardly be so called, and indeed in *v.* 40 are referred to as "far off." The word may mean "warriors" (the similar word "war" or "battle" 2 Sam. xvii. 11 and often). Corn. suggests, "famous," the term used in *v.* 23. The verse should be connected with *v.* 6, as appears from *v.* 12—even on the Assyrians, warriors clothed with blue.

6. *captains and rulers*] Or, governors and satraps, cf. Neh. iv. 14, v. 15.

7. *with all their idols*] The alliance with Assyria brought in Assyrian idolatry, cf. 2 Kings xxiii. 11, where horses and chariots of the sun are mentioned, and also the altars on the roofs, where incense was burnt to the host of heaven, *v.* 12, Jer. xix. 13.

8. Samaria intrigued with Assyria and Egypt alternately, or different parties simultaneously. Hos. vii. 11, "Ephraim is like a silly dove, without understanding; they call unto Egypt, they go unto Assyria."

9. *I have delivered*] **I delivered.** The Assyrians overthrew Samaria in 722 B.C. Menahem was supported on the throne by Assyria (2 Kings xv. 19); and Hoshea, the last king, was dethroned on account of his intrigues with Egypt (2 Kings xvii. 4).

10. *famous among women*] lit. *a name to women*, i.e. a notorious example to women to take warning from, *v.* 48, xxxvi. 3, xvi. 41.

And when her sister Aholibah saw *this*, she was more 11
corrupt in her inordinate love than she, and in her whoredoms more than her sister in *her* whoredoms. She doted 12
upon the Assyrians *her* neighbours, captains and rulers
clothed most gorgeously, horsemen riding upon horses, all
of them desirable young men. Then I saw that she was 13
defiled, *that* they took both one way, and *that* she increased 14
her whoredoms: for when she saw men pourtrayed upon
the wall, the images of the Chaldeans pourtrayed with vermilion, girded with girdles upon their loins, exceeding in 15
dyed attire upon their heads, all of them princes to look
to, *after* the manner of the Babylonians of Chaldea, the

11—21. THE INFIDELITIES OF JUDAH WITH ASSYRIA, BABYLON AND EGYPT.

11. On the greater excesses of Judah cf. xvi. 47, 51; Jer. iii. 8, 11.

12. her *neighbours*] The order is: the Assyrians, governors and satraps, warriors clothed...See on *v.* 5. The intervention of Assyria in the affairs of Judah was caused by the appeal of Ahaz for help against Syria and Ephraim, 2 Kings xvi. 7. On the disastrous consequences of Ahaz's folly cf. Is. vii. 17—25.

14. *and* that *she increased*] Rather: **And she added to her whoredoms**, with full stop at *v.* 13. It was certainly the custom in Babylonia to draw figures of men and the like upon the walls; it is not probable, however, that such figures of Chaldean warriors had actually been seen in Jerusalem. The prophet combines the Babylonian custom with the reports of Chaldean military splendour current in Judah. Even when Babylon was still a vassal state of Assyria Hezekiah entered into intrigues with it, Is. xxxix. In later times it was the rivalry between Babylon and Egypt that drew Judah into the whirl of imperial politics, and left her from the time of the battle of Carchemish and the defeat of Egypt subject to Babylon (B.C. 604).

15. *girded with girdles*] The "girdles" were properly not belts or sashes, but articles of clothing, tunics or waist-cloths (Is. xi. 5). "It appears, however, from the monuments that the Assyrians used what was originally the waist-cloth as an ornamental sash" (note from Prof. W. R. Smith).

exceeding in dyed attire] The word "exceeding in" means redundant; it is used of the curtains that "hung over" the sides of the tabernacle (Ex. xxvi. 12, 13), and possibly "dyed attire" may mean "turbans," from being *wound* (Frd. Del. Baer *Ez.* p. xii.). The idea would be that the high turbans folded back and hung down.

all of them princes] Or, heroes. The term is used of the choice warriors in chariots, Ex. xiv. 7; xv. 4, but also more generally.

after *the manner of*] Perhaps: *the likeness of* the Babylonians. It

16 land of their nativity: and as soon as she saw them with her eyes, she doted upon them, and sent messengers unto
17 them into Chaldea. And the Babylonians came to her into the bed of love, and they defiled her with their whoredom, and she was polluted with them, and her mind was alienated
18 from them. So she discovered her whoredoms, and discovered her nakedness: then my mind was alienated from
19 her, like as my mind was alienated from her sister. Yet she multiplied her whoredoms, in calling to remembrance the days of her youth, wherein she had played the harlot in
20 the land of Egypt. For she doted upon their paramours, whose flesh *is as* the flesh of asses, and whose issue *is like*
21 the issue of horses. Thus thou calledst to remembrance the lewdness of thy youth, in bruising thy teats by the Egyptians for the paps of thy youth.
22 Therefore, O Aholibah, thus saith the Lord GOD; Behold, I will raise up thy lovers against thee, from whom thy mind is alienated, and I will bring them against thee on every

is doubtful if the word "likeness" can ever be rendered "in the manner of" or "like" (Is. xiii. 4). Here "likeness" resumes "images" *v.* 14.

16. Read: **and she doted upon them after the sight of her eyes**—i.e. with delight and desire (Is. xi. 3).

17. *alienated from them*] The figure lies in the revulsion of sated passion; the thing in the weariness of the Babylonian alliance and yoke, cf. ch. xvii.

18. "Discovered" is uncovered, revealed.

19. Judah being situated between the two great empires of Babylon and Egypt and coveted by both, was naturally a hotbed of intrigue by partizans on both sides. The influence of the Egyptian party was great even in the Assyrian age (Is. xxx.—xxxi.), and the imposing and pretentious power of the Nile valley continued to delude the politicians of Judah throughout the period of Chaldean supremacy (ch. xxix.—xxxii.; Jer. ii. 18, xxxvii. 5 seq.; Lam. iv. 17).

21. *calledst to remembrance*] **didst recall**, i.e. renew, cf. xxxviii. 8.

for the paps] By a slight change of reading (*k* for *n*), **when thy teats were bruised by them of Egypt, when the breasts of thy youth were pressed** (*v.* 3).

22—35. CHASTISEMENT OF THE ADULTERESS.

22. *thy lovers*] the nations once in alliance with her, *v.* 9; ch. xvi. 37; Jer. xxx. 14; Lam. i. 19. In Hos. ii. the "lovers" are the Baals.

23. On these peoples cf. Del. *Parad.*, pp. 182, 236, 240. According to this writer the names appear in the inscriptions as Pukûdu,

side; the Babylonians, and all the Chaldeans, Pekod, and 23 Shoa, and Koa, all the Assyrians with them: all of them desirable young men, captains and rulers, great lords and renowned, all of them riding upon horses. And they shall 24 come against thee *with* chariots, wagons, and wheels, and with an assembly of people, *which* shall set against thee buckler and shield and helmet round about: and I will set judgment before them, and they shall judge thee according to their judgments. And I will set my jealousy against 25 thee, and they shall deal furiously with thee: they shall take away thy nose and thine ears; and thy remnant shall fall by the sword: they shall take thy sons and thy daughters; and thy residue shall be devoured by the fire. They shall also strip thee out of thy clothes, and take away 26 thy fair jewels. Thus will I make thy lewdness to cease 27 from thee, and thy whoredom *brought* from the land of Egypt: so that thou shalt not lift up thine eyes unto them, nor remember Egypt any more. For thus saith the Lord 28 GOD; Behold, I *will* deliver thee into the hand *of them* whom thou hatest, into the hand *of them* from whom thy mind is alienated: and they shall deal with thee hatefully, 29

Sutu or Su and Kutu or Ku, and are names of peoples lying east of the Tigris and on the confines of Elam or Persia.

"Captains and rulers," governors and satraps, *vv.* 6, 12. "Great lords," heroes, *v.* 15.

and renowned] Perhaps: chiefs. The word is parallel to "princes" Numb. i. 16, lit. "called men," cf. Am. vi. 1.

24. with *chariots*] The term is entirely unknown; LXX. *from the north*. Boettcher suggested the word "multitude" (xxvi. 10), a sense which Frd. Del. (Baer, *Ez.* p. xi.) thinks can be reached through the Assyr., the present word remaining unchanged. For people **peoples**.

set judgment] i.e. commit it unto them, Deut. xi. 26; 1 Kings viii. 46.

according to their judgments] lit. *with* their judgments, which are cruel and savage, *v.* 25.

25. "Jealousy" differs little from fury, ch. xvi. 38.

take away thy nose] Reference is either to the ancient practice (as in Egypt) of mutilating the adulteress, or to the habit of disfiguring the captives, cf. xii. 13; xvi. 40.

26. Cf. xvi. 39.

27. brought *from...Egypt*] i.e. continued since the time they were in the land of Egypt, cf. xvi. 41; xxii. 15.

29. *deal...hatefully*] **in hatred**. "Labour" is wealth, the fruit of labour. "Discovered" is exposed.

and shall take *away* all thy labour, and shall leave thee naked and bare: and the nakedness of thy whoredoms shall be discovered, both thy lewdness and thy whoredoms. 30 *I will* do these *things* unto thee, because thou hast gone a whoring after the heathen, *and* because thou art polluted 31 with their idols. Thou hast walked in the way of thy 32 sister; therefore will I give her cup into thine hand. Thus saith the Lord God; Thou shalt drink *of* thy sister's cup deep and large: thou shalt be laughed to scorn and had in 33 derision; *it* containeth much. Thou shalt be filled *with* drunkenness and sorrow, *with* the cup of astonishment and 34 desolation, *with* the cup of thy sister Samaria. Thou shalt even drink it and suck *it* out, and thou shalt break the sheards thereof, and pluck off thine own breasts: for I 35 have spoken *it*, saith the Lord God. Therefore thus saith the Lord God; Because thou hast forgotten me, and cast me behind thy back, therefore bear thou also thy lewdness and thy whoredoms.

31. *her cup*] That which she drank, Is. li. 22, 23; Jer. xxv. 15, 16.
32. *sister's cup deep*] i.e. which is deep. The words "thou shalt... derision" are parenthetical; LXX. omits.
33. *and sorrow*] Or, affliction.
34. Cf. Ps. lxxv. 8; Is. li. 17.
break the sheards] **gnaw** the sherds. The act of plucking out her own breasts is that of one intoxicated to madness, Jer. xxv. 16. The words are wanting in LXX. Beating the breasts and tearing the cheeks was a sign of excessive grief (*Hamasa*, p. 373). "The women rent the breast of their dress, went half-naked, tore their faces, and beat their skin till it was lacerated with shoes (*Aghani*, xiv. 101, 28; xv. 139, 6; *Hudh*. 139, 3)," Well., *Skizzen*, iii. p. 160.
35. *bear thou...lewdness*] Here "bear" means endure the punishment of it, *v*. 49.

36—49. NEW EXPOSURE OF THE IMMORALITIES OF OHOLAH AND OHOLIBAH (*vv*. 36—44), AND THREAT OF THEIR PUNISHMENT (*vv*. 45—49).

The passage is not a continuation of *v*. 1—35, but an independent description, parallel to these verses.
(1) *vv*. 36, 37. The adulteries, that is, idolatries, and bloodshed of which the two women are guilty.
(2) *vv*. 38, 39. Their profaning the house of Jehovah, and breaking his Sabbaths—the former particularly in their entering his house fresh from the sacrifice of their children.

The LORD said moreover unto me; Son of man, wilt 36 thou judge Aholah and Aholibah? yea, declare unto them their abominations; that they have committed adultery, 37 and blood *is* in their hands, and with their idols have they committed adultery, and have also caused their sons, whom they bare unto me, to pass for them through *the fire*, to devour *them*. Moreover this they have done unto me: 38 they have defiled my sanctuary in the same day, and have profaned my sabbaths. For when they had slain their 39 children to their idols, then they came the same day into my sanctuary to profane it; and lo, thus have they done in the midst of mine house. And furthermore, that ye have 40 sent for men to come from far, unto whom a messenger *was* sent; and lo, they came: for whom thou didst wash *thyself*, paintedst thy eyes, and deckedst thyself with orna-

(3) *vv*. 40—44. Their alliances with idolatrous nations and receiving their gods, under the figure of a harlot receiving and entertaining men.
(4) *vv*. 45—49. Their punishment with the death of an adulteress at the hands of righteous men.—The text in some passages is extremely difficult.

36. *yea, declare*] **then** declare.
37. *that they have committed*] **for** they have. The blood on their hands is that of their children whom they sacrifice. See xvi. 20, 21.
38. *the same day*] The phrase is more fully explained in *v.* 39. LXX. omits in both places.
39. The particular profanation of the Lord's house lay in this that those who had sacrificed their children entered it. The children were no doubt offered to Jehovah, under whatever conception or name, and the worshippers felt no incongruity in entering his house. Jer. vii. 9 *seq*.
midst of mine house] It is not meant that children were sacrificed *in* the house; their sacrifice was combined with other service in the house.
40—44. These verses hardly refer to political alliances merely; *v.* 41 suggests idolatrous worship. As the foreign gods came in, however, through intercourse with the nations which served them they are spoken of as being sent for by messengers (cf. *v.* 16). The whole is presented under the figure of an harlot receiving men from all quarters. The passage has great resemblance to Is. lvii. 9 *seq*.
40. *that ye have sent*] Perhaps: and furthermore *they* sent. The change of person occurs later. The word "they sent" is wanting in LXX.
wash thyself] i.e. bathe thyself.
paintedst thy eyes] This refers to the practice of colouring the edges of the eyelids with a dark powder (stibium), which made the eye

41 ments, and satest upon a stately bed, and a table prepared before it, whereupon thou hast set mine incense and mine
42 oil. And a voice of a multitude being at ease *was* with her: and with the men of the common sort *were* brought Sabeans from the wilderness, which put bracelets upon
43 their hands, and beautiful crowns upon their heads. Then said I unto *her that was* old *in* adulteries, Will they now

itself appear large and brilliant, 2 K. ix. 30; Jer. iv. 30. The word *kahal* is Arab., and the root of Alcohol; the Heb. is *pûch* (Is. liv. 11); Job's daughter bore the name Keren-hap-puch, horn of paint.

41. *a table prepared*] i.e. spread.

hast set mine incense] **didst set.** The words indicate that service of other gods is referred to under the figure of the harlot's entertainment.

42. *being at ease*] If the reading be correct "at ease" must refer to careless living, a sense which the word has not elsewhere. LXX. renders: and a sound of music they raised; but though the word "multitude" may mean sound or noise when joined to songs (xxvi. 13; Am. v. 23), it can hardly of itself mean music. LXX. may have read "they sang" for "at ease;" "and with a loud noise (Dan. x. 6) they sang"—a sense not suitable seeing the musicians must have been the harlots themselves, Is. xxiii. 15, 16. For the idea of multitude cf. Jer. v. 7 end. If music were referred to the words would be better attached to the previous verse.

was with her] Rather: **therein** or **therewith.** LXX. om.

and with the men...Sabeans] and **with men.** For Sabeans Heb. text reads "drunkards," as *marg.*, and from the nature of the passage, which speaks of a general practice, reference to any particular nation is less probable. Read as R.V. "and with (in addition to) men...were brought drunkards from the wilderness; and they put bracelets" &c. Even for these vulgar guests the harlots, so indiscriminate was their whoredom, put bracelets on their hands and decked themselves. The idea that it was "men of the common sort" who adorned the harlots with bracelets as their hire (A.V. &c.) has little to recommend it, cf. xvi. 31 *seq.* (the verb "they put" is *mas.* because *fem.* is not in use, Esth. i. 20). Even in Muhammed's days the Arabs were addicted to drunkenness. LXX. om. "drunkards," which might be a duplicate of "brought," and certainly the mention of *two* classes here is rather improbable, the common sort and those brought from the wilderness might rather be the same, viz. the vulgar and petty peoples in contrast to the larger and nobler such as Babylon. The omission makes the clause difficult to construe. Corn. reconstructs the clause after Prov. vii. 16, making it a description of the "bed of love" (*v.* 17), but with little probability. If the adulterous act be anywhere referred to it is in *v.* 43.

43. *unto* her...*old* in *adulteries*] *Old* is worn out, e.g. of clothes, Josh. ix. 4, 5, and the verb of the body, in the decay of nature (Gen. xviii. 12, of Sarah). The construction of A.V. is unusual; the words commit whoredoms with her, and she *with them?* Yet 44 they went in unto her, as *they* go in unto a woman that playeth the harlot: so went they in unto Aholah and unto Aholibah, the lewd women.

And *the* righteous men, they shall judge them after the 45 manner of adulteresses, and after the manner of *women* that shed blood; because they *are* adulteresses, and blood *is* in their hands. For thus saith the Lord GOD; *I will* bring 46 up a company upon them, and *will* give them to be removed and spoiled. And the company shall stone them 47 with stones, and dispatch them with their swords; they shall slay their sons and their daughters, and burn up their houses with fire. Thus will I cause lewdness to cease out 48 of the land, that all women may be taught not to do after your lewdness. And they shall recompense your lewdness 49 upon you, and ye shall bear the sins of your idols: and ye shall know that I *am* the Lord GOD.

might be read as an exclamation: She that is aged committeth adulteries! or, With her that is aged shall they commit adulteries! Ew., reading "aged" as a noun, To perdition with adulteries! None of these senses is very natural. LXX., as in some other places, appears to assume a contraction, which it expands, Do they not commit adultery with these?

The meaning put by A.V., R.V. upon the rest of the verse can hardly be drawn from the words, which are extremely obscure. The natural sense is: "now shall her whoredom commit whoredom even itself" (Hitz.); but the idea that what the faded harlot can no more do herself her vicious propensity continues to do, though true in itself, is scarcely to be expected here. LXX., which had nearly our present text before it, disposes the letters differently: And she too has gone a whoring after the manner (with the doings) of a harlot. So Syr., And according to the doings of harlots have they committed whoredom.

44. *Yet they went*] **and** they. The verse sums up all that precedes.

the lewd women] The form of *plur.* "women" does not occur again, though the usual one in Assyr. LXX., *to work* lewdness.

45—49. JUDGMENT ON THE ADULTEROUS WOMEN.

45. the *righteous*] **righteous** men. The prophet carries on the figure of the punishment of adulteresses. They are judged by righteous men. He has not in his mind the nations, the actual executors of judgment in the case of Israel. The word "righteous" throws no light on Is. xlix. 24.

46. Cf. xvi. 40.

to be removed] maltreated.

48. *be taught*] **take warning** (the form *nithpa.*, cf. Deut. xxi. 8).

24 Again in the ninth year, in the tenth month, in the tenth day of the month, the word of the LORD came unto me, 2 saying, Son of man, write thee the name of the day, *even* of this same day: the king of Babylon set himself against Jerusalem this same day. 3 And utter a parable unto the rebellious house, and say unto them, Thus saith the Lord GOD; Set on a pot, set *it* on, and also pour water into it: 4 gather the pieces thereof into it, *even* every good piece, the thigh, and the shoulder; fill *it with* the choice bones. 5 Take the choice of the flock, and burn also the bones under

CH. XXIV. THE RUSTED CALDRON SET UPON THE COALS.

The passage, of date Jan. 587, is the prophet's last oracle against Jerusalem. It consists of two parts:

First, *vv.* 1—14. A parable of a rusted caldron set upon the fire—the siege and capture of the city.

Second, *vv.* 15—27. On the death of his wife the prophet abstains from all mourning—a sign of the silent stupefaction which the news of the city's fall will occasion.

1—14. THE RUSTED CALDRON SET ON THE FIRE.

(1) *vv.* 1—5. A caldron is to be set on the fire, filled with water, pieces of flesh cast into it and fuel piled under it that it may boil furiously. The caldron is Jerusalem; the pieces of flesh the inhabitants; the fire and boiling the siege with its terrible severities. The pieces of flesh shall be pulled out of the caldron indiscriminately, symbol of the universal dispersion when the siege is over.

(2) *vv.* 6—8. Explanation: these sufferings are judgments for the sins of the city, its bloodshed and uncleanness, which are public and open. This blood and filthiness cleaves to it like rust to a caldron.

(3) *vv.* 9—14. Rising anew into tones of menace the divine voice commands that the caldron be set empty upon the coals that its rust and foulness may be molten and consumed. This must signify the ruin in which the city shall long lie, and the dispersion in which her inhabitants shall pine away, till her warfare be accomplished and her iniquity pardoned.

1. The same date of the commencement of the siege is given 2 K. xxv. 1; Jer. lii. 4. In later times the day was kept as a fast, Zech. viii. 19.

3. *Set on a pot*] the caldron.

4. *the pieces thereof*] those belonging to the caldron, which are to be boiled in it.

5. *burn also the bones*] **a pile also of wood under it.** If "pile" could be read as a verb, *and pile also wood*, the construction would be easier. In spite of the versions *wood* must be substituted for "bones."

it, *and* make it boil well, and let them seethe the bones of it therein.

6 Wherefore thus saith the Lord God; Woe to the bloody city, to the pot whose scum *is* therein, and whose scum is not gone out of it! bring it out piece by piece; let no lot fall upon it. 7 For her blood is in the midst of her; she set it upon the top of a rock; she poured it not upon the ground, to cover it with dust; 8 that *it* might cause fury to come up to take vengeance; I have set her blood upon the top of a rock, that *it* should not be covered. 9 Therefore thus saith the Lord God; Woe to the bloody city! I will even make the pile for fire great. 10 Heap on wood, kindle the fire, consume the flesh, and spice it well, and let the bones be burnt. 11 Then set it empty upon the coals thereof, that the brass of it may be hot, and may burn, and *that* the filthiness of it may be molten in it, *that* the scum of it

make it boil well] Lit. make boil its boilings. The word "boilings" does not occur again; possibly by changing a letter "boil *its pieces*," parallel to *its bones* in next clause.

let them seethe] **let the bones thereof be seethed.** Naturally here and *v.* 4 "bones" include the flesh upon them. They are those of such parts as leg and shoulder.

6. Explanation: the caldron is Jerusalem, the bloody city.

whose scum] **rust.**

bring it out] i.e. the caldron as having contents.

let no lot fall] The contents (the inhabitants) shall be pulled out indiscriminately. The dispersion is alluded to.

7. *top of a rock*] **a bare rock.** Job xvi. 18, "O earth cover not my blood." Blood uncovered cries for vengeance. Cf. Lev. xvii. 13; Deut. xii. 16. On the idea of the openness of Jerusalem's sin cf. Is. iii. 9, "They declare their sin as Sodom, they hide it not."

8. *I have set her blood*] In *v.* 7 it was Jerusalem herself who left her bloodshed uncovered; here, as usual in the prophet, this is an appointment of God, that he may bring up judgment because of it.

9—14. Rising anew into tones of threatening the divine voice commands fuel to be heaped under the caldron, and to set it empty upon the coals, that its brass may glow in the fire and its rust be consumed.

9. *I will even*] **I too will** make. LXX. wants the clause "woe... city," cf. *v.* 6.

10. *consume the flesh*] **boil** (or, do) **well,** as R.V.

spice it well] Probably: make thick (stew) the broth.

bones be burnt] Either "burnt" is used inexactly of the powerful action of the heat in boiling, or, less naturally, the contents of the pot are supposed to suffer directly from the fire. LXX. omits.

11. *scum of it*] **Rust.** When the contents of the caldron have been

₁₂ may be consumed. She hath wearied *herself with* lies, and her great scum went not forth out of her: her scum *shall be* ₁₃ in the fire. In thy filthiness *is* lewdness: because I have purged thee, and thou wast not purged, thou shalt not be purged from thy filthiness any more, till I have caused ₁₄ my fury to rest upon thee. I the LORD have spoken *it:* it shall come to pass, and I will do *it*; I will not go back, neither will I spare, neither will I repent; according to thy ways, and according to thy doings, shall they judge thee, saith the Lord GOD.

¹⁵₁₆ Also the word of the LORD came unto me, saying, Son of man, behold, I take away from thee the desire of thine eyes with a stroke: yet neither shalt thou mourn nor weep, ₁₇ neither shall thy tears run down. Forbear to cry, make no mourning *for* the dead, bind the tire of thine head upon

seethed and emptied out of it—the siege and dispersion—the caldron itself shall be set empty upon the coals that its filth and rust may be molten and consumed—a figure for the purifying judgments continued long after the destruction of the city.

12. As the words stand they seem to read: *she hath wearied* my *labours*, and her great rust goeth not out from her; *let her rust be in the fire!* Previous efforts to purify Jerusalem have been in vain, her uncleanness will go out only by fire (*v.* 13); cf. Is. xliii. 24. LXX. omits first clause, which might be a duplicate of words immediately preceding.

13. *In thy...lewdness*] Or, because of thy lewd filthiness, cf. xvi. 27, thy lewd way.

shalt not be purged...more] i.e. shalt never be purged, till, &c., or purged so as to be again clean, till, &c.

caused...to rest] **appeased**, v. 13, viii. 18, xvi. 42.

14. *shall they judge*] Cf. xxiii. 49. LXX. and the versions, *I will* judge, which LXX. then amplified into an additional verse, somewhat in terms of xxii. 5. The words, though found by the translator in his MS., are hardly original.

15—27. THE PROPHET'S ABSTENTION FROM MOURNING ON THE DEATH OF HIS WIFE—A SYMBOL OF THE STUPEFACTION OF THE PEOPLE AT THE NEWS OF THE FALL OF THE CITY.

16. *with a stroke*] The word need not be pressed to mean a sudden unexpected death, apart from all previous sickness.

thy tears run down] wanting in LXX.

17. *Forbear to cry*] **sigh in silence**; lit. sigh, be silent.

mourning for *the dead*] Another order was to be expected; two accus. must be assumed.

the tire of thine head] The "tire" is not necessarily the priestly

thee, and put on thy shoes upon thy feet, and cover not *thy* lips, and eat not the bread of men. So I spake unto the people in the morning: and at even my wife died; and I did in the morning as I was commanded. And the people said unto me, Wilt thou not tell us what these *things are* to us, that thou doest *so?* Then I answered them, The word of the LORD came unto me, saying, Speak unto the house of Israel, Thus saith the Lord GOD; Behold, I *will* profane my sanctuary, the excellency of your strength, the desire of your eyes, and that which your soul pitieth; and your sons and your daughters whom ye have left shall fall by the sword. And ye shall do as I have done: ye shall not cover *your* lips, nor eat the bread of men. And your tires *shall be* upon your heads, and your shoes upon your feet: ye shall not mourn nor weep; but ye shall pine away for your iniquities, and mourn one towards another. Thus Ezekiel is unto you a sign: according to all that he hath done shall ye do: and when this cometh, ye shall know that I *am* the Lord GOD.

Also, thou son of man, *shall it* not *be* in the day when

tiara, but the ordinary headdress (*v.* 23), which would probably be white. Putting off the shoes was a sign of calamity, 2 Sam. xv. 31, and also covering the lower part of the face up to the upper lip. Mic. iii. 7; Lev. xiii. 45.

the bread of men] Jer. xvi. 7, "Neither shall men break bread for them to comfort them for the dead, neither shall men give them the cup of consolation to drink for their father or for their mother."

18. The death of the prophet's wife was no doubt an actual occurrence. And there is nothing improbable in his demeanour after it, with the view of attracting the attention of his fellow-captives. At the same time his tendency to idealize occurrences precludes absolute certainty.

21. *excellency of your strength*] i.e. your proud boast, or, your boasted stronghold (*v.* 25). The temple is referred to.

that which...pitieth] Or, spareth, i.e. holds dear, xxxvi. 21; Job xx. 13.

23. *pine away for*] in your iniquities; xxxiii. 10; Lev. xxvi. 39.

mourn one towards] moan. The unparalleled severity of the stroke will paralyse grief and prevent it expressing itself.

24. *is...a sign*] **shall be.**

25—27. When tidings come of the city's fall, verifying the prophet's predictions and giving confirmation to all the principles which he had long declared, his mouth will be opened, he will have confidence to speak and more willing listeners before him.

I take from them their strength, the joy of their glory, the desire of their eyes, and that whereupon they set their
26 minds, their sons and their daughters, *that* he that escapeth in that day shall come unto thee, to cause *thee* to hear *it*
27 with *thine* ears? In that day shall thy mouth be opened to him which is escaped, and thou shalt speak, and be no more dumb: and thou shalt be a sign unto them; and they shall know that I *am* the LORD.

25. *their strength*] i.e. stronghold; the thing in which they placed confidence.

joy of their glory] the glorious (or beautiful) thing in which they delighted. Both expressions allude to the temple, &c.

set their minds] their **hearts**,—that which is the object of their desire, Ps. xxiv. 4.

26. *that escapeth in that day*] **on that day he that is escaped shall come.** The phrase "on that day" is used with considerable latitude, to indicate the period marked by any great event and following it.

cause thee...thine *ears*] Perhaps more general: to cause it to be heard with the ears—not the prophet's only but also those of the exiles.

27. *opened to him*] Or, **with** him, i.e. when he comes. Cf. iii. 26, 27, xxxiii. 22. The last words of this verse recur to the prophet's demeanour *vv.* 16—18.

SECOND DIVISION. CH. XXV.—XLVIII. PROPHECIES OF THE RESTITUTION OF THE KINGDOM.

FIRST SECTION. CH. XXV.—XXXII. PROPHECIES AGAINST THE NATIONS.

The prophecies of Ezekiel against the nations form a single collection in the Book precisely as the similar oracles of Jeremiah (ch. xlvi.—li.) and of Isaiah (ch. xiii.—xxvii.). In the Book of Ezekiel they occupy the proper ideal place, being an introduction to the positive prophecies of Israel's restoration (ch. xxiii.—xxxix.). Israel occupies a place of universal significance in the history of the world, for it is the people of Jehovah, who is God alone. He who is God alone has become God of Israel, and it is through Israel that he is known to the nations, and through Israel and her history that he will fully reveal himself to the peoples of the world. This perfect manifestation of himself will be seen in Israel's restoration, when his glory shall be revealed and all flesh shall see it together (Is. xl. 5). But this restoration of Israel cannot be without great judgments on the nations who have hitherto harassed her or seduced her. These judgments will awaken the nations to the knowledge who the God of Israel is—they shall know that he is Jehovah; and they will ensure that in the future his people shall not be troubled or led astray. All the prophets have the presentiment of a general judgment upon the world immediately preceding the incoming of the perfect kingdom of the Lord. The idea is shared by

Ezekiel, though, as usual, he develops it into much further details than his predecessors had occasion to do.

The *place* of these prophecies in the Book of Ezekiel is important, because it suggests the place which the judgments on the nations had in his scheme of thought, and his construction of the history of redemption. So far as the prophecies themselves are concerned they belong either to the last years of Israel's existence as a nation, or to the period immediately following the downfall of the state. The prophecies are seven in number, being against (1) Ammon, (2) Moab, (3) Edom, (4) the Philistines (ch. xxv.), (5) Tyre (ch. xxvi.—xxviii.), (6) Sidon (xxviii. 20—26), (7) Egypt (xxix.—xxxii.). Those against the first six countries seem immediately posterior to the destruction of Jerusalem; those against Egypt belong to the time from the 10th to the 12th year of Jehoiachin's captivity, that is, the year before the capture of the city, the year in which it was taken, and the year after, with the exception of the passage ch. xxix. 17—21, belonging to the 27th year of Jehoiachin's captivity, which is probably a later insertion.

Chastisement overtakes the nations for two sins. First, because of their demeanour towards Israel, the people of Jehovah. Either they had taken part in Jerusalem's destruction (Edom, xxv. 12, the Philistines, xxv. 15), or had rejoiced over it, whether out of malice (Ammon, xxv. 3), jealousy (Moab, xxv. 8), or for selfish reasons (Tyre, xxvi. 2); or else they had been a snare to Israel, inspiring false trust and seducing her from the true God (Egypt, xxix. 6). And secondly, because of their ungodly pride and self-deification (Tyre, ch. xxviii., Egypt, xxix. 3). This conduct of the nations and these feelings bring them into relation with Jehovah, either mediately through Israel the people of the true God, whom they injured or despised or seduced; or immediately and in a wider way in their not recognising him as God,—him who was God alone. Hence in all cases his judgments upon them have this purpose and result—they shall know that I am Jehovah.

The prophet has a very lofty consciousness of God, which he expresses by the word "Jehovah." To be Jehovah is to be God alone, and all which he who is God alone is. It is from this conception of the God of Israel that the prophet speaks. But he estimates the conduct and feelings of the nations as if they also had or should have the same consciousness of Jehovah, as if they knew him as the prophet himself does. Other prophets speak in the same way, e.g. Is. x. 6, 7. His way of thinking arises from the fact that the one true God was God of Israel. He whom the nations knew as Jehovah, the God of Israel, was the one living God. And when they did despite to his people, it was not a nationality among other nationalities that they injured, nor a mere tribal god whom they scorned, they were moving in a far higher plane than this, they were doing despite to the people of him who was God alone, and were injurious to the one living God. Again, Jehovah being God over all, pride of heart in the nations or their rulers, and self-deification, as when the prince of Tyre said, I am God (xxviii. 2), or when the Pharaoh said, My river is mine,

25 The word of the Lord came again unto me, saying, Son
² of man, set thy face against the Ammonites, and prophesy

I have made it (xxix. 3), was blasphemy against him. This self-exaltation detracted from him who is alone exalted (Is. ii. 11). This is the prophet's conception. In a certain way his manner of thinking may do an injustice to the nations, who might not know that Jehovah, God of Israel, was God alone. The question is not quite simple. For this pride and self-deification of rulers and nations was a sin against God, it was on the part of man a lifting-up of himself against what the human mind feels to be above it. And it is not just quite clear that Israel's neighbours were altogether guiltless in not knowing Jehovah to be God alone. He was in the world, though the world knew him not. The Light had appeared. How far men everywhere are responsible for not coming to the Light when it has anywhere appeared is a question not to be settled just offhand (John xviii. 37, 38). The prophet appears to intimate that the neighbouring nations were not unaware of Israel's pretensions to be different from themselves (xxv. 8). The superiority claimed by Israel was a religious one (Deut. xxxii. 31), and when the prophet represents the nations as aware of it, he is not to be thought as speaking merely from his own point of view (Numb. xxiii. 21—23; Lam. iv. 12).

Ch. xxv. contains prophecies directed against four peoples: *vv.* 1—7, Ammon; *vv.* 8—11, Moab; *vv.* 12—14, Edom; and *vv.* 15—17, the Philistines.

1—7. Prophecy against Ammon.

The name of this people is usually the children of Ammon (Beni Ammon). This is the name both of the people and the country (in the latter case construed as *fem. vv.* 3, 10). Ammon was recognised by Israel as a distant member of the same family with themselves (Gen. xix. 38). At an early period the people was settled on the E. of the Jordan, between the Arnon and the Jabbok (Judg. xi. 13), but before the Exodus they had been dispossessed of this territory by Amorites from the W. of the Jordan, and pushed eastward towards the desert (Numb. xxi. 21), though they could not forget their ancient claims to their former seat, even when Israel had wrested it from the Amorites (Judg. xi. 19; cf. Josh. xiii. 25). The relations of Ammon to Israel were for the most part unfriendly. In the times of the Judges they harassed the tribes E. of the Jordan, and were crushed by Jephthah (Judg. x.—xi.). Saul signalised his early reign by defeating their king, who had laid siege to Jabesh in Gilead (1 Sam. xi.). Owing to the affront offered to his ambassadors David invaded the country and took cruel vengeance on the inhabitants (2 Sam. x. 1, xi. 14, xii. 26). The Ammonites continued when opportunity offered to carry on a savage warfare with the tribes across the Jordan (Am. i. 13); and when these were carried away by the Assyrians they naturally in company with Moab seized the depopulated country (Jer. xlix. 1; Zeph. ii. 8). During the struggle of Judah with Babylon they shewed

vv. 3—7.]   EZEKIEL, XXV.   181

against them; and say unto the Ammonites, Hear the 3
word of the Lord GOD; Thus saith the Lord GOD; Because thou saidst, Aha, against my sanctuary, when it was
profaned; and against the land of Israel, when it was desolate; and against the house of Judah, when they went into
captivity; behold therefore, I *will* deliver thee to the men 4
of the east for a possession, and they shall set their palaces
in thee, and make their dwellings in thee: they shall eat thy
fruit, and they shall drink thy milk. And I will make Rabbah 5
a stable for camels, and the Ammonites a couching place for
flocks: and ye shall know that I *am* the LORD. For thus 6
saith the Lord GOD; Because thou hast clapped *thine* hands,
and stamped with the feet, and rejoiced in heart with all thy
despite against the land of Israel; behold therefore, I will 7
stretch out mine hand upon thee, and will deliver thee for a
spoil to the heathen; and I will cut thee off from the people,
and I will cause thee to perish out of the countries: I will
destroy thee; and thou shalt know that I *am* the LORD.

the old mischievous animosity (2 Kings xxiv. 2), and after the fall
of the city the treacherous murder of Gedaliah the Babylonian governor
by Ishmael was instigated by their king (Jer. xl. 14). After the Return
Ammonites are again found obstructing the pious aspirations of the
restored community (Neh. iv. 3; cf. ii. 10, 19), and true to their old
instincts they appear on the side of the Syrians in the Maccabean war
of independence (1 Macc. v. 6).

3. *when it was desolate*] i.e. desolated. For the demeanour of the
nations on the destruction of Jerusalem, cf. Ez. xxi. 28, xxxv. 13,
xxxvi. 20; Obad. 12; Lam. ii. 15, 16.

4. *men of the east*] lit. *children of the east*, the nomad tribes of the
Arabian desert, Jud. vi. 3.

set their palaces] their **encampments**, Judg. vi. 1—6.

drink thy milk] Ammon, lying toward the desert, was a pastoral
country.

5. *Rabbah a stable*] Rabbah, "great city," was the capital (Am.
i. 14); in later times it bore the name of Philadelphia, and its site
is probably marked by the ruins called Ammân. The word "stable"
is usually rendered habitation, but sheepcote, 2 Sam. vii. 8. It may
mean a place where animals are housed or where they pasture, cf. Is.
v. 17, xxxii. 14; Jer. xxxiii. 12; Zeph. ii. 14, 15.

6. *clapped* thine *hands*] A gesture of malicious delight, Lam. ii. 15.

7. *a spoil to the heathen*] the **nations** (the reading *baz* to be adopted),
cf. xxvi. 5, vii. 21, xxiii. 46. For people **peoples**.

know that I am *the Lord*] The statement is hardly to the effect that
the Ammonites shall be converted to the worship of the true God,

8 Thus saith the Lord God; Because that Moab and Seir do say, Behold, the house of Judah *is* like unto all the
9 heathen; therefore behold, I *will* open the side of Moab

They shall recognise that there is one Most high, ruling in the kingdom of men (Dan. iv. 17), and that it is he who is shaping their history; possibly also that this God is Jehovah, God of Israel. The prophet does not pursue the destinies of the nations beyond this recognition, nor state what it implies. It is to be observed, however, that Israel restored, though occupying only the land west of the Jordan, enjoys profound peace on all sides. The nations that swell the army of Gog (ch. xxxviii.) are not Israel's historical neighbours, but peoples from the uttermost parts of the earth.

8—11. Prophecy against Moab.

The Moabites, like the Ammonites, were recognised by Israel as a kindred people (Gen. xix. 30). Technically the border of Moab on the N. was the Arnon, but they had pretensions to the district lying beyond this stream at least as far as the head of the Dead Sea, and these pretensions they often asserted. Practically the tribes of Reuben and Gad seem to have been unable to make good their claim to this territory by dispossessing the Moabites. The peoples appear to have mixed together, and frequently Moab is found in possession of the fertile district and the numerous cities which covered it (Mesha's Inscrip.). The country was subdued by David, and on the division of the kingdom fell as a dependency to northern Israel, to which it paid a yearly tribute of 200,000 fleeces of wool (2 Kings iii. 4), though making frequent struggles for independence (2 Kings i. 1, iii. 5, xiii. 20). Unlike the Ammonites, who continued a half-nomad people, the Moabites became more a settled nation, and appear to have attained to a considerable degree of civilization. Their language was closely allied to Hebrew, and the art of writing appears familiar as early as the beginning of the 9th century (Mesha's Inscrip.). After the intervention of the Assyrians in western Asia Moab with the neighbouring peoples became tributary to that power. Hostilities between Israel and Moab were too frequent, and along with Ammon they helped towards the downfall of Judah at the hands of the Chaldeans (2 Kings xxiv. 2; Zeph. ii. 8). Their warfare was characterized by inhuman excesses (Am. ii. 1), and the people are stigmatised as proud and boastful (Is. xv. xvi.; Zeph. ii. 8—10). Moab is referred to after the return (Ezr. ix. 1; Neh. xiii. 1; the ref. Is. xxv. 10 is of uncertain date and meaning), and as late as Dan. xi. 41.

8. *Moab and Seir*] LXX. omits *and Seir*. Ezek. elsewhere always says "mount Seir" (xxxv. 2, 3, 7, 15), and Edom, with which mount Seir is joined (xxxv. 15), has a special prophecy directed against it (*vv.* 12—14). The phrase "like unto all the nations" implies knowledge of some claim to preeminence on the part of Judah. Moab rejoices that these pretensions have received a signal refutation.

9. *open the side*] Lit. *the shoulder* of Moab, i.e. the border or territory of Moab conceived as looking towards other countries, as from the cities, from his cities *which are* on his frontiers, the glory of the country, Beth-jeshimoth, Baal-meon, and Kiriathaim, unto the men of the east with the Ammonites, and will give them in possession, that the Ammonites may not be remembered among the nations. And I will execute judgments upon Moab; and they shall know that I *am* the LORD.

Thus saith the Lord GOD; Because that Edom hath dealt

"shoulder" has hardly reference to the shape of the Moabite territory (Is. xi. 14). To open the side is to give invaders access to the country (Nah. iii. 13).

from the cities...frontiers] Perhaps: *at* the cities, at his cities in every quarter. The prep. *from* seems to indicate position, *by* or *on* the cities, i.e. where they are. Others take it in a privative sense: *stript of* the cities. The three towns named are given as examples of the glory of Moab. Beth-Jeshimoth lay at the N.E. of the head of the Dead Sea, Numb. xxxiii. 49; Josh. xii. 3, xiii. 20; it is supposed to be Suweimeh, at the mouth of the Jordan. Baal-meon, Num. xxxii. 3, 38, more fully Beth-baal-meon (Josh. xiii. 17), and in another form, Bethmeon (Jer. xlviii. 23), lay further inland, a little S. of Heshbon; supposed to be Mâ'in. Kirjathaim lay somewhat further south (Num. xxxii. 37; Josh. xiii. 19; Jer. xlviii. 1, 23); supposed to be El Kureyat.

10. Read, with full stop at *v.* 9: **Unto the children of the East will I give it for possession together with** the children of Ammon (*v.* 4). Moab and Ammon alike shall become a possession of the wandering Bedawin. The name of Ammon shall disappear from among the nations, and Moab shall be visited with severe judgments.

12—14. PROPHECY AGAINST EDOM.

The relations of Edom to Israel were changeful. Subdued by David it shook off the yoke under Jehoram (2 Kings viii. 20). Reconquered by Amaziah and Uzziah (2 Kings xiv. 7, 22), it rebelled under Ahaz (2 Kings xvi. 6; 2 Chr. xxviii. 17), and from this time was probably independent. Edomites seem to have taken part in the capture of Jerusalem by the Chaldeans, or at least to have been active in cutting off the fugitives (Ob. *v.* 10—14), and for their part in this they incurred the lasting hatred of Israel (Obad., Lam. iv. 21; Is. xxxiv. 5 *seq.*, lxiii. 1—6; Joel iii. 19; Ps. cxxxvii. 7; Mal. i. 2. Cf. Jer. xlix. 7 *seq.*). During the exile the Edomites took possession of part of the land of Israel (xxxv. 10); and in the time of the Maccabean war of independence, like the Ammonites, they shewed their hereditary enmity to Israel (1 Macc. v. 3, 35). John Hyrcanus finally subdued them and incorporated them in the state of Israel. Ultimately, like Moab and Ammon, the name of Edom disappears from history, all the three peoples being known by the general name of Arabs,—Children of the East—as Ezek. had prophesied.

against the house of Judah by taking vengeance, and hath
13 greatly offended, and revenged himself upon them; therefore
thus saith the Lord GOD; I will also stretch out mine hand
upon Edom, and will cut off man and beast from it; and I
will make it desolate from Teman; and they of Dedan shall
14 fall by the sword. And I will lay my vengeance upon Edom
by the hand of my people Israel: and they shall do in Edom
according to mine anger and according to my fury; and
they shall know my vengeance, saith the Lord GOD.
15 Thus saith the Lord GOD; Because the Philistines have
dealt by revenge, and have taken vengeance with a despite-
16 ful heart, to destroy *it for* the old hatred; therefore thus
saith the Lord GOD; Behold, I *will* stretch out mine hand
upon the Philistines, and I will cut off the Cherethims, and
17 destroy the remnant of the sea coast. And I will execute

12. *hath greatly offended*] Israel as the people of the true God was inviolable (Jer. ii. 3), except when Jehovah employed the nations to chastise it. Too often the nations exceeded their commission, cherishing purposes of their own (Is. x. 6 *seq.*), and themselves incurred guilt by their excess (Is. xlvii. 6; Zech. i. 15).

13. *they of Dedan shall fall*] **and unto** (as far as) **Dedan shall they fall.** Teman in the N. of Edom (Gen. xxxvi. 11; Am. i. 11; Jer. xlix. 7, Ob. 9), and Dedan to the south; the latter probably only bordered on Edom (Gen. x. 7; Is. xxi. 13; Jer. xxv. 23).

14. *the hand of my people*] Cf. Ob. 18, "the house of Jacob shall be a fire...and the house of Esau for stubble, and they shall burn among them and devour them." Is. xi. 14; Zeph. ii. 9.

know my vengeance] that it is I who take vengeance upon them (*v.* 4); Is. xxxiv. 8.

15—17. PROPHECY AGAINST THE PHILISTINES.

15. *with a despiteful heart*] Lit. *with despite in soul*, as *v.* 6, i.e. the deepest despite of heart, chaps. xvi. 57, xxxvi. 5.

destroy it for *the old hatred*] Rather: **to destroy with perpetual hatred**, cf. xxxv. 5; Am. i. 11. The power of the Philistines was conclusively broken by David, but references to their rancour and injuriousness when opportunity occurred run through all the literature of Israel, Am. i. 6 *seq.*; Is. ix. 12; Zeph. ii. 5; Ob. 19; Joel iii. 4; Zech. ix. 5.

16. *the Cherethims*] the **Cherethites**. The name was given to the inhabitants of the Philistine coast, Zeph. ii. 5, "woe to the inhabitants of the sea-coast, the nation of the Cherethites...the land of the Philistines." Cf. 1 Sam. xxx. 14; 2 Sam. viii. 18; Jer. xlvii. 4.

the remnant] Cf. Am. i. 8; Is. xiv. 30; Zeph. i. 4.

great vengeance upon them with furious rebukes, and they shall know that I *am* the LORD, when I shall lay my vengeance upon them.

And it came to pass in the eleventh year, in the first *day* of the month, *that* the word of the LORD came unto me, saying, Son of man, because that Tyrus hath said against Jerusalem, Aha, she is broken *that was* the gates of the

26

2

17. *with furious rebukes*] Wanting in LXX. No agents are mentioned as the destroyers of the Philistines.

CH. XXVI.—XXVIII. PROPHECY AGAINST TYRE.

The three chapters xxvi.—xxviii. are occupied with Tyre, containing threats of her destruction in various forms.

First, ch. xxvi. Literal prophecy of Tyre's destruction at the hands of Nebuchadnezzar.

Secondly, ch. xxvii. Dirge over the downfall of Tyre under the figure of a gallant ship steered into dangerous waters and suffering shipwreck.

Thirdly, ch. xxviii. The pride and fall of the prince of Tyre.

CH. XXVI. PROPHECY OF TYRE'S DESTRUCTION.

The prophecy has these divisions:

(1) *vv.* 1—6. The sin of Tyre, and therefore her downfall.
(2) *vv.* 7—14. The instrument of her destruction, Nebuchadnezzar.
(3) *vv.* 15—18. Dismay of the princes at the news of her ruin. Their sorrow and lament over her.
(4) *vv.* 19—21. Repetition and confirmation of the threat against her. She shall be plunged into eternal darkness, with those dead of old, never more to rise among the living.

1. *first day of the month*] The 11th year of Jehoiachin's captivity was that in which Jerusalem was taken. On the 9th day of the 4th month of this year the city was stormed, and on the 10th day of the 5th month it was destroyed (Jer. lii. 6, 12). The present prophecy assumes the destruction of the city (*v.* 2). The month is not stated. If the 11th year be read in xxxiii. 21 (see there), fugitives announcing the fall of the city reached the prophet on the 5th of the 10th month of that year. The prophecy is probably later than this date, and the month may be the 11th or 12th.

2. The sin of Tyre: her rejoicing over the calamity of Judah, in the hopes that it will further her interests.

Aha, she is broken] Rather: **aha! the gate (door) of the peoples is broken, it is turned unto me.** ("Door" is plur. having leaves, or by attraction of peoples.) The idea appears to be that Jerusalem or Judah was a door barring the entrance to Tyre, which being broken and turned or opened towards Tyre the nations would stream with their commerce towards her. The kingdom of Judah lay across the great commercial

people: she is turned unto me: I shall be replenished, *now*
3 she is laid waste: therefore thus saith the Lord GOD; Behold, I *am* against thee, O Tyrus, and will cause many nations to come up against thee, as the sea causeth his
4 waves to come up. And they shall destroy the walls of Tyrus, and break down her towers: I will also scrape her
5 dust from her, and make her like the top of a rock. It shall be *a place for* the spreading of nets in the midst of the sea: for I have spoken *it*, saith the Lord GOD: and it shall
6 become a spoil to the nations. And her daughters which *are* in the field shall be slain by the sword; and they shall know that I *am* the LORD.

7 For thus saith the Lord GOD; Behold, I *will* bring upon Tyrus Nebuchadrezzar king of Babylon, a king of kings,

routes from the south, and no doubt intercepted much of the merchandise that otherwise would have reached Tyre, and probably exacted custom on that which was allowed to pass. The natural sense of "door of the nations" would be door *into* the nations (Nah. iii. 13; Zech. xi. 1), and the idea would be that the door was now opened for Tyre to enter. The sense remains the same: that which stood between Tyre and the nations is removed.

3. The punishment of Tyre. Many nations shall be brought up against her (*v.* 3); her dust shall be scraped from her into the sea, leaving her a naked rock, a place for drying nets (*vv.* 4, 5), and her dependent cities on the mainland shall be laid waste (*v.* 6).

3. *the sea causeth his waves*] The comparison is powerful. It is not the succession, but the multitude and overwhelming power of the waves that is referred to.

4. *like the top of a rock*] like **a naked rock**, ch. xxiv. 7. Tyre stood upon a small island of rock separated from the mainland by a narrow strait. She shall be swept from her place, and her dust scraped into the sea, leaving her island site a bare rock, cf. *v.* 12.

5. The threat is repeated *v.* 14.

6. *daughters...in the field*] i.e. her dependent towns on the mainland, ch. xvi. 46, xxx. 18. Tyre at this time was at the head of the Phœnician confederation of cities, cf. xxvii. 8—11.

7—14. JEHOVAH'S INSTRUMENT IN TYRE'S DESTRUCTION, NEBUCHADNEZZAR.

The description is graphic: the advance of the assailant with his great army (*v.* 7); the siege with the powerful train of engines (8, 9); the assault, and capture and sack of the city (10—12), which is left a joyless ruin, a naked rock in the midst of the sea, never again to be built (13, 14).

7. The correct spelling, Nebuchadrezzar (xxix. 18, xxx. 10), the

from the north, with horses, and with chariots, and with horsemen, and companies, and much people. He shall slay 8 with the sword thy daughters in the field: and he shall make a fort against thee, and cast a mount against thee, and lift up the buckler against thee. And he shall set engines of 9 war against thy walls, and with his axes he shall break down thy towers. By reason of the abundance of his horses their 10 dust shall cover thee: thy walls shall shake at the noise of the horsemen, and of the wheels, and of the chariots, when he shall enter into thy gates, as men enter into a city wherein is made a breach. With the hoofs of his horses shall he 11 tread down all thy streets: he shall slay thy people by the sword, and thy strong garrisons shall go down to the ground. And they shall make a spoil of thy riches, and make a prey 12 of thy merchandise: and they shall break down thy walls, and

name being Nabû-Kudurri-usur, "Nebo protect the crown!" Schrader *KAT*, p. 361 (on 2 K. xxiv. 1).

a king of kings] **the** king. Ezr. vii. 12; Dan. ii. 37. Already the king of Assyria had said, "Are not my princes altogether kings?" Is. x. 8, xxxvi. 4.

and companies, and] and **a company, and.** LXX. reads: company *of* much people (very many nations), which may be the meaning of the Heb.

8. The cities and villages, dependencies of Tyre in the mainland, naturally are the first to suffer. Then the siege of the insular city itself is taken in hand. The order is precise: first the "fort" or moveable tower from which the archers shot so as to counteract the defensive efforts of the besieged (cf. iv. 2); then the "mount" or embankment, which in this case was a dam thrown across the narrow strait, in order to gain access to the walls; then the "buckler" or shield, i.e. probably the testudo or roof of shields under cover of which the besiegers operated, and finally (*v.* 9) the battering engines.

9. *engines of war*] or, engines of assault, i.e. battering engines. "Axes" is lit. swords, i.e. irons.

10 *seq.* The assault and capture and sack of the city. The description is graphic in the extreme. When the conqueror enters the dust following the march of his cavalry shall cover the city; the walls shall shake at the rushing of his chariots in the streets; and the city shall be given up to slaughter and plunder.

11. *thy strong garrisons*] thy **strong** (or, proud) **pillars.** The word is almost always used of a pillar having religious meaning, particularly the obelisk dedicated to Baal (2 Kings x. 26). The rendering "pillars of thy strength," those in which Tyre confided and thought her strength to lie (Ges.), is rather out of the way here; more naturally, her proud or majestic pillars, cf. xxiv. 21, 25.

destroy thy pleasant houses : and they shall lay thy stones
13 and thy timber and thy dust in the midst of the water. And
I will cause the noise of thy songs to cease; and the sound
14 of thy harps shall be no more heard. And I will make thee
like the top of a rock : thou shalt be *a place* to spread nets
upon; thou shalt be built no more: for I the LORD have
spoken *it*, saith the Lord GOD.
15 Thus saith the Lord GOD to Tyrus; Shall not the isles
shake at the sound of thy fall, when the wounded cry, when
16 the slaughter is made in the midst of thee? Then all the
princes of the sea shall come down from their thrones, and
lay away their robes, and put off their broidered garments:
they shall clothe themselves with trembling; they shall sit
upon the ground, and shall tremble at every moment, and
17 be astonished at thee. And they shall take up a lamentation for thee, and say to thee, How art thou destroyed, *that
wast* inhabited of seafaring men, the renowned city, which
was strong in the sea, she and her inhabitants, which cause
18 their terror *to be* on all that haunt it. Now shall the isles

14. *the top of a rock*] a naked rock, *v.* 4.

15—18. COMMOTION AMONG THE PRINCES OF THE SEA CAUSED
BY HER FALL; THEY MOURN AND TAKE UP A LAMENT OVER
TYRE (17, 18).

15. *the isles shake*] the coast-lands, the island-like countries on the seaboard.
the sound of thy fall] might mean "at the report of thy fall," but here by a strong hyperbole the prophet appears to represent the crash of the city's fall and the cries of the wounded as being heard in the neighbouring coasts, ch. xxvii. 28, xxxi. 16; cf. Jer. xlix. 21.

16. In token of mourning the princes of the sea, the rulers of the principalities and cities on all sea-coasts, shall descend from their thrones, lay aside their royal robes and sit on the ground (Lam. ii. 10).
clothe themselves] Or, *be clothed*, i.e. be enveloped in, be wholly tremblings; cf. vii. 27.

17, 18. Lament of the princes over Tyre.
17. *of seafaring men*] lit. inhabited *from the seas.*
cause their terror] Rather: caused. A.V. "all that haunt it" has taken the ref. to be to the sea, which is almost necessary, though the present text is literally *all her inhabitants,* referring to the city. The phrase "caused their terror to be" occurs several times in ch. xxxii. 17 *seq.* with a different construction (*b* for *l*), but the sense here can hardly be different, viz., made their terror felt. To say, however,

tremble *in* the day of thy fall; yea, the isles that *are* in the sea shall be troubled at thy departure. For thus saith the 19 Lord GOD; When I shall make thee a desolate city, like the cities that are not inhabited; when *I* shall bring up the 20 deep upon thee, and great waters shall cover thee; when I shall bring thee down with them that descend into the pit, with the people of old time, and shall set thee in the low

that Tyre and her inhabitants made their terror felt by all her inhabitants is very unnatural. The pronoun must refer to the "seas." The phrase "inhabited from the seas" is also peculiar; "inhabited" means having inhabitants, not drawing inhabitants.

18. *the isles*] See on *v.* 15. The form of plur. nowhere else occurs, and appears to be adopted in order to gain a parallelism to "isles" (ordinary form) in the next clause. The phrase "at thy departure," lit. *outgoing* is strange; but might have a parallel Ps. cxliv. 14.

The elegy seems confined to *v.* 17, but probably through explanatory amplifications that have crept into the text, *v.* 18 has also been drawn into it. LXX. reads in a shorter form:

17. How art thou destroyed from the sea—the renowned city!
   She that brought her terror—on all her inhabitants.
18. And the isles shall be terrified—at the day of thy fall.

v. 18 can hardly refer to the *memory* of Tyre's fall, but to the fall itself, xxvii. 27 (xxxii. 10), which being represented as future, is unsuitable to the dirge in the mouth of the princes. The verse hardly belongs to the dirge but forms the transition to the next strophe, *vv.* 19—21. In the phrase "all her inhabitants" it seems necessary with A.V. (Ew.) to refer "her" to the sea, or with Corn. to alter the pronoun in order to gain this sense.

19. Tyre shall be overwhelmed in the great waters, and brought down to the pit, with them dead from of old; she shall never be inhabited nor found any more.

20. *when I shall bring*] Rather in connexion with *v.* 19: when I shall make thee a desolate city…**then I shall bring thee down.** The prophet regards Tyre's sinking beneath the waters as her entrance upon the descent into the pit, the place of the dead, just as frequently elsewhere (ch. xxxii.) he makes the grave the entrance into the underworld of the dead. Cf. Is. xiv. 11, 19.

that descend into the pit] Rather: **them that are gone down into the pit, unto** the people. The common phrase "they that go down to the pit" should be rendered: *that are gone down* (past). Ezek. always says *with* them that are gone down, xxviii. 8, xxxi. 14: cf. Is. xiv. 19, xxxviii. 18.

The "people of old time" are those dead from of old, xxxii. 27; Lam. iii. 6; Ps. cxliii. 3; hardly with more definite ref. to the Flood, Job xxii. 15.

low parts of the earth] the **nether parts**, i.e. in the underworld of

parts of the earth, in places desolate of old, with them that go down to the pit, that thou be not inhabited; and I shall 21 set glory in the land of the living; I will make thee a terror, and thou *shalt be* no *more:* though thou be sought for, yet shalt thou never be found again, saith the Lord GOD.

the dead (xxxi. 14, xxxii. 18—24; Lam. iii. 55; Ps. lxiii. 9), which was held to be situated in the bowels of the earth or under the earth.

in places desolate of old] According to the textual tradition (Baer, *Ezek.*) the true reading is *like* places..., so LXX., Vulg. The prophet gives Tyre a personality; when buried under the sea she goes down into the abode of the dead, and possibly he regards the "places desolate of old" as also gone down and gathered in the underworld. For "that go down," *that are gone down.*

and I shall set glory] Such an antithesis is entirely unnatural; something further must be said of Tyre in continuation of "thou shalt not be inhabited." Either: *nor set* (thy) *glory*, (reading 2 fem., with final *y* otiose), a phrase, however, nowhere else occurring; or else the reading presumably before LXX. must be accepted: **nor arise** (stand forth) **in the land of the living** (tithyaççebi).

21. *make thee a terror*] lit., terrors or *destructions*—I will utterly destroy thee, xxvii. 36, xxviii. 19; cf. Ps. lxxiii. 19. On "make" cf. xvi. 38.

The passage xxix. 17—21 states that Nebuchadnezzar received no adequate reward for the service against Tyre which he served for Jehovah. History records his thirteen years' siege of Tyre, but is silent as to the issue of it. It is not known (1) whether he took the city, or (2) whether it capitulated, or (3) whether he retired from it. On the whole the second supposition may be most probable. At any rate neither the king nor his army received wages for his service. The prophecy was not literally fulfilled. Now

1. All prophecy is moral, is based on moral considerations. What the prophet aims his threats against is not the prosperity of Tyre, but its pride of heart, which was rebellion against Jehovah, God over all. The humiliation of Tyre was morally as good as its ruin, in so far as it shewed that there were higher forces in the world than itself.

2. Prophecy is always ideal in its delineations. Its threats and promises are alike hyperbolical whether they concern Israel or the nations. And in regard to fulfilment the same general principles must be applied to all prophecies, those of redemption and those of calamity alike. The former are not fulfilled at once, nor at all literally, neither need we expect immediate or literal fulfilment of the latter. At the same time in regard to both it must be maintained that the prophets *imagined* the fulfilment as they describe it. This, however, is part of their idealism; the moral element is always the main thing in their prophecies. What they predict is the exhibition of Jehovah's moral rule of the world; the *form* in which they clothe this exhibition may not be quite that given in history.

The word of the LORD came again unto me, saying, Now, 27 thou son of man, take up a lamentation for Tyrus; and say 2 unto Tyrus, O thou that art situate at the entry of the sea, 3 *which art* a merchant of the people for many isles, Thus saith the Lord GOD; O Tyrus, thou hast said, I *am* of perfect beauty. Thy borders *are* in the midst of the seas, 4 thy builders have perfected thy beauty. They have made 5 all thy *ship* boards of fir trees of Senir: they have taken

CH. XXVII. DIRGE OVER THE DOWNFALL OF TYRE.

The lament represents Tyre under the figure of a gallant, richly-laden ship, steered by her pilots into dangerous waters and suffering shipwreck. The passage has three main divisions:
(1) *vv.* 1—11. The ship, her timbers, furnishings and manning.
(2) *vv.* 12—25. The wares and merchandise with which the nations lade her.
(3) *vv.* 26—36. Her shipwreck: consternation of seafaring men (*vv.* 26—31); their lament over her (*vv.* 32—36).

vv. 1—11. TYRE AS A GALLANT SHIP.

2. For the phrase "take up a lamentation" cf. xix. 1, xxvi. 17, xxviii. 12, xxxii. 2. The word is technical for the dirge.

3. *entry of the sea*] lit. *entries*, reference possibly being to the two harbours of Tyre, one of which was to the N.-E. of the island, called the Sidonian harbour, because looking towards Sidon; and the other on the S. or S.-E. of the island, the exact position of which is uncertain owing to the silting which has taken place. See plate in Rawlinson, *Phœnicia*, p. 71.

people for many isles] **peoples unto many coasts**, or, countries, cf. *vv.* 3, 6, 15. Her traffic with the peoples extended to many and distant coastlands.

4. *borders...midst of the seas*] lit. *heart* of the seas, a phrase which appears to mean not "far out at sea," but, in the deep waters of the sea, ch. xxviii. 2, 8; Ex. xv. 8; Jon. ii. 3; Ps. xlvi. 2. The term "borders" seems to mean station, moorings (*v.* 25). The proud ship was conscious of her beauty. The ship is a figure for the maritime city, the mistress of trade, built upon an ocean rock, as if moored in the sea. The city was without doubt beautiful (ch. xxviii. 12); a similar phrase is used of Jerusalem, Ps. l. 2 (Ps. xlviii. 2); Lam. ii. 15.

vv. 5, 6 the ship's timbers.

made thy ship *boards*] **built thy planks**. The word is *dual*, referring to the two ribs of the ship, corresponding to one another.

fir trees of Senir] Or, *cypresses*. The tree is mentioned as furnishing, along with the cedar, the principal material for building the Temple, 1 Kings v. 8. Senir was the Amorite name of Hermon, which the Sidonians called Sirion (Deut. iii. 9). According to Schrader (*KAT*. on Deut. iii. 9; 1 Kings v. 13) both names were used by the

6 cedars from Lebanon to make masts for thee. *Of* the oaks of Bashan have they made thine oars; the company of the Ashurites have made thy benches *of* ivory, *brought* out of the
7 isles of Chittim. Fine linen with broidered work from Egypt was that which thou spreadest forth to be thy sail; blue and purple from the isles of Elishah was that which covered
8 thee. The inhabitants of Zidon and Arvad were thy mariners: thy wise *men*, O Tyrus, *that* were in thee, *were*

Assyrians. The name Hermon possibly signifies "sacred" mountain, being due to its ancient sanctuary. Senir, and Sirion, is supposed to mean "coat of mail."

On "mast" cf. Is. xxxiii. 23. Whether an actual cedar was ever used to be the mast of "some great ammiral" may be uncertain; the prophet, though more exact than most prophets, is also a poet.

6. The oars of the great ship were made of oaks of Bashan; cf. Is. ii. 13; Zech. xi. 2. The term "oars" occurs in another form, *v.* 27, but probably with no difference of meaning. The rest of *v.* 6 should read: **thy deck they made of ivory** (inlaid) **in sherbin wood from the isles of Chittim** (the words bath teasshur should no doubt be read *bitheasshur*, in theasshur). This tree is mentioned as growing in Lebanon, Is. xli. 19, lx. 13; it is usually considered to be the tree called in Arabic sherbīn, a species of cedar. Others contend for box or larch. The term "deck" is literally "board," e.g. of the boards of the sanctuary, Ex. xxvi. 15 *seq.* Chittim is Cyprus, called after the town Kition (Larnaka), but probably the name embraced the coasts of Asia Minor and Greece or perhaps even of Italy (Dan. xi. 30; 1 Macc. i. 1, viii. 5).

7. The rigging and furnishing of the ship. Her sail (ancient ships usually had but one) was embroidered byssus, fine linen, out of Egypt (xvi. 10). Render: **broidered byssus of Egypt was thy sail, to serve to thee for a pennon.** The flag proper seems not to have been used in ancient navigation, its purpose was served by the sail, as for example at the battle of Actium the ship of Antony was distinguished by its purple sail. The word seems to mean sail, Is. xxxiii. 23. On "broidered" cf. ch. xvi. 10, 13, 18.

that which covered thee] lit. *thy covering* (in Is. xiv. 11 a coverlet, cf. Is. xxiii. 18), either an awning, or more probably a cabin, the sides and roof of which were of the fine stuffs named.

the isles of Elishah] In Gen. x. 4 Elishah is one of the sons of Javan, i.e. Ionia or Grecian Asia. The Targ. renders "country of Italy." Ges. combines the name with Elis, and understands the Peloponnesus in general, which was certainly noted for the dyes referred to in the verse.

8 *seq.* The manning of the ship. The inhabitants of Sidon and Arvad were her rowers, and her own wise men her steersmen.

thy mariners] **rowers.** Sidon lay to the N. of Tyre, about half way between it and Beirut, and was probably the oldest Phœnician town, Tyre being a colony. Sidon is the firstborn of Canaan (Gen. x. 15), and

thy pilots. The ancients of Gebal and the wise *men* thereof 9
were in thee thy calkers: all the ships of the sea with their
mariners were in thee to occupy thy merchandise. They 10
of Persia and of Lud and of Phut were in thine army, thy
men of war: they hanged the shield and helmet in thee;

is called Great Sidon in Josh. xix. 28. It is frequently referred to in Homer (e.g. *Il.* 7. 290), who does not mention Tyre. At a later time Tyre eclipsed her mother in power and wealth. Arvad (Aradus) lay greatly more to the N. It was built on a small island, over two miles from the mainland, and, being without natural harbours, piers were laboriously constructed of huge blocks of stone, 16 feet long by 7 broad, quarried on the island. It was dependent for water upon the mainland, but when its supply was cut off recourse was had to a powerful spring of fresh water which was known to rise under the sea in the channel between the town and the mainland. This spring was isolated and the water brought by a tube to the surface. The spring is said still to exist. Arvad, now Ruwād, or, Ruweideh, is often mentioned in the Assyrian Annals. Tiglath-pileser I. (c. 1100) embarked on ships of Arvad and sailed out into "the great sea," Del., *Parad.* p. 281 (the same expression is used by another king of himself, Schrader, *KAT.* p. 184, on 1 K. v. 13, cf. p. 104). See chart of Arvad, Rawl., *Phœn.* p. 74.

9. *ancients of Gebal*] The **elders**, a title of honour or office, the magistrates. Probably also the "wise men thereof" is a semi-official title (cf. *v.* 8). The power of Tyre was exerted over all her dependencies (xxvi. 17), in which men of the highest position entered all ranks of her service. Gebal (the classical Byblos, now Jubeil) is situated not far from the river Adonis (Ibrahim) somewhat over 20 miles N. of Beirut (Josh. xiii. 5; 1 Kings v. 18, R.V.). The town was devoted to the worship of Beltis (Astarte) and Adonis, cf. on ch. viii. 14. The name appears in the Assyrian inscriptions, Del., *Parad.* p. 283.

thy calkers] Marg. stoppers of chinks, carpenters.

to occupy thy merchandise] **to handle thy wares.** The representation is that the great ship was attended on by all the ships of the sea with their sailors, who served her and delivered her wares to her, or were occupied about them (*v.* 27).

10. Her men of war.

Her mercenaries were drawn from all quarters of the world. The people called here "they of Persia" appears along with Cush and Phut, African peoples, in the army of Gog, ch. xxxviii. 5, in which, however, northern nations as Gomer and Togarmah are also mustered. The host of Gog includes the nations lying on the outskirts of the known world, and Persia might be named among them, though the first certain mention of that country is in Ezr. iv. 5, ix. 9, &c. Others have thought here of some African people. Lud is named, ch. xxx. 5, along with Cush and Phut, as allies of Egypt (Jer. xlvi. 9); and in Gen. x. 13 Ludim is the firstborn of Mizraim (Egypt). In Is. lxvi. 19 Lud is named after Tarshish, and probably some people lying on the African coast, W. of Egypt, is referred to. Phut (Gen. x. 6) is son of Ham,

11 **they set forth thy comeliness.** The men of Arvad with thine army *were* upon thy walls round about, and the Gammadims were in thy towers: they hanged their shields upon thy walls round about; they have made thy beauty perfect.

and brother of Cush (Ethiopia), Mizraim (Egypt) and Canaan (Phœnicia). In Ez. xxx. 5 (Jer. xlvi. 9; Nah. iii. 9) the people is an ally of Egypt. LXX. renders Lybians. The inhabitants of western Egypt, or those on its western border may be referred to.

they hanged the shield] The great ship is still spoken of. A figure of a ship so adorned and dressed with weapons hung on its sides is given in Layard, *Nineveh*, II. p. 388. The practice of hanging weapons on buildings was not unknown in Israel, Song iv. 4 (1 Macc. iv. 57).

11. *with thine army*] It is scarcely possible to render: *men of Arvad, they were* thine army. Some proper name seems required: the men of Arvad and of... Cornill conjectures Hethlon (xlvii. 15, xlviii. 1), others, Cilicia.

the Gammadims] A proper name is certainly to be expected, but no place, Gammad, is known. Some have suggested "they of Gomer," but an adj. is not formed from Gomer; Corn., Zemarites, Gen. x. 18. Others take the word as an appellative: *brave warriors*.

12—25. THE MARKET OF TYRE.

Several things are to be observed in this passage: 1. The representation is not that Tyre is traded with by the nations, though this is the fact lying under the figures employed. The nations are not customers of Tyre. Tyre neither buys nor sells, nor does she exchange one article for another. The nations are *her* merchants, who bring to her wares from every land; or they are her dependents, and the merchandise which they bring is a tribute which they render her (*v.* 15). They are her subjects, ministering to her luxury, bringing wares to her, and enriching her. The counterpart to this idea is that she enriches many peoples by bestowing her wealth upon them (*v.* 33). 2. The passage is artistic. Two words are employed for "to trade," "to be a merchant." The words have little difference of sense and are generally used alternately, e.g. one word in *vv.* 12, 15, 16, 18, 21, the other in *vv.* 13, 15, 17, 20, 22 *seq*. Two words also are used in the sense of *wares* or goods, though hardly differing in meaning. These also are used alternately so as to diversify the phraseology, e.g. the one in *vv.* 12, 14, 16, 18, 22, the other in *vv.* 13 (15), 17, 19, with other variants of the same sense. Gesen. attributed various senses to these words, as: 1, traffic, trading, 2, fair, market-place, and 3, gain, wealth. The words do not appear to differ in meaning, and neither of the two probably has any other sense than the general one of wares. 3. Again, the language is diversified by the adoption of a variety of constructions. The word "give," which receives an extraordinary extension of usage in Ez. and in later Heb. in general (cf. its use in the Apocalypse), is employed in the sense of put, bring, render, &c. That it ever means to "sell" (Ges.) is without evidence. The various constructions employed are seen in *vv.* 12, 22 (acc.

vv. 12—14.] EZEKIEL, XXVII. 195

Tarshish *was* thy merchant by reason of the multitude of all 12
kind of riches; with silver, iron, tin, and lead, they traded
in thy fairs. Javan, Tubal, and Meshech, they *were* thy 13
merchants: they traded the persons of men and vessels of
brass in thy market. They of the house of Togarmah 14

and prep. *b*, cf. *vv.* 13, 17); in *vv.* 16, 18 (double prep. *b*), and in *v.* 14 (double accus.). These different constructions probably all express the same general meaning.

There is much uncertainty in the text, e.g. for "sons of Dedan," *v.* 15, LXX. reads, sons of the Rhodians, and for Aram (Syria) *v.* 16, Syriac reads Edom (so LXX. "man"), in both cases by interchange of the similar letters *d* and *r*. *V.* 19 is certainly out of order, and *v.* 24 exceedingly obscure. Owing to these obscurities the precise order followed in the enumeration of the nations is involved in some uncertainty. 1. *vv.* 12—14, the prophet names the nations lying in the widest circle around Tyre, beginning with the furthest west, Tarshish (Spain), and pursuing a line along the north, Javan (Ionia), Tubal (N. of Asia Minor), and Togarmah (Armenia). 2. If Rhodians be read in *v.* 15, a narrower circle of the Mediterranean coasts would be described. 3. *vv.* 16—19, if Edom be read for Aram, the line traced is from S. to N., along the eastern trade route, Edom, Judah, Damascus. 4. In *v.* 19 Uzal seems certainly to be the name of a place (A.V. "going to and fro") in the S. of Arabia, the other names are Arabian, Dedan, Kedar, Sheba and Raamah. 5. The names in *v.* 23 *seq.* are more obscure, and it is not certain whether this be the previous line carried further N. or a new line.

12. The name Tarshish (Tartessus) was given to the district of country lying outside the Straits of Gibraltar on the lower Baetis, the Guadalquiver (Wadi el Kebīr, great river).

with silver...in thy fairs] Rather apparently: **silver...they brought as thy wares.** There is no evidence that the word means "fairs;" in *vv.* 27, 34 the things so named fall into the waters of the sea. The representation is that all things brought to Tyre were hers, the nations offered them to her as tribute (*v.* 15). Spain was famous for the metals mentioned; cf. for silver, Jer. x. 9. Probably Tarshish served as an entrepôt for such products found further north, as in the Cassiterides (Scilly Islands) and Cornwall.

13. These three countries, Javan, Tubal and Meshech are usually named together, Gen. x. 2; Ezek. xxxii. 26, xxxviii. 2, xxxix. 1; Is. lxvi. 19. The first is the Ionians, the Greeks of Asia Minor, and the two last have usually been identified with the Moschi and Tibareni, lying to the S. and S.E. of the Black Sea. Copper and "souls of men" i.e. slaves, form the contribution of these countries. That Javan traded in slaves appears from Joel iv. 6; cf. Am. i. 6, 9.

they traded...in thy market] **they brought as thy wares souls of men**, &c. The nations are the servants of Tyre, and what they bring is *her* wares.

14. *house of Togarmah*] Usually supposed to be Armenia or part of it. Togarmah lay in the extreme N. of the world known to the

13—2

traded in thy fairs with horses and horsemen and mules.
15 The men of Dedan *were* thy merchants; many isles *were* the merchandise of thine hand: they brought thee *for* a
16 present horns of ivory and ebeny. Syria *was* thy merchant by reason of the multitude of the wares of thy making: they

prophet, and the people appears in the army of Gog with other nations from the ends of the earth (ch. xxxviii. 6; cf. Gen. x. 2). Others think of Phrygia or Cappadocia. All these countries were noted for breeding horses.

traded in thy fairs with horses] **brought as thy wares**, or, commodities, **horses**, &c. *Horsemen* can hardly have been an article of traffic; if the word be original war horses may be intended; 2 Sam. i. 6. The ancients did not use the horse for labour. LXX. omits *mules*, a somewhat similar word, and possibly (as Corn. conjectures) only two words should be read: horses and mules.

15. *men of Dedan*] lit. sons of Dedan; LXX. sons of *the Rhodians* (*r* being read for *d*, as often). Dedan occurs again *v.* 20, in connexion with Arabian tribes, and in xxv. 13 it appears to be placed S. of Edom, being either part of that country or bordering on it (cf. Jer. xlix. 8, xxv. 23; Is. xxi. 13). Here, however, Dedan is connected with coast lands and must be another. Hence it has usually been placed on the Persian Gulf. Ivory and ebony, the articles in which it traded, might be Indian products. On the other hand the Phœnicians certainly had colonies in Rhodes; and if Rhodians were the true reading the "isles" would be the coasts of the Mediterranean.

merchandise of thine hand] If "merchandise" be the right reading the abstract term is used for "merchants." The phrase "of thy hand" means under thee, doing thy service, cf. *v.* 21.

horns of ivory] Tusks of elephants, so called from their resemblance to horns. Ebony, the other article referred to, was brought from India and Ethiopia. The African ebony was most esteemed. If Rhodians be read reference would be to the traffic between Phœnicia and the interior of Africa, the intermediaries of which were Rhodes and the sea-coasts of the Mediterranean. Rawlin. (*Phœnicia*, p. 287) mentions that many objects in ivory have been found in Cyprus.

brought thee for *a present.* Rather: **horns of ivory...they rendered to thee as tribute**, lit. rendered as thy tribute. Tyre is the mistress to whom the nations are subject, and the merchandise they bring is a tribute which they render to her.

16. For Syria (Aram) the Syr. reads Edom, and so in effect LXX. (interchange of *d* and *r* as *v.* 15). If Edom be read the line pursued would be from S. to N., Edom, *v.* 16, Judah, *v.* 17, Damascus, *v.* 18. The verse is otherwise peculiar in beginning with a precious stone, then passing on to stuffs and ending with precious stones.

wares of thy making] Rather; **by reason of the multitude of thy works**, i.e. not those wrought by Tyre, but those which the nations wrought and brought to her, all of which are considered hers.

occupied in thy fairs with emeralds, purple, and broidered work, and fine linen, and coral, and agate. Judah, and the 17 land of Israel, they *were* thy merchants: they traded in thy market wheat of Minnith, and Pannag, and honey, and oil, and balm. Damascus *was* thy merchant in the multitude 18 of the wares of thy making, for the multitude of all riches; in the wine of Helbon, and white wool. Dan also and 19 Javan going to and fro occupied in thy fairs: bright iron,

occupied in thy fairs] Rather: **emeralds...they brought as thy wares.** The "emerald" according to others is the carbuncle. "Coral" may be "pearls." The two things may have been confused; both were fished in the Persian Gulf. The "agate" may be the ruby. The precious stones might seem in favour of Edom, but the fine linen is more naturally the Syrian byssus. LXX. omits all the textile fabrics with the exception of broidered work; and the text must be held uncertain.

17. Judah and the land of Israel furnished Tyre with wheat, honey, oil and balsam.

traded in thy market wheat] **they brought as thy wares wheat.** Minnith is supposed to be the Ammonitish place of that name (Judg. xi. 33). There is something unnatural, however, in Judah and Israel bringing an Ammonitish product to Tyre. It is their own productions that the nations bring, or at least the articles are assumed to be their own. LXX. renders "ointments;" and Corn. conjectures "spices" (Gen. xliii. 11; Is. xxxix. 2; 2 Kings xx. 13). The term "pannag" is otherwise unknown; R.V. marg. suggests a kind of confection (Targ.), while Corn. conjectures "wax" (donag). The "honey" referred to is no doubt that of bees, not grape honey. The "balm" mentioned, a product of Gilead (Jer. viii. 22), and of Palestine (Gen. xliii. 11), was not the genuine balm, which was peculiar to Arabia, but an odoriferous resin (LXX. Vulg.) exuding from the mastix tree (Pistaccia lentiscus).

18. *wares of thy making*] **the multitude of thy works,** i.e. the works done for Tyre, all of which are hers.

multitude of all riches] or, **because of every kind of riches.**

wine of Helbon] This is repeatedly mentioned as a choice wine in the Assyrian inscriptions (Schrad. *KAT.* p. 425). The Persian kings also preferred it on their table. Cf. Hos. xiv. 7, Song viii. 11. The place is identified with Chalbûn, N.E. of Damascus.

white wool] Possibly, wool of *Zachar*, though a place of this name is unknown.

19. *Dan also and Javan*] This is certainly incorrect; none of the verses begins with *and* or also, and any reference to Dan is out of the question. The word rendered "going to and fro" was translated by Ges. "spun," i.e. *yarn* (and so R.V.): *Wedan and Javan brought as thy wares yarn*. The word is more probably a proper name and to be rendered *from Uzal*. Uzal (Gen. x. 27) is supposed to be

20 cassia, and calamus, were in thy market. Dedan *was* thy
21 merchant in precious clothes for chariots. Arabia, and all
the princes of Kedar, they occupied with thee in lambs, and
22 rams, and goats: in these *were they* thy merchants. The
merchants of Sheba and Raamah, they *were* thy merchants:
they occupied in thy fairs with chief of all spices, and with
23 all precious stones, and gold. Haran, and Canneh, and

identical with San'āa, the capital of Yemen in S. Arabia. LXX.
omits *wedan* and for Javan reads "wine" (a similar word). The
text is probably in disorder. In all other cases the phrase "brought
as thy wares" ends the verse, and possibly the first words of *v.* 19
should be attached to *v.* 18. So LXX. which reads *v.* 19, "from Uzal
(Azel) came wrought-iron" &c. Corn. follows LXX., supplying all
the words after Helbon out of the Assyrian wine lists: wine of Helbon
and Zimin and Arnaban they brought to thy market. From Uzal
came wrought iron &c. As the verse stands it may read: "Wedan and
Javan of Uzal furnished thy wares; bright iron, cassia and calamus
were among thy goods"—though the most serious objections occur to
the rendering. The "bright iron" may refer to sword blades, for
which Yemen was famous. The calamus or sweet cane (Jer. vi. 20;
Is. xliii. 24) supplied one of the ingredients of the holy oil for anointing
the priests (Ex. xxx. 23, 24), and so did the cassia.

20. On Dedan cf. *v.* 15; Gen. xxv. 3; Ezek. xxv. 13.
precious clothes for chariots] Or, **saddle cloths for riding.**

21. *occupied with thee*] Lit. *were the merchants of thy hand*, i.e.
serving thee. Cf. Is. lx. 7, "all the flocks of Kedar shall be gathered
unto thee." The Arab nomads were rich in flocks. Kedar (Gen.
xxv. 13, second son of Ishmael) was an important people toward the
N. of Arabia. In Is. lx. 7 they are named along with the Naba-
theans; in Jer. xlix. 28 they are threatened with destruction by
Nebuchadnezzar, as they were threatened at an earlier time with an
attack from the Assyrians (Is. xxi. 16). Outside of scripture they are
mentioned first in the inscriptions of Assurbanipal (667—626 B.C.),
where they are represented as dwelling between the gulf of Akaba
and Babylon. Cf. the ref. Jer. ii. 10.

22. *merchants of Sheba*] The abode of this people was in the S.W.
of Arabia, the ruins of their capital Marib still remain, six days' journey
E. of San'āa, the capital of Yemen. Their caravans (Job vi. 19) traded
to Syria and other countries with gold, precious stones and aromatics
(1 Kings x. 2, 10; Is. lx. 6; Jer. vi. 20; Ps. lxxii. 10, 15).

occupied in thy fairs] **they brought chief of all spices...as thy
wares.** Raamah was son of Cush and father of Sheba and Dedan
(Gen. x. 7). Raamah probably lay on the Persian Gulf.

23. The places named may be regarded as an extension of the
line from S. to N. in *vv.* 19—22, though the names are given rather
in the order W. to E. Harran in Mesopotamia, two days' journey
S.E. of Edessa, on a branch of the Euphrates, was a sacred city and

Eden, the merchants of Sheba, Asshur, *and* Chilmad, *were* thy merchants. These *were* thy merchants in all sorts of 24 things, in blue clothes, and broidered work, and in chests of rich apparel, bound with cords, and made of cedar,

place of pilgrimage, and also an emporium of trade. The defeat of Crassus by the Parthians took place there. Canneh may be Calneh (Gen. x. 10; Am. vi. 2), otherwise Calno (Is. x. 9), a city in Babylonia. Its site has not been identified. Von Gutschmidt (*Ency. Brit.*, art. Phœnicia) identifies Canneh with Cænæ. Eden, spelled somewhat differently from the Eden of Paradise, is elsewhere named in connexion with Haran, Is. xxxvii. 12 (2 Kings xix. 12), and said to be in Telassar (Tel Asshur).

the merchants of Sheba] It is strange that these should be mentioned again (v. 22). For "Eden...Sheba" LXX. reads: *these were thy merchants*, i.e. Haran and Canneh. It has been supposed that the merchants of Sheba frequented the fairs of Haran and thence made their way westward along the trade route to Phenicia.

Asshur and *Chilmad*] LXX. reads *and* between the words. Asshur if taken in its usual sense would be Assyria. Others think of Sura, or Essurieh, on the Euphrates. G. Smith conjectured that Chilmad was Kalwâdha near Bagdad. LXX. renders Charman, which suggests Caramania. The rendering: "Asshur was as thine apprentice in traffic" (Hitz. Corn.), besides being a conceit, misses the whole idea of the chapter.

24. The first half of the verse may read: **These were thy merchants with splendid apparel, cloaks of purple and broidered work.** The second half is obscure owing to the occurrence of some words not found elsewhere.

in chests of rich apparel] The term rendered "chests" occurs Esth. iii. 9, iv. 7 in the sense of "treasures," from root to hide, lay up, a sense common to all the dialects. In Eth. it means to wind in graveclothes for purposes of burial, but has no special reference to clothing or textile fabrics. The sense "chests" is without evidence. A term virtually the same as that rendered "rich apparel" occurs in Assyrian of stuffs for clothing (Schr. *KAT.* pp. 213—16); and a similar word is used of the night heavens, according to Jensen (*Babylonian Cosmog.* p. 6 *seq.*) from the mixed colour, blue-gray. It appears used of fabrics woven of differently coloured materials.

bound with cords] This would refer to the "chests," but this is not probable. More likely: **with cords twined and durable**, the "cords" themselves being the article of commerce. "Cords" can hardly be thread. The rendering "made of cedar" is altogether unlikely, some sense like strong, firm or durable is more probable. The cords were probably of wool as well as of flax, of divers colours, and used for fastening hangings or other purposes, Est. i. 6. The Babylonian weaving was very celebrated, cf. xvi. 10, xxiii. 6, also the "Babylonish garment," Josh. vii. 21.

25 among thy merchandise. The ships of Tarshish did sing of thee *in* thy market: and thou wast replenished, and made 26 very glorious in the midst of the seas. Thy rowers have brought thee into great waters: the east wind hath broken 27 thee in the midst of the seas. Thy riches, and thy fairs, thy merchandise, thy mariners, and thy pilots, thy calkers, and the occupiers of thy merchandise, and all thy men of war, that *are* in thee, and in all thy company which *is* in the midst of thee, shall fall into the midst of the seas in the day 28 of thy ruin. The suburbs shall shake at the sound of the

25. The "ships of Tarshish" here are deep-sea ships, great ships trading to the most distant coasts, Is. ii. 16; Ps. xlviii. 7.

did sing of thee] For this Ges. suggested "were thy caravans" from a verb signifying to travel (Is. lvii. 9). The camel has been called the ship of the desert, but conversely to call an east indiaman a caravan is too brilliant for the prophet. Probably by a slight change of reading: the ships of Tarshish *did serve thee with* (in) thy wares (*vv.* 13, 17 &c.), cf. Is. lx. 9, 10, and above *v*. 9. So Aquila (Field).

made very glorious] Rather: and **wast heavily laden**. The figure of a mistress served by all nations, who bring wares and riches to her from all lands, passes here again into the idea of the vessel deeply laden with cargo, and therefore more easily shipwrecked and broken in dangerous waters.

26—31. THE VESSEL STEERED BY HER PILOTS INTO DANGEROUS WATERS, IS SHIPWRECKED AND HER CARGO AND CREW CAST INTO THE SEA (*vv*. 26, 27). DISMAY AND LAMENTATION OF ALL SEAFARING MEN (*vv*. 28—31).

26. The allegory does not need interpretation. How far her statesmen precipitated the fall of Tyre is unknown; it was the east-wind that broke her in the heart of the sea—a force above that of men (Ps. xlviii. 7).

27. *and thy fairs*] thy **wares**. The verse is interesting for the enumeration which it gives both of the crew and cargo. The cargo is described in three words: riches, wares and merchandise—the last two words meaning the same thing virtually, though differing in shade of idea. The verse shews that any such rendering as "fair," "market" for these terms cannot be sustained, the things are here said to fall into the heart of the seas, cf. *vv*. 33, 34. The crew consists of (1) sailors, (2) pilots, (3) calkers (carpenters), (4) handlers of the wares, and (5) men of war.

and in all thy company] **even all thy.**

28. *the suburbs*] According to tradition (Baer, *Ezek*.) the term here is differently pointed from that rendered "suburbs," e.g. ch. xlv. 2. The latter term means the free space surrounding a city or building. If the sense of the present word were the same reference would be to

cry of thy pilots. And all that handle the oar, the mariners, 29 *and* all the pilots of the sea, shall come down from their ships, they shall stand upon the land; and shall cause their 30 voice to be heard against thee, and shall cry bitterly, and shall cast up dust upon their heads, they shall wallow themselves in the ashes: and they shall make themselves utterly 31 bald for thee, and gird them with sackcloth, and they shall weep for thee with bitterness of heart *and* bitter wailing. And in their wailing they shall take up a lamentation for 32 thee, and lament over thee, *saying*, What *city is* like Tyrus, like the destroyed in the midst of the sea? When thy wares 33 went forth out of the seas, thou filledst many people; thou didst enrich the kings of the earth with the multitude of thy riches and of thy merchandise. *In* the time when *thou shalt* 34 *be* broken by the seas in the depths of the waters, thy merchandise and all thy company in the midst of thee shall fall. All the inhabitants of the isles shall be astonished 35 at thee, and their kings shall be sore afraid, they shall be troubled *in their* countenance. The merchants among the 36

the lands or coasts in the vicinity of Tyre, a sense far from natural. Jerome conjectured "fleets" (Ew.). In Is. lvii. 20 the verb describes the violent action of the waters of the sea (Am. viii. 8), and A. V. marg. suggests *waves* here—the waves shall quake at the cry of thy pilots.

29. All seafaring men raise a lamentation over the shipwreck of the gallant vessel.

30. *heard against thee*] **over** thee. On first sign of sorrow cf. Job ii. 12, and on second Jer. vi. 26; Mic. i. 10; Est. iv. 1.

31. For these signs of grief cf. ch. vii. 18; Is. xv. 2, xxii. 12; Jer. xvi. 16, xlvii. 5; Mic. i. 16.

32—36. Lament over Tyre.

The lament appears to be in elegiac metre. The word "wailing" is a contracted form (ni = nehi).

What city] Rather: **who is like** Tyre.

like the destroyed] The form is very obscure, but nothing better has been proposed.

33. *thy wares went forth*] i.e. when they were landed from the sea on many shores many peoples were filled, cf. Is. xxiii. 3 (R.V.).

34. *the time when* thou shalt be] Rather: **what time thou art broken**; or with further change of points: *now art thou broken from the seas...thy merchandise...are fallen*. The reading "time" is difficult, though cf. Jer. ii. 17.

36. *among the people*] **peoples.** "Hiss" here is hardly the expres-

people shall hiss at thee; thou shalt be a terror, and never *shalt be* any more.

3 The word of the LORD came again unto me, saying, Son
2 of man, say unto the prince of Tyrus, Thus saith the Lord GOD; Because thine heart *is* lifted up, and thou hast said, I am a God, I sit *in* the seat of God, in the midst of the seas;

sion of malicious joy, rather of astonishment and dismay, or other vivid emotion, 1 Kings ix. 8.
shalt be a terror] lit. terrors, i.e. destructions—thou shalt be utterly destroyed, cf. xxvi. 21.

CH. XXVIII. THE FALL OF THE PRINCE OF TYRE.

The chapter has three parts:
(1) *vv.* 1—10. The sinful pride of the prince of Tyre and his destruction.
(2) *vv.* 11—19. Lament over his fall and expulsion from the garden of God.
(3) *vv.* 20—26. To this is added a prophecy against Sidon.

1—10. THE SIN OF THE PRINCE OF TYRE (*vv.* 1—5), AND HIS DESTRUCTION (*vv.* 6—10).

The prince of Tyre of the time was probably Ithobal II. It is not, however, any individual prince that the prophet threatens, but the ruler of Tyre, who is the embodiment of the spirit of the proud commercial city. The sin with which the prophet charges the prince is pride of heart and self-deification. The prince—who is but the impersonation of the spirit of the community—was very wise, wiser than Daniel (*v.* 3). His wisdom expressed itself and found scope in his commerce and manufactures and in his arts. These produced wealth and splendour, which led to ungodly arrogance (*vv.* 4, 5): the prince said, I am God, I dwell in the abode of God (*v.* 2). For this deifying of himself in his own mind he shall be brought down. Strangers, the most terrible of the nations, shall assail him, and he shall die the death of the uncircumcised—those whose bodies are unburied or unhonoured in their burial.

2. am *a God*] **I am God.** Ezekiel speaks from his own point of view, which recognizes but one God, not from that of polytheism. The prince set his heart as the heart of God; he felt and acted as if divine. There is not the slightest allusion, of course, to actual worship being paid to the prince; it is his own feeling alone, his pride and self-exaltation, that is referred to.
I sit in *the seat of God*] Naturally the prince speaks of his own abode, Tyre; but he regards it as divine. He is God and it is the seat of God. There is no doubt allusion to the idea that there was a seat of God or the gods; the prince identified Tyre with it. The beauty and splendour of the place, its richness and renown, possibly

yet thou *art* a man, and not God, though thou set thine heart as the heart of God: behold, thou *art* wiser than Daniel; *there is* no secret *that* they can hide *from* thee: with thy wisdom and with thine understanding thou hast gotten thee riches, and hast gotten gold and silver into thy treasures: by thy great wisdom *and* by thy traffick hast thou increased thy riches, and thine heart is lifted up because of thy riches: therefore thus saith the Lord God; Because thou hast set thine heart as the heart of God; behold therefore, I *will* bring strangers upon thee, the terrible of the nations: and they shall draw their swords against the beauty of thy wisdom, and they shall defile thy brightness. They shall bring thee down to the pit, and thou shalt die the deaths of *them that are* slain in the midst of the seas. Wilt thou yet say before him that slayeth thee, I *am* God? but

also its isolation, make it something not of the earth. In Is. xiv. the king of Babylon affects to seat himself beside the Most High, here the prince of Tyre identifies himself with God.

3. *wiser than Daniel*] Cf. on ch. xiv. 14. The language appears ironical. It does not follow from the allusion that the story of Daniel was known in Tyre.

no secret...hide] Or, no secret *is hidden*. In xxxi. 8 the word seems to mean "be equal to," "come up to." This sense would require a personal subject, which might be got if the term "no secret," lit. *no closed*, could be taken as Numb. xxiv. 3, 5 closed of eyes, i.e. inspired. The versions differ widely from one another.

v. 4 *seq.* The wisdom of the prince, who is but the incarnation of the spirit of the city, displayed itself in his commercial enterprise, in his skill in arts and manufactures, for which the Tyrians were famous, and thus he amassed such riches and surrounded himself with such splendour that he deemed himself God (*v.* 6). Already Homer calls the Sidonians *poludaidaloi* (*Il.* 23. 743).

v. 7 *seq.* His chastisement because of his self-deification. As Nebuchadnezzar affected to set himself in the sides of the North but was brought down to the sides of the pit, the prince of Tyre shall die an ignominious death. The "terrible" i.e. most terrible of the nations are the Chaldeans, cf. the prophet's contemporary Hab. i. 6—10. See ch. vii. 21, 24, xxx. 11, xxxi. 12, xxxii. 12.

the beauty of thy wisdom] The beauty is not regarded as the product of his wisdom, but rather as the expression of it, that in which it clothes itself. Cf. *v.* 12.

defile thy brightness] **profane**, cf. *v.* 17. The term "profane" is used on account of the prince's assumption of divinity.

8. *deaths of...slain*] The **death**.

thou *shalt be* a man, and no God, in the hand of him that
10 slayeth thee. Thou shalt die the deaths of the uncircumcised

9. *but thou* shalt be] Rather: **whilst thou art man, and not God.**
The last clause "in the hand," &c. is wanting in LXX.

10. *deaths of the uncircumcised*] the **death.** The term uncircumcised is employed by the prophet not in its usual sense but in reference to the dead, who suffer death from the sword, and whose bodies either lie unburied and dishonoured or are flung indiscriminately into the earth with no funeral honours. Deprivation of burial did not hinder the dead persons from descending into Sheol, the place of the dead, but the dishonour done them here followed them there, and they were subject to reproach. Cf. the same representation Is. xiv. 19, 20, where it is an entire misconception to consider "stones of the pit" to refer to a paved mausoleum, and thus a sumptuous burial. The stones of the pit are the lowest pit.

12—19. LAMENT OVER THE FALL OF THE PRINCE OF TYRE.

The passage is of extreme difficulty partly from the obscurity of several expressions in it, which do not occur again, and partly from allusions not now intelligible. The general drift of the passage is plain. (1) *vv.* 12—15. The prince of Tyre is represented as a glorious being placed in Eden the garden of God. He was the perfection of beauty, was set on the mountain of God, and was perfect in his ways from the day he was created till iniquity was found in him. (2) *vv.* 16—19. He fell from his high place through pride because of the multitude of his riches, and was therefore expelled from the garden of God.—Towards the end of the passage the allegory of a being in paradise is departed from and the actual circumstances of the prince and his city are more literally referred to. The text of LXX. diverges in important particulars from the Heb.

Particular difficulties, however, are numerous. 1. The expression "sealest up the sum," *v.* 12 is very obscure. For the participle "sealest" the ancient versions read signet or *ring*. That there is reference to a ring seems plain from *v.* 13. 2. Again the cherub is referred to. There can be no doubt that the prophet has in his mind the story of Paradise (Gen. ii. iii.). The cherub naturally belongs to the Paradise of God. In the Heb. text, as at present pointed (though the pointing is very anomalous) the prince is compared to the cherub, or said to be or have been the cherub. The text, however, permits the reading *with* or *beside* the cherub (*v.* 14, so LXX.). The prince sinned and was expelled from the garden of God where he was placed. The idea of the prophet is that pride and self-deification was the sin of the prince and caused his expulsion. This, however, in Ezek. is the sin of all the foreign princes or nations, Egypt no less than Tyre, and cannot be held part of a tradition of the Fall, or of paradise. That the prophet does refer to a fall and expulsion from paradise or destruction of the transgressor seems plain (*vv.* 16, 17). But any fall of the cherub is not hinted at anywhere in the Old Test.; on the contrary the cherubs are

by the hand of strangers: for I have spoken *it*, saith the Lord GOD.

Moreover the word of the LORD came unto me, saying, 11 Son of man, take up a lamentation upon the king of Tyrus, 12 and say unto him, Thus saith the Lord GOD; Thou sealest up the sum, full *of* wisdom, and perfect in beauty. Thou 13 hast been in Eden the garden of God; every precious stone

represented as watchers and protectors of the garden of God against men (Gen. iii. 24). There are references in the Old Test. to the sin of higher beings (e.g. Gen. vi. 1; Is. xxiv. 21), but the prophet's allusions to the cherubs in other places make it very improbable that he should think of them as sinning. 3. It is probable, therefore, that it is the history of the first man that floats before his mind. The term "created" applied to the prince would hardly be used of the cherub. It is not unlikely, however, that Ezek. is in possession of traditions regarding Paradise more ample than those in Gen. or different from them. At the same time the divergences may be due to his own tendency to idealize. The prince of Tyre is represented as wiser than all men, even than Daniel; and in Job xv. 7, 8 the first man born is spoken of as possessing supernatural wisdom. The prophet might have before his mind that Wisdom which was the first of God's works of old (Prov. viii.), and his architect in creation, and who realized herself in the symmetry of the universe.

12. *king of Tyrus*] The prophet appears to use the terms king and prince (nagîd, or nasî') indifferently. LXX. of Ezek. reserves the term "king" for the rulers of Babylon and Egypt, except in general expressions like "kings of the earth," or, of the nations (xxvii. 33, 35, xxxii. 10).

sealest up the sum] The term "sum" only again ch. xliii. 10 of the construction or idea of the temple, there rendered "pattern." The verb is used of the work of God in ordering creation by weight and measure, Job xxviii. 25; Is. xl. 12, 13. The phrase "thou sealest" is pointed as part. *art the sealer of*, but some MSS. and the ancient Versions read *art the sealring of*. To "seal" has always the natural sense, or means to close up, fasten up; it seems nowhere to mean to round off, complete or consummate. LXX. omits "full of wisdom," and the first words are in parallelism to "the perfection of beauty." This would suggest that the first words describe what the prince is or was, not what he did. The term rendered "sum" may mean *symmetry* (perfection), and the whole: *thou wast the sealring of symmetry* (perfection), *and the perfection of beauty*. In this case the prince is compared to a sealring of exquisite workmanship. On the other hand if part. be read, "thou wast the sealer of symmetry," the conception of something impressing symmetry (upon all things) seems expressed. There might then be an allusion to the Wisdom; cf. the comparison of light to a seal Job xxxviii. 14.

13. *Thou hast been*] **thou wast** in Eden. The term rendered "cover-

was thy covering, the sardius, topaz, and the diamond, the beryl, the onyx, and the jasper, the sapphire, the emerald, and the carbuncle, and gold: the workmanship of thy tabrets and of thy pipes was prepared in thee in the day that
14 thou wast created. Thou *art* the anointed cherub that covereth; and I have set thee *so:* thou wast upon the holy

ing" does not occur again. Possibly "emerald" and "carbuncle" should be transposed. These precious stones are mentioned in sets of three, being nine in number, to which LXX. adds three more, the ligure, the agate and the amethyst, as in the high-priest's breastplate (Ex. xxviii. 19), while Syr. reduces the number to eight. Possibly the original number may have been very much smaller.

thy tabrets and of thy pipes] It is obvious that timbrels and pipes are out of place here. It is also probable that the preceding words *and gold* should be disjoined from the list of precious stones. Render: **and of gold was the workmanship of thy sockets and grooves.** Reference is unmistakeably to the setting of precious stones, and while possibly a person might be supposed to be covered or clothed with the jewels mentioned, the phrase "thy sockets" seems to recall the figure of the ring. The phrase "was prepared" is wanting in LXX. and the last words "in the day that thou wast created" should probably go to the next verse.

14. *Thou* art *the anointed*] The word "thou" is pointed here anomalously as Num. xi. 15; Deut. v. 24. It may more naturally be read *with* or beside. The terms rendered "anointed" and "that covereth" are wanting in LXX. (also in *v.* 16). No meaning can be attached to anointed cherub, probably: cherub **with spreading wings.** The other phrase "that covereth" is used to describe the cherubim over the mercy-seat whose wings covered it and (at least in the temple of Solomon) extended from wall to wall of the most holy place (Ex. xxv. 20, xxxvii. 9; 1 Chr. xxviii. 18). In these passages LXX. renders the word rightly "overshadowing."

I have set thee] **I set** thee.

holy mountain of God] Different representations of the abode of God were current; it was sometimes spoken of as a mountain and sometimes as a garden. The mountain here is the same as the garden of *v.* 13, cf. *v.* 16. It is the abode of God, where the cherub was and where the prince was placed on the day when he was created. The allusion to the mount of assembly in Is. xiv. 13 is obscure. The combinations of Del. (*Parad.*) and Jeremias (*Bab. Assyr. Vorstellungen vom Leben nach dem Tode*) are controverted by Jensen, who makes it probable that Arâlu, the "mountain of the countries," is not a special mountain *on* the earth, but the earth itself conceived as a mountain, under which lay the primary ocean. Neither is there the slightest foundation for the supposition that the prophet compares the prince of Tyre to a Gryph guarding treasure upon the mountain of God.

mountain of God; thou hast walked up and down in the midst of the stones of fire. Thou *wast* perfect in thy ways 15 from the day that thou wast created, till iniquity was found in thee. By the multitude of thy merchandise they have 16 filled the midst of thee *with* violence, and thou hast sinned: therefore I will cast thee as profane out of the mountain of God: and I will destroy thee, O covering cherub, from the midst of the stones of fire. Thine heart was lifted up be- 17

hast walked up and down] **didst walk** in the midst of (the) stones of fire. The "stones of fire" might be flashing precious stones (Assyr. *aban ishâti*, precious stone, Frd. Del., *Par.* p. 118); more probably there is some reference to the phenomena attending the divine presence and manifestation, ch. i. 13, x. 6, cf. Is. vi. 6; Ps. xviii. 14. Among the Muhammedans the shooting stars are held to be thunderbolts hurled at the eavesdropping demons who pry into the divine secrets.

15. The sin and fall of the prince. The terms "the day when thou wast created" are very unsuitable if applied to the cherub. The sons of God existed before creation, Job xxxviii. 7.

16. *By the multitude*] Or, in the multitude.

they have filled] Or, **thy midst** (heart) **was filled with wrong, and thou didst sin.** LXX., thou didst fill.

therefore I will cast] therefore **have I cast.** The destruction of the prince is described as completed, lit. therefore have I profaned thee (casting thee) out of the mountain.

and I will destroy thee] More probably: **and the** (covering) **cherub hath destroyed thee** (driving thee) **from the midst of the stones of fire.** The construction as 1st pers. *I have destroyed* is possible, but quite improbable. The cherub is rather regarded as active in the expulsion from Paradise; in Gen. iii. 24, he is represented as barring the return of those whom God had expelled.

With the words wanting in LXX. put in square brackets the verses would read: " Thou art the (a) seal of symmetry, [full of wisdom], and the perfection of beauty. 13 Thou wast in Eden the garden of God; every precious stone was thy covering, the sardius, the topaz and the diamond, the beryl, the onyx and the jaspar, the sapphire, the carbuncle and the emerald; and gold was the workmanship of thy sockets and grooves in thee in the day that thou wast created" [they were prepared]. Or, drawing the last words to the beginning of *v.* 14.—14 "In the day that thou wast created I set thee with the [outspread, the covering] cherub, thou wast in the holy mountain of God, in the midst of the stones of fire [thou didst walk]. 15 Thou wast perfect in thy ways from the day that thou wast created, till iniquity was found in thee. 16 In the multitude of thy traffic thy midst was filled with wrong [LXX. thou didst fill], and thou didst sin: therefore I have profaned thee (and cast thee) from the mountain of God; and the [covering] cherub hath destroyed thee (driving thee) from the midst of the stones of fire."

17. The prince's sin was self-exaltation because of his beauty and

cause of thy beauty, thou hast corrupted thy wisdom by reason of thy brightness: I will cast thee to the ground, I will lay thee before kings, that *they* may behold thee. Thou hast defiled thy sanctuaries by the multitude of thine iniquities, by the iniquity of thy traffick; therefore will I bring forth a fire from the midst of thee, it shall devour thee, and I will bring thee to ashes upon the earth in the sight of all them that behold thee. All they that know thee among the people shall be astonished at thee: thou shalt be a terror, and never *shalt* thou *be* any more.

wisdom. The prince is but the representative of the city and its inhabitants; the beauty of the one (xxvii. 3) and the wisdom of the other (xxvii. 8, 9) are attributed to him. The prophet's own deep humility before Jehovah makes him recoil from the self-exaltation of men elsewhere.

corrupted thy wisdom] i.e. lost thy wisdom over, or amidst, thy splendour. The tenses "I will cast" &c. are all perfects, the threat taking the form of an accomplished judgment.

that they *may behold thee*] i.e. as a spectacle to feast their eyes upon.

18. *defiled thy sanctuaries*] **profaned**. The phrase occurs ch. vii. 24; here, however, where the prince is spoken of, "sanctity" or personal sacredness rather than "sanctuary" seems the sense required. It is doubtful if the word can bear this meaning. LXX. reads: because of the multitude of thine iniquities in the wrong of thy traffic *I have profaned* thy sanctuaries, and I have brought forth a fire. The tenses are all in the perfect of threatening, and the threats here pass away from the prince and apply more to the city. On "fire" cf. ch. xix. 14.

bring thee to ashes] **have brought**, perf. of threatening. Any reference to the Phenix, consumed in a self-kindled fire, has little probability. The idea of the city, of the spirit and activity of which the king is the embodiment, tends more and more to take the place of the idea of the king. This is evident from the closing words *v.* 19, which are identical with those referring to the city, ch. xxvii. 36. For people read **peoples** as usual.

19. *shalt be a terror*] Cf. xxvi. 21, xxvii. 36.

20—26. PROPHECY AGAINST SIDON.

See on ch. xxv. 1. The passage has three parts:

(1) *vv.* 20—23. The Lord shall send great judgments on Zidon, by which means he shall get his greatness and holiness recognised, and they shall know that he is God. (2) *v.* 24. Thus shall all that vex Israel round about come to an end and cease. (3) *vv.* 25, 26. Israel when restored shall thus dwell securely, all that were hostile to her having been removed; and she shall know Jehovah her God to be God alone. These words suggest the explanation both of the judg-

Again the word of the LORD came unto me, saying, Son 20
of man, set thy face against Zidon, and prophesy against it, 21
and say, Thus saith the Lord GOD; Behold, I *am* against 22
thee, O Zidon; and I will be glorified in the midst of thee:
and they shall know that I *am* the LORD, when I shall have
executed judgments in her, and shall be sanctified in her.
For I will send into her pestilence, and blood into her 23
streets; and the wounded shall be judged in the midst of
her by the sword upon her on every side; and they shall
know that I *am* the LORD. And there shall be no more a 24
pricking brier unto the house of Israel, nor *any* grieving
thorn of all *that are* round about them, that despised them;
and they shall know that I *am* the Lord GOD. Thus saith 25
the Lord GOD; When I shall have gathered the house of
Israel from the people among whom they are scattered, and
shall be sanctified in them in the sight of the heathen, then
shall they dwell in their land that I have given to my servant
Jacob. And they shall dwell safely therein, and shall build 26
houses, and plant vineyards; yea, they shall dwell with con-

ments upon the nations and of the position which they occupy in the prophet's Book. See introd. to ch. xxv.

21. In Gen. x. 15 Zidon is the firstborn of Canaan, and it was probably the parent city of Tyre, which lies twenty miles further south. The modern town bears the name Saida. See chart of Sidon in Rawl. *Phenic.* p. 66.

22. *be glorified*] Or, *get me glory* (honour). So for "be sanctified" get me sanctifying, or shew myself holy. To get sanctifying for himself is to get recognition as God alone, and that which God alone is. To "get glory" is a part of to get sanctifying.

23. *wounded...be judged*] Rather: **shall fall**, or, fall thick, if the word be read as an intensive. The judgments on Zidon shall bring home to her that there is a great God and that He has sent them. This God is Jehovah God of Israel, God alone. The prophet speaks from his own belief.

24. "Brier" is "thorn" ch. ii. 6 (slightly different form). The term "pricking" is used of the leprosy (Lev. xiii. 51, fretting).

25. Read **peoples** for people.
sanctified in them] i.e. *through them*, in their restoration. Jehovah is sanctified through the chastisement of the nations who distress His people, and He is sanctified through His people's restoration. On "sanctify" cf. *v.* 22.

my servant Jacob] Cf. ch. xxxvii. 25; the phrase already in Jer. xxx. 10, and frequently in Is. xl.—lxvi.

26. *dwell safely*] Or, with confidence, *feeling* secure, Jer. xxiii. 6;

fidence, when I have executed judgments upon all those that despise them round about them; and they shall know that I *am* the LORD their God.

Am. ix. 14; Is. lxv. 21; Ezek. xxxiv. 27, xxxviii. 8, xxxix. 26. An illustration of the promise is seen in ch. xxxviii.—ix.

know that I am *the Lord*] This oft-repeated phrase is not a mere formula. The prophet's idea is that Jehovah does all, brings all calamities, causes all catastrophes and revolutions in states, and guides the fortunes of Israel in the sight of the nations, with one great design in view—to make himself, the true and only God, known to all mankind.

CH. XXIX.—XXXII. PROPHECY AGAINST EGYPT.

With the exception of the passage ch. xxix. 17—21 the prophecies against Egypt belong to a time shortly anterior to the fall of Jerusalem or shortly after it. Ch. xxix. is dated about seven months before the capture of the city; ch. xxx. 20 *seq.* about four months, and ch. xxxi. about two months before that event, while ch. xxxii. falls somewhat more than a year and a half later than the destruction. The active participation of Egypt in the affairs of Israel all this time, the hopes reposed in her by the people (Lam. iv. 17), and the disappointments caused by her, explain the large space devoted by the prophet to her character and her destinies in the purposes of Jehovah.

The general thought prevailing in the prophecy is the same as that in other parts of Ezekiel's book, viz. that Jehovah, God of Israel, is the one true God, and that all the movements among the nations, the overthrow of some and the triumphs of others, are his operations, and that they are but parts of a general rule and direction of the world, the design of which is to make himself known to all the nations as the one living and true God. The two sins for which Egypt, represented by Pharaoh, is chastised are, first, pride of heart which recognizes no God above it, which says, My River is mine, I have made it (xxix. 3); and second, the deceptive fascination which the imposing and pretentious power of the Nile valley exerted on the people of God, seducing them away from trust in Jehovah alone (cf. Is. xxx. 1—5, xxxi. 1—3), and proving always a delusive support (xxix. 6, 7). This reed which, so far from supporting, pierced the hand that leant on it, must be broken for ever, that in the future (the new age about to dawn) the people of Jehovah may no more be tempted to trust in it.

Egypt, however, is a different kind of power both from the petty peoples like Edom and Moab, and from Tyre the great commercial mart of the nations. The smaller nations suffer because of their despite against Israel, and in suffering they learn what Jehovah is. Tyre did not affect to be a conqueror. She was the lady at whose feet the nations laid their tribute of precious ores and jewels, rich cloths and sweet perfumes. The prince of Tyre prided himself upon his wisdom, his skill in seamanship and commerce, his brilliant ingenuity in the arts, and on his beauty and splendour. The sin of Tyre was this ungodly pride of mind, and this wholly secular devotion to trade. But Egypt is a world power. It rules nations (xxix. 15). It is a great cedar, envied by the trees in the garden of God (xxxi. 9), in the branches of which all the fowls of heaven nest, and under the shadow of which all the beasts of the field bring forth (xxxi. 6). It aspires to universal dominion. Hence in treating of it the prophet's mind takes a wider sweep. He thinks of Jehovah as God over all, and of his operations as embracing the world. The judgment of Egypt is the day of the Lord (xxx. 3); it is the time of the Gentiles. Hence its overthrow is felt over the world (xxxii. 10). Creation shudders; the waters stand motionless (xxxi. 15). Jehovah is known to the ends of the earth (xxx. 19, 26).

Each of the four chapters is formed in the main upon the same model, containing first, a general threat of destruction upon Egypt, represented by the Pharaoh, under some allegorical designation (e.g. the crocodile); secondly, a more particular detail of the instrument whom Jehovah shall use (the king of Babylon), the destruction of the country and the dispersion of its inhabitants; to which, thirdly, in several of the chapters a description is added of the effect on the nations and all creation which these terrible convulsions shall produce. These events shall be done on the stage of the world, with mankind as spectators; Jehovah shall brandish his sword in the eyes of the nations, and nature and men will shudder (xxxii. 10). Ch. xxxii. ends with a dirge chanted over the interment of Pharaoh, which is one of the most weird passages in literature.

CH. XXIX. GENERAL THREAT OF JUDGMENT ON PHARAOH AND HIS PEOPLE.

(1) *vv.* 1—7. Pharaoh is presented under the allegory of a great crocodile inhabiting the waters of the land, and the population as fishes. Jehovah with his hook shall draw him out of his waters, with his fishes cleaving to his scales, and shall cast his carcase upon the desert, where the fowls and the beasts shall batten on him. The causes of this judgment on Pharaoh and his people are, his ungodly pride (*v.* 3), and the fact that he has always proved a delusive confidence to Israel, seducing them from their single trust in Jehovah (*vv.* 6, 7).

(2) *vv.* 8—12. Explanation of the allegory. A great conqueror, stirred up by Jehovah, will overthrow Pharaoh, destroy his people and desolate his land. The inhabitants shall be scattered into all countries, and Egypt shall remain utterly desolate, trodden by the foot neither of man nor beast, for the space of forty years.

(3) *vv.* 13—16. At the end of forty years Egypt shall be restored, but only to attain the rank of a mean power, meaner than all the kingdoms of the earth. It shall no more rule over nations, and no more from its imposing greatness be a temptation to the people of Jehovah to put their trust in it. The term of forty years is considered by the prophet the time of Chaldean supremacy. At the end of this period the world shall be revolutionised.

(4) *vv.* 17—21. A passage of date 570 B.C., probably inserted after

29 In the tenth year, in the tenth *month*, in the twelfth *day* of the month, the word of the LORD came unto me, saying, 2 Son of man, set thy face against Pharaoh king of Egypt, 3 and prophesy against him, and against all Egypt: speak, and say, Thus saith the Lord GOD; Behold, I *am* against thee, Pharaoh king of Egypt, the great dragon that lieth in the midst of his rivers, which hath said, My river *is* mine 4 own, and I have made *it for* myself. But I will put hooks in thy jaws, and I will cause the fish of thy rivers to stick unto thy scales, and I will bring thee up out of the midst of thy rivers, and all the fish of thy rivers shall stick unto thy 5 scales. And I will leave thee *thrown* into the wilderness, thee and all the fish of thy rivers: thou shalt fall upon the open fields; thou shalt not be brought together, nor

the prophecies against Egypt had been reduced to writing—hardly after the book had been published—and suggested by the termination of Nebuchadnezzar's thirteen years' siege of Tyre. It consists of a promise to Nebuchadnezzar that Egypt shall be given him as a recompense for the service which he served in Jehovah's behalf against Tyre, for which service he failed at Tyre to obtain the adequate reward.

1—7. Pharaoh under the allegory of the crocodile, and the population as fishes. Jehovah draws him out of the waters with his hook and flings him on the land.

3. *the great dragon*] i.e. the crocodile. Conversely the present Arabs with some humour name the crocodile "Pharaoh."
midst of his rivers] The Nile arms and canals.
My river is mine] The Nile. The prophet is well aware what the Nile is to Egypt, and he represents Pharaoh, who, just like the prince of Tyre, is the impersonation of the spirit and disposition of the people of Egypt, as equally well aware. The Nile is the life and the wealth of the land. And Pharaoh in his pride claims to be the creator, the author of it. To the prophet's profoundly religious mind this is blasphemous arrogance.
made it for *myself*] A peculiar construction, but not impossible, cf. Zech. vii. 5.
4. *with hooks*. This is suggested by the monster inhabiting the waters. Possibly the crocodile was occasionally caught with hooks, as Herodotus affirms (cf. ch. xxxii. 3), although Job xli. 1 seems to doubt the practicability of it. On "hooks," ch. xxxviii. 4; Is. xxxvii. 29.
fish of thy rivers] A figure for the population of the country of rivers; hardly merely for the army of Pharaoh.
5. *will leave thee* thrown] I will **throw thee down upon**.
brought together] does not differ from "gathered," meaning "buried," cf. Jer. viii. 2, xvi. 4, xxv. 33. The great dragon's carcase shall be

gathered: I have given thee for meat to the beasts of the field and to the fowls of the heaven. And all the inhabitants of Egypt shall know that I *am* the LORD, because they have been a staff of reed to the house of Israel. When they took hold of thee by thy hand, thou didst break, and rent all their shoulder: and when they leaned upon thee, thou brakest, and madest all their loins to be at a stand. Therefore thus saith the Lord GOD; Behold, I *will* bring a sword upon thee, and cut off man and beast out of thee. And the land of Egypt shall be desolate and waste; and they shall know that I *am* the LORD: because he hath said, The river *is* mine, and I have made *it*. Behold therefore, I *am* against thee, and against thy rivers, and I will make the land of Egypt utterly waste *and* desolate, from the tower of

flung upon the fields, which means death to the water monster; and the fowls and beasts shall feed on it. It is not necessary to allegorize the fowls and beasts, they belong to the figure of the carcase, ch. xxxix. 17 *seq.*; Is. xviii. 6; Jer. vii. 33, xxxiv. 20.

6. The people of Egypt shall learn as of old who it is that sends such judgments upon them.

staff of reed] A staff or stay which was but a reed, and broke when leant upon (*v.* 7). Cf. Is. xxxvi. 6; 2 Kings xviii. 21. The figure of the reed was natural when speaking of Egypt.

7. *took hold...by thy hand*] Rather: **take hold of thee with the hand**, as Heb. marg. All the verbs are better put in the present: **take hold...dost break.. dost rend**, &c.

madest...to be at a stand] Rather: **makest** all loins **to shake** (reading him'adta for ha'amadta, Ps. lxix. 24).

8—12. For this irreligious self-exaltation Egypt shall be made a desolation from Migdol to Syene, even to the border of Ethiopia.

8. The name of the conqueror of Egypt is not indicated in this preliminary threatening. The sword that comes on Egypt is the sword of the Lord, cf. xiv. 17, xxxii. 11, 12, 13. The land shall be utterly desolated, man and beast swept away. It need not be said that these prophetic threatenings have always an element of the ideal in them.

9. The ungodly overweening pride of Egypt is chiefly mentioned as the cause of its humiliation. It is a common idea that pride draws forth the judgment of Jehovah, who is alone exalted (Is. ii. iii.). The prophet assumes that this pride is irreligious and an offence against Jehovah. However sedulously devoted the Egyptians might be in serving their own gods, their religion did not prevent this self-deification, which was an offence against him who was God alone.

10. *the tower of Syene*] Rather: **from Migdol unto Syene**—from Lower Egypt to the southern border of Upper Egypt. Migdol is said to have been situated 12 miles S. of Pelusium, upon the N. border of Lower Egypt (Ex. xiv. 2; Jer. xliv. 1, xlvi. 14; Num. xxxiii. 7).

11 Syene even unto the border of Ethiopia. No foot of man shall pass through it, nor foot of beast shall pass through it,
12 neither shall it be inhabited forty years. And I will make the land of Egypt desolate in the midst of the countries *that are* desolate, and her cities among the cities *that are* laid waste shall be desolate forty years: and I will scatter the Egyptians among the nations, and will disperse them through
13 the countries. Yet thus saith the Lord GOD; At the end of forty years will I gather the Egyptians from the people
14 whither they were scattered: and I will bring again the captivity of Egypt, and will cause them to return *into* the land of Pathros, into the land of their habitation; and they
15 shall be there a base kingdom. It shall be the basest of the kingdoms; neither shall it exalt itself any more above the nations: for I will diminish them, that *they* shall no
16 more rule over the nations. And it shall be no more the confidence of the house of Israel, which bringeth *their*

Syene (ch. xxx. 6), the modern Assouan, on the S. border of Upper Egypt. Cush or Ethiopia lay to the south of Pathros or Upper Egypt; its capital lay near the 4th Cataract, between Abu Hamed and old Dongola.

11. *No foot of man*] See xxxii. 13, cf. xxxiii. 28, xxxv. 7; Jer. ii. 6. The desolation of Egypt shall continue forty years, the period of Chaldean supremacy (*cf.* iv. 6).

12. Cf. xii. 15, xxvi. 19, xxx. 7.

13. After forty years of desolation Egypt shall be restored, though only to the rank of a humble kingdom. It shall no more rule over the nations (*v.* 15); and no more be a confidence to the house of Israel, seducing them away from trust in Jehovah alone.

Yet thus saith] For thus. Ezekiel considers forty years—a general expression like Jeremiah's seventy years—to be the period of Babylonian supremacy in the world. At the end of this period a change in the aspect of the world shall supervene under Jehovah's guidance; Israel will be restored (ch. iv. 6), and the other nations subject to Babylon shall be reinstated. Egypt shall be restored though only to be a humble state in comparison of her former greatness. For people **peoples**.

14. *land of Pathros*] i.e. Upper Egypt or the Thebaid, ch. xxx. 14; Is. xi. 11; Jer. xliv. 15. The name is said to mean "south land."

their habitation] their **origin**, or birth, cf. xvi. 3. For the phrase "bring again the captivity" i.e. probably *turn the fortunes*, cf. xvi. 53.

a base kingdom] i.e. a low or humble state, ch. xvii. 6, 14.

16. *the confidence*] Cf. Is. xxx. 2, 3, xxxvi. 4, 6.

bringeth iniquity to remembrance] The phrase occurs again Num. v. 15; 1 Kings xvii. 18; Ezek. xxi. 23, 24, and appears to mean *to*

iniquity to remembrance, when they shall look after them: but they shall know that I *am* the Lord GOD.

And it came to pass in the seven and twentieth year, in 17

accuse before God. The phrase here is scarcely in apposition to "confidence," but is rather parallel to that word and a further description of Egypt—*no more a confidence* and *a reminder of iniquity*. Egypt was a seduction to Israel, leading them to trust in it and distrust Jehovah; it was an accuser of Israel before Jehovah, calling Israel's iniquity to his mind. The iniquity lay primarily in trusting in Egypt, but it might be wider and more general (1 Kings xvii. 18).

when they shall look] Rather: **in their turning after them**—in Israel's turning to the Egyptians for help. Cf. xxiii. 27, and on x. 11. In the happy time of Israel's restoration not only shall attack and enmity on the part of the surrounding nations be removed, but all temptation also to look to any for salvation but their God alone.

they shall know] seems said of Israel. See last note.

That Ezekiel names a term of forty years as the period of Chaldean supremacy, and looks for the turn of the world's affairs in Jehovah's hand in so short a space of time is in conformity with the manner of representation in all the prophets. To all the day of the Lord is near (Joel ii. 1; Zeph. i. 1; Is. vii.). In Is. xxiii. seventy years are named as the period of Tyre's humiliation, at the end of which time she shall be remembered and dedicate her hire to the Lord. In Jeremiah this period is the duration of the captivity of Judah. Such numbers as forty, seventy are general. They imply however that the prophets conceived of the time as comparatively short. It is less easy to suggest an explanation of this mode of conception. What has been named "perspective" in prophecy offers no explanation, for this so-called perspective is but another name for the thing to be explained. The explanation is to be sought rather on these lines: 1. The prophets deal with principles, with what might be called absolute conceptions. Such conceptions are good and evil, Jehovah and the false gods, true religion and idolatry, the kingdom of Jehovah and the power of the heathen world. What the prophets depict is usually a conflict of these principles, and every conflict which they perceive seems to them the absolute and final one, because it is a conflict of principles. True religion comes out of the struggle victorious—the Kingdom is the Lord's. 2. Moving thus among principles the mind of the prophets either took no note of time, or else as they deal in general with great movements of their own day, these present or imminent movements assume an absolute moral and religious meaning. They appear the embodiment of the principles which fill the prophetic mind. Consequently their issue is the final decision, which therefore appears at hand. When the prophets embody their general conception of the nearness of the final crisis in numbers, these numbers are usually round, and express merely a powerful religious presentiment.

vv. 17—21. A later passage of date 570, sixteen years after the fall of Jerusalem, written probably after Nebuchadnezzar's thirteen

the first *month*, in the first *day* of the month, the word of
18 the LORD came unto me, saying, Son of man, Nebuchadrezzar king of Babylon caused his army to serve a great service against Tyrus: every head *was* made bald, and every shoulder *was* peeled: yet had he no wages, nor his army, for Tyrus, for the service that he had served against
19 it: therefore thus saith the Lord GOD; Behold, I *will* give the land of Egypt unto Nebuchadrezzar king of Babylon; and he shall take her multitude, and take her spoil, and take her prey; and it shall be the wages for his army.
20 I have given him the land of Egypt *for* his labour wherewith he served against it, because they wrought for me,
21 saith the Lord GOD. In that day will I cause the horn of the house of Israel to bud forth, and I will give thee the

years' siege of Tyre had come to an end, and inserted among the prophecies relating to Egypt already collected. Nebuchadnezzar had served a great service for Jehovah against Tyre, for which neither he nor his army had received wages. Jehovah will recompense him for his service against Tyre by giving him the land of Egypt.

18. On spelling of Nebuchadnezzar cf. xxvi. 7, xxx. 10.

every head made bald] Not by the *length* of time but by the hard service, the rubbing of the armour or the burdens borne on head and shoulder. Arabic poets refer to the baldness caused by the headpieces. The siege of Tyre lasted thirteen years, but while this is well attested history is silent as to the issue of the siege. Whatever the issue was Neb. and his army did not reap adequate reward from it—he had no wages for his service done for Jehovah.

19. *take her multitude*] i.e. carry away. Others: her wealth, or abundance, but wrongly, cf. xxx. 4, 10, 15, xxxi. 2, 18. The words rather disturb the vigorous "spoil her spoil" (xxxviii. 12, 13), and are wanting in LXX.

20. for *his labour*] Rather: **as his recompense for which he served.**

because they wrought] Or, *for that which* they wrought for me. The subject is still Neb. and his army; it was Jehovah's work in which they served against Tyre.

21. The passage concludes with a promise to Israel.

In that day] An indefinite term common in all the prophets. The ref. is to the general time when Neb. shall have humbled Egypt. After that shall the time of Israel's prosperity come in. Cf. Is. iv. 2, xi. 10, xix. 18, 19.

the horn of the house] I will cause **a horn to bud forth to the house** of Israel. The "horn" is the symbol of power (Lam. iv. 3); with the budding of the horn power waxes or is exhibited. The ref. is general, to the restoration of Israel to prosperity and influence,

opening of the mouth in the midst of them; and they shall know that I *am* the LORD.

The word of the LORD came again unto me, saying, Son 30 of man, prophesy and say, Thus saith the Lord GOD; Howl 2 ye, Woe worth the day! For the day *is* near, even the day 3 hardly particularly to the raising up of the personal Messiah (Ps. cxxxii. 17). On figure cf. 1 Kings xxii. 11; Am. vi. 13; Jer. xlviii. 25; 1 Sam. ii. 1.

the opening] **opening** of. The prophet felt his mouth closed by the incredulity of the people, and the improbability, as it seemed to them, of his predictions. His mouth was opened and he had boldness of speech when his anticipations were verified. It is the causing of a horn to bud to Israel that will give the prophet opening of the mouth. All his prophecies since the exile had been prophecies of Israel's restoration, and Israel's restored felicity will fulfil them. The phrase give thee opening of the mouth means little more than give verification to thy words. The idea of the prophet's own presence when this occurs is hardly to be pressed.

CH. XXX. FURTHER PROPHECIES AGAINST EGYPT.

Ch. xxx. consists of two prophecies, the first of which, *vv.* 1—19, in all probability belongs to the same date as xxix. 1—16, that is, about seven months before the fall of Jerusalem; and the second, *vv.* 20—26, is dated four months before the capture of the city. The second prophecy seems to have been suggested by some actual reverse inflicted on Pharaoh, called "breaking his arm" (*vv.* 21, 22), and further disaster is threatened against him.

Unlike the petty nations lying around Israel Egypt is a world power. Its influence is felt over all nations, and its history and destinies interest and affect the world. When Jehovah interposes to deal with it mankind and nature feel his presence. His interposition is the day of the Lord, a day of darkness and terror over all. When Egypt is judged creation wraps herself in a pall.—Like the other prophecies in Ezekiel the chapter is filled up with details within its general frame. The main ideas, however, are these: 1. Egypt with her many allied nations, whose troops compose her vast and many-coloured army, shall be overthrown. 2. Her great cities, the centres of her life and restless activity, shall be cast to the ground, and her teeming population scattered among all the nations. 3. Her idols and all her idolatries shall cease, and her native princes (closely connected with her priesthood and worship) shall be cut off. And Jehovah shall be known.

2. *Howl ye*] The day of the Lord is one of terror and lamentation, Am. v. 20; Is. xiii. 6; Zeph. i. 7, 14; Joel ii. 1 *seq.*

3. *the day is near*] The "day" of the Lord is never in the prophets a mere calamity or judgment from God. It is the time of Jehovah's final interposition in the world to do judgment, to chastise evil, and give the crowning victory to his own cause. This day has a

of the LORD *is* near, a cloudy day; it shall be the time of
4 the heathen. And the sword shall come upon Egypt, and
great pain shall be in Ethiopia, when the slain shall fall in
Egypt, and they shall take *away* her multitude, and her
5 foundations shall be broken down. Ethiopia, and Libya,
and Lydia, and all the mingled people, and Chub, and the
men of the land that is in league, shall fall with them by
6 the sword. Thus saith the LORD; They also that uphold

universal bearing: particularly, it falls in terror and calamity upon the heathen, the foes of Jehovah's kingdom, but also upon the sinners in Zion, those who are at ease and settled on their lees (Zeph. i. 12), on the proud and the oppressors of the poor (Is. ii. 12). The presentiment of this day is common to all the prophets, and the knowledge of it exists among the people (Am. v. 18). The feeling of its nearness, however, was awakened in various ways: either by great convulsions among the nations or calamities, in which Jehovah was so visibly operating that his final interposition seemed at hand (Is. xiii.; Zeph. i. 7; Joel ii. 1); or, by a moral condition of the world which it was felt he must intervene to chastise and put an end to (Is. ii., iii.). Naturally the convulsions or calamities which awakened the presentiment of the nearness of the day passed over and the day was deferred, but this does not justify the supposition that the prophets mean merely a great calamity or judgment by the day of the Lord.

the time of the heathen] the **nations**, the foes of Jehovah's kingdom and people, when Jehovah shall be revealed to them and they shall be judged. Is. ii., iii., xiii. 22; Jer. xxvii. 7; Ezek. vii. 7, xxii. 3.

4. *great pain*] **anguish**, a late word, cf. *v.* 9.

her multitude] Ch. xxix. 19; cf. *vv.* 10, 15, ch. xxxi. 2. Her "foundations" is suggested by the idea of a building overthrown. Reference is hardly to the allies and mercenaries on whom Egypt relied in war, rather to the classes and institutions in which the strength of the state lay.

5. See on xxvii. 10; Heb. is **Cush** and **Phut** and **Lud**. For Cush LXX. reads Persians as xxvii. 10, for Phut Cretans, and for Lud Lydians.

the mingled people] perhaps **foreigners**. In Jer. xxv. 24 these so named ('ereb) are represented as having kings and dwelling in the desert (cf. 1 Kings x. 15), and in *v.* 20 they are named next to the kings of Uz. On the other hand in Jer. l. 37 they are spoken of as being in the midst of Babylon. Hence the sense of "mercenaries" has been suggested. In the present passage some distinct people seems intended.

the land that is in league] Lit., *children of the land of the covenant*. Reference can hardly be to the land of Israel, or to refugees from Israel in Egypt. Either some definite country is meant, the name of which would be suggested by the prophet's description, or "land" is used collectively—all allied lands. The name Chub does not occur

Egypt shall fall; and the pride of her power shall come down: from the tower of Syene shall they fall in it by the sword, saith the Lord God. And they shall be desolate in 7 the midst of the countries *that are* desolate, and her cities shall be in the midst of the cities *that are* wasted. And 8 they shall know that I *am* the Lord, when I have set a fire in Egypt, and *when* all her helpers shall be destroyed. In that day shall messengers go forth from me in ships to 9 make the careless Ethiopians afraid, and great pain shall come upon them, as *in* the day of Egypt: for lo, it cometh. Thus saith the Lord God; I will also make the multitude 10 of Egypt to cease by the hand of Nebuchadrezzar king of Babylon. He and his people with him, the terrible of the 11 nations, *shall be* brought to destroy the land: and they shall draw their swords against Egypt, and fill the land *with* the slain. And I will make the rivers dry, and sell the land 12 into the hand of the wicked: and I will make the land waste, and all that is therein, by the hand of strangers: I the Lord have spoken *it*. Thus saith the Lord God; I 13 will also destroy the idols, and I will cause *their* images to

again; LXX. Libyans, and in Nah. iii. 9 the Lubim appear beside Cush, Egypt and Phut.

6. *the tower of Syene*] **from Migdol to Syene**; cf. xxix. 10.
7. A frequently recurring expression; cf. xxix. 12.
8. "Fire" is a frequent figure for war and its desolations, *vv.* 14, 16, ch. xv. 5, xx. 47, xxxix. 6.
9. *messengers...in ships*] Cf. Is. xviii. 2. The word "ships" again Numb. xxiv. 24; Is. xxxiii. 21.

go forth from me] This means more than that messengers go in ships from Egypt, where Jehovah is present. He sends them; his intervention in Egypt is designed to alarm the world, and bring himself to its knowledge.

as in *the day*] **in the day** (om. as) Is. xxiii. 5.
10. The instrument whom Jehovah uses is here named for the first time, except in the later passage, ch. xxix. 17—21.
11. *terrible of the nations*] Cf. ch. xxviii. 7, xxxi. 12, xxxii. 12.
12. *make the rivers dry*] Cf. Is. xix. 5, 6. The expression is scarcely figurative (Is. xliv. 27); the drying up of her rivers would be the severest calamity that could befall Egypt, as indeed in all her history whenever her canal system has been allowed to fall into disrepair the country has sunk into wretchedness.

hand of the wicked] Or, *of evil men*, ch. vii. 24; Jer. xv. 21; cf. Is. xix. 4 "a cruel lord."
13. *destroy the idols*] On "idols" ch. vi. 5. The clause fails in LXX.

cease out of Noph; and there shall be no more a prince of
the land of Egypt: and I will put a fear in the land of
14 Egypt. And I will make Pathros desolate, and will set fire
15 in Zoan, and will execute judgments in No. And I will
pour my fury upon Sin, the strength of Egypt; and I
16 will cut off the multitude of No. And I will set fire in
Egypt: Sin shall have great pain, and No shall be rent
17 asunder, and Noph *shall have* distresses daily. The young
men of Aven and of Phi-beseth shall fall by the sword: and

their *images to cease*] Lit., their not-gods, a favourite term of
Isaiah's, e.g. xix. 1, 3, though found only here in Ezek. For "not-
gods" (elīlim) LXX. renders "magnates" (elim), which no doubt
gives a good parallelism to the next clause; cf. Is. xxxiv. 12.
put a fear] Cf. Is. xix. 16, Egypt "shall fear because of the
shaking of the hand of the Lord of hosts, which he shaketh over it."
Noph (in Hos. ix. 6 Moph) is Memphis, the most important city of
lower Egypt, lying on the left bank of the Nile, somewhat south of
the modern Cairo. Is. xix. 13; Jer. ii. 16, xliv. 1, xlvi. 14.

14. Pathros is upper Egypt, or its capital, xxix. 14. Zoan, or
Tanis, the modern San, on the south shore of lake Menzaleh, according to Numb. xiii. 22 built seven years after Hebron, cf. Ps. lxxviii.
12, 43.

15. Sin, called here the "bulwark of Egypt," is usually identified
with Pelusium, which lying on the N.-E. frontier of the country might
be considered the key to it.
multitude of No] i.e. No-Amon (Nah. iii. 8) or Thebes, the capital
of Upper Egypt, Jer. xlvi. 25.

16. *rent asunder*] i.e. broken through by armed assault, cf. xxvi.
10 (last words).
have *distresses daily*] **distresses** (or adversaries) **in the day-time**;
cf. Zeph. ii. 4, "they shall drive out Ashdod at noonday" (Jer. xv. 8).
The construction is unnatural, and the text may be in some confusion.
LXX. reads differently.

17. *young men of Aven*] i.e. On or Heliopolis, "city of the sun,"
Jer. xliii. 13; cf. Gen. xli. 45. The obelisk known as Cleopatra's
Needle belonged to the sun temple in On; and in the vicinity of the
ruins near the village Matariyeh stands the sycamore under which
tradition affirms that the Holy Family rested in their flight to Egypt.
The modern name is Ain Shems (sun-fountain) a few miles N.-E.
of Cairo.
Phi-beseth shall fall] i.e. Bubastos or Bubastis, Egyptian Pa Bast,
house of Bast or Pasht, the goddess to whom the cat was sacred, and
who herself was represented under the aspect of the cat. The cat
mummies were here preserved. The place lay on the Pelusiac arm of
the Nile; the ruins, bearing the name Tell Basta, are not far from
the modern Zagazig. Herod. mentions that at a yearly festival held
here as many as 700,000 people would assemble.

these *cities* shall go into captivity. At Tehaphnehes also 18 the day shall be darkened, when I shall break there the yokes of Egypt: and the pomp of her strength shall cease in her: *as for* her, a cloud shall cover her, and her daughters shall go into captivity. Thus will I execute judgments in 19 Egypt: and they shall know that I *am* the LORD.

And it came to pass in the eleventh year, in the first 20 *month*, in the seventh *day* of the month, *that* the word of the LORD came unto me, saying, Son of man, I have broken 21 the arm of Pharaoh king of Egypt; and lo, it shall not be

18. Tehaphnehes, spelled somewhat differently Jer. ii. 16. Jer. xliii. 8 speaks of a royal palace there, and xlvi. 14 it is named along with Memphis as a chief city in Egypt. Its site is probably the modern Tell Defenneh (Daphnae), near the Pelusiac arm of the Nile, south of lake Menzaleh, about 30 miles S.-W. of the ancient Pelusium.

the yokes of Egypt] must here be those imposed by Egypt, a sense not very suitable to the connexion. A different pointing would give sceptres (LXX.) or staves—but "staves" in the sense of supports is more than doubtful (cf. Is. xiv. 5).

her daughters] may be literal (cf. v. 17, young men of On), or said figuratively of her towns.

19. The purpose of these convulsions among the nations is that Jehovah the true God may be known; and this purpose will not fail.

20—26. A NEW PROPHECY AGAINST EGYPT, FOUR MONTHS BEFORE THE FALL OF JERUSALEM.

Pharaoh seems to have quite recently suffered a defeat (*v.* 21), and a complete disaster to his power is threatened (*v.* 22). This idea is expressed in a figure: one of his arms has been irremediably broken, it cannot be healed so as again to grasp the sword (*v.* 21). But both arms shall be broken, the strong one as well as the disabled one, and the sword shall fall out of his hand (*v.* 22). But Jehovah will make strong the arms of Nebuchadnezzar, and put his own sword into his hand, which he shall stretch out over Egypt. It is Jehovah's sword that Neb. wields, and Egypt shall be scattered among the nations.

21. *broken the arm*] While the Chaldeans were besieging Jerusalem the army of Pharaoh Hophra (Apries) advanced and compelled them to raise the siege, Jer. xxxvii. 5; cf. xxxiv. 21. The Egyptians were repulsed and the siege renewed. It is possible that breaking the arm of Pharaoh refers to this circumstance. At all events the distinction between the two arms, and the threat that both the sound and the fractured one shall be altogether broken, suggest that an actual past occurrence is referred to in the figure of *v.* 21.

bound up to be healed, to put a roller to bind it, to make it
22 strong to hold the sword. Therefore thus saith the Lord
God; Behold, I *am* against Pharaoh king of Egypt, and
will break his arms, the strong, and that which was broken;
23 and I will cause the sword to fall out of his hand. And
I will scatter the Egyptians among the nations, and will
24 disperse them through the countries. And I will strengthen
the arms of the king of Babylon, and put my sword in his
hand: but I will break Pharaoh's arms, and he shall groan
before him *with* the groanings of a deadly wounded *man*.
25 But I will strengthen the arms of the king of Babylon, and
the arms of Pharaoh shall fall down; and they shall know
that I *am* the Lord, when I shall put my sword into the
hand of the king of Babylon, and he shall stretch it out
26 upon the land of Egypt. And I will scatter the Egyptians
among the nations, and disperse them among the countries;
and they shall know that I *am* the Lord.

a roller to bind it] i.e. a bandage. For the word cf. xvi. 4, Job xxxviii. 9.

23. The consequence of breaking Pharaoh's arms will be the utter defencelessness of the people of Egypt, which shall be scattered into all lands. In *v.* 26 their dispersion is looked at from the other side, and said to follow from Jehovah's strengthening the arms of the king of Babylon.

24. *groan before him*] Pharaoh shall groan before Nebuchadnezzar as a wounded man groans. The figure is well pursued. The "arm" sometimes means the "helper," but here the two champions appear as if engaged in a personal combat. Jehovah strikes down the arms of Pharaoh, and the sword falls from his grasp; he strengthens the arms of Nebuchadnezzar, putting his own sword into his hand. And thus the king of Egypt, mortally wounded, groans before his adversary from his death-stroke. Cf. xxviii. 9.

26. See on *v.* 23.

Ch. XXXI. Pharaoh under the figure of a great cedar cut down and flung upon the ground.

The passage has three parts:
(1) *vv.* 1—9. Pharaoh, the impersonation of the spirit and might of Egypt, was a lofty cedar, with spreading branches, and its top in the clouds. All the fowls lodged in the branches, and all the beasts brought forth their young under it. Its waters nourished it and made it great. The trees in the garden of God did not equal it; all the trees of Eden envied it.

(2) *vv.* 10—14. The great tree shall be cut down by the mighty

And it came to pass in the eleventh year, in the third 31 month, in the first day of the month, *that* the word of the LORD came unto me, saying, Son of man, speak unto 2 Pharaoh king of Egypt, and to his multitude; Whom art thou like in thy greatness? Behold, the Assyrian *was* a 3 one of the nations, and thrown upon the ground. Its bulk shall fill the mountains and valleys of the land. All the nations shall depart from under the shadow of it; and the fowls and beasts of the field shall feed on it. Its heart was lifted up because of its great height, therefore it shall be cut down, that none of the trees lift themselves up and put their head among the clouds.

(3) *vv.* 15—18. Nature shall shudder and put on blackness over the fall of Pharaoh. And the great trees of the garden of God that are gone down to the pit shall be comforted when Pharaoh and his auxiliaries descend among them.

The allegory is easily read. The mighty cedar, burying its head in the clouds, is the proud king and his powerful state, aspiring to a greatness that belongs to heaven. The fowls and beasts lodging under the shadow of the tree are the nations of the earth seeking his protection and subject to him (Dan. iv. 12). The trees in the garden of God are other mighty states impersonated in their rulers. The universal meaning which was given to the judgment on Egypt by representing it as the day of the Lord in ch. xxx. is suggested here in other ways, by the imposing height of the cedar, unapproachable by other trees in the garden of God; by the fowls and beasts of the field lodging in the tree—all nations seeking the protection of the Pharaoh; and by the shock which all nature receives when the great tree is cut down and flung upon the ground; and finally by the commotion occasioned in Sheòl when Pharaoh descends among the dead (ch. xxxii.; Is. xiv.). In some points the allegory has incongruities, as was natural. Pharaoh is a great cedar, but it is his waters—the Nile—that nourish him, and give him an altitude to which the trees of Eden cannot aspire. The cedar is in Lebanon, the home of cedars, but also by the great deep, and probably too in Eden (*v.* 11). The trees, once in Eden, descend into Sheòl with those that are gone down to the pit.

1. The date is about two months before Jerusalem fell.

2. *his multitude*] The population of Egypt; hardly merely his army.

Whom art thou like] The question seems to imply that none can be compared to him; he is unapproached in his greatness; cf. *v.* 18.

3. *the Assyrian was a cedar*] It is evident that the Assyrian has nothing to do here; any comparison of Egypt to Assyria is without motive. Besides *v.* 3 is repeated in *v.* 10, and spoken of Egypt (cf. *v.* 18). The word "asshur" here is the name of a tree, either the same as teasshur (ch. xxvii. 6), or this form should be read. Render: *Behold a stately cedar in Lebanon* (lit. a teasshur of a cedar); or, behold

cedar in Lebanon with fair branches, and with a shadowing shrowd, and of a high stature; and his top was among the 4 thick boughs. The waters made him great, the deep set him up on high with her rivers running round about his plants, and sent out her little rivers unto all the trees of the field. 5 Therefore his height was exalted above all the trees of the field, and his boughs were multiplied, and his branches became long because of the multitude of waters, when he shot 6 forth. All the fowls of heaven made their nests in his boughs, and under his branches did all the beasts of the field bring forth their young, and under his shadow dwelt all 7 great nations. Thus was he fair in his greatness, in the length of his branches: for his root was by great waters. 8 The cedars in the garden of God could not hide him: the fir trees were not like his boughs, and the chesnut trees

a sherbin, a cedar in Lebanon—the more general "cedar" being added after the species.

a shadowing shrowd] The "shroud," usually "forest," must refer to the closely interwoven branches, hardly to the underwood. The phrase is wanting in LXX.

the thick boughs] The **clouds**, so *v.* 10, 14; cf. xix. 11.

4. *set him up on high*] i.e. made him grow lofty. There is probably, however, the figure of a parent nourishing his offspring. The words "made great" and "set on high" are rendered "nourished and brought up" children, Is. i. 2; cf. xxiii. 4. The waters rear the tree as their child. The waters are those of Egypt.

with her rivers running] The construction is anomalous, and *with* expresses accompaniment, not instrumentality. It is easiest to read (with LXX.): *she* (the deep) *made her rivers to run round...and sent out.* Or possibly: as for her rivers, they ran, &c.

his plants] Rather: **her plantation**, "her" referring to the "deep," which nourished the plantation, though this is not quite natural.

her little rivers] Marg. conduits, the small canals for irrigation. The plenteous waters nourished the great tree and the other trees alike.

5. *his boughs were multiplied*] Wanting in LXX.

when he shot forth] When he **sent them forth**, i.e. his branches, cf. xvii. 6, 7. Others: when it (the deep) sent them (the waters) forth; cf. *v.* 4.

6. The "fowls" and "beasts" are as much figurative as the tree; they are probably interpreted by "nations" in the end of the verse; cf. xvii. 23; Dan. iv. 12, 14. But see Jer. xxvii. 6.

8. *could not hide him*] Probably: **equal him**, compare with him (cf. the common particle "over against" or "alongside of," i. 20, xlviii. 13, &c.).

chesnut trees] Probably: **plane** trees, Gen. xxx. 37; cf. Ps. civ. 16;

were not like his branches; nor any tree in the garden of God was like unto him in his beauty. I have made him ⁹ fair by the multitude of his branches: so that all the trees of Eden, that *were* in the garden of God, envied him.

Therefore thus saith the Lord GOD; Because thou hast ¹⁰ lifted up thyself in height, and he hath shot up his top among the thick boughs, and his heart is lifted up in his height; I have therefore delivered him into the hand of the ¹¹ mighty one of the heathen; he shall surely deal with him: I have driven him out for his wickedness. And strangers, ¹² the terrible of the nations, have cut him off, and have left him: upon the mountains and in all the valleys his branches are fallen, and his boughs are broken by all the rivers of the land; and all the people of the earth are gone down from

Numb. xxiv. 6. The trees in the garden of God are naturally the most lofty.

9. *have made him fair*] **I made** him fair. But the idea of his beauty being conferred by God is foreign to the connexion. His stateliness was due to his great waters, beside which he was planted; it was the fruit of *nature*, which in this passage is rather contrasted with God. The words are wanting in LXX., and may be a marginal gloss on "beauty," which a reader attributed to God. If the words be omitted, the last clause of *v.* 8 should probably be closely connected with *v.* 9: "and no tree in the garden of God was like unto him, because of (in) the multitude of his branches."

10—14. BECAUSE OF HIS PRIDE IN HIS HEIGHT HE SHALL BE CUT DOWN. NEBUCHADNEZZAR, THE MIGHTY ONE OF THE NATIONS, SHALL HEW HIM TO THE GROUND, AND THE BEASTS SHALL FEED ON HIM. SUCH JUDGMENT MUST OVERTAKE ANY GREAT TREE THAT EXALTS ITSELF INTO THE HEAVENS.

10. *the thick boughs*] the **clouds.**
11. *have...delivered*] **I will deliver.**
mighty one of the heathen] of the **nations**, Nebuchadnezzar.
for his wickedness] The traditional reading is: *according to* his. On "driven out" cf. Gen. iii. 24. The whole clause, "I have...... wickedness" appears to fail in LXX.

12. The tenses in *vv.* 12, 13 are perfects of threatening: the fut. would be plainer in *v.* 12 as A.V. *v.* 13. On "terrible" cf. xxviii. 7.
have left him] **cast him down**, ch. xxxii. 4; Am. v. 2. His great trunk covers the land and fills the watercourses. The nations who dwelt under his shadow, seeking his protection, have fled away from him (Dan. iv. 11). For people, **peoples.**

13 his shadow, and have left him. Upon his ruin shall all the fowls of the heaven remain, and all the beasts of the field
14 shall be upon his branches: to the end that none of all the trees by the waters exalt themselves for their height, neither shoot up their top among the thick boughs, neither their trees stand up in their height, all that drink water: for the are all delivered unto death, to the nether parts of the eartl in the midst of the children of men, with them that go down to the pit.
15 Thus saith the Lord God; In the day when he wen down to the grave I caused a mourning: I covered th deep for him, and I restrained the floods thereof, and the

have left him] **and** (or, for) **they have cast him down.** The words seem emphatic repetition from the beginning of the verse.
13. *his ruin*] i.e. his fallen trunk and branches, ch. xxxii. 4, xxxi: 17; Is. xviii. 6.
14. The downfall of Pharaoh is a chastisement for his pride an' a warning.
for their height] Or, **in** their. It is not merely pride of hea because of the height, it is the height itself, the shooting up the top among the clouds—aspiring to a greatness belonging only to heaven—that is the sin.
thick boughs] the **clouds.**
neither their trees stand up] Rather: **and that their mighty ones** (those of the nations) **stand not up** (or, forward, i.e. display themselves) in their height. The phrase "all that drink water" is a circumlocution for "trees," fed by water.
nether parts of the earth] i.e Sheòl, the place of the dead, deep down in the earth, or under it.
the children of men] i.e. men in general, common men. The meaning is hardly that expressed in Ps. xlix. 10, that all die, the wise as well as the fool and the brutish, and that the "mighty ones" have no privilege over common men in this respect; the death referred to here is rather the violent death, the death of them slain with the sword, attended with no funeral honours. Cf. ch. xxxii. 17 *seq.*
them that go down] them that **are gone down** to the pit. So everywhere. The allegory of the tree here passes over into the reality.
15. Creation puts on mourning and is paralysed at Pharaoh's fall. Lebanon is covered with blackness, and all the trees faint.
down to the grave] to **Sheòl,** the place of the dead.
caused a mourning] Rather: **I caused to mourn, I covered** the deep for him. The term "covered" (wanting in LXX.) is used as in xxxii. 7, "cover the heaven, and make the stars thereof black," having the same meaning as "caused to mourn." The "deep" and the "floods" (rivers in *v.* 4) are those mentioned in *v.* 4, but though the ref. is to the Nile and the waters of Egypt, a universal magnitude

great waters were stayed: and I caused Lebanon to mourn for him, and all the trees of the field fainted for him. I ¹⁶ made the nations to shake at the sound of his fall, when I cast him down to hell with them that descend into the pit: and all the trees of Eden, the choice and best of Lebanon, all that drink water, shall be comforted in the nether parts of the earth. They also went down into hell with him unto ¹⁷ *them that be* slain with the sword; and *they that were* his arm, *that* dwelt under his shadow in the midst of the heathen. To whom art thou thus like in glory and in ¹⁸

is given to these, they are the "deep" absolutely. This deep which had nourished the great cedar is covered with mourning and paralysed by his fall, she is motionless, her waters congeal.

caused Lebanon to mourn] Lit. *made* Lebanon *black*, in mourning. The prophet's representation naturally is not quite consistent. The home of Pharaoh, as a cedar, is Lebanon, but it is the waters of Egypt, magnified here into the "deep" absolutely, that nourish him. Hence both the deep and Lebanon, with all the trees thereon, mourn and faint (Is. li. 20) over his fall. What the language primarily expresses is the idea of the world-wide importance of the Egyptian power, so that, as the greatest forces of nature minister to its growth, all creation is affected by its fall. Cf. xxxii. 9, 10.

16. *at the sound of his fall*] See on xxvi. 15; cf. xxxii. 10.

to hell...into the pit] to Sheòl with them that **are gone down** to the pit, ch. xxxii. 18; Is. xiv. 15. The nations living on the earth shake with terror (ch. xxvi. 15) at the noise of his fall; while those already gone down to the pit are "comforted" that one so mighty has fallen as well as themselves, xxxii. 19, 31; Is. xiv. 10. The language does not imply that those comforted were hostile to Pharaoh.

the trees of Eden] The figure of "trees" for states, or for the representatives of states like Pharaoh, is continued. The term Eden is used generally to suggest great trees or the place where trees are found, for the next words describe the trees as the "choice of Lebanon."

choice and best] An anomalous construction, which is obviated in LXX. by the want of "best."

drink water] i.e. trees nourished by water, *v*. 14.

17. *They also...into hell*] **These also are gone down into Sheòl**, ref. being to the "trees of Eden," *v*. 16.

were *his arm*, that *dwelt*] **and his arm, that dwelt.** His "arm" is his helpers (xvii. 9). The construction is difficult (read probably cons. plur. of part. for "that dwelt;" om. of rel. improbable); cf. xxxii. 15. LXX. points "his seed" for "his arm," but that "seed" could mean underwood (Corn.) has no probability.

18. The question implies that Pharaoh had no peers. Yet though incomparably greater than the other trees his fate shall be the same as theirs—he shall be brought down with them to the nether parts of the

greatness among the trees of Eden? yet shalt thou be brought down with the trees of Eden unto the nether parts of the earth: thou shalt lie in the midst of the uncircumcised with *them that be* slain with the sword. This *is* Pharaoh and all his multitude, saith the Lord GOD.

32 And it came to pass in the twelfth year, in the twelfth month, in the first *day* of the month, *that* the word of the 2 LORD came unto me, saying, Son of man, take up a lamentation for Pharaoh king of Egypt, and say unto him, Thou art like a young lion of the nations, and thou *art* as a whale in the

earth. LXX. reads the first half of the verse thus: To whom art thou like? Go down, and be brought down with the trees of Eden to the nether parts of the earth, cf. xxxii. 19.

midst of the uncircumcised] The term is applied to those slain with the sword, and buried indiscriminately with no funeral rites, ch. xxviii. 10; cf. xxxii. 19, 21, 24, &c.

CH. XXXII. FINAL PROPHECY AGAINST PHARAOH.

The chapter contains two parts:
First, *vv.* 1—16. A lament over Pharaoh.
Second, *vv.* 17—32. A funeral dirge over the interment of him and his multitude.

The line of thought in *vv.* 1—16 resembles that in the other chapters:
(1) *vv.* 1—6. Pharaoh, represented as a dragon in the waters, is dragged out by the net of Jehovah, and flung upon the land, where all fowls and beasts feed on him. His carcase fills the land and his blood the water-courses.

(2) *vv.* 7—10. Shock of nature and commotion among the nations, even the most distant and unknown to Egypt, over his fall.

(3) *vv.* 11—16. The instrument of his destruction is the king of Babylon. The overthrow of Pharaoh and his people shall be complete. The land shall be desolate and life shall cease in it; no foot of living creature, man or beast, shall trouble its waters, which shall run smooth and dead.

1. The prophecy is dated the first of the twelfth month of the twelfth year, nearly a year and seven months after the fall of Jerusalem. Syr. reads *eleventh* year.

2. *art like a young lion*] Perhaps: *wast likened to*, though the construction is exceedingly hard (cf. xxxi. 18). So far as the form of words goes the meaning might rather be: O lion of the nations *thou art undone* (Is. vi. 5; Hos. x. 15), the root being another. The prophet has a fondness, however, for using the Niph. (Cf. xiv. 4, 7, xix. 5, xxxiii. 30, xxxvi. 3.) The words can hardly mean: thou thoughtest thyself a young lion. Cf. xxxviii. 13.

and thou art] **whereas thou wast** as a dragon (monster) in the rivers, lit. *seas;* cf. Is. xix. 5, xxvii. 1; Job xli. 23. The construction seems to imply an antithesis between this clause and the previous one.

seas: and thou camest forth with thy rivers, and troubledst the waters with thy feet, and fouledst their rivers. Thus 3 saith the Lord GOD; I will therefore spread out my net over thee with a company of many people; and they shall bring thee up in my net. Then will I leave thee upon the 4 land, I will cast thee forth upon the open field, and will cause all the fowls of the heaven to remain upon thee, and I will fill the beasts of the whole earth with thee. And 5 I will lay thy flesh upon the mountains, and fill the valleys *with* thy height. I will also water with thy blood the land 6 wherein thou swimmest, *even* to the mountains; and the rivers shall be full of thee. And when *I* shall put thee out, 7 I will cover the heaven, and make the stars thereof dark; I will cover the sun with a cloud, and the moon shall not

camest forth with] **didst break forth in** thy rivers. The term "break forth" is used of coming forth out of the womb (Ps. xxii. 9; cf. Job xxxviii. 8), and also of those in ambush breaking out of their hiding-place (Judg. xx. 33). The term describes not the origin of the monster but his activity; cf. "didst foul." Ew. conjectured for "in thy rivers," *with thy nostrils*—thou didst spout (cause spray) with thy nostrils; cf. Job xli. 18—20. The object of the verb is wanting here, however, and the verb though used of Jordan (Job xl. 23) is employed intransitively. Cf. however, Mic. iv. 10.

their rivers] Or, streams—those of the waters. The vitality of the monster and his violent activity are suggested by his troubling the waters and fouling the streams. Cf. the opposite idea, *vv.* 13, 14.

3. Jehovah shall drag him out with his net by means of many peoples (*vv.* 11, 12). On figure, cf. xii. 13, xvii. 20; Hos. vii. 12. For **people** read **peoples**.

4. *will leave thee*] **Will cast thee down**; cf. xxix. 5. See xxxi. 13, xxxix. 17 *seq*.

5. Cf. xxxi. 12. Other suggestions for "height" have little probability.

6. *land wherein thou swimmest*] Probably: **and I will water the earth with the outflow of thy blood**, lit. with thy outflow from thy blood. It is possible that "from thy blood" is an explanatory gloss to "with thy outflow." Cf. Is. xxxiv. 3.

7. *put thee out*] i.e. extinguish thee. Pharaoh is regarded as a brilliant luminary; cf. Is. xiv. 12, "How art thou fallen from heaven, O shining one, morning star!" It is doubtful if there is any ref. to the constellation of the dragon. The dragon (Job iii. 8, ix. 13, xxvi. 12) is not a constellation but a purely ideal representation of the eclipse or the storm-cloud which swallows up the lights of heaven. The phenomena in the verse are those usually characteristic of the dissolution of nature on the day of the Lord (Is. xiii. 10; Joel ii. 31, iii. 15; Am. viii. 9);

8 give her light. All the bright lights of heaven will I make dark over thee, and set darkness upon thy land, saith the
9 Lord God. I will also vex the hearts of many people, when I shall bring thy destruction among the nations, into the
10 countries which thou hast not known. Yea, I will make many people amazed at thee, and their kings shall be horribly afraid for thee, when I shall brandish my sword before them; and they shall tremble at every moment, every man for his own life, in the day of thy fall.
11 For thus saith the Lord God; The sword of the king of
12 Babylon shall come *upon* thee. By the swords of the mighty will I cause thy multitude to fall, the terrible of the nations, all of them: and they shall spoil the pomp of Egypt, and
13 all the multitude thereof shall be destroyed. I will destroy also all the beasts thereof from besides the great waters; neither shall the foot of man trouble them any more, nor
14 the hoofs of beasts trouble them. Then will I make their waters deep, and cause their rivers to run like oil, saith the
15 Lord God. When I shall make the land of Egypt desolate,

but here they express rather the shock which creation receives when one so great meets with destruction.

8. *bright lights*] Lit. luminaries of light.

upon thy land] Possibly with LXX.: upon *the earth*. The extinction of the lights in heaven referred to in the previous clause suggests a more general darkness than one over Pharaoh's own land.

9. *vex the hearts*] Or, **trouble**. The precise feeling is not grief, and certainly not anger (A. V. marg.); in *v.* 10 it is dismay, and then terror for themselves. For people **peoples**.

bring thy destruction among] Hardly means "bring the news" of thy destruction; the destruction itself occurs among the nations, they observe it; cf. "brandish my sword before them," *v.* 10.

into the countries] **unto countries**. The effect of Pharaoh's fall shall be felt by nations lying beyond the horizon of his knowledge; cf. Is. lv. 5.

10. Read **peoples**, as always. Cf. xxvi. 16, xxvii. 35.

11. It is the king of Babylon who shall execute the Lord's judgment upon Egypt.

12. *terrible of the nations*] Cf. on xxviii. 7, xxix. 19.

13. The desolation of Egypt shall be complete, man and beast swept away; cf. Zeph. i. 3. These pictures both of desolation and felicity are always ideal; cf. xxix. 11.

14. The waters of Egypt, no more troubled by the foot of man or beast, shall run smooth like oil.

make their waters deep] Rather: **make to settle**, become clear; cf. noun, xxxiv. 18. No more trampled they shall settle and run smooth.

and the country shall be destitute of that whereof it was full, when I shall smite all them that dwell therein, then shall they know that I am the LORD. This *is* the lamentation 16 wherewith they shall lament her: the daughters of the nations shall lament her: they shall lament for her, *even* for Egypt, and for all her multitude, saith the Lord GOD.

15. The end of this desolating judgment shall be that Jehovah shall be known. This is the purpose and the effect of all his interpositions among the nations. Ex. vii. 5, xiv. 4, 18.

16. Lit. *It is a lamentation and they shall chant it* (LXX. thou shalt chant it); *the daughters of the nations shall chant it; over Egypt and over all her multitude shall they chant it.* The daughters of the nations, in *v.* 18 the daughters of the famous nations, chant the dirge because professional wailers were chiefly women; cf. Jer. ix. 17, "call for the mourning women...and let them take up a wailing for us."

17—32. DIRGE SUNG AT THE INTERMENT OF EGYPT AND ITS MULTITUDE.

Several things are observable in this remarkable passage:

1. It is a funeral dirge primarily over the multitude or nation of Egypt; and so in the case of the other nations referred to, Asshur, Elam and the rest. These peoples are all gone down to Sheòl, uncircumcised, slain with the sword. There in the world of the dead each people has an abode to itself. Around one chief grave the graves of the general mass are gathered. The chief grave is probably that of the prince, though the prince is considered the genius, the embodiment of the spirit and being of the nation. The prophet regards the nations, even when no more existing on earth, as still having a subsistence in the world of the dead (cf. on Sodom, ch. xvi.). They are beings, who, having once lived, continue throughout all time. Though passed from the stage of history they still subsist in Sheòl. This idea of the continued existence, not of individuals only but of nationalities, suggests a conception of the meaning of history upon the earth which is not only weird but almost disturbing.

2. The prophet uses two words for the world of the dead, "the pit" and Sheòl. The former name seems suggested by the grave, which is regarded as the entrance to Sheòl, and indicates what kind of place Sheòl is. It is a vast burying-place, deep in the earth, and full of graves. The nationalities spoken of have, like Egypt, all fallen by the sword, and the scene on earth is transferred to the world below. The nation and its prince are represented as slain on the battle-field, and the graves that crowd the field, the prince or genius of the nation in the midst, and those of the multitude around, are let down so to speak into Sheòl beneath, where they abide. This scene of overthrow, the final experience of the nation on earth, expresses the meaning of the nation's history and the verdict of God upon it, and it is consequently transferred to the

world of the dead and made eternal. In this respect the idea of the prophet in regard to nations coincides with the general view of the Old Testament regarding individuals; the judgment of God regarding a man's life becomes manifest at the close of it on earth, and the state of death but perpetuates the manner of the end of life.

3. For, of course, the prophet desires to express by his representation a moral truth. The nations which he mentions are those that have come into conflict with Israel, although their sin is regarded as more general than this. They are chiefly the contemporary peoples whom Nebuchadnezzar, under commission from Jehovah, was to destroy, though Asshur belongs to an earlier time. Although, therefore, the nations can hardly be supposed to fall under a common judgment, the day of the Lord, the effect is the same. Their fate is the judgment of Jehovah upon them, his verdict in regard to their life as nations. Their common sin is violence: they put their terror in the land of the living. And their fate is but the nemesis of their conduct: taking the sword they perish by it. The history of nations is the judgment of nations. But the nations like individuals continue to subsist, they bear their shame in Sheòl for ever.

4. The text of the passage is in considerable disorder. The LXX. offers a briefer and smoother text, though it is also marked by singular blunders (cf. *vv.* 29, 30). It can hardly be doubted that the Hebrew is to some extent overgrown with glosses. The meaning too is in some parts obscure. The passage has affinities with Is. xiv., but the representations there are in some respects different, and care must be taken to allow each passage to speak for itself. It is doubtful if any ideas to be called specially Babylonian be found in either of the prophets. There are two points in the interpretation of some difficulty: 1. There are two names for the world of the dead, "the pit" and Sheòl; are they different in meaning? or, do they indicate, if not strictly a different locality in the underworld, a different condition? The usage of other passages appears decidedly against any distinction. The term "pit" is used of what we so call, e.g. of the pit into which Joseph was cast (Gen. xxxvii. 24), of the "dungeon" into which Jeremiah was thrown (Jer. xxxviii. 6 *seq.*), and the like (Jer. xli. 7). The ideas of the people regarding the world of the dead were formed by looking into the grave and from the condition of the body in death. The world of the dead was created by the shuddering imagination out of these things. Apparently the name "pit" was given to the underworld because the grave was the mouth of it. The "pit" is used in parallelism with Sheòl, and in the same sense, e.g. Ps. xxx. 3, lxxxviii. 3, 4. 2. Another question closely connected is this. Certain persons called the mighty ones (*vv.* 21, 27) are referred to and spoken of as being in Sheòl (A.V. hell), and the question is, are these persons, though in Sheòl, in a condition in some measure different from those like Pharaoh and his multitude, slain by the sword? Unfortunately in both verses the Heb. and Greek disagree. In *v.* 27 Heb. reads: they (Meshech and Tubal) *shall not lie* with the mighty ones, while LXX. omits the *not*, making their destiny the same.

It came to pass also in the twelfth year, in the fifteenth 17 *day* of the month, *that* the word of the LORD came unto me, saying, Son of man, wail for the multitude of Egypt, and 18 cast them down, *even* her, and the daughters of the famous nations, unto the nether parts of the earth, with them that go down into the pit. Whom dost thou pass in beauty? go 19 down, and be thou laid with the uncircumcised. They shall 20 fall in the midst of *them that are* slain by the sword: she is delivered *to* the sword: draw her and all her multitudes. The strong among the mighty shall speak to him out of the 21

17. The month is not specified, but presumably the same month as that named in *v.* 1 is intended, the twelfth. The present passage would in that case date a fortnight later than *vv.* 1—16. LXX. reads *first* month of twelfth year; if this reading were followed the year in *v.* 1 must be read eleventh (with Syr.).

18. The lament is primarily over the multitude or nationality of Egypt.

cast them down, even *her*] Probably: and **sink them down, thou and the daughters of famous nations**. In *v.* 16 the daughters of the nations were spoken of as chanting the dirge over Pharaoh and his multitude. The prophet (LXX. *v.* 16) and these daughters together chant the lament. They are said to "sink the multitude down" because in their lament they describe their sinking down. The reading "thou" for "her" implies no change in the consonantal text, and the "daughters of famous nations" cannot be those that are interred, but those who inter. It is Pharaoh and his multitude who are let down into the pit (cf. *v.* 31).

them that go down] that **are gone down**, xxvi. 20, xxxi. 16.

19. *Whom...pass in beauty*] i.e. surpass; Ew., pass in fortune. Probably the meaning is very much, To whom art (wast) thou superior? The multitude of Egypt or the Pharaoh as the genius of the nation is addressed, hardly his dead body (Sm.).

go down] i.e. to the grave, or pit. "Uncircumcised" has in all the passage the sense of dishonoured, profaned in death, and differs little from slain with the sword, *vv.* 21, 24. The pass. imper. "be thou laid" is very rare, Jer. xlix. 8.

20. *she is delivered* to *the sword*] Rather: **the sword is put forth**, lit. *given*, a peculiar phrase and wanting in LXX.

draw her] i.e. Egypt down into the pit. The simple "draw" leaves rather much to be understood, and LXX. reads the clause differently: and all his multitude shall lie.

21. The Pharaoh and his multitude are supposed here to have descended into Sheôl, and the "mighty ones" already there address them (Is. xiv. 8, 10) or speak of them.

The strong among the mighty] lit. the *strong of the mighty*, where "strong" is not a class among the mighty, but identical with them—

midst of hell with them that help him: they are gone down,
22 they lie uncircumcised, slain by the sword. Asshur *is* there
and all her company: his graves *are* about him: all of them
23 slain, fallen by the sword: whose graves are set in the sides
of the pit, and her company is round about her grave: all
of them slain, fallen by the sword, which caused terror in
24 the land of the living. There *is* Elam and all her multitude

the strong mighty ones (gen. of appos.). In LXX. "strong" is wanting as in *v*. 27. The word "strong" is that rendered *mighty one* of the nations, xxxi. 11. It is probably entirely different (though the same in spelling) from the word *God*, xxviii. 2, and from the phrase "mighty God," Is. ix. 6, x. 21.

speak to him] Or, *of* him. The words that follow seem spoken in regard to Pharaoh—though such a meaning is rather flat.

that help him] **his helpers,** auxiliary nations. The meaning must be that the mighty speak to (of) Pharaoh and his helpers, hardly that Pharaoh's helpers already gone down join the mighty in mocking Pharaoh.

In LXX. these three verses stand in a different order, viz. *vv*. 20 *a*, 20 *b* (read differently), 21 *a*, 19, and the first three words of *v*. 20 again,—"They shall fall with him in the midst of them that are slain with the sword, and all his multitude (strength) shall lie down. And the mighty (lit. giants, *v*. 27) shall say unto thee: Be thou in the depth of the pit; to whom art thou superior? go down, and lie with the uncircumcised, in the midst of them that are slain with the sword." Probably neither text presents the original, though the general meaning of both is the same. It is in favour of Heb. that it begins with the interrogation, and rather against the LXX. that it makes the address rather prolix. The "mighty" who speak are in any case those already in Sheòl, and not persons upon the earth such as the Babylonians (Hitz.).

22, 23. Asshur.

her company] In ref. to the other peoples "multitude" is used. The term "company" may be used of the many nationalities in the Assyrian empire, cf. xxiii. 24.

his graves...him] The gender varies as the country (fem.) or king, as representative of the people, is thought of. The ref. here is to the king. LXX. uses the *mas.* pron. throughout. The text here is shorter in LXX., but no difference of sense arises.

23. *sides of the pit*] i.e. the depths or bottom of the pit.

caused terror] Cf. xxvi. 17, 20. This phrase must mean that Asshur inspired terror into the nations by his might; to suppose that the meaning is that the *fate* of Asshur by the judgment of God caused terror (Hitz.) is altogether false, cf. *vv*. 24, 25, 26, 27, 32.

24, 25. Elam.

Elam, said to mean Highlands, lay E. of the Tigris, and touched Assyria and Media on the N., Media and Persia on the E., and on the

round about her grave, all of them slain, fallen by the sword, which are gone down uncircumcised into the nether parts of the earth, which caused their terror in the land of the living; yet have they borne their shame with them that go down to the pit. They have set her a bed in the midst of the 25 slain with all her multitude: her graves *are* round about him: all of them uncircumcised, slain by the sword: though their terror was caused in the land of the living, yet have they borne their shame with them that go down to the pit: he is put in the midst of *them that be* slain. There *is* 26 Meshech, Tubal, and all her multitude: her graves *are* round about him: all of them uncircumcised, slain by the sword, though they caused their terror in the land of the living. And they shall not lie with the mighty *that are* 27 fallen of the uncircumcised, which are gone down *to* hell

S. the Persian Gulf. An early expedition of Elam into the land of the Jordan is referred to Gen. xiv. 1 *seq.* The country was incorporated into the Assyrian empire, in the armies of which it served (Is. xxii. 6, cf. xi. 11), and on the fall of this empire it probably asserted its independence. It appears independent in the time of Jeremiah, who threatens it with destruction at the hands of Nebuchadnezzar (Jer. xlix. 34, 39).

yet have they borne] **and have borne.** Their shame is that which adheres to them as slain with the sword and unhonoured. The consequences of their life shewed themselves in the manner of their death, and abode upon them. Cf. xxxvi. 6, 7.

them that go down] that **are gone down.**

25. *though their terror*] **for** their terror...**and they have borne,** &c. The verse is greatly a repetition of *v.* 24, and is wanting in LXX., except the words "in the midst of the slain," which are attached to *v.* 24. The words "that are gone down to the pit" usually close the verse, *vv.* 18, 24, 29, 30; and if the verse be retained the last clause should probably be omitted as an accidental repetition of the first clause, due to the copyist's eye straying from "pit" in 25 to "pit" in 24. The three words retained in LXX. cannot stand by themselves.

26. MESHECH AND TUBAL. See on xxvii. 13; cf. xxxviii. 2.

her graves...him] On genders cf. *v.* 22.

though they caused] **for** they caused.

27. *they shall not lie*] LXX. Syr. omit the neg.: *and they are laid with the giants.* Ew. would retain the neg., reading as an interrogation with an affirmative sense: and shall they not lie with...?, which is not very natural.

fallen of the uncircumcised] LXX. fallen *of old.* This reading has considerable probability, although the other reading might stand. Some scholars would also alter "fallen" (nophelim) into Nephilim

with their weapons of war: and they have laid their swords under their heads, but their iniquities shall be upon their bones, though *they were* the terror of the mighty in the land of the living. Yea, thou shalt be broken in the midst of the uncircumcised, and shalt lie with *them that are* slain with

(cf. R. V. Gen. vi. 4); an unnecessary change. For "hell" read **Sheôl**.

they have laid their swords] **they laid** (indeterminate subj.)—equivalent to the passive: and their *swords were laid*.

but their...shall be] **and** their iniquities **were**. The reference is still to the "mighty;" to change the subject spoken of, making the clause refer to Meshech and Tubal, is most unnatural.

though they were *the terror*] **because the terror of the mighty was in the land**. The clause explains the preceding, as for ex. why their iniquities were upon their bones, and would certainly be easier if the reading had been: because the terror *of their might* was, as the Syr. reads, precisely as in *vv.* 29, 30. So Hitz. Corn. (Possibly *geburam* should be read; cf. Hos. xiii. 2, and often with fem. nouns.)

Verse 27 is difficult. The reading "they shall not lie with the mighty" suggests the idea that the mighty who fell of old, and went down to Sheôl in full armour, and had their swords laid under their heads, occupy a more honourable place in Sheôl than such a rout as Meshech and Tubal, who are counted unworthy to lie beside them. This idea is not probable in itself, and cannot be reconciled with other parts of the verse. The last clause "because the terror of the mighty (or, of their might) was in the land of the living" ascribes the same sin to these mighty as is charged against Asshur and the rest (*vv.* 23, 24, &c.), and for which they bear their shame. Again, the phrase "their iniquities were upon their bones" can have no other meaning than that their evil and violence were interred with their bones, and continued to cleave to them—that they went down unhouselled, disappointed, unaneled, cut off in the blossom of their sin. The conjecture of Corn. "their *shields* were upon their bones" is altogether destitute of probability. LXX. renders "giants," as it does Gen. vi. 4, and possibly it thought of the antediluvian race. The prophet may have had this race in his mind, but more probably his reference is a wider one (cf. xxxii. 12, xxxix. 18, 20). Even if he referred to the giants before the Flood, it is anything but likely, with Gen. vi. before him and with his moral temper, that he would assign an honourable place in Sheôl to those violent desperadoes. The weird touch "went down to Sheôl in their weapons of war, and had their swords laid under their heads," probably means that the manner of their death and burial was in keeping with the violence and bloodshed which was the occupation of their life. The usages and sentiments of chivalry were not yet known to Ezekiel. The clause should, therefore, probably be read positively.

28. *Yea, thou shalt*] **thou also shalt**. The Pharaoh is addressed. The phrase "shalt be broken" is wanting in LXX.—"thou also shalt the sword. There *is* Edom, her kings, and all her princes, 29 which with their might are laid by *them that were* slain by the sword: they shall lie with the uncircumcised, and with them that go down to the pit. There *be* the princes of the 30 north, all of them, and all the Zidonians, which are gone down with the slain; with their terror *they are* ashamed of their might; and they lie uncircumcised with *them that be* slain by the sword, and bear their shame with them that go down to the pit. Pharaoh shall see them, and shall be 31 comforted over all his multitude, *even* Pharaoh and all his army slain by the sword, saith the Lord God. For I have 32 caused my terror in the land of the living: and he shall be

lie in the midst of the uncircumcised, with them that have been slain with the sword."

29. Edom. Cf. xxv. 12.

with their might] Possibly, *because of*—the words might and mighty being used in a bad sense. Otherwise the words might signify: *notwithstanding* their might.

are laid by them] i.e. **with**, or, **beside** them. The term "laid," lit. given, means rather put, *consigned*.

them that go down] that **are gone down**.

30. The princes of the North and the Sidonians. The former are probably those of the Syrian states, and the Sidonians represent the Phœnician principalities in general.

with their terror] Rather, in close connexion with the preceding, **gone down with the slain, because of** (notwithstanding) **their terror** (coming) **from their might** (they are) **ashamed.** The term "ashamed" is wanting in LXX., and it occurs only here.

31. *comforted over all his multitude*] The Heb. order is: over all his multitude, slain with the sword, even Pharaoh and all his army, saith, &c. The words "slain with...his army" are wanting in LXX. On "comforted," cf. xiv. 22, xxxi. 16. Pharaoh will be "comforted" by the sight of all these nations in the pit, suffering the same humiliation as himself and his multitude.

32. *I have caused my terror*] So Heb. marg., Heb. text, *his* terror, as all the versions except Vulg. Throughout the passage "to cause terror" is uniformly employed of the conduct of the various nations when on the stage of history. If used of Jehovah here it would be intended to express a vivid contrast—it is *he* who ultimately puts his terror on the world when he interposes to overthrow these tyrannical and violent nations; cf. Is. viii. 13. This somewhat sensational antithesis is not natural, and does not harmonise with the next clause. If *his* terror be read, the power of Pharaoh and the terror he caused would be attributed to Jehovah. But this is an idea out of harmony with the whole representation, which ascribes the supremacy of the peoples named to their own violence or to the gifts of nature. It is just the point insisted on in

laid in the midst of the uncircumcised with *them that are slain with the sword*, *even* Pharaoh and all his multitude, saith the Lord GOD.

all these chapters on the nations that their power was a self-exaltation and rebellion against Jehovah, and for this they perish by the sword and are doomed to eternal dishonour. It seems almost imperative to retain *his* terror, and alter the verb to the 3rd pers.—*for he caused his terror*... therefore he shall be laid, &c. So probably Targ., which paraphrases as in *vv*. 23, 24, 25, 26. Similarly Jer. in his Comm. on Ezek.; and so in copies of the Lat.

SECOND SECTION. CH. XXXIII.—XXXIX. PROPHECIES OF ISRAEL'S RESTORATION AND ETERNAL PEACE.

Only one date appears in connexion with these prophecies, that in xxxiii. 21. Though this date does not stand at the beginning of ch. xxxiii. *seq*., it may be held to indicate the time generally to which the whole seven chapters are to be assigned. There is something suspicious, however, in the date of the arrival of the fugitives—fifth day of tenth month of twelfth year—nearly, a year and a half after the fall of the city. The Syr. read or suggested eleventh year, which would leave about six months for the news of the city's fall to be carried by messengers to the exiles in Babylon, and this date is now very generally accepted. The various chapters may not all belong to the same period. The dates throughout the book are little else than rubrics of a very general kind, under which, in default of more precise details, a number of discourses, extending over considerable periods, have been grouped. The occupation of part of the country by Edom (xxxv. 36) would not take place just close upon the fall of the kingdom; and perhaps the state of despondency of the people and their sense of sinfulness (xxxiii. 10) was one which the fall of the country and the confirmation of the predictions of the prophet took some time to create in their minds. The precise dates are of little consequence, it is the general situation alone that is important. The fall of the city is presupposed (xxxiii. 21), the overthrow of the royal house (xxxiv.), the extinction of the nationality (xxxvii.), the dispersion of the people among all nations (xxxvi. 16 *seq*.), the occupation of part of the country by Edom and the neighbouring tribes (xxxv.; cf. Jer. xli.), and the complete prostration of men's minds under their calamities and the unbearable burden of the sin that had occasioned judgments so unparalleled (Lam. i. 12, ii. 13, 20, &c.). Only the prophet stood erect, while all others were overwhelmed in despair. The greatness of the blow had stunned them, and, as the prophet had foreshewn (xxiv. 23), a stupor had fallen on them. Yet the Lord had not made a full end of Israel. The old era was closed, but a new era was about to open, and a new Israel about to arise. It is of this new era that the prophet has now to speak, and of the hopes of the new Israel and of the conditions of being embraced in it. It is in these chapters that the prophet's contributions to Old Testament theology are chiefly to be found. The passage contains these general conceptions:—

First, ch. xxxiii. The function of the prophet in preparation for the new age. It is to awaken the moral mind, to create the sense of individual worth and responsibility, and to shew that the conditions of belonging to the new Israel are moral only. This chapter defines the place of the individual human mind, and its duties; the following chapters describe rather the divine operations in bringing in the new and perfect kingdom of the Lord.

Second, ch. xxxiv. The royal house, the shepherds of the people, had destroyed alike themselves and the flock (xvii., xix. 14). The Lord himself will take in hand the gathering of his scattered sheep together, and the feeding of them henceforth; he will appoint his servant David to lead them.

Third, ch. xxxv.—vi. The land, the mountains of Israel, usurped by aliens, shall be rescued from their grasp and given again to the people as of old. The reproach of barrenness shall no longer cleave to it; the mountains of Israel shall shoot forth their branches and yield their fruit to the people, and man and beast shall be multiplied.

Fourth, ch. xxxvii. The nation is dead and its bones bleached, but there shall be a resurrection of the dead people and a restoration of them to their own land. Two kingdoms shall no more exist there, but the Lord's people shall be one, and his servant David shall be prince over them for ever.

Fifth, ch. xxxviii.—ix. The peace of his people shall be perpetual. The Lord shall be their everlasting defence. When the armies of Gog come up from the uttermost regions of the earth, with all the nations which have not heard Jehovah's fame nor seen his glory, to assail his people, drawn by the hope of boundless plunder, they shall be destroyed by fire out of heaven.

CH. XXXIII. THE FUNCTION OF THE PROPHET.

Though the prophet seems the chief figure in the chapter, he is really but the medium through whom the principles of the new kingdom of God and the conditions of entering it are enunciated. These principles are: (1) that God desires that men should live. (2) The new Israel shall be composed of members who enter it individually. (3) The condition of entering on man's part is repentance. (4) Man is free to repent—to do good or do evil. The righteous may fall from his righteousness and sin; and the sinner may turn from his evil and do righteousness. He that doeth righteousness shall live; and the soul that sinneth shall die. These principles of the worth and freedom of the individual man, though latent in many parts of the Old Testament, had never been stated so explicitly before. They are no more than what all men will now allow. If pressed indeed and regarded as exhaustive (as everything in this prophet is pressed to his disadvantage), they might seem to ascribe more power to man than he possesses. But in subsequent chapters the prophet lays sufficient emphasis upon the operation of God in regenerating the individual mind and in founding the new kingdom. It would be a novelty indeed if an Old Testament writer were found ascribing too much to man and too

33 Again the word of the Lord came unto me, saying, Son
2 of man, speak to the children of thy people, and say unto
them, When I bring the sword upon a land, if the people of
the land take a man of their coasts, and set him for their
3 watchman: *if* when he seeth the sword come upon the land,

little to God. There is a certain vagueness in the prophet's delineation. It is evident that he is moving among religious principles, and that the enunciation of them is his chief interest; the time and circumstances in which they shall operate are left indefinite. When he says that the righteous shall live and the sinner die, the question, When? naturally occurs. No precise answer is given. But there floats before his view an approaching crisis. The advent of the new era presents itself as a moment of trial and decision; it is like the approach of war upon a people (*vv*. 1—6). The remarkable passage ch. xx. 33—44 may be compared in supplement of the present chapter.

The chapter contains these parts:

(1) *vv*. 1—6. Illustration taken from life—the part of the watchman in war. It is his duty to blow the trumpet when danger is coming. If he does so, the fate of those who hear will lie at their own door. If he fails, the blood of those that perish will be on his head.

(2) *vv*. 7—9. Such is the place of the prophet: the same his duties and responsibilities.

(3) *vv*. 10—20. This is the place of the prophet, but the state of the people's mind is such that his warnings may be addressed to deaf ears. Their calamities have stunned and paralysed the people; they feel lying under an irrevocable doom, entailed upon them by their past history—our sins be upon us, we pine away in them; how, then, shall we live? Nothing is reserved for them but to bear the inexhaustible penalty of their past evil, until, like those in the wilderness, they fall prostrated beneath it. In answer to this stupor of despair comes the voice from heaven with two consoling words: first, that Jehovah has no pleasure in the death of the sinner, but desires that all should turn and live; and secondly, it is not by that which men have been that they shall be judged, but by that which they shall become. The past writes no irrevocable doom over men.

(4) *vv*. 21—29. Fugitives from Judaea arrive among the exiles saying, the city is smitten. This confirmation of all the prophet's past predictions opens his mouth and gives him boldness to address his countrymen. He proceeds to pass judgment on those left in the land, and to state anew that the conditions of inheriting the land are only moral.

(5) *vv*. 30—33. The confirmation which the fall of the city gave to the prophet's past predictions awakened the interest of his fellow exiles in him and his words.

1—6. The illustration—duty of the watchman in war.

2. *of their coasts*] of **their number**, from among them, cf. 2 Kings ix. 17.

he blow the trumpet, and warn the people; then whosoever 4 heareth the sound of the trumpet, and taketh not warning; if the sword come, and take him away, his blood shall be upon his own head. He heard the sound of the trumpet, 5 and took not warning; his blood shall be upon him. But he that taketh warning shall deliver his soul. But if the 6 watchman see the sword come, and blow not the trumpet, and the people be not warned; if the sword come, and take *any* person from among them, he is taken *away* in his iniquity; but his blood will I require at the watchman's hand. So thou, O son of man, I have set thee a watchman 7 unto the house of Israel; therefore thou shalt hear the word at my mouth, and warn them from me. When I say unto 8 the wicked, O wicked *man*, thou shalt surely die; if thou dost not speak to warn the wicked from his way, that wicked *man* shall die in his iniquity; but his blood will I require at thine hand. Nevertheless, if thou warn the 9 wicked of his way to turn from it; if he do not turn from his way, he shall die in his iniquity; but thou hast delivered thy soul.

Therefore, O thou son of man, speak unto the house of 10 Israel; Thus ye speak, saying, If our transgressions and our

3. The trumpet was the signal of danger, Hos. viii. 1; Am. iii. 6; Jer. vi. 1.

4, 5. He that heareth the trumpet and taketh not warning, his blood shall be on his own head; he is responsible for his own death, which shall not be laid at the door of the watchman.

6. Although in *v.* 2 Jehovah is said to bring the sword upon the people (xiv. 17), and presumably for their sin, the language of the present verse leads over from the illustration to the thing meant to be illustrated.

7—9. Similar to the part of the watchman is that of the prophet. Cf. ch. iii. 17 *seq.* The evil, corresponding to the sword in the illustration, in regard to which the prophet is to warn the people, is left undefined. As in the case of all the prophets, however, the turning point in the fortunes of the exiles appeared to Ezek. of the nature of a divine interposition and judgment, and it is this general idea that colours his language. Except in the two or three passages, xiii. 5, xxx. 3, cf. xxxviii. 19, the day of the Lord is not referred to in Ezek.

10—20. Despondency of the people, making the prophet's appeals to them of none effect. Removal of the despair by two gracious words from the Lord.

10. *If our transgressions*] Better, direct: our transgressions...**are**

sins *be* upon us, and we pine away in them, how should we
11 then live? Say unto them, *As* I live, saith the Lord GOD, I
have no pleasure in the death of the wicked; but that the
wicked turn from his way and live: turn ye, turn ye from
your evil ways; for why will ye die, O house of Israel?
12 Therefore, thou son of man, say unto the children of thy
people, The righteousness of the righteous shall not deliver
him in the day of his transgression: as for the wickedness
of the wicked, he shall not fall thereby in the day that he
turneth from his wickedness; neither shall the righteous be
able to live for his *righteousness* in the day that he sinneth.

upon us. The people had come to regard their calamities as due to their sins and evidence of them. They had come round to the prophet's view of their history, for they saw his predictions fulfilled. But the new view came with a crushing weight upon them. The calamities of their country were unparalleled (Lam. i. 12, ii. 13, 20, iii. 1, iv. 6, 9), and equally unparalleled must have been their guilt (Lam. i. 9, 14, ii. 14, iv. 13, v. 7). And their calamities seemed final, their sin was expiable only by their complete destruction.

we pine away] Or, waste away. The word expresses not mental but physical wasting away, ending in complete dissolution. See the very similar figures, Is. x. 18, xvii. 4; cf. Ezek. iv. 17, xxiv. 23; Lev. xxvi. 39.

11. Jehovah's answer to the people's despondency and despair of "life." These verses must be estimated from the point of view of the people's despair of life, to which they are an answer. The passage is not directly an affirmation of the rectitude of God, although this is indirectly affirmed in answer to the people's objection, founded on traditional ways of thinking, that the Lord's ways are not equal. The divine rectitude is not the point of view from which the prophet looks; he speaks in answer to the people's despondency. And his answer is twofold: first, God's desire is that men should live; and secondly, the past is not irrevocable. Not according to what men have been but according to what they shall be or become, will God judge them.

12. It would have been enough to illustrate the earnest exhortation, Turn ye, why will ye die? (*v.* 11) by the assurance that if the wicked turns his past sins will not be remembered against him (*v.* 16). But the prophet states the truth in a more general form. His purpose is to teach also the general truth that the past of one's life does not of necessity determine the future either in itself or in the judgment of God. This, next to the assurance of God's gracious will regarding men (*v.* 11), was the truth most needed to comfort the people and awaken them out of the stupor which lay on them into a moral life and activity again.

It is merely to distort the prophet's words to say that he teaches

When I shall say to the righteous, *that* he shall surely live; 13
if he trust to his own righteousness, and commit iniquity,
all his righteousnesses shall not be remembered; but for his
iniquity that he hath committed, he shall die for it. Again, 14
when I say unto the wicked, Thou shalt surely die; if he
turn from his sin, and do that which is lawful and right; *if* 15
the wicked restore the pledge, give again that he had robbed,
walk in the statutes of life, without committing iniquity; he

that a man's past life goes for nothing, and that he will be judged
merely according to what he is found doing "at the moment" of the
judgment. The prophet is not speaking of moments. He speaks to
men overwhelmed by a judgment of God which seemed to leave no
hope for the future, and he lays down the principle needful for the
moral awakening of the people that the past is not irrevocable, that a
future of possibility lies before them. It is too true that the evil of a
man's past life prolongs itself into the future and that sin cannot at
once be done with. Yet we "believe in the forgiveness of sins;" and
this is the truth which the prophet desires to teach his countrymen,
overwhelmed with the thought of their own evil past. When he says
the righteous shall "live" he means by living the complex thing,
having the favour of God and having an external felicity corresponding
to this.

Old Testament prophets and saints were hardly able to conceive
the first of these two things existing apart from the second. And
the prophet probably still considers them inseparably connected.
And hence, when teaching that the son shall not suffer for the sins of
the father, and that the righteous shall "live" and the wicked "die,"
he has been charged with inculcating a doctrine more false to reality
than the old one which it was designed to supersede. But here again
a certain injustice is done to the prophet. No doubt when he uses the
word "live" he employs it in the pregnant sense, viz. to enjoy the
favour of God and to have this favour reflected in outward felicity.
But just as Jeremiah relegates the principle that the children shall not
suffer for the sins of the father to the new era about to dawn, so Ezek.
agrees with him. Neither prophet is laying down a new principle
which is to obtain in the world, the world going on as it had done
before. Ezek. feels himself, as all the prophets do, on the threshold of
a new Epoch, the era of the perfect kingdom of God, and it is in
this new era that the principle which he enunciates shall prevail.
See at the end of ch. xviii.

13. Cf. iii. 20, xviii. 24.
14. Cf. iii. 18, xviii. 27.
that which is lawful] Lit. as marg., (just) judgment and justice.
15. Instances of a return to righteousness on the part of the
wicked, cf. xviii. 7; Ex. xxii. 1, 4; Num. v. 6, 7.
the statutes of life] By walking in which a man shall live, ch. xiii.
21, xx. 11; Lev. xviii. 5. As elsewhere "life" is used in the preg-

16 shall surely live, he shall not die. None of his sins that he hath committed shall be mentioned unto him: he hath done
17 that which is lawful and right; he shall surely live. Yet the children of thy people say, The way of the Lord is not equal:
18 but *as for* them, their way is not equal. When the righteous turneth from his righteousness, and committeth iniquity, he
19 shall even die thereby. But if the wicked turn from his wickedness, and do that which is lawful and right, he shall
20 live thereby. Yet ye say, The way of the Lord is not equal. O ye house of Israel, I will judge you every one after his ways.

21 And it came to pass in the twelfth year of our captivity, in the tenth *month*, in the fifth *day* of the month, *that* one that had escaped out of Jerusalem came unto me, saying,
22 The city is smitten. Now the hand of the Lord was upon

nant sense of enjoyment of the favour of God and the external prosperity which is the reflection and seal of it.

16. Cf. xviii. 22.

shall be mentioned] Or, **remembered against** him, as *v.* 13.

17. Cf. xviii. 25, 29.

18, 19. These verses sum up the whole principles of the passage, cf. xviii. 26, 27. On *v.* 20 cf. xviii. 25, 29.

21, 22. Fugitives from Judaea arrive among the exiles announcing that the city had fallen. This confirmation of all the prophet's anticipations, which the exiles had received with so much incredulity, opened his mouth, gave him confidence to speak before his fellow exiles. And he announces what shall be the fate of those left in the land (*vv.* 23—29).

21. The date here given is about a year and a half after the city's fall. Considering the constant intercourse between the mother country and the exiles this period is very long. Some MSS. as well as the Syr. read *eleventh* year, leaving about six months for the news to travel by messenger. (Eleven and twelve are easily confused in Heb.).

our captivity] That of Jehoiachin, ch. i. 2. "One that had escaped," lit. the *fugitive*, may refer to one or more, cf. xxiv. 26.

22. Though the date is inserted here, it is probably to be understood as applicable to the whole chapter, for *vv.* 1, 2 the prophet is commanded to speak publicly to the children of his people. In the evening he felt the hand of the Lord upon him, he fell into an excitation. Thoughts such as those in *vv.* 1—20 of the new Israel that God would create and of the conditions of belonging to it filled his mind. He was well aware that the city's fall was inevitable, to him it was as good as fallen. And full of the new thoughts of the future he felt himself standing before his fellow exiles with an impulse strong upon him to speak to them of this future in the name of the Lord. In the

me in the evening, afore he that was escaped came; and had opened my mouth, until *he* came to me in the morning; and my mouth was opened, and I was no more dumb. Then the word of the LORD came unto me, saying, Son of man, they that inhabit those wastes of the land of Israel speak, saying, Abraham was one, and he inherited the land: but we *are* many; the land is given us for inheritance. Wherefore say unto them, Thus saith the Lord GOD; Ye 23 24 25

morning the fugitives arrived with the confirmation of all his past predictions.

until he *came to me*] **should come** : against his coming, Ex. vii. 15.
no more dumb] i.e. silent, Ps. xxxix. 2; Is. liii. 7.

23—29. The confirmation by the fugitives of all his previous predictions gave the prophet boldness to speak anew, and what he says is but a continuation of that which he had said before, and had been so literally confirmed. He had predicted the city's fall because of its sins, and his prophecy had been verified; those remaining in the land continue in the sins for which the city fell, and its fate shall certainly overtake them. The judgment must be carried out till the offences cease. But the teaching of these verses is the natural supplement also to that in *vv.* 1—20. Those remaining in the land presume that they shall inherit the land because they are in it, notwithstanding their evil conduct: the inheritance of the land will be given on different conditions (*vv.* 1—20, cf. xxxvi. 25—38, xxxvii. 23).

24. Regarding those remaining in the land even before the fall of the city, cf. xi. 5—12, 14—21; Jer. xxiv. Those remaining in the land express their confident hopes. Though reduced in numbers they are still many in comparison of the single individual Abraham. Yet he was multiplied in such a way as to take possession of the land; much more may they hope yet to assert their claims to it. They perhaps hardly argued on mere natural probabilities; they felt themselves the heirs of the promises made to Abraham, and in spite of disasters hoped that Jehovah would fulfil them to them. They display the same temper as the people had always shewn; they have a faith in Jehovah but no knowledge of what Jehovah is (Am. v. 14; Hos. iv. 1; Jer. iv. 22, v. 2, 4). Another prophet of this age applies the strange history of Abraham and his multiplication to comfort "the few men of Israel" who followed after righteousness, Is. li. 2.

inhabit those wastes] The ruined cities chiefly, *v.* 27; but cf. xxxvi. 4.

the land is given us] Words of confident anticipation.

25. The claim of the remnant is repudiated by Ezek. with indignation. They persist in the sins for which their country fell, and the same judgment shall overtake them.

eat with the blood, and lift up your eyes toward your idols,
26 and shed blood: and shall ye possess the land? Ye stand
upon your sword, ye work abomination, and ye defile every
one his neighbour's wife: and shall ye possess the land?
27 Say thou thus unto them, Thus saith the Lord GOD; As
I live, surely *they* that *are* in the wastes shall fall by the
sword, and him that *is* in the open field will I give to the
beasts to be devoured, and *they* that *be* in the forts and in
28 the caves shall die of the pestilence. For I will lay the
land most desolate, and the pomp of her strength shall
cease; and the mountains of Israel shall be desolate, that

ye eat with the blood] i.e. eat flesh slaughtered in such a way that
the blood remains in it. According to the law animals had to be
slaughtered in such a way as to drain away the blood, which was
poured into the ground, where not dashed upon the altar. An example of a prohibited way of slaughtering was breaking the neck, Is.
lxvi. 3. Cf. Lev. xvii. 10, xix. 26; Deut. xii. 16; 1 Sam. xiv. 32. See
on xviii. 6, 11, 15, xxii. 9.
lift up your eyes] See xviii. 6. On "shed blood" xxii. 6, 9.
26. *stand upon your sword*] Hardly means, the footing on which
ye deal with men is the sword; but probably, ye occupy yourselves
with the sword, cf. xliv. 24.
work abomination] The term is mostly applied to religious practices
contrary to the pure religion of Jehovah. On the other sin named
cf. xviii. 6, xxii. 11. Verses 25, 26 are wanting in LXX. The passage
is vigorous and apart from the anomalous form "ye work" (where
fem. n is due to following *t*) altogether unsuspicious. The omission in
LXX. may have arisen from the eye of the translator straying from the
words "Lord God" *v.* 25 to the same words *v.* 27.
27. The "wastes" are the desolate cities; those that still hover
about these ruins shall be slain by the enemy. The "open field"
is the country, now depopulated and "the possession of wild beasts;"
and the "forts," coupled with caves, are the natural fastnesses of
the land. Those taking refuge there shall die of the pestilence, due
to crowding and famine. The remnant shall be exterminated from
the land.
28. Cf. vii. 24, xxiv. 21, xxx. 6, 7. The "mountains of Israel"
are the mountain land of Israel.

30—33. DEMEANOUR OF THE PEOPLE TOWARDS THE PROPHET.

The confirmation which the fall of the city gave to the prophet's
past predictions awakened the interest of his fellow exiles in him and
his words. They congregated together in knots under the shadow of
the walls and in the doors of the houses discussing his sayings. Recent
events had given him a more prominent place in their thoughts. There

none shall pass through. Then shall they know that I am 29 the LORD, when I have laid the land most desolate because of all their abominations which they have committed.

Also, thou son of man, the children of thy people still 30 are talking against thee by the walls and in the doors of the houses, and speak one to another, every one to his brother, saying, Come, I pray you, and hear what *is* the word that cometh forth from the LORD. And they come unto thee as 31 the people cometh, and they sit before thee *as* my people, and they hear thy words, but they will not do them: for with their mouth they shew much love, *but* their heart goeth after their covetousness. And lo, thou *art* unto them as a 32 very lovely song *of* one that hath a pleasant voice, and can play well on an instrument: for they hear thy words, but they do them not. And when this cometh to pass, (lo, it 33 will come) then shall they know that a prophet hath been among them.

was something also in the new truths he was uttering, in his outlook into the future and in his appeals to the individual mind, causing each to turn his eyes inward upon himself, that touched them and awakened a certain reality of concern. Still it was in the main curiosity rather than genuine seriousness that led them to listen to him. There was a certain charm, more perhaps in the kind of future presented by the prophet than in his manner of presenting it, which was like sweet music; but though they listened the drift of their minds was too steadily set in another direction to be changed.

30. *are talking against thee*] **the children of thy people who talk of thee.** The construction has a certain inconsequence in it. On "talk" cf. Mal. iii. 16. The "walls" afforded a shade, under which men gathered for conversation.

one to another] The form "one" is Chaldee rather than Heb. The clause says the same thing as next clause and is wanting in LXX.

31. On "come unto thee" cf. viii. 1, xiv. 1, xx. 1.

as my people] The construction is very hard. LXX. omits.

with their mouth...love] The language is peculiar, but can hardly have any other sense. LXX. Syr. read: *for falsehood is in their mouth and their heart &c.* The term "covetousness" or gain has, especially in later books, the general sense of advantage, self-advancement, Is. lvi. 11.

32. *lovely song* of *one*] lit. a lovely song; one that hath. The comparison "like a lovely song" is as usual inexact; "like" merely indicates the circumstances—as when there is a lovely song. The prophet is compared to the singer as A. V.

33. *when this cometh*] **but when it cometh to pass.** The general *it* (fem. as usual in general references) is the judgment or crisis, the

34 And the word of the Lord came unto me, saying, Son of man, prophesy against the shepherds of Israel, prophesy, and say unto them, Thus saith the Lord God unto the shepherds; Woe *be* to the shepherds of Israel that do feed themselves! should not the shepherds feed the flocks? Ye eat the fat, and ye clothe you with the wool, ye kill them that are fed: *but* ye feed not the flock. The diseased have ye not strengthened, neither have ye healed that which was sick, neither have ye bound up that which was broken,

idea of which underlies all the prophet's words and is presupposed in them. Cf. ii. 5.

Ch. XXXIV. The former selfish shepherds of the flock, and the future good shepherd.

The past history of the people and their future is presented under the common allegory of a flock. The shepherds are the rulers.

(1) *vv.* 1—10. The evil shepherds of Israel fed themselves and not the flock. And thus the sheep were scattered over all the earth. The Lord will rid his sheep out of the hand of these shepherds.

(2) *vv.* 11—16. Jehovah himself will undertake the care of his sheep. He will seek them out and gather them from all the nations, and will bring them again to the mountains of Israel, where they shall feed in plentiful pasture.

(3) *vv.* 17—22. He will judge also between sheep and sheep, between the strong and the weak. The strong shall no more push with the horn and thrust with the shoulder; neither shall they alone eat the good pasture and drink the clear water. These pushing rams and he-goats are the magnates, whose oppression of the common people is so common a theme in the early prophets.

(4) *vv.* 23—31. The Lord will raise up a good shepherd to rule his flock, even his servant David. And in those days to come the earth shall be transfigured: showers shall bless the land and the earth shall yield her increase. And the peace of the people shall be perpetual: they shall no more fear the heathen abroad, and no more suffer from scarcity at home.

2. *the shepherds*] i.e. the rulers. The term is chiefly used in later writings (Jer. ii. 8, iii. 15); it occurs, however, in Zech. ix.—xi., the date of which is disputed. On Zedekiah cf. ch. xvii., and on his immediate predecessors, Jer. xxii. 10—30. In general, Jer. xxiii., xxv. 32 *seq.*

unto the shepherds] Possibly this is a marginal heading which has crept into the text, cf. Jer. xxiii. 9, and the reading may be, *thus saith the Lord God, Woe be to...* For flocks, **flock**.

3. *Ye eat the fat*] LXX. the *milk* (the consonants are the same). Cf. Is. vii. 22; Zech. xi. 16.

4. Five classes are here mentioned, in *v.* 16 only four, the "diseased"

neither have ye brought again that which was driven away, neither have ye sought that which was lost; but with force and with cruelty have ye ruled them. And they were scattered, because *there is* no shepherd: and they became meat to all the beasts of the field, when they were scattered. My sheep wandered through all the mountains, and upon every high hill: yea, my flock was scattered upon all the face of the earth, and none did search or seek *after them*.

Therefore, ye shepherds, hear the word of the LORD; *As* I live, saith the Lord GOD, surely because my flock became a prey, and my flock became meat to every beast of the field, because *there was* no shepherd, neither did my shepherds search for my flock, but the shepherds fed themselves, and fed not my flock; therefore, O ye shepherds, hear the word of the LORD; Thus saith the Lord GOD; Behold, I *am* against the shepherds; and I will require my flock at their hand, and cause them to cease from feeding the flock; neither shall the shepherds feed themselves any more; for I will deliver my flock from their mouth, that they may not be meat for them.

For thus saith the Lord GOD; Behold, I, *even* I, will both search my sheep, and seek them out. As a shepherd seeketh out his flock in the day that he is among his sheep *that are* scattered; so will I seek out my sheep, and will deliver them out of all places where they have been scattered in the cloudy and dark day. And I will bring them out from the people, and gather them from the countries, and

---

being wanting, and "strengthen" used here of the diseased is said there of the sick. The "broken" is the hurt or bruised; the "lost" that which has wandered away of itself, in distinction from that "driven away" by violence.

5. The allegory is simple enough. Owing to the evil and selfish government of the rulers the people became the prey of all the nations round about them. The figure of the flock indicates, however, the affection of Jehovah for his people and his compassion over their sufferings.

11—16. JEHOVAH HIMSELF WILL UNDERTAKE THE CARE OF HIS FLOCK.

11. *search my sheep*] i.e. search for, or, search out.
13. Read **peoples** as usual.

will bring them to their own land, and feed them upon the mountains of Israel by the rivers, and in all the inhabited places of the country. I will feed them in a good pasture, and upon the high mountains of Israel shall their fold be: there shall they lie in a good fold, and *in a fat pasture shall they feed upon the mountains of Israel.* I will feed my flock, and I will cause them to lie down, saith the Lord God. I will seek that which was lost, and bring again that which was driven away, and will bind up that which was broken, and will strengthen that which was sick: but I will destroy the fat and the strong; I will feed them with judgment. And *as for* you, O my flock, thus saith the Lord God; Behold, I judge between cattle and cattle, between the rams and the he goats. *Seemeth it a small thing unto you* to have eaten up the good pasture, but ye must tread down with your feet the residue of your pastures? and to have drunk of the deep waters, but ye must foul the residue with your feet? And *as for* my flock, they eat that which ye have trodden with your feet; and they drink that which ye have fouled with your feet.

14. Jehovah first seeks out his sheep (*v.* 11), then he delivers them out of the places where they are scattered (*v.* 12), then he leads them into their own land (*v.* 13), where he feeds them upon the mountain heights of Israel (*vv.* 14, 15).

16. The Lord's treatment of his flock will be in all things the reverse of the treatment given them by the evil shepherds.

with judgment] i.e. just judgment; *in rectitude and justice.* Cf. such demands as those in Is. i. 17, iii. 15, v. 8; Mic. ii. 1—2, iii. 1—4.

17. Not only shall the cruel shepherds be removed and the flock delivered out of their hands and fed by the Lord himself, the injuries inflicted by members of the flock on each other shall no more prevail. The strong shall no more push the weak or drive them from the good pasture.

between cattle and cattle] between **sheep and sheep,** even **the rams and the he-goats.** The "rams" and "he-goats" explain the second word "sheep." Jehovah will judge between one class (the poor and weak) and another (the rams). Cf. xxii. 27, 29; Am. ii. 7, iii. 9, iv. 1.

18. The words are addressed to the rams and he-goats—the magnates and ruling classes.

deep waters] **clear** (lit. settled) waters, cf. xxxii. 14.

Therefore thus saith the Lord GOD unto them; Behold, 20
I, *even* I, will judge between the fat cattle and between the
lean cattle. Because ye have thrust with side and with 21
shoulder, and pusht all the diseased with your horns, till
ye have scattered them abroad; therefore will I save my 22
flock, and they shall no more be a prey; and I will judge
between cattle and cattle. And I will set up one shepherd 23
over them, and he shall feed them, *even* my servant David;
he shall feed them, and he shall be their shepherd. And I 24
the LORD will be their God, and my servant David a prince

23—28. Instead of the many worthless shepherds of old there shall
in the future be one good shepherd, even David, and Jehovah shall in
truth be God of Israel.

23. *my servant David*] The meaning cannot be that David would in
person revive and reappear. It is more doubtful whether the prophet
means that the line or family of David would again occupy the throne
or that a single person would be king. It is possible that this question
was not strictly before his mind; it is the character of the ruler that he
thinks of. The oriental mind hardly distinguishes between an ancient
personage and one who appears in his power and spirit; when it compares it identifies. The new prince over the people will be David, the
servant of the Lord. Both the person and the reign of David were
idealized. He was not in general terms but in truth the man after
God's own heart. His rule was not merely extensive, it was universal. He gave the people victory and secured them peace—he was
a leader and commander of the peoples (Is. lv. 4; Ps. xviii. 43).
Such shall be the king of the restored community when Jehovah is
indeed the God of Israel. For it is to be noted that in Messianic
prophecy it is Jehovah who *saves* the people (*v.* 22 and preceding
verses); then he appoints a shepherd over the restored community,
who feeds them in righteousness and peace. The Messiah is the
king of the saved community, whom he rules in the fear of the Lord
with all royal and godly qualities; and the virtues of his character,
fruit of the spirit of the Lord, communicate themselves to those whom
he rules (Is. xi.). It is possible that the phrase "one shepherd" is
to be interpreted as in xxxvii. 24, with the meaning that the two
kingdoms shall be one, and that this is part of the meaning of the
term "David," cf. Hos. i. 11, iii. 5; Am. ix. 11. See more fully ch.
xxxvii.

24. *I the Lord...their God*] This is the goal towards which all
movements strive; when this is reached perfection is attained and
the covenant with its aims fully realized, cf. xxxvii. 27; Jer. xxxi. 31;
Ex. xxix. 45. The meaning of the words is very profound, implying
closer fellowship and deeper feelings accompanying it than can well
be expressed.

David a prince] David is here called "prince"; in xxxvii. 22, 24 he

25 among them; I the LORD have spoken *it*. And I will make with them a covenant of peace, and will cause the evil beasts to cease out of the land: and they shall dwell 26 safely in the wilderness, and sleep in the woods. And I will make them and the places round about my hill a blessing; and I will cause the shower to come down in his 27 season; there shall be showers of blessing. And the tree of the field shall yield her fruit, and the earth shall yield her increase, and they shall be safe in their land, and shall know that I *am* the LORD, when I have broken the bands of their yoke, and delivered them out of the hand of those 28 that served themselves of them. And they shall no more be a prey to the heathen, neither shall the beast of the land devour them; but they shall dwell safely, and none shall 29 make *them* afraid. And I will raise up for them a plant of renown, and they shall be no more consumed with hunger in the land, neither bear the shame of the heathen any

is named "king" (though LXX. avoids the term). The term "prince" is common in Ezek., and does not imply a dignity inferior to that of royalty.

25. *a covenant of peace*] a covenant securing everlasting peace and therefore implying the removal of all that would injure or disturb them. In Hos. ii. 20 the sense is somewhat different: Jehovah makes a covenant for them with the beasts of the field, that they shall not hurt. In Hos. "beasts" is used literally (cf. Is. xi. 6), here figuratively, meaning foes, heathen assailants, though the figure of the flock is still maintained (Lev. xxvi. 6). The "wilderness" is the uncultivated pasture land as distinguished from that under tillage, covered with crops or fruit-trees (Carmel). Even in the "woods," the parts covered with bush, the haunts of wild beasts, the flock shall sleep safely.

26. *make them...a blessing*] i.e. altogether blessed, Gen. xii. 2; Is. xix. 24, as the last words of the verse imply. Cf. construction xvi. 38, xxvii. 36, xxviii. 19, xxxiii. 28. The language of the clause is not very natural; LXX. reads: and I will set them round about my hill (the word "blessing" wanting).

showers of blessing] i.e. bringing blessing, not, composed of blessing, v. 27, Joel ii. 23—27; Lev. xxvi. 4.

27. *bands of their yoke*] i.e. the yoke bound upon them, Lev. xxvi. 13; Jer. ii. 20, where read "thou hast broken."

29. *a plant of renown*] a *plantation* of renown, lit. for a name, i.e. a plantation which shall be (or, so as to be) renowned; cf. for the phrase xxxix. 13; Is. lv. 13. The ref. is not to the person of the Messiah, but to the luxuriant fertility and vegetation of the earth in the Messianic age. Comp. Ps. lxvii., lxxii. 16; Am. ix. 13; Hos. ii.

more. Thus shall they know that I the LORD their God 30
am with them, and *that* they, *even* the house of Israel, *are*
my people, saith the Lord GOD. And ye my flock, the 31
flock of my pasture, *are* men, *and* I *am* your God, saith the
Lord GOD.

Moreover the word of the LORD came unto me, saying, 35
Son of man, set thy face against mount Seir, and prophesy 2

21; Joel ii. 23 *seq*. The land of Israel was subject to droughts and famine (xxxvi. 15, 30; 1 Kings xvii. *seq*.; Jer. xiv. 1—6, 18; Joel i.). In the regeneration this reproach shall no more fall on it, ch. xxxvi. 3, 6, 15.

30. am *with them*] LXX. omits *with them*, reading: that I the Lord am their God, and they...my people—the usual antithesis. The people's consciousness of salvation shall be, so to speak, a double one, that Jehovah is their God and that they are his people. The two things might seem identical, but the second suggests a feeling regarding themselves which belongs to the perfect enjoyment of salvation.

31. *ye my flock*...are *men*] Omit "are men" with LXX. and read: *and ye are my flock...pasture, and I am your God*.

CH. XXXV.—XXXVI. THE LAND.

After the review of the dark history of the "shepherds" of the people in the past and the promise of the good shepherd who shall rule the restored community, securing protection and peace to them for ever, there follows a similar oracle in regard to the Land of Israel. The passage has three divisions:—

First, Ch. xxxv. Negatively, a threat against Edom. Edom had shewn despite to the people all through their history: particularly, first, it had expressed malicious joy over the desolation of the country at the time of its great calamity, which it had helped forward (*v.* 5, 11—15); and secondly, it had arrogated to itself the right to take possession of the country, though it was Jehovah's abode (*vv.* 10, 12). Therefore desolation shall overtake the mountain of Seir; it shall be made desolate when all the earth rejoices (*vv.* 14, 15).

Secondly, Ch. xxxvi. 1—15. Positively, an oracle in behalf of the mountain land of Israel. It shall be delivered out of the hand of the heathen who are round about, and they shall bear their shame (*vv.* 1—7).

Thirdly, *vv.* 16—38. The redemptive principles illustrated in all this—not for Israel's sake but for his own name's sake it is that Jehovah doeth all these things for his people.

CH. XXXV. THREAT AGAINST EDOM.

1. On Edom cf. xxv. 12 *seq*.
2. *set thy face against*] Cf. ch. vi. 2.

3 against it, and say unto it, Thus saith the Lord GOD; Behold, O mount Seir, I *am* against thee, and I will stretch out mine hand against thee, and I will make thee most
4 desolate. I will lay thy cities waste, and thou shalt be
5 desolate, and thou shalt know that I *am* the LORD. Because thou hast had a perpetual hatred, and hast shed *the blood of* the children of Israel by the force of the sword in the time of their calamity, in the time *that their* iniquity *had*
6 an end: therefore, *as* I live, saith the Lord GOD, I will prepare thee unto blood, and blood shall pursue thee: sith thou hast not hated blood, even blood shall pursue thee.
7 Thus will I make mount Seir most desolate, and cut off
8 from it him that passeth out and him that returneth. And I will fill his mountains *with* his slain *men:* in thy hills, and in thy valleys, and in all thy rivers, shall they fall *that are*

3. *stretch out mine hand*] Ch. vi. 14. Edom shall be made a complete desolation, and it shall realize whose hand it is that falls so heavily upon it (*v.* 4).

5. The causes of the judgment on Mount Seir. These causes are three: first, its perpetual hatred of Israel, xxv. 15; Am. i. 11; second, its malicious joy over the downfall of Israel and the part it took in the destruction of the people in the day of their calamity, when the consequences of their guilt fell upon them, Obad. *vv.* 10—14; and third, Edom's invasion of the land and seizure of it as their own, though the Lord dwelt in it (*v.* 10).

hast shed...of the sword] and **didst deliver the children of Israel over into the hands of the sword.** Jer. xviii. 21; Ps. lxiii. 10.

time iniquity had *an end*] Lit. time *of the iniquity of the end.* The "iniquity of the end" is either, the final punishment of iniquity, or, the iniquity whose punishment was seen in the end (of the state). Cf. ch. vii. The phrase again xxi. 30. The ref. is to the destruction of Jerusalem; so the "calamity" referred to is the downfall of the city and state, as Ob. *v.* 13; cf. Ps. cxxxvii. 7, "the day of Jerusalem."

6. *prepare thee unto blood*] **make thee blood** (cf. xvi. 38, and on xxxiv. 26), i.e. all blood—give thee over to universal slaughter. The clause "I will...pursue thee" is wanting in LXX.

sith thou hast not hated] The words might mean: *surely thou hast hated* (hatest) blood, and blood shall..., a sense not very clear, but probably similar to xi. 8, "Ye fear the sword, and I will bring the sword." LXX. reads: ye have sinned even unto blood (xxii. 4).

7. *passeth out...returneth*] A phrase like "shut up and free," used to denote all classes, cf. "the shod and the barefoot" in Arab. LXX. has altered into "man and beast," the usual phrase after "cut off," e.g. xxv. 13.

slain with the sword. I will make thee perpetual desola- 9
tions, and thy cities shall not return: and ye shall know
that I *am* the LORD. Because thou hast said, These two 10
nations and these two countries shall be mine, and we will
possess it; whereas the LORD was there: therefore, *as* I 11
live, saith the Lord GOD, I will even do according to thine
anger, and according to thine envy which thou hast used
out of thy hatred against them; and I will make myself
known amongst them, when I have judged thee. And thou 12
shalt know that I *am* the LORD, *and that* I have heard all
thy blasphemies which thou hast spoken against the mountains of Israel, saying, They are laid desolate, they are given
us to consume. Thus with your mouth ye have boasted 13
against me, and have multiplied your words against me: I
have heard *them*. Thus saith the Lord GOD; When the 14
whole earth rejoiceth, I will make thee desolate. As thou 15
didst rejoice at the inheritance of the house of Israel, because

9. *cities shall not return*] Probably, *shall not be inhabited* (Heb. text *teshabnah*). The pointing "return" possibly reposes on xvi. 55.

10. In aggravation of their historical bearing towards Israel and their participation in her overthrow, Edom has proceeded to lay hands upon the territory of the two houses of Israel, although it is the place of the Lord's abode and consecrated by his presence.

These two nations] Judah and Israel.

whereas the Lord] Or, *although* the Lord was there. The ref. appears to be to the time when the people were in the land, and the Lord dwelt in it in the midst of them, consecrating it by his presence. This relation of his to the land was unalterable; and Edom had "profaned" his holy abode.

11. Amos i. 11 also uses the word "anger" of Edom's demeanour. LXX. reads the verse in a shorter form.

amongst them] i.e. Israel, or, those who behold it. LXX. *in thee* (Edom, changing one letter), which is more pointed, cf. *v.* 12. For "have judged," better, **shall judge**.

12. *all thy blasphemies*] Or, **contumelies**, 2 Kings xix. 3.

14. *When the...rejoiceth*] Probably: *to the rejoicing of* the whole earth will I make thee desolate. This gives the requisite antithesis to *v.* 15: as Edom rejoiced over the destruction of Judah, the whole earth will be overjoyed at her desolation.

15. The clause "as thou didst...do unto thee" is wanting in LXX.

As Edom had been active in the destruction of Judah, their own desolation must follow. The author of the Lamentations has a presentiment that the next great act of divine judgment will be on Edom (Lam. iv. 22; cf. Is. xxxiv., lxiii. 1—6). The great empires which brought destruction upon Jerusalem were acting under commission

it was desolate, so will I do unto thee: thou shalt be desolate, O mount Seir, and all Idumea, *even* all of it: and they shall know that I *am* the LORD.

from Jehovah and the work was according to his will. But in the first place there is a difference between the work itself and the spirit in which it is done. Jehu received commendation for his act in cutting off the seed of Ahab, but later his house was extirpated for the guilt of this same "blood of Jezreel" (Hos. i. 4). The Assyrian was entrusted with a commission against the ungodly nation; but he meant not so, it was in his heart to cut off nations not a few (Is. x. 7), and the decree that he should be broken upon the mountains of Israel went out against him (Is. xiv. 25). Nebuchadnezzar was the "servant" of the Lord, but because Babylon laid her yoke heavily on the aged of the people, not considering the issue of such things, bereavement and widowhood shall come upon her in one day (Is. xlvii. 6—8). Here the prophet reprobates both the actions and the spirit of Edom, and threatens that Jehovah will recompense it into their bosom. In ancient modes of thought the people and their god were one. The people were but the reflection of the god, they were the people of Chemosh or Milcom or Jehovah. All wars were religious wars, wars against a god who animated and gave strength to his people (Ex. xii. 12). Edom's despite was to some extent in the strict sense directed against Jehovah. In truth they knew Jehovah only as the God of Israel, but it was he whom they knew, though they might not have such knowledge of him as Ezek. had attained to. But it is possible to be guilty of great sins against God, even though they are done unwittingly and without full knowledge of that which he is.

And in the second place, Edom received no commission from Jehovah against his people. Their place in history and among the nations of the earth gave them no significance in relation to Israel, or in Jehovah's providence embracing all the world. The contact of Israel with the nations exercising universal empire over the earth, if it did not suggest conceptions of Jehovah's universal power and dominion to the prophets, at least gave them occasion for expressing to the people and to all time such conceptions; and this period of Israel's history lent a breadth and elevation to prophecy to which in political conditions such as existed in earlier times it could never have attained. The transportation of colonies of Israelites also into the Assyrian and Babylonian empires, besides purifying the religion of the people from its dependence on ritual observance and making it more inward among those who continued to adhere to it, leavened the populations of these heathen nations with truer conceptions of Deity and religion. The writers of this age often refer to the strangers joining themselves to the covenant of the Lord (Is. xiv. 1, 2, lvi. 1—8), and no doubt the same influence was exerted by Israel, if not to the same extent, in Babylon and the countries of the East, as we are familiar with in later times in Rome and the empire of the West. In such respects Edom had no importance, and hardly entered into the larger designs of Jehovah with respect to his people and mankind.

Also, thou son of man, prophesy unto the mountains of 36
Israel, and say, Ye mountains of Israel, hear the word of
the LORD: thus saith the Lord GOD; Because the enemy 2
hath said against you, Aha, even the ancient high places
are ours in possession: therefore prophesy and say, Thus 3
saith the Lord GOD; Because *they* have made *you* desolate,
and swallowed you up on every side, that ye might be a
possession unto the residue of the heathen, and ye are taken
up in the lips of talkers, and *are* an infamy of the people:
therefore, ye mountains of Israel, hear the word of the Lord 4
GOD; Thus saith the Lord GOD to the mountains, and to
the hills, to the rivers, and to the valleys, to the desolate

CH. XXXVI. POSITIVE PROPHECY IN BEHALF OF THE LAND.

(1) *vv.* 1—7. The mountain land of Israel shall be delivered out of the hand of the heathen round about, who have usurped it. These nations shall bear their shame.
(2) *vv.* 8—15. The land shall in the age to come be luxuriantly fruitful. The reproach that it ate up its inhabitants shall no more fall upon it.
(3) *vv.* 16—38. The redemptive principles illustrated in these blessings of the future, and in all Israel's history. Not for Israel's sake but for his own name's sake it is that Jehovah will accomplish these things.

1 *seq.* Deliverance of the mountains of Israel from the nations who have usurped it. The passage is the reversal of all that which was threatened in ch. vi.

mountains of Israel] i.e. mountain land of Israel, vi. 2, xvii. 22, xxxiii. 28, &c.

2. Cf. xxv. 3, xxvi. 2.

ancient high places] "High places" is not used here in the usual religious sense of rural sanctuaries, but said of the mountain-land of Israel, cf. Deut. xxxii. 13; Mic. iii. 12. On ancient or "eternal" as an epithet of mountains cf. Gen. xlix. 26; Deut. xxxiii. 15; Ps. xxiv. 7. For "high places" LXX. reads "wastes," cf. perpetual desolations, xxxv. 9.

3. *Because*...] lit. *because, because*, xiii. 10. The passage throughout betrays passionate feeling on the part of the prophet. His patriotism is aglow as the loved mountains of his native land rise before his mind; cf. the pathetic words in reference to the exiled king, xix. 9. Hence the excitation and solemnity displayed in introducing the prophecy, which itself is expressed (*v.* 7 *seq.*) only after four or five commands to utter it (*vv.* 3, 4, 5, 6). For made desolate *gaped for* might be read, Is. xlii. 14.

and ye are taken up] Or, and **are come up upon the lips**, Deut. xxviii. 37; Lam. ii. 15; Dan. ix. 16 (niph. not unusual in this verb, Jer. xxxvii. 5).

wastes, and to the cities that are forsaken, which became a prey and derision to the residue of the heathen that *are* 5 round about; therefore thus saith the Lord GOD; Surely in the fire of my jealousy have I spoken against the residue of the heathen, and against all Idumea, which have appointed my land into their possession with the joy of all *their* heart, with despiteful minds, to cast it out for a prey. 6 Prophesy therefore concerning the land of Israel, and say unto the mountains, and to the hills, to the rivers, and to the valleys, Thus saith the Lord GOD; Behold, I have spoken in my jealousy and in my fury, because ye have 7 borne the shame of the heathen: therefore thus saith the Lord GOD; I have lifted up mine hand, Surely the heathen that *are* about you, they shall bear their shame.

8 But ye, O mountains of Israel, ye shall shoot forth your branches, and yield your fruit to my people of Israel; for 9 they are at hand to come. For behold, I *am* for you, and I 10 will turn unto you, and ye shall be tilled and sown: and I will multiply men upon you, all the house of Israel, *even* all of it: and the cities shall be inhabited, and the wastes shall

---

5. *fire of my jealousy*] "Jealousy" is injured self-consciousness; it is the reaction of Jehovah's sense of himself against the injurious conduct of Edom and the nations in relation to him or that which is his, cf. *my* land.

to cast it out] The expression is difficult both in grammar (as xvii. 9) and meaning. To take "cast it (the land) out" in the sense of cast out the inhabitants is not quite natural, though cf. xxiv. 6. The reading may be faulty.

6. *borne the shame of the heathen*] The shame cast on them by the heathen, cf. *v.* 15, xxxiv. 29.

7. *lifted up mine hand*] The gesture of taking an oath, xx. 5. Strictly the rendering is *I lift up*, so *I speak*, *vv.* 5, 6.

bear their shame] As Israel has borne the shame of the reproaches and taunts of the heathen, so they, when their destruction cometh (as it is near), shall bear the shame of it.

8—15. Positive promise to the mountain-land of Israel. In the age of the regeneration, which is at the door, it shall be luxuriantly fruitful (*vv.* 8, 9), and populous (*vv.* 10—12); it shall no more kill its inhabitants with scarcity (*vv.* 13, 14), nor any more be subject to the reproach of the nations on this account (*v.* 15).

8. *at hand to come*] The presentiment of the prophet is that the restoration of the people and the age to which all these promises which he gives (ch. xxxiii.—xxxvii.) belong is close at hand.

10. Cf. *v.* 33; Is. lviii. 12, lxi. 4; Zech. viii. 12.

be builded: and I will multiply upon you man and beast; 11 and they shall increase and bring fruit: and I will settle you after your old estates, and will do better *unto you* than at your beginnings: and ye shall know that I *am* the LORD. Yea, I will cause men to walk upon you, *even* my people 12 Israel; and they shall possess thee, and thou shalt be their inheritance, and thou shalt no more henceforth bereave them of men. Thus saith the Lord GOD; Because they 13 say unto you, Thou *land* devourest up men, and hast bereaved thy nations; therefore thou shalt devour men no 14 more, neither bereave thy nations any more, saith the Lord GOD. Neither will I cause *men* to hear in thee the shame 15 of the heathen any more, neither shalt thou bear the reproach of the people any more, neither shalt thou cause thy nations to fall any more, saith the Lord GOD.

11. Jer. xxxi. 27, xxxiii. 12, 13; Hos. ii. 23; Zech. viii. 4, 5. On "old estates," i.e. former condition, cf. xvi. 55.

your beginnings] i.e. early or former estate, Job viii. 7, xlii. 12. The phrase "increase and bring fruit (multiply)," common in some parts of Pent. (Priests' Code), is wanting in LXX.

12. *bereave them of men*] Properly the term means to bereave of children, here it is used generally, to bereave the people, i.e. destroy its members, Jer. xv. 7.

13. Comp. the report of the spies, Numb. xiii. 32, "the land is a land that eateth up the inhabitants thereof." The land whose population perishes of scarcity is regarded as itself devouring them. It is doubtful if there is any reference to such things as the unhealthy situation of the land (2 Kings ii. 19), or even to the wars by which the country had been decimated. The true meaning is given *v.* 30.

bereaved thy nations] thy **nation**, i.e. population, and so *vv.* 14, 15. The *plur.* could hardly refer to the two nations, Israel and Judah (xxxv. 10), although it might possibly be used like "peoples" of the nation considered as made up of a number of portions (Hos. x. 14). The land of Israel was subject to droughts (Jer. xiv. 1; 1 K. xvii. *seq.*, Am. iv. 7), to blasting and mildew (Am. iv. 9), as well as to the scourge of locusts (Joel i.). Comp. the struggles with famine which the returned exiles had, Hag. i. 10, 11, ii. 17.

15. Read **peoples** for people, as usual.

cause thy nations to fall] Rather: **bereave thy nation** any more. The same word is read *v.* 14, but corrected in Heb. marg., and the same correction should be made here (shakal=bereave, kashal=fall). The clause is wanting in LXX.

16—38. NOT FOR ISRAEL'S SAKE BUT FOR HIS OWN NAME'S SAKE DOES JEHOVAH DO ALL THIS IN BEHALF OF HIS PEOPLE.

The passage is remarkable and deserves to be studied almost more

16 Moreover the word of the LORD came unto me, saying,

than any other part of Ezek. when one is seeking to understand his general conceptions. It exhibits his philosophy of history (cf. ch. xx.), and also describes with great beauty the principles of Jehovah's redemption of his people, and how step by step this shall be accomplished. The prophet reviews the history of the people from the beginning, running it out till it is lost in its eternal issues, and shewing how it will read to all the nations of the earth the true lesson of that which Jehovah, the God of Israel, is, and leave ineffaceable impressions on the mind of his own people.

First, *vv*. 16—24. The history with its significance up to Israel's final restoration.—The people defiled the land with their idolatries and bloodshed (*v*. 17), therefore the fury of Jehovah was kindled and he poured it out upon them, scattering them among the nations (*vv*. 18, 19). By these disasters which the people brought upon themselves they "profaned" Jehovah's name among the heathen. The nations, ignorant of the nature of Jehovah, and incapable of divining the moral principles of his rule of the world and of his people, attributed the calamities of Israel to the feebleness of their God, who was unable to defend them, saying, these are the people of Jehovah, and they are gone forth out of his land. Thus the greatness and power of Jehovah, who is God alone, was detracted from, and the knowledge of him by the nations—which he wills in all that he does to convey to them—was delayed or frustrated (*v*. 20). Therefore for the sake of his holy name he will interpose and turn the fortunes of his people, that he may be sanctified in the eyes of the nations and known by them to be God omnipotent (*vv*. 21—24, cf. *vv*. 35, 36).

Secondly, *vv*. 24—38. The history of Jehovah's restoration of his people and their full redemption in its successive steps, with the eternal impressions which this history will engrave upon the people's minds.—In the prophet's view Jehovah must vindicate himself in the eyes of the nations by the restoration of Israel, not because he is a mere tribal god who will do something for his people, but because he is God alone, and his manifestation of himself to the nations of the world is the goal towards which all history runs.

Jehovah "sanctifies" himself in the sight of the nations not only by convincing them of his power, but even more if possible by displaying his moral rule of his people (cf. xxxix. 23, 24), and by the spiritual regeneration which he works among them (*v*. 25 *seq*.). But though this great thought of Jehovah's revelation of himself in the sight of the nations be attractive to the prophet, having touched upon the redemption of Israel he becomes absorbed in these internal operations of Jehovah among his own people, which he pursues in all their details, and the wider thought of their influence on the heathen is not reverted to till *vv*. 35, 36. (1) Jehovah will take his people from the nations and bring them again to their own land (*v*. 24). (2) Then he will sprinkle clean water upon them and wash them from all their past impurities (*v*. 25). (3) He will also regenerate them, giving them

Son of man, when the house of Israel dwelt in their own land, they defiled it by their own way and by their doings: their way was before me as the uncleanness of a removed woman. Wherefore I poured my fury upon them for the blood that they had shed upon the land, and for their idols *wherewith* they had polluted it: and I scattered them among the heathen, and they were dispersed through the countries: according to their way and according to their doings I judged them. And when they entered unto the heathen, 17 18 19 20

a new heart and a new spirit, putting indeed his own spirit within them (*vv.* 26, 27). (4) In this spirit they shall walk in his statutes and judgments, and thus shall inherit the land for ever, which the Lord will greatly bless (*vv.* 27—30). (5) Surrounded thus on all sides by the tokens of Jehovah's goodness, and looking at themselves and at their past doings with the new mind which the Lord will give them (*v.* 26), they shall loathe themselves because of all their former impurity and evil, for it is not for what they have been that Jehovah does this to them (*vv.* 31, 32). (6) Thus when Israel's captivity is brought back the nations shall learn the true meaning of their dispersion, and the nature of Jehovah their God, who disperses and restores (*vv.* 33—36).

16—23. Israel's past history and the principles which it illustrates.

17. When in their own land the people defiled it with their doings. The land was "holy" being sanctified by Jehovah's presence in it. The sins of the people, idolatry and bloodshed, desecrated it and made it unclean. Holy embraces "clean" under it, as the general does a particular, Jer. ii. 7; Lev. xviii. 25. Ezek., however, seems to call all sins "uncleanness." This way of speaking and thinking could hardly have arisen except under the influence of a law of ceremonial defilements (which were *real* defilements) and purifications.

uncleanness of a removed] the **uncleanness of a woman's impurity**. Lev. xv. 19. The comparison expresses the extreme of loathing, ch. vii. 20.

18. The effect of these sins was to awaken the fury of Jehovah. The "blood" may be murder from violence or judicial murder, so often reprobated in the earlier prophets, or it may be the sacrifice of children, xvi. 36, xxiii. 37.

19. The consequences of Jehovah's wrath—the people were scattered by him among all the nations, vii. 3, xviii. 30.

20. These disasters which the people of Jehovah brought on themselves led to the desecration of his name among the heathen. The nations judged him weak and unable to protect his people. In the eyes of the nations the interests of the god and his people were one; if a people was subdued by another it was because its god was too feeble to protect it. Naturally the idea of a god exercising a moral

whither they went, they profaned my holy name, when *they* said to them, These *are* the people of the LORD, and
21 are gone forth out of his land. But I had pity for mine holy name, which the house of Israel had profaned among
22 the heathen, whither they went. Therefore say unto the house of Israel, Thus saith the Lord GOD; I do not *this* for your sakes, O house of Israel, but for mine holy name's sake, which ye have profaned among the heathen, whither
23 ye went. And I will sanctify my great name, which was profaned among the heathen, which ye have profaned in the midst of them; and the heathen shall know that I *am* the LORD, saith the Lord GOD, when I shall be sanctified

rule over his own people would not yet occur to them. That Jehovah so rules is the lesson which the history of Israel, its dispersion and restoration, is intended to read to the nations of the earth. This lesson was one which Israel itself was slow to learn, and when Amos (iii. 2) read it to them, it was perhaps as strange to some as it might be to the heathen.

they profaned] i.e. Israel. Israel by bringing their dispersion upon themselves led to the desecration of Jehovah's name by the nations, and hence they are said directly to have profaned his name (*v.* 21).

when they *said to them*] when **it was said of them**, These are... and they are gone forth..., i.e. though the people of Jehovah, they have been driven into exile out of the land—he has not been able to protect them.

21. Cf. xx. 9, 14.

22. *do not* this *for your sakes*] Not for what Israel has been or deserved. The ref. is to Israel's past history; such a meaning as that it is not for any interest which he has in Israel or in order to benefit them that Jehovah delivers them, but only to magnify his own name, is entirely extraneous to the passage and a distortion of its sense. Cf. Is. xliii. 22—28, xlviii. 9—11. "Name" is not equivalent to person, but is a reflection or expression of the person; hence all that is due to the person or can be said of it, is due to the name and can be employed of it.

23. *sanctify my great name*] To sanctify is the opposite of to profane. As the latter term means to detract from the power, majesty or purity of Jehovah, or from any of those attributes which belong to his godhead, to sanctify is to manifest or make these attributes conspicuous. Hence the effect of Jehovah's sanctifying his name is that the heathen know him to be Jehovah—God alone and all that which he is who is God alone. In *v.* 22 "holy name," here "great name"; "greatness" is an element in "holiness."

be sanctified in you] Or reflexive: shew myself holy—where "holy" embraces the attributes of Deity as a whole. Israel is the

in you before their eyes. For I will take you from among ²⁴ the heathen, and gather you out of all countries, and will bring you into your own land.

Then will I sprinkle clean water upon you, and ye shall ²⁵ be clean: from all your filthiness, and from all your idols, will I cleanse you. A new heart also will I give you, and a ²⁶ new spirit will I put within you: and I will take away the stony heart out of your flesh, and I will give you a heart of flesh. And I will put my spirit within you, and cause you ²⁷

subject *through* which Jehovah shews himself to be God, i.e. by his operations in Israel in the sight of the nations.

24 *seq.* These operations are his restoration and regeneration of Israel. It is certainly possible that the more internal operations of Jehovah on Israel (*v.* 25 *seq.*)—his washing them with clean water and putting a new spirit within them that they shall walk in his statutes, are considered part of Jehovah's sanctifying of himself in the sight of the nations. They do express better what Jehovah is than a mere exhibition of power, cf. xxxix. 23, 24; Is. lxi. 3, lxii. 2. At the same time this more general idea seems to pass from the prophet's mind in the delight with which he dwells on Israel's religious regeneration. The wider idea is at any rate returned to in *v.* 33 *seq.*

25. Dogmatically, sprinkling with clean water might seem merely to express the idea of the forgiveness of past sins. The figure is taken from the washings by which ceremonial defilement was removed, and the figure is part of the idea. By their relation to the idols and service of them the people contracted uncleanness. And when the kind of service which this was is considered, the debasing forms which it took, and the immoralities which accompanied it or formed part of it (Hos. iv. 13, 14), the depth of defilement will be understood and the strong figure *v.* 17 will not appear too strong.

26. *A new heart*] The "heart" is used here generally of the nature. Formerly their heart was strong, obdurate, unimpressible and rebellious (ii. 4, iii. 7); now they shall receive a "heart of flesh," impressible and soft, sensitive to the divine admonitions and will. The phrase shews that in the Old Testament no idea of corrupt inclination attaches to the term "flesh" (xi. 19). According to usage "spirit" expresses the ruling principle in the mind, the force that gives direction and motion to the current of thought and conduct, or that prevailing current itself. The heart is more passive and receptive and but responds to influences, the spirit is active and regulative. Jer. xxxii. 37—39.

27. *put my spirit*] This great promise is one which does not appear prominently in the prophets till the exile. In Is. xi. the Messianic king has the spirit of Jehovah in all the manifoldness of his operation, and in xxxii. 15 the hope is expressed that "the spirit shall be poured on us from on high" (though the passage is held by some to be later than Is.); but it is in exile and post-exile times that the idea is first

to walk in my statutes, and ye shall keep my judgments, 28 and do *them*. And ye shall dwell in the land that I gave to your fathers; and ye shall be my people, and I will be 29 your God. I will also save you from all your uncleannesses: and I will call for the corn, and will increase it, and lay no 30 famine upon you. And I will multiply the fruit of the tree, and the increase of the field, that ye shall receive no more 31 reproach of famine among the heathen. Then shall ye

expressed with great certainty, e.g. Ezek. xxxvi. 27, xxxvii. 14; Joel ii. 28; Zech. iv. 6 (xii. 10). Jeremiah does not use the expression, though his promise that Jehovah will write his law on men's hearts seems to have much the same sense, or at least it expresses the "new spirit" of Ezek., and in the New Testament this new spirit is the spirit of God. There always attaches to "spirit" the idea of power in operation, the spirit of God is God exerting power.

to walk in my statutes] Being endowed with the spirit of God they will walk in his statutes, for these are expressions of his spirit. The spirit of God will appear both as an inward impulse to fulfil God's will, and as a power to do it. In the Old Testament the spirit of God, even the prophetic spirit, is usually a dynamic influence, an elevation of the natural human faculties. The "statutes and judgments" are not the mere external enactments of the law; they embrace all the moral laws to which Ezek. so often refers (e.g. ch. xviii., xxii., xxxiii.), and it is doubtful if the prophet refers specially to written laws at all.

28. Again, the consequence of walking in Jehovah's statutes will be that they shall inherit the land for ever, cf. xxviii. 25, xxxvii. 25. The promise attached to the fifth commandment—the first commandment with promise—belongs to the commandments given to Israel as a whole. The keeping of them was the condition of remaining in the land. When the people disregarded them they were driven out, and only when their former sins were forgiven could they be restored (Is. xl. 2). It may be a question whether there be now any connexion between Israel and the land of Canaan. If there be, the condition of restoration to it is faith and obedience on the part of the people. A restoration of Jews still in unbelief to Canaan, even if it should occur, could have no meaning so far as the redemptive providence of God is concerned, and would not enter into any relation with the Old Testament scriptures. Comp. the order stated *v.* 33.

29. *save you from...uncleannesses*] Or, **I will save** (deliver) **you out of your...** The phrase "save out of" is pregnant, meaning "save you by purifying you from"..., hardly, save you from the consequences of... Cf. xxxvii. 23, and reading there.

call for the corn] Cf. xxxiv. 27, 29; Hos. ii. 21; Jer. xxxi. 12 (cf. 2 Kings viii. 1).

30. Cf. xxxiv. 27 *seq*.

31. Cf. vi. 9, xvi. 61, 63. Omit the words "in your own sight," ch. xx. 43.

remember your own evil ways, and your doings that *were* not good, and shall lothe yourselves in your own sight for your iniquities and for your abominations. Not for your 32 sakes do I *this*, saith the Lord GOD, be it known unto you: be ashamed and confounded for your own ways, O house of Israel. Thus saith the Lord GOD; In the day that I shall 33 have cleansed you from all your iniquities, I will also cause *you* to dwell in the cities, and the wastes shall be builded. And the desolate land shall be tilled, whereas it lay desolate 34 in the sight of all that passed by. And they shall say, This 35 land that was desolate is become like the garden of Eden; and the waste and desolate and ruined cities *are become* fenced, *and* are inhabited. Then the heathen that are left 36 round about you shall know that I the LORD build the ruined *places, and* plant that that was desolate: I the LORD have spoken *it*, and I will do *it*. Thus saith the Lord GOD; 37

32. The verse is closely connected with the preceding: ye shall remember your former evil, for not for your sakes do I this—not because of your good deserving (*v.* 22); on the contrary their own ways when thought upon could only cause them shame. In Lev. xxvi. 45 "for their sakes" means "to their benefit," on their behalf.

33—36. The prophet returns to the lessons which Israel's history, the author of which is their God, will read to the nations of the world. When they behold the desolated land of Israel become like the garden of Eden they shall form another judgment regarding Jehovah, and know that which he is, and the meaning of the history of his people.

33. The order stated here is of course a necessity: as the sins of the people caused them to be cast out of their land, their forgiveness must precede their restoration to it. In the prophets events are not events merely, they are exhibitions of moral principles. So in Is. xl.—lxvi. the restoration of Israel to Canaan is preceded by the atonement of their sins by the servant of the Lord (Is. xl. 2).

36. *I...build...plant*] Perhaps; **have builded...planted**. The words hardly express a general characteristic of Jehovah, but refer to the fact that it is he who has restored Israel—comp. last words of the verse. Reflecting on Jehovah's restoration of the people the nations will recognise not merely his power, but also the deeper principles which underlie his government of his people.

37, 38. A single point in the Lord's restoration of Israel is made prominent, the multiplication of the people. The terrible threats of the diminution of their numbers (*v.* 12), and of the destruction both of those remaining in the land and those going into exile, were no doubt to a great extent fulfilled (Lam. v.). The scanty population of Jerusalem is referred to by Nehemiah nearly a century after the first exiles returned (vii. 4). The old promise that they should be as the

I will yet *for* this be inquired of by the house of Israel, to do *it* for them; I will increase them *with* men like a flock. 38 As the holy flock, as the flock of Jerusalem in her solemn feasts; so shall the waste cities be filled *with* flocks of men: and they shall know that I *am* the LORD.

sand of the sea is here repeated, cf. *vv.* 10, 11, 33; Jer. xxxi. 27; Hos. i. 10; Zech. ii. 4.

37. *yet...be inquired of*] Almost: *I will let myself be inquired of*, which embraces not merely the enquiry or request on the part of the people, but the response to it on the part of the Lord. Cf. xiv. 3, xx. 3, 31. As usual "this" refers to what follows—the multiplication of the people.

38. *the holy flock*] i.e. the sacrificial sheep. The solemn feasts (where solemn has its proper sense of "customary," appointed) may be the three great yearly festivals, though in point of fact Ezek. does not refer to Pentecost, or the feast of weeks, in his concluding chapters. The comparison shews that already in pre-exile times enormous numbers of sacrificial animals were brought to Jerusalem for offerings at the feasts.

flocks of men] lit. *sheep-flocks in men*. The word "flock" in Heb. is not generalized so as to express a great number—it means a sheep-flock, and is explained by "men."

Probably no passage in the Old Testament of the same extent offers so complete a parallel to New Testament doctrine, particularly to that of St Paul. It is doubtful if the Apostle quotes Ezek. anywhere, but his line of thought entirely coincides with his. The same conceptions and in the same order belong to both—forgiveness (*v.* 25); regeneration, a new heart and spirit (*v.* 26); the spirit of God as the ruling power in the new life (*v.* 27); the issue of this, the keeping of the requirements of God's law (*v.* 27; Rom. viii. 4); the effect of being "under grace" in softening the human heart and leading to obedience (*v.* 31; Rom. vi., vii.); and the organic connexion of Israel's history with Jehovah's revelation of himself to the nations (*vv.* 33—36; Rom. xi.). The prophet's idea of the divine pedagogic is not precisely the same as that of the Apostle, and the present passage has in some particulars to be supplemented from ch. xvi. As put here it is Israel's historical experiences, their dispersion and restoration, with the thoughts which these suggest, that impress the nations and teach them what Jehovah is.

CH. XXXVII. THE PEOPLE.

The last step in the reconstruction of the new Israel is the resurrection of the people. The nation is dead, and its bones scattered and dry. But it shall rise from the dead; the bones shall come together and the spirit of life from Jehovah shall enter into them and they shall live. The passage has two parts:—

The hand of the LORD was upon me, and carried me out 37
in the spirit of the LORD, and set me down in the midst of
the valley which *was* full *of* bones, and caused me to pass 2
by them round about: and behold, *there were* very many in
the open valley; and lo, *they were* very dry. And he said 3
unto me, Son of man, can these bones live? And I answered,

First, *vv.* 1—14 the resurrection of the people Israel from death, and restoration to their own land.

Second, *vv.* 15—28 the union of the two houses of Israel, Judah and Ephraim, when restored under one head, even David.

1—14. THE VISION OF ISRAEL'S RESURRECTION FROM THE DEAD.

The vision seems suggested by the saying current among the people, "our bones are dried, our hope is lost; we are wholly cut off." This idea and feeling of the people takes form in the vision which the prophet saw in the valley. The language of the people is figurative: they speak of the nationality, which is no more,—it is dead and its bones scattered and dry. And this idea regarding the nationality, figuratively expressed by the people, is embodied to the prophet in a vision. Hence the passage is not a literal prophecy of the resurrection of individual persons of the nation, dead or slain; it is a prophecy of the resurrection of the nation, whose condition is figuratively expressed by the people when they represent its bones as long scattered and dry. Perfect consistency is not maintained by the prophet: in *vv.* 1, 2 the dry bones are represented as lying on the face of the valley, very many and very dry; in *v.* 12 they are represented as buried and brought up out of their graves. Hosea had already used the figure of resurrection for the resuscitation of the nation (vi. 2, xiii. 14); but, though the language used both here and by Hosea shews familiarity with the idea of the raising again of individuals, this is not what is prophesied. In Is. xxvi. 19; Dan. xii. the actual resurrection of individual members of Israel is predicted, cf. Job xiv. 13 *seq.*

1. *The hand of the Lord*] The prophetic ecstasy from the Lord, ch. i. 3. On "spirit" of the Lord cf. iii. 14, viii. 3, xi. 24. The "valley" is probably that mentioned early in the Book, iii. 22.

2. *the open valley*] lit. *on the face of the valley*. The bones were strewed over the valley in vast numbers, and they appeared bleached and dry. Their great number no doubt was suggested by the actual fact that vast multitudes of the people had been slain with the sword or had otherwise perished; and their "dryness" expresses at least the utter deadness of the nation and the apparent hopelessness of its revival, if not that it had been long dead (*v.* 11).

3. To the question, Can these bones live? the prophet, looking at them, could not answer Yea (even to the Apostle attainment unto the resurrection of the dead was something ineffably lofty, Phil. iii. 11), and yet in the presence of him who put the question he could not answer No (Rom. iv. 17—21; Heb. xi. 19). With reverence he answers, Thou knowest (Rev. vii. 14).

4 O Lord God, thou knowest. Again he said unto me, Prophesy upon these bones, and say unto them, O ye dry 5 bones, hear the word of the Lord. Thus saith the Lord God unto these bones; Behold, I *will* cause breath to enter 6 into you, and ye shall live: and I will lay sinews upon you, and will bring up flesh upon you, and cover you with skin, and put breath in you, and ye shall live; and ye shall know 7 that I *am* the Lord. So I prophesied as I was commanded: and as I prophesied, there was a noise, and behold a shaking, 8 and the bones came together, bone to his bone. And when I beheld, lo, the sinews and the flesh came up upon them, and the skin covered them above: but *there was* no breath 9 in them. Then said he unto me, Prophesy unto the wind, prophesy, son of man, and say to the wind, Thus saith the Lord God; Come from the four winds, O breath, and 10 breathe upon these slain, that they may live. So I prophesied

vv. 4—6. The prophet is bidden prophesy to the bones and promise them life from Jehovah.
5. The act of putting breath within them, being the main and final step of giving them life, is mentioned first as if it embraced all.
6. Then follow the details of their becoming actual men of flesh and blood.
vv. 7—10. As the prophet spoke there was a great sound and the bones came together, bone to his bone, and they became clothed with flesh; but as yet there was no breath of life in them.
7. *behold a shaking*] The word is rendered "rushing" (iii. 12). The noise is that occasioned by the rising and rushing of the bones together. The previous word "noise" is wanting in LXX., which reads simply: and it came to pass as I prophesied that behold a rushing.
9. The order described in the creation of man (Gen. ii.) is observed here: first the body was formed and then the breath of life was breathed into it.
Prophesy unto the wind] Or, *breath*. In Heb. the same word means wind, breath and spirit. The sign of life, the breath, is seen to be identical with the wind or air, and by an intensification of meaning common to many languages the "breath" becomes the principle of life, or the living principle itself, the spirit. The poet truly says (etymologically) the spirit does but mean the breath; but though the words be identical the ideas are different. The breath needful to be life in the vast multitude now created must be furnished by wind coming from all quarters of the heavens.
upon these slain] Or, **into** the slain. What is needful to make living men of them is breath in their nostrils. That which God did himself to the individual man when created, even breathe into his nos-

as he commanded me, and the breath came into them, and they lived, and stood up upon their feet, an exceeding great army. Then he said unto me, Son of man, these bones are 11 the whole house of Israel: behold, they say, Our bones are dried, and our hope is lost: we are cut off for our parts. Therefore prophesy and say unto them, Thus saith the 12 Lord God; Behold, O my people, I *will* open your graves, and cause you to come up out of your graves, and bring you into the land of Israel. And ye shall know that I *am* the 13 Lord, when I have opened your graves, O my people, and brought you up out of your graves, and shall put my spirit 14 in you, and ye shall live, and I shall place you in your own land: then shall ye know that I the Lord have spoken *it*, and performed *it*, saith the Lord.

trils the breath of life, is here accomplished by the wind from the four quarters of the heavens at his command breathing into the innumerable multitude. The wind from the four corners of the heavens is but a symbol of the universal life-giving spirit of God (*v.* 14).

vv. 11—14. Explanation of the vision.

11. *The whole house of Israel*] viz. Judah and Ephraim.

our hope is lost] Those who speak are the living members of the nation, and it is of the nationality that they speak. The destruction and dissolution of the nation appeared to them final. It could no more be revived than the dry bones could be made to live. This feeling often appears in exile writings, e.g. Is. xl.—lxvi. (xlix. 14 &c.) cf. the singular struggling against the idea, Lam. iii. 20 *seq.*

for our parts] A rendering of the ethical dat., which merely gives vividness to the words "we are cut off," or expresses the feeling of those who speak by reflecting the action back upon the subject. The term "cut off" (otherwise uncommon) is used also of the servant of the Lord, Is. liii. 8.

12. The figure is varied here, the people are regarded as dead and buried and their revival is an opening of their graves. The phrase "bring you into the land of Israel" shews, however, that the language is still used figuratively of the resuscitation of the dead nation and not literally of the resurrection of deceased individuals.

14. The symbol of the wind breathing into the slain is here explained: it is the spirit of Jehovah that gives life, Ps. civ. 30. The connexion shews that the spirit of the Lord here is merely the life-giving spirit, and not the regenerating spirit, as in xxxvi. 27—though the distinction is merely part of the figure. The resuscitation of the dead nation could come about only through their moral regeneration, and hence in Is. xl.—lxvi. this is part of the work of the Servant of the Lord (Is. xlix. 8—12, lxi. 1).

The passage is of great interest, apart from its own beauty, as casting light upon the condition of the people's mind. The prophet

15 The word of the Lord came again unto me, saying,
16 Moreover, thou son of man, take thee one stick, and write upon it, For Judah, and for the children of Israel his companions: then take another stick, and write upon it, For Joseph, the stick of Ephraim, and *for* all the house of Israel
17 his companions: and join them one to another into one
18 stick; and they shall become one in thine hand. And when the children of thy people shall speak unto thee,

is fond of quoting expressions from the mouth of the people (e.g. xi. 3, xii. 22, 27, xvi. 44, xviii. 2, 25, 29, cf. xxxiii. 17, 20, xx. 49, xxxvi. 20 &c.), and probably the words here used were actually heard. They shew a state of despondency quite natural and one no doubt greatly prevalent. Indeed in all the prophets of this age the hope that exists is hope only in Jehovah, which believes that in spite of past disasters their God will yet save the people. It is only by giving moral significance to Israel's calamities on the one hand, and on the other by animating the revolutions and commotions among the nations with Jehovah's purpose, that the faith of the prophets themselves is sustained. The prophetic hopes of this period are based on dogmatic presuppositions, e.g. that Jehovah is the true and living God and that there is none else; that Israel is his people and has his true revelation among them, which is imperishable and which must accomplish the purpose for which it was given and become effectual in making a true people of the Lord (Is. lv.); and that the purpose of the one God must embrace all the nations of the earth, between whom and Jehovah Israel is the link of communication. The prophetic views as to how Jehovah shall use Israel to give the nations the knowledge of himself differ. In Is. xl. *seq.* Israel becomes the light of the nations—having the true knowledge of God it imparts it to the heathen. In Ezekiel it is their own observation and reflection on Israel's history that reveals to the nations Jehovah's true nature. In all, however, the work of redemption is the work of Jehovah. Here his restoration of Israel is reanimation of the dead through his life-giving spirit.

15—28. Prophecy of the reunion of the restored Israel into one kingdom, ruled by one king, even David.

(1) *vv.* 15—23. Symbol of the union of Judah and Israel into one kingdom, with its explanation.

(2) *vv.* 24—25. There shall be one king over the new nation, even David.

(3) *vv.* 26—28. Jehovah's covenant with the people shall be everlasting, and his presence will sanctify them.

16. *one stick*] i.e. staff, or rod, equivalent to sceptre, Numb. xvii. 2; so *vv.* 17, 19, 20.

children of Israel] After the fall of the northern kingdom the name Israel was often used of Judah, the only remaining part of it. Here Israel of the north is called Joseph or Ephraim.

saying, Wilt thou not shew us what thou meanest by these? say unto them, Thus saith the Lord GOD; Behold, I *will* take the stick of Joseph, which *is* in the hand of Ephraim, and the tribes of Israel his fellows, and will put them with him, *even* with the stick of Judah, and make them one stick, and they shall be one in mine hand. And the sticks whereon thou writest shall be in thine hand before their eyes. And say unto them, Thus saith the Lord GOD; Behold, I *will* take the children of Israel from among the heathen, whither they be gone, and will gather them on every side, and bring them into their own land: and I will make them one nation in the land upon the mountains of Israel; and one king shall be king to them all: and they shall be no more two nations, neither shall they be divided into two kingdoms any more at all: neither shall they defile themselves any more with their idols, nor with their detestable things, nor with any of their transgressions: but I will save them out of all their dwelling places, wherein they have sinned, and will cleanse them: so shall they be my people,

19. Explanation of the symbolical action.
put them with him] lit. *join them unto it*, even *unto the stick of Judah*. The construction is rather unnatural (for *eth*, cf. xiv. 22, xliii. 17, others would read *el*).
in mine hand] Vulg. reads *in his hand* (so Ew.), i.e. Judah's, and LXX. actually *in the hand of Judah*. LXX. either read *his* hand and interpreted it of Judah, or took the final *y* of *my* hand as an abbreviation for Yehudah. On the one hand the united staff or sceptre might be given into the hand of Judah as the ruler of the one kingdom was to be David (Am. ix. 11; Hos. iii. 5). On the other hand there is no trace in the passage of any preeminence of Judah over Israel of the north.
20. This symbolical action may have been actually performed, though the supposition is scarcely necessary, cf. xii. 3.
22. This promise runs throughout all prophecy. The disruption of the state was felt even by Hosea, a native of the north, to have introduced a schism into the one kingdom of Jehovah, and to have broken the unity of the consciousness of the community, to which the consciousness of the one God corresponded. Hos. i. 11, viii. 3, 4; Is. xi. 13; Jer. iii. 18. The one God, the husband of the community, required that the community should also be one, with a single affection and service. Cf. xxxiv. 23, 24.
23. Cf. xxxvi. 25.
all their dwelling places] More probably: out of all their **backslidings**. So LXX., cf. xxxvi. 29.

24 and I will be their God. And David my servant *shall be* king over them; and they all shall have one shepherd: they shall also walk in my judgments, and observe my statutes, 25 and do them. And they shall dwell in the land that I have given unto Jacob my servant, wherein your fathers have dwelt; and they shall dwell therein, *even* they, and their children, and their children's children for ever: and my 26 servant David *shall be* their prince for ever. Moreover I will make a covenant of peace with them; it shall be an everlasting covenant with them: and I will place them, and multiply them, and will set my sanctuary in the midst of 27 them for evermore. My tabernacle also shall be with them:

24. *David my servant*] Cf. xxxiv. 23, 24. Here the term "king" is applied to the ruler of the future (*v.* 22); in other places "prince." The words seem used indifferently, cf. xix. 1, xxii. 25. Cf. xxxvi. 27.

25. Cf. xxxvi. 28.

Jacob my servant] Jacob is here the patriarch himself, not as in Is. xl. *seq.* a name for the people. He is referred to as the ancestor of Israel in Hos. xii. 12, as Abraham in Is. xxix. 22. Cf. ch. xxxiii. 24; Is. xli. 8, li. 2, lxiii. 16.

their prince for ever] It is not at all probable that "David my servant" means either the Davidic house or a line of kings. But possibly the point whether the king would be one person living for ever is not before the prophet's mind. It is the quality of the new people and the new ruler that he specially refers to; the point whether generation after generation of the people shall dwell in the land and prince succeed prince is hardly in his mind. The unity of the people and the unity of the ruler, one such as David; the character of the people (*v.* 24) and their perpetual possession of the land—these are the elements of the prophet's idea, and further questions are not touched. In xliii. 7, xlv. 8, a succession of princes appears presupposed, but the idea hardly belongs to the present passage.

26. *a covenant of peace*] Cf. xxxiv. 25; Is. lv. 3; Jer. xxxii. 40.

my sanctuary] The name given by the prophet to the temple as the dwelling place of Jehovah (*v.* 27) and specially sanctified or made holy by his presence.

27. *My tabernacle also*] And **my dwelling place...and I will be.** The words repeat the idea in *v.* 26. The last words of the Book are, "The Lord is there." The phrase *with* them, i.e. by or beside them (cf. ii. 6), might mean *over* them, reference being to the situation of the temple, high above the city (xl. 2), but this has little probability. It would be more natural to take *over* in the ideal sense of a "protection" to them. The sanctuary, however, does not protect, it sanctifies, although being sanctified Jehovah will protect them (ch. xxxviii.—xxxix.). The expression "I will be their God" varies the idea of his dwelling place being with them, xi. 20, xiv. 11, xxxvi. 28.

yea, I will be their God, and they shall be my people. And 28 the heathen shall know that I the LORD do sanctify Israel, when my sanctuary shall be in the midst of them for evermore.

28. The presence of Jehovah makes the house wherein he dwells a sanctuary (holy place), and the presence of his sanctuary (he being there, xlviii. 35) among the people sanctifies them or makes them "holy"—a term which expresses two things: being the possession of Jehovah, and being in disposition and life all that the people of Jehovah must be. The idea that Jehovah's presence "sanctifies" the people is common. Jehovah's dwelling-place being among the people for ever the nations shall know that he "sanctifies" them. To sanctify is not to protect, it is to make the people his own and worthy of him, but this implies protection. Jer. ii. 3, "Israel was a holy thing to the Lord, the first fruit of his increase, all that ate him up incurred guilt." The ideas in this verse lead naturally over to the episode of Gog's invasion, the issues of which so remarkably illustrate them.

The restoration of Israel includes the tribes of the north as well as Judah. All the prophets of this age regard the northern exiles as still existing, cf. Jer. iii. 12—15: Is. xlix. 5, 6, and the strong passage Is. xliii. 5—7 "every one called by my name," i.e. every member of the people of the Lord. Cf. the present prophet's disposition of all the tribes in the holy land, ch. xlviii.

CH. XXXVIII., XXXIX. INVASION OF THE RESTORED ISRAEL IN THE LATTER DAYS BY GOG AND ALL THE NATIONS LYING IN THE OUTSKIRTS OF THE WORLD, AND ISRAEL'S PROTECTION BY JEHOVAH.

These two chapters are closely connected with ch. xxxvii. 28, "the nations shall know that I Jehovah do sanctify" Israel. This recalls to the prophet's mind the invasion of Gog, a great and final attack on Israel by the nations, and he introduces the description of it here, as it illustrates so conspicuously what is said in xxxvii. 21—28. For the invasion of Gog is an episode out of connexion with the restoration of the people, which has formed the theme of the preceding chapters (xxxiii.—xxxvii). It lies far in the future (*v.* 8, 16), long after Israel has been restored, and when it has dwelt long in peace in its own land (*v.* 8, 11). The sedulous care with which the land is purified from the carcases of Gog's host, every bone being carefully collected and the whole buried beyond the Jordan, is sufficient evidence of the holiness of Israel and the land at the time of Gog's attack (xxxix. 11—16).

The prophet is not the author of the idea of this invasion. It has been predicted of old by the prophets of Israel, prophesying over long periods (xxxviii. 17, xxxix. 8). Neither is it probable that the idea was one read out of certain prophecies merely by Ezekiel. More likely it was an idea widely entertained. The former prophecies on which the belief was founded are not to be supposed to have contained the *name* of Gog, any more than the prophecies applied by the author of Is. xl. *seq.* to the career of Cyrus need have referred to him by name.

The conception is rather shadowy and vague. The time is indefinite, it is far into the years to come; the nations who cluster around the standard of Gog, himself a somewhat nebulous personage, are those lying in the uttermost regions of the world, which had been heard of but never seen. The most distant north and the most distant south send their contingents to swell the innumerable host, and the far-off commercial peoples Sheba and Dedan and Tarshish follow his camp (*vv.* 3, 5, 6, 13). The description seems almost a creation, the embodiment of an idea—the idea of the irreconcilable hostility of the nations of the world to the religion of Jehovah, and the presentiment that this must yet be manifested on a grander scale than has ever yet been. Hence the supernatural magnitude of the outlines of the picture (*vv.* 9, 16, 20). The main idea of the prophet, however, is quite perspicuous. With the exception of Ethiopia, a somewhat general name for the most distant south, none of the historical nations appear under Gog's banner. These nations that came into connexion with Israel during her history have already learned to know Jehovah (ch. xxv.—xxxii.). They have not been exterminated, but his glory has been revealed to them and they no more trouble the peace of the restored Israel (xxxvi. 36). But the nations lying in the outskirts of the earth, as another prophet expresses it, "have not heard Jehovah's fame neither have seen his glory" (Is. lxvi. 19), and he who is God alone must reveal himself to all flesh, for he has sworn by himself that to him every knee shall bow (Is. xlv. 23). Such is the meaning of this last act in the drama of the world's history. As it is Jehovah's final revelation of himself to all the nations of the earth, it is accompanied by all those terrors and convulsions in nature which in earlier prophets usually signalize the day of the Lord (xxxviii. 19—23). This indeed is peculiar in Ezek. that he places Jehovah's great and last revelation of himself *after* the restoration of his people to peace and felicity, while in the earlier prophets it precedes or accompanies their restoration; as it does even in prophets after him (Is. xl. 5; Ps. cii. 16). In this order he is followed by the Apocalypse (Rev. xix. 11, xx. 7). Besides the display of Jehovah's might in the overthrow of Gog and in the terrible convulsions of nature, his moral being and rule is also revealed through his people, for his protection of them now that they are holy and true casts light to the nations on his former dispersion of them (xxxix. 23).

Gog is styled prince of Rosh, Meshech and Tubal, nations lying in the extremities of the north (*v.* 15). Other nations are joined to these, lying in the furthest south (*v.* 5). And in the train of these warriors come the hosts of far-off commercial peoples, camp followers intent on gain (*v.* 13). It is, therefore, self-evident that the Chaldeans are not represented under the name of Gog. The Chaldeans are Jehovah's mandatories, commissioned to chastise his people, and humble the ungodly pride of such nations as Egypt and Phenicia, and Ezekiel's prophecies contain no threats against Babylon. He intimates indeed that the supremacy of that power is but temporary, naming 40 years

And the word of the LORD came unto me, saying, Son of 38
man, set thy face against Gog, the land of Magog, the chief [2]
prince of Meshech and Tubal, and prophesy against him,

as the term when a new condition of the world will arise, which presupposes her decline and fall. But the invasion of Gog appears to him to be far away in the indefinite future, long after the promises of the Lord to his people have been fulfilled, and this fulfilment must be preceded by the overthrow of the Chaldean power.

The passage extends to ch. xxxix. 24, where the prophet resumes the point of view occupied in ch. xxxiii.—vii. prior to the Restoration of Israel.

CH. XXXVIII. THE INVASION OF GOG, AND HIS DESTRUCTION.

(1) *vv.* 1—9. Gog's enterprise regarded as the purpose and operation of Jehovah. The Lord will bring Gog forth with all his allies. He is commanded to hold himself in readiness to go up against Israel.

(2) *vv.* 10—13. Gog's enterprise regarded as due to his own evil purposes. Evil thoughts shall come into his mind, and he will resolve to invade Israel, to spoil a spoil and to get him much prey. The merchant nations shall follow his camp intent on gain.

(3) *vv.* 14—19. Gog's coming up and his bringing up have the same result or purpose eventually: Jehovah shall be "sanctified" in (through) him, and the nations shall know that he is God.

(4) *vv.* 17—23. Gog's attack had long been predicted by former prophets. On that day Jehovah will reveal himself in all his majesty and shake terribly the earth. All creation shall be terror-stricken before him, and all that is lofty on the earth shall be thrown down (Is. ii. iii.). He will bring destruction on Gog, causing a supernatural panic in his host and turning the sword of the confederates against one another, and overwhelming them in tempests of hail and fire from heaven. Thus will the nations fear his holy name.

1—6. THE GREAT ARRAY OF GOG WHICH JEHOVAH SHALL LEAD FORTH.

2. *set thy face against Gog*] Cf. xxxv. 2, 3. The meaning of the word Gog is obscure. Schrader (*KAT.* on the passage) refers to the name of the Lydian king Gyges, given as Gu-gu in the Assyr. inscriptions, on the one hand, and on the other to Gagi, name of the ruler of a country in the east, the situation of which is uncertain. This land apparently lay north of Assyria (Frd. Del. *Par.* p. 246—7).

Gog, the land of Magog] i.e. in sense: Gog in (of) the land of Magog. Gog is the prince and Magog his country (xxxix. 6). (In construction Magog is *acc.* of direction or in loose apposition to Gog, hardly *gen.* after the proper name).

the chief prince] More probably: **the prince of Rosh**, Meshech &c., although a people or country Rosh may be impossible to identify. Of course any connexion between the name and Russian is to be rejected. Frd. Del. (*Par.* p. 322) refers to the land of Rāsh (māt Ra-a-shi) of

3 and say, Thus saith the Lord GOD; Behold, I *am* against thee,
4 O Gog, the chief prince of Meshech and Tubal: and I will turn thee back, and put hooks into thy jaws, and I will bring thee forth, and all thine army, horses and horsemen, all of them clothed with all sorts *of armour, even* a great company *with* bucklers and shields, all of them handling swords:
5 Persia, Ethiopia, and Libya with them; all of them *with*
6 shield and helmet: Gomer, and all his bands; the house of Togarmah *of* the north quarters, and all his bands: *and*
7 many people with thee. Be thou prepared, and prepare for thyself, thou, and all thy company that are assembled unto
8 thee, and be thou a guard unto them. After many days

the inscriptions, situated on the borders of Elam on the Tigris. The geography of the prophet is no doubt vague and general, but this position as well as that of Gagi referred to above appears to lie too far east. The rendering "chief prince" would imply an unusual construction (chief-priest is different), and it is difficult to guess what chief prince or over-lord could mean. On Meshech, Tubal, cf. xxvii. 13, xxxii. 26.

3. *chief prince*] Cf. on *v.* 2.

4. *I will turn thee back*] Either: I will *turn thee about*, or, I will *lead thee*. The sense entice or "decoy" (Ew.) has scarcely evidence (Is. xlvii. 10). The clause "and I will turn...jaws" is wanting in LXX. Putting hooks into the jaws suggests unwillingness and compulsion (ch. xxix. 4; 2 Kings xix. 28), whereas Gog comes up of his own accord. This, however, is not quite conclusive, as Jehovah is leading him on to his destruction.

with all sorts of armour] Rather: **clothed gorgeously** (cf. xxiii. 12), or, in full armour (R.V.). The host of Gog is probably not exclusively cavalry, though these are specially mentioned; and besides their vast numbers their splendid uniforms and heavy armour are vividly pictured.

5. Cf. on xxvii. 10, xxx. 5.

6. Cf. xxvii. 14; Gen. x. 2. His "bands," xii. 14.

north quarters] lit. *sides of the north*, i.e. the furthest north, Is. xiv. 13. Gomer, Assyr. Gimir, is usually identified in name with the Kimmerians. Schrader (*KAT.* in loc.) and others understand Cappadocia.

7—9. INJUNCTION TO GOG TO BE IN READINESS FOR THE LATTER DAYS WHEN JEHOVAH SHALL LEAD HIM FORTH.

7. *a guard unto them*] The term means something to be kept or observed, a rallying point; Gog shall be the leader of the people—though the word hardly means strictly "standard" (Ew.). For "unto them" LXX. reads "unto me," giving the meaning that Gog shall be kept "in reserve" by Jehovah for his future operations (*v.* 8).

thou shalt be visited: in the latter years thou shalt come into the land *that is* brought back from the sword, *and is* gathered out of many people, against the mountains of Israel, which have been always waste: but it is brought forth out of the nations, and they shall dwell safely all of them. Thou 9 shalt ascend and come like a storm, thou shalt be like a cloud to cover the land, thou, and all thy bands, and many people with thee.

Thus saith the Lord God; It shall also come to pass, *that* 10 at the same time shall things come into thy mind, and thou shalt think an evil thought: and thou shalt say, I will go up 11 to the land of unwalled villages; I will go *to* them that are at rest, that dwell safely, all of them dwelling without walls, and having neither bars nor gates, to take a spoil, and to 12

8. *thou shalt be visited*] Not in the frequent sense of visited with punishment, but in the sense of recalled to mind in order to be employed (cf. usage xxiii. 21). Others: *mustered*, which is not very natural; and the meaning "thou shalt receive orders" (from Jehovah) can hardly be supported from usage. From the position of the prophet the invasion of Gog seems to belong to the far-distant future, to a time after the people have been restored and have enjoyed long peace and great felicity. For many people, **peoples**, and so *vv.* 9, 15, 22.

always waste] i.e. long time waste, cf. Is. xlii. 14, lviii. 12. "Always" is a natural exaggeration for the exile period, which seemed endless, see xxxvi. 2, cf. xxxv. 9.

dwell safely] Or, in confidence. The term always expresses the feeling of security.

9. *like a storm*] Cf. on the figure Is. xxi. 1, xxviii. 2; Jer. iv. 13. The rapidity of the movements of Gog (Hos. viii. 1), and their destructiveness, as well as the infinite masses of his host (Num. xxii. 5; Jud. vi. 5) are expressed by the comparison with the storm and cloud.

10—13. GOG'S INVASION PROMPTED BY HIS OWN EVIL PURPOSES.

10. *It shall also come to pass*] Read: **It shall come to pass at that time that things shall come** &c. The "also" of A.V. suggests an additional thing to *vv.* 1—9, whereas it is only the same thing from another point of view. *Vv.* 10 *seq.* are *parallel* to *vv.* 1—9, not a consequence e.g. of *v.* 4.

shall things come] lit., words, i.e. purposes. Is. viii. 10, "speak a word and it shall not stand." Cf. xiv. 3.

think an evil thought] As marg. **conceive an evil purpose.**

11. Cf. Deut. iii. 5; 1 Sam. vi. 18; Jud. xviii. 27. "Safely," i.e. in confidence, *v.* 8.

12. On "take a spoil" cf. xxix. 19; Is. x. 6. The phrase "turn the hand upon" is always used in a hostile sense (Is. i. 25). Verses 11,

take a prey; to turn thine hand upon the desolate places *that are now* inhabited, and upon the people *that are* gathered out of the nations, which have gotten cattle and goods, that
13 dwell in the midst of the land. Sheba, and Dedan, and the merchants of Tarshish, with all the young lions thereof, shall say unto thee, Art thou come to take a spoil? hast thou gathered thy company to take a prey? to carry away silver and gold, to take *away* cattle and goods, to take a
14 great spoil? Therefore, son of man, prophesy and say unto Gog, Thus saith the Lord GOD; In that day when my people
15 of Israel dwelleth safely, shalt thou not know *it*? And thou shalt come from thy place out of the north parts, thou, and many people with thee, all of them riding upon horses, a

12 give the prophet's idea of the condition of the restored community and of the state of the world in those days which permits it. He does not furnish details, but previous prophecies (ch. xxv.—xxxii.) describe how all the nations formerly hostile to Israel are humbled or taken out of the way. The period of Israel's restoration is a time of universal peace. Only distant nations on the outskirts of the world, that have never entered upon the stage of history, remain unaware of the fame and glory of the God of Israel (Is. lxvi. 19). The same circle of ideas appears in the passage relating to the period of a thousand years in the Apocalypse: outside the historical world there remain distant nations unaffected by the kingdom of Christ.

midst of the land] of the **earth**, lit. the *navel* of the earth, i.e. the mountain-land of Israel, the centre of the earth, cf. *v*. 5. The prophet speaks of the world as known in his day.

13. The merchant peoples are roused to excitement by the enterprise of Gog; probably it is the hope of gain by trafficking with him for his spoil that excites them—hardly envy at the rich harvest lying before him. On Sheba xxvii. 22; Dedan xxvii. 20; Tarshish xxvii. 12.

all the young lions] Cf. xix. 3, 5, xxxii. 2. The term might be thought not very suitable to a troop of camp followers intent merely on traffic. The term is probably used generally to describe the eminence of these merchant people—hardly to represent them as *thirsting* for gain, as lions for prey!

14—16. THE PURPOSE AND ISSUE OF GOG'S INVASION: THAT THE NATIONS MAY KNOW JEHOVAH, WHEN HE IS SANCTIFIED IN GOG.

14. *shalt thou not know* it] It is the peaceful and unprotected condition of the people, along with their wealth, that tempts Gog to invade them. LXX., however, reads: shalt thou not *stir thyself up*, or, arise, which gives a more vigorous sense (Is. xli. 25; Jer. vi. 22), though the Heb. is quite good. "Safely," **in confidence.**

15. Cf. *vv*. 4, 6, xxxix. 2. For many people, **peoples.**

great company, and a mighty army: and thou shalt come up 16
against my people of Israel, as a cloud to cover the land;
it shall be in the latter days, and I will bring thee against
my land, that the heathen may know me, when I shall be
sanctified in thee, O Gog, before their eyes.

Thus saith the Lord GOD; *Art* thou he of whom I have 17
spoken in old time by my servants the prophets of Israel,

16. Cf. *v.* 9.

shall be sanctified] Or, get me sanctifying, i.e. recognition as
"holy"—"holy" having the meaning of all that which God alone is.
The rendering "shew myself holy" is less natural, though the meaning
is virtually the same. Jehovah shews his great deeds in the sight of
the nations, and thus they recognise his Godhead, cf. *v.* 23. He gets
him sanctifying "in" or through Gog, as the object on whom his great
operations of power are manifested.

In these verses Jehovah is represented on the one hand as bringing
up Gog in order that he may be sanctified in him in the sight of the
nations; and on the other hand Gog is represented as coming up of
his own will, prompted by evil purposes, by the hope of an easy conquest and by lust of spoil. The first representation must not be
pressed as if this case of Gog were something special, as if Jehovah
for no object but to shew his power brought up against his people a
leader and nation from the ends of the earth, who otherwise would
have remained in peace in their distant abodes. Because such a view
of the episode of Gog forgets in the first place the other side of the
representation, viz. that Gog comes up of his own will, and with evil
intent. It is the hope of an easy conquest and lust of spoil that animates him as well as the merchant peoples who follow in his train.
This spirit of irreligious traffic on the part of these peoples is reprobated by the prophet and represented as antagonistic to the religion of
Jehovah, just as it is in the case of Tyre (xxvi.—xxviii.). And secondly
the view forgets the general teaching of the prophet, to the effect that
Jehovah is in truth the author of all the great movements in the world,
and that his operations have one great end in view, to reveal himself
as that which he is to the nations of the world. His raising up Gog
with this view is not a special thing, but one among many other
similar things. To signalize it as something distinct and lift it out of
the general current of the prophet's conceptions creates an untrue impression of his teaching.

17—23. This invasion of Gog has been long predicted. It shall be
the occasion of a final manifestation of himself by Jehovah to creation
and the nations, which shall inspire universal awe, and leave in the
minds of all mankind the knowledge of Jehovah, and that which he is.

17. The question gives vividness to the fact of Gog's invasion
having been long predicted, and identifies him with the subject of
these predictions. These former prophecies had not named Gog; the
identification is matter of inference,

which prophesied in those days *many* years, that *I* would bring thee against them? And it shall come to pass at the same time when Gog shall come against the land of Israel, saith the Lord GOD, *that* my fury shall come up in my face. 19 For in my jealousy *and* in the fire of my wrath have I spoken, Surely in that day there shall be a great shaking in the land 20 of Israel; so that the fishes of the sea, and the fowls of the heaven, and the beasts of the field, and all creeping things that creep upon the earth, and all the men that *are* upon the

those days many *years*] The construction is peculiar, but this is probably the sense. Gog, though not by name, had formed the subject of repeated predictions by many prophets. The prophecies referred to are probably such as Zeph. i. (iii. 8), which agrees with Ezek. *v.* 20 in mentioning the fishes of the sea (again only Hos. iv. 3), and Jer. iii.—vi. (Is. xvii. 12 *seq.*). The age of Joel may be later than Ezek., and passages like Joel iii., Zech. xiv., possibly repose rather on him, or at all events shew the continued prevalence of the same ideas, which indeed passed as current conceptions into the Apocalyptic prophecy dating from this age. The passage Mic. iv. 11 *seq.* is also of uncertain date. It is possible that the invasion of the Scythians may have suggested the prophecies of Zeph. and Jer., though the supposition is less necessary in the case of the latter prophet. It is not likely, however, that Ezekiel's renewal of the prophecy was occasioned by any fresh movements among these northern nations occurring in his time (Sm. Kuen.), because he regards the inroad of Gog as an event to happen in the far distant future.

18. *come to pass at the same time*] Rather: come to pass in that day, in the day when Gog &c.

come up in my face] lit. in my *nostril*. The idea is not that of the inflammation of the face from anger, but that of a fiery breath appearing in the nostrils. Deut. xxxii. 22; Ps. xviii. 8.

19. *have I spoken*] i.e. *do I speak;* cf. xxi. 36, xxxvi. 5, xxxix. 25. The word "shaking" is the usual one for earthquake, but the general term is better here, *v.* 20, cf. Hag. ii. 6, 7.

20. The terror of creation before the majesty of Jehovah shall be universal, and all that is high shall be brought down. The passage agrees with the usual prophetic descriptions of the day of the Lord, cf. Zeph. i. 1 *seq.*; Is. ii.—iii.; Jer. iv. 23—26. It describes Jehovah's final manifestation of himself in his fury and jealousy. In the earlier prophets this manifestation of his majesty by Jehovah usually precedes or accompanies the final restoration of his people, here it is postponed until long after they have entered upon the rest of God in their own land. In other words that which earlier writers view as one scene, comprising Jehovah's revelation of himself and the final restoration of his people, is resolved into two, one of which takes place long after the other. The same difference is observable in the New Test. between the representation of the Apocalyptist and that of the other writers.

face of the earth, shall shake at my presence, and the mountains shall be thrown down, and the steep places shall fall, and every wall shall fall to the ground. And I will call *for* 21 a sword against him throughout all my mountains, saith the Lord GOD: every man's sword shall be against his brother. And I will plead against him with pestilence and with blood; 22 and I will rain upon him, and upon his bands, and upon the many people that *are* with him, an overflowing rain, and great hailstones, fire, and brimstone. Thus will I magnify 23 myself, and sanctify myself; and I will be known in the eyes of many nations, and they shall know that I *am* the LORD.

Therefore thou son of man, prophesy against Gog, and 39

the steep places] the **clefts** of the hills. In Song ii. 14 the term is rendered "stairs," but it is parallel to "clefts of the rock," and has the same general meaning.

21. *every man's sword*] sign of a supernatural panic caused by Jehovah, Jud. vii. 22; 1 Sam. xiv. 20. LXX. has read first clause: I will summon against him all terrors (i.e. a panic).

22. *I will plead*] i.e. contend. Jehovah's pleadings are often great acts of judgment, Is. lxvi. 16; Jer. xxv. 31. Cf. Ez. v. 17, xiv. 19; Is. xxix. 6, xxx. 30; Ps. xi. 6, for similar judgments.

23. Thus will Jehovah magnify himself—manifest his greatness and power; and sanctify himself—shew himself to be "holy," i.e. one who is God, xxxvi. 23. Then shall he be known as that which he is by all the nations of the earth.

CH. XXXIX. RESUMPTION OF THE PROPHECY AGAINST GOG.

(1) *vv.* 1—7. Renewal of the prophecy: Gog shall be broken on the mountains of Israel by a divine interposition.

(2) *vv.* 8—15. For seven years the wood of his weapons shall suffice the people for fuel. It will take seven months to bury his dead. His burial-place shall be beyond the Jordan, east of the Dead Sea; and the land shall be carefully purified of every bone of his host.

(3) *vv.* 16—24. Jehovah invites the fowls of the heaven and the beasts of the earth to a great feast, a sacrificial meal which he shall slay for them. They shall eat the flesh of princes and mighty men, be sated with fat and drunk with blood. And this interposition of Jehovah to protect his restored and now righteous people shall teach the nations that Israel's former expulsion from the land was due to their iniquity.

(4) *vv.* 25—29. The prophet, abandoning the point of view of Gog's invasion in the future, occupied by him in these two chapters, returns to the position he occupied in predicting Israel's restoration (ch. xxxiii.—xxxvii.), which he prophesies anew.

say, Thus saith the Lord GOD; Behold, I *am* against thee,
2 O Gog, the chief prince of Meshech and Tubal: and I will
turn thee back, and leave but the sixth part of thee, and will
cause thee to come up from the north parts, and will bring
3 thee upon the mountains of Israel: and I will smite thy
bow out of thy left hand, and will cause thine arrows to
4 fall out of thy right hand. Thou shalt fall upon the mountains of Israel, thou, and all thy bands, and the people that
is with thee: I will give thee unto the ravenous birds of
every sort, and *to* the beasts of the field to be devoured.
5 Thou shalt fall upon the open field: for I have spoken
6 *it*, saith the Lord GOD. And I will send a fire on Magog,
and among them that dwell carelessly in the isles: and they
7 shall know that I *am* the LORD. So will I make my holy
name known in the midst of my people Israel; and I will
not let *them* pollute my holy name any more: and the
heathen shall know that I *am* the LORD, the Holy One in
Israel.

1. Cf. xxxviii. 2, 3.
chief prince] **prince of Rosh**, Meshech, &c., xxxviii. 2.
2. *turn thee back...sixth part*] Perhaps: **turn thee about and lead thee**. The word "lead" does not elsewhere occur. A.V. derived from numeral "six."
3. The northern warriors were bowmen.
4. Cf. *v.* 17, xxxviii. 21.
6. Magog is the name of the country of Gog.
in the isles] the **countries**, i.e. the distant lands of the earth. The armies of Gog and his allies are annihilated on the mountains of Israel, but the judgment extends simultaneously to their distant abodes, that the ends of the earth may know and fear the Lord.
7. *will not let* them *pollute*] will not **let my holy name be profaned**, lit. *I will not profane.* Jehovah's holy or divine name was profaned,—his majesty and power were detracted from—when Israel his people were subjected by the heathen and dispersed abroad from their own land (xxxvi. 20). Israel's sins constrained Jehovah to cast them out of his land, and thus to profane his holy name. Now they are another people, a new heart has been given them, and his signal protection of them in their defenceless condition (xxxviii. 11) from so extreme a danger (xxxviii. 4—6) will reveal both to Israel and the nations what Jehovah is, and what are the principles on which he rules his people (*v.* 23). Thus shall his name be sanctified—he shall be known to be God alone, all powerful and righteous.—While Isaiah says "Holy One of Israel," Ezek. says *in* Israel, a usage which shews that the element "of Israel" forms no part of the conception of "holiness."

Behold, it is come, and it is done, saith the Lord GOD; 8
this *is* the day whereof I have spoken. And they that dwell 9
in the cities of Israel shall go forth, and shall set on fire and
burn the weapons, both the shields and the bucklers, the
bows and the arrows, and the handstaves, and the spears,
and they shall burn them with fire seven years: so that they 10
shall take no wood out of the field, neither cut down *any*
out of the forests; for they shall burn the weapons with
fire: and they shall spoil those that spoiled them, and
rob those that robbed them, saith the Lord GOD. And it 11
shall come to pass in that day, *that* I will give unto Gog
a place there of graves in Israel, the valley of the passengers
on the east of the sea: and it *shall* stop the *noses of the*

8. The words vividly bring into the presence of the speaker the great catastrophe. Rev. xvi. 17, xxi. 6.

9. The wood of the weapons of Gog's warriors shall serve the people of Israel as fuel for seven years, they shall go neither to gather faggots for fire in the fields nor to cut down any wood out of the forests (*v.* 10).

set on fire and burn] **make fire of the weapons and burn them**—i.e. they shall use them as fuel. The "handstaves" are probably those with which the animals ridden upon or others were driven.

burn them with fire] **make fire of them.**

10. *burn the weapons*] **make fire with** the weapons. Such abundance of fuel shall the weapons supply, that firewood shall neither be gathered in the field nor cut down out of the forests.

11. Gog's burial-place shall be east of the Dead Sea.

a place there of graves] a **place for a grave**, lit. *a place where a grave* may be. For "there" LXX. reads *name*—a place of renown (name), a grave in Israel.

valley of the passengers] In *vv.* 14, 15 the word is used of those appointed to go through the land in search of the scattered bones. The term cannot have that sense here. Ew. conjectured that it was a term applied to the hosts of Gog, *the invaders*, from their overflowing the country (Is. viii. 8). The reading of *v.* 14, however, which would be the strongest support of this view, is doubtful. The expression is probably a proper name; the "valley of the passers through" may have been so named as the usual route of communication between the east and west of the sea. Others by altering the points read "the (or, a) valley of Abarim" (Hitz. Corn.).

shall *stop the* noses] **it shall stop them that pass through** (or, the passengers). The valley shall be filled up with the graves of the innumerable hosts of Gog, so that the way of passers through shall be barred. A.V. has no probability. Neither LXX. nor Syr. read the words "those that pass through;" the former renders: and they shall build up the mouth of the valley round about.

passengers: and there shall they bury Gog and all his multitude: and they shall call *it* The valley of Hamon-gog.
12 And seven months shall the house of Israel be burying of
13 them, that *they* may cleanse the land. Yea, all the people of the land shall bury *them;* and it shall be to them a renown the day that I shall be glorified, saith the Lord GOD.
14 And they shall sever out men of continual employment, passing through the land to bury with the passengers those that remain upon the face of the earth, to cleanse it: after the
15 end of seven months shall they search. And the passengers *that* pass through the land, when *any* seeth a man's bone, then shall he set up a sign by it, till the buriers have buried

Hamon-gog] i.e. Gog's multitude.
12. It shall take all Israel (*v.* 13) seven months to bury Gog's dead. The bones scattered over the land defiled it, for it was holy to the Lord, and they must be gathered and interred, cf. *vv.* 14, 16.
13. *a renown*] Or, *a glory* (lit. a name), viz. that they have seen their last enemy destroyed by their God. The triumph is theirs, being his, Ps. cxlix. 9.
the day that...glorified] i.e. *on* the day (at the time) when I shall be glorified (or, glorify myself).
14. When the remains that are visible shall all have been buried, men shall be appointed whose continual task it shall be to go through the land to search for any bones that may have been overlooked. When they find a bone they shall set up a sign beside it that the buriers may come and inter it (*v.* 15).
of continual employment] lit. continual men (same phrase as "continual" burnt-offering),—men constantly occupied.
with the passengers] The words should probably be omitted with LXX. Read: **to bury those that remain**, &c. After seven months have been consumed in burying the masses of the dead everywhere visible, occasional bodies or bones may still be left, having escaped notice. These shall be diligently searched for by the "continual men." Those who would retain the words "them that pass through" (passengers of A.V.) here read, *to bury them that pass through* (i.e. the invaders), even *those that remain* (cf. R.V.). The construction is unnatural, and any play of words between two classes of "passers through," viz. invaders and searchers, has no probability. In *v.* 15 "those that pass through," i.e. the searchers, are distinguished from the buriers, and a reader finding "buriers" in the present verse assumed that they were different from the searchers, and added "with those that pass through" (the searchers) on the margin.
15. Render with R.V., **And they that pass through the land** (the searchers) **shall pass through; and when any seeth a man's bone, then shall he set up** (lit. build) **a sign** (or pillar), &c. On Hamon-Gog cf. *v.* 11.

it in the valley of Hamon-gog. And also the name of the 16
city *shall be* Hamonah. Thus shall they cleanse the land.

And thou son of man, thus saith the Lord GOD; Speak 17
unto every feathered fowl, and to every beast of the field,
Assemble yourselves, and come; gather yourselves on every
side to my sacrifice that I do sacrifice for you, *even* a great
sacrifice upon the mountains of Israel, that ye may eat flesh,
and drink blood. Ye shall eat the flesh of the mighty, and 18
drink the blood of the princes of the earth, of rams, of
lambs, and of goats, of bullocks, all of them fatlings of
Bashan. And ye shall eat fat till *ye* be full, and drink blood 19
till *ye* be drunken, of my sacrifice which I have sacrificed
for you. Thus ye shall be filled at my table *with* horses 20

16. *name of the city...Hamonah*] Or, **a city.** Hamonah is *fem.* of
Hamon, multitude, and presumably of the same meaning. The words,
however, are enigmatical and alien to the connexion. The last clause,
"and they shall cleanse the land," suggests the previous mention of some
action which has this result. The Versions, however, are in agreement
with Heb. text. If the text be correct, the prophet's meaning is that a
city shall also be built in commemoration of Gog's overthrow; naturally
this city must be supposed situated near the valley of Hamon-Gog, because its name Hamonah (multitude), if the city were situated elsewhere,
would not of itself suggest any connexion with Gog.

vv. **17** *seq.* The great sacrificial feast provided by Jehovah for the
fowls of heaven and the beasts of the field. They shall eat the flesh of
the mighty and drink the blood of princes of the earth (17—20). And
thus shall that which Jehovah is be made known both to Israel and the
heathen; and the nations shall understand, from Jehovah's defence of
his godly people now, why it was that aforetime he inflicted such evils
upon them and cast them out of his land (21—24).

17. *to my sacrifice*] The eating of flesh was of rarer occurrence in
ancient times than it is now. All slaughtering of animals was a sacrificial act. The blood and some parts of the victim were given to
Jehovah; and the rest eaten before him by the company. Hence the
terminology here: Jehovah's slaughter of his enemies is to afford a sacrificial feast. Cf. Zeph. i. 8; Is. xxxiv. 6.

18. The actual victims sacrificed were princes and mighty men; here
they are described as rams and goats—the usual animals sacrificed.
Jer. li. 40.

fatlings of Bashan] Bashan was a pastoral country, producing the
fattest and greatest beasts. Cf. Deut. xxxii. 14; Am. iv. 1; Is. xxxiv.
6, 7; Ps. xxii. 12.

20. *my table*] It is the Lord that holds the sacrificial feast here
(*v.* 19), and it is his table to which he invites the fowls and beasts.

horses and chariots] It is scarcely necessary to point with LXX.
horse *and rider;* "chariot" suggests that those borne in the chariot are

and chariots, with mighty *men*, and *with* all men of war, saith
21 the Lord God. And I will set my glory among the heathen,
and all the heathen shall see my judgment that I have
22 executed, and my hand that I have laid upon them. So the
house of Israel shall know that I *am* the Lord their God
23 from that day and forward. And the heathen shall know that
the house of Israel went into captivity for their iniquity:
because they trespassed against me, therefore hid I my face
from them, and gave them into the hand of their enemies:
24 so fell they all by the sword. According to their uncleanness
and according to their transgressions have I done unto
them, and hid my face from them.
25 Therefore thus saith the Lord God; Now will I bring
again the captivity of Jacob, and have mercy upon the whole
26 house of Israel, and will be jealous for my holy name; after

intended. The term rendered "chariot" seems used, however, of "riding-beasts," e.g. the ass and the camel, Is. xxi. 7, 9; and there is no intimation elsewhere that Gog's army rode in chariots: they were horsemen and bowmen.

21. The great discomfiture of Gog will reveal Jehovah's power to the nations. None but God alone could deal so wonderfully. Cf. xxxviii. 16, 23.

22. And Israel from that day will feel secure in the protection of Jehovah their God; all misgivings which the past might create will disappear, and they shall know that now Jehovah is indeed their God.

23. Jehovah's dealing with his people Israel is the great lesson which he reads to the heathen; it is the history of Israel in the hand of Jehovah their God that reveals to the nations what Jehovah is. For the nations knew Jehovah only as God of Israel, and it was thus only through Israel that he could reveal himself to them. This last great event in the history of Israel, Jehovah's signal defence of them now that they are his people in truth, casts light on his former hiding of his face from them. Deeper elements than mere power enter into his rule of his people; a conception of God is suggested to the nations unlike any they had hitherto entertained—there is a God who is omnipotent and who rules the nations in righteousness, the God of Israel.

24. *have I done unto them*] **did I do** unto them.

vv. **25** *seq.* The prophet returns to the point of view occupied in ch. xxxiii.—xxxvii., before the restoration of Israel. The transition is suggested by the words I hid my face from them (*v.* 24). This shall no more be (*v.* 29); they shall be restored, and dwell safely in their land (*v.* 26), and Jehovah shall be their God in truth.

25. *bring again the captivity*] Cf. xvi. 53, xxix. 14.

jealous for my holy name] little different from "my divine name." The prophet represents Jehovah as acting from the sense of that which

that they have borne their shame, and all their trespasses whereby they have trespassed against me, when they dwelt safely in their land, and none made *them* afraid. When I have brought them again from the people, and gathered them out of their enemies' lands, and am sanctified in them in the sight of many nations; then shall they know that I *am* the LORD their God, which caused them to be led into captivity among the heathen: but I have gathered them unto their own land, and have left none of them any more there. Neither will I hide my face any more from them: for I have poured out my spirit upon the house of Israel, saith the Lord GOD.

he is. The representation is to be explained from the profound sense which the prophet, and other prophets, had of the Godhead of Jehovah, with all that Godhead meant. Cf. xx. 9, 14, 22, 44.

26. *after that...borne*] Rather: **And they shall bear their shame.** The phrase "bear shame" is not used in the sense of bearing the outward disgrace (xxxii. 24, 25, 30, xxxiv. 29, xxxvi. 7), but in the sense of bearing the inward feeling of unworthiness, which the undeserved goodness of Jehovah creates (xvi. 52, 54). The word "bear" is written defectively and by a change of a "tittle" might mean "forget." While "forget their shame" however might well be said, shame meaning reproach (Is. liv. 4), "forget their trespasses," implying complete obliteration of the unhappy past, is so powerful an idea that it causes surprise. Either idea is beautiful; whether the idea be that the redeemed people sit in abashed gladness, the memory of former evil adding depth to the gladness, or whether it be that the assurance that Jehovah is their God (*v.* 22) is so exalted that the memory of former sad days is wholly wiped out by it.

when they dwelt...afraid] **when they dwell with confidence...and none maketh them afraid.** Reference is to the time of restoration.

27. The verse is closely connected with the preceding: none maketh them afraid; when I have brought...and have been sanctified in (or, through) them. Cf. xxxvi. 23, 24, xxxviii. 16. For people, **peoples.**

28. Read: And **they shall know...in that I caused them...and will gather...and will leave.** The words: and I will gather, &c. to the end are wanting in LXX., which also points the first clause differently.

29. *poured out my spirit*] This states in brief all the regenerating influences more fully dwelt upon in xxxvi. 25—31. Cf. Joel ii. 28; Zech. xii. 10. On first clause, Is. liv. 8—10; Jer. xxxi. 3 *seq.*

THIRD SECTION. CH. XL.—XLVIII. FINAL CONDITION OF THE REDEEMED PEOPLE.

This concluding section of Ezekiel's prophecy is in many ways remarkable, and the main idea expressed by it needs to be carefully attended to.

The passage is separated by an interval of twelve or thirteen years from the latest of the other prophecies (except the brief intercalation, xxix. 17 *seq*.). It stands therefore apart from the rest of the Book, with the ideas of which it is not easy in some parts to reconcile it. Some scholars indeed (Stade, *Hist*. II. 37) consider that in the interval Ezekiel had broken with his former conceptions. There does seem a discrepancy between the place assigned to the "Prince" in this passage and the more elevated part which the Lord's "servant David" plays in earlier chapters.

On the whole, however, the passage can be only understood if we keep before our minds all the teaching of the earlier part of the Book, and also suppose that the prophet had it vividly before his own mind. This passage contains no teaching. All that the prophet wished his people to learn regarding the nature of Jehovah and the principles of his rule, his holiness, his wrath against evil and his righteous judgments, has been exhausted (iv.—xxiv.). All that he desired to say about the revelation of Jehovah's glory to the nations, that they may know that "he is Jehovah," and may no more exalt themselves against him in self-deification, and no more disturb or seduce his people, has been said (xxv.—xxxii.). And the great operations of Jehovah's grace in regenerating his people, and in restoring them to their own land, have been fully described (xxxiii.—xxxvii.). All this forms the background of the present section. The last words of i.—xxxix. are: "And I will hide my face from them no more; for I have poured out my Spirit upon the house of Israel, saith the Lord God." The people are washed with pure water, a new heart and spirit is given to them, the spirit of Jehovah rules their life, and they know that Jehovah is their God.

Therefore the present section gives a picture of the people in their final condition of redemption and felicity. It does not describe how salvation is to be attained, for the salvation is realized and enjoyed; it describes the people and their condition and their life now that their redemption has come. This accounts for the strange mixture of elements in the picture—for the fact that there is "so much of earth, so much of heaven" in it. To us who have clearer light the natural and the supernatural seem oddly commingled. But this confusion is common to all the prophetic pictures of the final condition of Israel redeemed, and must not be allowed to lead us astray. We should go very far astray if on the one hand fastening our attention on the natural elements in the picture such as that men still exist in natural bodies, that they live by the fruits of the earth, that death is not abolished, that the "Prince" has descendants, and much else, we should conclude that the supernatural elements in the picture such as the elevation of Zion above the mountains (cf. Is. ii.), the change in the physical condition of the region of the holy city (cf. Jer. xxxi. 38; Zech. xiv. 10), and the issue of the river from the Temple spreading fertility around it and sweetening the waters of the Dead Sea (Zech. xiv. 8, Joel iii. 18), were mere figures or symbols, meaning nothing but a higher spiritual condition after the restoration, and that the restoration described by Ezekiel is no more than that one which might be called natural, and which took place under Zerubbabel and later. Ezekiel of course expects a restoration in the true sense, but it is a restoration which is complete, embracing all the scattered members of Israel, and final, being the entrance of Israel upon its eternal felicity and perfection, and the enjoyment of the full presence of Jehovah in the midst of it. The restoration expected and described by the prophet is no more the restoration that historically took place than the restoration in Is. lx. is the historical one. Both are religious ideals and constructions of the final state of the people and the world. Among other things which gave rise to what appears to us an incompatible union of natural and supernatural were two fundamental conceptions of the Hebrew writers. They could not conceive of a life of man except such a life as we now lead in the body. This bodily life could be lived nowhere but upon the earth, and it could be supported only by the sustenance natural to man. Ezekiel considers death still to prevail in the final state. In this he is followed by some prophets after him (Is. lxv. 20), who do not expect immortality but only patriarchal longevity, a life like the "days of a tree," while others assume that death will be destroyed (Is. xxv. 7, 8). The other conception was that true religious perfection was realized only through Jehovah's personal presence among his people, when the tabernacle of God was with men. The words with which Ezekiel closes his Book are: "And the name of the city from that day shall be, *The Lord is there.*" To us a bodily life of man upon the earth such as we now live, and a personal presence of Jehovah in the most real sense in the midst of men, appear things incompatible. To the Hebrew mind they were not so, or perhaps in their lofty religious idealism the prophets did not reflect on the possibility of their ideals being realized in fact. The temptation, however, to allegorize the prophetic pictures of the final state, and to evaporate from them either the natural or the supernatural elements, must be resisted at all hazards.

Consequently we should go equally far astray on the other hand if fastening our attention only on the supernatural parts of Ezekiel's picture, such as the personal presence of Jehovah, the stream that issues from the Temple, and other things, we should conclude that the whole is nothing but a gigantic allegory; that the temple with its measurements, the courts with their chambers, the priests and Levites with their ministrations—that all this to the prophet's mind was nothing but a lofty symbolism representing a spiritual perfection to be eventually reached in the Church of God of the Christian age. To put such a meaning on the Temple and its measurements and all the details enumerated by the prophet is to contradict all reason. The Temple is real, for it is the place of Jehovah's presence upon the earth; the ministers and the ministrations are equally real, for his servants serve him in his Temple. The service of Jehovah by sacrifice and offering is considered to continue when Israel is perfect and the kingdom the Lord's even by the greatest prophets (Is. xix. 19, 21, lx. 7, lxvi. 20; Jer. xxxiii. 18).

There can be no question of the literalness and reality of the things in the prophetic programme, whether they be things natural or supernatural, the only question is, What is the main conception expressed by them? It would probably be a mistake to suppose that the picture given by the prophet in this section is a picture of the life in all its breadth of Israel redeemed. Many sides of the people's life do not come into consideration here. For the prophet's view regarding these his previous chapters must be consulted. The Temple, the ministrants and their ministrations and also the Prince and people are all here spoken of from one point of view. As already said the section is not a description of the way by which salvation is to be attained, it is a picture of salvation already realized and a people saved. The sacrifices and ministrations are not performed in order to obtain redemption, but at the most to conserve it. They have two aspects: first, they are worship, service of Jehovah; and secondly, they have a prophylactic, conservative purpose, to secure that the condition of salvation be in no way forfeited. The salvation and blessedness of the people consists in the presence of Jehovah in his Temple, among men. His people, though all righteous and led by his spirit, are not free from the infirmities and inadvertencies incidental to human nature. But as on the one hand, the presence of Jehovah sanctifies the Temple in which he dwells, the land which is his, and the people whose God he is, so on the other hand any uncleanness in the people, the land or the Temple, disturbs his Being and must be sedulously guarded against or removed. It was former uncleannesses that caused the Lord to withdraw from his House (viii.—xi.); and it is only when it is sanctified that he returns to it (xliii.). Hence the care taken to guard against all "profaning" of Jehovah, and to keep far from him anything common or unclean. First, the sacred "oblation," the domain of the priests, Levites, prince and city is placed in the centre of the restored tribes, Judah on one side of it and Benjamin on the other (xlv. 1—8, xlviii. 8 *seq.*). In the midst of this oblation is the portion of the priests, that of the Levites lying on one side, and that of the city on the other. In the middle of the priests' portion stands the Temple. This is a great complex of buildings, around which on all sides lies a free space or suburbs. Then comes a great wall surrounding the whole buildings, forming a square of five hundred cubits. Within this wall is an outer court; and within this an inner court, accessible only to the priests, even the prince being debarred from setting his foot in it. In this inner court stands the altar, and to the back of it the Temple House. The House has also a graduated series of compartments increasing in sanctity inwards—an outer apartment or porch, an inner or holy place, and an innermost, where the presence of Jehovah abides. Only the priests can serve at Jehovah's table, the altar, and enter the house, and only the Levites can handle the sacred offerings of the people, whether to slay them or boil them for the sacrificial meal. All these arrangements have one object in view, to guard against disturbance to the holiness of Jehovah, who dwells among his people.

This, however, suggests another point. It has been remarked in disparagement of the prophet that he makes little reference to moral law in this section, occupying himself with mere "ceremonial." The objection forgets two things: first, that the background to this final picture of the people's condition is formed by the whole great passage, ch. xxxiii.—xxxvii. It is a people forgiven and sanctified, and led

In the five and twentieth year of our captivity, in the **40** beginning of the year, in the tenth *day* of the month, in the

by the spirit of God which the prophet contemplates in ch. xl. *seq.* He does not inculcate morality, because he feels that morality is assured (xxxvi. 25—29). It is true that the people is not perfect, but they only err from inadvertency. But secondly, these errors of inadvertency disturb the Divine holiness equally with offences which we call moral. The distinction of moral and ceremonial is unknown to the Law, and if possible more unknown is the idea of a factitious "ceremonial" which has a moral symbolical meaning. The uncleannesses and the like which we now call "ceremonial" were held real uncleannesses and offensive to God, and the purifications were not symbolical but real purifications. These things which we name ceremonial belong rather to the aesthetic in our view than to the moral, but in Israel they were drawn in under the *religious* idea equally with what was moral.

CH. XL.—XLIII. THE NEW TEMPLE.

The passage contains these divisions:—

First, xl. 1—27. Preface (*vv.* 1—4); description of the gateway into the outer court with its various chambers, and of the outer court itself with its buildings.

Second, xl. 28—47. Description of the gateway into the inner court with its chambers, and of the inner court itself.

Third, xl. 48—xli. 26. Description of the House or Temple itself with the annexed buildings.

Fourth, ch. xlii. Description of the other buildings in the inner court, with the dimensions of the whole.

Fifth, xliii. 1—12. Entry of Jehovah into the House thus prepared for him, to dwell there for ever.

Sixth, xliii. 13—27. Description of the altar of burnt-offering in the inner court, and of the rites to be performed in order to consecrate the whole edifice.

CH. XL. 1—27. THE OUTER GATEWAY AND COURT.

In the 25th year of Jehoiachin's captivity, which was the 14th year after the fall of the city (B.C. 572), the prophet fell into a prophetic trance (*v.* 1); he seemed transported to the land of Israel and set down upon a high mountain, on which was a great building (*v.* 2). At the gate of the building there stood a man with a line of flax in his hand and a measuring reed (*v.* 3). The prophet is commanded closely to observe all that is shewn him, and to declare it to the house of Israel.

1. *our captivity*] that of Jehoiachin, in which the prophet himself had been carried away (B.C. 597). With the exception of ch. xxix. 17—21, dating from the 27th year (B.C. 570), these chapters are the latest part of the Book.

the beginning of the year] In post-biblical Heb., the words mean

fourteenth year after that the city was smitten, in the selfsame day the hand of the LORD was upon me, and brought me
2 thither. In the visions of God brought he me into the land of Israel, and set me upon a very high mountain, by which
3 *was* as the frame of a city on the south. And he brought me thither, and behold, *there was* a man, whose appearance *was* like the appearance of brass, with a line of flax in his hand, and a measuring reed; and he stood in the gate.
4 And the man said unto me, Son of man, behold with thine eyes, and hear with thine ears, and set thine heart upon all that I shall shew thee; for to the intent that *I* might shew *them* unto thee art thou brought hither: declare all that
5 thou seest to the house of Israel. And behold a wall on

the first day of the year, and so possibly here. The phrase does not otherwise occur. The ecclesiastical year or old style began with the month Abib (March—April), and is that referred to here.

selfsame day] ch. xxiv. 2. On "hand of the Lord," cf. i. 3.

brought me thither] The word "thither" must refer to the "city which was smitten." LXX. omits, connecting vv. 1 and 2 and leaving out "brought he me," v. 2: "he brought me in the visions of God to the land of Israel."

2. *visions of God*] ch. i. 1, viii. 3, xi. 24.

a very high mountain] The site is the ancient hill of Zion, but it is now exalted above the hills, Is. ii. 2; Zech. xiv. 10, cf. xvii. 22, xx. 40.

by which...frame of a city] lit. **upon which was as it were a building of a city**, i.e. a city-like, or, citadel-like building. The ref. is to the Temple, with its complex of buildings (v. 3).

on the south] The pre-exile Temple at any rate occupied the southern slope of the hill, and possibly Ezek. recalls this. For "on the south" LXX. read *fronting* me (neged for negeb).

3. there was *a man*] The "man" is not to be identified with Jehovah himself, who brought the prophet to him. It is scarcely necessary to enquire who the man is. He is a creation of the prophet's own mind, a living symbol of the revelation of God. This revelation personified has the attributes of Jehovah himself; hence the man is like bright brass (i. 7), and speaks with authority (v. 4). Cf. xliv. 2, 5.

a line of flax] For measuring greater dimensions (xlvii. 3), as the reed usually for smaller.

in the gate] Or, *at*. The east gateway is meant, v. 6.

4. The man, like the Lord himself, addresses the prophet as "child of man," cf. v. 3, xliv. 5. The prophet is commanded to see and hear and lay to heart all that is revealed to him, for he has to declare it to the house of Israel, xliii. 10.

5. A wall surrounded the whole temple buildings (xlii. 20). This

the outside of the house round about, and in the man's hand a measuring reed of six cubits *long* by the cubit and a hand breadth: so he measured the breadth of the building, one reed; and the height, one reed. Then came he unto the gate which looketh toward the 6 east, and went up the stairs thereof, and measured the threshold of the gate, *which was* one reed broad; and the other threshold *of the gate, which was* one reed broad. And 7 wall was a reed broad or thick and a reed high. The reed was six cubits, each cubit being a cubit and a handbreadth, i.e. a handbreadth larger than the lesser cubit in use. This larger cubit was probably about 18 inches, and the reed 9 feet. Others, the Egyp. ell, 20½ in.

by the cubit and] Six cubits long, **each of one cubit and,** &c.

6—16. THE OUTER GATEWAY ON THE EAST SIDE.

As the Temple lay east and west, the eastern gateway was the natural entrance. Through it Jehovah entered to take up his abode in the new House (xliii. 4); it was therefore to be kept shut (xliv. 1, 2). The measurements of this gate are given in detail, *vv.* 6—16; those of the N. and S. gateways are said to be similar.

6. The threshold. After measuring the surrounding wall the man entered the gateway. On the outside of the entrance, ascending to it, were steps, seven in number, as is stated in connexion with N. and S. gateways (xl. 22, 26). Thus the gateway was elevated above the ground outside, and on the same level with it was the outer court. Again, from the outer court an ascent of eight steps went up to the gateway leading into the inner court (xl. 31), and the inner court was on the same level as the gateway. Finally, an ascent of ten steps led up to the entrance to the house itself (xl. 49), which thus stood on a raised platform above the inner court which surrounded it. According to xli. 8 the ten steps to the house were equal to six cubits of elevation; if the steps leading up to the gateways were of the same dimensions they would together amount to nine cubits, so that the elevation of the house above the level outside the surrounding wall (*v.* 5) would be 15 cubits. The whole structure formed three terraces, each rising above the other inwards.

the threshold] The space between the steps and the guardrooms is called threshold, being just the breadth of the wall, 6 cubits. Fig. 1 *a*.

and the other threshold] This is no translation of the original, which syntactically is scarcely translateable. The words are probably a gloss suggested by the fact that there was a second threshold (*v.* 7). The definition "broad" is suspicious, because, though in general the smaller dimension might be named breadth, and the larger one length, the prophet going from E. to W. calls measurements in that direction "length" (*v.* 7), and the direction N. to S. "breadth," even should it be the larger dimension (*v.* 11). The words are wanting in LXX.

every little chamber *was* one reed long, and one reed broad; and between the little chambers *were* five cubits; and the

Read *v.* 6 thus: **and he measured the threshold of the gate one reed.**

7. The guardrooms. Fig. 1 *bb*.

every *little chamber* was] And **the guardroom was**—sing. used collectively. These chambers were used as sentry-boxes or guard-

FIG. 2. TEMPLE HOUSE.

FIG. 1. OUTER GATEWAY.

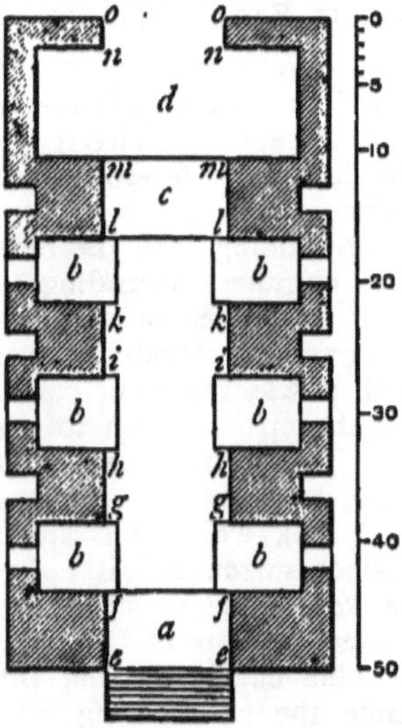

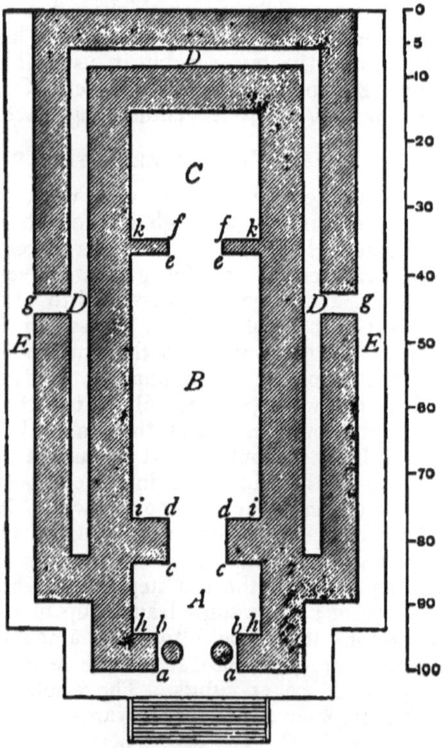

rooms (1 Kings xiv. 28), where the temple officers were stationed to preserve order and keep the house. Of these guardrooms there were three on each side of the gateway (*v.* 10). They were without doors towards the gateway inside, being merely protected on that side by a barrier or fence (*v.* 12), this allowing the keepers full view of the gateway. They were provided with windows (*v.* 16), and possibly at the back with doors leading into the outer court (cf. *v.* 13). The measurements 6 cubits long and broad refer to the inner area.

between the little chambers] Between **the guardrooms was five cubits.** Between two guardrooms a wall-front of five cubits faced

threshold of the gate by the porch of the gate within *was* one reed. He measured also the porch of the gate within, 8 one reed. Then measured he the porch of the gate, eight 9 cubits; and the posts thereof, two cubits; and the porch of the gate *was* inward. And the little chambers of the gate 10 eastward *were* three on this side, and three on that side; they three *were* of one measure: and the posts had one measure on this side and on that side. And he measured 11 the breadth of the entry of the gate, ten cubits; *and* the

the gateway. Of these wall-fronts there were only two, because the guardrooms were but three. Fig. 1, *gh, ik*.

threshold of the gate] Beyond the three guardrooms and the two intervening wall-fronts there was another space called a threshold, of the same dimensions as the first (*v.* 6), leading into the large apartment called the porch (*v.* 9). Fig. 1, *c*.

porch of the gate within] Or, *toward the inside*, R.V., toward the house, though the correction is hardly necessary in syntax (xli. 25). The sense is the same in either case: the porch, fig. 1, *d*, of the outer gate lay at the inner end of the building, looking into the court, while the porch of the inner gates lay at the outer end of the gate-building.

8, 9. These verses should read: **And he measured the porch of the gate, eight cubits; and the posts thereof,** &c.—the words "within (*v.* 8)...gate" (*v.* 9) being omitted. The copyist's eye when he came to the word *gate v.* 8 went back to the same word *v.* 7, the clause following which he repeated. Some MSS. and all the ancient Versions, except Targ., omit. Fig. 1, *mn*.

the posts thereof] Possibly: the **post**—sing. used collectively. The posts are the projecting wall-fronts or jambs on either side of the exit or door from the porch into the outer court, Fig. 1, *no*. The thickness of this jamb was two cubits.

was inward] Or, *toward the inside* (*v.* 7), i.e. on the end of the gateway building toward the interior, and looking into the outer court. This is specially mentioned because in the inner gateway buildings the porch was on the side away from the house.

10. The measurer, having passed through the whole length of the gateway E. to W., and named each particular thing on one side of it, viz. threshold (*v.* 6), guardroom (*v.* 7), wall space between guardrooms (*v.* 7), inner threshold to porch (*v.* 7), porch and its posts (*v.* 8, 9), with their dimensions, now states that there were three guardrooms on each side, all of the same size, and also some other points. For little chambers, **guardrooms.**

the posts had one measure] Probably the "posts" here are not the jambs of the door of the porch (*v.* 9), but the wall-fronts or spaces between the guardrooms (*v.* 7), Fig, 1, *gh, ik*. There were two of these on each side of the passage, each measuring five cubits.

11. *breadth of the entry*] The "breadth"—the measure from N. to S.—of the outside entrance was 10 cubits, Fig. 1, *ee, ff*; and this was

12 length of the gate, thirteen cubits. The space also before the little chambers *was* one cubit *on this side*, and the space *was* one cubit on that side: and the little chambers *were* 13 six cubits on this side, and six cubits on that side. He measured then the gate from the roof of *one* little chamber to the roof of another: the breadth *was* five and twenty 14 cubits, door against door. He made also posts *of* three-

the breadth of the passage all along, except perhaps before the guardrooms, the barrier in front of which on both sides contracted it from 10 to 8 cubits (*v*. 12).

length of the gate] the **gateway.** This statement that the length of the gateway was 13 cubits is very obscure. The length of the gateway was 50 cubits (*v*. 15). "Length" is a measurement from E. to W., and cannot be taken in the sense of "height." It has been suggested that possibly the whole gateway of 50 cubits was not covered; that it consisted of a covered portion at each end, with an unroofed space in the middle, and that this covered portion is here referred to. But no ground appears for calling one part of the passage the gateway; and further the guardrooms and intermediate spaces were provided with windows, a fact which suggests that the whole was roofed over. LXX. read or perhaps interpreted "breadth," which is equally obscure.

12. *space...before the little chambers*] A **barrier before the guardrooms, one cubit,** Fig. 1, *fg, hi, kl*. The meaning appears to be that the barrier took away a cubit on each side from the passage, reducing it from 10 to 8 cubits opposite the guardchambers. The height of the barrier would probably not be very great. The measure of "a cubit" can hardly be the height, as all the measurements refer here to breadth.

13. The gate building was 25 cubits across, i.e. from the outside N. to the outside S. The measurement is made from roof to roof of the guardrooms. LXX. read or substituted "wall" for roof. The meaning is clear. The measurement inside was three cubits less, viz. passage 10, a guardroom on each side 6+6, in all 22, leaving for each back wall 1½ cubits, *vv.* 21, 25, 29.

door against door] Or, *opposite to* door. Possibly each guardroom on both sides of the gateway had a door in the back wall opening into the outer court. Others less naturally suggest three doors of the gate lengthways, viz. that before first threshold, that before inner threshold, and the exit out of the porch.

14. Verse 14 is obscure. In the first place "he made" is suspicious, everywhere else it is "he measured." In the second place the number 60 cubits is incomprehensible. The idea that the "posts" were prolonged into pillars of such a height is altogether improbable. Besides, the "posts" are accurately distinguished from pillars, for which another word is employed (*v*. 49). It is to be observed that the measurer first passes in from E. to W. along one side of the gateway, mentioning the different things with their dimensions of which it was composed. Having reached the porch at the inner end he returns,

score cubits, even unto the post of the court round about the gate. And from the face of the gate of the entrance 15 unto the face of the porch of the inner gate *were* fifty cubits. And *there were* narrow windows to the little chambers, and 16 to their posts within the gate round about, and likewise to

noting that the two sides of the gateway were in all respects alike. Then from *v.* 11 onwards he gives measurements of the *breadth* of various parts of the gateway, the entrance (*v.* 11), the contraction opposite the guardrooms (*v.* 12), and finally the breadth of the whole gate building (*v.* 13). While, however, the breadth of all other parts of the gateway has been given, that of the "porch" at the inner end has not been mentioned, though its length from E. to W., Fig. 1, *mn*, was stated to be 8 cubits (*v.* 8, 9). It is probable, therefore, that *v.* 14 supplies this measurement. Render: **and he measured the porch, 20 cubits**—reading *porch* (ailam), for *posts* (ailim), and, 20 for 60, in both cases with LXX. The 20 are inside measurement, N. to S.; 22 might have been expected, for the back wall of the guardrooms was 1½ cubits, but a chamber like the porch used for assemblies and feasts (xliv. 3) might well have a wall of 2½ cubits thick, as in point of fact the wall to the W. was two cubits (*v.* 9).

even unto the post...gate] At any rate with present pointing: *and unto* (touching on) *the post was the court...gate*. It is probable, however, that "post" is either repetition of *unto*, and should be struck out, or else that it is a consequence of the false reading "posts" in first clause, and should be read "porch" as there (so in *v.* 37). The latter is more probable: *and unto* (adjoining) *the porch was the court, round about the gate.* The omission of prep. before "gate" is difficult, but cf. acc. 1 Kings vi. 5, and the more remarkable case Ezek. xliii. 17. LXX. read differently, and Syr. wants the clause.

15. Measurement of the whole length of the gate-building, 50 cubits.

the face of the gate] i.e. the outside front.

face of the porch of the inner gate] i.e the front of the porch at the inner end of the gate. Either "inner gate" means inner part of the gate, or "inner" means (lying) towards the inside, as LXX. From the outside front of the gate to the inner front, lying on the court, was 50 cubits. The sense is clear though the text may need slight emendation.

16. The description of the gateway building concludes with a ref. to the way in which it was lighted.

narrow windows] Heb. *closed*, i.e. fastened, not capable of being opened like ordinary windows (2 Kings xiii. 17). Windows were usually openings with lattice-work. Here they may have been loopholed, widening out toward the inside. For little chambers, **guardrooms**.

to their posts] i.e. those of the guardrooms. The ref. is to the 5 cubit thick wall fronts between the guardrooms. Cf. *v.* 10.

the arches: and windows *were* round about inward: and upon *each* post *were* palm trees.

17 Then brought he me into the outward court, and lo, *there were* chambers, and a pavement made for the court

to the arches] Probably: and **to the porch thereof**, i.e. of the gate. There are three words in this chapter which need to be distinguished: (1) "post" (ail), the meaning of which is certain from *v.* 9. It means the front face (thickness) of a wall that projects forward (*v.* 9), especially the jamb (on each side) of an entrance, e.g. xl. 48, of the entrance to the porch of the house, and xli. 3 of the entrance to the house itself, cf. 1 Kings vi. 31. It seems also certainly used of the front (thickness) of any wall that springs forward, the side of which bounds a space, and so of the fronts of the walls which bounded the guardrooms (previous note and *v.* 10). (2) The second is "porch" (ulam), the meaning of which is also clear. It refers to the large apartment which lay at the inner end of the outer gate (*v.* 8, 9), and at the outer end of the inner gate, and also to the apartment which formed the outmost of the three divisions of the house (*v.* 48). (3) The third word is that rendered "arch" (ailam), R.V. marg., colonnade. The term occurs only in this chapter. The punctuators always make it plur., though the text appears to make it sing.: except xl. 16, 30 (fem. plur.; in xli. 15 mas. pl. of ulam). These plurals are of doubtful authenticity. In regard to the word it appears, (1) that it is clearly distinguished from "post" (ail), xl. 21, 24, 29, 33, 36. (2) The LXX. does not know the pronunciation *ulam*, uniformly transliterating *ailam*. (3) Even Heb. uses *ailam* in the sense of *ulam* (porch), e.g. certainly xl. 31, 34, 37 (and probably xl. 23, 26), where it is said that the "porch" (ailam) was towards the outer court. There is no evidence that the word has any other sense than "porch." The pronunciation ailam (êlam) is Assyr. also, the word meaning "anything in front" (Frd. Del., Baer *Ezek.*).

and windows] Probably: and *the windows*.

each *post* were *palm trees*] The "post" here is that of *v.* 9, viz. the wall front or jamb on each side of the egress from the porch into the outer court, Fig. 1, *no*. This alone was decorated with palm trees.

17—27. MEASUREMENTS OF THE OUTER COURT AND REMAINING GATES.

17. *outward court*] **outer** court. The prophet passed out of the pathway, where he had hitherto been, into the outer court. Round about on the inside of the surrounding wall of this court (*v.* 5) was a pavement, probably of stone, Fig. 3, B, and on the pavement chambers, thirty in number, Fig 3, C. The chambers ran round the wall on three sides, the W. being occupied with other buildings (xli. 12). The chambers were probably used for meetings and feasts; the ancient high places had such a feast chamber (1 Sam. ix. 22), cf. Jer. xxxv. 4 (xxxvi. 10). It is not stated how the chambers were disposed, whether singly or in blocks. They were apparently of several stories (xlii. 6),

round about: thirty chambers *were* upon the pavement. And the pavement by the side of the gates over against the length of the gates *was* the lower pavement. Then he measured the breadth from the forefront of the lower gate unto the forefront of the inner court without, an hundred cubits east*ward* and north*ward*.

but did not occupy the corners of the wall, in which kitchens were situated (xlvi. 21—24).

18. Render: **and the pavement was by the side of the gates, along the length of the gates, to wit, the lower pavement.** The

FIG. 3. TEMPLE COURTS.

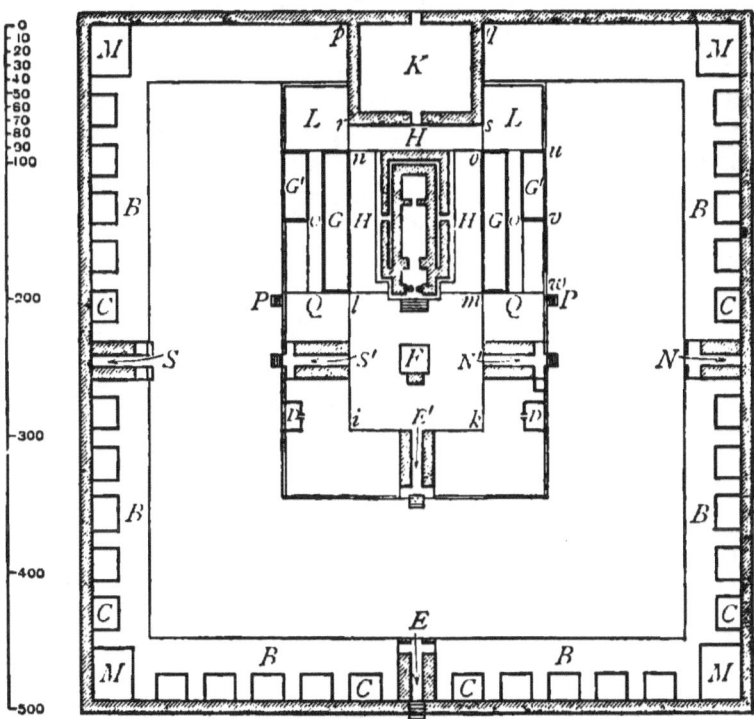

pavement is called "lower" because the outer court lay below the level of the inner (*v.* 34); it extended into the court along the whole length of the gateway, and was therefore (the outer wall being subtracted) 44 cubits broad.

19. The "lower" gate is the outer gate (on *v.* 18). From the inner front of this gate to the outer front of the gate of the inner court facing it was 100 cubits.

*east*ward *and* north*ward*] Or, *on the east and on the north*. The

20 And the gate of the outward court that looked toward the north, he measured the length thereof, and the breadth 21 thereof. And the little chambers thereof *were* three on this side and three on that side; and the posts thereof and the arches thereof were after the measure of the first gate: the length thereof *was* fifty cubits, and the breadth five and 22 twenty cubits. And their windows, and their arches, and their palm trees, *were* after the measure of the gate that looketh towards the east; and they went up unto it by seven 23 steps; and the arches thereof *were* before them. And the gate of the inner court *was* over against the gate toward the north, and toward the east; and he measured from gate to gate an hundred cubits.

24 After that he brought me toward the south, and behold a gate toward the south: and he measured the posts thereof 25 and the arches thereof according to these measures. And *there were* windows in it and in the arches thereof round about, like those windows: the length *was* fifty cubits, and 26 the breadth five and twenty cubits. And *there were* seven steps to go up to it, and the arches thereof *were* before them: and it had palm trees, one on this side, and another 27 on that side, upon the posts thereof. And *there was* a gate

words are loosely appended, the points being stated from which the measurements were taken, viz. E. and N. (*v.* 23).

20. The dimensions of the N. gate were as those of the E. gate.
21. *the little chambers*] **guardrooms.**

and the arches thereof] **the porch thereof.** Probably all the words, guardroom, post, porch, should be read in the sing. as collectives (Heb. text). The difference is unimportant except in regard to "porch."

22. The outer gate was elevated above the ground outside, and reached by a flight of seven steps.

arches thereof were *before them*] Probably: **and the porch thereof was to the inside,** i.e. at the inner end of the gate, looking toward the interior of the whole temple-buildings, cf. *vv.* 31, 34, 37.

23. Render: **and there was a gate in the inner court,** as *v.* 27, lit. *the inner court had a gate,* &c. For "and toward the east" LXX. reads: just as the gate looking toward the east (*v.* 19).

24. *and the arches*] the **porch.** LXX. more fully: he measured the guardrooms thereof and the posts &c., as *vv.* 29, 33, 36.

25. *arches thereof*] **in the porch** thereof.
26. *arches...before them*] **the porch thereof was to the inside,** cf. *v.* 22. The palm trees belong exclusively to the "posts," i.e. the jambs of the egress from the porch into the court.

in the inner court toward the south: and he measured from gate to gate toward the south an hundred cubits.

And he brought me to the inner court by the south gate: 28 and he measured the south gate according to these measures; and the little chambers thereof, and the posts thereof, and 29 the arches thereof, according to these measures: and *there were* windows in it and in the arches thereof round about: *it was* fifty cubits long, and five and twenty cubits broad. And the arches round about *were* five and twenty cubits 30 long, and five cubits broad. And the arches thereof *were* 31 toward the utter court; and palm trees *were* upon the posts thereof: and the going up to it *had* eight steps.

And he brought me into the inner court toward the east: 32 and he measured the gate according to these measures. And the little chambers thereof, and the posts thereof, and 33 the arches thereof, *were* according to these measures: and *there were* windows therein and in the arches thereof round about: *it was* fifty cubits long, and five and twenty cubits broad. And the arches thereof *were* toward the outward 34 court; and palm trees *were* upon the posts thereof, on this side, and on that side: and the going up to it *had* eight steps.

28—37. THE INNER COURT AND ITS GATEWAYS.

The measurement of the outer court was finished at the S. gate. Opposite to this was the S. gate of the inner court at a distance of 100 cubits (*v.* 27), and the measurement of the inner court naturally begins with the S. gate. The gates of the inner court were similar in all respects to those of the outer court, except that in the former the "porch" lay at the outer end of the gateway, looking into the outer court (*vv.* 31, 34, 37).

29. *arches thereof*] porch thereof.

30. The verse is wanting in LXX. and some MSS., and in others deleted. No object belonging to the gateways has hitherto been mentioned to which the measurements can apply. The verse may have arisen from an inaccurate repetition of the measurements given in previous verse.

31. Render: **and the porch thereof was toward the outer court**, cf. *vv.* 34, 37.

palm trees...posts] Cf. *vv.* 16, 26.

33. *little chambers...arches*] **guardroom...porch**, the last at least in the sing.

34. *arches thereof*] **porch**.

35 And he brought me to the north gate, and measured *it*
36 according to these measures; the little chambers thereof, the posts thereof, and the arches thereof, and the windows to it round about: the length *was* fifty cubits, and the
37 breadth five and twenty cubits. And the posts thereof *were* toward the utter court; and palm trees *were* upon the posts thereof, on this side, and on that side: and the going up to
38 it *had* eight steps. And the chambers and the entries thereof *were* by the posts of the gates, where they washed the burnt offering.
39 And in the porch of the gate *were* two tables on this side, and two tables on that side, to slay thereon the burnt offer-
40 ing and the sin offering and the trespass offering. And at

36. As before for little chambers...arches, read **guardroom...porch.**

37. *the posts...utter court*] Probably: **and the porch thereof was toward the outer court,** cf. *vv.* 31, 34. So LXX. The "posts" are mentioned immediately after, and said to be decorated with palm trees, *vv.* 16, 26, 31.

38—43. Sacrificial appointments connected with the inner gate.

The verses are in some respects obscure. The text of LXX. differs in some points, but is hardly consistent with itself. The arrangements for slaughtering spoken of are of course connected with the inner gateway, but points not clear are: (1) which gateway, the N. or the E.? And (2) the position of the tables, *v.* 40; were they situated in the inner court at the long sides of the gateway, or in the outer court in front of the gateway, on either side of the steps leading up to it?

38. Read: **and a chamber, and the entry thereof** (was) **in the porch of the gate.** The plur. *gates* can hardly be right. It is not probable that slaughtering took place at more than one gate. LXX. reads *gate* (sing.) and also *porch* for posts, cf. *v.* 37. The chamber whose entry was from the porch must have been contiguous to the porch, but is not further described.

where they washed] Not the usual word Lev. i. 9. Both words Is. iv. 4; 2 Chr. iv. 6. LXX. thinks here of a drain or runnel for carrying off the sacrificial blood.

39. The verse states what was *in* the porch, in antithesis to *v.* 38. Possibly the words "to slay thereon" are used generally, not of the actual slaughtering, but of the manipulation of the flesh of the victims. In *v.* 41 it is said that there were eight tables on which they slew, four of which were certainly outside the porch. If the burnt, sin and trespass offerings (LXX. omits burnt offerings here) were slain *in* the porch, there would remain only the peace offerings to slay outside.

40. *at the side without*] Side, lit. *shoulder*, is used generally of the side of the gate projecting lengthways into the court (*v.* 18), or of the side lengthways of a wall (xli. 2). According to this interpretation the

the side without, as one goeth up to the entry of the north gate, *were* two tables; and on the other side, which *was* at the porch of the gate, *were* two tables. Four tables *were* 41 on this side, and four tables on that side, by the side of the gate; eight tables, whereupon they slew *their sacrifices*. And the four tables *were* of hewn stone for the burnt 42 offering, of a cubit and a half long, and a cubit and a half broad, and one cubit high: whereupon also they laid the instruments wherewith they slew the burnt offering and the sacrifice. And within *were* hooks, a hand broad, fastened 43

tables would be at the sides of the gate *in* the inner court. Others think that the "shoulders" might be the front parts of the gate-building on either side of the steps leading up to it, and that thus the tables would stand in the outer court, two at each angle formed by the steps and the front of the gate. This use of "shoulder" is less natural, but cf. xlvii. 1, 2; 1 Kings vii. 39.

as one goeth up...north gate] For *as one goeth up* (oleh) might be read *at the stairs* (olah, as R.V. mar.). The difficulty lies in the word north or northwards. A.V. renders "the north gate" which is most natural. Others think of the E. gate and render: *and on the side without, on the N. as one goeth up to the entry of the gate*, i.e. on the left hand of the person going up. But this is extremely improbable. Such a designation of the left hand of a *person* has no examples, besides that here the word "north" is too far distant from the other word "one going up." A possible rendering would be: by the stair, at the entry to the gate northwards, i.e. on the N. side of the entry (Lev. i. 11). On the whole "the N. gate" of A.V. is most probable, but the language hardly decides which gate is meant. See after *v.* 43.

side which was *at the porch*] **side of the porch**, lit. belonging to the porch.

42. Read: **and there were four tables for the burnt offering, of hewn stone.** The phrase "for the burnt offering" is very indefinite. These stone tables seem too small to slay the offerings upon, and the end of the verse intimates that instruments for slaughtering were laid on the stone tables.

whereupon also they laid] **whereupon they laid.** The construction is peculiar.

43. *within* were *hooks*] The word rendered *hooks* occurs in the sense of cattlepens (Ps. lxviii. 14), a meaning precluded here by the dimension, a handbreadth. Such hooks fitted up "within," i.e. in the porch, might be used for hanging the carcases upon in order to flay them (Targ.). The meaning "hooks" is not certain. LXX. assumes that the stone tables are still referred to and points differently, reading lip or border for "hooks:" "and they shall have a border of hewn stone inwards round about of a span broad." Cf. xliii. 13, 17.

round about: and upon the tables *was* the flesh of the offering.

44 And without the inner gate *were* the chambers of the singers in the inner court, which *was* at the side of the north gate; and their prospect *was* toward the south: one at the side of the east gate *having* the prospect toward the north.

45 And he said unto me, This chamber, whose prospect *is* toward the south, *is* for the priests, the keepers of the charge

flesh of the offering] Except in a clause of xx. 28 (wanting in LXX.) the word "offering" is not used by Ezek. The present clause seems to say little. LXX. reads: "and over the tables above (they shall have) coverings, to protect them from the wet and from the heat"—which has a suspicious resemblance to Is. iv. 6.

The verses 38—43 are no doubt in some disorder. They suggest several questions not easily settled. Upon the whole it is improbable that slaughtering took place at more than one gate. The word "northwards" indeed (*v.* 40) seems decisive of this point. Either the N. gate is intended, or the N. side of the E. gate, no other gate having a N. side. There are several things in favour of the N. gate:

(1) In *vv.* 35—37 the prophet was at the N. inner gate, and no intimation is given that he was transported to another gate in *v.* 38. (2) In the Law slaughtering is ordered to be performed on the N. side of the altar in the case of the burnt, sin and trespass offerings (Lev. i. 11, iv. 24, 29, 33, vi. 25, vii. 2, xiv. 13); no injunction is given in the case of the peace-offering (iii. 2, 8, 13). It is probable that the prophet's legislation and that of the Levitical books will be in harmony. (3) In ch. viii. 5 the "altar-gate" is certainly the N. gate. (4) The E. gate, both inner and outer, was to be kept shut except on sabbaths and new moons (xlvi. 1), or on other occasions when the prince wished to offer a freewill offering (xlvi. 12). In favour of the E. gate there is the supposed meaning of *v.* 40; but the rendering, "on the N. of one going up to the entry," is hardly tenable (*v.* 40). Ew. indeed for "gates" *v.* 38 would read "east gate"— a purely arbitrary amendment. And altogether unhappy is his proposal to read for *without* (michuçah), *v.* 40, "runnel" (meruçah)—the verb to "run" being never used of the running of water or fluids.

44—46. Chambers for the priests who keep the house and serve the altar. Fig. 3, D.

44. This *v.* must be corrected according to *vv.* 45, 46 as follows: **and without the inner gate were two chambers in the inner court, one at the side of the N. gate, and its prospect was toward the S.; and one at the side of the S. gate, having its prospect towards the N.** So LXX. The phrase "without the inner gate" means that the chambers were in the inner court, not in the gateway itself.

45. *charge of the house*] "House" is used generally of the whole temple buildings. Here those having the charge of the house are called "priests," elsewhere the charge of the house is assigned to the Levites,

of the house. And the chamber whose prospect *is* toward 46
the north *is* for the priests, the keepers of the charge of the
altar: these *are* the sons of Zadok among the sons of Levi,
which come near to the LORD to minister unto him. So he 47
measured the court, an hundred cubits long, and an hundred
cubits broad, foursquare; and the altar *that was* before the
house.
And he brought me to the porch of the house, and 48
measured *each* post of the porch, five cubits on this side, and
five cubits on that side: and the breadth of the gate *was*
three cubits on this side, and three cubits on that side.
The length of the porch *was* twenty cubits, and the breadth 49

cf. ch. xliv. 15—31. This charge embraced several duties: e.g. that of keeping the gates (xliv. 11); and that of slaying the sacrifices (xliv. 11) and preparing the sacrificial meal for the people (xlvi. 24).
46. The other chamber was for the ministrants at the altar; these were the sons of Zadok, xliv. 15—31.
47. Measurements of the inner court.
Lines drawn along the inner fronts of the inner gates, and along the front of the house, gave a square of 100 cubits. In this space stood the altar in front of the house, and being high it could be seen through the gates. The place between the temple and the altar was especially sacred. On altar cf. xliii. 13—17. The square, Fig. 3, *iklm*; the altar, Fig. 3, F.

XL. 48—XLI. 4. MEASUREMENTS OF THE TEMPLE HOUSE, IN ITS THREE PARTS, PORCH, HOLY PLACE AND MOST HOLY PLACE.

48, 49. The porch. Fig. 2, A.
48. *post of the porch*] The "post" is as before the front or jamb of the advancing wall on each side of the entrance. This wall was 5 cubits thick. Fig. 2, *ab*.
breadth of the gate was *three cubits*] The "gate" here means the two bits of wall (N. to S.) on either side, the fronts of which formed the posts or jambs of the entrance, Fig. 2, *bh*. The language is brief; LXX. either read or judged that the reading should be: *and the breadth of the entrance was fourteen cubits, and the side pieces of the entrance of the porch were three cubits on one side and three cubits*, &c. These measures are correct and probably original, for 14 (entrance, Fig. 2, *aa*, *bb*) +6 (3+3)=20, the extent of the porch N. to S. (*v*. 49).
49. Here "length" is the larger dimension N. to S. (1 Kings vi. 3), Fig. 2, *hh*; and breadth the smaller E. to W.; Fig. 2, *bc*.
breadth eleven cubits] **twelve** cubits, as LXX. The number eleven cannot be reconciled with the other measurements. The length of the house E. to W. was 100 cubits, i.e. 5 (wall, *v*. 48) + 12 (porch, here) + 6 (wall of holy place, xli. 1) + 40 (holy place) + 2 (wall of holiest, xli. 3) + 20 (holiest, *v*. 4) + 6 (wall, *v*. 5) + 4 (annexe, *v*. 5) + 5 (outer wall of annexe, *v*. 9) = 100.

eleven cubits; and *he brought me* by the steps whereby they went up to it: and *there were* pillars by the posts, one on this side, and another on that side.

41 Afterward he brought me to the temple, and measured the posts, six cubits broad on the one side, and six cubits broad on the other side, *which was* the breadth of the
2 tabernacle. And the breadth of the door *was* ten cubits; and the sides of the door *were* five cubits on the one side, and five cubits on the other side: and he measured the length thereof, forty cubits: and the breadth, twenty cubits.
3 Then went he inward, and measured the post of the door, two cubits; and the door, six cubits; and the breadth of
4 the door, seven cubits. So he measured the length thereof,

and...by the steps whereby] and **by ten steps they went up to it**; so LXX. Beside the posts stood two pillars, one on either side of the entrance. These would narrow in some measure the entrance of 14 cubits. These pillars correspond to the Jachin and Boaz of Solomon's temple (1 Kings vii. 21).

XLI. **1, 2.** Measurement of the "temple," the holy place, Fig. 2, B.

1. The "posts" or jambs of the entrance wall were 6 cubits thick, Fig. 2, *cd*.

breadth of the tabernacle] Heb. *tent*. The word does not occur in the prophet except in the compounds Oholah and Oholibah. Read: other side: **the breadth of the posts**.

2. The entrance way between the posts N. to S. was 10 cubits. Fig. 2, *cc, dd*.

sides of the door] i.e. the pieces of wall running N. to S. on each side of the entrance, Fig. 2, *di*, that is, $10+5+5=20$, breadth of the house. The length (E. to W.) of the "temple" or holy place was 40 cubits.

3, 4. The most holy place, Fig. 2, C.

3. The wall was 2 cubits thick, Fig. 2, *ef*.

breadth of the door, seven cubits] The actual door or entrance Fig. 2, *ee, ff*, was 6 cubits (preceding clause); the present statement, therefore, refers to the walls on either side of the entrance (N. to S.). LXX. read or rightly interpreted: *and the entrance six cubits; and the side pieces of the entrance seven cubits on one side and seven cubits on the other.* Fig. 2, *fk*. That is $6+7+7=20$, breadth of the house as before (*v.* 4). It is to be observed that while Ez., being a priest, enters the holy place along with the guide he refrains from entering the most holy place, which the angel alone enters.

4. The most holy place was a square of 20 cubits.

twenty cubits; and the breadth, twenty cubits, before the temple : and he said unto me, This *is* the most holy *place*. After he measured the wall of the house, six cubits; and 5 the breadth of *every* side chamber, four cubits, round about

before the temple] *in front of.* The "temple" is the holy place, 1 Kings vi. 3, 5.

CH. XLI. 5—11. THE SIDE CHAMBERS OR ANNEXE TO THE HOUSE.

The text in some places is confused, but the general meaning is clear. Round about the wall of the house on three sides (N., W. and S.) were built side-chambers in three stories, thirty chambers in each story, Fig. 2, D. The chamber on the ground floor was 4 cubits wide (N. to S.), but in the second story the width was greater than in the first, and in the third story greater than in the second. The reason of this greater wideness of the upper stories was that the wall of the house on which the chambers were built diminished in thickness as it ascended. This wall was 6 cubits thick at the base (*v.* 5), but it was let in at two points as it ascended. The same arrangement had place in Solomon's temple— "on the outside he made rebatements in the wall of the house round about" (1 Kings vi. 6). The effect of this decrease in the thickness of the wall (in Solomon's temple a cubit each time) was that the chambers in the second and third stories became so much broader. In consequence of this narrowing of the wall of the house at two points two ledges ran round the wall on three sides, and on these ledges the beams that supported the second and third stories of the side-chambers rested, without being let into the wall (*v.* 6). The wall of the side-chambers was thus on one side the wall of the house; on the other side they had a wall of their own, 5 cubits thick (*v.* 9). The whole structure, house and side chambers, was built upon a raised platform, 6 cubits higher than the level of the inner court (*v.* 8). The buildings, however (temple and side-chambers), did not quite cover the platform: a margin of 5 cubits ("that which was left," *vv.* 9, 11) remained free outside the side-chambers, on two sides (N. and S.), Fig. 2, E; and from this free space the doors into the side-chambers opened, one on the N. and another on the S., Fig. 2, *g* (*v.* 11). Further, on the walls of the inner court, N. and S., were chambers for the priests, Fig. 3, GG', and between the temple-platform and these cells ran a passage or court of 20 cubits ("the separate place," *v.* 12). This court ran round the house-platform on three sides (N. W. S.), Fig. 3, H. The way in which one story of the side-chambers communicated with another is described only generally (*v.* 7); in Solomon's temple the communication is supposed to have been by a spiral staircase, or more probably by a ladder and trap-doors. It is evident that the prophet reproduces in the main the arrangements of the temple, hence he refers to the several things, even when first mentioning them, as *the* so and so, assuming that they are well known.

5. The wall of the house at its base was 6 cubits thick, and the breadth (N. to S.) of the side-chambers on the basement was 4 cubits.

6 the house on every side. And the side chambers *were* three, one over another, and thirty *in* order; and they entered into the wall which *was* of the house for the side chambers round about, that *they* might have hold, but they
7 had not hold in the wall of the house. And *there was* an enlarging, and a winding about still upward to the side chambers: for the winding about of the house *went* still

If the rebatements in the wall of the house were the same here as in Solomon's temple, the second story would be a cubit broader than the ground floor, and the third a cubit broader than the second (1 K. vi. 6), i. e. 4, 5 and 6 cubits. In Solomon's temple the side-chambers were larger, measuring 5, 6 and 7 cubits.

6. The Heb. would naturally read: "and the side-chambers were side-chamber against side-chamber three and thirty times"—which would give 33 chambers. Apart from syntax this is not probable. LXX. and some other versions give a different order: "and the side-chambers, side-chamber against side-chamber, were thirty, three times" (cf. 1 K. vii. 4, 5). It is probable that the chambers were thirty; those in the outer court were also thirty (xl. 17), and Josephus is cited as witness for this number (Boett., Corn.).

wall...of the house for the side chambers] It must not of course be supposed that the house had two walls,—a separate one for the chambers. The word "entered into" must either be taken as a noun: *and there were intakes in the wall of the house for the side chambers;* or it must be altered into some other word having this sense (1 K. vi. 6, LXX. uses the same word here as there)—*and there were rebatements* &c.; or some word of this meaning has fallen out before "entered into." LXX. has rendered the word "times," doubly, "thrice" "twice." If the word "times," lit. *steps*, could have the required meaning of intakes, it might be supposed that being written twice it had fallen out. But this is doubtful.

might have hold] It is self-evident that the second and third stories must have been supported in some way by the wall of the house, which was their own wall on one side, and mere contact with a perpendicular wall could be no support. The beams had support on the wall, but were not let *into* the wall in holes.

7. What the verse means to say is that the side-chambers widened in the second and third stories through the retreating of the wall of the house. The present text being assumed it might read: "and there was a widening of the side-chambers and an encompassing (by them) ever upwards; for the encompassing of the house was (the more) ever upwards, round about the house"—the meaning being that the higher the three story building rose the broader it grew and the closer it encompassed the house, i.e. appeared to encroach upon the house owing to the retreat of the wall. Another sense of the present reading would be got if the word rendered "encompass" could be supposed to be something which the house did, viz. "turn," turn in, retreat. The sense

upward round about the house: therefore the breadth of the house *was still* upward, and so increased *from* the lowest *chamber* to the highest by the midst. I saw also the height 8 of the house round about: the foundations of the side chambers *were* a full reed of six great cubits. The thickness 9

would remain the same. LXX. omits "encompassing" after "widening" and instead of "for the encompassing" &c. it reads: *according to the appendage* (projection, i.e. the ledge) *out of the wall*—giving the same general meaning.

the breadth of the house] The words mean: the house became broader upwards—an impossible sense. Either "house" must be omitted with LXX., or the clause read: and it broadened toward the house (or, inwards) ever upward. Subject is the side building.

and so increased] The words state how the various stories communicated with one another, according to the clear statement, 1 K. vi. 8. Read: **and from the lowest one went up to the highest and to the middle story**, or possibly with R.V., *by* the middle story. LXX. perspicuously: that they might go up from the chambers below to the upper chambers, and from the middle chambers to the third story. Syr. is equally distinct.

8—11. THE RAISED PLATFORM UPON WHICH THE HOUSE AND THE SIDE-CHAMBERS STOOD.

The house and the annexe stood on a platform raised a full reed, or 6 cubits above the level of the inner court (*v.* 8). The platform was reached in front of the house by a flight of 10 steps (xl. 49) from the court. The outside wall of the annexe was 5 cubits thick (*v.* 9). A space of 5 cubits of the platform remained unoccupied by the buildings (*v.* 11), Fig. 2, E. Then came a free space of 20 cubits running round the platform (*v.* 10), Fig. 3, H. Finally came other buildings in the inner court, one behind the house on the W. (*v.* 15), Fig. 3, K; and others on both sides of it, N. and S. (xlii. 1 *seq.*), Fig. 3, GG'.

8. *I saw also*] An uncommon form; usually it is said, *and there appeared*, which LXX. probably read here[1]. For "height" (gobah) probably "raised pavement" (gabbah, Gabbatha, John xix. 13) should be read (cf. footnote)—**and the house appeared as having a raised pavement round about**, lit. there appeared (belonging) to the house &c., cf. ch. x. 8. All that was seen of the platform was the passage of 5 cubits round about the building (*v.* 11). "House" includes both the temple proper and the side-chambers. This is supplemented by saying that the foundations of the side-chambers were 6 cubits high—of course house and side-chambers were on the same level.

six great cubits] as R.V., marg., **six cubits to the joint**, or angle, i.e.

---

[1] The curious word in LXX. καὶ τὸ θραελ appears a transliteration of this reading with following prep. *l* attached, וְתִרְאָ֖ל (fem. apoc. impf. niph.); cf. for form and construction ch. x. 8; and for short final vowel the spelling Abimael, Gen. x. 28. Therefore a fem. noun should be read as subj. (gabbah).

of the wall, which *was* for the side chamber without, *was* five cubits: and *that* which *was* left *was* the place of 10 the side chambers that *were* within. And between the chambers *was* the wideness of twenty cubits round about 11 the house on every side. And the doors of the side chambers *were* toward *the place* that *was* left, one door toward the north, and another door toward the south: and the breadth of the place that was left *was* five cubits round about.

probably to the point where the vertical line of the height of the platform cut the level of the court. The words cannot be a description of the kind of cubit, nor, since the foundations are being described, can there be any reference to the height within of the side-chambers or to the point of junction of one story with another.

9. The outside wall of the side-chambers was 5 cubits; and there was left a part of the raised platform not covered by buildings (*v.* 11).

that *which* was *left* was] This clause is in some disorder; and must be connected with *v.* 10. The text clearly distinguishes between "that which was left" (munnach), i.e. the outer margin of the raised platform left free of buildings, which was 5 cubits broad (*v.* 11), Fig. 2, E, and the "separate place" (gizrah), Fig. 3, H, i.e. the court running round the whole house buildings or the raised platform on which they stood, which was 20 cubits broad (*vv.* 10, 13, 14)—although LXX. renders both by the same word. In *v.* 9, "that which was left" cannot differ from the same in *v.* 11, where it is undoubtedly the remainder of the raised platform. Some words have fallen out in *v.* 9. It is easiest perhaps to supply the words "five cubits" from Syr. and read: *and that which was left was 5 cubits; and between* (*bêth* for *bên*) *the side-chambers of* (belonging to) *the house,* 10 *and the cells* was a breadth of 20 cubits, &c. All the versions agree as to *v.* 10, but "between the cells" cannot mean between something else and the cells. The "cells" or chambers here are undoubtedly those on the N. and S. walls of the inner court (xlii. 1, *seq.*), which were separated from the house buildings by the court of 20 cubits, Fig. 3, GG'.

11. The verse states plainly that the place that was left, i.e. the margin of platform unoccupied by buildings, was 5 cubits broad, Fig. 2, E. and that the doors of the side-chambers opened upon it, one on the N. and another on the S. side, Fig. 2, *g.* It is evident that the side-chambers could have doors nowhere else, for their wall on one side was the wall of the house, in which doors could not be permitted; and the measurements seem to shew that the margin of raised basement did not go round the house on the west. In Solomon's temple there was probably only one door, on the S. side, 1 Kings vi. 8.

12. THE BUILDING BEHIND THE HOUSE ON THE WEST, Fig. 3, K.

To the west of the house proper, but divided from it by the 20 cubits of the "separate place" (Fig. 3, H), was a large building, 70 cubits

Now the building that *was* before the separate place *at* 12
the end toward the west *was* seventy cubits broad; and
the wall of the building *was* five cubits thick round about,
and the length thereof ninety cubits. So he measured the 13
house, an hundred cubits long; and the separate place, and
the building, with the walls thereof, an hundred cubits long;
also the breadth of the face of the house, and of the 14
separate place toward the east, an hundred cubits. And 15

broad (E. to W. Fig. 3, *rp, sq*), and 90 long (N. to S. Fig. 3, *rs, pq*)—
breadth being the smaller and length the larger dimension here. The
wall of the building all round was 5 cubits thick. The measurements
70 and 90 are inside. The uses which this building served are not
specified, they were probably general.

before the separate place] i.e. the court of 20 cubits broad (Fig. 3, H),
which ran round the house. "Before" is opposite to or facing.

13—15. General measurements of length and breadth of buildings.
—These measurements form three squares of 100 cubits. First, the
inner court forms a square of 100 cubits when lines are drawn along the
front of the house and in front of the inner ends of the gates, Fig. 3, *iklm*.
Secondly, the house buildings form a square of 100 cubits, when the
20 cubits of "separate place" N. and S. of them are included,
Fig. 3, *lmno*. And thirdly, the building W. of the house buildings
forms a square of 100 cubits when the twenty cubits of "separate place"
are added to its dimensions from E. to W., Fig. 3, *nopq*.

13. Two measurements of 100 cubits E. to W.

house an hundred cubits long] namely, 5 (wall of porch, xl, 48) + 12
(porch, xl. 49) + 6 (wall of holy place, xli. 1) + 40 (length of holy place,
xli. 2) + 2 (wall of holiest, xli. 3) + 20 (length of holiest, xli. 4) + 6 (wall
of house, xli. 5) + 4 (side-chambers, *v.* 5) + 5 (wall of side-chambers,
xli. 9) = 100. Here it is evident that on the W. of the house the margin
or "that which was left" of the raised basement does not appear. It
existed only on two sides N. and S., where the doors of the side-
chambers opened from it; on the W. the "separate place" skirted the
wall of the side-chambers.

separate place, and the building] The "building" here (though spelled
differently) can be no other than that mentioned *v.* 12, Fig. 3, K. The
"separate place" or court of 20 cubits, Fig. 3, H, being added to this
building formed a length of 100 cubits, viz. 20 (separate place) + 5 + 5
(two walls of building) + 70 (interior of building) = 100, Fig. 3, *np*.

14. Two measurements of 100 cubits from N. to S.
The front of the house buildings, the "separate place" on each side
of them being included, gives 100 cubits, namely, 20 (breadth of house)
+ 6 + 6 (side walls) + 4 + 4 (side-chambers) + 5 + 5 (walls of side-chambers) + 5 + 5 (remainder of raised basement) + 20 + 20 (separate place) =
100, Fig. 3, *lm*.

he measured the length of the building over against the separate place which *was* behind it, and the galleries thereof on the one side and on the other side, an hundred cubits,

15. The "length" here is reckoned from N. to S.

which was *behind it*] Rather: **behind which it was**. The building, while lying "over against" the "separate place," was behind it, i.e. to the W. of it. If this construction be not adopted the meaning is, which (building) was behind it (the separate place)—an independent clause. The length of the building as it lay along the "separate place" N. to S. was 100 cubits, i.e. 90 (interior, *v.* 12) + 5 + 5 (side walls, *v.* 12) = 100, Fig. 3, *rs*. The term rendered "galleries" is of uncertain meaning. It occurs only xli. 15, 16 and xlii. 3, 5. If the reading be right here it can mean nothing else but walls, or something equivalent to walls and occupying the same space, according to *v.* 12. Syriac uses a term by which it also renders the "walls" of the altar, *v.* 22.—The verse should end at the word *cubits*.

15 *b seq*. DESCRIPTION OF THE INSIDE OF THE HOUSE, WITH ITS ORNAMENTATION.

The details of measurement were exhausted in *v.* 15 *a*. The prophet proceeds now to describe the interior of the house in two particular points: (1) the woodwork with which the house in its walls, &c., was covered, 15 *b*—16 *a*; and (2) the ornamentation of this woodwork, 16 *b seq*. The text is in some disorder, and the unknown term rendered "galleries" causes perplexity, though two general statements are plainly made, viz. that the whole interior of the house was covered with wood, and that this woodwork from floor to roof was ornamented in the holy place and in the holiest with cherubs and palms (in the porch perhaps with palms only). With no more changes than are absolutely necessary *vv.* 15 *b*—16 *a* might read: "and the temple (i.e. holy place), and the inner house (holiest), and the porch of the court (more probably, and its outer porch), 16 and the thresholds, and the closed windows and the galleries round about the three of them, opposite the threshold (i.e. towards the interior) were veneered with wood (or, were polished wood) round about." This would state generally that the whole interior was wainscotted. But the jump from "thresholds" (A.V. door-posts) to "closed windows" in *v.* 16 is unnatural. It is probable that "thresholds" should be read with LXX. *cieled* (or, wainscotted). It is certainly probable that the roofing is described; the word read by LXX. (saphan) is always used of the roof-work in the description of Solomon's temple (1 Kings vi. vii., unless vii. 7 be an exception, a clause wanting in LXX.); and LXX. understood it so here (*v.* 20). Further the mention of the closed windows, which must have been toward the roof, in immediate connexion, is in favour of the roof-work. What the "galleries" were is obscure. LXX. either did not read the word or rendered it "narrow openings" (slit windows). A.V. "on their three stories" should be **to the three of them** (the holy place, holiest and porch, *v.* 15). Pointed thus the reading is: *and the temple and the inner house* (holiest) *and the porch of the court* (or, and its outer porch) *were covered with a*

with the inner temple, and the porches of the court; the door posts, and the narrow windows, and the galleries round about on their three *stories*, over against the door, cieled with wood round about, and *from* the ground up to the windows, and the windows *were* covered; to *that* above the door, even unto the inner house, and without, and by all the wall round about within and without, *by* measure. And *it was* made *with* cherubims and palm trees, so that a palm tree *was* between a cherub and a cherub; and *every* cherub had two faces; so that the face of a man *was* toward the palm tree on the one side, and the face of a young lion toward the palm tree on the other side: *it was* made through all the house round about. From the ground roof-work, and they three had their closed windows and their galleries round about.

16. *over against the door*] the **threshold**. It looks as if some words had fallen out of the text here. LXX. reads: *and the house and the adjoining parts were wainscotted with wood round about* (and the floor). The present Heb. text, even if read, *and over against the threshold was a wainscotting of wood*, is too short to give the necessary sense—"over against the threshold" would be rather obscure as an expression for the whole interior of the house. The words "over against the threshold" can hardly be regarded as a definition of the locality of the "galleries," as if these were borders or gangs (dado) going round the foot of the walls (Sm.).

vv. 16 *b seq.* The ornamentation of the interior. Here also there is some obscurity: *and from the floor unto the windows* (and the windows were covered), 17 *and unto above the door, and unto the inner house and without, and on all the walls round about in the inner* (house) *and the outer* [were measures and], 18 *there were made cherubs and palm-trees, so that*, &c. The words in parenthesis "and the windows," &c., may not be original. The phrase "and without" hardly refers to the porch, rather to the outer house or holy place; because it does not appear that cherubs were carved on the wall of the porch. The word "measures" is wanting in LXX. If genuine the term "measures" might possibly imply that the wall was panelled into compartments, and that in each of these was carved a cherub and palm. The term is used once of garments (Ps. cxxxiii. 2) from the meaning to spread out or cover, but could hardly be used of a casing or wainscotting of wood. Boettcher suggested "carvings," a sense which would add nothing to the general meaning. *V.* 20 is rather in favour of the omission of the word.

vv. 18, 19. Only the two chief faces of the cherub were represented, that of a man and of a lion.

20. The prophet is to be conceived as standing in the holy place, and when he speaks of the "door" he evidently refers to the end walls and

unto above the door *were* cherubims and palm trees made, and *on* the wall of the temple.

21 The posts of the temple *were* squared, *and* the face of the sanctuary; the appearance *of the one* as the appearance 22 *of the other*. The altar *of* wood *was* three cubits high, and the length thereof two cubits; and the corners thereof, and the length thereof, and the walls thereof, *were of* wood: and

not to the side walls. It remains obscure whether it be the "door" of the holiest or that of the holy place to which he refers.

and on *the wall...temple*] The word "temple" is marked as suspicious by dots over it, and is omitted in some MSS. and in the ancient versions. The clause is to be connected with *v.* 21.

21. *the posts...squared*] The text is very uncertain, the versions deviating from Heb. and from one another. The word "temple" (*v.* 20) being omitted the words read: *and the wall*, 21 *of the temple was square door-posts*—a construction scarcely possible to express the idea that the wall *had* square door-posts. Syriac read: and the wall of the temple was four-square—omitting "door-posts." LXX.: and the holy place (holiest) and the temple opened (spread out) four-square—reading "holy place" for wall, and "opened" for door-posts. It is probable that something is said of the holiest, because the next clause refers to an article that stood in front of it. It is also probable that the "door" referred to *v.* 20 is that from the holy place into the holiest. But the witnesses leave us uncertain whether something be said about the wall or about the door-posts. If of the first the reading may be: *and the wall of the holiest was four-square* (Hitz., Corn.). Reference, however, might be to the door-posts. In Solomon's temple those of the holy place appear to have been four-cornered, and those of the holiest five-cornered (1 Kings vi. 31, 33).

face of the sanctuary...the other] This has no probability. The clause is rather to be connected with *v.* 22. Perhaps: **and in front of the sanctuary** (the holiest) **was the appearance as the appearance 22 of an altar of wood, three cubits the height thereof**, &c. So LXX. and partly Syr. In the holy place in front of the holiest there stood an object having the appearance of an altar of wood. The present text might read: "and (as for) the front of the sanctuary, the appearance was as the appearance," i.e. it had the appearance which is well known and does not need further description—a form of speech common enough in Shemitic, but quite improbable here.

22. The altar was 3 cubits high and 2 long. LXX. adds that it was 2 broad.

the length thereof...of wood] and **the base** thereof, a simple emendation, after LXX.; cf. Ex. xxvi. 19 *seq*. The altar had corners, probably somewhat raised, but not horns. It was wholly of wood, and is called the table which is before the Lord. The term table is applied to the altar of burnt-offering xliv. 16 (cf. Mal. i. 7, 12). This is quite natural, as the flesh was the bread of Jehovah (xliv. 7). Ezek. does not

he said unto me, This *is* the table that *is* before the LORD. And the temple and the sanctuary had two doors. And 23 24 the doors had two leaves *apiece*, two turning leaves; two *leaves* for the one door, and two leaves for the other *door*. And *there were* made on them, on the doors of the temple, 25 cherubims and palm trees, like as *were* made upon the walls; and *there were* thick planks upon the face of the porch without. And *there were* narrow windows and palm 26 trees on the one side and on the other side, on the sides of the porch, and *upon* the side chambers of the house, and thick planks.

name any other object in the holy place besides this table, and it is probable that he refers here to the altar-like table of shewbread, the cakes on which would also be considered an offering of bread for the Lord.

23—26. The doors of the holy place and the holiest.

The temple or holy place and the holiest had each a two-leaved door; and each of the leaves was again divided into two leaves.

23. *two doors*] i.e. each had a double or two-leaved door.

24. *And the doors*] i.e. the leaves of the door had again two leaves, so that the doors as a whole of the holy place and holiest were each composed of four small leaves, like a screen.

25. The doors of the holy place were carved with cherubs and palm trees just as the walls (*v.* 17 *seq.*).

thick planks upon the face] The word rendered "thick planks" ('*ab*) occurs again 1 Kings vii. 6 in connexion with a porch, but is of uncertain meaning. Here it is said to lie outside the porch and in front of it, and might be the "landing" at the top of the flight of steps. Others think of an overhanging on the front of the roof, to protect the entrance. But in 1 Kings vii. 7 the '*ab* fronts the pillars, as here it faces the porch. Therefore perhaps: "and a landing of wood in front of the porch on the outside." No doubt "without" might describe the lie of the porch in reference to the house and not the lie of the '*ab* in reference to the porch; in which case the '*ab* would be something between the holy place and the porch, and in fact the description in *v.* 26 refers to the *inside* of the porch. Still this is less probable.

26. For narrow windows, **closed.** The "sides" (lit. shoulders) are the side walls of the porch, but whether the walls on both sides of the entrance be meant, or the end-walls (N. and S.), cannot be decided. There should be a full stop at *porch*. The next statement is incomplete: and the side-chambers of the house and the landings....

CH. XLII. OTHER BUILDINGS OF THE INNER COURT.

The Chapter has three divisions:

First, *vv.* 1—12. The chambers in the inner court.
Secondly, *vv.* 13, 14. The uses of these chambers for the priests.

42 Then he brought me forth into the utter court, the way toward the north: and he brought me into the chamber

Thirdly, *vv.* 15—20. Measurements of the outer wall and area of the whole temple buildings.
1—12. The chambers in the inner court.
In the inner court on the two sides N. and S. of the house or temple proper were erected blocks of cells for the use of the priests, where they ate the holy things and deposited their sacred garments. They are those referred to xli. 10. The block on the N. side is fully described (*vv.* 1—9), and that on the S. of the house is said to be similar in all respects (*vv.* 10—12). The block on the N. extended from the "separate place" to the N. wall of the inner court, a breadth of 50 cubits, all the space available. The block of cells had two wings, one 100 cubits long running along the "separate place," Fig. 3, G, the other 50 cubits long, Fig. 3, G', running along the N. wall of the inner court—both measurements E. to W. Between the two wings of the block ran a walk of 10 cubits broad and 100 cubits long, i.e. the whole length of the longer wing, Fig. 3, O, and on this walk the doors into the chambers opened, i.e. looked to the N. (at least in the longer wing). The chambers were built in three stories, but those of the third story were narrower than those of the other two, because a "gallery" in the uppermost story took up some space. The chambers had no pillars like those in the outer court. There was an entrance-way leading to the chambers from the outer court, through the wall of the inner court, but its precise situation is not indicated.

1—3. These verses may read consecutively: "And he brought me forth into the inner court, the way toward the north; and he brought me unto the chambers that were over against the separate place, and that were over against the (wall-) building toward the north, 2 (even) in front of the length of 100 cubits with the doors toward the north; and the breadth was 50 cubits, 3 over against the 20 cubits belonging to the inner court, and over against the pavement belonging to the outer court, gallery (being) over against gallery in the third story."

1. *the utter court*] LXX. the *inner* court. Something may be said for both. On the one hand the entrance-way to the chambers was from the outer court, and the prophet might have been first brought to the outer court and then by this way to the chambers in the inner court. This, however, is rather a complicated movement, and is not indicated; and perhaps the "inner" of LXX. has most probability. The position of the prophet is pretty clear, it was on the E. of the chambers, to the N. of the longer wing and facing it, Fig. 3, Q. LXX. reads "eastward" for "the way."

into the chamber] **unto the chambers.** The word is sing. as collective. The "separate place" is the 20 cubits broad court running round the house on its three sides, Fig. 3, H. The longer wing of the block of cells ran along this "separate" place its whole length of 100 cubits, Fig. 3, G. The "building toward the N." is the wall of the outer court with its blocks of cells (xl. 5), Fig. 3, B, C. As there was nothing that *was* over against the separate place, and which *was* before the building toward the north. Before the length of 2 an hundred cubits *was* the north door, and the breadth *was* fifty cubits. Over against the twenty *cubits* which *were* 3 for the inner court, and over against the pavement which *was* for the utter court, *was* gallery against gallery in three *stories.* And before the chambers *was* a walk of ten cubits 4

between the wing of chambers on the N. wall of the inner court and this "building" or wall of the outer court with its cells, except the mere level of the court, the one is said to be over against the other.

2. *V.* 2 states the precise place where the prophet was brought to—it was in front of, or so as to face, the longer wing of chambers, or the walk of 100 cubits before them, i.e. he was slightly to the N. of this longer wing, and to the E. of the whole block. This seems more natural than to suppose the "length of 100 cubits" to be the separate place. Probably, Fig. 3, Q.

was *the north door*] As above: **with the doors toward the north** (*v.* 4). This is rather hard in construction, and for "with the doors" might be read: *on the side* toward the N. (peath for pethaḥ). So LXX. The breadth N. to S. of the whole block of chambers was 50 cubits (cf. *v.* 4).

3. The breadth of the block having been mentioned in *v.* 2, *v.* 3 adds in what directions this breadth extended or lay on either hand (N. and S.), viz. towards the 20 cubits of the separate place (Fig. 3, H) on the S., and toward the pavement running round the wall of the outer court (xl. 17) on the N. (cf. *v.* 1), Fig. 3, B. The term "gallery" is obscure, but here it seems to mean a passage running round the chambers, in front of them, and so taking away from their area.

in three stories] More naturally: **in the third story**, lit. in *the thirds*, i.e. third chambers (Gen. vi. 16). What is meant by "gallery over against gallery" is rather obscure. Most naturally the galleries or gangways round the highest story would be supposed to lie towards the interior of both wings, i.e. on the "walk" of 10 cubits running between the wings (Fig. 3, O), because if they lay toward the outside of the wings respectively it is difficult to see how they could be said to lie "over against" or to face one another, for in that case both wings of the chambers in the third story would lie between them. It is altogether unnatural to suppose that by the second "gallery" any galleries in the chambers of the outer court on the one side, or any galleries in the structure of the house proper on the other, are referred to.

4—6 may be read: "And before the chambers was a walk of 10 cubits breadth inward, with a length of 100 cubits; and their doors were toward the north. 5 Now the upper chambers were shorter; for the galleries took away from them compared with the lower and middle (chambers) in room. 6 For they were in three stories, and they had not pillars like the pillars of those in the outer court; therefore" &c.

breadth inward, a way of one cubit; and their doors toward
5 the north. Now the upper chambers *were* shorter: for the
galleries were higher than these, than the lower, and than
6 the middlemost of the building. For they *were* in three
stories, but had not pillars as the pillars of the courts:
therefore *the building* was straitened more than the lowest
7 and the middlemost from the ground. And the wall that
was without over against the chambers, towards the utter
court on the forepart of the chambers, the length thereof
8 *was* fifty cubits. For the length of the chambers that *were*

4. *inward*] i.e. between the two wings (Fig. 3, O). Or possibly: (leading) *into the inner court*.
a way of one cubit] A mere error of transcription for: *a length of 100 cubits*. So LXX., Syr. In *v.* 16 "cubit" and "hundred" (both having the same three letters) have again been confused. The doors of the chambers were to the N., i.e. opened upon this passage of 10 cubits, between the wings.

5. The uppermost story was contracted by the gallery, so that its area was smaller than that of the other two stories.

6. *the pillars of the courts*] LXX. reads: pillars of *the outer ones*, i.e. the chambers in the outer court. Probably there is a transcriptional error here, cf. xli. 15.
was straitened] lit. *there was* (room) *taken away from the lowest...from the ground*. The last words seem in apposition with "lowest," and refer to the ground area. The verse indicates that the chambers in the outer court had pillars, and that the three stories were all of the same dimensions.

7—9. The shorter wing of chambers. Read together the verses run: "And the wall that was without, beside the chambers which were toward the outer court, facing the (other?) chambers, the length thereof was 50 cubits. 8 For the length of the chambers that were toward the outer court was 50 cubits; but those toward the temple were 100 cubits. 9 And below these chambers was the entrance-way on the east when one goeth to them from the outer court, at the beginning of the wall of the court"—the first words of *v.* 10 being connected with *v.* 9.

7. *wall...without*] i.e. not forming part of the block of cells, but extending eastward from the end of the shorter wing, and therefore said to be beside the cells that lay towards the outer court. Fig. 3, *vw*.
on the forepart] *in front of* or *facing*—still said of the wall (Fig. 3, *vw*). The "chambers" seem to be those of the longer wing. The piece of wall would face them; but the words might be (though less likely) a second specification of the position of the piece of wall referred to in regard to the shorter wing (cf. *v.* 2). The length of this piece of wall was 50 cubits. The reason is stated in *v.* 8.

8. The shorter wing of chambers lying toward the outer court was 50 cubits long. Fig. 3, *uv*.

in the utter court *was* fifty cubits: and lo, before the temple *were* an hundred cubits. And from under these 9 chambers *was* the entry on the east side, as one goeth into them from the utter court. The chambers *were* in the 10 thickness of the wall of the court toward the east, over against the separate place, and over against the building.

and lo,...the temple] The exclamation *and lo!* is rather unnatural, a slight change of punctuation gives, *but those*. The expression "before the temple" is difficult. Usually "temple" means merely the holy place. The phrase "before" the temple makes no difficulty, "before" means merely "facing," and does not imply the "front" of the temple in the technical sense. The LXX. (so Ew. Corn.) reads differently: *and these* (the shorter wing, Fig. 3, G') *faced the others* (the longer, Fig. 3, G), *together* 100 *cubits*—"together" referring to the shorter wing and wall (Fig. 3, *uv + vw*).

9. *under these chambers*] i.e. the shorter wing.

10. *thickness of the wall*] Probably: *at the beginning* (or, head) *of the wall* (cf. v. 12). The "wall" is that piece of wall referred to *v*. 7, and the "beginning of it" is the point where the way enters from the outer court, Fig. 3, P. In xlvi. 19 this is stated to have been at the shoulder (the long side) of the N. gate. It is said that the doors into the chambers were from the "walk" of 100 cubits long fronting the longer wing (Fig. 3, O), and possibly also that this walk led into the inner court (*v*. 4), consequently the entrance-way from the outer court must have lain as far east as the end of this "walk," which it led to and so reached the chambers. The area of 100 × 50 on which the cells stood, though not wholly covered by the cells, must have been in some way marked off from the general level of the court, and the entrance-way from the outer court was on the east front of it; and it was probably in this entrance-way that the prophet had his position (*vv*. 1—9), Fig. 3. Q.

10—12. The corresponding chambers on the south side of the temple-house. The text is undoubtedly in great confusion; and has been amended in various ways. Taken as nearly as possible as it stands it reads: "Towards the south, over against the separate place and over against the (wall-) building, there were chambers, 11 with a way before them, like the appearance of the chambers which were towards the north, as long as they and as broad as they, and according to all their goings out, and according to their fashions. And according to their doors, 12 so were the doors of the chambers that were toward the south; there was a door at the beginning of the way, to wit the way before the corresponding (?) wall, on the east as one entereth into them."

10. For "east" must be read **south**, according to *vv*. 12, 13 and the whole scope; cf. xliv. 44. The "building" as in *v*. 1 is the wall of the outer court with its stories of cells, Fig. 3, B, C. On the one side the chambers faced the separate place, and on the other side the shorter wing looked towards the buildings in the outer court.

11 And the way before them *was* like the appearance of the chambers which *were* toward the north, as long as they, *and* as broad as they: and all their goings out *were* both according to their fashions, and according to their doors.

12 And according to the doors of the chambers that *were* toward the south *was* a door in the head of the way, *even* the way directly before the wall toward the east, as *one* entereth into them.

13 Then said he unto me, The north chambers *and* the south chambers, which *are* before the separate place, they *be* holy chambers, where the priests that approach unto the LORD shall eat the most holy *things:* there shall they lay the most holy *things*, and the meat offering, and the sin offering, and the trespass offering; for the place *is* holy.

11. *way before them*] The term "way" here seems used of the 10 cubits broad walk running between the two wings of the block of chambers (*v*. 4), Fig. 3, O. LXX. renders "walk" as there. For "appearance" LXX. reads *measures*. The "they" and "their" refer to the chambers on the north side of the court (*vv*. 1—9); those on the south side were like them in all particulars.

12. As the text reads it is easiest to attach the last words of *v*. 11 to *v*. 12. The sense resulting from this change is not very natural. Possibly *v*. 11 should end as A.V., in which case *v*. 12 must be amended: *and the doors of the chambers were toward the south*. In this point they differed from the other chambers, the doors of which were towards the north (*v*. 4).

The term rendered "corresponding" is quite unknown. In the Targ. and post-biblical Heb. a similar word appears to mean suitable, excellent —the appropriate wall. The word is no doubt corrupt. LXX. "reed."

13, 14. Uses to which the chambers were put.

These cells serve two purposes: the priests shall eat in them the most holy things; and they shall deposit there the sacred garments when they put them off to go into the outer court among the people. The "most holy things" were the portion of the meal-offering not consumed on the altar (Lev. ii. 3, 10, vii. 9—11, x. 12), and the flesh of the sin and trespass offerings, except the flesh of the sin-offering for the high-priest and congregation, which was burnt outside the sacred buildings (Lev. vi. 30, vii. 6).

before the separate place] *over against*, as *vv*. 1, 10, i.e. the longer wing on the N. and on the S. Nothing specially is said as to the uses of the shorter wing.

lay the most holy things] Naturally the meal-offering had to be baked before being eaten, and the flesh of the sacrifices boiled. Being most holy things they must be kept in a holy place.

When the priests enter *therein*, then shall they not go out 14
of the holy *place* into the utter court, but there they shall
lay their garments wherein they minister; for they *are* holy;
and shall put on other garments, and shall approach to
those things which *are* for the people.

Now when he had made an end of measuring the inner 15
house, he brought me forth toward the gate whose prospect
is toward the east, and measured it round about. He 16
measured the east side with the measuring reed, five hun-

14. *the priests enter* therein] Omit *therein*. The ref. is not to the holy cells, but to the house or more probably the inner court, in which the altar stood.

go out of the holy place] probably the whole inner court is meant, with its contents, house and chambers, seeing it is contrasted with the outer court.

things...*for the people*] Or, **that which is for the people**—the outer court.

15—20. MEASUREMENTS OF THE WHOLE COMPLEX OF THE TEMPLE BUILDINGS ON THE OUTSIDE.

The measuring angel began by measuring the height and thickness of the outside surrounding wall (xl. 5); then he entered the outer gate, passing into the outer court, the measurements of which were made (xl. 6—27); then he entered the inner court, containing the house and cells, all of which he measured (xl. 28—xlii. 14). These measures being completed, the angel now returns to the outside by the way he entered, the eastern gate, and finishes by measuring the compass of the whole temple buildings outside. This building, its surrounding wall being measured, forms a square of 500 cubits.

15. *measured it*] i.e. whole building, along the outer wall.

16. *five hundred reeds*] Rather: **cubits.** Five hundred reeds, the reed being 6 cubits, would give a measurement of 3000 cubits. No allusion is made to such a space surrounding the house buildings anywhere else. On the contrary in xlv. 2 the area of the temple buildings is said to be 500 cubits square, and the free place about it 50 cubits. LXX. omits the word "reeds" everywhere in these verses, expressly giving "cubits" in *v.* 17. In *v.* 20 (Heb.) allusion is made to the *wall*, and "reeds" is omitted. That the outer wall of the temple buildings formed a square of 500 cubits appears from measurements given elsewhere. Taking the direction N. to S. we have 50 (outer gate, xl. 21) + 100 (gate to gate, xl. 23) + 50 (inner gate, xl. 36) + 100 (inner court, xl. 47) + 50 (inner gate) + 100 (gate to gate) + 50 (outer gate) = 500. Or going from E. to W. the result is the same: 50 (outer gate) + 100 (gate to gate) + 50 (inner gate) + 100 (inner court) + 100 (house, xli. 13) + 100 (building behind house, xli. 13) = 500.

17 dred reeds, with the measuring reed round about. He
measured the north side, five hundred reeds, with the
18 measuring reed round about. He measured the south side,
19 five hundred reeds, with the measuring reed. He turned
about to the west side, *and* measured five hundred reeds
20 with the measuring reed. He measured it by the four
sides: it had a wall round about, five hundred *reeds* long,
and five hundred broad, to make a separation between the
sanctuary and the profane *place*.

43 Afterward he brought me to the gate, *even* the gate that
2 looketh toward the east: and behold, the glory of the God
of Israel came from the way of the east: and his voice *was*

round about] The word is wanting in *v.* 18, and *v.* 19 reads: he
turned about and *measured*. LXX. reads in the latter way in all the
verses 16, 17, 18, attaching the word to the beginning of the following
verse, no doubt rightly, cf. a similar case 1 S. xiv. 21. In LXX. also
vv. 18 and 19 are transposed, the natural order round the wall being
followed.

20. *sanctuary...profane* place] Rather: **between that which was
holy and that which was profane** (common). Holy and profane are
used here relatively, just as *v.* 13 the inner court is relatively holy in
contrast with the outer to which the people had access. Cf. xliii. 12,
where the limits of the house are said to be "most holy." In xlv. 4
the priests' land surrounding the temple is called holy, and in xlviii. 12
most holy.

CH. XLIII. ENTRY OF JEHOVAH INTO THE HOUSE.

The measurements of the whole temple buildings being completed,
the prophet sees Jehovah return to it by the E. gate, by which he had
seen him leave it (ch. xi.). The vision of the glory of the Lord was
like that seen on former occasions (ch. i. and x.). The chapter has
three divisions:—

(1) *vv.* **1—12.** Entry of Jehovah into his house.
(2) *vv.* **13—17.** Measurements of the altar of burnt-offering.
(3) *vv.* **18—27.** Sacrifices and ceremonies to be employed in dedicating the altar.

1—12. The glory of Jehovah enters the house by the E. gate. The
sound of his chariot was as the sound of many waters, and his glory
lightened the earth (*vv.* 1—4). The prophet hears one speaking to him
from the house and saying that the defilements to which the house had
been exposed through idolatries and the burial of kings near it shall
henceforth cease (*vv.* 6—9). The prophet is commanded to make
known the fashion and ordinances of the house to the people (*vv.* 10—12).

2. *and his voice*] and **the sound of him was like the sound**.
Reference is to the sound made by the cherubim in their flight.

like a noise of many waters: and the earth shined with his
glory. And *it was* according to the appearance of the 3
vision which I saw, *even* according to the vision that I saw
when I came to destroy the city: and the visions *were* like
the vision that I saw by the river Chebar; and I fell upon
my face. And the glory of the LORD came into the house 4
by the way of the gate whose prospect *is* toward the east.
So the spirit took me up, and brought me into the inner 5
court; and behold, the glory of the LORD filled the house.
And I heard *him* speaking unto me out of the house; and 6
the man stood by me. And he said unto me, Son of man, 7
the place of my throne, and the place of the soles of my

3. *And* it was *according to*] **And the appearance which I saw was
like the appearance which I saw when I came**—the word "appearance"
at the beginning of the verse being omitted.
I came to destroy] Reference is to ch. viii.—xi. and the destruction
of the city there seen in vision by the prophet. He was carried to Jerusalem to witness the destruction, and he calls this his coming to destroy
it. Vulg., when *he* (Jehovah) *came*.
the visions were *like the vision*] like the **appearance**. The words
"and the visions" are rather unnatural; LXX. reads: and the vision of
the chariot which I saw was like &c. The "chariot," i.e. the whole
theophany of cherubim and wheels is often spoken of in later times
(e.g. Ecclesus. xlix. 8), but is nowhere named in the Bible (cf. 1 Chr.
xxviii. 18). The reading of LXX. is probably a gloss in explanation of
the Heb., which is awkward. Possibly the word "visions" should be
omitted :...the city, *and like the appearance that I saw by the river Chebar*.
Cf. iii. 23, where LXX. interpolates "according to the vision."
4. The glory of the Lord enters the house by the E. gate, by which
he had departed from it, x. 19, xi. 22, 23.
5. The prophet, who hitherto was at the E. gate outside (*v.* 1), is
brought by the spirit into the inner court, from which he perceived the
house to be filled with the glory of the Lord.
6. *heard* him *speaking*] *One* speaking.
and the *man*] Possibly: and **a man**. No doubt the same man is
meant as before. The prophet was transported into the inner court by
the spirit, not led as in other instances by the man, who, however,
reappears at his side. The man is merely the divine voice and word
personified and interposed between the Lord and the prophet, hence
though Ezekiel appears to hear one speaking from the house, the voice
immediately takes the shape of a man beside him.
7. *the place of my throne*] **this is the place of my throne...for ever:
and the house of Israel shall no more defile.** No change of reading
is implied but the emphatic position of "the place" &c. requires to be
expressed by some such word as "this is," or, "Behold." On "soles

feet, where I will dwell in the midst of the children of Israel for ever, and my holy name, shall the house of Israel no more defile, *neither* they, nor their kings, by their whoredom, nor by the carcases of their kings *in* their high places. 8 In their setting of their threshold by my thresholds, and their post by my posts, and the wall between me and them, they have even defiled my holy name by their abominations that they have committed: wherefore I have consumed 9 them in mine anger. Now let them put away their whoredom, and the carcases of their kings, far from me, and I will wheel in the midst of them for ever.

10 Thou son of man, shew the house to the house of Israel, that they may be ashamed of their iniquities; and let them 11 measure the pattern. And if they be ashamed of all that

of my feet" cf. Is. lx. 13, lxvi. 1; Lam. ii. 1; Ps. cxxxii. 7; 1 Chr. xxviii. 2.

by their whoredom] Their idolatries, cf. ch. viii.

in *their high places*] Probably: **in their death**, i.e. when dead, Lev. xi. 31, 32. So some MSS., Targ., by change of one vowel. The ref. is to the burial of the kings in the vicinity of the temple. The passages Lev. xxvi. 30; Jer. xvi. 18, to which appeal is made, do not sustain the idea that "carcase" could be used as a mere name of opprobrium for idols (Ps. cvi. 28 is of doubtful meaning). In the former passage the hewn down idol is a carcase just as the slain man is; and in Jer. xvi. 18 the use of the word "dead body" is not figurative. It is true that there is no record of kings being buried close to the temple, but their sepulchres were in such vicinity that in comparison with the new ideal of holiness they could not but be held to bring defilement to the dwelling-place of Jehovah, the living God. *V.* 9 seems conclusive for this rendering.

8. Ref. is to the fact that the royal palace and the first temple stood virtually within the same enclosure and were one ensemble of edifice. See the sketch in W. R. Smith's Art. Temple, *Encyc. Brit.*

and the wall between] **with but the wall between me and them; and they defiled....**

10—12. The prophet is commanded to shew to Israel the fashion and ordinances of the house that they may observe them.

10. *ashamed of their iniquities*] i.e. in disregarding the ordinances of the Lord's house, in defiling it (*v.* 7, 8), and in committing its services to the hands of uncircumcised aliens (xliv. 7), and the like.

measure the pattern] LXX. has, "and its appearance and its pattern." Cf. xlii. 11, where "measures" and "appearance" were also interchanged.

11. The verse seems overgrown with amplifications or repetitions. LXX. omits: "and the comings in thereof and all the forms thereof." The second "and all the forms thereof" seems an accidental misreading

they have done, shew them the form of the house, and the fashion thereof, and the goings out thereof, and the comings in thereof, and all the forms thereof, and all the ordinances thereof, and all the forms thereof, and all the laws thereof: and write *it* in their sight, that they may keep the whole form thereof, and all the ordinances thereof, and do them. This *is* the law of the house; Upon the top of the mountain 12 the whole limit thereof round about *shall be* most holy. Behold, this *is* the law of the house.

And these *are* the measures of the altar after the cubits: 13 The cubit *is* a cubit and a hand breadth; even the bottom *shall be* a cubit, and the breadth a cubit, and the border thereof by the edge thereof round about *shall be* a span:

and consequent duplication of the following "and all the laws thereof." Cf. xliv. 5, where the "ordinances" and "laws" of the house again come together.

12. *Upon the top...mountain*] Add: *shall it be;* the whole &c.

13—17. THE ALTAR OF BURNT-OFFERING IN THE INNER COURT.

The altar was a large structure, built of stone, and rose in terraces, contracting by means of two inlets towards the top. It consisted: (1) of a basement, with a border or moulding on the top or edge of it. (2) Two cubits above this basement or socket, in which the altar proper stood, was the first inlet, a cubit broad, so that there ran a ledge of a cubit round about the altar on its four sides (*vv.* 13, 14). (3) Four cubits above this first inlet came the second inlet or contraction, also a cubit broad, so as to form in like manner a ledge of a cubit round about the altar (*v.* 14). (4) Then four cubits upwards from this ledge was the altar area or platform proper, the "hearth of God," having horns rising up at the four corners (*v.* 15). The area of this altar-hearth was a square of 12 cubits (*v.* 16). At the higher inlet the area was 14 cubits square (*v.* 17). Probably, therefore, at the lower inlet the area was 16 cubits square and the basement 18 cubits. Thus the structure had the appearance of four square blocks, each narrower in area than the one below it, and each thus appearing set into the one under it as into a socket. Such structures built in stages were common in the architecture of the East; see examples in Rawlin. *Phœnicia*, p. 166 *seq.*

13. THE BASEMENT OF THE ALTAR.

13. *bottom* shall be *a cubit*] lit. its bottom a cubit, i.e. in depth or height, and so in breadth. The bottom, lit. *bosom*, appears to be the basement in which the altar proper was set; it was a cubit high and extended a cubit in breadth beyond the first block or stage of the altar proper. The idea that the "bosom" means a drain or gutter running round the foot of the altar to carry away the blood seems without any

14 and this *shall be* the higher place of the altar. And from the bottom *upon* the ground *even* to the lower settle *shall be* two cubits, and the breadth one cubit; and from the lesser settle *even* to the greater settle *shall be* four cubits, and the 15 breadth *one* cubit. So the altar *shall be* four cubits; and 16 from the altar and upward *shall be* four horns. And the altar *shall be* twelve *cubits* long, twelve broad, square in the 17 four squares thereof. And the settle *shall be* fourteen *cubits* long and fourteen broad in the four squares thereof; and the border about it *shall be* half a cubit; and the bottom thereof *shall be* a cubit about; and his stairs *shall* look toward the east.

support. This basement extended a cubit all round beyond the lowest stage of the altar proper, and on the outer edge of this space of a cubit there was a border of a span, probably, in height. This border may have been a moulding, or possibly a very low parapet or close screen, running round the outer edge of the ledge of one cubit. Either would suggest the idea of a bosom in which the altar proper was placed.

higher place of the altar] the **elevation.** The word is that rendered "eminent place" xvi. 24, 31, 39 (see notes), and refers to the basement on which the altar proper stood. Cf. xli. 8. LXX. divides the letters differently, reading: *this is the height of the altar*, and attaching the clause to the following verse. This appears to be unnecessary.

14. Two cubits up from the basement the fabric underwent the first contraction, being let in a cubit. Thus a ledge of a cubit broad was formed running all round the altar. A.V. appears to call this bench or ledge a "settle." The altar narrowed in dimension not gradually like an obelisk, but at two places. Cf. the similar way in which the wall of the house retreated, xli. 6.

At a height of four cubits above the first inlet came another, of the same breadth of a cubit, so that a second ledge of a cubit broad was formed round the altar on its four sides.

15. *So the altar*] **And** the altar, lit. the hearth of God (Is. xxix. 1). The word here is spelled harel (mount of God?), and in the next clause ariel (hearth of God). LXX. spells both alike, and probably they do not differ. The form ariel is also Moabite (Mesha inscr. l. 12, 17). From the second ledge up to the altar-hearth or platform was a distance of four cubits, and from the altar area rose four horns, one at each corner. LXX. for "four" reads "a cubit"—as the height of the horns.

16. The preceding measurements have referred to height. Those referring to breadth or area are now given. The altar-hearth or platform was 12 cubits square.

four squares thereof] **four sides** thereof. So *v.* 17.

17. The "settle" referred to here is the higher or greater one (*v.* 14). Its area was a square of 14 cubits. The verse appears to say that this uppermost ledge had a border and an "enclosure" or setting just as the

And he said unto me, Son of man, thus saith the Lord 18
God; These *are* the ordinances of the altar in the day when
they shall make it, to offer burnt offerings thereon, and to
sprinkle blood thereon. And thou shalt give to the priests 19
the Levites that *be* of the seed of Zadok, which approach
unto me, to minister unto me, saith the Lord God, a young
bullock for a sin offering. And thou shalt take of the blood 20

basement had. If so the "setting" or bosom was that for the Harel arising out of the block, and its size, a cubit, is simply the ledge itself. There is no ground at least to suppose that the "border" and setting refer to the altar-hearth—from which the measurer has descended and come down at any rate as far as the uppermost ledge. It may be made a question whether in the last half of *v.* 17 he has not descended to the foot of the edifice, and whether the "border" and "bosom" be not those already referred to in connection with the basement (*v.* 13). For (1) the measurements are the same—a span (*v.* 13) being equivalent to half a cubit (*v.* 17). (2) Immediately after mention of the "border" and bosom or setting the "steps" are referred to by which the altar as a whole was ascended, which seems to imply that the speaker conceived himself upon the ground (*v.* 17.) (3) Further in *v.* 20 blood is to be put upon the horns of the altar-hearth, upon the four corners of the upper ledge (settle) and upon the "border" round about; and it is certainly natural that the blood should be put on all the stages of the altar, the top, the middle and the basement.

For squares read **sides**; for bottom **basement**; and by *stairs* is meant steps. The whole height of the altar was probably 12 cubits and the basement a square of 18. Thus height of basement 1 (*v.* 13) + 2 (lowest block) + 4 (higher block) + 4 (block of altar-hearth) + 1 (horn) = 12. On breadth see preliminary remark to *vv.* 13—17.

18—27. Sacrifices and ceremonies by which the altar was consecrated and inaugurated.

The general purpose of the altar is to offer burnt-offerings upon and to sprinkle blood thereon. The statement in *vv.* 19, 20 is somewhat elliptical, the writer's object being to advert specially to the difference between the sin-offering on the first day and that on the following days. Hence he describes the ritual of the sin-offering on the first day fully, omitting to refer to the burnt-offering, which he mentions only in connexion with the second and following days. And when in *v.* 25 it is said that a goat for sin-offering and a young bullock and a ram were offered for seven days, the difference between the sin-offering on the first day (a bullock) and that for the following six days (a goat) is not adverted to, the burnt-offering being the same all the seven days.

18. The general purpose of the altar. The burnt-offering was wholly consumed on the altar, of the other offerings only the fat.

19. The phrase "saith the Lord" adds solemnity to the statement that only the sons of Zadok shall minister at the altar (xliv. 15 *seq.*).

thereof, and put *it* on the four horns of it, and on the four corners of the settle, and upon the border round about: 21 thus shalt thou cleanse and purge it. Thou shalt take the bullock also of the sin offering, and he shall burn it in the appointed place of the house, without the sanctuary. 22 And on the second day thou shalt offer a kid of the goats without blemish for a sin offering; and they shall cleanse 23 the altar, as they did cleanse *it* with the bullock. When thou hast made an end of cleansing *it*, thou shalt offer a young bullock without blemish, and a ram out of the flock 24 without blemish. And thou shalt offer them before the LORD, and the priests shall cast salt upon them, and they shall offer them up *for* a burnt offering unto the LORD. 25 Seven days shalt thou prepare every day a goat *for* a sin offering: they shall also prepare a young bullock, and a 26 ram out of the flock, without blemish. Seven days shall they purge the altar and purify it; and they shall consecrate

20. Blood was to be put on the four horns of the altar hearth, on the four corners of the (upper) settle, and on the border; see on *v*. 17. To "cleanse" is to purify from sin, to "un-sin," if such a word could be formed; and to "purge" is usually rendered "to make atonement for."

21. The sin-offering was burnt wholly in a place outside the whole temple area, i.e. outside the space enclosed by the 500 cubits square wall (xlii. 16 *seq*.), possibly in the space of 50 cubits (xlv. 2) lying round the outer wall. Cf. Ex. xxix. 14; Lev. iv. 11, vi. 23, xvi. 27; Heb. xiii. 11.

22. The sin-offering for the second and following days was a he-goat—so read for "kid of the goats." On "cleanse" cf. *v*. 20. The ceremonies with the blood and the burning outside were no doubt the same as those on the first day, *vv*. 20, 21.

23. The burnt-offering, following the sin-offering, was a young bullock and a ram.

24. The burnt-offering was wholly consumed on the altar, salt being sprinkled on the flesh, Lev. ii. 13; Mark ix. 49.

25. The statement is somewhat general; strictly the he-goat was offered only on six days (*v*. 19), but the burnt-offering was the same all the seven.

26. The ceremonial of consecrating the altar lasts seven days. On to "purge" cf. *v*. 20.

consecrate themselves] consecrate it, i.e. the altar, lit. fill its hand (or, hands). The phrase is properly said of the priests, to install; here of the altar, to inaugurate it. Originally the expression had probably a literal meaning, to put the things to be offered into the hands of the priests (Lev. viii. 25 *seq*.), but later it came to be used

themselves. And when *these* days are expired, it shall be, 27
that upon the eighth day, and *so* forward, the priests shall
make your burnt offerings upon the altar, and your peace
offerings; and I will accept you, saith the Lord God.

Then he brought me back the way of the gate of the 44
outward sanctuary which looketh *toward* the east; and it

generally in the sense of initiate, consecrate (Ex. xxviii. 41, xxix. 9, 29, 33, 35; Lev. vii. 37; Num. iii. 3; Judg. xvii. 5, 12), cf. Ex. xxxii. 29. Wellh. *Hist.* p. 152, argues that the priest's hand was originally "filled" with money (Jud. xvii.). The phrase "fill the hand" of one appears also in the general meaning "to invest with office" in Assyrian; Fd. Del. *Heb. Lang.* p. 20, *Prolegomena*, p. 48.

In all the above passage it is the altar not the priests that is consecrated. The consecration of the altar appears to carry with it that of the whole sanctuary. The altar needs atonement not because it is a work of human hands, but because it belongs to the things of the world. The sin of the world has defiled all things, penetrating even to the precincts of that where Jehovah abides as he is in himself (Heb. ix. 23). The passage can scarcely be compared with Ex. xxix. and Lev. viii. because there the ceremonies refer to the consecration of the priests chiefly and little to the altar. Cf. Ex. xxix. 36; Lev. viii. 11, 15, 33. In these passages the altar is said to have been anointed with oil, a ceremony wanting in Ezek.; the sin-offering was a young bullock *each* day and the burnt-offering simply a ram each day.

CH. XLIV.—XLVI. ORDINANCES REGARDING THE TEMPLE.

These ordinances define who shall minister in it, priests and Levites (ch. xliv.); the revenue of the priests, the Levites and the prince, with the duties devolving on the prince in upholding the ritual (xlv. 1—17); the special and daily services in the temple, and the special offerings of the prince (xlv. 18—xlvi.).

CH. XLIV. THOSE WHO SHALL MINISTER IN THE TEMPLE.

The passage contains these parts:

(1) *vv.* 1—3. An ordinance regarding the eastern gate: it shall be kept shut because by it the Lord entered into the house.

(2) *vv.* 4—14. Precepts regarding the subordinate ministrants, who keep the gates of the house and perform such offices as slaughtering the victims. These subordinate services shall no more be performed, as they have been to the desecration of them, by uncircumcised foreigners (*vv.* 4—9). But the Levites, who ministered as priests at the high-places when Israel went astray from Jehovah, shall perform such services. For their former sin they shall bear their iniquity and be excluded from the holy functions of the priesthood proper, though permitted to take part in the service of the house in a subordinate place (*vv.* 10—14).

(3) *vv.* 15—31. Precepts regarding the priests (i.e. those who

2 *was* shut. Then said the LORD unto me; This gate shall be shut, it shall not be opened, and no man shall enter in by it; because the LORD, the God of Israel, hath entered in
3 by it, therefore it shall be shut. *It is* for the prince; the prince, he shall sit in it to eat bread before the LORD; he shall enter by the way of the porch of *that* gate, and shall go out by the way of the same.
4 Then brought he me the way of the north gate before the house: and I looked, and behold, the glory of the LORD filled the house of the LORD: and I fell upon my face.
5 And the LORD said unto me, Son of man, mark well, and behold with thine eyes, and hear with thine ears all that I say unto thee concerning all the ordinances of the house of the LORD, and all the laws thereof; and mark well the entering in of the house, with every going forth of the
6 sanctuary. And thou shalt say to the rebellious, *even* to the house of Israel, Thus saith the Lord GOD; O ye house

minister at the altar), e.g. that they shall be the sons of Zadok alone (*vv.* 15, 16); regarding their garments in their ministrations (*v.* 17 *seq.*); their marriage (*v.* 22); their functions as teachers of the people and judges (*vv.* 23, 24); their preservation from defilement by contact with the dead (*vv.* 25—27), and their maintenance (*v.* 28 *seq.*).

vv. 1—3. The prophet is brought to the outside of the outer gate, which he observes to be shut. It must be kept shut because the glory of the Lord entered by it into the house. None shall enter by it.

3. The only exception is in favour of the prince. He shall eat bread in this gate, i.e. partake of the sacrificial meal there. Though not expressly stated it is implied that the meal shall be partaken of in the porch of the gate, which looked into the outer court. The statements in ch. xlvi. make it probable that even the prince did not enter through the E. gate from the outside, but passed into the outer court through some other gate, and entered the porch from the court.

vv. 4—9. The former practice of employing uncircumcised foreigners to minister and to keep the charge of the house shall absolutely cease.

4. The prophet is brought by way of the N. gate into the inner court before the house. From his position in front of the house he beholds the glory of the Lord filling the house, and falls on his face.

5. He is commanded to give heed to all the ordinances and laws regulating the future service of the house.

entering in of the house] The phrase to the end of the verse is a general designation for all the functions of the house, those who shall be permitted to enter it (*vv.* 10—14), with the manner of their going in and coming out (*vv.* 17—21).

6. The "rebellious," lit. rebellion, a term frequently used in ch. i.—xxiv. (e.g. ii. 5, iii. 9, xii. 2, xvii. 12, xxiv. 3), but dropped since

of Israel, let it suffice you of all your abominations, in 7 that ye have brought *into my sanctuary* strangers, uncircumcised in heart, and uncircumcised in flesh, to be in my sanctuary, to pollute it, *even* my house, when ye offer my bread, the fat and the blood, and they have broken my covenant because of all your abominations. And ye have 8 not kept the charge of mine holy *things*: but ye have set keepers of my charge in my sanctuary for yourselves.

Thus saith the Lord GOD; No stranger, uncircumcised 9 in heart, nor uncircumcised in flesh, shall enter into my sanctuary, of any stranger that *is* among the children of Israel. And the Levites that are gone away far from me, 10

the fall of the city. Recollection of the former abominations practised in the sanctuary again brings it to the prophet's lips.

7. into my sanctuary *strangers*] i.e. foreigners. What is reprobated is not of course allowing foreigners to present sacrifices to Jehovah, which they might do (Lev. xvii. 10, 12; Numb. xv. 14), but allowing them to *officiate* in the offering, and in general in the ministry of the sanctuary. It is not ascertainable to what extent these uncircumcised heathen were permitted to fill the subordinate offices about the house, such as those of keepers of the gates and assistants to the priests, but just as the kings employed foreign mercenaries as guards (who were employed even in the temple, 2 Kings xi. 7), it appears that persons not Israelites and not incorporated in Israel by the necessary rites, were employed in the house. They were probably captives taken in war and the like (Josh. ix. 27; 1 Sam. ii. 13; Zech. xiv. 21; cf. Ezr. viii. 20, ii. 58). This is regarded by the prophet as a profanation of the house and an infraction of the covenant between Jehovah and Israel. It is the latter from the nature of the case. Israel was the people of the Lord and his service must be performed by Israel. These heathen were uncircumcised both in flesh and heart, their service was purely mercenary, and without religious reality. For "and they have broken" LXX. reads, and *ye have* broken, which is more exact.

because of all] Perhaps: *in addition to* all your abominations.

8. *ye have set keepers*] Some would read: ye have *set them* keepers. This of course is the meaning. The change is hardly supported by LXX (as Well. p. 122).

9—14. Such services shall not be performed by foreigners any more, but by the Levites who formerly ministered at the high-places. Because of their sin in leading the house of Israel astray they shall bear their iniquity and be excluded from the priesthood.

10. *And the Levites*] **But the Levites which went away far from me...after their idols, they shall bear their iniquity,** 11 **and shall be ministers** &c. The clause "they shall be ministers" explains how these Levites shall bear their iniquity—they shall be degraded from the priestly office and reduced to the place of subordinate servants. To

when Israel went astray, which went astray away from me
11 after their idols; they shall even bear their iniquity. Yet
they shall be ministers in my sanctuary, *having* charge at
the gates of the house, and ministering to the house: they
shall slay the burnt offering and the sacrifice for the people,
and they shall stand before them to minister unto them.
12 Because they ministered unto them before their idols, and
caused the house of Israel to fall into iniquity; therefore
have I lift up mine hand against them, saith the Lord God,
13 and they shall bear their iniquity. And they shall not come
near unto me, to do the office of a priest unto me, nor to
come near to any of my holy *things*, in the most holy *place*:
but they shall bear their shame, and their abominations
14 which they have committed. But I will make them keepers
of the charge of the house, for all the service thereof, and
15 for all that shall be done therein. But the priests the
Levites, the sons of Zadok, that kept the charge of my

"bear iniquity" is to bear the penalty of it, ch. iv. 4. On "idols,"
ch. vi. 4.

which went astray] Most naturally refers to Israel, cf. *v.* 15; though
it might refer to the Levites, cf. xlviii. 11.

11. The verse is closely connected with *v.* 10 (note on *v.* 10). The
services which the Levites shall be allowed to perform are such as
having charge of the gates, slaying the burnt-offering, and the peace-
offering for the people and in general ministering to them, e.g. cooking
the sacrificial flesh for their meals (xlvi. 24). To "stand before" is to
serve, Numb. xvi. 9.

12. *caused...to fall...iniquity*] lit. as marg.: *were a stumbling-block
of iniquity unto.* Ch. vii. 19, xiv. 3, 4, xviii. 30. On "idols," *v.* 10.
lift up mine hand] i.e. sworn, xx. 5.

13. *v.* 13 is closely connected with *v.* 12...bear their iniquity, and
they shall not come near unto me.

in the most holy place] Rather: **unto the things that are most
holy.** The words are in apposition with "my holy things."

14. *But I will make*] **And** I will. The prophet as was natural to him takes a severe view of the conduct of the priests of the
high-places, laying much of the blame of Israel's defection upon them
(*v.* 12).

15, 16. The priests of the family of Zadok alone shall be priests in
the new Temple. These continued faithful to Jehovah when the pro-
vincial priests went far from him. The judgment of the prophet may
be to some extent a comparative one. The worship at Jerusalem never
sank to the level of the licentiousness and corruption prevailing at the
rural sanctuaries, though undoubtedly the record of the reform of
Josiah reveals great corruptions at Jerusalem also (2 Kings xxiii.).

sanctuary when the children of Israel went astray from me, they shall come near to me to minister unto me, and they shall stand before me to offer unto me the fat and the blood, saith the Lord GOD: they shall enter into my 16 sanctuary, and they shall come near to my table, to minister unto me, and they shall keep my charge.

And it shall come to pass, *that* when they enter in at the 17 gates of the inner court, they shall be clothed with linen garments; and no wool shall come upon them, whiles they minister in the gates of the inner court, and within. They 18 shall have linen bonnets upon their heads, and shall have linen breeches upon their loins; they shall not gird *themselves* with any thing that causeth sweat. And when they 19 go forth into the utter court, *even* into the utter court to the people, they shall put off their garments wherein they ministered, and lay them in the holy chambers, and they shall put on other garments; and they shall not sanctify the people with their garments. Neither shall they shave 20

How far these were introduced by the kings, such as Manasseh, despite the opposition of the priests, cannot be ascertained. The reforms of Hezekiah most probably, and certainly those of Josiah, were promoted by the priests (2 Kings xxii.). The family of Zadok dates from Solomon, who deposed Abiathar on account of his favouring the pretensions of Adonijah and installed Zadok in his place. Since those remote times the Zadokites had served in the temple, and upon the whole the prophet's favourable judgment of them is no doubt justified (cf. 2 Kings xi.; Is. viii. 2).

16. *near to my table*] The altar of burnt-offering is no doubt meant, cf. on xli. 22.

vv. 17—19. The garments of the priests.—In the service of the sanctuary they shall wear only linen clothing, drawers and head-dresses. In Ex. xxviii. 39, 42, xxxix. 27; Lev. xvi. 4, the coats and bonnets of the priests are byssus (possibly cotton).

18. Sweat is regarded as uncleanness.

19. The sacred garments shall be worn only in the inner court, and in service. Before going out into the outer court the priests shall put them off and deposit them in the sacred cells, xlii. 13, 14.

sanctify the people] i.e. by bringing that which is holy in contact with them. The enactment is not a precaution against defilement of the holy garments, at least in form, though it may be a precaution against confusion of the sacred and the common. Cf. xlvi. 20; Ex. xxix. 37, xxx. 29; Lev. vi. 27. The words "even *into the utter court*" are probably an accidental repetition. LXX. omits.

20. The priests shall poll or cut the hair of their heads, and neither shave their heads bald nor let the hair flow loose. Shaving the head

their heads, nor suffer *their* locks to grow long; they shall
21 only poll their heads. Neither shall any priest drink wine,
22 when they enter into the inner court. Neither shall they
take for their wives a widow, nor her that is put away: but
they shall take maidens of the seed of the house of Israel,
23 or a widow that had a priest before. And they shall teach
my people *the difference* between the holy and profane, and
cause them to discern between the unclean and the clean.
24 And in controversy they shall stand in judgment; *and* they
shall judge it according to my judgments: and they shall
keep my laws and my statutes in all mine assemblies; and
25 they shall hallow my sabbaths. And they shall come at no
dead person to defile *themselves:* but for father, or for
mother, or for son, or for daughter, for brother, or for sister

bald was a sign of mourning (Lev. xxi. 5, 10, cf. Ezek. xxiv. 17),
and forbidden both to priests and people as a practice of the heathen
(Deut. xiv. 1); though the prophets frequently refer to it as a token of
disaster and mourning; Is. iii. 24, xxii. 12; Jer. xvi. 6; Am. viii. 10;
Mic. i. 16. Lev. x. 6 indicates that letting the hair flow loose and
dishevelled was also a sign of grief. The phrase appears used both of
this practice and of the Nazirite custom of allowing the hair to remain
uncut (Numb. vi. 5, cf. Numb. v. 18).

21. On this prohibition cf. the narrative Lev. x. 1—9.

22. The marriage of the priests. They shall marry only virgins, or
the widows of former priests. In Lev. xxi. 14 marrying a widow of
any kind is forbidden to the high-priest, but no restriction is imposed
on the priests (*v.* 7). Ezek. makes no allusion anywhere to a high-
priest.

23, 24. General duties of the priests towards the people. They
shall teach the people to distinguish between the holy and the common,
between the clean and the unclean, cf. xxii. 26; Lev. x. 10; Hag. ii.
11; Mal. ii. 7.

24. They shall also act as judges in causes that arise among the
people. It is not certain that Ezek. commits the office of judge to the
priests exclusively, cf. xlv. 9. In Deut. xvii. 8 *seq.*, xix. 17, xxi. 5 the
priests sit in difficult cases along with the judges who shall be in those
days (cf. Deut. xxi. 19, xxii. 15; Ex. xviii. 21, 22). In Ezekiel's final
state of the kingdom of the Lord, however, only cases of misunder-
standing, not of wrong, would arise. Finally it is the duty of the
priests to see that the laws and statutes of the Lord be observed at all
the **appointed seasons** (A.V. assemblies), or sacred occasions (xlv. 17
seq.), and that the sabbath be sanctified, cf. xxii. 26.

25—27. Regulations for their necessary contact with the dead.
They shall approach the dead bodies only of their nearest relatives,
father, mother, son, daughter, brother and unmarried sister. From
the defilement caused by this contact they must purify themselves

that hath had no husband, they may defile themselves.
And after he is cleansed, they shall reckon unto him seven 26
days. And in the day that he goeth into the sanctuary, 27
unto the inner court, to minister in the sanctuary, he shall
offer his sin offering, saith the Lord GOD. And it shall be 28
unto them for an inheritance: I *am* their inheritance: and
ye shall give them no possession in Israel: I *am* their
possession. They shall eat the meat offering, and the sin 29
offering, and the trespass offering; and every dedicate thing
in Israel shall be theirs. And the first of all the firstfruits 30
of all *things*, and every oblation of all, of every *sort* of your
oblations, shall be the priests': ye shall also give unto the

before resuming their service in the inner court. It is curious that no
reference is made to the priest's wife among the relatives with whose
dead bodies they may defile themselves. The same omission occurs
Lev. xxi. 1—3. In Ez. xxiv. 15 it is understood that he would naturally shew tokens of mourning for his wife. The two things, however,
are not identical, and Ezek. was not an acting priest. According to
Lev. xxi. 11 the high-priest was not to defile himself by going near any
dead body whatever. How defilement was contracted is explained
Numb. xix. 14.

26. *after he is cleansed*] i.e. the priest. The length of time during
which he shall remain unclean is not stated. In ordinary cases he who
touched a dead body was unclean seven days (Numb. xix. 11). After
his cleansing the priest must count seven days, which would imply
exclusion from his official duties for 14 days.

27. Before resuming his functions the priest presents a sin-offering.

28—31. The maintenance of the priest. He shall have no inheritance among the people: the Lord is his inheritance. He shall eat the
meat-offering, the sin- and trespass-offering; everything put to the ban
shall be his, and the best of all the first-fruits and of all the dues.

28. *it shall be...inheritance*] This cannot refer to the sin-offering
(*v.* 27), which was burnt entire outside the sanctuary. To translate:
This shall be their inheritance (viz.) *I am their inheritance*, making the
words "I am" &c. subject is too artificial. The balance of sentence
seems to require, *they shall have no inheritance*, I am &c., corresponding to the second half of the verse. So Vulg., cf. Numb. xviii. 20;
Deut. x. 9, xviii. 1, 2; Josh. xiii. 14 &c.

29. Cf. Lev. ii. 3, vii. 9—11, for the meat-offering; Lev. vi. 18, vii.
6, 7; Num. xviii. 9, 10, for the sin- and trespass-offerings; and for that
put to the ban or "devoted" to Jehovah, Lev. xxvii. 28; Num. xviii.
14. For "dedicated" as marg. *devoted*.

30. *And the first*] Or, *the best*. Cf. Ex. xxiii. 19, xxxiv. 26; Numb.
xviii. 13; Deut. xviii. 4.

and every oblation] The word sometimes rendered *heave offering*.
Numb. xv. 19, xviii. 19. It means a part taken from a larger whole,

priest the first of your dough, that he may cause the bless-
31 ing to rest in thine house. The priests shall not eat *of* any
thing that is dead of itself, or torn, whether it be fowl or
beast.

45 Moreover, when ye shall divide *by lot* the land for inheritance, ye shall offer an oblation unto the LORD, a holy

cf. xlv. 1, &c., where the portion of land dedicated to the use of the priests and Levites is so called.

of your dough] The term occurs again only Numb. xv. 20, 21; Neh. x. 37, and is of doubtful meaning. LXX., dough; Targ. Syr., baking trough; others, *coarse meal*. On the "blessing," Mal. iii. 10; Prov. iii. 9, 10.

31. On this prohibition Ex. xxii. 31; Lev. xxii. 8. Cf. Lev. xvii. 15. The injunctions in *v*. 30 are very general. The prophet presupposes former customs familiar to the people, which he desires to continue. Everywhere in these chapters his directions are in the main a reproduction of a past customary and understood practice.

CH. XLV. 1—17. THE PORTIONS OF LAND ASSIGNED FOR MAINTEN-
ANCE TO THE PRIESTS, LEVITES AND PRINCE RESPECTIVELY;
WITH THE DUES WHICH THE PEOPLE SHALL PAY THE PRINCE,
IN RETURN FOR WHICH HE SHALL PROVIDE THE RITUAL.

(1) *vv*. 1—8. The oblation (terumah) of land for maintenance of priests, Levites and prince, and for the city.

(2) *vv*. 9—12. Regulations as to just standards of weight, measure and coinage.

(3) *vv*. 13—17. Dues to be paid the prince in respect of his being at the charge of providing the materials of ritual.

In the centre of the country a portion of land shall be measured off 25,000 long and 20,000 broad. The measure is no doubt cubits, not reeds, though this is stated only in regard to the free place around the sanctuary (*v*. 2). Length is the measure E. to W., and breadth that from N. to S. This region is to be divided into two parallel strips E. to W., one of 25,000 long and 10,000 broad, which shall be for the priests (*v*. 4), and another N. of this, of the same length and breadth, which shall be for the Levites (*v*. 5). Parallel to this on the S. side of the priests' domain, of the same length (25,000) with it and 5000 broad, there shall be a portion of land for the possession of the city. In the midst of it the city shall be situated (*v*. 6). These three portions thus form a square of 25,000. Finally the land from the E. side of this square to the Jordan, and from the W. side of it to the sea shall be for a possession to the prince (*vv*. 7, 8).

1. *divide* by lot] So the phrase originally signified, but probably it came to mean merely "divide" or assign portions to. Ezek. definitely fixes the positions of the tribes, and each tribe appears to have the same extent of territory assigned to it.

offer an oblation] Cf. xliv. 30.

holy portion of the land] i.e. *out of*, or *from* the land.

portion of the land: the length *shall be* the length *of* five and twenty thousand *reeds*, and the breadth *shall be* ten thousand. This *shall be* holy in all the borders thereof round about. Of this there shall be for the sanctuary five 2 hundred *in length*, with five hundred *in breadth*, square round about; and fifty cubits round about *for* the suburbs thereof. And of this measure shalt thou measure the length 3 of five and twenty thousand, and the breadth of ten thousand: and in it shall be the sanctuary *and* the most holy *place*. The holy *portion* of the land shall be for the priests 4 the ministers of the sanctuary, which shall come near to minister unto the LORD: and it shall be a place for their houses, and a holy place for the sanctuary. And *the* five 5 and twenty thousand of length, and *the* ten thousand of breadth, shall also the Levites, the ministers of the house, have for themselves, for a possession *for* twenty chambers.

breadth...ten thousand] Grammar as well as context seems to require **twenty thousand**, cf. *vv.* 3, 5, xlviii. 10, 18. In *v.* 3 this "measure" is divided into two portions each 10,000 broad. So LXX. For *reeds*, no doubt, **cubits**.

2. In this sacred territory, more particularly, in the half of it assigned to the priests (*vv.* 3, 4), shall the sanctuary be situated, a square of 500, surrounded by a free space of 50 cubits on all sides. The 500 are certainly cubits, cf. xlii. 20.

the suburbs thereof] What the "suburbs" are appears from Numb. xxxv. 4; it is an open space around the walls of an enclosure, a city or building, held to belong to the building or city, but not occupied by it. It is the liberties of a city or the precincts of an edifice, xlviii. 15, 17.

3. The portion of the sacred land assigned to the priests shall consist of a tract 25,000 long by 10,000 broad.

sanctuary and *the most holy*] **sanctuary**, (even) **the most holy thing**. The whole area of land is holy, the sanctuary most holy.

4. Read: **An holy portion of the land is it, it shall be for**, &c.

holy place for the sanctuary] Lit. *a sanctuary for the sanctuary*. The use of "sanctuary" in the sense of sacred territory can hardly be supported by evidence, though the idea of a sacred territory around a sacred house or locality is a common one in the East. LXX. reads: a place for houses set apart for their sanctity, i.e. possibly: houses set apart for them (the priests), they being holy. No satisfactory emendation has been proposed.

5. Read: **and five..., and ten... shall the Levites have**. (The Keri is unnecessary).

for *twenty chambers*] Probably with LXX.: **for cities to dwell in**. Cf. same words Numb. xxxv. 2; Josh. xiv. 4. In *v.* 6 Jerusalem, with

6 And ye shall appoint the possession of the city five thousand broad, and five and twenty thousand long, over against the oblation of the holy *portion*: it shall be for the whole house
7 of Israel. And *a portion shall be* for the prince on the one side and on the other side of the oblation of the holy *portion*, and of the possession of the city, before the oblation of the holy *portion*, and before the possession of the city, from the west side westward, and from the east side eastward: and the length *shall be* over against one of the
8 portions, from the west border unto the east border. In the land shall be his possession in Israel: and my princes shall no more oppress my people; and *the rest of* the land shall they give to the house of Israel according to their tribes.

9 Thus saith the Lord GOD; Let it suffice you, O princes

its suburbs, is assigned a tract of land only half of this given to the Levites.

6. The city possesses a strip of land 5000 cubits broad and 25,000 long, running parallel to the portion of the priests, cf. xlviii. 15. The city shall stand in the midst of this tract, which it entirely covers N. to S., cf. xlviii. 16, 17.

7. The domain of the prince. A portion of land shall fall to the prince equal in breadth (N. to S.) to the whole square assigned to the priests, Levites and city (viz. 25,000), and extending on both sides of this square to the borders of the country, to the Jordan on the E., and the sea on the W.

and the length...portions] **and in length answerable to one of the portions**, as R.V. The "portions" here are the tracts of land assigned to the tribes respectively (ch. xlviii.). These stretched across the country from the Jordan to the sea. The portion of the prince in like manner stretches across the whole country, only it is interrupted in the middle by the 25,000 square tract assigned to priests, Levites and city. Cf. xlviii. 21.

8. *In the land...possession*] **In the land it shall be to him for a possession**, lit. in respect of the land. Others: *for a domain* it shall be..., for a possession. The *art.* must then be omitted, and the use of "land" in this sense is unnatural.

my princes] The language *my* is unusual. In *v.* 9, "princes of Israel," and so LXX. here. It is possible that Israel was represented in MS. merely by the initial letter, which is the same as the last letter of "princes" (cons.), and that one of the letters fell out.

the rest of *the land*] Read: **oppress my people, but shall give the land to the house**. On the oppressions of the princes, cf. xxii. 25, xxxiv.; Jer. xxii. 17.

of Israel: remove violence and spoil, and execute judgment and justice, take away your exactions from my people, saith the Lord God. Ye shall have just balances, and a just ephah, and a just bath. The ephah and the bath shall be of one measure, that the bath may contain the tenth part of a homer, and the ephah the tenth *part* of a homer: the measure thereof shall be after the homer. And the shekel *shall be* twenty gerahs: twenty shekels, five and twenty shekels, fifteen shekels, shall be your maneh. This *is* the oblation that ye shall offer; the sixth *part* of an ephah of a

9—17. The dues to be given the prince, and his obligations to provide the materials for the ritual.

v. **9** *seq.* The former unjust and irregular exactions of the princes shall cease. These exactions had not only been oppressive in their nature, but unjust and arbitrary from want of a fixed standard in weights, measures and currency.

9. *take away your exactions*] Lit. *remove your expulsions* from my people. Ref. probably to unjust extrusion of persons from their possessions, of which the early prophets often complain, Is. v. 8; Mic. ii. 9, iii. 2, 3, and the story of Naboth, 1 Kings xxi.

10. Cf. Lev. xix. 35, 36; Deut. xxv. 13—15; Mic. vi. 10, 11 (the accursed scanty ephah); Prov. xi. 1, xvi. 11, xx. 10. From this it appears that the words of Am. viii. 5 "making the ephah small and the shekel large" are more than a figure.

11. The homer is assumed as the standard both for liquid and dry measures. The ephah was a tenth of the homer, dry measure; and the bath a tenth of the homer, liquid measure, Is. v. 10.

12. Cf. Ex. xxx. 13; Lev. xxvii. 25; Numb. iii. 47, xviii. 16. The verse at present is without meaning. Read after LXX. (cod. Alex.): **and the shekel shall be twenty gerahs; five** (shekels) **shall be five, and ten shekels ten, and fifty shekels shall be your maneh** (mina). The text is grammatically suspicious, and the way in which "fifteen" is supposed to be expressed, viz. "ten and five" is without parallel. The statement that "five shekels shall be five," &c., does not imply that there were five and ten shekel pieces, but means that just weighing of money shall prevail, and five go for five, no more and no less. The passage has been fully discussed by Bertheau (*Zur Gesch. der Israeliten*, pp. 8—14), whose table of money weights may be given (p. 14):

Talent	1				
Maneh	60	1			
Shekel	3,000	50	1		
Beka	6,000	100	2	1	
Gera	60,000	1000	20	10	1.

Cf. Ex. xxxviii. 25; Lev. xxvii. 3, 16; Josh. vii. 21; 1 Kings x. 17; Ezr. ii. 69; Neh. vii. 71.

13. *oblation...offer*] The people are addressed. The due which

homer of wheat, and ye shall give the sixth part of an
14 ephah of a homer of barley: concerning the ordinance of
oil, the bath *of* oil, *ye shall offer* the tenth part of a bath out
of the cor, *which is* a homer of ten baths ; for ten baths *are*
15 a homer: and one lamb out of the flock, out of two
hundred, out of the fat pastures of Israel; for a meat
offering, and for a burnt offering, and for peace offerings, to
16 make reconciliation for them, saith the Lord GOD. All the
people of the land shall give this oblation for the prince in
17 Israel. And it shall be the prince's part *to give* burnt
offerings, and meat offerings, and drink offerings, in the
feasts, and in the new moons, and in the sabbaths, in all
solemnities of the house of Israel : he shall prepare the sin
offering, and the meat offering, and the burnt offering,
and the peace offerings, to make reconciliation for the
house of Israel.

they shall pay the prince is one sixtieth in grain. For, of an homer, rather: **out of** an homer.
 14. The cor was another name for the homer, 1 Kings v. 2, 25; 2 Chr. ii. 9, xxvii. 5.
 which is *a homer...baths*] **ten baths are an homer.** The words are wanting in LXX. The due in oil was one-hundredth part.
 15. The due out of the flock was one in two hundred.
 the fat pastures] lit. *the watered* land of Israel (Gen. xiii. 10). LXX. reads, *out of all the families* of Israel. These dues from the flock and from the soil were for purposes of sacrifice and offering (*v.* 17).
 16. A.V. margins on this verse ought to be deleted. The words "all the people of the land" are anomalous grammatically; LXX. omits "of the land."
 17. In return for these dues paid him by the people the prince shall be charged with providing the sacrifices for public worship.
 he shall prepare] **provide.**
 The "feasts" were the three great festivals, passover or unleavened bread (easter), the feast of weeks, or pentecost, and the feast of in-gathering or tabernacles at the end of the vintage. Ezekiel, however, seems to give no place to pentecost.
 all solemnities] i.e. stated seasons. A reconciling or "atoning" efficacy appears attributed by the prophet to all the various kinds of sacrifices.

CH. XLV. 18—XLVI. 24. THE OFFERINGS TO BE MADE AT THE
  FEASTS AND OTHER APPOINTED SEASONS.

 (1) xlv. 18—25. Offerings at the feasts.
 (2) xlvi. 1—11. Offerings for the sabbaths and new moons.
 (3) *v.* 12. Voluntary offerings of the prince.

Thus saith the Lord GOD; In the first *month*, in the first 13 *day* of the month, thou shalt take a young bullock without blemish, and cleanse the sanctuary: and the priest shall 19 take of the blood of the sin offering, and put *it* upon the posts of the house, and upon the four corners of the settle of the altar, and upon the posts of the gate of the inner court. And so thou shalt do the seventh *day* of the month 20 for every one that erreth, and for *him that is* simple: so shall ye reconcile the house. In the first *month*, in the 21

(4) *vv.* 13—15. The daily burnt-offering.
(5) *vv.* 16—18. Case of the prince alienating any part of his landed estate to his children or servants.
(6) *vv.* 19—24. Kitchens for boiling the offerings eaten by the priests, and those partaken of by the people.

XLV. 18—25. OFFERINGS AT THE FEASTS.

18—20. The stated atonement for the sanctuary twice in the year— on the first day of the first month (*v.* 18); and on the first day of the seventh month (*v.* 20). The sin-offering on both occasions shall be a young bullock *to cleanse*, better: **to make atonement for the** sanctuary (xliii. 20).

19. Ceremonial with the blood. The blood shall be put on the door-posts of the house (xli. 21), on the four corners of the great "settle" of the altar (xliii. 20), and upon the door-posts of the gateway of the inner court—which gateway is not specified, probably that at which the victims were slaughtered. Gateway, however, might be used collectively.

20. *seventh* day *of the month*] The text can hardly be so rendered. Probably: **in the seventh month, on the new moon** (i.e. the first day). LXX. fully: in the seventh month, on the first day of the month. An atonement was made for the sanctuary, purifying it from the defilements of the people, at the beginning of each half-year. No mention is made of burnt-offerings, but cf. xlvi. 6, 7.

every one that erreth] i.e. not for any particular person had in view, but for the people on account of there being among them persons who have erred unwittingly or through simplicity, i.e. natural slowness which may not have apprehended the exact requirements of duty. Ezekiel is speaking of the people in their perfect condition, when, of course, only such mistakes will be committed as are due to inadvertence and the limitations to which the mind of man is subject.

reconcile the house] **make atonement for.** Cf. Lev. xvi. 16, 18.

21. THE FEASTS. THE PASSOVER ON THE FOURTEENTH OF THE FIRST MONTH.

feast of seven days] So no doubt Heb. should be read, with the ancient versions. At present it reads: a feast of weeks of days. Ezekiel

fourteenth day of the month, ye shall have the passover, a feast of seven days; unleavened bread shall be eaten.
22 And upon that day shall the prince prepare for himself and for all the people of the land a bullock *for* a sin offering.
23 And seven days of the feast he shall prepare a burnt offering to the LORD, seven bullocks and seven rams without blemish daily the seven days; and a kid of the
24 goats daily *for* a sin offering. And he shall prepare a meat offering *of* an ephah for a bullock, and an ephah for a ram,
25 and a hin of oil for an ephah. In the seventh *month*, in the fifteenth day of the month, shall he do the like in the feast *of* the seven days, according to the sin offering, according to the burnt offering, and according to the meat offering, and according to the oil.

46 Thus saith the Lord GOD; The gate of the inner court that looketh *toward* the east shall be shut the six working days; but on the sabbath it shall be opened, and in the
2 day of the new moon it shall be opened. And the prince shall enter by the way of the porch of *that* gate without,

omits all ref. to the so-called feast of weeks, i.e. pentecost, seven weeks after the unleavened bread, when the sickle was put into the grain.

22. *prepare for himself*] **provide**, v. 17.
23. *kid of the goats*] **a he goat**. For prepare, **provide**, so v. 24.
25. Feast of tabernacles on the fifteenth day of the seventh month. Render: **in the seventh month, on the fifteenth day of the month, in the feast, shall he do the like, the seven days**. The "feast" is that of tabernacles, the feast *par excellence* of the year, concluding the yearly round of festivals (Is. xxix. 1). For this feast the prince makes the same provision as for the feast of unleavened bread (*v.* 23).

XLVI. 1—7. OFFERINGS FOR THE SABBATH AND NEW MOON.

The prince was under obligation, besides providing for the great festivals of unleavened bread or passover and tabernacles (xlv. 21, 25), and for the special new moons in the first and seventh months (xlv. 18, 20), to furnish offerings also for the sabbaths and the ordinary new moons. The east gate of the inner court was kept shut six days of the week (the outer was always shut), but opened on the sabbaths and also on the new moons (*v.* 1). On these days the prince came by way of the porch and advanced as far as the door-posts of the inner gate, where he worshipped while the priests were offering the burnt and peace-offerings (*v.* 2). The gate remained open till the evening. While the prince could come as far as the threshold of the inner gate the people stood without before the inner east gate to worship (*v.* 3).

2. *porch of* that *gate without*] **porch of the gate without**. It is

and shall stand by the post of the gate, and the priests shall prepare his burnt offering and his peace offerings, and he shall worship at the threshold of the gate: then he shall go forth; but the gate shall not be shut until the evening. Likewise the people of the land shall worship *at* the door of 3 this gate before the LORD in the sabbaths and in the new moons. And the burnt offering that the prince shall offer 4 unto the LORD in the sabbath day *shall be* six lambs without blemish, and a ram without blemish. And the meat offer- 5 ing *shall be* an ephah for a ram, and the meat offering for the lambs as he shall be able to give, and a hin of oil to an ephah. And in the day of the new moon *it shall be* a young 6 bullock without blemish, and six lambs, and a ram: they shall be without blemish. And he shall prepare a meat 7 offering, an ephah for a bullock, and an ephah for a ram, and for the lambs according as his hand shall attain unto, and a hin of oil to an ephah. And when the prince shall 8 enter, he shall go in *by* the way of the porch of *that* gate, and he shall go forth by the way thereof.

difficult to decide whether "without" describes porch or gate. If porch, then the porch of the inner gate is meant, which lay "without," i.e. towards the outer court (xl. 31, 34, 37). If "without" refers to gate, then the porch of the outer gate is meant. In the latter case the prince would cross the outer court from the porch of the outer gate and enter the inner gate, cf. xliv. 3. Neither is it certain whether the "posts" and "threshold" are those at the outer end of the inner gate, or those at the end opening into the inner court. The technical "threshold" lay at the inner end, inasmuch as the inner gate was the outer gate reversed (xl. 6). It is possible that the prince was allowed to enter the inner gateway and advance to the inner end of it so as to have a full view of the operations of the priests at the altar, without, however, being permitted to set his foot in the inner court. In this case "porch" would be that of the inner gate (as A.V.).

4—6. On the sabbath the burnt-offering shall be six lambs and a ram, and the meal-offering an ephah of flour for the ram and what the prince thinks good for the lambs; and the libation a hin of oil.

7. For the new moons the burnt-offering shall be a young bullock, and the same meal-offering and libation as for the sabbath.

8, 9. The gates by which prince and people shall come in and go out. The prince shall come in by way of the porch of the gate, and shall go out the same way, i.e. probably the porch of the inner east gate, and he shall go back as he entered, without passing into the inner court. The people shall not go out by the gate at which they came in, but by the opposite gate—those entering by the N. gate shall leave by the S. and conversely.

9 But when the people of the land shall come before the LORD in the solemn feasts, he that entereth in *by* the way of the north gate to worship shall go out *by* the way of the south gate; and he that entereth *by* the way of the south gate shall go forth *by* the way of the north gate: he shall not return *by* the way of the gate whereby he came in, but 10 shall go forth over against it. And the prince in the midst of them, when they go in, shall go in; and when they go 11 forth, shall go forth. And in the feasts and in the solemnities the meat offering shall be an ephah to a bullock, and an ephah to a ram, and to the lambs as he is able to give, and 12 a hin of oil to an ephah. Now when the prince shall prepare a voluntary burnt offering or peace offerings voluntarily unto the LORD, *one* shall then open him the gate that looketh *toward* the east, and he shall prepare his burnt offering and his peace offerings, as he did on the sabbath day: then he shall go forth; and after his going forth *one*

the solemn feasts] **appointed seasons.**
10. *shall go forth*] So must be read, the prince being subject. Heb. text reads: *when they go forth they shall go forth* (i.e. prince and people; R.V. to make this plain supplies *together*). This is a very unnatural reading. Read in either way the words mean that the prince and people come in and go out simultaneously. This would suggest that the worshipping of the prince and people was contemporaneous with the act of the priests in offering, and that when this act was over the people dispersed and the prince departed. The Syr. followed by Corn. reads: *but the prince in their midst, by the gate at which he came in shall he go out*—finding a repetition of *v.* 8, giving a freedom to the prince denied to the people (*v.* 9).
11. General regulation in regard to the meal-offering, it shall be the same both at the feasts proper (xlv. 21, 25) and at the solemnities or stated seasons, such as new moons, &c.
12. Regulation when the prince presents a free-will offering. The east (inner) gate shall be opened for him on such occasions as on the sabbaths and new moons. Cf. Lev. vii. 16, xxxiii. 28; Numb. xv. 3, xxix. 39; Deut. xii. 6; Am. iv. 5.

13—15. THE DAILY OFFERING.

There shall be a daily offering, a lamb for a burnt-offering, with one-sixth of an ephah of flour and the third part of a hin of oil for a meal-offering. This shall be presented every morning. In earlier times the daily offering in practice appears to have been a burnt-offering in the morning and a meal-offering in the evening (2 Kings xvi. 15, cf. 1 Kings xviii. 29, 36). In Numb. xxviii. 3, 8 the daily offering is a lamb morning and evening, with one-tenth of an ephah of flour

shall shut the gate. Thou shalt daily prepare a burnt 13
offering unto the LORD *of* a lamb of the first year without
blemish: thou shalt prepare it every morning. And thou 14
shalt prepare a meat offering for it every morning, the sixth
part of an ephah, and the third *part* of a hin of oil, to
temper with the fine flour; a meat offering continually *by*
a perpetual ordinance unto the LORD. Thus shall they 15
prepare the lamb, and the meat offering, and the oil, every
morning *for* a continual burnt offering.

Thus saith the Lord GOD; If the prince give a gift unto 16
any of his sons, the inheritance thereof shall be his sons'; it
shall be their possession by inheritance. But if he give a 17
gift of his inheritance to one of his servants, then it shall be
his to the year of liberty; after, it shall return to the prince:
but his inheritance shall be his sons' for them. Moreover 18
the prince shall not take the people's inheritance, by
oppression to thrust them out of their possession; *but* he
shall give his sons inheritance out of his own possession:
that my people be not scattered every man from his
possession.

and one-fourth of a hin of oil morning and evening for meal-offering;
to which is to be added one-fourth of a hin of wine for drink-offering.
Ezek. nowhere refers to wine in the offerings.

13. *thou shalt...prepare*] LXX. *he shall* prepare; so *v.* 14. Cf.
xlv. 17.

14. *to temper*] Probably as R.V. **to moisten**, or, besprinkle the
fine flour. Song v. 2, *drops* of the night.

**16—18. CASE OF THE PRINCE ALIENATING ANY PART OF HIS
LANDED PROPERTY TO HIS SONS OR SERVANTS.**

If given to his sons the gift shall remain with them as their inheritance (*v.* 16); if given to any of his servants it shall revert to the
prince at the year of liberty (*v.* 17).

17. *year of liberty*] In Jer. xxxiv. 14 the year of liberty is that
of the freeing of the bondservant in the seventh year; and this year
may be meant here. Cf. Is. lxi. 1. Otherwise the year of Jubilee,
the fiftieth year, is referred to, when all landed property that had been
alienated reverted to its original owner, Lev. xxv. 10, xxvii. 24.

but his inheritance...them] lit. but (or, only as for) his inheritance,
his sons, it shall be theirs, i.e. the portion of his inheritance which the
prince may bestow on his sons shall remain theirs, without reverting
to the prince (*v.* 16). LXX., Syr. more clearly: *the inheritance of his
sons*, it shall be theirs.

19 After, he brought me through the entry, which *was* at the side of the gate, into the holy chambers of the priests, which looked toward the north: and behold, there *was*
20 a place on the two sides westward. Then said he unto me, This *is* the place where the priests shall boil the trespass offering and the sin offering, where they shall bake the meat offering; that *they* bear *them* not out into the utter court, to
21 sanctify the people. Then he brought me forth into the utter court, and caused me to pass by the four corners of the court; and behold, in every corner of the court *there*
22 *was* a court. In the four corners of the court *there were* courts joined *of* forty *cubits* long and thirty broad: these
23 four corners *were* of one measure. And *there was* a row *of*

19—24. THE KITCHENS FOR THE PRIESTS (*vv.* 19, 20), AND PEOPLE (*vv.* 21—24).

The kitchens for cooking the sin and trespass offering and baking the meal-offering, the holy things to be consumed by the priests (xliv. 29), were situated in the inner court at the furthest part of the court westward, to the west of the holy cells (xlii. 1—14), and on both sides of the erection called the "building" (xli. 12, 13) which lay behind the house, Fig. 3, L. The inner court on the west reached back to the boundary wall of the outer court, which on that side was the wall of the inner court, and in the two corners, N. and S., the priests' kitchens were placed. The prophet is brought to those on the N. side; those on the S. were similar.

19. *through the entry*] the *entrance way*, viz. that mentioned xlii. 9. Since xliv. 4 the prophet had been before the house. The holy chambers are those described, xlii. 1—14.

a place on the two sides] **a place in the innermost part westward**; i.e. at the western extremity of the court. In Fig. 3 the kitchens, LL, should probably be extended back to the wall.

to sanctify the people] Cf. xliv. 19.

21—24. The kitchens for cooking the sacrificial meals of the people. These were situated in the four corners of the outer court. In each of the four corners was a small enclosure or court 40 cubits long and 30 broad (*v.* 21, 22); and in these were situated the kitchens, where the "ministers of the house," the subordinate officials (xliv. 10—14), boiled the people's offering for their sacrificial meal (*v.* 23, 24), Fig. 3 M.

22. *courts joined*] The term "joined" is obscure, not occurring elsewhere. Possibly: enclosed courts. LXX. appears to have read: *small* (the words differ in one letter).

these four corners] lit. *the four of them had one measure*, they being *in the corners*. The word in the corners, or, cornered, is deleted in the Heb. tradition by points over it, and not rendered in LXX. and Vulg.

building round about in them, round about them four, and *it was* made *with* boiling places under the rows round about. Then said he unto me, These *are* the places of 24 them that boil, where the ministers of the house shall boil the sacrifice of the people.

Afterward he brought me again unto the door of the 47 house; and behold, waters issued out from under the threshold of the house eastward: for the forefront of the house *stood toward* the east, and the waters came down from under from the right side of the house, at the south *side* of the altar. Then brought he me out *of* the way of the gate 2

23. The description is brief. The "row" is probably not a series of separate buildings running round the court, but a continuous course of building, in which at the bottom ("under" the row) were recesses in which were the hearths where the pots were set in which the sacrifices were cooked. The hearth usually consisted of some stones within which the fire was put and upon which the pot was set.
20. The "ministers" are the subordinate officials—the Levites.

CH. XLVII. THE STREAM THAT ISSUED FROM THE TEMPLE.

The chapter contains two parts:—
(1) *vv.* 1—12. The stream issuing from the temple, that fertilized the desert and sweetened the waters of the Dead Sea.
(2) *vv.* 13—23. The boundaries of the holy land; and the privileges of strangers attaching themselves to the tribes.
1—12. The river issuing from the temple. The prophet saw a stream issuing from beneath the threshold of the house, which pursued its way eastward, passing the altar on the south side and emerging into the open on the right hand of the outer east gate. A thousand cubits from the gate the waters were ankle deep, but speedily they became a river so deep that it could be crossed only by swimming (*vv.* 3—5). A luxuriant nature attended the course of the stream; trees grew on every side, ever green and with unfailing fruit, the leaves of which possessed a healing virtue (*vv.* 7, 12). The desert place to the east became transformed, and the bitter waters of the Dead Sea into which the river flowed were made sweet, and swarmed with life like the great sea on the west. Fishermen peopled the shores from En-gedi to En-eglaim; only the marshes by the seaside remained salt (*vv.* 6—12).
1. From the outer court (xlvi. 23) the prophet was brought again to the door of the house. There he saw waters issuing from beneath the threshold on the right, that is the south side, which flowed east, passing the altar on the south side.
2. The eastern gates being shut (xliv. 2, xlvi. 1) the prophet is led out by the N. gate, round to the outer E. gate, at which he beheld the stream emerge into the open at the S. side of the gate.

northward, and led me about the way without unto the utter gate *by* the way that looketh east*ward;* and behold, there ran out waters on the right side. And when the man that had the line in his hand went forth east*ward*, he measured a thousand cubits, and he brought me through the waters; the waters *were* to the ankles. Again he measured a thousand, and brought me through the waters; the waters *were to* the knees. Again he measured a thousand, and brought me through; the waters *were* to the loins. Afterward he measured a thousand; *and it was* a river that I could not pass over: for the waters were risen, waters to swim in, a river that could not be passed over.

6 And he said unto me, Son of man, hast thou seen *this?* Then he brought me, and caused me to return to the brink of the river. Now when I had returned, behold, at the bank of the river *were* very many trees on the one side and on the other. Then said he unto me, These waters issue out toward the east country, and go down into the desert, and go into the sea: *which* being brought forth into the sea, the waters shall be healed. And it shall come to pass, *that*

by *the way that looketh*] **which looketh,** viz. the gate.

3. A thousand cubits from the place of emergence the waters were ankle deep.

4, 5. Successive measurements shewed a depth to the knees, the loins, and finally an impassable river. The word rendered "river" is the usual one for "brook" or wady, viz. a stream with its valley or gorge.

6. *to the brink*] Perhaps: **along** the brink. *River* is brook or wady as *v.* 5.

7. Both banks of the wady, as is everywhere seen, were covered with trees.

8. The direction of the stream was eastward, towards the region which is desert, and towards the Dead Sea.

the east country] lit. circle, or, *district*, the same word as Galilee (Is. ix. 1). Cf. Joshua xxii. 10, 11, "the circuits of the Jordan."

unto the desert] **the Arabah,** what is now called the Ghor, the depression of the Jordan valley, the Dead Sea, and southward as far as the gulf of Akaba; Deut. i. 1, iii. 17; Josh. xviii. 18. The "sea" into which the waters flow is the Dead Sea.

brought forth into the sea] The construction is difficult. For "into the sea" LXX. read "the waters." This would necessitate a further change: into the sea, *unto the bitter* waters, and the waters, &c.; so Corn. after Syr., putrid waters.

every thing that liveth, which moveth, whithersoever the rivers shall come, shall live: and there shall be a very great multitude of fish, because these waters shall come thither: for they shall be healed; and every *thing* shall live whither the river cometh. And it shall come to pass, *that* the 10 fishers shall stand upon it from En-gedi even unto En-eglaim; they shall be a place to spread forth nets; their fish shall be according to their kinds, as the fish of the great sea, exceeding many. But the miry places thereof 11 and the marishes thereof shall not be healed; they shall be given to salt. And by the river upon the bank thereof, on 12 this side and on that side, shall grow all trees for meat, whose leaf shall not fade, neither shall the fruit thereof be consumed: it shall bring forth new fruit according to his months, because their waters they issued out of the sanctuary:

9. *every thing...moveth*] **every living creature which swarmeth** (or, creepeth). The word is used of the smaller animals, particularly the smaller aquatic creatures—these shall come to life and swarm in the waters of the Dead Sea. This sea is entirely destitute of life.

the rivers shall come] lit. the *two rivers*. The dual is difficult to explain; LXX. sing. The representation is different in Zech. xiv. 8, where one stream goes to the Dead Sea and another to the western sea.

because these waters] with different interpunction: **multitude of fish**; **for when these waters come thither they** (the waters of the sea) **shall be healed and there shall be life, whithersoever the river cometh.**

10. En-gedi, the modern Ain Jidy, kid's well, situated about the middle of the west shore of the Dead Sea. En-eglaim has not been identified; it probably lay N. toward the mouth of the Jordan. It has been supposed to be Ain Feshkah, Robinson ii. 489. The word differs in spelling from Eglaim, Is. xv. 8, which probably lay to the south of the sea.

11. The marshes around the sea shall not be sweetened, but left as beds for digging salt. The saltness of the Dead Sea is due to the strata of salt rocks which surround it.

12. *according to his months*] **every month.** For issued, issue. The fruit of these trees shall not " be consumed" i.e. fail; it shall renew itself every month, and the leaves shall be ever green and possess a healing virtue. Ps. i. 3; Rev. xxii. 2.

This beautiful representation of the healing stream, issuing from the temple and fertilizing the desert as well as changing the bitter waters of the Dead Sea into sweet, so that they yield abundant sustenance to men, rests on some natural and some spiritual conceptions common in Ezekiel's days. One natural fact was this, that there was a fountain connected with the temple-hill, the waters of which fell into the valley east of the city and made their way towards the sea; and long ere

and the fruit thereof shall be for meat, and the leaf thereof for medicine.

13 Thus saith the Lord GOD; This *shall be* the border, whereby ye shall inherit the land according to the twelve

this time the gentle waters of this brook, that flowed fast by the oracle of God, had furnished symbols to the prophets (Is. viii. 6). Such waters in the east are the source of every blessing to men. The religious conceptions are such as these : that Jehovah himself is the giver of all blessings to men, and from his presence all blessings flow. He was now present in his fulness and for ever in his temple. Hence the prophet sees the life-giving stream issue from the sanctuary. Another current idea was that in the regeneration of men, when the tabernacle of God was with them, external nature would also be transfigured. Then every good would be enjoyed and there would be no more evil nor curse. The desert would blossom like the rose, and the field that aforetime was thought fruitful should be accounted no better than bush. The barren land toward the east and the bitter waters of the sea were a contradiction to the ideal of an external nature subservient in all her parts to man in the fellowship of God. Therefore the desert shall be fertilized and the waters of the sea healed, and all things minister to man's good. But "good" to the Israelite was not exclusively spiritual, it was also material. It would be an error to regard this fertilizing, healing stream in the light of a mere symbol for blessings which we call "spiritual." It is well fitted in other connexions to be such a symbol; but to take it so here would be to overstep the limits of the Old Testament and anticipate a later revelation. As yet the Israelite had no conception of a transcendent sphere of existence for men in the fellowship of God, such as we name heaven. Man's final abode even in his perfect state was considered to be still on the earth. God came down and dwelt with men; men were not translated to abide with God. But God's presence with men on earth gave to earth the attributes of heaven. Yet man's needs remained, and God's presence was the source of all things necessary to supply them. When he had the needful blessings the Israelite saw in them the tokens and the sacraments of God's favour and presence with him; and conversely when God was near him he was assured that he should want no good thing (Ps. xxxiv. 9).

13—21. THE BOUNDARIES OF THE NEW HOLY LAND.

On the east the boundary shall be the Jordan from Hazar Enon on the north to the salt sea on the south, for in the time of restitution the promised land shall be confined to Palestine west of the Jordan, according to the oath sworn by God unto the fathers (Gen. xii. 7, xiii. 15, xvii. 8, xxviii. 13). On the west the boundary shall be the Mediterranean sea. The boundaries on the N. and S. are particularly defined, the towns being mentioned by which they run, but the places named are mostly unknown. The boundaries are in the main the same as those laid down in Num. xxxiv.

tribes of Israel: Joseph *shall have two* portions. And ye 14
shall inherit it, one as well as another: *concerning* the which
I lifted up mine hand to give it unto your fathers: and this
land shall fall unto you for inheritance. And this *shall* 15
be the border of the land toward the north side, from the
great sea, the way of Hethlon, as *men* go to Zedad; Hamath, 16

13. The tribe of Joseph, being composed of two great families, shall have "portions," i.e. two lots (perhaps *dual* should be read). There still remained twelve tribes, therefore, even when Levi was provided for by the sacred Terumah or oblation.

15. The northern border. The two ends of the line of delimitation on the N. are the great sea on the west and Hazar Enon on the east. The line passes from west to east, bending, towards its termination at least, towards S.E. In its way it skirts the territory of Hamath and that of Damascus.

as men go to Zedad] In *v.* 20 and xlviii. 1 the reading is "as one goeth to Hamath," a frequent phrase, sometimes rendered "the entering into Hamath" (Josh. xiii. 5), or "the entering in of Hamath" (Jud. iii. 3; 1 K. viii. 65), or "the entrance of Hamath" (Numb. xxxiv. 8). In 1 K. viii. 65 the phrase seems to mean the southern boundary of Hamath. Unfortunately the point on the western sea from which the line starts is not specified, as the situation of Hethlon is unknown. The entrance to Hamath must be either the mouth of the Bukāʿ, the great plain between the Libanus on the W. and the Anti-libanus on the E., by which one goes N. to Hamath, or it must be the plain between the North end of the Libanus and the Nusairīyeh mountains, opening from the sea and running east. This would throw the boundary-line north of Tripoli, and south of Arvad. In Josh. xiii. 5, the land of the Giblites, i.e. Gebal (Byblus) to the N. of Beirut, is regarded as part of Israel's possession. In Numb. xxxiv. 8, where the northern boundary is described, the reading is the "entrance of Hamath," Zedad being mentioned afterwards. Except in 1 Chron. v. 9 the phrase is only used of Hamath. Following xlviii. 1, and Numb. xxxiv. 8, the place of Zedad and Hamath may be changed, as LXX. also seems to have read Hamath before Zedad.—15 "And this shall be the boundary of the land: on the N. side, from the great sea by the way of Hethlon, where the way goeth unto Hamath, by Zedad, 16 Berothah, Sibraim, which is between the border of Damascus and the border of Hamath, even unto Hazar-hattikon, which is by the border of Hauran." If we could suppose the entry to Hamath not the southern one by the plain of Cœle Syria, but the western one from the sea to the N. of Tripoli, Hethlon might be the modern Heitela (Robinson's Map, 1852). Zedad has been supposed to be Sadad, S. of Emesa (Homs) and not far from Riblah. With Berotha, cf. Berothai, 2 Sam. viii. 8. In Numb. xxxiv. 9 Ziphran seems to occupy the place of Sibraim here. In Numb. the line appears to run E. as far as Zedad, and then to change its direction to the S. till it ends at Hazar Enan.

Berothah, Sibraim, which *is* between the border of Damascus and the border of Hamath; Hazar-hatticon, which *is* by the
17 coast of Hauran. And the border from the sea shall be Hazar-enan, the border of Damascus, and the north northward, and the border of Hamath. And *this is* the north
18 side. And the east side ye shall measure from Hauran, and from Damascus, and from Gilead, and from the land of

17. The verse repeats and sums up *vv.* 15, 16, with special reference to the countries lying on the N. of the northern border of Israel. In *v.* 17 Hazar Enon is named as the extremity of the Northern boundary, in *v.* 16 Hazar hattikon (the middle Hazar). The places must be identical, whether hattikon be a misreading or not. LXX. reads Saunan, Cod. Alex. Eunan, and in xlviii. 1, Numb. xxxiv. 9, Enon here is spelled Enan. In *v.* 16 the place is said to be on the border of Hauran. *V.* 17 may read: "and so the border shall be from the sea to Hazar Enon on the border of Damascus, and north northwards the border of Hamath: this is the north side" (reading *this* as *v.* 20 and possibly with omission of *and* before "border of Hamath," words wanting in LXX.). The boundary is first stated generally as going from the sea to Hazar Enan, and then in the contrary direction north, Hamath being the country to the N. It is not certain that Hauran is the district now so called, but it is probable. Wetzstein (Del. Psalms iii. 439, Eaton's Trans.), identifies the village of Hadar at the East foot of Hermon with Hazar Enan. In all likelihood the end of the boundary line is hereabouts; in Deut. iii. 8 Hermon is the northernmost point of conquest, and Ezek. would probably follow this. The northern boundary followed an easterly course from the sea, Hamath lying on the N., then a southerly course having Damascus on the E., till it terminated at Hazar Enon between Damascus and Hauran. But at what point of the sea it started, and in what latitude the line to the east ran is obscure. The identifications of Hethlon with Heitela and of Zedad with Sadad would give the latitude of Emesa (Homs), which is very far north; see Porter, *Five Years in Damascus*, II. 354 *seq.* and map. More likely the prophet fancied the starting-point on the W. to be about Tyre.

18. The eastern border.
In *v.* 16 the eastmost point of the north border was said to be Hazar Enon on the border of Hauran. The E. boundary will therefore start from this point. The verse may read: "and the east side: from between Hauran and Damascus, between Gilead and the land of Israel shall be the Jordan, from the (north) boundary to the eastern sea, even unto Tamar; this is the east side." The line starts from Hazar Enon, a place lying where Damascus and Hauran adjoin one another (*v.* 16). Instead of Hazar Enon, however, the point of contact between Damascus and Hauran is named as the starting-point (for the last two *umibben* read *ben* and *uben*). From this point the line runs south; its course is the Jordan between Gilead and the land of Israel. The order Hauran, Damascus, Gilead is entirely incomprehensible (for Hauran lay S. of

Israel *by* Jordan, from the border unto the east sea. And *this is* the east side. And the south side southward, from 19 Tamar *even* to the waters of strife *in* Kadesh, *the* river to the great sea. And *this is* the south side southward. The 20 west side also *shall be* the great sea from the border, till *a man* come over against Hamath. This *is* the west side. So shall ye divide this land unto you according to the tribes 21 of Israel.

And it shall come to pass, *that* ye shall divide it *by lot* for 22 an inheritance unto you, and to the strangers that sojourn among you, which shall beget children among you: and they shall be unto you as born in the country among the children of Israel; they shall have inheritance with you among the tribes of Israel. And it shall come to pass, 23 *that* in what tribe the stranger sojourneth, there shall ye give *him* his inheritance, saith the Lord GOD.

Now these *are* the names of the tribes. From the north 48 end to the coast of the way of Hethlon, as *one* goeth to

Damascus) if R.V. be followed. The phrase "ye shall measure" is no doubt a misspelling for "unto Tamar" (LXX. Syr., *d* for *r*), from which the southern border starts in *v.* 19. Tamar probably lay S. of the Dead Sea. The Onomasticon (Ed. *Lagarde*, p. 85) says: one day's journey from Mampsis as you go to Aelia (?Elath) from Hebron. Robinson identifies Mampsis with Malatha, in his view el Milh.

19. The southern boundary. Read: "and the southside southward: from Tamar on to the waters of Meriboth-Kadesh, to the brook (of Egypt), and unto the great sea; this is the south side southward." The delimitation on the S. is more fully described Numb. xxxiv. 3—5; Josh. xv. 1—4. There Kadesh is called Kadesh-Barnea, here Meriboth Kadesh (elsewhere Meribah), i.e. waters *of strife* of Kadesh, Numb. xxvii. 14. The brook of Egypt is the Wady el Arish. The line striking this brook follows its course to the sea.

20. The western boundary—"and the west side: the great sea, from the (south) border as far as over against where one goeth unto Hamath; this is the west side."

21—23. The land so bounded shall be divided equally among the tribes; and strangers sojourning in Israel shall inherit just as those born in the land. The stranger shall have his inheritance among the members of the tribe in which he sojourns.

CH. XLVIII. THE DISPOSITION OF THE TRIBES IN THE LAND.

(1) *vv.* 1—7. The tribes north of the sacred oblation of land.
(2) *vv.* 8—22. The oblation in its various divisions: for the priests, the Levites, the city and the prince.

Hamath, Hazar-enan, the border of Damascus northward, to the coast of Hamath; for these are his sides east *and* 2 west; a *portion for* Dan. And by the border of Dan, from 3 the east side unto the west side, a *portion for* Asher. And by the border of Asher, from the east side even unto the 4 west side, a *portion for* Naphtali. And by the border of Naphtali, from the east side unto the west side, a

(3) *vv.* 23—29. The tribes situated south of the oblation.
(4) *vv.* 30—35. The gates of the city.

All the tribes are now settled on the West of the Jordan. The land is divided into zones running from E. to W. of the country, one of which falls to the lot of each tribe. The dimensions of the zone are not mentioned, neither is there any indication whether the greater or less breadth of the country from the Jordan to the sea was taken into account. The oblation of land given to the priests and Levites lay not strictly in the middle of the country, but in the neighbourhood of Jerusalem, and therefore more toward the south; hence seven tribes are located to the north of the oblation and five to the south of it. Of the tribes beyond Jordan the half of Manasseh is now united with the other half, forming one tribe, and receiving one portion; while Gad and Reuben are provided with new settlements, the former in the extreme south, and the latter in the northern half of the country. Judah and Benjamin change places, the former lying to the north of the oblation and the city, and the latter to the south. In other respects the position of the tribes remains nearly what it was, except that Issachar and Zebulun have to be provided for in the south. It is perhaps accidental that the children of Leah and Rachel occupy the centre, while the sons of the handmaids are placed at the extremities.

1—7. The tribes to the north of the sacred oblation.

1. Dan on the furthest north. The verse as it stands has probably some confusion of text. It may read: "now these are the names of the tribes: on the furthest north, along side of the way to Hethlon, as one goeth to Hamath, as far as Hazar Enan on the border of Damascus, even on the north along side of (the land of) Hamath—he shall have the east side (and) the west side: Dan one (portion)." First the boundary line W. to E. is specified from the sea to Hazar Enan (xlvii. 16, 17), and then is mentioned the country bounding the portion on the north, viz. Hamath. The *he* in "he shall have" is Dan, already in the writer's mind. We might have expected "he shall have the east side even unto the west side," or from the east side, &c., as in the following verses. The former in LXX.

2—7. After Dan in the furthest North bordering on the land of Hamath comes Asher (*v.* 2), Naphtali (*v.* 3), the whole reunited tribe of Manasseh (*v.* 4), Ephraim (*v.* 5), Reuben transferred from the other side of the Jordan (*v.* 6), and finally Judah (*v.* 7).

2. *a* portion for *Asher*] **Asher one portion.** And so in each of the following verses.

	Dan	
	Asher	
	· Naphtali	
	Manasseh	
	Ephraim	
	Reuben	
	Judah	

Prince's portion	Domain of Levites			Prince's portion
	Priests' domain	☐ Sanctuary		
	City land	City	City land	

	Benjamin	
	Simeon	
	Issachar	
	Zebulun	
	Gad	

5 *portion for* Manasseh. And by the border of Manasseh, from the east side unto the west side, a *portion for*
6 Ephraim. And by the border of Ephraim, from the east side even unto the west side, a *portion for* Reuben.
7 And by the border of Reuben, from the east side unto the west side, a *portion for* Judah.
8 And by the border of Judah, from the east side unto the west side, shall be the offering which ye shall offer *of* five and twenty thousand *reeds in* breadth, and *in* length as one of the *other* parts, from the east side unto the west side:
9 and the sanctuary shall be in the midst of it. The oblation that ye shall offer unto the LORD *shall be of* five and twenty thousand *in* length, and *of* ten thousand *in*
10 breadth. And for them, *even* for the priests, shall be *this* holy oblation; toward the north five and twenty thousand *in length*, and toward the west ten thousand *in* breadth, and toward the east ten thousand *in* breadth, and toward the

---

8—22. The oblation or Terumah in the centre of the country. This oblation is a tract of 25,000 cubits broad, N. to S., and in length equal to the portions of the tribes E. to W. This oblation is first specified in its whole extent (*v.* 8); then the portion of it to be assigned to the priests is described (*vv.* 9—12); then the portion of the Levites (*vv.* 13, 14); then the part of the oblation belonging to the city (*vv.* 15—20); and finally the portion of the oblation which shall constitute the inheritance of the prince (*vv.* 21, 22).

8. *the offering*...reeds in *breadth*] The **oblation** (xlv. 1)...**cubits in breadth**, i.e. N. to S. This is the breadth of the whole part subtracted from the territory of the country, and devoted to the priests, the Levites, the city and the prince. In length it goes from the Jordan to the sea, just "as one of the other parts," i.e. the portions of the tribes. The sanctuary shall be situated in the centre of this oblation, viz. in the portion assigned to the priests—that assigned to the Levites being on the north and that assigned to the city on the south.

9—12. The domain assigned to the priests. This is mentioned first, not because it actually borders on Judah—the Levites border on Judah—but because it is most important.

9. *ten thousand* in *breadth*] LXX. **twenty** thousand. This reading assumes that *v.* 9 refers to the portion assigned to priests and Levites together. So *v.* 13 end. The length E. to W. is 25,000, because the prince's domain lies between it and the Jordan on the one side, and between it and the sea on the other.

10. *And for them...priests*] **And for these shall be the holy oblation, even for the priests: on the north...and on the west...and on the east...and on the south.**

south five and twenty thousand *in* length: and the sanctuary of the LORD shall be in the midst thereof. *It shall be* for 11 the priests that are sanctified of the sons of Zadok; which have kept my charge, which went not astray when the children of Israel went astray, as the Levites went astray. And *this* oblation of the land that is offered shall be unto 12 them *a thing* most holy by the border of the Levites. And 13 over against the border of the priests, the Levites *shall have* five and twenty thousand *in* length, and ten thousand *in* breadth: all the length *shall be* five and twenty thousand, and the breadth ten thousand. And they shall not sell of it, 14 neither exchange, nor alienate the firstfruits of the land: for *it is* holy unto the LORD.

And the five thousand, that are left in the breadth over 15 against the five and twenty thousand, *shall be* a profane *place* for the city, for dwelling, and for suburbs: and the city shall be in the midst thereof. And these *shall be* the 16 measures thereof; the north side four thousand and five hundred, and the south side four thousand and five hundred, and on the east side four thousand and five hundred, and the west side four thousand and five hundred. And the 17 suburbs of the city shall be toward the north two hundred

11. *that are sanctified of the sons*] Lit. the priests, the sanctified thing, from the sons. Possibly the words should be divided differently: *it shall be for the priests that are sanctified, the sons* of Zadok. On the erring of the Levites, cf. xliv. 10.

12. Read: **And it shall be to them as an oblation out of the oblation of the land, a thing most holy, by,** &c. Cf. xlv. 3 *seq.*

13. The portion of the oblation of land assigned to the Levites.— The portion of the Levites is of the same extent as that of the priests, 25,000 long (E. to W.) by 10,000 broad (N. to S.). It runs "over against," i.e. along side of the priests' domain, and lies to the north of it.

14. Seems to apply to the united domain of priests and Levites.

the firstfruits] Possibly: this *first-fruits*, or, *best*—the term being applied to the holy oblation in distinction from the rest of the land.

15—20. The portion of the oblation assignable to the city.—The remaining 5000 in breadth (N. to S.) shall belong to the city, with the same length as the portions of the priests and Levites, viz. 25,000, as it is said "over against (i.e. in length) the 25,000." On "suburbs," cf. xlv. 2—they are the free place round the city.

16. The city shall be a square of 4500 cubits.

17. The "suburbs" or free space round the city shall be 250 cubits on all the four sides. Adding the 250 on the N. and on the S. of the

and fifty, and toward the south two hundred and fifty, and toward the east two hundred and fifty, and toward the west 18 two hundred and fifty. And the residue in length over against the oblation of the holy *portion shall be* ten thousand eastward, and ten thousand westward: and it shall be over against the oblation of the holy *portion;* and the increase 19 thereof shall be for food unto them that serve the city. And they that serve the city shall serve it out of all the tribes of 20 Israel. All the oblation *shall be* five and twenty thousand by five and twenty thousand: ye shall offer the holy 21 oblation foursquare, with the possession of the city. And

city to the 4500 it appears that the whole *breadth* of the 5000 assigned to the city was occupied by it and its suburbs from N. to S.

18. As the city with its suburbs was a square of 5000 cubits, there remained of the 25,000 in length assigned to it a portion 10,000 long on the E. and another equally long on the W. In their length these portions lay "over against," i.e. along, the holy portion of the priests.

that serve the city] The words are very difficult. It is plain that the 10,000 cubits of land E. and W. of the city serve to supply the inhabitants of the city with food. The restored land is a land of husbandmen, and those who dwell in the city live from the city's domain. Either "serve" or "cultivate," must be taken in the sense of inhabit and the words be read: for food to them that *inhabit the city*, 19 and they *that inhabit the* city &c.; though such a usage has no parallel. Or, the word "city" must be taken in a general sense of the city and its domain of land: for food *to the tillers of the city*, 19 *and they that till the city* &c.

19. *that serve the city*] Those who render *inhabit* (Hitz.) consider that the verse states directly who the inhabitants of the city shall be: "and as for the inhabitants of the city, they shall inhabit it (reading *fem.*) out of all the tribes of Israel." On the other supposition: "and they that till the city shall till it (the domain of land) out of all the tribes of Israel." This rendering also states, though indirectly, that the city shall be common to all the tribes of Israel, and that whoever comes to sojourn there shall live by the land belonging to the city. However the words be translated there is no ref. to *two* classes of persons—citizens and labourers.

20. The verse means that the holy oblation when the possession of the city is included forms a square of 25,000 by 25,000.

21, 22. The domain of the prince. The domain of the Levites, priests and city formed a square of 25,000 cubits in the heart of the country. The portion of the prince shall be the land from the E. of this square to the Jordan, and from the W. of it to the sea. The "five and twenty thousand" here is the breadth N. to S.; the prince's domain shall be of the same breadth and be "over against" the square on the E. and W.

the residue *shall be* for the prince, on the one side and on the other of the holy oblation, and of the possession of the city, over against the five and twenty thousand of the oblation toward the east border, and westward over against the five and twenty thousand toward the west border, over against the portions for the prince: and it shall be the holy oblation; and the sanctuary of the house *shall be* in the midst thereof. Moreover from the possession of the Levites, 22 *and* from the possession of the city, *being* in the midst *of that* which is the prince's, between the border of Judah and the border of Benjamin, shall be for the prince.

As for the rest of the tribes, from the east side unto the 23 west side, Benjamin *shall have* a *portion*. And by the 24 border of Benjamin, from the east side unto the west side, Simeon *shall have* a *portion*. And by the border of Simeon, 25 from the east side unto the west side, Issachar a *portion*. And by the border of Issachar, from the east side unto the 26 west side, Zebulun a *portion*. And by the border of 27 Zebulun, from the east side unto the west side, Gad a *portion*. And by the border of Gad, at the south side 28

over against the portions] Or, **by the side of the portions, it shall be for the prince; and the holy oblation, and the sanctuary of the house shall be in the midst thereof.** The "portions" here are those of the tribes, which run from the Jordan to the sea; the prince's domain shall run alongside of them, i.e. Judah's on the N. and Benjamin's on the S. And the holy oblation lies between the two halves of the prince's domain.

22. *Moreover from the possession*] **And** from. The verse gives again the breadth of the prince's possession, by stating the two limits N. (the Levites) and S. (the city) of the central oblation. All the land lying between these limits, in other words between the tribes of Judah and Benjamin, shall belong to the prince.

being in the midst] i.e. lying between the two halves of the prince's portion.

23—29. THE TRIBES LYING SOUTH OF THE OBLATION.

First, Benjamin, which changes places with Judah, and bounds the oblation on the south (*v.* 23). The two tribes that formed the ancient kingdom of Judah still have the prerogative of lying nearest the sanctuary. Then Simeon, formerly located in the south (*v.* 24). Then successively Issachar (*v.* 25), Zebulun (*v.* 26), and finally Gad (*v.* 27). The two former are brought down from the north, and Gad from beyond the Jordan.

southward, the border shall be even from Tamar *unto* the waters of strife *in* Kadesh, *and to the* river toward the great
29 sea. This *is* the land which ye shall divide *by lot* unto the tribes of Israel for inheritance, and these *are* their portions, saith the Lord GOD.
30 And these *are* the goings out of the city: on the north
31 side, four thousand and five hundred measures. And the gates of the city *shall be* after the names of the tribes of Israel: three gates northward; one gate of Reuben, one
32 gate of Judah, one gate of Levi. And at the east side four thousand and five hundred: and three gates; and one gate
33 of Joseph, one gate of Benjamin, one gate of Dan. And *at* the south side four thousand and five hundred measures: and three gates; one gate of Simeon, one gate of Issachar,
34 one gate of Zebulun. At the west side four thousand and five hundred, *with* their three gates; one gate of Gad, one
35 gate of Asher, one gate of Naphtali. *It was* round about

28. The southern border is again given as stated in xlvii. 19.
and to the *river*] to **the brook** (of Egypt), **unto the great sea.** Cf. xlvii. 19.

30—35. THE CITY WITH ITS TWELVE GATES, NAMED AFTER THE TRIBES. Cf. Rev. xxi. 12 *seq.*

30. *goings out of the city*] i.e. the extensions on all sides.
measures] **in measure**, i.e. extent. The 4500 are naturally *cubits*. The city lies foursquare, each side being 4500. But on each side is a free place of 250 cubits, so that the city forms a square of 5000 cubits.
31. The measurement proceeds from W. to E. The gate Reuben was thus the westmost on the north of the city; Judah in the centre and Levi towards the east.
32. Of the three gates on the east side Benjamin's was in the centre, Joseph's to the north and Dan's to the south.
33. Those on the south were Simeon, Issachar and Zebulun, tribes now all located in the south of the country. For "measures," **in measure** or extent.
34. The gates on the west were those of Gad, Asher and Naphtali.
35. The whole circumference of the city was 18,000 cubits, or somewhat under six miles. Josephus (*Bell. Jud.* v. 4, 3) reckoned the bounds of Jerusalem in his day at 33 stadia, or about four miles. For measures, **cubits**.

eighteen thousand *measures:* and the name of the city from *that* day *shall be,* The LORD *is* there.

The LORD is there] Cf. Rev. xxi. 3, "And I heard a great voice out of the throne saying, Behold the tabernacle of God is with men, and he shall dwell with them and they shall be his people, and God himself shall be with them and be their God." The prophet beheld the Lord forsake his temple (xi.), and he beheld him again enter it (xliii.); now he abides in it among his people for ever. The covenant ran that he should be their God and they his people; this is perfectly fulfilled in his presence among them. The end in view from the beginning has been reached.

INDEX.

Abarim, valley of, 283
Abraham, 245
Adonis, meaning of name, 58; worship of, 58, 193
Almighty, 11
allegory, of the crocodile, 211; of the cedar-tree, 222, 223; of the shepherd and flock, 248, 249; of the foundling child, 101; of the history of Israel, 105; of the lions, 134, 135; of the rusted caldron, 174; of the fall of Tyre, 200; of the prince of Tyre, 204
altar, gate of, 55; the brazen, 62; of burnt offering, description of, 325—327
amber, 4
Ammon, prophecy of Ezekiel against, 158, 180
Amorites, the, 102
annexe of the Temple, 307
apparel, rich, 199
Arabs, 183
arrows, 156; divination by, 156
Asher, portion of the tribe of, 354
Ashera, the, 54
Asshur, 199, 234
Assurbanipal, inscriptions of, 198
Assyria, alliances of Israel with, 108; intrigues of Samaria with, 166; infidelities of Judah with, 167
Astarte, worship of, 193
atonement, 117
authors referred to, lv

Baal, worship of, 143
Babylon, 72, 80, 96, 119, 147: infidelities of Judah with, 167
badger's skin, 104
baldness, 216; a sign of mourning, 49, 334, 335
balm, 197
barber's razor, symbol of, 36
Bashan, 285
bath = tenth of a homer, 340

battering-rams, 29, 156, 187
beasts, definition of term, 56
Beirut, 351
Beltis = Astarte, 193
Benjamin, portion of the tribe of, 359
beryl, 8, 67, 207
Beth-Jeshimoth, 183
Beth-meon, 183
birth, 101
block-gods, xx, 5, 42, 56
blood, 97, 104, 261
Blumenlese of Dukes, quoted, 46
bond, 148
bones, vision of the valley of, 267; explanation of the vision, 269
bosom of the altar, 325
brazen altar, the, 62
breath = principle of life, 268
brier, 209
broken, 43
bulls, winged, in Assyrian temples, 67
burden, 79
burial, 204
buriers, 284
burnt-offerings, liv; details of, 327; description of altar of, 325—7
Buzi, father of Ezekiel, xvii
Byblos, centre of Adonis worship, 58
byssus, the, 104, 192, 197

caldron, 71; allegory of, 174
Calvin quoted, xxix
camels, 200
Canaan, land of, 101
Canneh = Caenae, 199
Cappadocia, 196
captains and rulers, 167, 169
carbuncle, 207
carrion, 34
cedar-tree, Pharaoh compared to a, 222, 223; allegory of, 222, 223
ceremonial, 291
chains, 51

INDEX

Chaldea, alliances of Israel with, 108, 110; duration of the supremacy of, 214, 215, 274, 275
Chaldean robbers, 51
chambers for the priests in the Temple, 315, 316
chambers of imagery, 57
chariots, 285, 323
chastening rod, 152
Chebar, river of, xx, 1, 2, 24
Chemosh, 256
Cherethites, the, 184
cherubim, description of, 65; derivation of word, 69; faces of, 67; vision of, xxix, 65—69
chests, 199
child, allegory of the foundling, 101
child of man, xxv, xlii, 15, 292
children, sacrifice of, 107, 144, 171
Chilmad, 199
Chittim = Cyprus, 192
Cleopatra's needle, 220
cor = homer, 340
cords, an article of commerce, 199
conduits, 224
courts of the Temple, plan of, 299
covenant of peace, 252, 272
Creatures, the four living, 5
crocodile, allegory of the, 211
crown of glory, 104
Cush, situation of, 214
cypresses = fir-trees of Senir, 191

daily offering, directions concerning, 344, 345
Damascus, 351, 352
Dan, tribe of, portion of, 354
Daniel, 96, 203
David, xxxvi, 248, 251, 272
dawn, 46
day of the Lord, 83, 217, 218
Dead Sea, the, 347, 348, 349
Dedan, 184, 196
detestable things, 75
diadem, 157
diamond, 207
dirge, on the downfall of Jerusalem, 45; on the princes of Judah, 134; on the downfall of Tyre, 185, 186, 191; on the fall of Egypt, 231
dissolution of the kingdom, picture of, 48
divination, 83; by arrows, 156
door, 185; of the inner gate, 54, 314
door-posts of the Temple, 314
dough, 336
drink offerings, 145
dry bones, vision of the, xxix; 267
Dukes quoted, 46
dumbness, 27, 28
dyed attire, 167

eagle, riddle of the great, 119
earthquakes, accompany the revelation of Jehovah, 280
ebony, 196
ecclesiastical year, 292
Eden, 227
Edessa, 198
Edom, prophecy of Ezekiel against, 183; relations to Israel, 183; threat against, 254
Egypt, alliances of Israel with, 108; idolatry of, 109; infidelities of Judah with, 167; prophecy against, 210; dirge on the fall of, 231
Elam, 234
elders, xx, xxii—iii, 57, 63, 92; of Judah, 53; idolatry of, 55
Elisha, isles of, 192
emerald, 207
En-gedi, 347 = Ain Jidy, 349
engines of war, 187
En-eglaim, 347, 349
ephah, 339
Ephraim, portion of the tribe of, 354
Ethiopia, 274
evil counsel, 71
Ewald quoted, xxvii
eyes, practice of painting, 171
Ezekiel, general characteristics of Book of, ix; themes of, ix; divisions of, ix—xvi; descent of, xvii; supposed descendant of Jeremiah, xvii; date of prophecies of, xvii; style of, xxv; tradition of the death of, xxx; his conception of Jehovah, xxxi—ii; compared with Jeremiah, xliv; attitude towards Israel, xliv; points of contact with ritual Law, liii; meaning of the name, 3; trance of, 53; prophecies against the nations, 178, 179; against Moab, 182; against Edom, 183; against Ammon, 158, 180; prophecy against Tyre, 185; parallelisms between S. Paul and, 266

false prophets, xxi, 85
fear, 9
feasts, of passover, 340; of weeks, or pentecost, 340; of tabernacles, 340
feet, of the four living creatures, 5
fire, 4, 37, 53, 208, 219; passing through the, 108, 143
firmament, the, 10, 65
first-fruits, 148, 356
food, unclean, 34
foolish prophets, 85
forts, 29, 187, 246
foundling-child, allegory of, 101
foxes, 86
free-will offering, directions concerning, 344
full end, a, 74

Gabbatha = raised pavement, 309
Gad, portion of the tribe of, 358
gallery in the Temple, 316, 317
Gammadims, the, 194

INDEX. 365

gate, of the altar, 55; the upper, 61
gates of the Temple, named after the twelve tribes, 360
Gebal, centre of Adonis worship, 58, 193
Geiger, quoted, xxx
gerah, 339
girdles, 167
glory of the Lord, 21, 55, 60, 64, 68, 322, 330; glory, crown of, 104
God, meaning of word, xxxix; visions of, xxxi, 1, 3, 12—14, 54, 59
Gog, prince of Rosh, 274; invasion and destruction of, 275; armies of, 277; burial-place of, 283
Guadalquiver, the, 195
guard-rooms of the Temple, 294, 300

Hamath, 351
Hamonah, city of, 285
Hamon-Gog, valley of, 284, 285
Hananiah ben Hezekiah, xxxi
handstaves, 283
Hauran, 352
Hazar-enan, 350, 351
healing stream, 347
heart = nature, 263
hearth of God, 325
heathen, 15, 51, 218, 258; permitted in the Temple, 331
Helbon, wine of, 197; = Chalbûn, 197
Heliopolis, 220
Hermon, meaning of name, 192
Hethlon, 351
Hezekiah, reforms of, 333
high places, 41, 108, 112, 118, 127, 257
hin, 33
Hittites, the, 102
Hitzig quoted, 21
hole, 56
Holy of holies, measurements of, 306
Holy land, boundaries of the new, 350, 351
holy, meaning of word, xxxix; sense in which used, 273, 279
holy place, measurements of, 305, 306
homer, 339
honey, 197
hooks, 212, 303
horn, the symbol of power, 216
horses, 196
house, 63; = Temple buildings, 304, 309
human sacrifices, 107, 144, 171

idolatry, of the elders, 55; of Israel, 105, 107; of Egypt, 109
idols, xxv, 42, 56, 75, 92, 219, 332
imagery, chambers of, 57
images, of men, 107
inner-gate, of the Temple, 297, 342
interior of the Temple, description of, 312—314
isles, 189; of Elishah, 192
Israel, sin of, xlviii; necessity for destruction of, 76; idolatry of, 105, 108, 109, 110
Issachar, portion of the tribe of, 358
Ithobal, ii, 202
ivory, 196

Jaazaniah, son of Shaphan, leader of the elders, 57
Jacob, 272
Javan = Ionia, 195
jealousy, 40, 54, 169, 258
Jehoahaz, xviii; captivity of, 134, 135
Jehoiachin, xviii, xxii, 2; captivity of, 135
Jehovah, 16; Ezekiel's conception of, xxxi—ii, 55; attributes of, xxxiii; worship of, in Egypt, 139; life-giving spirit of, 269; earthquakes accompany the presence of, 280; voice of, 322; His entry into the Temple, 322, 323
Jehu, 256
Jeremiah, supposed descent of Ezekiel from, xvii; influence of, on character of Ezekiel, xix; compared with Ezekiel, xliv
Jerome, quoted, 7, 11, 107
Jerusalem, capture of, xx; attitude of Ezekiel toward, xlv, xlvi; symbolical siege of, 29; judgment on, 40; vision of fall of, 52; compared to the vine, 100; further predictions regarding fall of, 137
Jewish history, its influence on Ezekiel's character, xviii
Job, 96
Joseph, tribe of, portion of, 351
Josephus quoted, xvii, xxx
Josiah, xviii
jubilee year, 345
Judah, dirge on the princes of, 134; portion of the tribe of, 359

Kedar, people of, 198; flocks of, 198
keepers of the gate, 331
kerchiefs, 90
Kinah, or Lament, xxv
kindred, 73
kings, burial of, in the Temple, 324
Kirjathaim = El Kureyat, 183
kitchens in the temple for the priests and people, 346, 347
Klostermann, quoted, xxviii
knees, weakness of, 49
Kuenen, quoted, xxxvii

Lament, or *Kinah*, xxv
lands, allotted to the priests, 336
Law, the ritual, points of contact between Ezekiel and, liii
Lebanon, 120, 226, 227; cedars of, 223, 224
Levites, 329, 347; ordinances concerning, 331; portion of the, 357
lions, allegory of the, 134, 135

INDEX.

Lord, xxxii
Lud, site of, 193
Luzzatto quoted, 21

Magog, country of, 275
Manasseh, 333; portion of the tribe of, 354
marriages of the priests, directions as to, 334
Mattaniah, son of Josiah, 120
Matthes, J. C., quoted, xxxvi
meal-offering, 320; directions concerning, 344
measurements, of the Temple, 295, 296
mensures = appearance, 313, 320, 324
Memphis, situation of, 220
men of the east, 159
mercenaries of Tyre, 193; of Egypt, 218
merchandise, 196
Meshech, 235
Messiah, the, prophecy concerning, 158, 252
Messianic kingdom, promise of, 123, 157
Migdol, 213, 219; situation of, 213
Milton quoted, 58
ministers = Levites, 347
Minnith, 197
Moab, prophecy of Ezekiel against, 182
Molech, worship of, 143
money-weight, table of, 339
morning, 46
mount, 29
Mount of Olives, 4, 70, 76
Mount Seir, 182
mountain of God, 206
mountains of Israel, 246, 257, 258, 278
mourning, 49; baldness a sign of, 334, 335

Naphtali, portion of the tribe of, 354
nations, 15, 19, 218, 225; prophecies of Ezekiel against the, 178, 179
Nebuchadnezzar, xx, 32, 80, 119, 156, 185; destroyer of Tyre, 186, 187; compared to an eagle, 121, 190, 203, 212, 216, 222
Nebuchadrezzar = Nebuchadnezzar, 186
Nile, the, 210, 212; its importance to Egypt, 212
Noah, 96
No = Thebes, 220
Noph = Memphis, 220
nose, 59

oars, 192
oblations, 148, 290, 335, 353, 356
offerings, liv, 145, 148, 304; details of burnt, 327, 328; trespass, 335; general directions as to, 340, 341; for the Sabbath and new moon, 342, 343; free will, directions, concerning, 344
Oholah, 164
Oholibah, 164
ointment, 197

Olives, mount of, 4, 70, 76
On = Heliopolis, 220
onyx, 207
ordinances, of the Temple, 329
Ovid, quoted, 106

painting the eyes, practice of, 171
pannag, 197
Passover, feast of, 340
Pathros = Upper Egypt, 214, 220
Paul, S., parallelisms between Ezekiel and, 266
peace, 88; covenant of, 252, 272
peace-offerings, liv, 145, 304
Pelatiah, 71, 73
peoples, 15, 19, 147, 181, 201, 225, 259
Pharaoh-Hophra, 221
Pharaoh-Necho, 135
Pharaoh, prophecy against, 210; allegory of the crocodile representing, 211, 212; likened to a cedar tree, 222
Phi-beseth, site of, 220
Philistines, 109, 112; prophecy against, 184
Phoenix, the, 208
Phrygia, 196
phylacteries, 90
plan, of the Temple, 294; of the Temple Courts, 299
planks, 315
porch, of the Temple, 298
portions, 338; of the tribes, 354, 359
precious stones, 206, 207
priests, chambers for, in the Temple, 315, 316; ordinances concerning, 329—336; garments of, 333; directions as to marriage, 334; duties towards the people, 334; contact with the dead, 334; maintenance of, 335; purification of, 335; land allotted to, 336; kitchens in the Temple for, 346, 347
prince, domain of, 337, 358
prison-houses, xx
prophecy, against Israel's idolatry, 40; warning against despising, 82; against Ammon, 158; of Israel's restoration, 238
prophetesses, 89; chastisements of, 91
prophets, date of canonising, xxxi; foolish, 85

Raamah, 198
Rabbah, site of, 181
Rabbath-Ammon, 155
rainbow, the, 12
raised pavement of the Temple, 309
ravines, 41
razor, symbol of, 36
rebellious house, xxv, xliv, 15
reed = 6 cubits, 321, 337
reed, Egypt compared to a, 213
reprover, 26
resurrection from the dead, 267
Reuben, portion of the tribe of, 354

Reuss, quoted, xvii, xxiii
Rhodians, the, 195, 196
Riblah, wilderness of, 44, 351
rich apparel, 199
riddle of the great eagle, 119; interpretation of, 122
righteousness, 127, 173
ritual Law, points of contact between Ezekiel and, liii
robber, 128; Chaldean, 51
Robertson-Smith, quoted, 58, 324
rod, blossoming, 47; passing under the, 147; chastening, 152
Rosh, situation of, 276
rulers, 167, 169
rusted caldron, allegory of the, 174

Sabbath, the, 141; a symbol of religion, 141
Sabeans = drunkards, 172
sacrifice, of children, 107, 144, 171; to Jehovah, 285
sacrifices, method and details of, 327
sacrificial appointments in the Temple, 302, 303
sails, 192
Saida = Sidon, 209
sales, nature of, 48
Samaria, fall of, 32; abominations of, 117; intrigues with Assyria, 166
sanctification, 273
sanctuary, 74, 151, 208, 272, 322, 337
sapphire, 207
sapphire throne, the, 11, 12
sardius, 207
Saul, xxxvi
Scythians, 280
searchers, 284
Seinecke quoted, xxx
Seir, mount, 182, 254
Senir, fir-trees of, 191
settle, of the altar, 326, 341
seven days, 22
Sheba, merchants of, 198
sheep, 248; sacrificial, 266
shekel, 339
Shemaiah, 88
Sheol = place of the dead, 226, 236; explanation of the name, 231, 232
shepherds, 248
shepherd and flock, allegory of, 248, 249
ships of Tarshish, 200
side-chambers of the Temple, 308
Sidon, prophecy against, 208
sign, 78
silver, 162, 195
Simeon, portion of the tribe of, 359
sin-offerings, 328
Sin = Pelusium, 220
Sion, hill of, 292
Sodom, abominations of, 117
sour grapes, 124, 125
spirit, 7, 9, 86; = ruling principle, 263

Stade quoted, 288
staff of bread, 34, 96
staff = sceptre, 270
statutes of life, lii
statutes and judgments, 140, 143, 264
stibium, 171
stiff-necked, 16
stream flowing from the Temple, 347
stumbling-block of iniquity, xxv, 23, 24, 50, 92, 154
suburbs, 200; of the Temple, 337, 358
sun-worshippers, 58, 59
Suweimeh = Beth-Jeshimoth, 183
sweat, regarded as uncleanness, 333
sweet savour, 44, 107, 145, 148
sword, of the Lord, 150, 151; of Babylon, 152
Syene, tower of, 213, 219
symbol, of siege of Jerusalem, 28; of iniquity of Israel, 30, 31; of scarcity during siege, 32; of the fate of the people, 36, 37; of the beard and razor, 36; of the judgments of God, 61
symbolical actions, characteristics of Book, xxv; representing siege of Jerusalem, 28
symbolical figures, characteristics of Book, xxv
Syria, connection with Israel, 116

tabernacles, feast of, 340
table of money-weight, 339
Tamar, situation of, 353
Tammuz, identical with Adonis, 58
Tarshish, situation of, 195; ships of, 200
Tehaphnehes, site of, 221
Tel-abib, xx, 14, 20; meaning of name, 21
Teman; 184
Temple, the, Ezekiel's reconstruction of, liii; sun-worshippers in, 59; particulars of worship in, 290; description of the new, 291; threshold of, 293, 313; plan of, 294; measurements of, 295, 296; inner gate of, 297; porch of, 298; arches of, 298; plan of the courts of, 299; guardrooms of, 294, 300; outer court of, 298; inner court of, 301; sacrificial appointments of, 302, 303; measurements of holy place and holy of holies, 305, 306; annexe of, 307; side-chambers of, 308; raised pavement of, 309; description of interior of, 312—314; door-posts of, 314; chambers for the priests in, 315, 316; walk in front of, 319; entry of Jehovah into, 322, 323; burial of kings in, 324; kitchens in, 346, 347; stream flowing from, 347; gates of, named after the tribes, 360
teraphim, 156
Thebes, 220
Theophany, the, 3; general description of, 12, 13, 14
thorn, 209

thorns and briars, 16
threshold, of the Temple, 293, 313, 343
throne, the sapphire, 11, 12
thunder, the voice of Jehovah, 66
Tiglath-Pileser, 193
tire, the, 176
Togarmah=Armenia, 195
topaz, 207
trance of Ezekiel, 53
trespass offering, 335
tribes, portions of, 351, 354—361
Tubal, 195, 235
turbans, 167
Tyre, xxvi; prophecy against, 185; dirge on downfall of, 185, 186, 191; market of, 194; allegory of the fall of, 200; allegory of the prince of Tyre, 204

uncircumcised, 233
unclean food, 34
upper gate, the, 61
Urijah, xix
usury, 127
Uzal, 198

valley, of Abarim, 283; of Hamon-Gog, 284, 285
vetches, 33
vine-tree, the, 98, 99; Jerusalem compared to, 100
vision of the dry bones, xxix, 267, 269; of the Cherubim, xxix, 65—69; of the new Temple, xxix, 290—322; of God, 3; general description of, 12—14; of the destruction of Jerusalem, 52; of the valley of dry bones, 267; of God, xxxi. 1, 3, 12—14, 54, 59, 292
visions, special characteristics of Book of Ezekiel, xxv
visitations, 61
voice of Jehovah, 323

walk, before the Temple, 319
wall, 78, 88, 247; of the Temple, 292, 293
wastes, 246, 257
watchman, xx, xxiv, 15, 23, 241
water, 120; sprinkling with, 263
weeks, feast of, 340
Wetzstein quoted, 33
wheat flour, 105
wheels, the four, 8, 66, 67
wine of Helbon, 197
winged bulls in Assyrian temples, 67
wood and stone, images of, 146, 147
wool of Zachar, 197
wrath, 48

year, of liberty, 345; of Jubilee, 345; ecclesiastical, 292
Yemen, Uzal capital of, 198

Zachar, wool of, 197
Zadok, family of, xvii, 3, 305, 330, 332
Zebulun, portion of the tribe of, 358
Zedad, 351
Zedekiah, xxvii, 77, 80, 119, 122
Ziphran, 351
Zunz quoted, xxx

CAMBRIDGE UNIVERSITY PRESS.

THE PITT PRESS SERIES.

** *Many of the books in this list can be had in two volumes, Text and Notes separately.*

I. GREEK.

Aristophanes. Aves—Plutus—Ranæ. By W. C. GREEN, M.A., late Assistant Master at Rugby School. 3s. 6d. each.
Aristotle. Outlines of the Philosophy of. By EDWIN WALLACE, M.A., LL.D. Third Edition, Enlarged. 4s. 6d.
Euripides. Heracleidae. By E. A. BECK, M.A. 3s. 6d.
——— **Hercules Furens.** By A. GRAY, M.A., and J. T. HUTCHINSON, M.A. New Edit. 2s.
——— **Hippolytus.** By W. S. HADLEY, M.A. 2s.
——— **Iphigeneia in Aulis.** By C. E. S. HEADLAM, M.A. 2s. 6d.
Herodotus, Book V. By E. S. SHUCKBURGH, M.A. 3s.
——— **Book VI.** By the same Editor. 4s.
——— **Books VIII., IX.** By the same Editor. 4s. each.
——— **Book VIII. Ch. 1—90. Book IX. Ch. 1—89.** By the same Editor. 3s. 6d. each.
Homer. Odyssey, Books IX., X. By G. M. EDWARDS, M.A. 2s. 6d. each. **Book XXI.** By the same Editor. 2s.
——— **Iliad. Book VI.** By the same Editor. 2s.
——— ——— **Book XXII.** By the same Editor. 2s.
——— ——— **Book XXIII.** By the same Editor. 2s.
Lucian. Somnium Charon Piscator et De Luctu. By W. E. HEITLAND, M.A., Fellow of St John's College, Cambridge. 3s. 6d.
——— **Menippus and Timon.** By E. C. MACKIE, B.A. 3s. 6d.
Platonis Apologia Socratis. By J. ADAM, M.A. 3s. 6d.
——— **Crito.** By the same Editor. 2s. 6d.
——— **Euthyphro.** By the same Editor. 2s. 6d.
Plutarch. Lives of the Gracchi. By Rev. H. A. HOLDEN, M.A., LL.D. 6s.
——— **Life of Nicias.** By the same Editor. 5s.
——— **Life of Sulla.** By the same Editor. 6s.
——— **Life of Timoleon.** By the same Editor. 6s.
Sophocles. Oedipus Tyrannus. School Edition. By R. C. JEBB, Litt.D., LL.D. 4s. 6d.
Thucydides. Book VII. By H. A. HOLDEN, M.A., LL.D. 5s.
Xenophon. Agesilaus. By H. HAILSTONE, M.A. 2s. 6d.
——— **Anabasis.** By A. PRETOR, M.A. Two vols. 7s. 6d.
——— **Books I. III. IV. and V.** By the same. 2s. each.
——— **Books II. VI. and VII.** By the same. 2s. 6d. each.
Xenophon. Cyropaedeia. Books I. II. By Rev. H. A. HOLDEN, M.A., LL.D. 2 vols. 6s.
——— ——— **Books III. IV. and V.** By the same Editor. 5s.
——— ——— **Books VI. VII. VIII.** By the same Editor. 5s.

London: Cambridge Warehouse, Ave Maria Lane.
20/2/92

II. LATIN.

Beda's Ecclesiastical History, Books III., IV. By J. E. B.
MAYOR, M.A., and J. R. LUMBY, D.D. Revised Edition. 7s. 6d.

———— **Books I. II.** [*In the Press.*

Caesar. De Bello Gallico, Comment. I. By A. G. PESKETT,
M.A., Fellow of Magdalene College, Cambridge. 1s. 6d. COMMENT. II.
III. 2s. COMMENT. I. II. III. 3s. COMMENT. IV. and V. 1s. 6d. COMMENT.
VII. 2s. COMMENT. VI. and COMMENT. VIII. 1s. 6d. each.

———— **De Bello Civili, Comment. I.** By the same Editor. 3s.

Cicero. De Amicitia.—De Senectute. By J. S. REID, Litt.D.,
Fellow of Gonville and Caius College. 3s. 6d. each.

———— **In Gaium Verrem Actio Prima.** By H. COWIE,
M.A. 1s. 6d.

———— **In Q. Caecilium Divinatio et in C. Verrem Actio.**
By W. E. HEITLAND, M.A., and H. COWIE, M.A. 3s.

———— **Philippica Secunda.** By A. G. PESKETT, M.A. 3s. 6d.

———— **Oratio pro Archia Poeta.** By J. S. REID, Litt.D. 2s.

———— **Pro L. Cornelio Balbo Oratio.** By the same. 1s. 6d.

———— **Oratio pro Tito Annio Milone.** By JOHN SMYTH
PURTON, B.D. 2s. 6d.

———— **Oratio pro L. Murena.** By W. E. HEITLAND, M.A. 3s.

———— **Pro Cn. Plancio Oratio,** by H. A. HOLDEN, LL.D. 4s. 6d.

———— **Pro P. Cornelio Sulla.** By J. S. REID, Litt.D. 3s. 6d.

———— **Somnium Scipionis.** By W. D. PEARMAN, M.A. 2s.

Horace. Epistles, Book I. By E. S. SHUCKBURGH, M.A.,
late Fellow of Emmanuel College. 2s. 6d.

Livy. Book IV. By H. M. STEPHENSON, M.A. 2s. 6d.

———— **Book V.** By L. WHIBLEY, M.A. 2s. 6d.

———— **Book IX.** By H. M. STEPHENSON, M.A. [*Nearly ready.*

———— **Book XXI.** By M. S. DIMSDALE, M.A. 2s. 6d.

———— **Book XXII.** By the same Editor. 2s. 6d.

———— **Book XXVII.** By Rev. H. M. STEPHENSON, M.A. 2s. 6d.

Lucan. Pharsaliae Liber Primus. By W. E. HEITLAND,
M.A., and C. E. HASKINS, M.A. 1s. 6d.

Lucretius, Book V. By J. D. DUFF, M.A. 2s.

Ovidii Nasonis Fastorum Liber VI. By A. SIDGWICK, M.A.,
Tutor of Corpus Christi College, Oxford. 1s. 6d.

Ovidii Nasonis Metamorphoseon Liber I. By L. D. DOWDALL,
M.A. [*In the Press.*

Quintus Curtius. A Portion of the History (Alexander in India).
By W. E. HEITLAND, M.A., and T. E. RAVEN, B.A. With Two Maps. 3s. 6d.

Vergili Maronis Aeneidos Libri I.—XII. By A. SIDGWICK,
M.A. 1s. 6d. each.

———— **Bucolica.** By the same Editor. 1s. 6d.

———— **Georgicon Libri I. II.** By the same Editor. 2s.

———— ———— **Libri III. IV.** By the same Editor. 2s.

———— **The Complete Works.** By the same Editor. Two vols.
Vol. I. containing the Introduction and Text. 3s. 6d. Vol. II. The Notes. 4s. 6d.

London: Cambridge Warehouse, Ave Maria Lane.

III. FRENCH.

Corneille. La Suite du Menteur. A Comedy in Five Acts. By the late G. MASSON, B.A. 2s.

—— **Polyeucte.** By E. G. W. BRAUNHOLTZ, M.A. [*In the Press.*

De Bonnechose. Lazare Hoche. By C. COLBECK, M.A. Revised Edition. Four Maps. 2s.

D'Harleville. Le Vieux Célibataire. By G. MASSON, B.A. 2s.

De Lamartine. Jeanne D'Arc. By Rev. A. C. CLAPIN, M.A. New edition revised, by A. R. ROPES, M.A. 1s. 6d.

De Vigny. La Canne de Jonc. By H. W. EVE, M.A. 1s. 6d.

Erckmann-Chatrian. La Guerre. By Rev. A. C. CLAPIN, M.A. 3s.

La Baronne de Staël-Holstein. Le Directoire. (Considérations sur la Révolution Française. Troisième et quatrième parties.) Revised and enlarged. By G. MASSON, B.A., and G. W. PROTHERO, M.A. 2s.

—— —— **Dix Années d'Exil. Livre II. Chapitres 1—8.** By the same Editors. New Edition, enlarged. 2s.

Lemercier. Fredegonde et Brunehaut. A Tragedy in Five Acts. By GUSTAVE MASSON, B.A. 2s.

Molière. Le Bourgeois Gentilhomme, Comédie-Ballet en Cinq Actes. (1670.) By Rev. A. C. CLAPIN, M.A. Revised Edition. 1s. 6d.

—— **L'École des Femmes.** By G. SAINTSBURY, M.A. 2s. 6d.

—— **Les Précieuses Ridicules.** By E. G. W. BRAUNHOLTZ, M.A., Ph.D. 2s. **Abridged Edition.** 1s.

Piron. La Métromanie. A Comedy. By G. MASSON, B.A. 2s.

Racine. Les Plaideurs. By E. G. W. BRAUNHOLTZ, M.A. 2s.

—— —— **Abridged Edition.** 1s.

Sainte-Beuve. M. Daru (Causeries du Lundi, Vol. IX.). By G. MASSON, B.A. 2s.

Saintine. Picciola. By Rev. A. C. CLAPIN, M.A. 2s.

Scribe and Legouvé. Bataille de Dames. By Rev. H. A. BULL, M.A. 2s.

Scribe. Le Verre d'Eau. By C. COLBECK, M.A. 2s.

Sédaine. Le Philosophe sans le savoir. By Rev. H. A. BULL, M.A. 2s.

Thierry. Lettres sur l'histoire de France (XIII.—XXIV.). By G. MASSON, B.A., and G. W. PROTHERO, M.A. 2s. 6d.

—— **Récits des Temps Mérovingiens I.—III.** By GUSTAVE MASSON, B.A. Univ. Gallic., and A. R. ROPES, M.A. With Map. 3s.

Villemain. Lascaris ou Les Grecs du XVe Siècle, Nouvelle Historique. By G. MASSON, B.A. 2s.

Voltaire. Histoire du Siècle de Louis XIV. Chaps. I.—XIII. By G. MASSON, B.A., and G. W. PROTHERO, M.A. 2s. 6d. PART II. CHAPS. XIV.—XXIV. 2s. 6d. PART III. CHAPS. XXV. to end. 2s. 6d.

Xavier de Maistre. La Jeune Sibérienne. Le Lépreux de la Cité D'Aoste. By G. MASSON, B.A. 1s. 6d.

London: Cambridge Warehouse, Ave Maria Lane.

IV. GERMAN.

Ballads on German History. By W. WAGNER, Ph.D. 2s.
Benedix. Doctor Wespe. Lustspiel in fünf Aufzügen. By KARL HERMANN BREUL, M.A., Ph.D. 3s.
Freytag. Der Staat Friedrichs des Grossen. By WILHELM WAGNER, Ph.D. 2s.
German Dactylic Poetry. By WILHELM WAGNER, Ph.D. 3s.
Goethe's Knabenjahre. (1749—1761.) By W. WAGNER, Ph.D. New edition revised and enlarged, by J. W. CARTMELL, M.A. 2s.
—— **Hermann und Dorothea.** By WILHELM WAGNER, Ph.D. New edition revised, by J. W. CARTMELL, M.A. 3s. 6d.
Gutzkow. Zopf und Schwert. Lustspiel in fünf Aufzügen. By H. J. WOLSTENHOLME, B.A. (Lond.). 3s. 6d.
Hauff. Das Bild des Kaisers. By KARL HERMANN BREUL, M.A., Ph.D., University Lecturer in German. 3s.
—— **Das Wirthshaus im Spessart.** By A. SCHLOTTMANN, Ph.D. 3s. 6d.
—— **Die Karavane.** By A. SCHLOTTMANN, Ph.D. 3s.
Immermann. Der Oberhof. A Tale of Westphalian Life, by WILHELM WAGNER, Ph.D. 3s.
Kohlrausch. Das Jahr 1813. By WILHELM WAGNER, Ph.D. 2s.
Lessing and Gellert. Selected Fables. By KARL HERMANN BREUL, M.A., Ph.D. 3s.
Mendelssohn's Letters. Selections from. By J. SIME, M.A. 3s.
Raumer. Der erste Kreuzzug (1095—1099). By WILHELM WAGNER, Ph.D. 2s.
Riehl. Culturgeschichtliche Novellen. By H. J. WOLSTENHOLME, B.A. (Lond.). 3s. 6d.
Schiller. Wilhelm Tell. By KARL HERMANN BREUL, M.A., Ph.D. 2s. 6d. **Abridged Edition.** 1s. 6d.
—— **Geschichte des Dreissigjährigen Kriegs.** By the same Editor. [*Nearly ready.*
Uhland. Ernst, Herzog von Schwaben. By H. J. WOLSTENHOLME, B.A. 3s. 6d.

V. ENGLISH.

Ancient Philosophy from Thales to Cicero, A Sketch of. By JOSEPH B. MAYOR, M.A. 3s. 6d.
An Apologie for Poetrie by Sir PHILIP SIDNEY. By E. S. SHUCKBURGH, M.A. The Text is a revision of that of the first edition of 1595. 3s.
Bacon's History of the Reign of King Henry VII. By the Rev. Professor LUMBY, D.D. 3s.
Cowley's Essays. By the Rev. Professor LUMBY, D.D. 4s.
Discourse of the Commonwealf of thys Realme of Englande. First printed in 1581, and commonly attributed to W. S. Edited from the MSS. by ELIZABETH LAMOND. [*In the Press.*
Milton's Comus and Arcades. By A. W. VERITY, M.A., sometime Scholar of Trinity College. 3s.
Milton's Ode on the Morning of Christ's Nativity, L'Allegro, Il Penseroso and Lycidas. By the same Editor. 2s. 6d.
Milton's Samson Agonistes. By the same Editor. 2s. 6d.
Milton's Paradise Lost. Books XI. XII. By the same Editor. [*In the Press.*

London: Cambridge Warehouse, Ave Maria Lane.

More's History of King Richard III. By J. RAWSON LUMBY, D.D. 3s. 6d.
More's Utopia. By Rev. Prof. LUMBY, D.D. 3s. 6d.
The Two Noble Kinsmen. By the Rev. Professor SKEAT, Litt.D. 3s. 6d.

VI. EDUCATIONAL SCIENCE.

Comenius, John Amos, Bishop of the Moravians. His Life and Educational Works, by S. S. LAURIE, A.M., F.R.S.E. 3s. 6d.
Education, Three Lectures on the Practice of. I. On Marking, by H. W. EVE, M.A. II. On Stimulus, by A. SIDGWICK, M.A. III. On the Teaching of Latin Verse Composition, by E. A. ABBOTT, D.D. 2s.
Stimulus. A Lecture delivered for the Teachers' Training Syndicate, May, 1882, by A. SIDGWICK, M.A. 1s.
Locke on Education. By the Rev. R. H. QUICK, M.A. 3s. 6d.
Milton's Tractate on Education. A facsimile reprint from the Edition of 1673. By O. BROWNING, M.A. 2s.
Modern Languages, Lectures on the Teaching of. By C. COLBECK, M.A. 2s.
Teacher, General Aims of the, and Form Management. Two Lectures delivered in the University of Cambridge in the Lent Term, 1883, by F. W. FARRAR, D.D., and R. B. POOLE, B.D. 1s. 6d.
Teaching, Theory and Practice of. By the Rev. E. THRING, M.A., late Head Master of Uppingham School. New Edition. 4s. 6d.

British India, a Short History of. By E. S. CARLOS, M.A., late Head Master of Exeter Grammar School. 1s.
Geography, Elementary Commercial. A Sketch of the Commodities and the Countries of the World. By H. R. MILL, D.Sc., F.R.S.E. 1s.
Geography, an Atlas of Commercial. (A Companion to the above.) By J. G. BARTHOLOMEW, F.R.G.S. With an Introduction by HUGH ROBERT MILL, D.Sc. 3s.

VII. MATHEMATICS.

Arithmetic for Schools. By C. SMITH, M.A., Master of Sidney Sussex College, Cambridge. 3s. 6d.
Elementary Algebra (with Answers to the Examples). By W. W. ROUSE BALL, M.A. 4s. 6d.
Euclid's Elements of Geometry. Books I. and II. By H. M. TAYLOR, M.A. 1s. 6d. **Books III. and IV.** By the same Editor. 1s. 6d.
———— Books I.—IV., in one Volume. 3s.
Solutions to the Exercises in Euclid, Books I—IV. By W. W. TAYLOR, M.A. [*In the Press.*
Elements of Statics and Dynamics. By S. L. LONEY, M.A. 7s. 6d.
   Part I. Elements of Statics. 4s. 6d.
   Part II. Elements of Dynamics. 3s. 6d.
An Elementary Treatise on Plane Trigonometry for the use of Schools. By E. W. HOBSON, M.A., and C. M. JESSOP, M.A.
[*In the Press.*

Other Volumes are in preparation.

London: Cambridge Warehouse, Ave Maria Lane.

The Cambridge Bible for Schools and Colleges.

GENERAL EDITOR: J. J. S. PEROWNE, D.D.,
BISHOP OF WORCESTER.

"*It is difficult to commend too highly this excellent series.*—Guardian.

"*The modesty of the general title of this series has, we believe, led many to misunderstand its character and underrate its value. The books are well suited for study in the upper forms of our best schools, but not the less are they adapted to the wants of all Bible students who are not specialists. We doubt, indeed, whether any of the numerous popular commentaries recently issued in this country will be found more serviceable for general use.*"—Academy.

Now Ready. Cloth, Extra Fcap. 8vo. With Maps.

Book of Joshua. By Rev. G. F. MACLEAR, D.D. 2s. 6d.
Book of Judges. By Rev. J. J. LIAS, M.A. 3s. 6d.
First Book of Samuel. By Rev. Prof. KIRKPATRICK, B.D. 3s. 6d.
Second Book of Samuel. By the same Editor. 3s. 6d.
First Book of Kings. By Rev. Prof. LUMBY, D.D. 3s. 6d.
Second Book of Kings. By Rev. Prof. LUMBY, D.D. 3s. 6d.
Book of Job. By Rev. A. B. DAVIDSON, D.D. 5s.
Book of Psalms. Book I. By Prof. KIRKPATRICK, B.D. 3s. 6d.
Book of Ecclesiastes. By Very Rev. E. H. PLUMPTRE, D.D. 5s.
Book of Jeremiah. By Rev. A. W. STREANE, B.D. 4s. 6d.
Book of Hosea. By Rev. T. K. CHEYNE, M.A., D.D. 3s.
Books of Obadiah & Jonah. By Archdeacon PEROWNE. 2s. 6d.
Book of Micah. By Rev. T. K. CHEYNE, M.A., D.D. 1s. 6d.
Haggai, Zechariah & Malachi. By Arch. PEROWNE. 3s. 6d.
Book of Malachi. By Archdeacon PEROWNE. 1s.
Gospel according to St Matthew. By Rev. A. CARR, M.A. 2s. 6d.
Gospel according to St Mark. By Rev. G. F. MACLEAR, D.D. 2s. 6d.
Gospel according to St Luke. By Arch. FARRAR, D.D. 4s. 6d.
Gospel according to St John. By Rev. A. PLUMMER, D.D. 4s. 6d.
Acts of the Apostles. By Rev. Prof. LUMBY, D.D. 4s. 6d.
Epistle to the Romans. By Rev. H. C. G. MOULE, M.A. 3s. 6d.
First Corinthians. By Rev. J. J. LIAS, M.A. With Map. 2s.
Second Corinthians. By Rev. J. J. LIAS, M.A. With Map. 2s.

London: Cambridge Warehouse, Ave Maria Lane.

THE CAMBRIDGE UNIVERSITY PRESS. 7

Epistle to the Galatians. By Rev. E. H. PEROWNE, D.D. 1s. 6d.
Epistle to the Ephesians. By Rev. H. C. G. MOULE, M.A. 2s. 6d.
Epistle to the Philippians. By the same Editor. 2s. 6d.
Epistles to the Thessalonians. By Rev. G. G. FINDLAY, B.A. 2s.
Epistle to the Hebrews. By Arch. FARRAR, D.D. 3s. 6d.
General Epistle of St James. By Very Rev. E. H. PLUMPTRE, D.D. 1s. 6d.
Epistles of St Peter and St Jude. By Very Rev. E. H. PLUMPTRE, D.D. 2s. 6d.
Epistles of St John. By Rev. A. PLUMMER, M.A., D.D. 3s. 6d.
Book of Revelation. By Rev. W. H. SIMCOX, M.A. 3s.

Preparing.

Book of Genesis. By the BISHOP OF WORCESTER.
Books of Exodus, Numbers and Deuteronomy. By Rev. C. D. GINSBURG, LL.D.
Books of Ezra and Nehemiah. By Rev. Prof. RYLE, M.A.
Book of Isaiah. By Prof. W. ROBERTSON SMITH, M.A.
Book of Ezekiel. By Rev. A. B. DAVIDSON, D.D.
Epistles to the Colossians and Philemon. By Rev. H. C. G. MOULE, M.A.
Epistles to Timothy & Titus. By Rev. A. E. HUMPHREYS, M.A.

The Smaller Cambridge Bible for Schools.

"*We can cordially recommend this series of text-books.*"—Church Review.

"*The notes elucidate every possible difficulty with scholarly brevity and clearness, and a perfect knowledge of the subject.*"—Saturday Review.

"*Accurate scholarship is obviously a characteristic of their productions, and the work of simplification and condensation appears to have been judiciously and skilfully performed.*"—Guardian.

Now ready. Price 1s. *each Volume, with Map.*

Book of Joshua. By J. S. BLACK, M.A.
First and Second Books of Samuel. By Rev. Prof. KIRKPATRICK, B.D.
First and Second Books of Kings. By Rev. Prof. LUMBY, D.D.
Gospel according to St Matthew. By Rev. A. CARR, M.A.
Gospel according to St Mark. By Rev. G. F. MACLEAR, D.D.
Gospel according to St Luke. By Archdeacon FARRAR, D.D.
Gospel according to St John. By Rev. A. PLUMMER, D.D.
Acts of the Apostles. By Rev. Prof. LUMBY, D.D.

London: Cambridge Warehouse, Ave Maria Lane.

The Cambridge Greek Testament for Schools and Colleges,

with a Revised Text, based on the most recent critical authorities, and English Notes, prepared under the direction of the

GENERAL EDITOR, J. J. S. PEROWNE, D.D.,
BISHOP OF WORCESTER.

Gospel according to St Matthew. By Rev. A. CARR, M.A.
With 4 Maps. 4s. 6d.

Gospel according to St Mark. By Rev. G. F. MACLEAR, D.D.
With 3 Maps. 4s. 6d.

Gospel according to St Luke. By Archdeacon FARRAR.
With 4 Maps. 6s.

Gospel according to St John. By Rev. A. PLUMMER, D.D.
With 4 Maps. 6s.

Acts of the Apostles. By Rev. Professor LUMBY, D.D.
With 4 Maps. 6s.

First Epistle to the Corinthians. By Rev. J. J. LIAS, M.A. 3s.

Second Epistle to the Corinthians. By Rev. J. J. LIAS, M.A.
[*Nearly ready.*]

Epistle to the Hebrews. By Archdeacon FARRAR, D.D. 3s. 6d.

Epistles of St John. By Rev. A. PLUMMER, M.A., D.D. 4s.

London: C. J. CLAY AND SONS,
CAMBRIDGE WAREHOUSE, AVE MARIA LANE.
Glasgow: 263, ARGYLE STREET.
Cambridge: DEIGHTON, BELL AND CO.
Leipzig: F. A. BROCKHAUS.
New York: MACMILLAN AND CO.

THE CAMBRIDGE BIBLE FOR SCHOOLS AND COLLEGES.

GENERAL EDITOR, J. J. S. PEROWNE,
BISHOP OF WORCESTER.

Opinions of the Press.

"*It is difficult to commend too highly this excellent series.*"—Guardian.

"*The modesty of the general title of this series has, we believe, led many to misunderstand its character and underrate its value. The books are well suited for study in the upper forms of our best schools, but not the less are they adapted to the wants of all Bible students who are not specialists. We doubt, indeed, whether any of the numerous popular commentaries recently issued in this country will be found more serviceable for general use.*"—Academy.

"*One of the most popular and useful literary enterprises of the nineteenth century.*"—Baptist Magazine.

"*Of great value. The whole series of comments for schools is highly esteemed by students capable of forming a judgment. The books are scholarly without being pretentious: and information is so given as to be easily understood.*"—Sword and Trowel.

"*The notes possess a rare advantage of being scholarly, and at the same time within the comprehension of the average reader. For the Sunday-School Teacher we do not know of a more valuable work.*"—Sunday-School Chronicle.

The Book of Judges. J. J. LIAS, M.A. "His introduction is clear and concise, full of the information which young students require."—*Baptist Magazine.*

II. Samuel. A. F. KIRKPATRICK, M.A. "Small as this work is in mere dimensions, it is every way the best on its subject and for its purpose that we know of. The opening sections at once prove the thorough competence of the writer for dealing with questions of criticism in an earnest, faithful and devout spirit; and the appendices discuss a few special difficulties with a full knowledge of the data, and a judicial reserve, which contrast most favourably with the superficial dogmatism which has too often made the exegesis of the Old Testament a field for the play of unlimited paradox and the ostentation of personal infallibility. The notes are always clear and suggestive; never trifling or irrelevant; and they everywhere demonstrate the great difference in value between the work of a commentator who is also a Hebraist, and that of one who has to depend for his Hebrew upon secondhand sources."—*Academy.*

I. Kings and Ephesians. "With great heartiness we commend these most valuable little commentaries. We had rather purchase these than nine out of ten of the big blown up expositions. Quality is far better than quantity, and we have it here."—*Sword and Trowel.*

II. Kings. "The Introduction is scholarly and wholly admirable, the notes must be of incalculable value to students."—*Glasgow Herald.*

"It would be difficult to find a commentary better suited for general use."—*Academy.*

The Book of Job. "Able and scholarly as the Introduction is, it is far surpassed by the detailed exegesis of the book. In this Dr DAVIDSON's strength is at its greatest. His linguistic knowledge, his artistic habit, his scientific insight, and his literary power have full scope when he comes to exegesis...."—*The Spectator.*

"In the course of a long introduction, Dr DAVIDSON has presented us with a very able and very interesting criticism of this wonderful book. Its contents, the nature of its composition, its idea and purpose, its integrity, and its age are all exhaustively treated of....We have not space to examine fully the text and notes before us, but we can, and do heartily, recommend the book, not only for the upper forms in schools, but to Bible students and teachers generally. As we wrote of a previous volume in the same series, this one leaves nothing to be desired. The notes are full and suggestive, without being too long, and, in itself, the introduction forms a valuable addition to modern Bible literature."—*The Educational Times.*

"Already we have frequently called attention to this exceedingly valuable work as its volumes have successively appeared. But we have never done so with greater pleasure, very seldom with so great pleasure, as we now refer to the last published volume, that on the **Book of Job**, by Dr DAVIDSON, of Edinburgh....We cordially commend the volume to all our readers. The least instructed will understand and enjoy it; and mature scholars will learn from it."—*Methodist Recorder.*

Psalms. Book I. "His commentary upon the books of Samuel was good, but this is incomparably better, shewing traces of much more work and of greater independence of scholarship and judgment....As a whole it is admirable, and we are hardly going too far in saying that it is one of the very ablest of all the volumes that have yet appeared in the 'Cambridge Bible for Schools'."—*Record.*

"Another volume of this excellent Bible, in which the student may rely on meeting with the latest scholarship. The introduction is admirable. We know of nothing in so concise a form better adapted for Sunday-School Teachers."—*Sunday-School Chronicle.*

"It is full of instruction and interest, bringing within easy reach of the English reader the results of the latest scholarship bearing upon the study of this ever new book of the Bible. The Introduction of eighty pages is a repertory of information, not drily but interestingly given."—*Methodist Recorder.*

"For a masterly summary of all that is known and much that is hazarded about the history and authorship of this book of religious lyrics we can point to that with which Mr KIRKPATRICK prefaces his new volume. From a perusal of this summary the student will be unimpressionable indeed if he rise not convinced of the vitality imparted to the Psalter by a systematic study of its literary character and historical allusions....In conclusion, we may say that for a work which is handy, and withal complete, we know none better than this volume; and we await with considerable interest the next instalment."—*Education.*

"It seems in every way a most valuable little book, containing a mass of information, well-assorted, and well-digested, and will be useful not only to students preparing for examinations, but to many who want a handy volume of explanation to much that is difficult in the Psalter. ......We owe a great debt of gratitude to Professor Kirkpatrick for his scholarly and interesting volume."—*Church Times.*

"In this volume thoughtful exegesis founded on nice critical scholarship and due regard for the opinions of various writers, combine, under the influence of a devout spirit, to render this commentary a source of much valuable assistance. The notes are 'though deep yet clear,' for they seem to put in a concentrated form the very pith and marrow of all the best that has been hitherto said on the subject, with striking freedom from anything like pressure of personal views. Throughout the work care and pains are as conspicuous as scholarship."—*Literary Churchman.*

Job—Hosea. "It is difficult to commend too highly this excellent series, the volumes of which are now becoming numerous. The two books before us, small as they are in size, comprise almost everything that the young student can reasonably expect to find in the way of helps towards such general knowledge of their subjects as may be gained without an attempt to grapple with the Hebrew; and even the learned scholar can hardly read without interest and benefit the very able introductory matter which both these commentators have prefixed to their volumes. It is not too much to say that these works have brought within the reach of the ordinary reader resources which were until lately quite unknown for understanding some of the most difficult and obscure portions of Old Testament literature."—*Guardian.*

Ecclesiastes; or, the Preacher.—"Of the Notes, it is sufficient to say that they are in every respect worthy of Dr PLUMPTRE's high reputation as a scholar and a critic, being at once learned, sensible, and practical....Commentaries are seldom attractive reading. This little volume is a notable exception."—*The Scotsman.*

Jeremiah, by A. W. STREANE. "The arrangement of the book is well treated on pp. xxx., 396, and the question of Baruch's relations with its composition on pp. xxvii., xxxiv., 317. The illustrations from English literature, history, monuments, works on botany, topography, etc., are good and plentiful, as indeed they are in other volumes of this series."—*Church Quarterly Review.*

Malachi. "Archdeacon Perowne has already edited Jonah and Zechariah for this series. Malachi presents comparatively few difficulties and the Editor's treatment leaves nothing to be desired. His introduction is clear and scholarly and his commentary sufficient. We may instance the notes on ii. 15 and iv. 2 as examples of careful arrangement, clear exposition and graceful expression."—*Academy.*

"**The Gospel according to St Matthew**, by the Rev. A. CARR. The introduction is able, scholarly, and eminently practical, as it bears on the authorship and contents of the Gospel, and the original form in which it is supposed to have been written. It is well illustrated by two excellent maps of the Holy Land and of the Sea of Galilee."—*English Churchman.*

"**St Mark**, with Notes by the Rev. G. F. MACLEAR, D.D. Into this small volume Dr Maclear, besides a clear and able Introduction to the Gospel, and the text of St Mark, has compressed many hundreds of valuable and helpful notes. In short, he has given us a capital manual of the kind required—containing all that is needed to illustrate the text, i.e. all that can be drawn from the history, geography, customs, and manners of the time. But as a handbook, giving in a clear and succinct form the information which a lad requires in order to stand an examination in the Gospel, it is admirable......I can very heartily commend it, not only to the senior boys and girls in our High Schools, but also to Sunday-school teachers, who may get from it the very kind of knowledge they often find it hardest to get."—*Expositor.*

"With the help of a book like this, an intelligent teacher may make 'Divinity' as interesting a lesson as any in the school course. The notes are of a kind that will be, for the most part, intelligible to boys of the lower forms of our public schools; but they may be read with greater profit by the fifth and sixth, in conjunction with the original text."—*The Academy.*

"**St Luke.** Canon FARRAR has supplied students of the Gospel with an admirable manual in this volume. It has all that copious variety of illustration, ingenuity of suggestion, and general soundness of interpretation which readers are accustomed to expect from the learned and eloquent editor. Anyone who has been accustomed to associate the idea of 'dryness' with a commentary, should go to Canon Farrar's **St Luke** for a more correct impression. He will find that a commentary may be made interesting in the highest degree, and that without losing anything of its solid value....But, so to speak, it is *too good* for some of the readers for whom it is intended."—*The Spectator.*

The Gospel according to St John. "The notes are extremely scholarly and valuable, and in most cases exhaustive, bringing to the elucidation of the text all that is best in commentaries, ancient and modern."—*The English Churchman and Clerical Journal.*

"(1) **The Acts of the Apostles.** By J. RAWSON LUMBY, D.D. (2) **The Second Epistle of the Corinthians,** edited by Professor LIAS. The introduction is pithy, and contains a mass of carefully-selected information on the authorship of the Acts, its designs, and its sources. ......The Second Epistle of the Corinthians is a manual beyond all praise, for the excellence of its pithy and pointed annotations, its analysis of the contents, and the fulness and value of its introduction."—*Examiner.*

"The Rev. H. C. G. MOULE, M.A., has made a valuable addition to THE CAMBRIDGE BIBLE FOR SCHOOLS in his brief commentary on the **Epistle to the Romans.** The 'Notes' are very good, and lean, as the notes of a School Bible should, to the most commonly accepted and orthodox view of the inspired author's meaning; while the Introduction, and especially the Sketch of the Life of St Paul, is a model of condensation. It is as lively and pleasant to read as if two or three facts had not been crowded into well-nigh every sentence."—*Expositor.*

"**The Epistle to the Romans.** It is seldom we have met with a work so remarkable for the compression and condensation of all that is valuable in the smallest possible space as in the volume before us. Within its limited pages we have 'a sketch of the Life of St Paul,' we have further a critical account of the date of the Epistle to the Romans, of its language, and of its genuineness. The notes are numerous, full of matter, to the point, and leave no real difficulty or obscurity unexplained."—*The Examiner.*

"**The First Epistle to the Corinthians.** Edited by Professor LIAS. Every fresh instalment of this annotated edition of the Bible for Schools confirms the favourable opinion we formed of its value from the examination of its first number. The origin and plan of the Epistle are discussed with its character and genuineness."—*The Nonconformist.*

Galatians. "Dr PEROWNE deals throughout in a very thorough manner with every real difficulty in the text, and in this respect he has faithfully followed the noble example set him in the exegetical masterpiece, his indebtedness to which he frankly acknowledges."—*Modern Church.*

"The introductory matter is very full and informing, whilst the Notes are admirable. They combine the scholarly and the practical in an unusual degree....It is not the young students in 'schools and colleges' alone who will find this Commentary helpful on every page."—*Record.*

"This little work, like all of the series, is a scholarly production; but we can also unreservedly recommend it from a doctrinal standpoint; Dr E. H. PEROWNE is one who has grasped the distinctive teaching of the Epistle, and expounds it with clearness and definiteness. In an appendix, he ably maintains the correctness of the A. V. as against the R. V. in the translation of II. 16, a point of no small importance."—*English Churchman.*

The Epistle to the Ephesians. By Rev. H. C. G. MOULE, M.A. "It seems to us the model of a School and College Commentary—comprehensive, but not cumbersome; scholarly, but not pedantic."—*Baptist Magazine.*

The Epistle to the Philippians. "There are few series more valued by theological students than 'The Cambridge Bible for Schools and Colleges,' and there will be no number of it more esteemed than that by Mr H. C. G. MOULE on the *Epistle to the Philippians.*"—*Record.*

Thessalonians. "It will stand the severest scrutiny, for no volume in this admirable series exhibits more careful work, and Mr FINDLAY is a true expositor, who keeps in mind what he is expounding, and for whom he is expounding it."—*Expository Times.*

"Mr FINDLAY maintains the high level of the series to which he has become contributor. Some parts of his introduction to the Epistles to the Thessalonians could scarcely be bettered. The account of Thessalonica, the description of the style and character of the Epistles, and the analysis of them are excellent in style and scholarly care. The notes are possibly too voluminous; but there is so much matter in them, and the matter is arranged and handled so ably, that we are ready to forgive their fulness....Mr FINDLAY'S commentary is a valuable addition to what has been written on the letters to the Thessalonian Church."—*Academy.*

"Of all the volumes of this most excellent series, none is better done, and few are so well done as this small volume....From beginning to end the volume is marked by accurate grammatical scholarship, delicate appreciation of the apostle's meaning, thorough investigation of all matters open to doubt, extensive reading, and deep sympathy with the spiritual aim of these epistles. It is, on the whole, the best commentary on the Thessalonians which has yet appeared, and its small price puts it within reach of all. We heartily recommend it."—*Methodist Recorder.*

"Mr FINDLAY has fulfilled in this volume a task which Dr Moulton was compelled to decline, though he has rendered valuable aid in its preparation. The commentary is in its own way a model—clear, forceful, scholarly—such as young students will welcome as a really useful guide, and old ones will acknowledge as giving in brief space the substance of all that they knew."—*Baptist Magazine.*

Hebrews. "Like his (Canon Farrar's) commentary on Luke it possesses all the best characteristics of his writing. It is a work not only of an accomplished scholar, but of a skilled teacher."—*Baptist Magazine.*

The Epistles of St John. By the Rev. A. PLUMMER, M.A., D.D. "This forms an admirable companion to the 'Commentary on the Gospel according to St John,' which was reviewed in *The Churchman* as soon as it appeared. Dr Plummer has some of the highest qualifications for such a task; and these two volumes, their size being considered, will bear comparison with the best Commentaries of the time."—*The Churchman.*

Revelation. "This volume contains evidence of much careful labour. It is a scholarly production, as might be expected from the pen of the late Mr W. H. SIMCOX....The notes throw light upon many passages of this difficult book, and are extremely suggestive. It is an advantage that they sometimes set before the student various interpretations without exactly guiding him to a choice."—*Guardian.*

"Mr SIMCOX has treated his very difficult subject with that conscious care, grasp, and lucidity which characterises everything he wrote."—*Modern Church.*

The Smaller Cambridge Bible for Schools.

"*We can only repeat what we have already said of this admirable series, containing, as it does, the scholarship of the larger work. For scholars in our elder classes, and for those preparing for Scripture examinations, no better commentaries can be put into their hands.*"—Sunday-School Chronicle.

"*Despite their small size, these volumes give the substance of the admirable pieces of work on which they are founded. We can only hope that in many schools the class-teaching will proceed on the lines these commentators suggest.*"—Record.

"*We should be glad to hear that this series has been introduced into many of our Sunday-Schools, for which it is so admirably adapted.*"—Christian Leader.

"*All that is necessary to be known and learned by pupils in junior and elementary schools is to be found in this series. Indeed, much more is provided than should be required by the examiners. We do not know what more could be done to provide sensible, interesting, and solid Scriptural instruction for boys and girls. The Syndics of the Cambridge

OPINIONS OF THE PRESS.

University Press are rendering great services both to teachers and to scholars by the publication of such a valuable series of books, in which slipshod work could not have a place."—Literary World.

"For the student of the sacred oracles who utilizes hours of travel or moments of waiting in the perusal of the Bible there is nothing so handy, and, at the same time, so satisfying as these little books..... Nor let anyone suppose that, because these are school-books, therefore they are beneath the adult reader. They contain the very ripest results of the best Biblical scholarship, and that in the very simplest form."—Christian Leader.

"Altogether one of the most perfect examples of a Shilling New Testament commentary which even this age of cheapness is likely to produce."
—Bookseller.

Samuel I. and II. "Professor KIRKPATRICK'S two tiny volumes on the First and Second Books of Samuel are quite model school-books; the notes elucidate every possible difficulty with scholarly brevity and clearness and a perfect knowledge of the subject."—*Saturday Review.*

"They consist of an introduction full of matter, clearly and succinctly given, and of notes which appear to us to be admirable, at once full and brief."—*Church Times.*

Kings I. "We can cordially recommend this little book. The Introduction discusses the question of authorship and date in a plain but scholarly fashion, while the footnotes throughout are brief, pointed, and helpful."—*Review of Reviews.*

Matthew. "The notes are terse, clear, and helpful, and teachers and students cannot fail to find the volume of great service."—*Publishers' Circular.*

Mark. Luke. "We have received the volumes of St Mark and St Luke in this series....The two volumes seem, on the whole, well adapted for school use, are well and carefully printed, and have maps and good, though necessarily brief, introductions. There is little doubt that this series will be found as popular and useful as the well-known larger series, of which they are abbreviated editions."—*Guardian.*

Luke. "We cannot too highly commend this handy little book to all teachers."—*Wesleyan Methodist Sunday-School Record.*

John. "We have been especially interested in Mr PLUMMER'S treatment of the Gospel which has been entrusted to his charge. He is concise, comprehensive, interesting, and simple. Young students of this inimitable book, as well as elder students, even ministers and teachers, may use it with advantage as a very serviceable handbook."—*Literary World.*

John. "A model of condensation, losing nothing of its clearness and force from its condensation into a small compass. Many who have long since completed their college curriculum will find it an invaluable handbook."—*Methodist Times.*

Acts. "The notes are very brief, but exceedingly comprehensive, comprising as much detail in the way of explanation as would be needed by young students of the Scriptures preparing for examination. We again give the opinion that this series furnishes as much real help as would usually satisfy students for the Christian ministry, or even ministers themselves."—*Literary World.*

THE CAMBRIDGE GREEK TESTAMENT
FOR SCHOOLS AND COLLEGES

with a Revised Text, based on the most recent critical authorities, and English Notes, prepared under the direction of the General Editor, THE BISHOP OF WORCESTER.

"*Has achieved an excellence which puts it above criticism.*"—Expositor.

St Matthew. "Copious illustrations, gathered from a great variety of sources, make his notes a very valuable aid to the student. They are indeed remarkably interesting, while all explanations on meanings, applications, and the like are distinguished by their lucidity and good sense."—*Pall Mall Gazette.*

St Mark. "Dr MACLEAR'S introduction contains all that is known of St Mark's life; an account of the circumstances in which the Gospel was composed, with an estimate of the influence of St Peter's teaching upon St Mark; an excellent sketch of the special characteristics of this Gospel; an analysis, and a chapter on the text of the New Testament generally."—*Saturday Review.*

St Luke. "Of this second series we have a new volume by Archdeacon FARRAR on *St Luke*, completing the four Gospels....It gives us in clear and beautiful language the best results of modern scholarship. We have a most attractive *Introduction.* Then follows a sort of composite Greek text, representing fairly and in very beautiful type the consensus of modern textual critics. At the beginning of the exposition of each chapter of the Gospel are a few short critical notes giving the manuscript evidence for such various readings as seem to deserve mention. The expository notes are short, but clear and helpful. For young students and those who are not disposed to buy or to study the much more costly work of Godet, this seems to us to be the best book on the Greek Text of the Third Gospel."—*Methodist Recorder.*

St John. "We take this opportunity of recommending to ministers on probation, the very excellent volume of the same series on this part of the New Testament. We hope that most or all of our young ministers will prefer to study the volume in the *Cambridge Greek Testament for Schools.*"—*Methodist Recorder.*

The Acts of the Apostles. "Professor LUMBY has performed his laborious task well, and supplied us with a commentary the fulness and freshness of which Bible students will not be slow to appreciate. The volume is enriched with the usual copious indexes and four coloured maps."—*Glasgow Herald.*

I. Corinthians. "Mr LIAS is no novice in New Testament exposition, and the present series of essays and notes is an able and helpful addition to the existing books."—*Guardian.*

The Epistles of St John. "In the very useful and well annotated series of the Cambridge Greek Testament the volume on the Epistles of St John must hold a high position... The notes are brief, well informed and intelligent."—*Scotsman.*

CAMBRIDGE: PRINTED BY C. J. CLAY, M.A. AND SONS, AT THE UNIVERSITY PRESS.

www.ingramcontent.com/pod-product-compliance
Lightning Source LLC
Chambersburg PA
CBHW020535300426
44111CB00008B/675